Victor and Lavinia
May all good attend you
Chetanananda
28.6.2009

Girish Chandra Ghosh

A Bohemian Devotee of Sri Ramakrishna

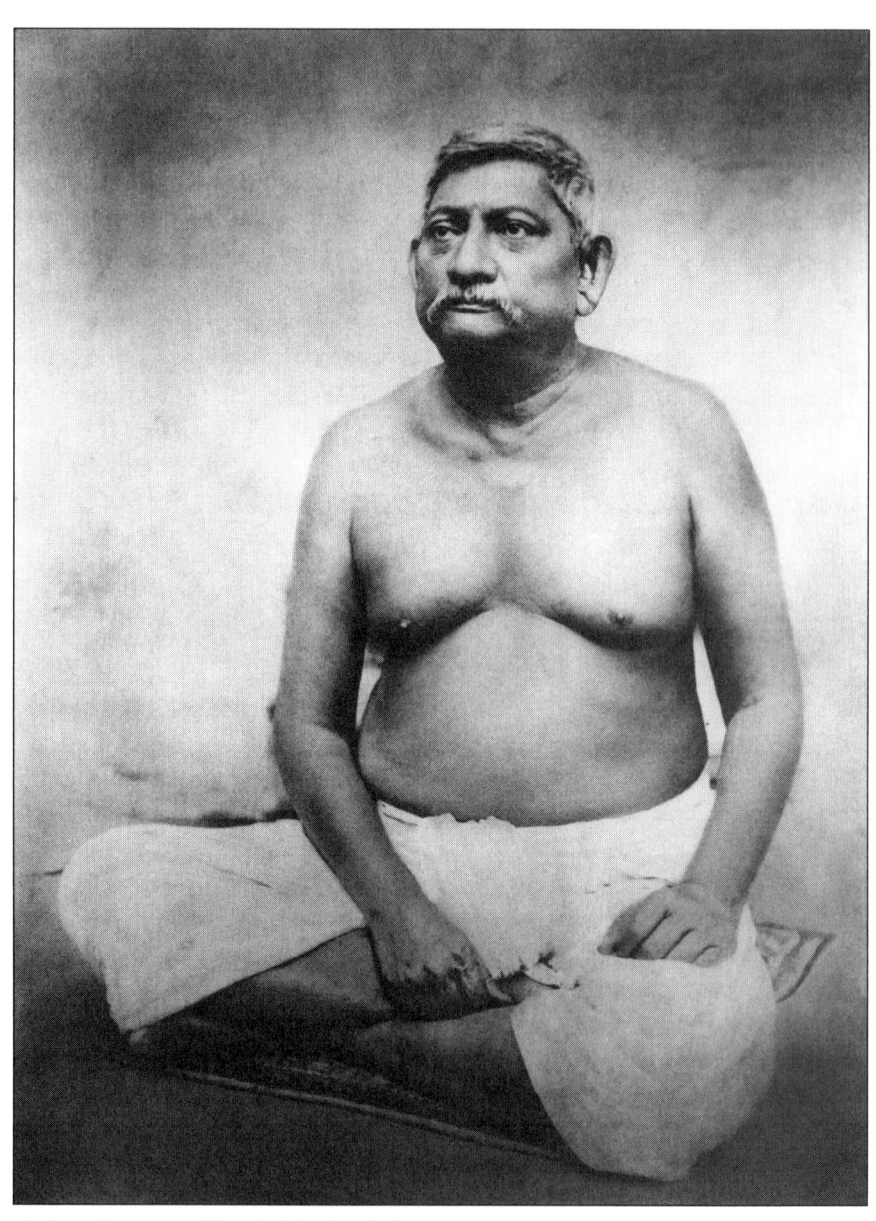
Girish Chandra Ghosh (1844–1912)

Girish Chandra Ghosh

A Bohemian Devotee of Sri Ramakrishna

Swami Chetanananda

Biographical Introduction

Christopher Isherwood

Vedanta Society of St. Louis

Copyright © 2009 Vedanta Society of St. Louis

All rights reserved. No part of this book may be used or reproduced in any manner whatsoever without permission in writing from the publisher, with the sole exception of brief quotations embodied in critical articles or reviews.

Library of Congress Cataloging-in-Publication Data

Chetanananda, Swami.
Girish Chandra Ghosh : a bohemian devotee of Sri Ramakrishna / Swami Chetanananda ; biographical introduction, Christopher Isherwood. -- 1st ed.
   p. cm.
Includes bibliographical references and index.
ISBN 978-0-916356-92-7 (hardcover : alk. paper) -- ISBN 978-0-916356-93-4 (pbk. : alk. paper)
1. Ghose, Girishchandra, 1844-1912. 2. Authors, Bengali--19th century--Biography. 3. Ramakrishna, 1836-1886--Disciples--Biography. 4. Theater--India--Bengal--History--19th century. I. Title.
PK1718.G4718Z615 2009
891.4'48409--dc22
[B]
                     2009015974

FIRST EDITION 2009

Cover design by Diane Marshall

Printed in the United States of America

Those who wish to learn in greater detail about the teachings contained in this book may write to:
Vedanta Society of St. Louis
205 S. Skinker Blvd.
St. Louis, MO 63105, U.S.A.

www.vedantastl.org

Contents

	List of Illustrations	6
	Preface	7
	Biographical Introduction by Christopher Isherwood	10
1.	"I Am a Sinner"	19
2.	Early Life to Adulthood (1844–1879)	23
3.	As an Accountant (1864–1879)	34
4.	As an Actor (1867–1879)	38
5.	As a Playwright and Actor (1880–1884)	50
6.	As a Playwright and Actor (1885–1912)	56
7.	As a Dramatic Director	87
8.	From Atheist to Devotee (1867–1873)	110
9.	Chaitanya Lila	118
10.	Prahlada Charitra	133
11.	Nimai Sannyas	142
12.	Brishaketu	147
13.	Daksha Yajna	157
14.	Sri Ramakrishna: Patron Saint of Bengali Stage	162
15.	Three Stars — Binodini, Tarasundari, and Tinkari	173
16.	Ramakrishna's Influence on Girish's Plays	225
17.	Reminiscenses of Ramakrishna	255
18.	Conversations with Ramakrishna	269
19.	The Power of Attorney	312
20.	Days with Ramakrishna	323
21.	Girish and Vivekananda	339
22.	Girish and Holy Mother	353

23. Girish and the Monastic Disciples of Ramakrishna	369
24. Girish and the Devotees of Ramakrishna	387
25. Further Glimpses of Girish	401
26. Interviews and Reminiscenses	411
27. Departure from the World Stage	454
References	469
Index	481

List of Illustrations

Girish Chandra Ghosh	2
National Theatre, Calcutta	46
Girish thinking of an acting plot	48
Girish in his late forties	49
Girish dictating a drama to Devendra Nath Majumdar	52
Girish in the role of Yogesh in *Prafulla* play	61
Girish as Pasupati in *Mrinalini*	72
Paresh Chandra Sen, Girish Ghosh, and Abinash Gangopadhyay	89
An Actor's Portfolio (22 pictures)	99-109
Binodini	128
Banabiharini as Nitai in *Chaitanya Lila*	129
Binodini, and Binodini as Mati Bibi in *Kapalkundala*	177
Tarasundari, and Tarasundari as Ayesha in *Durgeshnandini*	194
Tinkari	206
Ramakrishna at Bengal Photographer's Studio, Calcutta	254
Girish Ghosh resting in his living room	324
Swami Vivekananda in San Francisco	340
Holy Mother Sarada Devi, Calcutta	354
Girish with devotees and disciples of Ramakrishna	368
Back view of Girish's house	388
Surendra Nath Ghosh (Dani), Girish's son, and acting in costume	415
Girish at cremation ground, Calcutta	466

Preface

An author once asked Girish Chandra Ghosh for permission to write his biography. Girish responded: "Paint me as I am. Whoever wants to know me will find me in my writings."

People who read about Girish and his association with Ramakrishna are eager to learn more about him. Girish's flamboyant life is intriguing: He was one of the most attractive personalities among the devotees of Ramakrishna.

Many legends and rumours about Girish have travelled by word of mouth. We do not know the sources for most of them, nor do we have any way to verify their authenticity. This book presents the facts to the reader to help remove some of the misunderstandings surrounding his life. It also seeks to highlight Girish's genius and creativity to counter the desire that some people have to focus on his bohemian side — his carefree, wanton life, and his addiction to drugs and alcohol. In fact, some Westerners have half-seriously told me that Girish is their role model.

As far as I know, the present volume is the first English-language biography of this colourful bohemian. It is difficult to write a comprehensive biography of Girish. His genius was vast and his character was complex. On one hand, he was a daredevil, a drunkard, and a debauchee; on the other, he was a humble and staunch devotee of Ramakrishna. He was a paradox, difficult to comprehend.

When we read Girish's writings, we see glimpses of his far-reaching intellect and his knowledge of the ancient wisdom of India as well as of contemporary Western thought and literature. Girish's early works were first published in six volumes by his brother Atul Krishna Ghosh, between 1892 and 1900. After Girish's passing away, his collected works were published in ten volumes by his son Surendra Nath Ghosh, between 1928 and 1931. Much later, in 1969, Girish's complete works were published in five volumes by Sahitya Samsad of Calcutta. Altogether these volumes comprise 3,717 pages in small type. (See Chapter 6 for a complete list of Girish's writings.)

In his youth Girish led the life of a bohemian, disregarding conventional rules and social mores. He did not even finish school. Nonetheless, we marvel at his intellectual acumen and encyclopedic knowledge as well as his command of both Bengali and English. His extraordinary personality is evident in his powerful imagination and indomitable energy, his passion for acting and joy in serving others, his common sense and creativity, his faith and devotion, and his compassion for the poor and the fallen. He was simple and loving, yet he was also outspoken. He was compassionate, generous, and unselfish. Externally he was bold and masculine, but within he was tender and loving. On one occasion he offered to the Divine Mother his fame as a celebrated actor; on another, he surrendered his ego completely to his guru, Ramakrishna, by giving him his power of attorney.

As a bee collects nectar from different flowers and makes honey, so I have gathered material from many publications on and by Girish to give shape to this book. However, as paint, brushes, canvas, and an easel are not a painting, and heaps of sand, cement, brick, wood, and iron rods are not a building, so this collection of stories, incidents, dialogues, interviews, reminiscences, excerpts from diaries, and legends is not a complete biography of Girish.

This book describes Girish's early life, his life as an actor, playwright, and director, and his meeting with Ramakrishna and subsequent transformation under him. The reader will discover many hitherto unknown incidents in Girish's life, as well as his reminiscences of Ramakrishna, Holy Mother, Swami Vivekananda and other disciples and devotees that have long been scattered among numerous Bengali books, magazines, and diaries.

Apart from Girish's own works, there are several books about Girish in Bengali. I acknowledge my indebtedness to the authors of those works, especially to Abinash Chandra Gangopadhyay, who was Girish's secretary and attendant from 1899 to 1912. In 1927 Abinash wrote an authoritative biography in Bengali called *Girishchandra*. In his book he includes information that he collected from Girish himself and from Girish's sister Dakshinakali, his brother Atul, his son Surendra, and some of his friends.

While I was serving the Vedanta Society of Southern California (from 1971 to 1978), I asked Christopher Isherwood to give a lecture on Girish, which he delivered at the Santa Barbara temple on 7 December 1975. This lecture was transcribed and edited, and has been included here as a biographical introduction.

I gratefully acknowledge the Ramakrishna-Vivekananda Centre in New York and the Vedanta Society of Southern California in Hollywood for giving me permission to use some materials from their publications.

I am truly blessed that the Master has given me the opportunity to work on Girish's biography.

I wish to express my gratitude to my proofreaders, my typesetter, my designer, and those who corrected the manuscript on the computer. I also gratefully acknowledge the help that I received from my editors: Kim Saccio-Kent, a freelance editor in San Francisco; Linda Prugh, an English teacher in Kansas City; Pravrajika Shuddhatmaprana, a nun of the Vedanta Society of Southern California; Chris Lovato, Associate Professor, University of British Columbia, Vancouver. Ralph Hile also edited the manuscript and prepared the index. I am indebted to Sankar (Mani Sankar Mukherji, a famous novelist of Bengal) for supplying me with some valuable books on Girish, and Shankari Prasad Basu who encouraged me to complete this project.

Human beings cannot help but worship genius, because genius is a spark of the Divine. Krishna says in the Gita (10:41): "Whatever glorious or beautiful or mighty being exists anywhere, know that it has sprung from but a spark of My splendour." This book is the story of a genius. History cannot forget those who have had an impact on the cultural heritage of a nation. Girish's contribution is recorded in the pages of history and will be remembered for ages to come.

Chetanananda

St. Louis
Ramakrishna's birthday
27 February 2009

Biographical Introduction
Christopher Isherwood

I want to talk about Girish Chandra Ghosh, one of Bengal's greatest dramatists and poets, and one of Ramakrishna's greatest devotees. Since Girish Chandra Ghosh lived primarily in the world, it's good to begin by reminding ourselves of the situation in Calcutta in those days, the Calcutta of the mid-19th century, in which he lived. So I will start by reading two extracts from the book *Ramakrishna and His Disciples*, which just sketch something of the atmosphere between the British and the population of Calcutta at that time, and the general clash of ideas that was going on at that time which affected everybody in the city and the country.

> In those days the city of Calcutta was the seat of British rule in India and the main port of entry for the ideas and culture of the West. The changes that were taking place in India, for the worse and for the better, all had their beginnings there. In making the journey from Kamarpukur to Calcutta, Gadadhar [Ramakrishna] had passed from the timelessness of village life into the very midst of contemporary history.... The British had been peacefully established for more than seventy years. They had built an imposing European Quarter — "a city of palaces" one contemporary traveller called it; while another was reminded of St. John's Wood in London. Its architecture was predominantly neo-classical; the larger mansions had stately columns and massive porticos, and their rooms were vast, airy and scantily furnished in order to lessen the heat. Here, the social life was elegant and excessively formal. The high British officials rode around town in carriages with outriders; on their arrival at evening parties, servants would run ahead of them carrying flaming torches. Their families went to church and to the opera, their ladies drove out along the Esplanade and gossiped about each other, their sons played cricket. Despite the climate, everything was done to preserve the atmosphere of home. As for the Bengalis, they usually saw the insides

of these palatial homes only in the capacity of servants. And even when some wealthy high-caste families were occasionally invited to receptions, it was scarcely on a basis of friendly equality. Only recently (1852), British Calcutta society had been plunged into controversy because Lord Auckland, the Governor General, had actually permitted forty-five Bengali college boys to appear in his presence wearing shoes! As the century advanced, however, many of these barriers were gradually broken down.

The British in India at that period must have seemed strange, paradoxical beings to any detached observer. They were imperialists with bad consciences. They were builders of bridges, roads, hospitals, and schools — public benefactors who were nevertheless ceaselessly engaged in the piecemeal conquest of a nation. For the Indians, who did not want them, they sacrificed their health and their lives, going back to England prematurely aged, yellow-faced, on crutches, to die. Tens of thousands of them were buried in the country during the two centuries of their occupation. Many were altruistic, many were heroic, many were deeply devout and felt that they had accepted voluntary exile in this savage and unhealthy land in order to do God's work among the benighted. What almost none of them seem to have been aware of was that they were in the most religious country in the world; and in the presence of a spiritual culture which made their own sectarianism seem provincial indeed. Even Honoria Lawrence, wife of Sir Henry Lawrence, certainly one of the noblest and most dedicated Englishwomen in India, could write coldly: "There is something very oppressive in being surrounded by heathen and Mohammedan darkness, in seeing idol-worship all around, and when we see the deep and debasing hold these principles have on people, it is difficult to believe they can ever be freed of it."[1]

One of the many evils of foreign conquest is the tendency of the conquered to imitate their conquerors. This kind of imitation is evil because it is uncritical; it does not choose certain aspects of the alien culture and reject others, but accepts everything slavishly, with a superstitious belief that if you ape your conquerors you will acquire their superior power.

The British certainly had much to offer India that was valuable: medical science and engineering, the arts of the West, a clearly defined legal code. Unfortunately, they brought with them also two creeds — scientific atheism and missionary evangelism — diametrically opposed to each other yet equally narrow and dogmatic. These two creeds had done quite enough harm already in the West, where they were indigenous; exported to India, they had the added power of novelty and threatened to produce spiritual and cultural chaos. The young Indians who came into contact with them nearly all reacted violently. Either they lost belief in everything Hindu and got nothing from England in return but despair; or they were thrilled by the fanaticism and self-assurance of the missionaries and embraced a wretched version of Christianity which was both abject and self-seeking. (Since the missionaries had charge of most of the new educational facilities provided by the British, they got the opportunity to indoctrinate many of the most intelligent students of each generation.) Thus the young were growing up into cultural hybrids; laughed at and despised by the British because of their hopelessly silly efforts at imitation; condemned by orthodox Hindus of the old school as impious traitors to the religion and traditions of their race.[2]

I wrote this first of all because what has to be said about Girish Chandra Ghosh has a great deal to do with the concept of sin. Now, a little background on the facts of Girish's life.

Girish Chandra Ghosh was born in 1844, in the district of Baghbazar, Calcutta. His parents both died when he was still very young. He got married soon afterwards, but the marriage did not stabilize his life.

Girish was a person of great animal vitality, strength, ingenuity, force, drive, and indeed genius — a protean kind of talent. He was a poet, a dramatist, an actor, and he threw himself into everything with the utmost vitality. It was a function, an aspect, of this vitality that he was also exceedingly sensual; he had a considerable sex life, which was much discussed by everybody around him; and he drank enormously, took opium, and so forth. A modern poet has said: "A saint is easy to recognize; his constitution is designed for vice." He meant that in the case of somebody like Girish, without this energy he would not have had all the positive qualities as well as the negative ones.

His early life of doing a succession of boring office jobs was soon abandoned, and his spare time became divided between writing and amateur acting. He was also fond of playing practical jokes. I have always thought that people who play practical jokes are fundamentally very aggressive. This aggression appears in various forms later in his life. He was really a type of person who was fairly familiar already in 19th century Europe — that is to say, a bohemian artist. But he was not nearly such a familiar type in Calcutta, because the standards of Hinduism on the one hand and the standards of missionary Christianity on the other had attained a tremendous hold on people's feelings, and there was a great deal of puritanism which judged him to be a coarse, debauched man. This is all, however, the purely negative side of his character.

On the positive side, he was enormously productive. He started immediately to revive from the dead the dramatic life of Bengal. He began to write plays, both devotional in the most classic sense and written in a sort

Biographical Introduction 13

of Shakespearean style, and historical, and also contemporary plays on life in the 19th century, which were written in a kind of modern dialect style. In these plays he often played not only one but several parts, and before long, during his thirties or forties, he acquired a theatre, the Star Theatre, which exists to this day in Calcutta. In this theatre he was constantly putting on these new plays he had written. This was the situation at the time when he met Ramakrishna.

His meetings with Ramakrishna are very interesting, because this man, who was fundamentally enormously devotional and who was really looking for someone to help him throughout all the early part of his life, was not at all easily taken in, and was quite loath to accept any human being whatsoever as a guru, much less to accept any seeming human being as being an avatar.

Girish, in an article which he wrote later in life, described his state of mind before he met Ramakrishna:

> At such a crisis, I thought, "Does God exist? Does he listen to the prayers of man? Does he show the way from darkness to light?" My mind said, "Yes." Immediately I closed my eyes and prayed: "Oh God, if thou art, carry me across. Give me refuge. I have none!"... But I had nurtured doubt all these years. I had argued long, saying, "There is no God." ... Again I fell victim to doubt. But I had not the courage to say boldly, "God does not exist."[3]

There you see a sort of mirror image in a Bengali mind also of what I was reading just now: the influence of the scientific atheism imported on the one hand from the West and of the rigorous, Christian missionary puritanism on the other. He alternated. What he had, as a matter of fact, was a native spiritual vigour which far exceeded anything that was being offered by the missionaries of the conquering nation. He wrote:

> Everybody with whom I discussed my problem said unanimously that without instruction from a guru doubt would not go and nothing could be achieved in spiritual life. But my intellect refused to accept a human being as a guru.[4]

The first time Girish saw Ramakrishna he went to visit the house of an attorney who lived in his neighborhood. He had heard that this paramahamsa existed — this great holy man — these were already approaching the last years of Ramakrishna's life. It must have been around 1880 at least, and Ramakrishna left the body in 1886. Girish went to the house and Ramakrishna was sitting there in a high spiritual state and seemed almost unaware of his surroundings. Lamps were lighted — it being the evening — and Ramakrishna looked around and said, "Is it evening?" And Girish thought: "What a fake. He's putting on airs." You see, he was a very good tester in one way, because like all actors, he deeply suspected all kinds of behaviour at its surface level. He always looked to see what was underneath it — what it was all about. And I think that actors come to feel more and more, as they play different roles, a sort of instinctive sense of unreality at the surface of the personality of different people. They always think, "Well, that's all very well, but one can switch at any moment. What does it mean? What guarantee is there that this man is on the level?"

And it was indeed not for several years that Girish saw Ramakrishna again. This time he was much more favourably impressed, very largely because Ramakrishna, instead of sitting in utter meditative grandeur and ignoring everybody and expecting to be bowed to, was the very reverse. Every time he met anybody, he bowed down to them. This delighted Girish because it was out of character. It was out of the conventional role of the holy man. Of course, in India one could easily see so-called holy men in very large numbers which added to Girish's scepticism.

> Only a few days after this, on 21 September 1884, Ramakrishna and some of the devotees visited the Star Theatre, to see a play by Girish about the life of Chaitanya. Girish himself was strolling in the outer compound of the theatre when a member of Ramakrishna's party came to him and said: "The Master has come to see your play. If you'll give him a free pass, that will be very kind; otherwise we'll buy him a ticket." Girish answered that Ramakrishna need not pay for his seat, but that the others would have to. He then went to greet Ramakrishna in person. But, before he could bow to Ramakrishna, Ramakrishna bowed to him. Every time Girish bowed, Ramakrishna bowed; until Girish, fearing that this might continue all evening, bowed mentally instead of physically and led them all upstairs to a box. He then went home, as he was not feeling well. Thus Girish missed hearing Ramakrishna's delighted comments on the play and witnessing his frequent periods of ecstasy. When Ramakrishna was asked later how he had liked it, he answered, "I found the representation the same as the reality."[5]

This kind of remark made by people, as a rule, means very little, but you, with your false sense of reality, can imagine Ramakrishna saying that, knowing that he knew what the reality was. You can imagine that this was about the greatest compliment one could pay anybody. It takes a little imagination to imagine yourself in that position. Girish must have been aware by this time that he was in the presence of a very, very strange and extraordinary individual.

Three days later, Girish was sitting on the veranda of a friend's house when he saw Ramakrishna approaching along the street. They exchanged greetings. Girish felt a strong urge to join him, but did not. Then someone came to him with a message that the Master was asking for him. So Girish followed him into the house of Balaram, whom he was visiting. Ramakrishna was in a semiconscious state. As if in answer to Girish's previous scepticism, he murmured, "No, — this is not pretence; this is not pretence." Presently he returned to normal consciousness. Girish was always longing to find a guru, although, as we have seen, he obstinately refused to believe that any human being could stand in that relation to another. "What is a guru?" he now asked. And Ramakrishna answered: "He's like a procurer. A procurer arranges for the union of the lover with his mistress. In the same way, a guru arranges the meeting between the individual soul and his beloved, the Divine Spirit." Then he added: "You need not worry. Your guru has already been chosen."[6]

It is so typical of Ramakrishna that he always used words that related to a person's lifestyle. Then they began to talk about the theatre and so on, and Girish got rather embarrassed because Ramakrishna was praising the play again, and saying how remarkable it was. Then Girish began to get kind of aggressive and rude and said: "I don't care about the play and Chaitanya. I just wrote the play to make money." Ramakrishna just ignored this. Then later on he said to him: "You know, whatever you say, you do know something. There is something in you that recognizes the God-like. It is only if you can recognize the God-like that you can write about the God-like." And Girish was saying: "Oh, you know, after all it's nothing. I think I should give it up; it's silly, all this scribbling." And Ramakrishna said: "No, absolutely not. You should go on writing. That should be your work. You do a great deal of good by it."

So now began the curious duel, as it were, which Ramakrishna had with almost all of his disciples — very much so with Narendra (later Swami Vivekananda) — the duel between the forces in the other person which were resisting and Ramakrishna's open love and invitation to come to him. And this took various forms. Of course, the thing that strikes one when reading about Girish is really that he and Ramakrishna were, in a curious way, very much alike in certain respects. They were both very much children of Bengal. They were both very volatile and vivacious. They were born actors, loving dance and music.

When I myself went with Swami Prabhavananda to the Star Theatre in 1963 there was a modern play in Bengali. I didn't understand a word, but I didn't want to leave. I would have sat there for hours. The fascinating power of these people: there is something in the whole style of acting — in the enormous gusto — in the amusing gestures, the facial expressions. Something terrific was going on. It was actually a domestic farce, but you felt that this could be applied to anything — the enormous gusto of this performance — one could never tire of watching it. And you glimpsed there something of the extraordinary Bengali temperament which both of them had in different aspects.

Then there were the famous scenes where Girish took to visiting Ramakrishna very late at night and drunk. He was very fond of having tremendous moments of longing for Ramakrishna when he happened to be visiting with his various girlfriends and so on and would rush out to get a carriage, saying he had to see Ramakrishna. He arrived. Nothing could be more tiresome than arriving in the middle of the night, and this is so characteristic of Ramakrishna that he welcomed him completely and they began to dance. Now, I think there is a great significance in their dancing and the idea, again and again we hear of it, of how Ramakrishna stopped drunkards in the road — perfect strangers — and how he got out of the carriage and danced with them. And I think this takes us in a way to a sort of insight into the nature of so-called sin. What Ramakrishna profoundly understood was that all of our so-called vices are in fact frustrated attempts to find the truth or to find peace or to find release from something. You're frightened, you feel menaced, you have enemies, so if you're in a position to, you give the order to have a million people killed. Or again, on a smaller scale, you want to shut out reality because it is threatening or alarming. You long for some other kind of truth, you long for some kind of transcendental thing, and you proceed to take some form of drug or other — not to be wicked, not to be vicious; but because you want to find a release. You want to find an inner truth, a higher truth through the medium of this.

Of course nowadays we are much more sophisticated about things like this, and people do understand this to a greater extent. But you see, that was why Ramakrishna, looking at a drunkard dancing, could think: "Why, that's the same as ecstasy, only he's going about it in the wrong way. The drive behind it, the desire, is for a state of joy in the eternal." And therefore Ramakrishna felt a tremendous kinship with people who were in this condition.

However, there was an amusing scene when Girish did one of his midnight descents upon Ramakrishna, and asked, "Where's my bottle?" And Ramakrishna said, "Oh, that's quite all right." And it turned out that before Girish's carriage had left, Ramakrishna had sent a disciple out particularly to collect Girish's bottle, which he had left in the carriage. And he had it brought in, and said, "Here, drink some more." And Girish said: "Oh, I couldn't do that. Not here." And Ramakrishna said: "Go on! Make the most of it while you want to. You'll give it up one of these days." And he drank right in front of Ramakrishna. He had broken down the conventional puritanism, the outside layer; he had broken down the standards of mere respectability and its opposite, which we impose on everything.

Everybody in a way who is not respectable is in a minor state of grace in relation to people who are respectable, simply because there is a kind of truth in it. Even in disgrace there is a kind of truth. You find that in Russian novels with people who are always getting drunk and then repenting, or doing some other thing and then repenting, as in *The Brothers Karamazov*, for example. Then, of course, Ramakrishna himself was unconventional in another way. Ramakrishna was also scandalous. Girish once paid him the most marvellous compliment: He said to Ramakrishna, "Everything about you is illegal!" And what he meant by that was that he broke all the laws of orthodox Hinduism. There was a famous most scandalous scene where Ramakrishna was in the presence of the Mother in the shrine and a cat came in. And he suddenly realized that the Eternal is also in the cat, and he was about to offer the consecrated food to the deity, and he bowed down before the cat and gave the cat the food. Well, of course, people were absolutely horrified! They wanted to throw him out of his job as priest of the temple, although he had given one of the supreme demonstrations of what Vedanta is all about.

His demonstrations were invariably shocking just because they were so extremely graphic, so literal. Great spiritual figures in other religions did exactly the same thing. The great Christian saint Philip Neri is an example. He used to take the injunction, "Suffer the little children to come unto Me," literally, and he let them play on the high altar, where they were constantly knocking over the blessed sacrament! He said that the children were much more important. People were jolted by this sort of behaviour.

The danger of not being respectable is that you have to boast about it. Girish was indeed rather tiresome about this. He said things like, "I have drunk so many bottles of wine, that if you were to place one bottle on top of another they would reach the height of Mount Everest." It didn't prove anything except that Girish was accepting the kind of miserable, puritanical standards instead of looking at the thing the way his Master looked at it and as he gradually learned to look at it. The whole point of the life of Girish is: He came right through this, not so much with some kind of improvement in behaviour — although that, relatively speaking, did follow — not in becoming a "good boy" — but to a sort of devotion to Sri Ramakrishna about which Vivekananda himself said, "Nobody has devoted himself, has abandoned his will, so absolutely to the Master as Girish."

Girish asked for instructions from Ramakrishna: "What shall I do? Is there anything I can do?" Ramakrishna answered, "Try and call on God three times a day." Girish said: "I'm sorry. I can't promise to. I may forget." Then the Master said: "Do it twice a day. Do it once." "No, no, I can't promise anything," Girish told him. Then Ramakrishna said: "All right, then give me your power of attorney. I'll take it over. I'll be responsible for you. Now you have no will at all. You will only say, 'I do whatever the Lord wills.' Don't ever say again, 'I will do this' or 'I will not do that.'"

And Girish really began to live like this. This is something about which we, at this distance in time, can only take the word of observers. But it does seem that Girish in some way did turn into the kind of devotee who was really a saint. This was a sort of absolute throwing of himself at Sri Ramakrishna's feet. That was the way he lived. He outlived Sri Ramakrishna by twenty-six years; he was 68 years old in 1912 when he died, and he left behind him a tremendous tradition. When one thinks about it one always comes back to that tremendous line in the Bhagavad Gita: "The Lord is everywhere and always perfect. What does He care for our sins or our righteousness?"

Chapter 1

I Am a Sinner

At the Star Theatre in Calcutta on 14 December 1884 Girish Chandra Ghosh introduced himself to Ramakrishna with these words: "I am a sinner."

Ramakrishna replied: "The wretch who constantly harps on sin becomes a sinner."

Girish: "Sir, the very ground where I used to sit would become unholy."

Ramakrishna: "How can you say that? Suppose a light is brought into a room that has been dark a thousand years; does it illumine the room little by little, or all in a flash?"

Girish: "What will happen to this sinner?"

Ramakrishna sang in a tender voice:

Meditate on the Lord, the Slayer of hell's dire woes,
He who removes the fear of death;
Thinking of Him, the soul is freed from worldly grief
And sails across the sea of life in the twinkling of an eye.

Consider, O my mind, why you have come to earth;
What gain is there in evil thoughts and deeds?
Your way lies not through these: perform your penance here
By meditating long and deep on the everlasting Lord.

Ramakrishna: "'Sails across the sea of life in the twinkling of an eye.' One attains the vision of God if Mahamaya steps aside from the door. Mahamaya's grace is necessary."

Girish: "I still have that twist in my mind. Tell me what I should do."

Ramakrishna: "Give God your power of attorney.* Let Him do whatever He likes."[1]

There were few sins in which Girish had not indulged. He once said: "I have drunk so much wine in my life that if the wine bottles were placed one upon another, they would stand as high as Mount Everest."[2]

*For an explanation of "power of attorney," please see Chapter 19.

One day Ramakrishna asked Aswini Kumar Datta, a devotee: "Do you know Girish Ghosh?"

Aswini: "Which Girish Ghosh? The one who is in the theatre?"

Ramakrishna: "Yes."

Aswini: "I have never seen him. But I know him by reputation."

Ramakrishna: "A good man."

Aswini: "They say he drinks."

Ramakrishna: "Let him! Let him! How long will he continue that?"[3]

Girish gradually stopped drinking. He did not drink at all for the last twenty years of his life. Later, someone asked him: "The Master did not ask you to stop drinking. Why don't you drink?"

Girish: "Well, his permission has turned into prohibition in my case. Whenever a sinful thought arises, I see the Master appear in my mind."[4]

When Girish was drunk he had little control over his speech and behaviour. Even prostitutes hesitated to open their doors to him when he was in this condition.

"One night," said Girish, "in a euphoric and drunken mood, I was visiting a house of prostitution with two of my friends. But suddenly I felt an urge to visit Ramakrishna. My friends and I hired a carriage and drove out to Dakshineswar. It was late at night, and everyone was asleep. The three of us entered Ramakrishna's room, tipsy and reeling. Ramakrishna grasped both my hands and began to sing and dance in ecstasy. The thought flashed through my mind: 'Here is a man whose love embraces all — even a wicked man like me, whose own family would condemn me in this state. Surely this holy man, respected by the righteous, is also the Saviour of the fallen.'"[5]

Girish surrendered to Ramakrishna and gave him his power of attorney. Years later he would say, "Had I known that there was such a huge pit in which to throw one's sins, I would have committed many more." The story of Girish proves that today's sinner can be tomorrow's saint. Oscar Wilde said: "The only difference between the saint and the sinner is that every saint has a past, and every sinner has a future."

Girish played an important role in the divine drama of Ramakrishna. We also marvel at his genius — and how this one man acted in so many roles in his life. His classmate Reverend Kalicharan Bandyopadhyay said: "We knew from our childhood that Girish was a genius."

Many people consider themselves to be like the carefree bohemian Girish, who was a drunkard, a debauchee, a breaker of rules and norms. People are attracted to his dark side. It is true that Girish was wayward in his youth. He enjoyed life enormously and in his early days was a follower of the hedonistic philosophy, "Eat, drink, and be merry." He rebelled against traditional religion and against God.

But one should not overlook the positive and productive aspects of the man's character. Girish was frank and fearless, loving and generous, and sincere and honest. He was extremely outspoken and could not bear any kind of hypocrisy. He was endowed with gigantic willpower, tremendous physical strength, superb intelligence, a compassionate heart, and "one hundred and twenty-five percent faith" (as Ramakrishna said). Girish was also a prolific writer, poet, playwright, storyteller, actor, and director who came to be known as the father of the Bengali stage.

It is said that Buddha demonstrated his power of redemption through Ambapali; Christ, through Mary Magdalene; Chaitanya, through Jagai and Madhai; and Ramakrishna, through Girish. This book presents a portrait of Girish's transformation. At the beginning of this book Girish introduces himself by saying, "I am a sinner"; and at the end, he says: "The Master made me a god. Look at me, I am Ramakrishna's miracle."

Girish's life gives hope to the wayward and seemingly lost people of society. Moreover, his faith and devotion are so vibrant, tangible, and contagious that just reading about him awakens love and longing for God in the minds of spiritual aspirants.

The melting snow from the mountaintops forms different streams that flow through the plains and nourish human civilization. Similarly, the condensed spirituality of Ramakrishna flowed through his disciples and devotees, who shared that divine bliss with the people of the East and the West. Vivekananda and other disciples of Ramakrishna spread their guru's message all over the world. M. recorded *The Gospel of Sri Ramakrishna* and talked about his Master for nearly half a century. Girish presented the Master's ideas and teachings in some of his plays and writings, and carried his life-giving message even to the red-light districts of Calcutta. Girish believed that Ramakrishna was an avatar and that he went to the theatre not only to see a play but also to deliver the fallen people of society. (Actors and actresses were social outcastes at that time.)

Girish is now a legend in the religious tradition of Ramakrishna. People tell colourful stories about him; some even exaggerate or embellish those episodes. But it is more enjoyable to hear directly from Girish his own reminiscences that describe his struggle and suffering; his conflict and confession; his relationship with his guru, Ramakrishna, and his brother disciples and devotees; his acting career; his playwriting; and other aspects of his life.

Girish was extremely brave. He was not a coward. A coward tries to hide his dark side, and he blames others for his shortcomings. Girish never tried to hide his failings or defend his misdeeds. "True religion," according to Ramakrishna, "is to unite the mind and speech." Girish followed this teaching of his guru implicitly and that made him a great soul. Martin Luther said: "Sin is, essentially, a departure from God. The recognition of sin is the beginning of salvation."[6]

Chapter 2

Early Life to Adulthood
(1844–1879)

Girish Chandra Ghosh was born in Baghbazar, North Calcutta, on 28 February 1844. His father, Nilkamal, and mother, Raimani, had eleven children; Girish was the eighth child. Because Lord Krishna was his mother's eighth child, the Hindu tradition considers this child to be auspicious. Girish's uncle predicted: "This child will bring glory to our dynasty."

Girish said of his parents: "My father was an expert accountant and had tremendous managerial capacity and worldly wisdom. My mother was very gentle and had great devotion for God. She loved to listen to spiritual talk and was fond of reciting hymns of gods and goddesses. If any Vaishnava mendicant visited our home, my mother would give him money and request him to sing a devotional song. I inherited from my father a sharp intellect and pragmatic approach to life, and from my mother a love for literature and devotion to God."[1]

Girish's father was very practical and honest. Once a poor neighbour came to him for a job. Nilkamal agreed to employ him in his office on the condition that he deduct five rupees from his salary every month. The man agreed, but his relatives criticized Nilkamal's mean-mindedness. However, that man died after some years and his family fell into a dire financial crisis. Nilkamal called in the man's wife and told her: "Your husband deposited five rupees each month with me when he was working in my office. This amount that I am giving to you is his total savings, including interest."[2]

Another poor neighbour borrowed 500 rupees from Nilkamal to pay for his daughter's wedding. He agreed to pay fifteen rupees per month to clear the loan. This man was an alcoholic and he suffered from asthma. After paying back 450 rupees, he asked Nilkamal to write off the remaining fifty rupees. But Nilkamal demanded the entire amount and said: "You have money to buy alcohol. Don't you feel ashamed asking me to forgive your debt?" At last the loan was paid off. The man died within a year, leaving behind a few children. Nilkamal called the man's wife and said: "I asked your husband to stop drinking, but he did not listen to me. I knew that he would not live long. I am now giving you the five hundred rupees that he repaid me. Please clear your debts and use the remainder to raise your children." The neighbours were amazed by Nilkamal's generosity and farsightedness.[3]

On another occasion, a friend complained to Nilkamal about his wayward son, saying: "My boy did not finish school. He does not like to work or obey. He wanders around and spends his time fishing." Nilkamal told his friend: "Why don't you lease a couple of ponds and ask your son to grow fish and sell them? It will satisfy his hobby and be a good source of income for the family." That wayward young man eventually became a successful fish merchant and earned a lot of money.[4] Thus Nilkamal's practical advice helped his friends and neighbours.

Girish's mother was very devout; she served their family deity, Lord Sridhar (Vishnu), every day. Once Raimani saved a ripe jackfruit for the offering but one of her children — probably Girish — ate part of the fruit. During her devotions she noticed that someone had already eaten some of the fruit, so she did not offer it to the Lord. (According to the Hindu custom, food defiled in that manner cannot be offered to the deity.) That night she dreamt that a beautiful young child with a blue complexion said to her with a smile: "I love jackfruit. Why did you not offer it to me? It does not matter that it is defiled; I also dwell in your children. Tomorrow, offer that remaining piece of jackfruit to me."[5] Girish included this story in one of his writings.

Girish's uncle Ramnarayan was a very compassionate and humble person. Before he ate his lunch, he would first inquire whether his neighbours had had their meals. He was generous, jovial, and fond of drinking; Girish inherited these traits from his uncle.

Human character is not formed entirely by inherited qualities, good or bad. Place, time, education, tendencies inherited from previous lives, environment, and talent have considerable influence on a person's development. Genius also is not the product of inherited characteristics, nor can one attain it through self-effort. Genius is the flowering of a gifted, bright, and artistic intellect. As a flower's fragrance enhances its beauty, so does this gift from God make a man into a superman and an ordinary person into someone extraordinary.

Early Life to Adulthood (1844–1879)   25

When Girish was born, his mother became seriously ill. She developed puerperal diarrhoea and could not nurse her baby. A maidservant named Uma had a young child at that time, so she acted as wet-nurse to Girish. Because he received a great deal of affection from his family, Girish had tremendous self-esteem even as a child. He was very sensitive and would quickly become angry if he perceived even a small injustice, but his tantrums did not last long. As a boy, he was naughty and obstinate. If he was asked not to do a particular thing, he could not rest until he had done just that. With a smile, he later remarked about his temper: "It is because I was breastfed by that maidservant."

One afternoon Girish saw a cucumber in the family's garden. The child's aunt told him: "We shall offer this cucumber to Krishna. Don't touch it." Immediately Girish became desperate to eat that particular cucumber, but he was too afraid to say anything. He began to cry. When asked the reason for his tears, he said, "I am thirsty." But he would not drink water when it was offered.

That evening when Nilkamal returned from his office, he heard the story and then asked Girish why he would not drink water. Girish told his father that he wanted to eat that cucumber. When Nilkamal asked the servant to buy a cucumber from the market, Girish refused to eat it and demanded the one in their garden. Nilkamal then asked the servant to pick it and give it to the boy. Girish's aunt protested, saying to Nilkamal: "You should not give too much license to this boy and yield to all his demands. We have decided to offer that cucumber to the Lord." Nilkamal: "Look, this little boy is crying to eat it. I hope the Lord will be pleased." Girish ate the cucumber and then slept peacefully.

When a river is obstructed, the current becomes stronger and the water flows more vigorously. Similarly, Girish's energy and enthusiasm grew more intense if his wishes were curbed or someone thwarted his plans. His inner being would immediately declare war against the external force, and he would have no rest until he had overcome it. This willpower made Girish a great man. Girish said: "If anyone forbade me to do anything that was bad or difficult, my nature forced me to accomplish that thing immediately."[6] For example, once a friend of Girish's, who later became a judge of the Calcutta High Court, said to him, "It is impossible to translate into Bengali the conversations of the witches of Shakespeare's *Macbeth*." Immediately Girish decided to translate the whole play.[7] It was in his nature to rise to any challenge. If anyone would say, "Don't go there; there is a ghost," he would immediately run to see the ghost. He was fearless, independent, and proud of his strength. No one could pressure or intimidate him into beginning work, or quitting once he had started. He used to say, "A beast can be tamed by a whip, but not a human being." His attitude was that if he did not enjoy his work, then why should he do it? He did what he considered right, without caring if others criticized him.[8]

Girish was sent to the local primary school and then to the Oriental Seminary. He stayed there for only two years because the teacher caned the students. Girish had an inquisitive mind. He could not stop asking questions until he had understood the subject. Girish's argumentative nature and apparent arrogance irritated his teacher, so he sometimes punished Girish with lashes or by twisting his ears. Later on Girish remarked: "If those teachers had made me understand with sweet words rather than with beatings, perhaps I could have learned many things at the school."[9]

After leaving the Oriental Seminary, Girish entered the Hare School, where he studied for two years. Then he went to the Hindu School and finally the Paikpara School.

Girish was born with great feeling and imagination. His grandmother introduced him to the rich heritage of India's epics and mythology. In the evenings she would recount to him some of those ancient stories, and he would listen with rapt attention. Once she described Krishna's departure from Vrindaban, one of the most moving scenes in the Bhagavata. Krishna's uncle, Akrura, was sent to bring him to Mathura, much to the despair of the cowherd boys and girls of Vrindaban. When Krishna sat in the chariot, the boys began to cry, pleading with him, "O Krishna, do not leave us!" The girls held the wheels of the chariot, and some of them grabbed the reins of the horses. But Akrura paid them no heed. He took Krishna away from Vrindaban, and thus the days of joy that Krishna's playmates had known in his company came to an end. Girish listened to the story intently, with tears in his eyes. He then asked, "Did Krishna ever return to Vrindaban?" "No," replied his grandmother. Girish asked the question three times and each time got the same answer. He then burst into tears and ran away. The story upset him so much that for the next several evenings he refused to listen to any more tales.[10]

Girish always attended recitals of the Ramayana and the Mahabharata that were held near his home. Like his mother, he was fond of listening to the devotional songs of the Vaishnava minstrels. Although he did not care for his school studies, he memorized Krittivasa's *Ramayana* and Kashiram's *Mahabharata* in Bengali verse. In this manner his love for literature developed in early childhood, and even in his old age he could recite many passages from those great epics. He had a prodigious memory and mastered the Bengali language.

Girish later recalled an incident that occurred when he was attending the Paikpara School: "Once while going to school, I saw an English boy of eight chasing a jackal in the field of Chitpur. Anxious, I yelled out to him: 'Wait, wait! What are you doing?' When the boy stopped, I went to him and asked, 'Are you not afraid of the jackal?' The boy boldly replied: 'Oh no, no! Seeing me, the jackal is frightened!' I was amazed by that little boy's bravery and fearlessness. We inculcate the fear of ghosts and hobgoblins in the minds of our children, using fear to control their activities and make them as harmless as jellyfish. Regarding education, see the difference between the English people and us."[11]

Raimani's first child was a daughter, the second was a son; she then had five daughters. Girish was the eighth child. Raimani had three more sons, then died while giving birth to a stillborn baby.* Girish recalled: "One day we four brothers [Girish, Kanailal, Atulkrishna, and Kshirod] were playing with our playmates near the house. Generally a servant would come before evening to pick us up, but that day he did not show up. I wondered why he was so late. However, after some time, he came and took us home. As soon as I entered the house I found everyone sorrowful and there was a great commotion. Soon I heard the sound of a conch shell and I was told that I had another sister. But no sooner had the sound stopped than everyone began to cry. My mother had died while giving birth to a stillborn girl."[12] Girish was eleven years old when his mother died.

The eldest son, Nityagopal, married when he was in his teens but lost his wife before he reached the age of twenty. He was so grief-stricken that he became mentally ill. When he recovered, his father arranged another marriage for him; but unfortunately Nityagopal died within a year and a half. Girish was then eight years old and he loved his brother dearly. Now he began to experience the harshness of life. His grief-stricken father became sick. The doctor advised Nilkamal to take a boat trip on the Ganges, in the hope that it would help him to recover his health. Nilkamal rented a boat and took the trip, accompanied by Girish and other family members.

When the boat had almost reached Navadwip, the birthplace of Chaitanya, it was suddenly caught in a crosscurrent. As it whirled around

---

*Nilkamal Ghosh *m.* Raimani
1. Krishnakishori
2. Nityagopal
3. Krishnakamini
4. Krishnavamini
5. Dakshinakali
6. Krishnarangini
7. Prasannakali
8. Girish Chandra
9. Kanailal
10. Atulkrishna
11. Kshirod Chandra
12. Daughter (*stillborn*)

m. Pramodini (*died, 1874*)
1. Son (*died, 2 mos.*)
2. Surendranath (Dani)
3. Sarojini
4. Son (*died, after birth*)

m. Suratkumari (*died, 1888*)
1. Daughter (*died, 3 yrs.*)
2. Daughter (*died, 3 yrs.*)
3. Son (*died, 3 yrs.*)

in imminent danger of sinking, Girish clung tightly to his father's hand. Luckily the boatman was able to navigate the boat to safety. When they reached the shore, Girish's father said to him: "Why did you hold my hand? Don't you know that my life is dearer to me than yours? If the boat had started to sink, I would have snatched my hand from you and tried to save my own life. You would have been forsaken." Although Nilkamal was very loving and indulgent towards Girish, he wanted the boy to learn to be independent and rely on none but God. Speaking of this incident many years later, Girish said, "My father's cruel words hurt me terribly, but I learned that there is no one but God to hold onto in times of danger."[13]

Three years after his mother's death, when Girish was fourteen years old, his father died of blood dysentery at the age of fifty-two. Krishnakishori, Girish's eldest sister, was a widow, so she became the caretaker for the family and guardian of her four younger brothers. She had received some education and was extremely intelligent. Fortunately, their father had left sufficient means for their maintenance, so his children did not suffer from financial problems.

The next year, in 1859, Krishnakishori arranged Girish's marriage to Pramodini, whose father was Navin Chandra Sarkar of Shyampukur, Calcutta. Girish was then fifteen, so Navin Chandra became his guardian. In 1860 Girish returned to the Oriental Seminary to complete his education but he found that the school's discipline was too confining. Furthermore, its teaching methods did not satisfy his thirst for knowledge. In 1862 he took his final examination from the Paikpara School but failed. He then left school without having earned a degree. Brajabihari Som, one of Girish's classmates and a neighbour, recognized his friend's talent and potential. He encouraged Girish to continue his studies on his own and thus become a self-made man. Girish followed Braja's advice and the two remained close friends throughout their lives. Braja later became a sub-judge.[14]

Girish was born in a transitional period of Indian history. In Calcutta particularly, Western education and culture were being thrust upon Indian society, challenging traditional Indian culture and its religions. Consequently, the youth of Girish's generation grew up in an atmosphere of doubt, atheism, and cultural chaos. During that period, anyone who could speak and write English well was highly honoured. Girish therefore decided to master the English language. After his wedding in 1859, he spent his wife's dowry to buy classic works of English literature. For the next year he studied day and night behind closed doors, seldom going out even for walks. His friends lost contact with him.

Early Life to Adulthood (1844–1879)   29

Girish was a voracious reader throughout his life. He later became a member of the Asiatic Society and other well-known libraries in Calcutta. His reading included the Ramayana, the Mahabharata, the Puranas, and Bengali literature. As a youth he had taken as his role model Ishwar Chandra Gupta, a well-known Bengali poet; he now began to write poetry and songs. Girish recalled: "Once I went to listen to the Bengali song tournament [half-akhrai] at Bhagavati Ganguli's house near our home. I found a tremendous crowd there; it was hard to get into the hall. Meanwhile a man in ordinary clothes entered and all the distinguished people received him with great respect. Amazed, I asked, 'Who is this man?' I was told that he was Ishwar Gupta, who had come to compose songs in the tournament."[15] As Girish observed the man's popularity, the desire to become a poet arose in his mind. Ishwar Gupta died when Girish was fifteen years old.

As a young man, Girish translated many English poems into Bengali. Navinkrishna Basu, Girish's maternal uncle, was a physician. He eventually attained a high position in the British government by virtue of his sharp intellect and vast erudition. Girish learned from him the techniques of debate. Further, he gradually became well versed in history, logic, philosophy, zoology, and English literature. He also studied science and medicine. He did not care for superficial knowledge. His capacity for deep penetration into any subject, plus his keen observation of human character and his wonderful imagination, are what later made him a great poet and playwright.

Grief again began to haunt Girish. His sister Krishnarangini died within a year and a half of his marriage to Pramodini. A few years later, when he was 23, his wife gave birth to a son who died within a month. The next year he lost another sister, Krishnakamini, and then his brother Kanailal, with whom he had been very close. Girish's second son, Surendra, was born the next year, 1868. Surendra later became the great actor known as Danibabu. Four years later, Girish's daughter, Sarojini, was born. The following year Pramodini gave birth to a child who unfortunately did not survive, then she herself became seriously ill with puerperal diarrhoea. Girish's youngest brother, Kshirod Chandra, died soon after, followed by their sister Krishnavamini a few months later. Girish's wife then died, despite having received excellent care. Girish was then 30 years old, and his heart was perforated with grief. He saw darkness all around — no hope, no love. As a result, his rebellious nature raised its head.

Now, with little stability either in his family or in society to guide him, Girish drifted into drunkenness and debauchery. He became the leader of a group of mischief-makers in his neighborhood, and within a few years he became a menace. Yet side by side with his perverse behaviour, Girish would raise money to help the poor obtain food and medicine, or he would arrange for the cremation of those in his community who had died. Later, after he had studied homeopathic medicine, he began treating people himself.

Girish was a great student who learned each subject thoroughly. His eldest brother-in-law, Brajanath Sarkar, taught himself homeopathy. He read many books on the subject, then began treating himself and his family members. Girish became very enthusiastic about homeopathy and regularly visited Brajanath after work. When Brajanath died, Girish inherited his books and his medicines; he began to treat poor people in his neighbourhood. Once a neighbour had cholera, for which Girish gave him medicine. He stayed with the patient till midnight, then asked the patient's family members to inform him of the man's condition in the morning. No one showed up. Concerned, Girish went to the patient's house at 8:00 a.m. to find that the man was doing much better. He was greatly relieved.[16]

Girish would often watch people on the street through a small opening in his door. One afternoon when the men of the neighbourhood were away at their jobs, he observed an astrologer, in the guise of a monk, collecting information from a maidservant about the women of the household where she worked. The charlatan then visited that house claiming to be a fortuneteller, and the simple, curious women came to him to have their palms read. Girish could not tolerate such hypocrisy. He broke a branch from a flowering tree in his courtyard, ran to the house, and began to attack the astrologer. He did not stop chasing him until the man had left the area.[17]

Once a man drowned in Girish's neighbour's pond, but the dead man's relatives were too afraid to remove the floating corpse from the pond. When the police came, they decided to hire someone to take the body out. Girish could not resist such a challenge. He jumped into the pond and carried the swollen and disfigured body to shore. He then called some of his young friends and they took the body to the hospital so that an autopsy could be performed. He did not return home until the man had been cremated.

Hindus believe that it is auspicious to die on the bank of the holy river Ganges, so at that time there were many hospices for the dying in Calcutta. One day Girish was walking along the Ganges when he heard a piteous cry coming from a nearby hospice. He entered the hut and found a dying man on a cot, all alone. The man was asking for a little water. Girish immediately brought some Ganges water and poured it into his mouth. He then ran back home to get some milk. Meanwhile, a thunderstorm came up with torrential rain. Night fell. At that time, there were no street lights, so the city was completely dark. When the rain let up, Girish walked back to the dying man's room, carrying a glass of milk. The only light came from flashes of lightning streaking across the sky. When he reached the hospice, he saw that the door was closed. There was no response to his calls, so he pushed open the door, and as he entered, a hard, cold hand fell on his shoulder. As lightning illuminated the room, he saw the man's body huddled behind the door. Perhaps in a delirium, he had somehow made his way to the door, where he died. Girish touched the man's hand and concluded that he had died long before he arrived. Pained at this turn of events, Girish returned home.[18]

The terrible grief that Girish had suffered caused him to lose faith in God, and from 1866 to 1873 he went through a long period as an atheist, which he announced to all. It was his nature to publicly proclaim whatever he believed. Some of his young neighbours wanted to test Girish's renunciation of religion, so on the eve of Durga Puja (the day on which the goddess Durga is worshipped) they placed an image of Her in Girish's courtyard. The next morning, the house was thrown into an uproar. When Girish saw the image, he realized that some of his neighbours had put it there. The mischief-makers assembled to see what would happen. Girish returned to his room and drank a bottle of wine. He then took an axe and ran back to hack the clay image into pieces. Nobody dared come near him. His eldest sister cried out, forbidding him to desecrate the image. But would Girish listen? He chopped the image into pieces and buried them in the backyard. That night Girish had a high fever and his sister was very concerned. She prayed to the Divine Mother to forgive her brother, and she made a special offering to Her.[19]

In 1876, when he was 32, Girish married Suratkumari, the eldest daughter of Biharilal Mitra. Six months after the wedding Girish became ill with a virulent type of cholera. His physicians gave up all hope for his recovery. Girish was lying on his bed in a semiconscious state, surrounded by weeping relatives, when he had a vision: A resplendent woman appeared before him, wearing a red-bordered cloth. Her face was full of compassion and love. She sat near him and, putting something in his mouth, said, "Please eat this prasad [sanctified food] and you will be cured." Girish slowly regained consciousness, and from that moment his recovery began. He later recounted this mysterious vision to his brother disciples and added, "Sixteen years later [in 1891], when I first went to Jayrambati to see the Holy Mother [Sarada Devi], I found to my surprise and delight that the woman who had saved my life with the holy prasad was none other than Holy Mother herself."[20]

Girish was extremely honest. Once he lost some property in a legal battle because he would not give false testimony. This led his friends and relatives to consider him foolish and to make fun of him. When Girish was a child he would not deviate from the truth, even if he knew his mother would punish him.[21] Even at an early age Girish realized the ugly side of the world, which Swami Vivekananda referred to in his poem *To a Friend*:

> Be as one slothful, mean, and vile,
> With honeyed tongue but poisoned heart,
> Empty of truth and self-enslaved —
> Then thou wilt find thy place on earth.[22]

Later Girish used to tell stories of his rebellious days. Once he told Swami Subodhananda: "A Muslim family lived near our house and their chickens would sometimes fly onto our property. Whenever I could catch one, I would ask my cook to prepare chicken curry. I would then enjoy that curry with my drink. My Muslim neighbour asked me not to kill his chickens, but I paid no heed. At last he filed a suit against me in court. I got a summons from a judge to appear in court. But I engaged a lawyer and dressed like a devout Vaishnava — covering my body with a chadar [shawl] imprinted with Krishna's name, a tilak [holy mark] on my forehead, and a rosary in my hand. In this manner I appeared before the judge with my lawyer. The judge said to me: 'This Muslim gentleman says that you have killed his chickens.' As soon as I heard the word 'chicken,' I put my index fingers into my ears and cried out, 'Radhe-Krishna, Radhe-Krishna.' Again the judge repeated the statement, and I said loudly, 'Say Radhe, Radhe.' Then my lawyer told the judge, 'Your Honour, my client is a devout Vaishnava who does not eat any nonvegetarian food and cannot even bear those words. This man is trying to harass my client by bringing this false allegation.' There was no evidence, so the judge dismissed the case. I then chanted, 'Hari bol, Hari bol [Say Hari's name].' 'Jai Radhe, Sri Radhe [Victory to Sri Radha].'"[23] Thus Girish escaped the lawsuit.

When Girish began acting, he would return home at night in a drunken state. Sometimes, on the way, he would be stopped by the police. A Muslim policeman would quite often harass him, search his pockets, and steal his money. Girish wanted to teach him a good lesson. One night he carried with him the head of a pig, covered with a chadar. When the policeman stopped him, he threw the pig's head at him. It is taboo for Muslims to touch a pig, so the policeman ran away and never harassed Girish again.[24]

Chapter 3

As an Accountant (1864–1879)

Nilkamal, Girish's father, introduced the double-entry accounting system to corporate offices in Calcutta. Navin Chandra Sarkar, Girish's first father-in-law, learned bookkeeping from Nilkamal and became an accountant for the Atkinson Tilton Company. When Girish was twenty years old, Navin Chandra decided to train Girish to be a bookkeeper so that he could support his family. Accordingly, he gave him a job at the office where he worked. Girish worked there for nearly eight years and became a favourite of Mr. Atkinson.

Girish recalled: "I was then working at Mr. Atkinson's office. His company had an indigo business. One day the workers spread indigo on the roof of the warehouse to dry. That night I noticed heavy clouds and signs of imminent rain. There would be a tremendous loss of money if the indigo got soaked, so I hired a carriage and rushed back to the office. I then gathered some porters with the help of the office guards and paid them double wages to carry the entire batch of indigo into the warehouse. Mr. Atkinson was greatly relieved when he heard what I had done. However, when I submitted the bill for the labourers, Mr. Bancroft, his partner, was not happy. He thought that I was overcharging the company. But Mr. Atkinson appreciated my action and supported me. He told me to take three handfuls of money from the safe as a reward. Mr. Bancroft remained silent."[1]

When these men had another difference of opinion later on, Mr. Atkinson sold his shares to his partner and returned home to America. But Mr. Bancroft had lost the cooperation and sympathy of his workers, so he could not carry on his business for long. The company was put up for sale by auction and all the equipment and furnishings were sold. While working there, Girish had translated *Macbeth* into Bengali, and he had kept the manuscript in his desk drawer.[2] At the time of the auction, Girish was away from the office caring for his sick wife, Pramodini.

That precious manuscript was lost when the furniture was sold. Many years later, Girish retranslated *Macbeth*, and it was staged at the Minerva Theatre in Calcutta.

Girish worked in various capacities for different businesses over a period of fifteen years. He had indomitable energy, which he increasingly devoted to the theatre. It became common practice for him to work all day at the office then go to the theatre in the evening to act in a play, returning home at three or four o'clock in the morning.

Pramodini became very ill after giving birth to their stillborn daughter. Girish then regretted that he had been so occupied with the theatre, acting, and his wayward lifestyle, and had not paid sufficient attention to his wife, so he now went to work during the day and stopped acting at night. He also engaged the best doctors for his wife, and began to take care of her himself as well. At night he would study, and sometimes become so absorbed in his books that he did not notice when dawn appeared. Pramodini's illness turned more serious and the doctors lost hope. She died on 24 December 1874, leaving a son and a daughter. Girish was 30 years old. At first Girish was not much perturbed by her death, but over time his heart became tormented with grief. He considered himself an atheist, so he could not take solace in God. And because the Atkinson Tilton Company had failed, he could not turn his mind to that work to ease the pain.

The English poet Alfred Tennyson wrote:

But, for the unquiet heart and brain,
A use in measured language lies;
The sad mechanic exercise
Like dull narcotics, numbing pain.

As drugs and alcohol temporarily distract a person from pain and anguish, so does the effort to write poetry. To escape his agonizing grief, the rebel Girish began to write poems. His compositions during this period were full of melancholy.

That man is indeed unfortunate who loses his mother in childhood, his father in boyhood, and his wife in early manhood. Girish had suffered all three losses, and in addition, his employer had gone out of business. A thick, dark cloud of despair hovered over him. As God created grief to subdue man, so man created wine to subdue grief. Girish began to drink heavily.

After a short period, Girish took a job with Fribarger & Company. But the creative mind of a genius is never idle. Whenever his office duties allowed, he continued to write poems expressing his grief. Some time after taking this job, he went on a business trip to Bhagalpur, in Central India. One day while he was there he went for a walk with some friends and, in a boisterous mood, jumped into a deep ravine. When he tried to climb out he found he was unable to do so. His friends then attempted to rescue him, but they failed. One of them commented: "Now we are in *real* trouble. You are an atheist, and yet no one can save you now but God. Let us all pray together." Girish found himself joining wholeheartedly in the prayer, and strangely, just then he found a way out of the ravine. After he was safe he said to his friends: "Today I have called on God out of fear. If I ever call on Him again, it will be out of love; otherwise I will not call on Him, even at the cost of my life."[3]

Girish stayed in Bhagalpur for five months. The day before he was to return to Calcutta, everything he had brought with him was stolen. Helpless, he went to a friend and asked for a loan of ten rupees. His friend replied: "I shall not loan you ten rupees, but I shall give you five." Girish accepted the money with tears, as his pride was very much wounded. When that friend came to Calcutta, Girish went to him to repay the money. The friend said that he had given him the money and did not expect it to be repaid. But Girish put the rupees in front of him and left.[4]

Girish resigned from Fribarger & Company because he did not like taking the many business trips that the job required. In 1876 he became a head clerk and cashier of the Indian League. He worked there for a year, and then joined the Parker Company as an accountant. At one point Mr. Parker introduced a calling bell in his office. One day he rang for Girish. Girish heard the bell but did not respond. Mr. Parker sent an attendant to ask Girish whether he had heard the bell. Girish simply replied, "No, I didn't hear the bell," and continued with his work. The attendant's report angered Mr. Parker, and he went to Girish himself. "I was calling you. Why didn't you respond?" he asked. "I did not hear the bell," answered Girish. "And even if I did, how would I know that the bell was calling me? The bell never said, 'Girish, Girish.'" Becoming serious, he said: "Listen, sir. So far I have spoken to you as a gentleman; now I shall be frank. I am not your servant or bearer. I am not accustomed to standing and sitting according to a bell. I feel it is humiliating for a subordinate to be summoned by a bell. And when its employees are humiliated, a company loses its reputation."

Mr. Parker, as an Englishman, knew the value of human dignity and realized his mistake. He and Girish later became close friends. At one point Girish helped him with his business when it was failing. The company survived and Mr. Parker gave Girish a significant raise, far beyond his expectations.[5] However, Girish could not continue working for the company because at this time he became heavily involved in acting, writing plays, and theatrical management. Eventually, in 1879, he resigned from the Parker Company and became the manager of the Great National Theatre. Thus Girish ended his career as an accountant to focus exclusively on the theatre.

Chapter 4

As an Actor (1867–1879)

Regarded as the founder of the modern theatre in Bengal, Girish supported several theatres in Calcutta by acting and writing plays over a period of almost half a century. The *Bengalee* magazine wrote about Girish in 1912: "He was not only the founder of the Bengalee stage, but also its preserver. About forty-five years ago he appeared in the inimitable role of 'Nimchand' [in *Sadhabār Ekadāshi*, a social drama by Dinabandhu Mitra] before a cultured audience including the author, and when he awoke the next morning he found himself famous as an actor."[1]

If we want to study the life of Girish, it is important to know some of the history of Bengali theatre and folk arts and their status prior to his advent. Calcutta was then the capital of British India. For their own recreation and amusement, the English established the Chowringhee Theatre in 1813 and the Sans Soucci Theatre in 1839. But Westerners mainly patronized those theatres. Only on rare occasions would Indian aristocrats such as Prince Dwarakanath Tagore and others go there. The Bengalis enjoyed their own traditional entertainments: *yatra* (open-air theatre), *panchali* (poems celebrating the glory of a deity that are set to music), and *kavigan* (a song tournament between two composers). Bengali dramatists learned from the English theatre how to change the backdrop between acts. Excited by this novelty, they introduced it to their performances.[2]

In 1831 Navin Chandra Basu of Shyambazar, Calcutta, a very wealthy man, arranged a dramatic performance based on Bhartachandra Roy's *Vidyasundar*. There was no change of backdrop as in Western theatres; instead, he set different scenes in different locations in his palace, his garden, and other places. For example, the parlour of the palace served as the court of King Virsingha; near the pond the hero, Vidyasundar, sat under a bakul tree; in the garden was a small cottage for the heroine, Malini; and the backyard was the scene of a cremation ground; then there was an artificial tunnel from one spot to another, and so on. As the actors and actresses moved from one scene to another, so did the audience. This was something that people had never seen before. In addition, courtesans acted in the female roles, which surprised the audience. However, some puritans did not approve of courtesans appearing onstage, so they wrote letters to newspapers protesting this practice.[3]

In 1832 Professor Horace Hayman Wilson of the Sanskrit College translated Bhavabhuti's *Uttara-ramacharitam* (a drama about Ramachandra) from Sanskrit into English, and his students performed the play at Prasanna Tagore's garden house. Gradually students from the Hindu College and the Oriental Seminary were trained by Western professors to enact various plays of Shakespeare. As these dramas were in English, most Bengalis could not enjoy them. At that time there were no good Bengali plays that could be performed for the masses.

In Bengal during the middle of the nineteenth century, upper-class brahmins were permitted to have more than one wife. To gain prestige, many parents were eager to marry their daughters into upper-caste families. But the dreadful custom of polygamy degraded Bengali society and brought tremendous pain to the women involved. To assist in eradicating this practice, Kalichandra Roychoudhury, a wealthy philanthropist of the Rangpur district in Bengal, advertised in the *Rangpur Bārtābāha* newspaper: "If any scholar or playwright can write a play under the title *Kulin-kula-sarvaswa* (The High-Caste Bridegroom) in Bengali within six months, he or she will be awarded fifty rupees." Pandit Ramnarayan Tarkaratna wrote the play and collected the money. His play was first performed in 1857 at Jairam Basak's house in Pathuriaghata, Calcutta.

At this time, the English had two theatres in Calcutta: the Theatre Royal and the Opera House. The American actress Mrs. G.B.W. Lewis rented the Theatre Royal and started an acting troupe. An excellent actress, she attracted many high-ranking British government officials to her performances. She was a close friend of Mr. Atkinson, a fellow American, and she visited his office quite often while Girish was an accountant there. Mrs. Lewis made a good deal of money, and she engaged Girish to keep her personal accounts. As she liked Girish, she invited him to her theatre, where his talent gradually became manifest while watching the Western plays performed there. Mrs. Lewis was amazed when she heard his opinions about the Western actors and actresses.[4]

From 1857 to 1867, wealthy Bengalis in Calcutta staged plays in their homes. Competing for social status, these families would arrange theatrical performances in their luxurious homes and invite friends and dignitaries to attend. For example, Kalidasa's *Shakuntala* was enacted at Chatu Babu's house in Simla; Bhattanarayan's *Beni-samhār* at Kaliprasanna Singha's home; Madhusudan Datta's *Ratnāvali* and *Sharmisthā* at the Belgachia garden house of the Paikpara Maharaja; *Bidhavā-bibāha* at Gopallal Mallick's house in Sinduriapati under the direction of Keshab Chandra Sen; *Mālabikā-agnimitra*, *Vidyāsundar*, *Mālati-madhav*, and *Rukmini-haran* in Maharaja Jatindranath Tagore's house at Pathuriaghata; *Nava-nātak* at Dwarakanath Tagore's house at Jorasanko; *Krishna-kumāri* at the palace of Shobhabazar.[5]

These theatre patrons spent a huge amount of money to provide the stage, backdrops, and costumes, and to hire experienced actors and actresses. Many people were anxious to see these plays, but the wealthy hosts were afraid that crowds would cause problems at the performances, so they distributed free tickets to their relatives, friends, admirers, and distinguished guests. Middle-class play-lovers were excluded. Moreover, anyone who tried to sneak into the theatre hall was humiliated by the guards and thrown out. Girish told a story about how one of his neighbours procured a ticket for a play being performed at Jatindranath Tagore's house in Pathuriaghata. He showed that ticket to all the neighbours and surprised them by describing how artfully he had obtained it.

Girish came from a middle-class family and did not have much money, so he could not attend the plays performed in the houses of those aristocrats. Thus he developed an intense desire to start a public theatre. Eventually he found the opportunity to fulfill his wish through his neighbour Nagendra Nath Bandyopadhyay, who started a concert party in his house. When Girish expressed his idea of opening a public theatre to Nagendra, he responded enthusiastically.

It is very expensive to establish a theatre because it requires a stage, costumes, backdrops for the different scenes of plays, and so on. But *yatra* (open-air theatre) does not need a permanent stage or any backdrops. So in 1867 Girish, Nagendra Nath Bandyopadhyay, Dharmadas Sur, Radhamadhav Kar, and some other friends established an amateur yatra party in Baghbazar and performed *Sharmisthā*, a play by Michael Madhusudan Datta. As they needed some songs for that play, they went to the famous composer Priyamadhav Basu Mallick. But, despite repeated requests, he refused to provide any songs. Girish was disgusted. He said to his friend Umesh Chandra Choudhury: "Why so much hassle? Come, let us compose some songs." This was the first time Girish composed songs for a play — and he soon became famous for his compositions.

Sharmisthā was performed off and on in Baghbazar for almost a year. One day Girish said to Nagendra: "Look, we have been successful with this yatra. Now let us establish a theatre." Nagendra replied: "We need backdrops and expensive costumes. Where shall we get the money?" Girish came up with an idea: He proposed that they enact *Sadhabār Ekādashi*. This play required only ordinary clothes, not expensive costumes. And as for backdrops, they could find some cloth and paint backdrops themselves. Girish's passion inspired his young friends. Since he was the oldest among the group, they made him their leader and director of the party. Girish founded the Baghbazar Amateur Theatre group, which is considered the first public theatre in Bengal. He then recruited actors and actresses who had performed in *Sharmisthā* and started holding rehearsals at Arun Haldar's house in Baghbazar. At this time he had a full-time job at the Atkinson Company and was engaged in rehearsing from evening to midnight. He also composed a few songs to introduce the play. Then Ardhendu Sekhar Mustafi, a famous actor, joined Girish in the venture.

During Durga Puja in October 1869, the group performed *Sadhabār Ekādashi* in Prankrishna Haldar's house at Baghbazar. In this drama Girish played the role of Nimchand, a drunkard. Girish's portrayal was so realistic that through this role he first made a name for himself as an actor. He said to the stage manager before the performance: "I cannot portray a drunkard if I have to drink coloured water from a bottle onstage. I want genuine wine." The result was that even the writer of the play was overwhelmed by Girish's performance. He told Girish, "This role seems to have been written for you, and without you the play would not be a success."[6] The role of Nimchand involved reciting several long passages from English literature, which was not possible for an ordinary Bengali actor. Girish was fluent in English and the audience was spellbound listening to his British diction.[7]

At that time the young people of Bengal were blindly imitating Western culture, etiquette, language, and habits. They would quote Lord Byron, the celebrated English poet:

"Man being reasonable must get drunk.
The best of life is but intoxication."
"O pleasure, you are indeed a pleasant thing."

Young people believed that anyone who did not drink alcohol was uncivilized and uneducated. Drinking wine and enjoying the pleasures of the senses became their goal. Girish also fell victim to this Western influence.

But people of the older generation were shocked and they tried to save their children from this hedonism. The poet Pyarimohan Kaviraj wrote:

Don't drink, don't drink!

Don't touch, don't touch!
Wine is evil, a killer:
Listen to me, O dear brother.[8]

When the first two cantos of *Childe Harold's Pilgrimage* were published, Byron wrote in his memoir, "I awoke one morning and found myself famous."[9] Similarly, Girish became a celebrity overnight after the first performance of *Sadhabār Ekādashi*. After its initial success in Baghbazar, the play was performed in different venues throughout Calcutta. Observing the success of *Sadhabār Ekādashi*, some critics told Girish, "It is easy to act while listening to the prompter hiding behind the screen in a theatre, but it is not so easy in a yatra, where the stage is in the middle and the audience is seated all around it." This agitated Girish, and he took it as a challenge. He told his critics that he would produce a yatra ready for performance in eight days. Whenever he was challenged, his creative faculty prevailed. It was not his nature to do anything half-heartedly. He immediately consulted with his friends and decided to perform a yatra based on *Ushāharan* by Radhanath Mitra. That same night, he composed 26 songs for the play. He also hired two famous singers, a musician, and a popular actor. Rehearsals were held day and night. As promised, on the day of Jagadhatri Puja in 1869, the yatra was performed with great enthusiasm at Nagendra Bandyopadhyay's house in Baghbazar.[10]

In 1871, Girish and his party changed the name of their theatre company to the National Theatre and staged Dinabandhu Mitra's *Lilāvati* with great éclat. A permanent stage was built at Rajendranath Pal's house in Shyambazar; and Dharmadas Sur painted the backdrops with the help of an English sailor. Girish arranged to buy appropriate costumes for the play, and he himself was the director. He also performed in the role of Lalit, the main character. Although men acted in the female roles, it was a hit on the first night. Dr. Mahendralal Sarkar, Dinabandhu Mitra, and many other distinguished people were present. After the performance, Dinabandhu said to Girish: "I did not know that one could read my poem in such a magnificent way. Please accept my compliments at least."[11] *Lilavati* continued for five nights, but was interrupted by rain. The last performance was held during Durga Puja at Mathura Mohan Biswas's house at Shyambazar.[12]

On 7 December 1872 the National Theatre was officially inaugurated with Dinabandhu Mitra's *Nildarpan*. This play dramatized the exploitation of Indians by British indigo merchants. For this play tickets were sold to the public. At first Girish was against this, but he told his friends that he had no objection to the sale of tickets, provided the theatre was as well equipped as other professional companies. The National Theatre next staged Michael Madhusudan Datta's *Krishnakumāri*, a historical play about a Rajput princess. Girish's friends asked him to play King Bhimsingha, the main role. He agreed on the condition that he would not take any money and that his name would not be printed in the program. So "A distinguished amateur" was printed next to the name of his character. *Krishnakumāri* was premiered on 22 February 1873; Michael Madhusudan Datta was present on opening night. After the play he warmly greeted Girish and praised his acting. Raja Chandranath Roy Bahadur of Natore was so impressed with Girish's performance that he presented Girish with a royal costume and a sword.[13]

When Girish acted in any role, he would use his powerful imagination, intense concentration, and deep insight to identify with the character. As a result, the audience witnessed a living character on the stage. This God-given faculty made Girish a genius as an actor and a playwright, as well as a spiritual seeker. Abinash Gangopadhyay, Girish's biographer and secretary, commented on Girish's performance as Bhimsingha in the drama *Krishnakumāri*: "Losing his only daughter, Krishnakumari, Maharaja Bhimsingha became mad with grief. He shouted his enemy's name thrice: 'Mansingha — Mansingha — Mansingha!' When he uttered the name 'Mansingha' the first time, it was as if he was visualizing a shadow of his enemy; the second time, a luminous form; and the third time, a living form. Immediately he took his sword from its scabbard, and shouted, 'I shall destroy you right now!' Some spectators in the first row were so overwhelmed with fear that they fell off their chairs, and one lost consciousness."[14]

In Calcutta on 3 February 1873, Thomas George Baring, Earl of Northbrook and the Governor General of India, laid the foundation stone for a hospital. Dr. MacNamara then requested the local leaders to raise money to complete the construction. In response, Girish and his friends staged *Nildarpan* by Dinabandhu Mitra at Town Hall on 29 March 1873. This benefit performance raised 700 rupees for the hospital. Girish acted in the role of Mr. I.I. Wood, and his speech, movements, and gestures appeared to be those of a European.

On 31 March 1873, an art critic wrote in *The Englishman*: "On Saturday night the members of the Calcutta National Theatre performed in the Town Hall the play of 'Nil Darpan,' for the benefit of the Native Hospital. It is a great pity that so short a notice was given, as, on that account, very few Europeans were present. However, the natives mustered very strongly on the occasion and testified by their repeated plaudits how much they enjoyed the performance. The acting was exceedingly good throughout.

We hope the Management will give another performance shortly."[15]

On 10 May 1873, the National Theatre was about to perform a play based on Bankim Chandra Chattopadhyay's famous novel *Kapālkundalā* at Raja Radhakanta Dev's house in Calcutta. The audience filled the hall and the performers were ready to go onstage; but the manuscript of the play was missing. It was an embarrassing moment. The lead actors rushed to their director, Girish, and begged him to save the situation. Girish asked someone to bring a copy of *Kapālkundalā* from Raja's library. When it arrived, he told the cast members: "Have no fear. I shall hide in the wings and read you the parts. Go to the stage now." Girish's biographer wrote: "*Kapālkundalā* was staged smoothly and the audience did not realize the problem behind the scenes. Only Girish could have created and prompted the dialogue of the entire play."[16]

Girish was involved in several theatres throughout Calcutta. Sharat Chandra Ghosh, who established the Bengal Theatre, formed a committee with prominent people of Calcutta such as Ishwar Chandra Vidyasagar, Michael Madhusudan Datta, Umesh Chandra Datta, Pandit Satyavrata Samasrami, and others for setting up a public theatre. Vidyasagar had seen dramas such as *Bidhavā Bibāha* (Widow-Marriage) and *Nava Natak* (New Drama), and realized that plays like these could help eradicate social superstitions. When Sharat began to build the structure that would house the Bengal Theatre, Madhusudan started writing a play for it entitled *Māyākānan* (A Garden of Maya). But when Sharat tried to find some boys to play the female roles, Madhusudan told him: "The play will not be natural if boys act in the female roles. These parts should be played by women." At that time respectable women did not work in the theatre. After a long debate, the actors agreed to appear onstage with actresses whom they presumed would be courtesans. Vidyasagar, however, disapproved of this and left the committee. Shortly after Madhusudan finished the drama, he fell ill. He sold the copyright for *Māyākānan* to Sharat for 500 rupees, then died on 29 June 1873. When the Bengal Theatre opened on 16 August 1873, it presented Madhusudan's *Sharmisthā*, a play based on a love story from the Mahabharata. On 20 December 1873 the Bengal Theatre opened *Durgeshnandini*, a drama based on Bankim Chandra Chattopadhyay's book of the same name. Sharat acted in the role of Prince Jagat Singha and captivated the audience by riding a horse onstage.[17]

Bhuban Mohan Niyogi, a wealthy man of Calcutta, went to see a play in the Bengal Theatre, but he could not get a ticket because the house was full. He then decided to start his own theatre and consulted with some of his friends who were connected with the business. On 31 December

1873, they inaugurated the Great National Theatre by opening the play *Kāmya-kānan* (a forest of desire). Unfortunately, the gaslights in front of the stage started a fire on opening night. The audience ran out and the play was cancelled. Discouraged, the theatre owner and actors sought help from Girish. Girish wrote a play based on Bankim's *Mrinālini*, and when it opened on 14 February 1874, he performed the role of Pashupati.[18] He took no money for his work. Girish was a true worshipper of Nataraj Shiva, the presiding deity of the stage. The theatre was his altar; acting was his worship; and he gave joy to the devotees of Nataraj.

In 1875 and 1876 Girish was plunged into grief by several deaths in his family, including his first wife, and other troubles (see Chapter 2, p. 29). Finally, at the request of his relatives and friends, he married again and this lifted his spirits. During this period Girish withdrew from acting and stopped writing plays.

When the Prince of Wales (later Edward VII) visited Calcutta in 1876, Jagadananda Mukhopadhyay, a lawyer of the Calcutta High Court, invited the prince to his home and held a special Hindu reception in his honour. This created a tremendous uproar in Calcutta. Upendranath Das wrote a satire about Jagadananda called *Gajadananda*, and Girish wrote a few songs for it. On 19 February 1876, this play was performed at the Great National Theatre. British officials were upset because it caricatured a loyal subject of the empire and, indirectly, it criticized the government. They banned its performance and introduced the Dramatic Performance Control Bill on 25 March 1876, which states: "That whenever the Government was of the opinion that any dramatic performance was scandalous or defamatory, or likely to excite feelings of dissatisfaction towards the Government or likely to cause pain to any private party in its performance, or was otherwise prejudicial to the interests of the public, the Government might prohibit such performances."[19] This law caused many problems for the Bengali stage, and it restricted playwrights' freedom. Girish experienced the negative impact of this law when three of his plays were banned by the British.

In July 1877 Girish leased the Great National Theatre from its owner, Bhuban Mohan Niyogi, and changed its name to the National Theatre. He wrote a play based on *Meghnād-badh*, a poetical work of Michael Madhusudan Datta that describes the death of Meghnad, a heroic son of Ravana. Girish performed in the roles of Rama and Meghnad. The famous actress Binodini acted in the part of Pramila, wife of Meghnad. (See Chapter 15 for more on Binodini.) This play became a hit.[20]

Girish then wrote a play based on *Palāsir Yuddha*, a poetical work by Navin Chandra Sen about the Battle of Palāsi, in which the British

National Theatre, Beadon Street, Calcutta, 1873

defeated the Muslim ruler Siraj-ud-Daulla. Girish performed the role of Lord Clive and Binodini played the Queen of England. This play had a very long run. Navin Chandra Sen came to Calcutta to attend a performance. He was very pleased by Girish's interpretation, and the two men became lifelong friends.[21]

In the fall of 1877 Girish's first two musical dramas — *Āgamani* and *Akālbodhan* — were performed in the National Theatre. Both musicals are connected with the worship of Durga. Girish described in *Āgamani* Uma's visit to her parents, and in *Akālbodhan* Rama's worship of Durga. *Āgamani* was Girish's first completely original production, and he released it under the pen name Mukutacharan Mitra.[22]

When the National Theatre had become well established under Girish's leadership, an important decision was made. His brother Atulkrishna Ghosh was a lawyer, and he was apprehensive that Girish would be held responsible if the theatre failed or if it fell into debt. Because they were living as a joint family, Atulkrishna would also be responsible for the debt. For that reason, he asked his brother to either give up responsibility for the theatre or legally separate himself from the household. Girish gave up legal and financial responsibility for the theatre, and his brother-in-law Dwarakanath Deb assumed the building's lease.[23]

In January 1878 Kedarnath Chaudhury took over the lease from Dwarakanath and asked Girish to write plays based on Bankim Chandra Chattopadhyay's *Bishabriksha* (a social drama) and *Durgeshnandini* (a historical drama). Girish did so, and acted in the roles of Chandrasekhar and Jagat Singha, respectively. Later several other people leased the National Theatre, but they were not successful. In 1879 Bhuban Mohan, the theatre owner, went deeply into debt, so the National Theater was sold at auction. Pratapchand Jahuri bought it, then asked Girish to resign from his accounting job and accept a full-time job in his theatre. He offered Girish an initial 100 rupees per month, with the idea that the salary would increase as the theatre's profits improved. Observing Pratap's sincerity, enthusiasm, and practical business knowledge, Girish accepted his offer to become the manager and director of the National Theatre. Girish was then making 150 rupees per month at the Parker Company. When he went to Mr. Parker with his letter of resignation, the latter was reluctant to accept it. He was very fond of Girish and asked him to continue in both jobs. He even suggested that Girish come into the office at noon, but Girish did not relent. Mr. Parker finally accepted his resignation and gave him a diamond ring as a parting gift.

Girish thinking of an acting plot

Girish in his late forties

Chapter 5

As a Playwright and Actor
(1880–1884)

*E*verything that happens is part of God's great plan, and it became evident that He had a special plan for Girish. Girish was endowed with great talent and a powerful creative faculty, a strong body and tremendous energy, an indomitable mind and willpower, passion as well as a gigantic intellect. In the beginning, most people misunderstand genius, and they are astonished when they see it shining forth like a blazing fire. There is a saying: "Genius finds its own road and carries its own lamp."

At the age of 36, Girish began a new chapter in his life when Pratapchand Jahuri hired him to manage the National Theatre. Girish was made for his role as theatre manager, playwright, director, and actor. He was not born to be an accountant and lead an ordinary life. Jahuri recognized Girish's talent and gave him complete freedom, believing that by doing so his theatre would flourish. Girish immediately brought in the actors and actresses whom he had already worked with, as well as some new performers, and formed a strong and stable group. He sought out good plays for the stage and began by selecting *Hamir*, a historical drama. The playwright, Surendra Nath Majumdar, had based it on James Todd's *Rajasthan*, but he died shortly after completing it. Girish acquired the manuscript from Surendra's brother, Devendra, who later became his secretary. Girish added four songs to this drama and had backdrops and costumes made according to his specifications. *Hamir* opened on 1 January 1881, with Girish acting in the title role. It was received well but did not run long, as Surendra had been more a poet than a playwright.[1]

Plays written by Dinabandhu Mitra, Madhusudan Datta, and Bankim Chandra Chattopadhyay soon became well known to the Calcutta audience through the National Theatre. Girish offered prizes to encourage powerful writers to write new plays for the theatre. Meanwhile, he wrote two short musical dramas, *Māyātaru* (A Mystical Tree) and *Mohini Pratimā* (An Image of Love), and also a comedy, *Alādin*. *Māyātaru* was first performed on 22 January 1881 and *Mohini Pratimā* and *Alādin* opened on 16 April 1881. When Girish was unable to find a suitable drama, he wrote his first serious play *Ānanda Raho* (Be Happy), a historical-cum-mystical drama that opened on 21 May 1881. He acted in the main role of Vetal, a man who is always happy, unselfish, and benevolent. Girish incorporated some of his Western ideas into this play, but the Bengali critics did not give it good reviews.[2]

When Girish found that religious-minded Bengalis were not satisfied with historical dramas, he began to write plays based on the Hindu epics and the puranas. He wrote *Ravan-badh* (The Death of Ravana), based on the Ramayana, in irregular blank verse. Girish performed the role of Rama while the actress Binodini played Sita. This play touched the religious sentiments of the audience and successfully premiered on 30 July 1881.[3] Michael Madhusudan Datta had written *Meghnad-badh kāvya* in regular blank verse: fourteen letters in each line — but Girish wrote *Ravan-badh* in irregular blank verse.

Girish's writing career began when he was 36 and continued for thirty years. He was a prodigious writer, producing seventy-nine theatrical works, including dramas, satires, and musicals. In addition, he wrote many short stories, essays, novels, poems, and songs. His dramas dealt primarily with religious, social, historical, mythological, and patriotic subjects. His innovative spirit had a lasting effect on theatre in Bengal, and this is primarily why he became known as the Father of the Bengali stage. He avoided the traditional flowery language of the earlier theatre because of its heaviness and artificiality, and continued to use irregular blank verse in his dramas. This eventually became known as "Gairishi Chhanda," or Girish's metre.[4] Girish faced tremendous criticism from some orthodox scholars for his use of irregular blank verse, but others defended him. A genius is always misunderstood. But Dwijendra Nath Tagore supported him in *Bharati* magazine, saying: "We are in favour of Girish's new style of blank verse. His unrhymed metre is both free and sweet. We prefer the rhyme of the heart rather than the rhyme of prosody. Girish has helped us to achieve the goal."[5]

Girish realized that many of his actors and actresses were not highly educated, so he created the dialogue in his plays in such a way that his performers could easily pronounce the words and express them freely. The language of his plays is therefore natural, forceful, colloquial, poetic,

Girish dictating a drama to Devendra Nath Majumdar

and understandable. He felt that action and interaction comprise the life force of drama, and the spirit of a play is carried along by its language.[6]

Girish's mind worked so fast and so prodigiously that he required secretaries to take down his words; he could not write quickly enough himself. Absorbed in the flow of ideas, he would pace back and forth in his room and dictate all the dialogue for his plays in a loud voice, as if he were performing each role himself. His secretary always kept three pencils ready at hand; he could not use a pen and inkpot because there was never enough time to dip the pen into the pot. One time a secretary could not keep up with Girish's dictation and asked him to repeat what he had just said. This upset Girish because it interrupted his mood. He said: "Look, you just did great harm. I don't remember what I said, and now I don't know what I am going to say. If you miss any words, please put down dots and I shall fill them in later. It may not be exactly what I had said, but what I say afterwards would be correct."[7]

Amritalal Basu, Kedarnath Chaudhury, Amritalal Mitra, Devendra Nath Majumdar, and Devendra Nath Basu were among the secretaries who took dictation from Girish and helped him to record many of his theatrical works. Abinash Chandra Gangopadhyay was Girish's secretary for the last fifteen years of his life. Abinash was closely associated with Girish, so he was able to write an authentic biography of him.[8]

There are many stories about Girish's talent for writing. It is said that he could compose a drama in a couple of days. *Sitār Vanabāsh* (The Banishment of Sita) was written in one night.[9] Girish also wrote twenty-six songs for *Sadhabār Ekādashi* in one night.[10] Sister Devamata wrote in *Days in an Indian Monastery,* "One of the greatest, a six-act drama entitled *Vilwamangal the Saint,* was written in twenty-eight hours of uninterrupted labour."[11] Swami Subodhananda said, "We have seen Girish dictating three different dramas to three secretaries, one after another."[12] Girish dramatized *Kapālkundalā,* a famous novel by Bankim Chandra Chattopadhyay, in one night by dictating it to four secretaries.[13] When Girish was writing dramas based on the puranas or the epics for the National Theatre, he did not spend more than a week on each one. Abinash wrote: "Girish was an actor and at the same time a playwright. I observed that when he would dictate the dialogue of the various men and women characters, his voice would change accordingly, as if he were acting in all the roles. For this reason, the actors and actresses would feel at ease acting in Girish's dramas."[14]

In the 1880s religious dramas based on the epics and the puranas were very popular in Bengal. Having received favourable responses from audiences and critics alike, Girish wrote his third drama based on the Ramayana, *Sitār Vanabāsh* (The Banishment of Sita). He acted in the role of Rama, and Binodini and Kusumkumari acted in the roles of Lava and Kusha (Rama's sons), respectively. At that time a screen separated the women's seats from the men's. Many women flocked to see this play, and the theatre owner had to add more seats to their side of the theatre to accommodate them. Girish dedicated *Sitār Vanabāsh* to Ishwar Chandra

Vidyasagar. He showed his humility by dedicating most of his theatrical works to various prominent Bengalis and to his close friends and admirers.

Girish based his next drama, *Abhimanyu-badh* (The Death of Abhimanyu), on the Mahabharata. The hero Abhimanyu, one of Arjuna's sons, was attacked by seven warriors during the Mahabharata war and unjustly killed. According to the rules of war, any fight must be one-to-one. Girish portrayed Abhimanyu's character in a superb way — showing his love for his wife, Uttara, his affection for his mother, Subhadra, and his heroic attitude towards his enemies.

Girish then wrote *Lakshman-Varjan* (The Forsaking of Lakshman) based on a story in the Ramayana. It is a sad story about how Rama had to abandon his loving brother Lakshman. Girish acted in the role of Rama. The play debuted on 31 December 1881. Girish then wrote *Sitār Vibāha* (Sita's Marriage), which opened on 11 March 1882. In this Girish played the role of the sage Viswamitra. Girish's *Ramer Vanabāsh* (Exile of Rama) and *Sita-haran* (Abduction of Sita), also based on stories from the Ramayana, were performed on 15 April and 22 July 1882 respectively. Girish did not act in these two dramas, but Binodini played Kaikeyi in the former and Sita in the latter.

At this time Girish started to write a play based on *Meghnad-badh* (The Death of Meghnad). Michael Madhusudan Datta had written a long poem about Meghnad, the heroic son of Ravana, based on the Ramayana. Girish remarked: "Michael did not portray Rama's character well. While writing the plays based on the puranas and epics, I planned to write a play on *Meghnad-badh*. After writing a few pages, I gave up the idea, thinking that it would be in competition with Michael Madhusudan, whom I consider to be my literary guru."[15]

Girish was the manager of the National Theatre for two years, and during that period he wrote nine dramas and six musicals. He staged a new play almost every two months because theatregoers did not want to buy tickets for the same play twice. Readers may wonder how one can write a play and open it after two months of rehearsal. This was only possible for Girish because he had such God-given talent and willpower. Abinash, his biographer and secretary, marveled at how quickly he could work. This was a glorious period for the National Theatre. Pratapchand Jahuri, the owner, provided a wonderful stage with proper backdrops and gorgeous costumes, and Girish attracted excellent actors and actresses. He then trained them, and he also acted himself. Because Girish was well known, people flocked to see his plays in the National Theatre.

As a Playwright and Actor (1880–1884)

In 1933 Aparesh Chandra Mukhopadhyay wrote in his book *Rangalaye Tirish Vatsar* (Thirty Years Onstage): "The Bengali theatres were dependent on playwrights who could not supply enough plays to meet the demand. As a result the theatres could not stand firmly on their own feet. The theatres survived by using a few plays of Dinabandhu and sometimes transforming Bankim Chandra's novels into plays. Just as during a famine people eat bad food or rubbish — whatever is available — indiscriminately, so theatres lost their vitality by repeatedly staging the few available plays. Girish, the favourite son of the goddess of theatre, brought life to the dying Bengali stage. From the time he appeared, people realized that a theatre cannot thrive only on good acting; it also needs well-written plays. Good plays are the main food and life force of a theatre. Girish was behind several theatres in Bengal and saved them by feeding the audience nourishing and good food, that is, by writing wonderful plays. His original, imaginative, and creative ideas constantly brought a current of joy to the audience. Because of this, Girish became known as the 'Father of the Native Stage', and not its uncle. The stage had been running as if it had no guardian; it was shaky and near collapse. The immortal nectar that has kept the Bengali stage alive for the last fifty years was actually brought by Girish. So he alone should be glorified as the Father of the Bengali Stage."[16]

Chapter 6

As a Playwright and Actor
(1885–1912)

Girish was well versed in both Western and Indian dramatic forms. The classical Western drama has five parts: 1. Protasis, in which the characters are introduced and the arguments are explained; 2. Epitasis, in which the main action is developed; 3. Catastasis, the climax; 4. Periteteia, a sudden reversal of circumstances in a drama; 5. Catastrophe, the final event (death in a tragedy, or a marriage in a comedy).

According to ancient Indian tradition, a drama consists of five acts or stages: 1. A playwright begins a story or an event. 2. He introduces a situation that complicates or opposes the main story. 3. He creates a conflict between the main story or event and the opposing situation. 4. He sets up all obstacles to the plot and then clears them. 5. He shows the result, which may be tragic or comic.

Each act should cover an event occurring during only one day, and between any two acts there should not be a time difference of more than a year. There are nine kinds of *rasa* (sentiment or mood) in Indian drama: *sringara*, erotic; *vira*, heroic; *karuna*, pathetic; *raudra*, angry; *adbhuta*, astonishing; *bhayanaka*, terrible or dreadful; *bibhatsa*, monstrous; *hasya*, humorous; *shanta*, peaceful or calm. These rasas play against each other in a drama. For example, the erotic sentiment may be counteracted by the heroic, pathetic, angry, dreadful, or monstrous sentiments; the heroic mood may be counteracted by the dreadful or calm sentiments; and the pathetic mood may be opposed by the erotic or humorous sentiments.

In the plays of Shakespeare we get a glimpse of European society during the author's time. We see the scenes of fighting and murdering for power in *Hamlet, Macbeth, Othello, The Merchant of Venice,* and *Romeo and Juliet*. But in Indian Sanskrit dramas, we do not see this kind of fighting and killing. It seems that the ancient playwrights did not want to portray those terrible aspects of Indian society.

As a Playwright and Actor (1885–1912)

Girish was associated at various times with almost all of the theatres in Calcutta from 1869 to 1912. It is not possible to give details for all his plays, his activities in different theatres, and his many performances onstage. Instead, this chapter presents highlights from his career.

Girish based most of his dramas on stories from the Ramayana, the Mahabharata, and the Puranas, or the lives of the saints, historical events, or social issues. He tried to use the characters in his plays to inspire his audience with higher ideals. Girish said: "A playwright must be inspired by his national sentiment before writing a drama. He should deeply imprint in his mind the national character and environment; national actors and actresses; national religious, social, and political conditions; and the current national sentiment of the people. The Hindus from their childhood know the characters of Rama, Krishna, Bhishma, Arjuna, Bhima, and so on, and they appreciate the high ideals of those heroes. As a heroic character is cherished by a bellicose heroic nation, so a patient, self-sacrificing, religious character occupies the Hindu heart. The hearts of Hindus are saturated with religious sentiments, so one should write plays based on religion. Foreigners invaded India by the sword but could not destroy the religious sentiments in their hearts."[1]

Not only was Girish a playwright, he was also a talented poet. Some poets express ideas through words and sound and some through words and images. Girish belonged to the second group. Once Mahendra Datta asked him: "In *Buddhadev-Charit*, how did you create such vivid dialogue for Buddha when he was practising austerities under a tree? Your description differs from the Buddhist literature."

Girish replied: "Look, I was thinking of that scene for a few days. Suddenly one day I visualized an emaciated young man sitting under a tree. He was gasping, as if he were dying. His eyes were sunken into their sockets; his bones were covered only by skin. I was frightened seeing him. Then I noticed that the young man's lips had begun to move and he started speaking very faintly. Immediately I began to dictate those words and my secretary wrote them down."[2]

This is the dialogue that Girish is referring to Buddha: "My head is reeling, as if I shall soon die. I have not yet attained the Truth, and I have not been able to mitigate the sufferings of humanity. As long as I have this body, I shall seek the Truth. A flower blooms, spreads its fragrance all around, and then fades away. Does the flower have any fear of death? The tall trees invite the wind with their raised heads and sway their limbs out of joy; they are not afraid of death. I get this knowledge from the tree. Heat, cold, wind, and water are teaching me to endure everything. They always remain the same and do not forget to fulfill their respective duties. Then why should I forget my duty? I will be absorbed in deep meditation again. I have given up all other attachments. Why should I be attached to life?"[3]

Girish remarked that he would not have been able to describe Buddha's condition so vividly without having visualized that scene. When Girish was absorbed in any idea, he would lose outer consciousness. While giving dictation he could not repeat anything he had previously said because those ideas passed out of his mind as quickly as the pictures in a movie reel. For that reason, Girish could not write the words down himself: His secretaries had to take his dictation very quickly.

Buddhadev-Charit was performed at the Star Theatre (Beadon Street) on 19 September 1885, and it was very successful. A wealthy landlord named Nandalal Basu saw *Buddhadev-Charit* before Durga Puja, and he was so inspired by Buddha's nonviolence that he released all of the goats that he had bought to sacrifice during Durga Puja. From that year on he no longer carried out animal sacrifice in his home.[4]

A famous physician who was grief-stricken over his son's death also went to see *Buddhadev-Charit*. In this play Girish portrayed the story of a woman who had lost her son and came to Buddha to beg for the return of her son's life. Buddha asked her to bring him some black mustard seeds from a home where no one had died. When the woman could not find any such home, Buddha told her: "Now you see, no one can escape from the jaws of death." The woman replied: "Father, I shall subdue the grief of my heart as you advise, but my son was the joy of my eyes." The physician in the audience burst into tears when he heard that line "My son was the joy of my eyes." After the performance he went to Girish and said: "Sir, how do you know the hidden feelings of our heart? My friends and relatives have tried to console me again and again; they have explained how death is inevitable, but no one could understand how I feel. You have expressed it in that line, 'My son was the joy of my eyes.'"

Girish dedicated *Buddhadev-Charit* to Sir Edwin Arnold because he based the play in part on *The Light of Asia*. Sir Edwin came at this time to Calcutta, saw Girish's play, and profusely praised Girish's talent, effort, enthusiasm, and experience. Chapter 18 describes how Ramakrishna went into samadhi listening to a song from *Buddhadev-Charit*,* and Chapter 17 discusses how Swami Vivekananda was inspired by that same song.

Girish's satire *Bellik Bāzār* opened at the Star Theatre on 24 December 1886. He wrote it to mock the wayward, perverted, and self-serving people

---

* We moan for rest, alas! But rest we can never find; We know not whence we come, nor where we float away....

of Calcutta. This drama created a great stir. A critic named Akshay Sarkar wrote in the magazine *Navabibhākar Sādhārani*: "*Bellik Bāzār* exposes the perversity of our society. The acting was outstanding and true to life. The love for fun and frolic has entered our social system and degraded our moral values. This satire demonstrates how this perverted mentality is destroying our social norms and civility."[5]

*　　　　*　　　　*

Girish's *Rupa-Sanatan* brought a great deal of attention to the Star Theatre, which at that time was located at 68 Beadon Street in Calcutta. Observing the popularity of the Star Theatre, Gopallal Sil, a young man who had inherited a fortune from his family, decided that he wanted to start his own theatre. He secretly bought the land where the Star was located and gave notice to the theatre's owners to move. The owners — who were Girish's actors and disciples — realized that they would lose a legal battle with that wealthy young man. Girish advised them to sell the building to Gopallal Sil, but to keep the Star name. The sale proceeds would be used to buy land elsewhere and build a new Star Theatre. Gopallal paid 30,000 rupees for the building.

In July 1887, *Buddhadev-Charit* and *Bellik Bāzār* were performed at the Star Theatre on Beadon Street for the last time, to sold-out performances. The owners of the theatre then bought a plot of land on Cornwallis Street (now Bidhan Sarani) in Hatibagan, North Calcutta. Construction of the new Star Theatre began later that year.

It may be easy to buy a building, but that does not buy success in the art world. Gopallal Sil named his new theatre the Emerald. He remodeled the building and lured away some famous actors from the National Theatre by offering higher salaries. At that time electricity was not readily available in Calcutta, so Gopallal installed a power generator to light his theatre inside and out. The effect was stunning. On 8 October 1887, *Pandava Nirbasan* premiered in the Emerald Theatre. The audience was charmed by the exotic costumes of the actors and actresses and the special effects made possible by the electric lights. But within two months Gopallal felt he needed Girish. He had poured much money into the theatre but could not make it popular. Its productions were neither lively nor entertaining. Some people advised him: "Sir, if you want to succeed in the theatre business, hire Girish Ghosh; otherwise it will be like a sacrifice without Shiva." Thus Gopallal decided to hire Girish to manage his theatre, and he approached him with an offer.

At this time the construction of the new Star Theatre was in its final stage. The money that the owners had received from Gopallal Sil had been spent to buy the land and the beginning of construction. They had contributed some of their own money, but it was not enough to complete the building. They had started the project with Girish's encouragement and assistance, so he felt responsible for them. Moreover, it would be rather shameful if Girish accepted Gopallal's offer and left the Star to manage the Emerald. Girish rejected Gopallal's offer; but the latter did not give up. He offered Girish a 20,000-rupee cash bonus and a salary of 350 rupees per month.

Girish reconsidered. The 20,000 rupees would be enough to complete construction on the Star. His disciples would be able to manage it on their own with no difficulty; he had trained them well. In addition, Gopallal could pay higher wages, and he was threatening to hire away the Star's best actors and actresses if Girish refused to come to the Emerald. Under such conditions, Girish agreed to Gopallal's proposal and entered into a five-year contract with the Emerald.

Girish was a great lover of the Bengali stage, and extremely generous as well. He knew how wealthy theatre owners exploited actors and actresses. He gave 16,000 rupees in cash to his disciples so that they could complete construction on the new theatre, and he said to them: "You come from respectable families. For all these years you have been exploited by different theatre proprietors. Now by the grace of God you are free. I request that henceforth you see to it that no actors or actresses are harassed or exploited."[6]

Girish wrote *Purnachandra* and *Bishad* for the Emerald; these plays opened on 17 March 1888 and 6 October 1888, respectively. Within two years Gopallal Sil lost interest in the theatre and he leased the Emerald to four people. Girish took this opportunity to sever his contract and rejoin the Star as a manager.

While working for the Emerald, Girish lost his second wife. During these last two years he worked for the Star, he wrote plays like *Prafulla* that expressed the deep sorrow he felt at his wife's death.

Girish wrote *Prafulla* to show people the destructive power of alcohol and how it can ruin a man and his family. In this tragedy Girish portrayed a typical joint family of nineteenth-century Bengal.

The matriarch, Umasundari, is a widow with three grown sons: Yogesh (whom Girish played), Ramesh, and Suresh. Yogesh is married to Jnanada and they have a boy named Jadav. Ramesh is married to Prafulla and they are childless. Suresh is young and unmarried. After their father's death the whole family falls into dire poverty; however, Yogesh works hard and makes a fortune in business. Yogesh sees that his brothers are educated,

Girish in the role of Yogesh in *Prafulla* play

and he brings peace and prosperity to the household. He is truthful, dutiful, faithful, honest—a man of honour and integrity. However, when Yogesh is at the height of his career, his bank fails and all his money is lost. His business suffers and his clients humiliate him. He then begins drinking a little wine at night for relaxation, and gradually he becomes a terrible alcoholic.

The main sources of Yogesh's prosperity are his goodwill and honesty. He laments: "In this sorrowful world, God gives a little joy in the form of a good reputation. I don't have that anymore; I only have alcohol." His mother and wife cry and beg him to give up drinking, but he will not listen to them. Alcohol slowly poisons his brain. It ruins his health and wealth; it ruins his powers of discrimination and self-control; it ruins his concentration and the ability to work; and it ruins his character and stability. An alcoholic develops tremendously low self-esteem, leads a lonely and wretched life, and is despised by his friends and family. This awful addiction makes an alcoholic helpless, friendless, and sometimes homeless. When he comes back to his senses from time to time, he is grief-stricken seeing his pitiable condition and sometimes seeks help from God and well-wishers. The expiation of sin is repentance and wholehearted self-surrender to God. Girish's own life gives hope to alcoholics: One can get rid of this horrible disease by the grace of God or the guru.

Because of his alcoholic background, Girish depicted Yogesh's character so vividly that it was a great lesson for others. As a rubber ball bounces down the steps from the upper floor to the basement, likewise Yogesh drifts from his position of wealth to that of a homeless beggar. His brother Ramesh, a lawyer, becomes a monster and takes advantage of his weakened state. He lusts after his brother's wealth, and obtains his power of attorney by underhanded means so he can take control of his fortune. He also plots against his younger brother, Suresh, and has him sent to prison under false charges; he abducts his nephew and tries to poison him; he drives his mother insane, and has Yogesh declared senile. Finally, he evicts Yogesh and his wife from their family home. In the character of Ramesh, Girish showed how greed can make a man cruel, selfish, ungrateful, and dishonest.

Yogesh's drunkenness reaches its culmination when he comes to his wife and asks for money.

Jnanada scolds him: "Are you not ashamed of your behaviour?"

Yogesh replies: "I am shameless. I have been begging for money on the street for the last three days to buy alcohol. Do you think I have any shame?" He hits Jnanada and takes her money and jewellery. Jnanada cannot change her husband's drunken behaviour and later dies on the street. Sometime later, Yogesh comes home and sees a coin in his son's hand. He twists the boy's hand and grabs the coin. The entire play is full of sorrow. Girish made the audience feel how a single person's misconduct can turn a heavenly home into hell.

Prafulla, Ramesh's wife, is an oasis in the family. In her character Girish portrayed the ideal Indian woman. Prafulla is dutiful, pure, unselfish, loving, righteous, and does not hesitate to confront her husband. She cannot bear his cruel and greedy behaviour. Prafulla forces Ramesh to have Suresh released from prison, and she secretly helps her sister-in-law, Jnanada. One day Jnanada says: "If the British government closes all the taverns in town, then we can have a happy home."

Prafulla: "Let the government do it."

Jnanada: "The government will not listen to me. Moreover, the tavern owners pay the government a lot of money for their business."

The naïve Prafulla says: "Sister, I shall sell all my jewellery and give the proceeds to the government." This dialogue touches our hearts. In the midst of gloom, Girish showed a ray of light through Prafulla's unselfish character.

In the last act of the play Prafulla finally learns where her nephew, Jadav, is confined. She attempts to rescue him, boldly facing her husband: "You are a crook. Why and for whom are you destroying the whole family? You made your elder brother a street beggar; you sent your younger brother to jail; you drove your own mother mad; now you are destroying your innocent nephew. Why are you committing such horrible sins?"

Ramesh: "Prafulla, get out of my way or I'll kill you."

Prafulla: "Do you think that I fear death and will run away, leaving this innocent boy in the hands of a monster? I won't allow my husband to perform such a heinous act. I have taken refuge in dharma all through my life and I shall never deviate from it. I don't fear death. Know for certain that your efforts will fail. Every action has an end. God has endured much; He will endure no more. Be careful. I am a chaste woman. Listen to me if you want your own good. Never go against dharma. Don't kill this boy."

Ramesh: "Get out of here before I kill you."

Prafulla: "Is your heart made of stone? Shame on you! You want to kill this boy! Please honour my request. Don't commit any more sin."

Ramesh: "Then you will die."

Ramesh gags Prafulla and kills her. At that moment Suresh, a police officer, and others burst into the house. Ramesh is arrested. Yogesh and his mother come onto the scene and meet Suresh and Jadav. Yogesh has the last line: "Aha, Aha! Amār sājāno bāgān shukiye gālo — Alas, alas! My beautiful flower garden has withered away!"[7]

*   *   *

After *Prafulla*, Girish wrote two more plays for the Star Theatre. *Hāranidhi*, a social play with a happy ending, opened on 8 September 1889. *Chanda*, a historical play based on James Todd's *History of Rajasthan*, was first performed on 26 July 1890. Despite his wife's death and other family problems, Girish continued to write new plays for the Star, although he could not go to the theatre regularly. His young son became very sick, so he started spending more time with him; then he fell ill himself. During this difficult period the owners of the Star Theatre sent a letter of dismissal to Girish. He was shocked because it was he who had taught them acting, given them 16,000 rupees to build the Star, and written plays for them under a pseudonym when he was under contract with the Emerald.

However, Girish did not protest. He left the Star with dignity. It would have been difficult for him to live peacefully amongst such people, and it was better not to see the faces of such ungrateful creatures.

However, news of this created a commotion. Some of the Star's actors and actresses could not tolerate this ill-treatment of their guru. Fifteen famous performers left the Star Theatre and joined the City Theatre under the leadership of Nilmadhav Chakrabarty, where they staged *Vilwamangal, Buddhadev-Charit, Malinā-vikāsh, Bellik Bāzār*, and other plays written by Girish. He did not participate, because he was in Madhupur caring for his dying son. The owners of the Star brought a lawsuit against Girish and Nilmadhav in the High Court, claiming that the copyright to those dramas belonged to the Star. Girish returned to Calcutta and settled the case by paying the owners 5,000 rupees, which was given to him by Nagendra Bhusan Mukhopadhyay. Nagendra then hired Girish for his Minerva Theatre and began construction. While the Minerva was being built, Girish began to study science and then went to Kamarpukur and Jayrambati with Swami Niranjanananda.

We mentioned in Chapter 3 that Girish translated Shakespeare's *Macbeth* into Bengali while he was working for the Atkinson Company, but he left the manuscript in his office desk drawer. Girish was away from the office taking care of his sick wife when the company was sold at auction. Regrettably all the furniture was sold and the manuscript was irretrievable.

A creative mind never remains idle. Girish now began another translation of *Macbeth*, displaying his poetic and creative faculties in re-creating the witches' dialogue. Girish gathered suitable actors and actresses for this play, and the staging and rehearsals took seven months. The Bengali *Macbeth* premiered on 28 January 1893 at the Minerva Theatre. Girish acted in the role of Macbeth and the superstar Tinkari performed in the role of Lady Macbeth. He engaged Mr. Williard, a famous English painter, to create the drop scenes, and he produced wonderful work using water colours. Mr. Pim, an English dress designer, made the costumes. Girish did not hesitate to spend whatever it took to make this production perfect.

On the opening night of *Macbeth*, in the scene in which Macbeth appears after killing Duncan, Girish came onstage in the role of Macbeth with bloody hands. Seeing his terrible form, two elderly members of the audience fainted. In whatever role he performed, Girish became completely absorbed in that character. Once he explained how this is done: "A drunkard may be absorbed in drinking alcohol, but he cannot act in the role of a drunkard. A real actor divides his mind in two parts. In the first part he remains absorbed in his role, and with the second part he becomes a witness and observes how he is acting and speaking. However, the function of the first part is primary and the other part is secondary."[8] Girish became a successful actor by his identification with whatever character he portrayed. Moreover, he adopted the same technique while writing a play.

After seeing the play, the editor of *The Englishman* wrote: "A Bengali Thane of Cawdor is a lively suggestion of incongruity, but the reality is an admirable reproduction of all the conventions of an English stage."[9] Gurudas Bandyopadhyay, a classmate of Girish and a judge of the Calcutta High Court, commented: "To translate the inimitable language of Shakespeare was a task of no ordinary difficulty; but Babu Girish Chandra Ghosh has performed that difficult task very creditably on the whole, and his translation is in many places quite worthy of the original."[10]

Girish wrote several plays for the Minerva Theatre. In *Mukul-Munjarā*, Girish wrote about pure love, the power of love, and the signs of a true lover and beloved. *Abu Hussein*, a humorous musical play, was based on *Arabian Nights*. In *Saptamite Visarjan*, a satire, he depicted the contemporary social extravaganza. During this period Girish also wrote *Janā*, a play based on the Mahabharata (see Chapter 16), *Barodiner Bakhsis*, a satire; *Swapner Phul*, a musical; *Sabhyatār Pāndā*, a satire; *Karameti Bāi*, a drama that has as its theme devotion and knowledge; *Phanir Mani*, a musical; *Pānch Kane*, a satire; *Bejai Āoyāj*, a satire. In addition, Girish acted in some of his older plays, performing the role of Nimchand in *Sadhabār Ekādashi*, Kichak in *Pāndaver Ajnātavās*, Daksha in *Daksha Yajna*, Clive in *Palāshir Yuddha*, Yogesh in *Prafulla*, and Ram and Indrajit in *Meghnād-badh*.

After four years of working in the Minerva, Girish was forced to leave. Nagendra had started the theatre with a small investment, and he fell into debt because of the production expenses involved in building the sets and making the costumes. Girish was in charge of hiring, dismissing, and setting the salaries of the actors and actresses; and Nagendra managed the theatre's other financial affairs. There was sufficient income but Nagendra did not manage the money efficiently. Most of the theatre's income was consumed by interest payments on an old debt. The contractors who supplied the costumes came to Girish to be paid. Girish became exasperated and assumed responsibility for managing the theatre's monetary affairs by hiring Devendra Nath Basu to handle the distribution of cash. Nagendra did not like what Girish had done, nor did he agree with his advice. As a result, Girish left the Minerva, and most of the actors and actresses left also.

This news quickly spread, and the owners of the Star came to his house that very night. They were desperately seeking new plays, which only Girish could supply. They treated Girish affectionately and respectfully and created the new position of "Dramatic Director" for him. Girish truly loved the dramatic arts, and he had dedicated his soul to the theatre. Ramakrishna once said: "A holy person's anger is like a mark on the water; it disappears quickly." Girish forgave his disciples for their previous rude behaviour. He then rejoined the Star and staged his new play *Kālāpāhār*.*

On the occasion of Queen Victoria's 60th birth anniversary, Girish wrote the musical *Hirak Jubilee* (Diamond Jubilee) to show his respect for the noble queen. He then wrote *Pārasya Prasūn*, a musical based on *Arabian Nights*, and included some inspiring songs in it. Girish remarked: "One can compose a song based on any human mood."[11] One of the songs in this play is based on the Epicurean philosophy: "Happiness or enjoyment is the summum bonum of life."

> Why are you thinking today of what will happen tomorrow?
> Can anyone understand by only thinking of this world's play?
> Time passes while one thinks,
> But can anyone change one's condition?
> One plans today to be happy tomorrow; but it does not happen.
> The current of time flows with its ups and downs.
> One lives in fear who asks: What will happen tomorrow?
> Don't give up whatever you have now; enjoy your life.

*   *   *

Girish's next play for the Star was *Māyā-avasān* (The End of Maya), a social drama that was first performed on 18 December 1897. In *Kālāpāhār* Girish had incorporated Ramakrishna's life and teachings, and in *Māyā-avasān* he introduced Swami Vivekananda's philosophy: Destroy ignorance by means of knowledge. Girish acted in the role of Kalikinkar, the hero of the drama. He was a lover of truth and knowledge, and extremely compassionate to his fellow beings. He was particularly fond of modern science because it improves human life.

Kalikinkar's neighbour, Satkari, was a strange man. One night Kalikinkar was sleeping and Satkari entered his room. Awakened by some noise, Kalikinkar got up and asked Satkari why he had come:

Kalikinkar: "Please tell me what you want."
Satkari: "Sir, I didn't come for money."

---

* See Chapter 16 for more about this play.

Kalikinkar: "Then what do you want?"

Satkari: "I came to take the notebooks in which you record your scientific findings."

Kalikinkar: "What will you do with them?"

Satkari: "I know you have no attachment to money, women, or name and fame, but you are attached to those notebooks. I want to burn them."

Kalikinkar: "What will you gain from that?"

Satkari: "I learned from a French philosopher's writing that there is misery in human life and that none can escape it. So when I see others suffering as I do, I get a little peace; so I am happy during my suffering and happiness."

Kalikinkar: "You are right about those notebooks. They are very precious to me. Instead of sleeping, at night I look through a telescope to watch the movements of the stars; I peer through the microscope to study the behaviour of germs; I experiment with electricity and various chemicals without regard for my life and health. I note down everything in those notebooks. Do you know why? I think that if they are published, they will help others. But now I see this will not reduce human suffering even an iota."

Satkari: "Sir, let me go."

Kalikinkar: "Will you not take these notebooks?"

Satkari: "No, sir. I see you have no attachment to them."

Kalikinkar: "Do you think those who help others are foolish? Let me ask you another question: Is there more happiness or more misery in human life?"

Satkari: "It is the nature of waves to rise and fall. But if one examines life carefully, one will find more misery than happiness."

When Satkari left, Kalikinkar said: "The goal of this man is to harm others. How strange! But then, I have never seen this fellow sad, even for a day."

He then pondered: "I have served others and endured suffering for others. Enough! From now on let me think about myself. What is happiness? What is misery? Where is bliss? The mind becomes still like the flame of an unflickering lamp! I have heard about that absolute blissful state. Is it possible to attain that state where happiness and misery do not exist? Or is that state mere imagination? The life of the lamp will surely end. But does death extinguish the lamp of wisdom? That is impossible. Matter changes, and it is subject to destruction, but one cannot think of the destruction of consciousness. Where is the solution? The solution is in the sacrifice of the little self, or the ego."

Having attained this knowledge, Kalikinkar goes to his disciple and says: "I have come to give you my last advice. Please consider it carefully. Have you not heard the word 'self-sacrifice'? Previously I thought that it was a mere word; but now I know that there is real self-sacrifice. Real self-sacrifice does not terminate at death because the self will go with us. When one gives away oneself completely here in this world, that is real self-sacrifice."

Disciple: "Sir, I cannot understand what you mean."

Kalikinkar: "I always advised you to do good to others. I also dedicated my life to the welfare of others. But I did not get any peace. Why? I may have said: 'Perform unselfish action. Do your duty without motive.' But my ego did not give up the desire for results. I did good to others for the sake of personal happiness; I served others for religious merit; I helped others while desiring name and fame. Today I offer all selfish results to the Ganges and shall lose myself in serving others. I am now one with this world."

In *Maya-avasan* Girish infused Kalikinkar's character with the highest wisdom.

*   *   *

Girish at the Classic Theatre

In 1899 Girish joined the Classic Theatre as Dramatic Director at the request of his disciple Amarendra Nath Datta. Initially he did not write any new plays, but instead acted in *Prafulla* as Yogesh, in *Daksha Yajna* as Daksha, and in *Meghnad-badh* as Meghnad and Rama. He then wrote *Deldār*, a musical that premiered on 10 June 1899.

Girish next wrote his famous drama *Pāndava Gaurav*, which was first performed at the Classic on 17 February 1900. It was based on the story of King Dandi, which appears in the Puranas. The essential message of this drama is: "Dharma is the pole star in this world of maya; and the essence of dharma is to protect those who seek refuge in it." Dandi disobeyed Krishna and thus became his enemy. Dandi knew that it was impossible to defeat Krishna, so he took refuge in Krishna's sister Subhadra, who was married to Arjuna. She and the Pandavas gave shelter to Dandi and thus a war became inevitable between Krishna and his cousins the Pandavas. The Pandavas gave shelter to Dandi, so it was their dharma to protect him. Krishna sent Kanchuki, Dandi's elderly minister, to Subhadra to negotiate a solution that would prevent the war. In this drama Girish depicted both heroism and devotion and showed how God makes Himself small to glorify His devotees.

Girish acted in the role of Kanchuki whose character is truthful, simple, faithful, and fearless.

Girish's secretary Abinash left these wonderful reminiscences concerning *Pandava Gaurav*:

> Girish used to dictate his plays to me. It would take time to write the first two acts; he gathered his thoughts slowly and carefully. Sometimes it happened that after writing the first and even the second act, he would destroy the whole manuscript and start anew. The more his ideas and imagination were invigorated while developing the theme and characters, the more his dictation would speed up and the drama would take shape smoothly. While writing the *Pandava Gaurav* play at night I felt drowsy because I was not accustomed to passing sleepless nights. He was irritated by this, and I was ashamed. Thus we continued up to the third act. When I realized that Girish would be irritated if I became sleepy while writing the fourth act, I drank four cups of tea consecutively and my sleepiness was gone. When we finished the fourth act, it was 2:30 a.m.
>
> Girish said: "Let us stop here now. You go to sleep." I replied: "I don't feel sleepy at all. Let us continue writing." He said: "Well, I am ready. My thoughts are all arranged. If you want to continue, go ahead." Girish started the fifth act of the play. Inspired, he continued to dictate and I began to write with redoubled energy. The whole drama was completed. Finally, he composed the first three lines of the song: '*Hera hara-manamohini ke bale re kalo meye* — Look at the charming wife of Shiva. Who says that She is black?' Then he said: "Let us stop here today. Tomorrow I shall compose other songs for the play. You open the doors and windows, I feel hot." When I opened the doors and windows. I found bright sunshine outside. I looked at the clock and it was 8:00 a.m. Anxiously he said: "Go, go home. Take your bath, have lunch, and sleep the whole day. And come back again tonight."[12]

Girish had infinite energy. While writing his plays, he would lose all body-consciousness, forgetting food and sleep. As the yogis experience *chetana samadhi*,* Girish would have a similar experience while writing his plays. Mahendra Datta recalled:

> I noticed one thing in Girish: His facial expression, gaze, and voice would change slowly according to his thoughts. He lived in the realm of ideas, where he could visualize them vividly. But when his mind was in the lower plane he could not see them. It is said: "A great man is one who can transform himself in various ways."
>
> The creator of the Bengali stage, the incomparable, unrivalled actor Girish and the Girish at home were two different persons. In a domestic setting, Girish was jovial, social, and carefree. He was capable of brightening up a gathering with pleasant talk. That is the reason many people

---
*When one is absorbed in God or any idea, one functions unconsciously.

visited him and enjoyed talking to him. We observed that ten or twelve Girish Chandra Ghoshes lived in one body, and each one had a different nature. It is amazing that on one side he was intelligent, talented, a jnani, and a devotee, and on the other he was a man of lower status, a drunkard. People expressed their opinions seeing one of his sides; that is why he had both a good and a bad reputation, fame and disgrace. But the real Girish was a good man, a simple devotee.[13]

In November 1900 shortly after joining the Classic, Girish's only daughter suffered terribly from puerperal diarrhoea. He engaged all the best doctors but finally lost hope for her life. The day before she died, she said: "If my father goes to Tarakeswar Shiva and brings back the sanctified water then I may recover from this disease." Without a second thought, the next day Girish and Abinash went to Tarakeswar to offer worship. While Girish was at the temple office making a donation for the worship, an officer looked at him again and again. Finally he asked: "Sir, it seems I have seen you somewhere before." Girish replied: "I am Girish Ghosh who acts in the theatre." Before the officer could offer his hospitality, Girish entered the temple to offer worship to Lord Shiva. After performing his worship he left the temple in a grave mood — there was no glimpse of hope in his mind. Before Girish and Abinash returned to Calcutta, Girish's daughter died, leaving one daughter and three sons.[14]

On 10 May 1873, the National Theatre had been preparing to stage a play based on Bankim Chandra Chattopadhyay's famous *Kapalkundala* at Raja Radhakanta Dev's house in Calcutta. The audience filled the hall; the actors and actresses were in makeup; but the manuscript for the play was missing. The indomitable Girish took the novel in hand, improvised the dialogue, and stood behind the screen to prompt the actors and actresses with dialogue that he composed on the spot.*

Almost 30 years later, Girish decided again to stage *Kapalkundala*. He finished the entire play in one night by dictating it to four secretaries. Despite the speed in which it was composed, Girish's talent and imagination gave a wonderful shape to the work. It opened at the Classic on 31 May 1901.

Most of the actors and actresses in the Classic were Girish's disciples, so he selected the roles for them. In *Kapalkundala*, Kusumkumari was assigned the title role. But she wanted to play Matibibi, which Girish had earmarked for Tarasundari. Kusumkumari was disappointed. Realizing how she felt, Girish told her: "All roles in a drama are equally important and worthy of a talented actor or actress. When *Kapalkundala* was performed

---

* See Chapter 4, p. 44, for the full account.

in the National Theatre, Binodini acted in the role of Kapalkundala. Her acting was so wonderful and impressive that the audience applauded her many times. She never craved the glamorous role of Matibibi. A playwright may create a main character in a drama, but a skillful actor or actress can make a small role lively and earn high praise from the audience." To prove the truth of his statement, he himself performed in five insignificant roles in *Kapalkundala* — a manager, a guard, a drunkard, a porter, and a neighbour — over three nights. Although those roles were very different, he received tremendous applause for each one.[15]

In 1874 Girish had made Bankim Chandra's novel *Mrinālini* into a drama and acted in the role of Pashupati. In 1901 Girish recast the old manuscript for the Classic and created a new version that was performed in August of that year. Girish reprised the role of Pashupati, the commander-in-chief of Laxman Sen, a Hindu king. Pashupati conspired with Bakhtiar Khilji, a Muslim general, who promised to make him the king of Bengal if he betrayed Laxman Sen. Pashupati trusted Bakhtiar and did not order his army to fight when Bakhtiar attacked. Laxman Sen fled, but the general did not keep his promise. Bakhtiar told Pashupati: "One who is unfaithful is wretched. A traitor is not fit to sit on the throne of Bengal." He arrested Pashupati and set fire to his house, where his wife Manorama was. Pashupati was so distressed that he almost became mad.

A betrayer is always betrayed. Girish depicted the storm of sorrow in the mind of the imprisoned Pashupati. He lamented: "It is my bad karma that I lost my kingdom and now I am in prison. How can I forget Manorama? Dear Manorama, I didn't listen to you, so I lost everything. But how can I live without you? Who says that the world is sorrowful? What misery can there be in this world that can torment Pashupati? Arise, O hell-fire! Punish Pashupati for his sin. Is there any punishment in hell that could be fit for Pashupati? Is hell worse than my mind? One can combine thousands of hells that will not be equal to my heart. I am responsible for shedding the blood of my friends and relatives. Is there any love in Pashupati's heart? O love, go live in the tree! O love, go live in the stone! You have no place in Pashupati's heart."[16]

After two appearances in the role of Pashupati, Girish had to stop acting for some time. Abinash wrote about the production: "In the last scene of the fourth act, the Muslims set fire to Pashupati's house. Pashupati went to the temple to immerse the goddess in water. He was convinced that Manorama had been burned to death, and his heart was burning in grief. Meanwhile the stage director was throwing fireworks onto the stage from below and above and from right and left to create a special effect so

Girish as Pasupati in *Mrinalini*

the audience could see that Pashupati's house was on fire. In Pashupati's role Girish wore a turban, but the upper part was made with a thin cloth because he feared that his head would become too hot. On the second night an explosive substance began falling on his head and burnt his skin. Girish plaintively asked the stage manager to stop, but the excited audience was clapping and making so much noise that Girish's voice could not be heard by the stage manager and he continued his fireworks. With great patience and forbearance Girish finished his performance. When the play was over, the actors and actresses were distressed when they saw his burnt costume and the skin on his skull. But at the same time they all praised his infinite endurance. Later Girish's son Surendra became very famous by acting in the role of Pashupati."[17]

Regarding Girish's portrayal of Pashupati, the famous actor Amritalal Basu said: "Girish would have received royal honours in any country for his performance as Pashupati. I will never again hear such a sweet and deep voice and never again see such a genuine expression of suffering." The actress Binodini also commented: "Girish, as Pashupati in prison, would shout, 'O minister, tell me where shall I go? Where shall I put my feet?' And the next moment, seeing his burning house, he would cry out: 'My wife Manorama is at home! Let me go! Let me go and rescue her!' Even now when I recall that scene, how he would try to snatch away his hands forcefully from the guards, I get goose bumps on my body. In the last 50 years I have never seen acting like that a second time."[18]

In November 1904 Amarendra Datta could no longer manage the theatre competently, so he became insolvent and the Classic Theatre was closed. Girish was not paid for three months' work. He then returned to the Minerva Theatre, for which he wrote *Hara-Gauri*, a musical based on the Pauranic story of Shiva and Gauri. It opened on 4 March 1905.

Girish saw how middle-class families in Bengali society were tormented by the oppressive dowry system. The father would lose his savings, and the mother would lose her jewellery. They would even have to mortgage their home in order to marry off their daughters. Like heartless butchers, the bridegroom's shameless parents would humiliate the bride's family and extort money, cars, jewellery, and other goods. Girish could not bear this terrible social custom, so he wrote *Balidan* as a protest against it. He dedicated the play to his classmate Saradacharan Mitra, who was a judge in the Calcutta High Court. It premiered at the Minerva on 8 April 1905, and Girish performed the role of Karunamay, the main character.

Karunamay is a learned, intelligent, and truthful householder, and his wife, Saraswati, is a pious, dutiful, and loving woman. They have three daughters and one son. Karunamay is an office clerk and his monthly salary is 150 rupees. His first two daughters are now of marriageable age, but he has no money for their dowries — and without money, it is not possible to find respectable bridegrooms. Somehow he arranges the marriage of his first daughter to a man who is a drunkard and debauchee. His second daughter is wed to a man who already has one wife; the new bride cannot bear the shame and misery she endures, so she drowns herself. Burdened by grief and poverty, Karunamay cannot bear the humiliation he receives from wealthy and prominent men. He hangs himself, and then his wife suffers a heart attack and dies. The third daughter enjoys a happier fate: She is married to a noble soul who does not want a dowry.

In *Balidan* Girish vividly portrayed the suffering of girls from poor families. His protest against the dowry system is clearly expressed in the last line of the tragedy: *Bānglār kanyā-sampradān nai — balidān* (In the social system of Bengal, it is not a daughter's marriage — it is murder.)[19]

Aparesh Mukhopadhyay saw Girish's performance as Karunamay, and he described it in his memoirs:

> Girish was ill from asthma, so he suggested that Ardhendu act in the role of Karunamay a few nights. There was much difference between the acting of these two great actors in the same role: When the second daughter's drowned body was found, Karunamay said: "Here is my daughter. She has been located. She is so sweet and gentle! I know she will never run away!" Saying these lines Ardhendu would shed tears profusely and the audience also would cry.
>
> But when Girish acted in that role there were no tears in his eyes. It was as if all the water in his body had dried up; his blood circulation stopped; his gloomy eyes ceased blinking; his voice was dry, broken, and grave. Seeing this scene, the hearts of the audience were pierced, and they would wail loudly, as an unseen grief suddenly engulfed them like a cyclone. This Karunamay (Girish) pursued the audience even after the play. While they were on the street or at home, in a dark bedroom or having food, they would remain stupefied for a few days by the intense grief of Karunamay. When someone later asked Girish about the differences in performance between the two Karunamays, Girish remarked: "If Karunamay cries in that scene, he cannot hang himself."[20]

After writing this famous social drama, Girish set his mind on a historical drama. He began writing a play about Rana Pratap, the famous Rajput king who fought against the Mogul emperor. He wrote two acts, but the play was never completed. When he heard that D.L. Roy's *Rana Pratap* was being staged in the Star, he gave up his project. Suresh Chandra

Samajpati, the famous editor of the *Sāhitya* magazine, then asked Girish to write a drama based on Siraj-ud-Daulla, the last patriotic Muslim Nawab of Bengal.

Girish was a perfectionist. Before writing any play, he read and did extensive research on his subject, then meditated on the characters. He was able to make those characters live because of his wide experience, vast imagination, and god-given talent. Girish was a member of the Asiatic Society of Calcutta, so he had access to all of the books available on Siraj-ud-Daulla and the Muslim history of Bengal. After extensive study, Girish began to write.

Abinash recalled: "There would be two five-act dramas if Girish were to write *Siraj-ud-Daulla* from Siraj's early life. Because he expected the audience to lose patience, Girish resolved to complete Siraj's character study in one play. But he faced tremendous difficulty in translating this plan into action. He dictated two or three scenes and then mercilessly destroyed them. After a few efforts, his plots began to take shape and the writing continued steadily. Still it took two weeks to finish the first act, where he condensed the events in half of Siraj's life. It is amazing how in the remaining four acts Girish depicted historical facts and at the same time Siraj's evolution and heart-rending end. In this play he vividly portrayed Siraj's patriotism, his youthful wantonness, his sorrows, and the touching picture of his affectionate family life. Girish added two imaginary characters — Jahara and Karimchacha — to help connect and develop the story."[21]

Siraj-ud-Daulla premiered at the Minerva Theatre on 9 September 1905. Surendra Nath Ghosh, Girish's son, performed in the role of Siraj, and Girish portrayed Karimchacha.

In 1752 Siraj became the Muslim Nawab of Bengal, Bihar, and Orissa. He was a great ruler, but was betrayed by Mirjafar, his Muslim commander-in-chief. Mirjafar and a few Hindu conspirators deceived Siraj, secretly making a pact with the East India Company, which later formed the British government. Mirjafar promised that he would not order his army to fight against the British if they made him the Nawab. In addition, he would pay 17,700,000 rupees to the East India Company every year. In 1757 the British army, under the leadership of Lord Robert Clive, invaded Murshidabad, Siraj's capital. Siraj ordered Mirjafar, Mirmadan, Mohanlal, and all of his other generals to fight against the British. However, the main division of his army was loyal to Mirjafar, and it stood by without fighting. Mirmadan and Mohanlal fought heroically on the battlefield of Palasi and were killed. When the English entered the palace, Siraj exchanged his royal clothes with those of Karimchacha, a courtier, and fled through a secret passage, but he was later caught and murdered. India would not have been under British rule if Siraj-ud-Daulla, the last Nawab of Bengal, had been victorious. Even now, whenever this drama is enacted onstage, both Hindus and Muslims shed tears for Siraj.

Siraj-ud-Daulla created a sensation and stirred much patriotic feeling among the masses in Bengal. Balgangadhar Tilak, a national leader from Maharashtra, came to Calcutta at that time to attend the convention of the National Congress. Seeing the play, he went to meet Girish and praised him profusely. The Minerva Theatre was then being auctioned off by the High Court, so Girish encouraged the owners to buy it back for 59,400 rupees, and his *Siraj-ud-Daulla* alone raised more money than the amount they needed.

On 3 February 1906, the Indian nationalist Surendra Nath Bandyopadhyay wrote: "Both from the dramatic and the literary point of view, *Siraj-ud-Daulla* is destined to occupy a high and enduring place in our national literature. As a piece for the stage it is *non pareil*; and it requires no mean talent to interpret the diverse and complex characters that the gifted author has marshalled in it."[22]

On 17 February 1906, *The Statesman*, an English newspaper, published this item: "The Company at this theatre has been playing *Siraj-ud-Daulla* by G.C. Ghosh for the past five months with unabated success. The author himself takes the part of Karimchacha, Clive is represented by Mr. K. Mitter, and the remaining characters are well placed."[23]

Mahendra Nath Datta asked Girish about his description of the traitor in *Siraj-ud-Daulla*: "You have not seen Mirjafar, so how can you write about him so vividly?"

Girish replied: "What do you mean I have not seen him? He appeared in front of me. He had a thick bushy beard; he was rather old. Patches of leucoderma were visible on his hands, feet, and face. When he talked, the odour of onion and garlic issued from his mouth." Saying this, Girish contracted his face in abhorrence. It seemed as if Mirjafar had again appeared in front of him.[24]

When Girish was in his early 60s, *Balidan* and *Siraj-ud-Daulla* brought him great fame and tremendous popularity. Fame cannot be bought; it has to be earned by the sweat of one's brow. Girish was a hard worker, and he put his entire being into each drama to make it a grand success. Because of the stress on his body and mind brought on by this effort, Girish developed asthma. Despite his illness, however, Girish wrote a musical play, *Bāsar*, for the Minerva Theatre. He also dramatized *Durgeshnandini*, a famous novel by Bankim Chandra. *Durgeshnandini* was performed at the

Minerva in February 1906 and Girish acted in the role of Birendra Singha, the Rajput king.

After attaining phenomenal success in *Siraj-ud-Daulla*, Girish decided to write another historical drama based on the same events. In *Mirkasim*, the traitor Mirjafar becomes the Nawab of Bengal, but he himself is betrayed by the British and eventually loses his throne.

To appease the British demands for money, Mirjafar exhausts his treasury and cannot pay his army. The army is about to revolt and the whole country is in deep turmoil. Mirjafar, failing in health and lamenting his treachery, begins taking drugs and becomes mentally unstable. He hands his administration over to his son-in-law Mirkasim, who becomes the acting Nawab.

Mirkasim is a real patriot. He tries his utmost to free his country from the grip of the British. He builds an army and engages qualified generals, but ultimately is betrayed by both Muslims and Hindus. His defeat and death wipe out the last ray of hope for India's freedom. In the beginning the British came to India for business as the East India Company; they later occupied the whole country and made India a colony under the British Empire. Girish showed in *Siraj-ud-Daulla* and *Mirkasim* how greed for money and power, selfishness and conspiracy, lies and betrayal destroy a country's freedom.

Mirkasim premiered at the Minerva on 16 June 1906; it continued every Saturday for seven months; the audience attendance surpassed *Siraj-ud-Daulla*. Girish acted in the role of Mirjafar and his son Surendra was Mirkasim.

On 23 June 1906 the *Bengalee* published this report: "Babu Girish Chandra Ghose's new historical drama, *Mirkasim*, which was put on the boards of the Minerva Theatre for the first time on Saturday last, has been a phenomenal success, both from the histrionic and literary points of view. The tumultuous period that followed the accession of Mirkasim to the throne, the strenuous fight that the ruler had with the East India Company for the protection of the indigenous industries and the various stratagems resorted to by both sides to win their points, how, with remarkable fidelity and consummate art, they have been portrayed by Bengal's greatest playwright. The piece abounds with diverse and complex characters, all of them very skillfully marshalled to produce an excellent stage effect, which one must see to fully realize."[25]

On 17 November 1907, *The Statesman* reported: "The exceedingly lavish manner in which *Mirkasim* has been staged at the Kohinoor assists materially in enhancing the enjoyment of this piece, which deals with the incidents of the tumultuous period that followed the accession of Mirkasim to the throne and the strenuous fight that the ruler had with the East India Company for the protection of indigenous industries. The acting all round reaches a high water mark of excellence, and the huge audience testified their appreciation in a most unmistakable manner."[26]

Regarding Girish's intense imagination, Abinash recalled: "When Girish wrote any drama, he was absorbed in its theme, idea, and characters day and night. One day Swami Saradananda came to see him when he was writing *Mirkasim*. Overjoyed, Girish said: 'When did you come to Calcutta from Belur Math?' 'Three days ago,' replied Saradananda.

Girish: 'You are in Calcutta for three days and now you have come to see me? As long as you are in Calcutta, please visit me every day. I feel good when I see the disciples of the Master. For quite a few days I have not had any chance to talk about the Master. I need a little diversion; I am now writing *Mirkasim*. Uh! It is full of conspiracy — only conspiracy and betrayal! I am gasping for breath. I cannot bear it anymore. When I go to bed, I see Mirkasim in my dreams. He comes and moves his full-bearded face near mine.'"[27]

In the fall of 1906 Girish was very ill and suffering from asthma. The owners of the Minerva came to see him and said: "Sir, we are sorry you are not well. All of the other theatres are presenting new plays and we are unable to present anything new." Girish reassured them: "Don't worry. Let me see what I can do." On that day he began to read the works of Moliere, the famous French playwright. Within a few days he wrote a satire, *Yaisa-ka-Taisa*, based on Moliere's *L'Amour Medicin*, which was first performed at the Minerva on 1 January 1907. It proved to be a popular play and continued for a long period.

In the spring of 1907 Girish began writing another historical drama, *Chatrapati Shivaji*, which premiered at the Minerva on 16 August 1907. Shivaji was a great hero of Maharashtra, a devout Hindu and worshipper of Shiva and the Divine Mother Bhavani. His guru was Ramdas, and under his guidance Shivaji raised an army and established an ideal Hindu kingdom. Shivaji skillfully fought against Aurangazeb, the famous Mogul emperor, and kept him from extending his empire into South and West India. Girish's genius made all the characters in this drama come alive. The play generated tremendous national sentiment.

Girish then left the Minerva and joined the Kohinoor Theatre. After three weeks *Chatrapati Shivaji* was performed at the Kohinoor and Girish acted in the role of Aurangazeb. The story of Shivaji was so popular and patriotic that the owners of the Minerva and the Kohinoor both continued producing the same play in their theatres. All of the newspapers wrote favourable reviews of this play. The *Bangabasi* remarked: "In this world Girish is his own peer."[28] Surendra Nath Bandyopadhyay wrote in the *Bengalee*: "*Chatrapati* is one of the best and most powerful dramas ever produced on the Indian stage."[29]

The Statesman wrote: "The popularity of Babu Girish Chandra Ghose's powerful drama 'Chatrapati', which deals with some of the most striking incidents in the life of Shivaji, is manifest from the large audiences which are attracted to the Minerva Theatre on every occasion that this thrilling play is billed. Though it has been running for about ten weeks now, the large auditorium was crammed in every part, and early in the evening the sale of tickets had to be stopped, the large overflow helping to fill the adjacent playhouses."[30]

Siraj-ud-Daulla, Mirkasim, and *Chatrapati Shivaji* had roused so much nationalism that the British government became alarmed: It feared that a revolution might occur, so in January 1911, the government banned the printing and performing of these dramas. Girish was brokenhearted. Aparesh Mukhopadhyay recalled: "We had a hard time getting approval of the script for *Siraj-ud-Daulla* from the police department. Girish was present from 7:00 a.m. to 2:00 p.m. and had to change the wording in a few places before it was approved."[31]

Rebellious, Girish began writing *Jhansir Rani*, another play based on well-known historical events. The main character was Lakshmi Bai, who married the king of Jhansi. They had no children, but Lakshmi adopted a boy so that he could inherit the throne. The British government nullified the adoption and moved to occupy Jhansi. The heroic queen Lakshmi Bai decided to fight against the British. She commanded her army from horseback and was killed in battle. Her words, "*Meri Jhansi kabhi nehi diungi* — I will never give up my Jhansi," are recorded in the annals of Indian history.

Girish wrote two acts of *Jhansir Rani* before news of it reached the police. A high-ranking Indian officer came to Girish and said: "Sir, please don't write any more historical dramas. Your three plays — *Siraj-ud-Daulla, Mirkasim,* and *Chatrapati Shivaji* — have been banned, and the same fate will befall this one. Your pen emits fire, and this gives the British heartburn."[32] Thus Girish could not finish his drama. Writers and playwrights cannot express their thoughts freely in a country that is ruled by a dictator or a foreign government.

When Girish was working in the Classic Theatre in 1904, he had another disappointing experience. He had written *Satnam*, which was based on an incident in Indian history. The Mogul Emperor Aurangazeb imposed an unfair tax on the Hindus and forcefully converted Hindus to Islam. The Hindus revolted. Vaishnavi, a Rajput girl, saw her father killed by the Muslims, and she wanted revenge. She formed a warrior group named *Satnami* (Satnam was the name of their God). Vaishnavi was like a Hindu Joan of Arc. She and her followers harassed and defeated the Mogul army many times. Vaishnavi and her army were finally defeated by Aurangazeb. *Satnam* premiered at the Classic on 30 April 1904.

As *Satnam* was based on a conflict between Hindus and Muslims, Girish used some harsh words in his dialogue to make it seem authentic. But Muslims in Calcutta could not bear the performance. They protested in front of the Classic Theatre, and the play closed on the fourth night. It was not only a setback for Girish, but a death blow to the memory of an important event in Indian history. In every country, powerful dictators, politicians, and fanatics try to distort history and suppress the truth, but truth is indestructible and eventually prevails.

In 1908 there was a controversy in Calcutta about widow marriage, which had been legal since 1856. The owners of the Minerva Theatre came to Girish and requested him to write a drama on that subject. Although Girish was in favour of widow marriage, he did not express his personal opinion in the play. Rather, he gave all arguments in favour and against this social custom and left the decision to the audience. He called his play: *Shasti ki Shanti?* (Does widow marriage bring punishment or peace?) This interesting play was first performed at the Minerva on 7 November 1908.

In Calcutta Girish suffered from asthma every winter, so his doctors and friends suggested that he move temporarily to Varanasi during that season. During the winters of 1909 and 1910, he stayed at Ramprasad Chaudhury's garden house in Sigra, Varanasi, and escaped asthma attacks by the grace of Lord Shiva. Abinash, Girish's secretary, described Girish's daily routine in Varanasi:

> Girish stayed at Ramprasad's garden house, near the Central Hindu College. Early in the morning he would go for a long walk and then have breakfast. During his youth he had studied homeopathy and treated many people in Calcutta. In Varanasi he treated many patients in the morning and afternoon by prescribing homeopathic medicine. After lunch he would rest and then answer his mail. In the evenings many monks of the Ramakrishna Order, doctors, lawyers, actors, musicians, and many distinguished people would come to talk to him. His encyclopedic knowledge on religion, philosophy, literature, music, and acting

amazed the listeners. After supper, at 10:00 p.m., he would study and write till midnight. Here he wrote the plays *Shankaracharya* and *Tapobal*, and also some articles for the *Natya Mandir* magazine.[33]

It is hard for a genius to be confined within a limited circle of ideas, so Girish continually explored new themes for his plays. He had already written many social, religious, and historical dramas. Now he decided to write a drama based on Vedanta, in which he would focus on the life of Shankaracharya, an eighth-century philosopher. Swami Brahmananda encouraged him, and Girish took this as an order from the guru, because the scriptures say, "The son of a guru is regarded as the guru." Girish could not direct the drama because he was unwell and was living in Varanasi. His son, Surendra, performed in the title role, but he went to Varanasi first to rehearse the role with his father. *Shankaracharya* opened at the Minerva on 15 January 1910 and was crowned with success.

On 19 March 1910, the *Bengalee* paper reviewed the play:

> Our Indian Garrick, Girish Chandra, when still in the full vigour of youth, brought out his *Chaitanya Lila* and represented the life and teachings of Chaitanya. But it was an easy task comparatively, for Sri Gauranga's creed of love is in itself a fascinating subject, and treated by his masterly pen, it was destined to crown him with success. The creed of Shankaracharya is the creed of knowledge, which is proverbially dry. A student of Hindu Philosophy can hardly guess how Shankara's life and doctrine can form the subject-matter of a dramatic performance, especially in these times when levity on the stage is the order of the day. But our Girish Chandra has performed an apparently impossible task by infusing into the dry loves of the subject, balmy liveliness which has made the drama quite agreeable to every variety of taste. The play, in short, is an all-round masterpiece which adds a fresh laurel to the already overloaded brow of the dramatist.[34]

It is not possible to discuss here all of the plays that Girish wrote in his long career. This chapter has highlighted a few important dramas, and now we shall conclude by briefly discussing his last play, *Tapobal* (The Power of Austerity). This work is based on the Ramayana. The main characters are the sage Vasishtha, a knower of Brahman, and King Vishwamitra, who was aspiring to become a knower of Brahman by practising severe austerities. After obtaining many occult powers and divine weapons, Vishwamitra was tempted by a celestial maiden named Menaka. In *Tapobal*, Girish described the obstacles in spiritual life, and illustrated how Vishwamitra's ego and self-effort almost led him to failure. In the end Vasishtha's grace helped Vishwamitra reach the goal. This play celebrates the supremacy of brahminical power, which originates from sattva, over royal power, which comes from rajas.

On 2 December 1911, the *Bengalee* paper reviewed *Tapobal*:

> The Minerva Theatre has for the past few weeks commenced the representation of a new drama called Tapobal composed by the veteran dramatist Babu Girish Chandra Ghosh. The drama represents to the Indian audience the power of austerities as mentioned in the Vedas and Puranas. How the power of spiritual acquisition enables the votary to raise himself to the highest dignity, unsurpassed by all physical and intellectual acquisition, is what the author presents before the audience.
>
> The play is a grand success, the scenes and songs are all novel, and they are so very enchanting that without personal experience it is impossible to bring them home to the minds of all lovers of fine art. The audience is so carried away during the whole representation that they forget themselves and consider themselves to really be in the midst of these sights and scenes.[35]

Girish started his acting career in 1867, when he was 23 years old; and in 1877, at the age of 32, he began to write plays. His dual career continued until 1912 when he died at the age of 68. As long as he was alive, the Calcutta audience never lacked new theatrical works. The following list of Girish's accomplishments as an actor and playwright, exhibits the magnitude of his genius.

Girish's Original Plays

Play	First Performance	Theatre
1. Agamani	9 September 1877	National (*6 Beadon Street*)
2. Akalbodhan	13 September 1877	"
3. Dollila	4 March 1878	"
4. Mayataru	25 January 1881	Great National (*6 Beadon Street*)
5. Mohini Pratima	9 April 1881	"
6. Aladin	9 April 1881	"
7. Ananda Raho	21 May 1881	"
8. Ravan-badh	30 July 1881	"
9. Sitar Vanabas	17 September 1881	"
10. Abhimanyu-badh	26 November 1881	"
11. Lakshman Barjan	31 December 1881	"
12. Sitar Bibaha	11 March 1882	"
13. Braja-Bihar	1 April 1882	"
14. Ramer Vanabash	15 April 1882	"
15. Sitaharan	22 July 1882	"
16. Bhota Mangal	7 October 1882	"
17. Malin Mala	28 October 1882	"

As a Playwright and Actor (1885–1912)   83

Play	First Performance	Theatre
18. Pandaver Ajnatavas	13 January 1883	"
19. Daksha Yajna	21 July 1883	Star (*68 Beadon St.*)
20. Dhruva Charitra	11 August 1883	"
21. Nala-Damayanti	21 December 1883	"
22. Kamale Kamini	29 March 1884	"
23. Brishaketu	26 April 1884	"
24. Hirar Phul	26 April 1884	"
25. Srivatsa Chinta	7 June 1884	"
26. Chaitanya Lila	2 August 1884	"
27. Prahlad Charitra	22 November 1884	"
28. Nimai Sannyas	28 January 1885	"
29. Prabhas Yajna	3 May 1885	"
30. Buddhadev-Charit	19 September 1885	"
31. Vilwamangal Thakur	3 July 1886	"
32. Bellik Bazar	24 December 1886	"
33. Rupa-Sanatan	21 May 1887	"
34. Purnachandra	17 March 1888	Emerald (*68 Beadon Street*)
35. Nasiram	25 May 1888	Star (*Hatibagan*)
36. Bishad	6 October 1888	Emerald
37. Prafulla	28 April 1889	Star (*Hatibagan*)
38. Haranidhi	8 September 1889	"
39. Chanda	26 July 1890	"
40. Malina Bikash	13 September 1890	"
41. Mahapuja	24 December 1890	"
42. Macbeth	28 January 1893	Minerva
43. Mukul Munjara	5 February 1893	"
44. Abu Hussein	25 March 1893	"
45. Saptamite Visarjan	7 October 1893	"
46. Jana	23 December 1893	"
47. Baradiner Bakhsis	24 December 1893	Star (*Hatibagan*)
48. Swapner Phul	17 November 1894	Minerva
49. Sabhyatar Panda	25 December 1894	"
50. Karameti Bai	18 May 1895	"
51. Phanir Mani	25 December 1895	"
52. Panch Kane	5 January 1896	"
53. Kalapahar	26 September 1896	Star (*Hatibagan*)
54. Hirak Jubilee	20 June 1897	"
55. Parasya Prasun	11 September 1897	"
56. Maya-avasan	18 December 1897	"
57. Deldar	10 June 1899	Classic
58. Pandava Gaurav	17 February 1900	"
59. Maniharan	22 July 1900	Minerva
60. Nandadulal	17 August 1900	"
61. Ashrudhara	26 January 1901	Classic
62. Maner Matan	20 April 1901	"
63. Abhishaph	28 September 1901	"

Play	First Performance	Theatre
64. Shanti	7 June 1902	"
65. Bhranti	19 July 1902	"
66. Ayana	25 December 1902	"
67. Satnam	30 April 1904	"
68. Hara-Gauri	4 March 1905	Minerva
69. Balidan	8 April 1905	"
70. Siraj-ud-Daulla	9 September 1905	"
71. Basar	26 December 1905	"
72. Mirkasim	16 June 1906	"
73. Yaisa ka Taisa	1 January 1907	"
74. Chatrapati Shivaji	17 August 1907	"
75. Shasti ki Shanti?	7 November 1908	"
76. Shankaracharya	15 January 1910	"
77. Ashoka	3 December 1910	"
78. Tapobal	18 November 1911	"
79. Grihalakshmi	September 1912	"
80. Chataki	24 December 1927	"

Girish's Unfinished Plays
1. Anami Natak (4 acts)
2. Chol Raj
3. Nityananda Vilas
4. Mahammad Shah (2 acts)
5. Sadher Bau (1 act)
6. Jhansir Rani (2 acts)
7. Rana Pratap (2 acts)
8. Milan Kanan

Girish's Adaptations of Others' Works
1. Kapalkundala
2. Chandrashekhar
3. Durgeshnandini
4. Bishabriksha
5. Mrinalini
6. Sitaram
7. Palasir Yuddha
8. Bhramar
9. Madhavi Kankan
10. Meghnad-badh
11. Yamalaye Jivanta Manush

Other Writings
1. Fiction and short stories — 25
2. Kāvya (poetical works) — 1
3. Biography — 1
4. Articles on Ramakrishna, Vivekananda, religion — 18
5. Articles on drama — 14
6. Obituaries — 8
7. Articles on social affairs — 2
8. Articles on science — 2
9. Miscellaneous articles — 12
10. Songs — 1370

Girish's Career as a Manager and Director
1869-70: Baghbazar Amateur Theatre
1871-73: National Theatre
1874: Great National Theatre (6 Beadon Street)
July 1877-February 1883: National Theatre
May 1883-July 1887: Star Theatre (68 Beadon Street)
November 1887-October 1888: Emerald Theatre
January 1889-February 1891: Star Theatre (Hatibagan)

As a Playwright and Actor (1885–1912) 85

May 1892-March 1896: Minerva Theatre
March 1896-March 1898: Star Theatre (Hatibagan)
July 1898-December 1898: Classic Theatre (68 Beadon Street)
December 1898-March 1899: Minerva Theatre
March 1899-April 1900: Classic Theatre
April 1900-October 1900: Minerva Theatre
November 1900-November 1904: Classic Theatre
November 1904-June 1911: Minerva Theatre

Girish's Performances

Girish demonstrated his art of acting playing in 62 roles. Some important ones are listed below.

Play	Role
Sadhabar Ekadashi	Nimchand
Lilavati	Lalit
Krishnakumari	Bhim Singha
Nildarpan	Mr. Ud
Mrinalini	Pashupati
Akalbodhan	Ramachandra
Meghnad-badh	Rama and Meghnad
Palasir Yuddha	Lord Clive
Bishabriksha	Nagendranath
Durgeshnandini	Jagat Singha & Birendra Singha
Hamir	Hamir
Madhavi Kankan	Seven roles
Aladin	Kuhaki
Ananda Raho	Vetal
Ravan-badh	Ramachandra
Sitar Vanabash	Ramachandra
Abhimanyu-badh	Yudhisthir and Duryodhan
Lakshman Barjan	Ramachandra
Sitar Bibaha	Vishwamitra
Bhoat Mangal	Dancer
Pandaver Ajnatavas	Kichak and Duryodhan
Daksha Yajna	Daksha
Macbeth	Macbeth
Jana	Bidushak (Courtier)
Prafulla	Yogesh
Kalapahar	Chintamani
Maya-avasan	Kalikinkar
Bhramar	Krishnakanta
Pandav Gaurav	Kanchuki
Sitaram	Sitaram
Kapalkundala	Five roles
Bhranti	Rangalal
Ayana	Srishtidhar

Play	Role
Vilwamangal	Sadhak
Hara-Gauri	Hara
Balidan	Karunamay
Siraj-ud-Daulla	Karimchacha
Mirkasim	Mirjafar
Chatrapati Shivaji	Aurangazeb
Shankaracharya	Shiuli
Chandrashekhar	Chandrashekhar and three roles
Rakamfer	Jali

Girish's Works Translated into Other Languages
1. *Buddhadev-Charit* was translated into English and was later staged in the Court Theatre in London.
2. *Nala-Damayanti* was translated into French.
3. *Vilwamangal* was translated into English by Baikuntha Nath Basu and was edited by Sister Nivedita.
4. *Bishad* was translated into Hindi and was staged in Allahabad.

Serious readers of Girish will agree that his ideas are awe-inspiring and far-reaching. Observing the five large volumes of his writings, comprising 3,717 pages, and finding him acting in so many roles and managing so many theatres, one may wonder how it was possible for one person to accomplish so much in one lifetime! Without even finishing school, Girish remained absorbed in the ocean of knowledge like an ancient rishi, gathering gems that he distributed to humanity. Perhaps someone will be inspired to translate Girish's important works into English someday.

Chapter 7

As a Dramatic Director

Girish was not only a brilliant playwright and actor but also an outstanding director. As might be expected, Girish's innovations in the theatre were met with some opposition. His irregular blank verse was criticized by traditional writers. He was also vehemently attacked by puritans for engaging courtesans for women's roles in his dramas. Before this, men had generally performed in women's roles. Often the women Girish chose proved to be dedicated and talented actresses. They were poorly educated, but Girish trained them and wrote his dramas in simple language so that they could portray the characters with naturalness. The famous actress Tinkari said: "I was an illiterate girl. It was by his [Girish's] grace that I am now an actress."[1]

Contrary to his reputation, Girish was actually a very serious and disciplined man, and eventually he was able to gain respect and attention. In fact, Girish's waywardness was somewhat overemphasized. In *The Face of Silence* Dhan Gopal Mukerji revealed another side of him:

> Not only was he our greatest modern playwright, he was also a great actor and producer. It was he who revealed to the women of the underworld that they could change their lives for the better by taking up acting as a trade. Many wretched souls he saved by training them to act. Not only that, he also lifted up and revealed to the eyes of the public at least half a dozen actresses of the highest rank, who had hitherto been condemned to a life of vice while boys played the parts of women on the stage. Since Girish, all that has been changed.
>
> The other day in India when one of his star actresses, now an old woman, called on my wife and myself, she told us how "Father" — that is what she called Girish — worked. "He brought about a revolution in the life of womanhood in general. Women in terrible penury, instead of being forced down into the abyss of vice, were now rescued by the stage. But Father did not stop there. He brought us all in touch with the teachings of Ramakrishna.

> "He wanted us to come to the monastery during the hours of worship and pray to God. Some of us were afraid lest we soil the sacred grounds. Father answered: 'If Ramakrishna were living, he would teach you and me himself. He loves us. Didn't he come to earth for the fallen like ourselves?'"
>
> Our talks with many other old actors and actresses convinced us that Girish, by staying with his old Bohemian companions, did more spiritual good than if he had left them. After his soul's second birth, he did not act like a moral parvenue; he repudiated nothing of his past. Instead, he slowly permeated his friends and his writings with the spirit of Ramakrishna. And as for the Power of Attorney that he gave his guru, Turiyananda and others testify that he never violated it. All of them affirm, "Girish was the most religious of us all; he lived, as he said he would, by the promptings of the Indweller."[2]

Girish had experienced a wide range of intense emotions in his life. These experiences, especially grief, helped him to vividly express human emotions onstage. This ability is vital for playwrights, actors, and directors. Girish's heart was devastated by sorrow after sorrow. He found solace by writing poems and songs, and by meeting his guru, Ramakrishna. The more he faced illness and death in his family, the brighter his talent shone and the stronger his faith in Ramakrishna grew.

Girish said: "Without encountering pain and suffering in life, it is extremely difficult to become a poet or a playwright. A playwright has to experience the truth by facing various adverse circumstances. A real poet does not write a poem without experiencing it. By God's grace I have seen all types of characters — from low prostitutes and debauchees to a highly venerable avatar. This whole world is a vast stage and the theatre is its microscopic form."[3]

During the last part of the nineteenth century there were two great dramatic directors in Bengal: Girish Chandra Ghosh and Ardhendu Shekhar Mustafi. Abinash, Girish's biographer and secretary, compared the teaching methods of these two directors so that readers could understand Girish's unique genius. According to Abinash, Ardhendu was not a playwright: He directed plays written by others and assigned the various roles by observing the characters of the actors and actresses employed by the theatre in which he was working. Girish first formed his theatre ensemble, then wrote a play he deemed suitable for them, and finally cast and directed each role accordingly. Therefore, while helping to found the Bengali stage, Girish built both the chariot and the path.

Abinash recalled:

As a Dramatic Director   89

Left to right: Paresh Chandra Sen, Girish Ghosh, and Abinash Gangopadhyay (secretary)

We have watched and listened to the rehearsals of both Ardhendu and Girish. Ardhendu would instruct his students to imitate the character of the drama exactly the way he himself understood and imagined it. His motto was: 'I am giving you the script of the role. Now you follow the character as much as you can.' The students would find it difficult to proceed in this way, but somehow they tried to bring the play to the stage.

Girish's teaching method was completely different. Before rehearsing a new play, Girish would read the entire drama in front of the actors and actresses. While listening, they would visualize and imagine the personality and moods of all the characters of the drama. They could then easily understand the personality and status of each character and the effect of each character on the entire drama. As a small part and a large part of a machine have equal utility and effectiveness, so also in a dramatic plot a small role and a large role both have importance and necessity. One cannot understand this fully until one pays close attention to the entire drama.

In addition, Girish would focus on each role, especially the major ones, and then train the students according to their natural ability. First, he concentrated on the voice of the actors: It must be natural to them and also impressive to the audience. Second, he keenly observed the actors' physical gestures, manifestation of mood, facial expression, and movement of the eyes. He would then direct his students in such a way that their artistic faculty or acting ability might be enhanced more and more by practice. He never wanted his students to blindly imitate, thus relinquishing their originality. For example, he would represent to his students several interpretations of a particular character, and then ask them to follow the one that appealed to them most.

In this way the actors and actresses would become inspired when their acting talent manifested itself, because they had eliminated the difficulty of imitation. Moreover, their delightful performances would charm the audience. As a result of this kind of training, the audience would see a new style of acting from Girish's handpicked actors and actresses. The acting — from the character of an ordinary messenger to that of a king or queen — flowed simply, smoothly, and naturally till the end of the drama. Thus a drama that Girish directed was never stereotyped or hackneyed.

As Girish took special care in directing the drama, so also in writing the drama he would create the mood and the language while keeping the reciting and acting abilities of his main actors and actresses in mind. For this reason, the actors and actresses considered themselves to be fortunate to have any role in one of Girish's new dramas. They never before had such a golden opportunity, nor such wonderful training to display their acting skill with minimal effort.[4]

Aparesh Mukhopadhyay, an actor and playwright, wrote in his famous book, *Rangalaya Tirish Batsar* (30 Years in the Theatre): "Girish was our Dramatic Director. We were extraordinarily fortunate to learn acting under his guidance. It was a great boon, the pride and joy of my acting life."[5]

Aparesh described the rehearsal of *Rana Pratap*, a famous historical drama written by Dwijendralal Roy:

> We decided to stage this long drama within five days. Rehearsal started on Monday. Girish and Mr. Roy were present and each actor and actress had a copy of the book in hand. Girish asked Mr. Roy: "Sir, you start the rehearsal. As you are the author of this play, you prompt the parts." Mr. Roy replied: "My goodness! I can't do that. You are a wonderful director. Please, you conduct the rehearsal, and let me listen."
>
> Rehearsal began. Girish and Mr. Roy sat side by side on two chairs. The actors and actresses sat in front of them and everywhere there was

pin-drop silence. Whenever Girish would conduct a rehearsal, there was tremendous excitement in the gathering. Many writers, playwrights, and critics would come and sit quietly and watch Girish's art of direction. It was a glorious period for the Bengali stage. However, after listening to two hours of rehearsals, Mr. Roy left, saying, "It will be wonderful!"[6]

Aparesh also wrote about the writing and direction of *Siraj-ud-Daulla*:

Before writing any play, Girish would study all the available books on that subject. He first collected and studied all the books about Siraj and the history of Murshidabad [the capital of Siraj] and the East India Company [the British colonists], and then he began to write *Siraj-ud-Daulla*. At that time his room looked like a small library while he remained absorbed in studying the detailed history of Bengal. His method of writing was such that he would not give dictation to his secretary until he completely understood the theme. If someone asked him to write a new play, he would reply: "How can I write a play? I have no time to read."

When the script of *Siraj-ud-Daulla* was finished, we began to rehearse with great enthusiasm. This was Girish's method of rehearsal: Before giving any direction, he would read aloud the entire script of the play. The owner of the theatre, the actors, actresses, stage manager, make-up artists, and others would listen to him attentively. He would read each role exactly the way it was to be enacted. As a result, everyone could visualize each character. When the reading was over, Girish would ask everyone's opinion irrespective of whether they were learned or illiterate. He would not disregard even the opinion of an unlettered stagehand who changed the scenes on the stage. One day I asked Girish: "Sir, why are you asking the view of that illiterate person? What does he understand?"

Girish replied: "He may not be able to answer like a drama critic, and I did not ask his opinion from that standpoint; but on the whole he would be able to say whether the story appealed to his heart, which is free from ego and uncluttered by erudition. Look, the full moon brings joy to the learned as well as to the illiterate. I write dramas not only for learned pandits but for everyone. The goal of a drama is to give joy to all people — the pandit, the illiterate, men, and women. For that reason, one should introduce different moods in a drama. I consider his opinion to be of some value. If someone like him comes to see the play, he should not feel that the money he spent and the sleep he lost were for nothing."[7]

Nowadays some directors are so proud and sensitive that they cannot tolerate any criticism. Aparesh revealed Girish's humility and his understanding of human psychology.

In addition to his plays, Girish also wrote some important articles on the dramatic arts in Bengali, including "Acting and the Actor," "Women

Acting in Men's Roles," "Criticism of an Actress," "How to Become a Famous Actress," "The Appeal of an Actor," "The Stage," "The Modern Theatre," "Theatre: A Temple," "A Playwright," "Make-Up," and "Dancing."

In 1901 Girish wrote an article in the journal *Rangalaya* entitled "Women Acting in Men's Roles." Michael Madhusudan Datta had originally suggested that women could act in women's roles. Then Sharat Chandra Ghosh introduced the practice in his Bengal Theatre in 1873.[8] But it was Girish who brought a revolution in the theatre by recruiting talented girls from red-light districts and training them to be actresses. However, many puritans — even the great social reformer Ishwar Chandra Vidyasagar and the great poet Rabindra Nath Tagore — did not approve of this.[9] (See Chapter 4 for a discussion on how women were introduced to the Bengali stage.)

Girish analyzed the problem in *Rangalaya* from a director's point of view: In the beginning he used young girls to act in the roles of young boys, such as Dhruva in *Dhruva Charitra*, Chaitanya and Nityananda in *Chaitanya Lila*, but he did not think this approach was successful. Girish wrote: "As a boy cannot act well in a woman's role, so also a woman's acting as a man looks unnatural." Girish wrote that Binodini had performed the early life of Chaitanya very well, but she could not fully manifest the adult Chaitanya's god-intoxicated mood. Similarly, the famous French actress Sarah Bernhardt acted in the title role of Shakespeare's *Hamlet*. The audience saw Sarah as Hamlet on the stage: She dressed like a boy and pretended to be a boy. A woman was imitating a boy's naughtiness and playful mood. But she could not hide her bosom and although she was a famous actress, her performance in *Hamlet* was not successful.[10]

As a director, Girish selected courtesans to act in the roles of women in his dramas because at that time no girls from good families were permitted by their parents to act on the stage. In March 1906, a school headmaster wrote an article in *Rangalaya* criticizing the acting of the courtesans onstage because he thought it would increase immorality among young students. Girish wrote a long and logical rejoinder in the same magazine. Here is an excerpt:

> Is it possible for a headmaster to remove all the bad habits of his students and make the school flawless? A director of a theatre focusses his attention on training the actors and actresses to act well and give joy to the audience. The goal of good actresses is not to tempt the audience by casting glances at them; otherwise they would not be praised by the critics for their acting. If one wants to see flirtatious ladies, one need not spend

money to go to the theatre. That can be seen on the street and elsewhere. A lustful man thinks all women desire him, which is not true.

Once a gentleman from Calcutta went to Vrindaban and said to a brahmachari: "I see there is a lot of adultery going on here." The brahmachari replied: "Sir, you can see that frequently in Calcutta. Why have you spent money to come here? Please see Radha and Krishna in Vrindaban." When Sri Ramakrishna came to see the play, he would salute the actresses, saying, "My Blissful Mother." He even blessed an actress with these words, "Mother, be illumined."[11]

Finally, Girish appealed to *Rangalaya* readers:

We hope our theatres will be made pure by the touch of the feet of holy people. These actresses will replace their censured profession with this wonderful art of acting, and thus they will receive blessings from the holy people and praise from the public. My request to the critics is not to hate these women, but rather to be well-wishers of the theatre and give advice to the directors about how to remove blemishes from it. Our method of correction is different: There is no hatred, only compassion; no fault-finding, but rather seeing good qualities; mild rebuke for great mistakes; encouragement for good deeds. Only motherly affection — not erudition — can eradicate bad samskaras.[12]

Usually the playwright writes the script; the casting director selects the actors and actresses; and the director stages and directs the play. The set designer, the lighting technician, the sound technician, the special-effects director, the stage manager, the make-up artist, the wardrobe master, the choreographer, the music director, and other professionals come forward to complete the production. Girish was such a genius that he wrote over 90 plays, composed the songs for them, selected and directed the actors and actresses, managed the stage design, oversaw the costume design, and instructed the dancing and music teachers. He even gave financial advice to the theatre owners. Girish's positive, optimistic, and practical attitude made him a successful director, and every owner wanted him to work in his theatre.

In his memoirs Girish recorded his wide range of experiences regarding theatre, acting, and actors. He left this document as his legacy for future generations:

It is said that a poet is born and so is an actor. One cannot be an actor through schooling and training alone. Of course an actor needs training, but generally he needs good posture, good looks, and a sweet voice. A homely person cannot act in the role of a hero simply by applying make-up. In some plays, an ugly person is necessary, such as the hero of Victor Hugo's "Hunchback of Notre Dame." The role of a serious part needs the right kind of body; so also the role of a jester needs the appropriate body. A king uses a sweet voice when he talks to the queen, but he needs a commanding tone when he gives orders to his army. The language and accent of an actor can be an obstacle to acting. For example, the Bengali accent of an East Bengal person is not suitable for the Calcutta stage.

An actor should not perform carelessly or half-heartedly. The audience may be large or small, appreciative or inappreciative, but the actor must present his skill with sincerity. Sometimes we hear that a great actor has left a deep impression on the audience by acting in a particular role and that none can surpass him. Knowing this, a real actor should not be afraid to accept that role; rather, he should meet the challenge and devote his energy, sincerity, and ingenuity to it. Previously Miss Siddons became famous in acting the role of Lady Macbeth; later Sarah Bernhardt also became famous in acting the same role. In our country, Rama and Lakshmana are changed every year in the *Ramlila*. So also in England Romeo and Juliet are changed every year and the audience then sees something new in those characters. This novelty originates from different actors and actresses becoming absorbed in the characters in different ways. This is how they charm the audience.

Sometimes ambitious actors and actresses fight for the main roles of a drama without knowing which role will suit them. If they do not get their desired roles, they become angry with the director. Suppose they get their desired roles: They will not be able to satisfy the audience. Ego is the main obstacle to an actor's meditation on his role. Sarah Bernhardt fully acknowledged this in her autobiography.

Finally, an actor's first duty is to wander in the realm of ideas and imagination and lift the audience to that realm. How does he do it? Meditation is the answer. Second, the actor must practise according to his meditation. Third, the actor's dress and make-up are very important. Sometimes we noticed that an actor's acting may not be up to the mark, but he receives an ovation from the audience because of his wonderful costume and make-up.[13]

As a director, Girish realized that absorption in one's role is not enough to make a good actor. He said: "While acting, an actor divides his mind and focusses it in two ways: With one half of his mind he remains absorbed in his own role, and with the other half he becomes a witness. At that time he watches how he is absorbed in his role, the delivery of his speech, the reaction and dialogue of his co-actors, and whether his voice is reaching the last row of the theatre. An actor learns this technique through training and practice."[14]

Upendranath Vidyabhusan, a witness to Girish's acting and an art critic and author, wrote:

> Drama is a visual form of literature. When Girish dictated the dialogue for each character, his voice and facial expression would change accordingly, as if he was acting in that role. He was extremely skillful in modulating his voice as well as in applying his make-up. He could mesmerize the audience by presenting various moods in a particular scene. In fact there was not another single all-round talented director in India like Girish, and it is hard to say how many like him were in Europe and America. Someone may ask: where did he get such training, skill, and erudition regarding drama?
>
> Well, he was deeply interested in plays and acting from his early youth. Wherever there was any theatrical performance or any discussion about drama, he would go there, leaving all his duties. In addition, he would attentively study innumerable books on drama and acting and try to act according to the guidelines of those books. To learn archaeology and history he became a member of the Asiatic Society. But he was not satisfied with reading books; he regularly visited well-known scientists and theologians, such as Dr. Mahendralal Sarkar and Father Eugene Lafont. He read all dramas published in Europe and Asia during his lifetime. He also studied the English translation of the plays published in the French, Belgian, Norwegian, Spanish, and German languages. Girish's personal library was packed with books on drama and acting. No professors of our universities were as well versed in the science and art of acting as Girish. He was truly a unique acting director.
>
> First he would select an actor and his role in the play, and then explain to him everything about that particular role. He would also make clear the meaning of difficult words if there were any in that role, and finally he would ask the actor to memorize the lines. During the rehearsal of that role, Girish would teach the actor the physical movements, facial expressions, modulation of voice, and mood needed for that role. Girish actually was the pioneer of many novel methods of acting on the Bengali stage.[15]

From October 1869 to February 1912, Girish dominated the Bengali stage as an actor, playwright, and dramatic director. During this period he also trained many young actors and actresses, who loved and respected him as their guru. Even some of Girish's contemporaries — Mahendralal Basu, Amritalal Mukhopadhyay, and Matilal Sur — regarded him as their guru. Only a jeweler knows the value of a jewel. Because Girish was a great actor himself, he recognized talent in others. For example, once while watching a yatra performance, Girish was struck by the powerful voice of one of the actors. He brought the actor, Amritalal Mitra, to the Star Theatre, where he trained him and gave him important roles in many of his plays. Amritalal became a superstar of the Bengali stage.

Girish also found some wonderfully talented young women in the red-light districts of Calcutta. Under his guidance, they became famous actresses: Binodini, Tinkari, Tarasundari, Basantakumari, Kiranbala, Pramadasundari, Nagendrabala, Narisundari, Kusumkumari, Sushilasundari, and others were all his students. He was like a loving father and compassionate guru to these actresses. Some writers have exaggerated Girish's sinful character, but the testimonies of these women reveal his true nature and the pure relationship he had with them.

Binodini wrote in her autobiography:

> In the theatre I was the right-hand person of Girish Babu and proud to be his first and main disciple. He was always anxious to fulfill even my smallest request. In every play, Girish Babu gave the main roles to me, Amrita Mitra, Amrita Basu, and to himself. With great care he taught me how to act. His method of teaching was wonderful. First he would explain the idea and mood of the role and then ask me to memorize the script. Whenever he had a little time, he would describe the fascinating stories and plays of Shakespeare, Milton, Byron, and Pope, and sometimes he would explain to us the art of acting from their works. If any famous actresses came to Calcutta from England, he would send us to watch their acting so that we could learn more. It was because of his training that when I acted on the stage, I would become one with that character and completely forget myself.[16]

Tinkari had very little education, but she acted in many of the main roles in Girish's plays, such as Lady Macbeth, Jana, Subhadra, and Sri. She attained much fame, wealth, and acclaim. In her reminiscences she wrote: "The most venerable Girish Babu trained me with special care, and for that reason, being an illiterate girl, I was able to achieve love and adoration from lovers of the theatre."[17]

Sushilasundari wrote: "We don't know about the genius of our guru Girish Chandra; we don't know anyone else who has written as many books as he did. We don't have the power or inclination to judge the pros and cons of his dramas. We are incapable of judging his good and bad qualities. But this much we know: he was a great soul; he was our guru, father, and trainer. He imparted a little light of wisdom in our hearts. He taught us to make our living by earning money by the sweat of our brows. He never hated us, but rather loved us immensely."[18]

Narisundari wrote: "The civilized people of society told me: 'As you are not born in a good family of society, you should go on living a sinful life, and we will hate and reprimand you by the power of our virtue.' Girish Babu was not this kind of virtuous man; he was a great soul. For that reason, he made this wretched girl act in the role of Nityananda in *Chaitanya Lila* and Pagalini in *Vilwamangal* and made me speak sweet, inspiring words."[19]

Basantakumari wrote: "Sitting at the feet of Girish Babu we learned not only acting but that great soul also touched our sorrowful hearts. He treated us as his affectionate daughters. His love, care, and inspiration sprinkled the water of peace on our burning lives."[20]

Hemendra Nath Dasgupta wrote: "Although Girish had slander showered on him because of his association with these actresses in the theatre, we heard directly from Binodini and other actresses about his stainless character. Girish was a serious person and if he had had no steadiness of character, he would not have been able to command love and respect from all types of people in the theatre."[21]

Girish wanted to make the theatre a temple of national education. He wrote: "We want to make people understand that the origin of art is the theatre: The playwrights write plays; the actors and actresses present a message through their acting; the singers create music; the painters paint the scenes; the sculptors decorate the stage; the scientists show the unreal as real by creating special effects. Thus we see that all kinds of art are evolving from the theatre."[22]

Girish was not only the founding father of the Bengali stage, but also a luminous star. The English are proud of Shakespeare; the Germans of Goethe; the French of Moliere; so the Bengalis are proud of Girish. In fact, such a versatile genius like him is extremely rare in the world: He was a talented playwright and poet, a thrilling actor, a wonderful composer of songs, a storyteller, an outstanding director and educator, an original thinker and philosopher, a great devotee, and a lover of the fallen and downtrodden in society. If Girish's works were to be translated from Bengali into English, people the world over would appreciate and benefit from this great nineteenth-century genius. During his lifetime, Girish was compared to David Garrick of England, an actor and playwright. King George III of England was Garrick's patron, but Girish relied only on his creative faculty, his charismatic personality, his indomitable energy, and the grace of his guru.

During the winter of 1909 Girish was suffering from asthma, so his doctors and friends advised him to leave Calcutta and go to Varanasi to improve his health. Accordingly, Girish stayed in Varanasi for a few months, and this helped him immensely. Because Girish was famous and had encyclopedic knowledge, many distinguished people in Varanasi came to see him to discuss religion, philosophy, drama, acting, and so on. Some of his admirers asked him to demonstrate how an actor's facial expressions change according to the change of moods in a play. He consented to do so. Although he was then 65 years old and not well, he satisfied his friends' curiosity. A photographer was engaged and he took some wonderful pictures of Girish, presented here.

An Actor's Portfolio 99

This series of portraits was taken of Girish in 1909 at Varanasi. The first is entitled "En Esse," or Girish in his essential nature. The subsequent poses form an actor's portfolio of emotional states.

Rumination

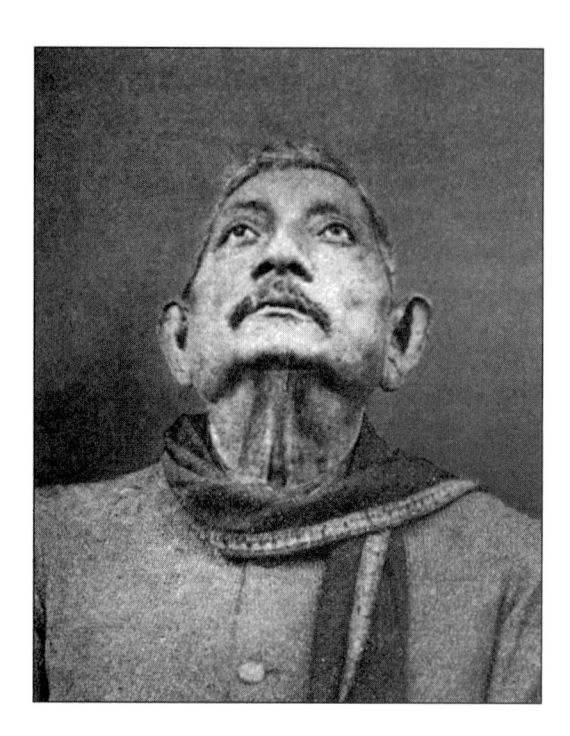

Contemplation

Deliberation

An Actor's Portfolio 101

Revulsion

Elation

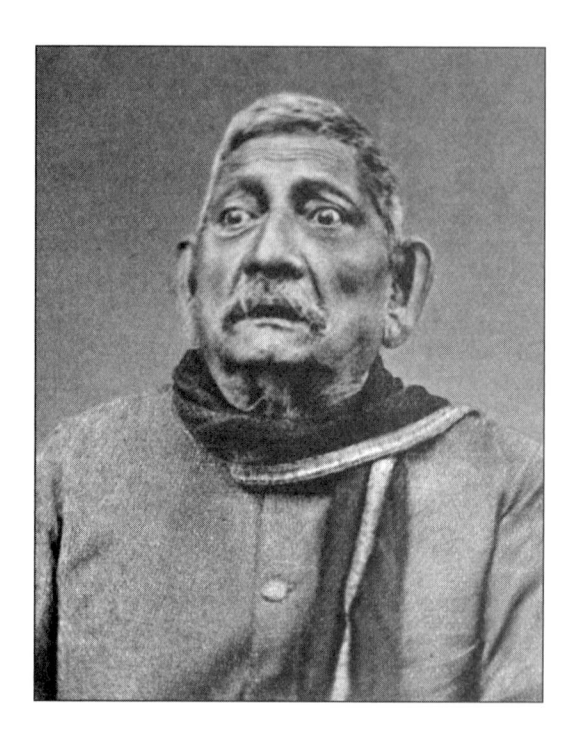

Frightened

Sinister motive

An Actor's Portfolio 103

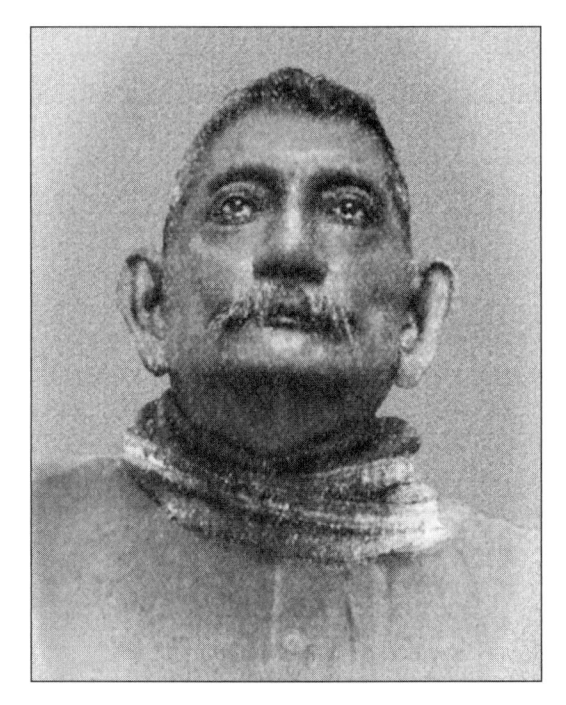

Infatuation

Enraptured

104 ◦⟶ Girish Chandra Ghosh

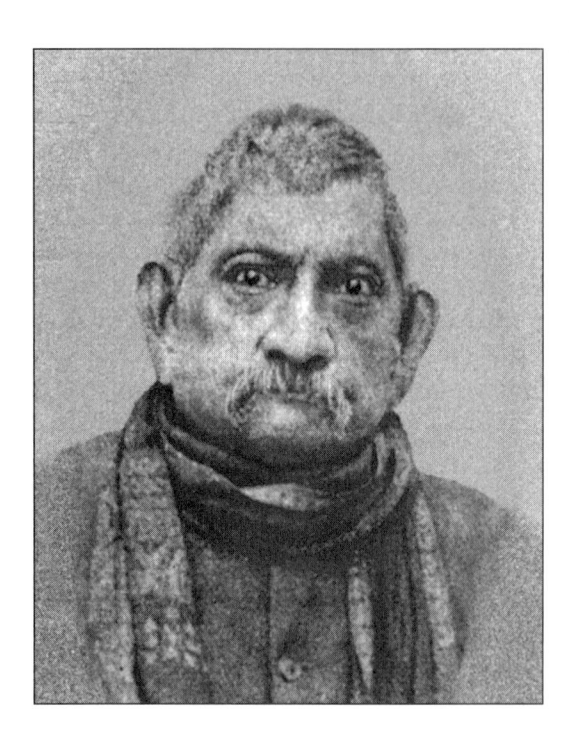

Determination

Displeasure

An Actor's Portfolio 105

Feigning grief

Terrified

106 — Girish Chandra Ghosh

Drunk

Simpleton

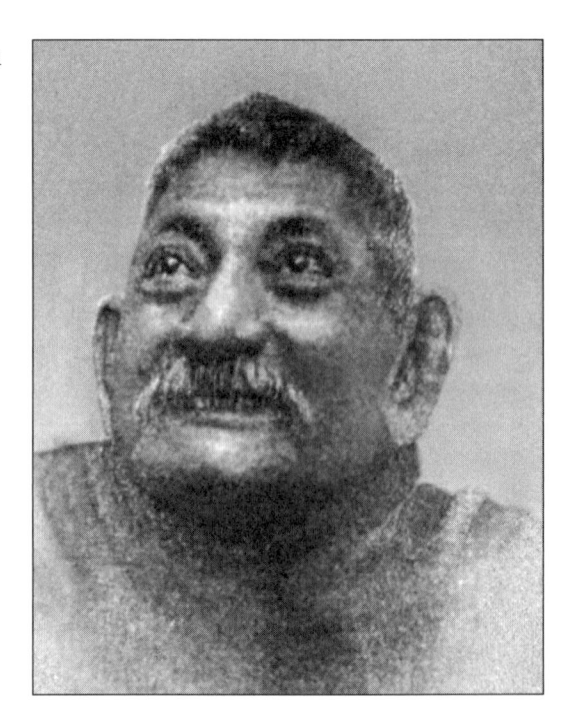

An Actor's Portfolio 107

Curious

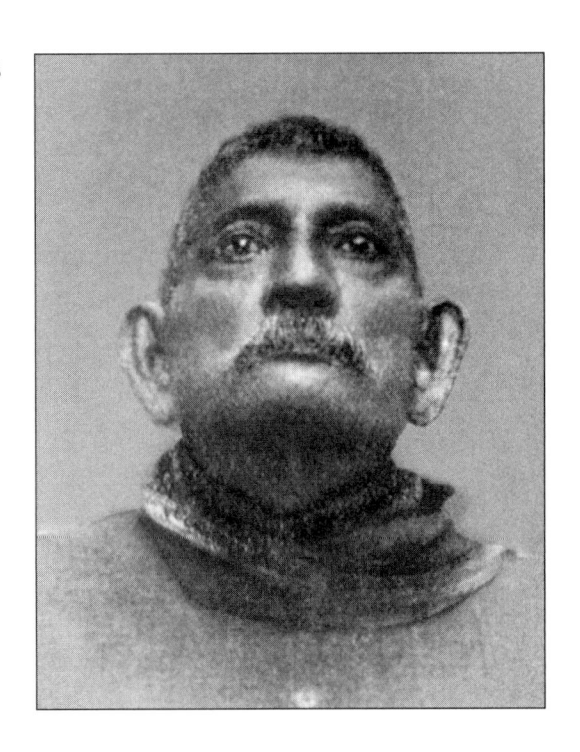

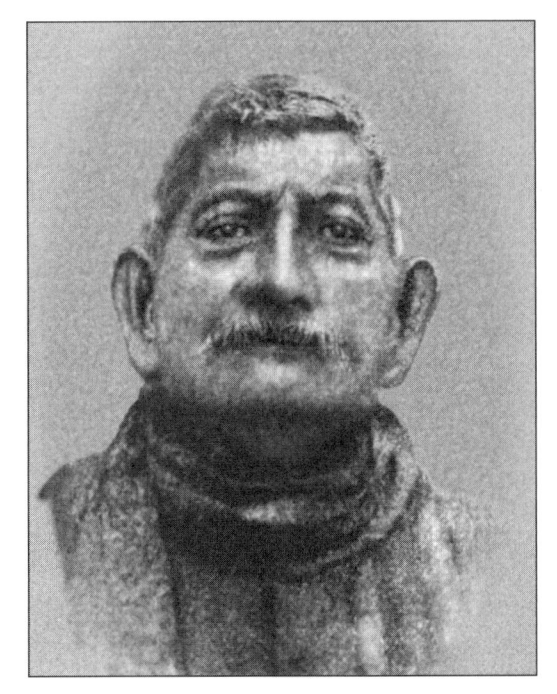

Joyous sympathy

108 — Girish Chandra Ghosh

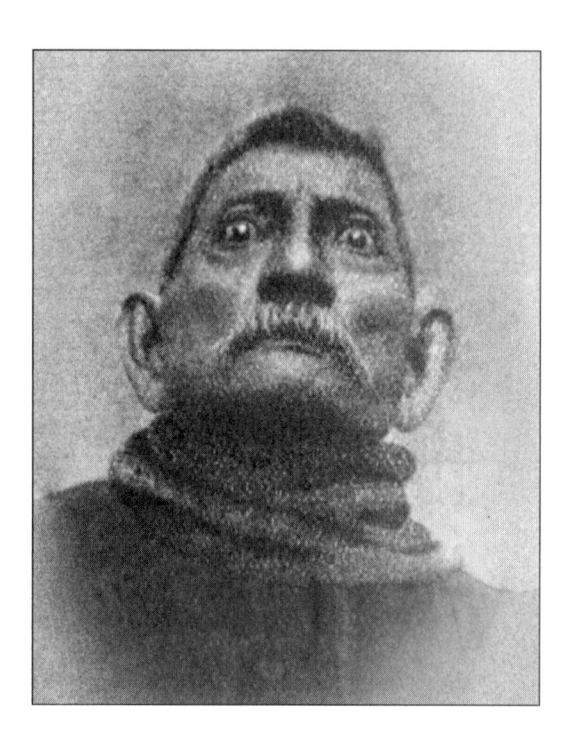

Shocked

Expectation

Introspection

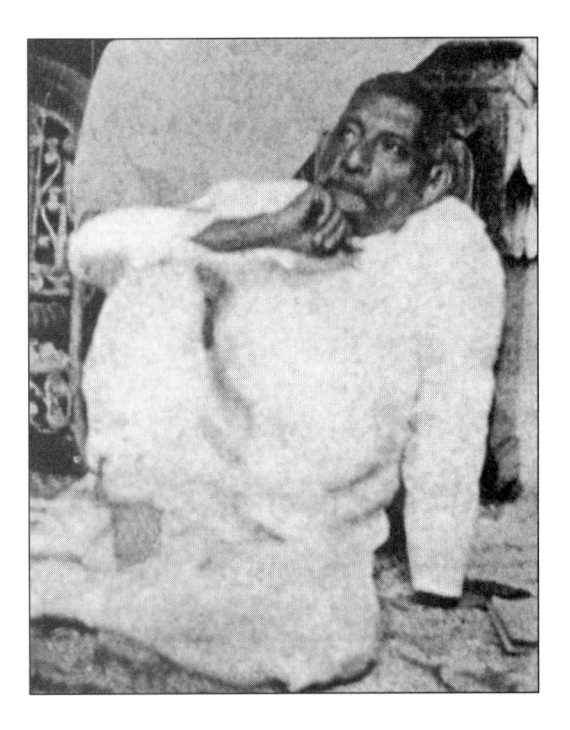

My play is done

Chapter 8

From Atheist to Devotee
(1867–1873)

*I*t is said that atheists keep religion alive because atheists think of God more often than so-called believers. Most of the time true atheists believe that God does not exist. Thus they think of God in a negative way. Napoleon said, "A man cannot become an atheist merely by wishing it." Francis Bacon wrote, "Atheism is rather in the lip than in the heart of man." This was true in Girish's life. His large ego and exuberant energy drove him to refuse God, challenge His existence, fight against His will, and ridicule His devotees. Girish was a born actor, and playing the role of an atheist forced him to think of God most of the time.

As described in Chapter 2, Girish became wayward as a young man because he had no guardian, and because he had suffered a series of tragedies. India was in transition at that time. Young people were greatly influenced by Western education and religion, and they started questioning their traditional religious beliefs. Some were so brainwashed by Western teachers and Christian missionaries that they lost faith in the Hindu religion. They were further confused by the advent of several new faiths such as the Brahmo Samaj, the Arya Samaj, the Hari Sabha, and others. Girish could not ascertain what was right or wrong in such religious chaos, so he did not have much faith in the Hindu religion. Gradually he became an atheist.

Although Girish led a wanton life, a hidden spiritual current flowed in his heart, as his close childhood friend Kalinath Basu witnessed. Kalinath, Girish's contemporary and neighbour, was a court inspector and later became the first Bengali superintendent of police. In 1867, when Kalinath was a railway police officer in Raniganj, Girish visited him and stayed at his house. Girish was then 23 years old. Here is the 14 February 1867 entry from Kalinath's diary: "At noon Girish and I, sitting on my couch, had a talk about moral conduct in life. Girish admitted that he was living a bad life and was denigrating himself. He wanted to correct himself. I am very sorry for him and wish his recovery. What a dreadful world — he says that he has no belief in the existence of the Almighty! I shall pray for him. Girish admits there is happiness in reliance on God. Oh, I must try to have that as much as possible. It is prayer I am after, now every day."[1]

Although Girish was a drinker, he did not like to see his friends drunk. Kalinath promised not to drink, but occasionally he did. On 24 February 1867 Kalinath's diary reads: "Girish reminded me that I signed my name in a covenant to the Temperance Society. I had forgotten, so I never thought of it. I am very sorry. I shall never drink but as prescribed by the Temperance Society. Thanks to Girish for the good he has done."[2]

The next day Kalinath wrote in his diary: "My servant stole something from my house last night. I decided to hand him over to the police and punish him according to law, but Girish pleaded with me, saying, 'It is better to forgive the servant's first offence instead of inflicting on him a heavy punishment.'" Kalinath was very strict regarding legal affairs, so Girish had to work hard to persuade him to forgive the servant.[3]

When Kalinath came to Calcutta, Girish went with him to attend the prayer meeting of the Adi Brahmo Samaj. Girish also attended the group's annual festival at which Devendra Nath Tagore, Reverend Becharam, and a preacher from East Bengal spoke. The next day, Girish went to Keshab Sen's house to hear his lecture. Keshab was the leader of the Brahmo Samaj, a rival group, and during his talk he made an uncharitable remark about the lecture of the East Bengal preacher who had spoken at the Adi Brahmo Samaj festival. Young Girish could not bear any kind of hypocrisy, so this pained him immensely. He realized that these religious leaders talked about universal brotherhood, but they harboured ill feelings for each other. From that day on he never visited the Brahmo Samaj again. While Kalinath was working at Monghyr, he met Keshab and became drawn to him. He then took initiation into the Brahmo faith from Keshab Sen. Kalinath died at the age of 38, so he did not live to see Girish's transformation under Ramakrishna's influence.[4]

In the early period of 1867 Girish reflected: "If God exists and religion is an indispensable aspect of human life, then it should be easily available like water, air, and light, which are things essential to life. 'The truth of religion is hidden in the cavity of the heart' — this scriptural statement is not reasonable." However, even during this atheistic period, he had unflinching devotion to his departed parents: Whenever he bathed in the Ganges, he would hold water in his cupped hands and offer it to them, reciting the Tarpan mantra. He thought: "Let me offer water. Who knows? It may truly help my parents." Girish's intense devotion to his parents helped him to endure grief, pain, and danger, and finally to achieve peace.

Girish later wrote about his early religious life:

> When we were students, because of the influence of English education, some became materialists, some Christians, some Brahmos. Seldom did we find anyone who had any faith in Hinduism. Among the Hindus also, there were many sects, such as Shakta, Vaishnava, and so on. Again, there were many sects among the Vaishnavas. Each sect was so intolerant of the other that they would pray for each other to go to hell. Moreover, the brahmin priests were degenerate: they used the wrong scripture to perform a shraddha ceremony. I have seen a priest go to answer the call of nature, then take the impure water from the jug with his finger, rub it on the mud wall, put a mark on his forehead, and then go to perform worship. Observing all these things, I lost faith in my religion.
>
> Again, I read English literature and found that the materialists are the greatest in learning and intelligence. Thus I would consider disbelief in God to be a sign of erudition. But the idea of God is deeply rooted in Indian life, so it is not easy to eradicate God from a Hindu's heart. Sometimes I would argue with my educated friends about the existence of God. Occasionally I visited the Brahmo Samaj, but I remained in the same darkness. I couldn't understand anything. Does God exist? If so, which religion should I follow? Mentally I prayed: "Lord, if you do exist, please show me the way." Gradually I realized that everything is false. If water, air, and light are freely available in our ephemeral life, then why should one search for religion, which is indispensable to eternal life? Materialists are learned and wise and whatever they say is true.[5]

Girish was born with tremendous strength and passion, and his nature never allowed him to do anything halfheartedly. He was a man of extremes. Moreover, he was so proud of his physical strength, learning, and intelligence that he did not care for anybody's opinion. Joseph Addison made a remark: "To be an atheist requires an infinitely greater measure of faith than to receive all the great truths which atheism would deny."[6] Girish studied all the books that supported atheism, and he would declare boldly and loudly, "There is no God." However, human life never passes evenly and smoothly. It encounters disease, grief, death of dear ones, bad days, accidents, persecution, humiliation, and so on.

As described in Chapter 2, Girish was attacked by cholera six months after he married his second wife, Suratkumari. He almost died, but his life was miraculously saved. Girish later described his condition: "At that time I lost my friends; I was trapped in the meshes of danger; my enemies were trying to ruin my life; and those people were trying to exploit my goodness. Seeing no way out, I pondered: 'Does God exist? Does He solve the problem if one sincerely prays?' I mentally prayed: 'O Lord, if You do exist, please show me a haven in this hopeless situation.' Krishna said in the Gita: 'If an afflicted person calls me, I give him shelter.' I realized the words of the Gita are true. As the sun removes darkness, so my sun of hope appeared and removed the darkness of my heart. I found a haven in the shoreless sea of danger."[7]

The curtain was beginning to fall on Girish's atheistic beliefs, yet his doubt persisted. He described his condition in some of the characters in his dramas. For example, in *Vilwamangal*, Somagiri says: "This world is a house of doubt. God is never perceptible by the senses. People only argue and guess about God. The more a person tries to concentrate on God, the more the cloud of doubt covers him."[8]

If a foreign particle enters the eye, one can have no rest until it is out. Similarly, at the age of 32, Girish's life became unbearable because he constantly carried that awful doubt in his mind. He felt breathless, as if this "doubt-demon" were choking him. Under such circumstances, he had no alternative but to seek help. People told him that doubt does not disappear without a guru's advice. So Girish reasoned with himself: "'Who is a guru?' The scriptures say: 'The guru is Brahma, the guru is Vishnu, and the guru is Shiva.' How can I say this of a man? Is there then no hope for me?"[9] Finally, Girish resolved that as Lord Shiva takes away all diseases, he should take refuge in Him.

Girish grew a beard and did not cut his hair; he also bathed in the Ganges every day. He began worshipping Lord Shiva and eating pure vegetarian food. During the festival of Shiva-ratri, he walked 40 to 50 miles to perform worship to Lord Shiva at Tarakeswar. He prayed: "O Lord Shiva, please destroy my doubt. If doubt does not go away without the advice of the guru, then You be my guru." God's grace always dawns in a longing heart. Soon after, Lord Shiva answered Girish's sincere prayer. Girish gradually began to feel that faith in God was becoming established in his heart. He told one of his relatives: "I am making one hundred years' spiritual progress in one day."[10]

After following this sadhana (spiritual discipline) for some time, Girish was desperate to have a direct vision of God. He heard that the Kalighat temple of Calcutta is a very holy place and that the Divine Mother fulfills one's sincere prayers there. Girish began to go to Kalighat every week on Tuesday and Saturday; he would sit near the sacrificial place in front of the temple and pray to the Divine Mother throughout the night. After following this routine for some time, a current of devotion began to flow in his heart. He would sing the glory of the Divine Mother, saying, "Kali Karālbadanā."*

Now Girish developed so much faith in Lord Shiva and the Divine Mother that he cured acute diseases by chanting the Mother's name with deep faith and tremendous willpower.

Amritalal Basu, a well-known actor, recorded his reminiscences about Girish's religious awakening:

> I was closely associated with Girish for forty-two years and learned many things about the art of acting from him. When I was young, he somewhat forced me to write a few plays and poems; I am sure without his encouragement I would not have gotten involved in the venture. I received my first acting lesson from Ardhendu Mustafi, who was my classmate and later became a famous actor and also a comedian. I respected Girish; I addressed him as "guru" because he was not only my acting teacher but much more.
>
> Our family was a very traditional one. We believed in God when we were children, and worship was incorporated into our play. During my youth I was greatly influenced by Keshab Chandra Sen and joined his Brahmo Samaj, which taught me to discard image worship as idolatry. When I joined the public theatre as an actor, I didn't feel any necessity to call on God. Gradually I lagged far away from the door of God and remained in darkness. Thus the days passed by. One day Girish and I left on foot for the theatre on Beadon Street. On the way we came to the Siddheswari Kali Temple at Baghbazar. Girish bowed down to the Divine Mother, but I just stood there. When we began to walk again, Girish asked me, "Didn't you bow down?" "No," I replied. Girish did not say anything. Then we reached Shobhabazar, Girish bowed down to the Lord Panchananda, and I turned my face in another direction. When we resumed our journey, Girish asked, "Why did you turn away?" I replied, "That deity is inauspicious." Girish: "Do you firmly believe that that is true?" I replied: "Everyone says that, so I believe it." Girish: "Very well! Hold onto that faith. Never look at the face of that deity."
>
> On that day we didn't talk about it anymore. A perplexity crept into my mind: "If I believed that deity to be inauspicious, then why should I not believe Him to be auspicious?"
>
> At that time a great change came over Girish's life. The strident atheist's tongue was then vibrating with the sound of "Mother, Mother." Girish would constantly chant "Mother, Mother, Ma Kali, Kali Karalbadana."

---

* The beginning of the meditation mantra of Kali: "We adore the terrible form of the Divine Mother Kali."

We noticed that when he did this his chest would swell with tremendous vigour and his face would beam with a supernatural power. At that time his faith was so firm that there was not a single doubt in his mind. Proudly he would say: "If I call on the Mother loudly and wholeheartedly and want anything, She will fulfill my desire immediately." In the civilized world one may consider this to be superstition, but with my own eyes I have seen Girish cure many chronic diseases within a short time by reciting a hymn to the Divine Mother. Later, one day while acting in the role of Pashupati in *Mrinalini*, he reached such a state that he promised that he would never ask for any power or anything from the Divine Mother, and he resolved never to manifest his powers again. He told us, "Call on the Mother, but don't ask for anything." Girish would recite the Mother's name and the actors and actresses would follow him. Imitating them, I chanted Mother's name but I didn't get any satisfaction in my heart. Rather, I felt emptiness.

One evening after rehearsal we were all seated onstage and Girish was talking about the glory of the Divine Mother. Meanwhile, I felt some kind of agonizing pain in my heart, and humbly said to Girish: "Sir, I used to be all right. But now that I follow you and call on Mother, I feel empty inside; I think it was better for me not to call on Her." Girish waited for a minute and then got up. He said to me, "Listen, come with me." There was a backdrop in the middle of the stage and behind that there was darkness. Girish sat there cross-legged and asked me to sit in the same way. He put his palms on my knees and asked me to do the same to him. He then began to repeat a hymn praising the Divine Mother as the killer of demons and I also recited it with him. I gradually developed goose bumps all over my body and I experienced a blissful current within. Shivering, I grabbed the feet of Girish and said in a choked voice: "O guru, you have made me call on Mother today. I have never experienced such peace, bliss, and ecstasy before." People know that Girish was my acting teacher, but I know he was my real spiritual guru.[11]

"Atheism is a disease of the soul," said Plato. But this disease does not stay in the human system eternally. It can be cured. A positive attitude can eradicate a negative attitude. Faith and lack of faith are all in the mind. Without the help of any guru, Girish uprooted atheism from his mind by his strong determination. Whenever he got a response from the Supreme Being, he wanted to be convinced by testing Him more. The following are some examples of how God's power became manifest through Girish as he developed the ability to heal others.

One day Girish was walking past the National Theatre when he met his old friend Gopal Chandra Mukhopadhyay, the editor of *Sāhitya Samhitā* and the playwright of *Kāmini-Kunja*.

Girish: "Hello, Gopal. I see your health has deteriorated immensely. I didn't recognize you."

Gopal: "I am suffering from dyspepsia. I can't digest any food. I even get acid when I take sago and barley. Without food I may soon die. It is better to die than to live this way."

Girish told Gopal, with a smile: "I shall cure your disease today." He asked someone to bring some *kachuri* (spicy fried bread) from the market. Then he told Gopal, "Please eat this food to your heart's content without fear." Observing his apprehension, Girish asked: "What are you afraid of? Please eat. Just now you said that you were going to die. Why not die after eating this food? Have faith in me. Today you will fully recover from your disease."

Reassured, Gopal ate the kachuri and then drank a glass of water. Finally, Girish said: "Know for certain that you are cured today. Eat whatever you like. Don't fear." After some days Gopal began gaining weight; he came to see Girish at the theatre and thanked him wholeheartedly.[12]

Devendra Nath Basu, Girish's cousin, recalled the following incident: "My friend Upendra Nath Mukhopadhyay had suffered from malaria for six months. Every other day, his temperature would rise at noon. I told this to Brother Girish. He gave me a grain of sago and said: 'You give this sago to Upen. Tell him that Brother Girish has given him this medicine and he will definitely be cured.' Accordingly I gave that sago to Upen on the day he would normally have had a fever. At noon Upen's eyes turned a little red and his forehead became warm. I told him: 'You won't get a fever today.' Upen soon began to perspire and his feverishness disappeared. That fever never returned. When he had had no fever for twelve days, I told him the full story."[13]

Surendra Nath Ghosh, Girish's son, told this story: "When I was a boy I had a pet bird and I would feed it regularly. One day I returned from school to find that the bird was dying. I began to cry. My father was then eating lunch. He asked, 'What happened?' I replied: 'Perhaps my bird was bitten by a poisonous worm. It may die.' My father was eating a mango. He took a mango peel and asked me to feed it to the bird. I said: 'The bird is dying. How will it eat?' He said emphatically, 'You just obey me.' I took the peel and put it near the bird's beak. Meanwhile my tutor arrived and I went to finish my homework. When the teacher left, I rushed to the bird and found it was all right and hopping around inside its cage."[14]

Girish gave up this power after he took refuge in Ramakrishna, as the Master did not like people using occult powers. Ramakrishna said:

"This kind of occult power eventually makes a person a charlatan. It is an obstacle to spiritual life."

Girish had another supernatural ability: He knew what was inside a letter without opening the envelope. He gave up this power also.

The curtain finally fell on Girish's doubts about God when he had the following vision. One night after a performance in the theatre, Girish was praying to the Divine Mother in a dark and solitary place. He felt that the room was filled with a divine effulgence and Someone was saying to him: "Girish, you wanted to see Me, so I have come. Look, you can see Me only by giving up all your hopes and desires, and driving the joys and pleasures of the world from your heart entirely. After seeing Me, a person never returns to the world [meaning that he merges into Cosmic Consciousness]."

Girish described what happened then: "When I heard that voice, I was scared to death. If I died who would look after my children? What would happen to those poor friends who depended on me? I closed my eyes and said: 'No, Mother, I don't want to see You now.' I then heard clearly: 'If you don't want to see Me, accept My boon. I never appear without giving something. Please ask for whatever you want.' When I was trying to imagine all the enjoyable objects of the world, my conscience revealed the horrible results of those things in my heart, which was stricken with fear of death. Frightened, I said, 'Mother, I don't want any boon.' I heard again the steady resonant voice: 'My visit always bears results. If you don't want any boon, why then did you call Me? Now take my curse: My open sword must fall on something. Tell me, which aspect of yours shall I destroy?' I was terrified. But my conscience reminded me that one should not give anything bad to a deity, so after deliberation I said: "Mother, I have a reputation as a star actor. Let your sword fall on it." The voice replied: 'So be it.' Afterwards I did not see or hear anything. The scriptures say: *krodhoapi devasya varena tulyah* — Even the anger of God is equal to a boon. I experienced that soon after, as my fame as a playwright gradually eclipsed my celebrity as an actor."[15]

It was after this auspicious experience that Girish met Ramakrishna.

By the time Girish was 40 years old he had written several religious dramas, including *Chaitanya Lila* (Life of Chaitanya), which opened the curtain on his relationship with the Master.

Chapter 9

Chaitanya Lila

In the early 1880s, Girish started to write plays based on the Ramayana, the Mahabharata, the Puranas, and the lives of the great saints of India. In 1884 he wrote *Chaitanya Lila* (The Divine Play of Chaitanya) which dramatized the early life of a great 15th century saint of Bengal. This was the first of five of Girish's plays that Ramakrishna saw performed between 1884 and 1885. This chapter discusses *Chaitanya Lila*. The other four plays — *Prahlada Charitra*, *Nimai Sannyas*, *Brishaketu*, and *Daksha Yajna* — are described in the chapters that follow.

Chaitanya Lila was first performed on 2 August 1884. A little more than one month later Ramakrishna attended a performance.

The Story of *Chaitanya Lila*

Chaitanya (1486-1533) was born Nimai Mishra in Navadwip, Bengal. His father, Jagannath, and mother, Sachi, were both very devoted to God; Jagannath died when Nimai was in school. Nimai was also called Gauranga because his body complexion was *gaur*, or golden. He was a very naughty boy but extremely intelligent. His elder brother, Viswarupa, left home and became a monk.

Nimai married twice. His first wife, Lakshmi, died from a snakebite. He then married Vishnupriya, who was very devoted to him. To support his family, Nimai ran a school. At first he was a logician, but after receiving spiritual initiation he became an ardent devotee of Krishna.

Nimai and his followers introduced kirtan to the public. They would sing and dance on the street glorifying Lord Krishna's name, but were often attacked by two drunkards and ruffians named Jagai and Madhai. One day they injured Nimai's closest associate, Nityananda, but he forgave them and requested them to chant God's name. Nimai eventually transformed Jagai and Madhai.

Over time Nimai came to understand that his mission was to carry the Lord's name from door to door and thus save humanity from endless suffering. He therefore asked his mother for permission to become a monk. He said to his weeping mother: "Mother, if you cry for Krishna, you will get everything, but if you cry for Nimai, you will lose him. Cut your attachment. Bless me, mother, so that your son can carry the Lord's name to all beings." Nimai left home the next day, and his wife lived the rest of her life as a nun.

Staging *Chaitanya Lila*

Here is a list of the main cast members:

Jagannath Mishra (Chaitanya's father)	Nilmadhav Chakrabarty
Sachi (Chaitanya's mother)	Gangamani
Nimai (Chaitanya)	Binodini
Vishnupriya (Chaitanya's wife)	Kiranbala
Nityananda (a disciple of Chaitanya)	Banabiharini
Advaita (a disciple)	Upendranath Mitra
Jagai (a ruffian)	Prabodh Ghosh
Madhai (a ruffian)	Amritalal Mitra

In addition to writing the play, Girish directed it. He engaged Benimadhav Adhikari as the music director. Adhikari was a devout Vaishnava and a great musician. He introduced the play with music and a devotional dance. The audience, which included sadhus, was overwhelmed watching Binodini dance in the role of Chaitanya. A current of devotion flowed on the stage, and Binodini's soul-stirring performance was perfect. While explaining Chaitanya's character and Binodini's acting Girish wrote:

> Inside he was Krishna and outside he was Radha; Purusha and Prakriti manifested in the same form. This dual personality revealed itself in Binodini when she portrayed Chaitanya onstage. When Chaitanya would lose consciousness, saying, "Where is Krishna? Where is Krishna?" in Binodini's performance one would see a woman pining for her beloved. Again, when Chaitanya blessed the devotees, Binodini's performance made her seem a superman. As they watched Binodini onstage, some people in the audience were so overwhelmed that they would rush to take the dust of her feet. Sri Ramakrishna blessed her, touching her head, saying, "Be illumined." Even hermits living in caves seek that blessing.[1]

Girish was brilliant, yet practical. When he discovered that there was not enough money to buy expensive costumes, he selected dramas that did not require costly royal dress. *Chaitanya Lila* required ordinary clothes, a few chadars with religious marks, some rosaries, and simple makeup. Later, Girish told the story of a painter whom he had engaged to make some backdrops for the play. Girish would guide the painter as he worked; during breaks, they would discuss the man's family situation and religious beliefs. The artist was a Bengali Vaishnava, and he was excited by the thought that his paintings would be used for a drama about his Chosen Deity, Gauranga. One day while talking about the glory of Gauranga, this simple and devout artist tearfully said: "Sir, how can I express the glory of Gauranga, the great saviour? He is so gracious to me! After a whole day of hard work, I return home, cook food, and offer it to my beloved deity. It is amazing that when I eat that prasad, I see that Gauranga has truly partaken of that food. I have seen the marks of his teeth on the chapati and the luchi. I am blessed by the grace of my guru. Without my guru's instruction, I could not have had this experience."[2]

The painter's story struck Girish's heart. Dumbfounded, Girish began to think: "How wretched I am! This ordinary fellow's religious belief gives him wonderful peace. And where am I? How far away I am from God!" Possessed by intense longing for God, Girish could not speak. He rushed to a room nearby, locked it, and began to cry to the Divine Mother, pouring out his anguish to Her.[3]

Chaitanya Lila became the talk of the town. This play attracted both the westernized young Bengalis and the shaven-headed Vaishnavas with marks on their foreheads to the Star Theatre, and there they both wept. Previously the puritanical Bengalis had despised the theatre as an immoral place because the actresses were courtesans. But after *Chaitanya Lila* opened, they considered the theatre to be a place of worship. After seeing this play, the people of Bengal became spiritually awakened and began to chant the Lord's name.

It is said that gossip spreads faster than the gospel, but *Chaitanya Lila* proved that the gospel actually spreads faster than gossip. News of *Chaitanya Lila* reached Navadwip, the birthplace of Chaitanya and the spiritual home of the Gaudiya Vaishnava sect. Pandit Brajanath Vidyaratna, a saintly Vaishnava, received an invitation to see the play. He told his son Pandit Mathuranath Padaratna: "I hear that *Chaitanya Lila* is being enacted at the Star Theatre in Calcutta. Perhaps Gauranga has come back. You go there and tell me about it after seeing the performance." Mathuranath went to Calcutta, and after seeing the play, he was so intoxicated with spiritual bliss that he rushed to take the dust of Girish's feet. Then he blessed Girish, saying, "May Gauranga fulfill all of your desires." Vijaykrishna Goswami, a well-known saint of Bengal, also saw *Chaitanya Lila* and then in a god-intoxicated mood got up from his seat and danced.[4]

The famous actor Amritalal Basu wrote about *Chaitanya Lila* satirically:

> The wicked actors and immoral actresses have finally spread religion in the country. Shame! Shame! This incident may appear in the mind, but one will commit sin if one admits it. It seems that when this worthless theatrical party began to glorify the greatness of Krishna on the abominable altar [theatre], the hearts of religious leaders were shaken a little, and the sleeping devout Hindus got up and began to spread the enchanting divine love of Gauranga. Innumerable kirtan parties have sprung up in cities and villages like mushrooms; the *Gita* and *Chaitanya-charitamrita* have gone through many editions. The Bengalis who had their education in England are not ashamed but rather have proudly begun to declare themselves Hindus.[5]

Mahendra Nath Datta, one of Swami Vivekananda's brothers, recalled the following incident:

> Girish was a bold and carefree soul, and he did not care for praise or blame. When *Chaitanya Lila* was enacted at the theatre, news spread that it was written by a very devout Vaishnava. Then many Vaishnava devotees — adorned with their distinctive garb, marks on their foreheads, rosaries around their necks — came from all over Bengal and even Navadwip to see Girish. But he acted till the late hours at night, then drank alcohol and went to bed in his parlour. After getting up he found the room full of people and they began to praise him, saying, "What a great devotee and Vaishnava you are!" Tired, Girish was disgusted with the flattery, so he devised a plan to get rid of those effusive devotees. He shouted, "Ish-ne [Ishan, Girish's servant], bring my bottle and glass." The Vaishnavas were watching Girish, with folded hands. In the meantime Ishan brought the bottle and glass. Girish opened the bottle, filled the glass, and began to drink in front of them.
>
> A devout Vaishnava asked: "Sir, are you sick? Are you taking medicine?" "No, it is not medicine," answered Girish. "I am drinking wine." Immediately the Vaishnavas said in an undertone: "Radhe Madhav! Radhe Madhav! This drunken fellow is a sinful heretic! We should leave this place right now." Girish jokingly said to them: "Have you not read *Srimad Bhagavat*? You will see it is written there: first *Srimad* and then *Bhagavat*."* The Vaishnavas could no longer tolerate the impious Girish, and everyone left at once. Later, Girish said: "I am Girish Ghosh of Baghbazar; and these fellows call me 'a great Vaishnava devotee!' I shall

---

* *Srimad Bhagavat* is the most famous Vaishnava scripture and it is read by all Vaishnavas. *Srimad* is used as an honorific for a sacred book or a holy person. However, in Bengali, *sri* means glorious and *mad* means wine. Girish therefore made a pun on the word *Srimad*.

tie a big *chalta* [a kind of heavy fruit, like a grapefruit] on each of their tufts. I am not afraid or ashamed of anything. Why should I care for others' opinions?"[6]

An elephant has two sets of teeth: the inner ones for masticating food and the external ones for protecting itself from enemies. Those Vaishnavas saw Girish's external behaviour. But, in fact, his heart was crying for a guru. *Chaitanya Lila* brought the guru to the door of his theatre. One day Ramakrishna heard about this play and expressed a desire to see it, but some of his conservative devotees objected because several of the roles were being played by women of ill repute. In those days women from respected families did not become actresses. Ramakrishna told the devotees: "I shall look upon them as the Blissful Mother Herself. What if one of them acts the part of Chaitanya? An imitation custard-apple reminds one of the real fruit."[7]

*   *   *

On 21 September 1884, Ramakrishna went to see *Chaitanya Lila* at the Star Theatre. M. recorded this in detail in *The Gospel of Sri Ramakrishna*:

About five o'clock that afternoon Sri Ramakrishna was on his way to Calcutta. M., Mahendra Mukherji, and a few other devotees accompanied him in Mahendra's carriage. Thinking of God, the Master soon went into an ecstatic mood. After a long time he regained consciousness of the world. He observed: "That fellow Hazra dares teach me! The rascal!" After a short pause he said, "I shall drink some water." He often made such remarks in order to bring his mind down to the sense plane.

Mahendra (*to M.*): "May I get some refreshments for him?"

M: "No, he won't eat anything now."

Master (*still in ecstatic mood*): "I shall eat."

Mahendra took the Master to his flour mill located at Hatibagan. After a little rest Sri Ramakrishna was to go to the theatre. Mahendra did not care to take him to his own house, for the Master was not well acquainted with his father. Priyanath, Mahendra's second brother, was also a devotee of the Master.

Sri Ramakrishna was sitting on a cot over which a carpet had been spread, and was engaged in spiritual talk.

Master (*to M. and the others*): "Once, while listening to the various incidents of the life of Chaitanya, Hazra said that these were manifestations of Shakti, and that Brahman, the All-pervasive Spirit, had nothing to do with them. But can there be Shakti without Brahman? Hazra wants to nullify the teachings of this place [*referring to himself*].

"I have realized that Brahman and Shakti are identical, like water and its wetness, like fire and its power to burn. Brahman dwells in all beings as the Bibhu, the All-pervasive Consciousness, though Its manifestation is greater in some places than in others. Hazra says, further, that anyone who realizes God must also acquire God's supernatural powers; that he possesses these powers, though he may or may not use them."

M: "Yes, one must have control over these supernatural powers!" (*All laugh.*)

Master (*smiling*): "Yes, one must have them in one's grasp! How mean! He who has never enjoyed power and riches becomes impatient for them. But a true devotee never prays to God for them."

Sri Ramakrishna washed his face. A smoke was prepared for him. He said to M.: "Is it dusk now? If it is, I won't smoke. During the twilight hour of the dusk you should give up all other activities and remember God." Saying this he looked at the hairs on his arm. He wanted to see whether he could count them. If he could not, it would be dusk.

About half past eight in the evening the carriage with the Master and the devotees drew up in front of the Star Theatre on Beadon Street. He was accompanied by M., Baburam, Mahendra, and two or three others. They were talking about engaging seats when Girish Chandra Ghosh, the manager of the theatre, accompanied by several officials, came out to the carriage, greeted the Master, and took him and the party upstairs. Girish had heard of the Master and was very glad to see him at the theatre. The Master was conducted to one of the boxes. M. sat next to him; Baburam and one or two devotees sat behind.

The hall was brilliantly lighted. The Master looked down at the pit and saw that it was crowded. The boxes also were full. For every box there was a man to fan those who occupied it. Sri Ramakrishna was filled with joy and said to M., with his childlike smile: "Ah, it is very nice here! I am glad to have come. I feel inspired when I see so many people together. Then I clearly perceive that God Himself has become everything."

M: "It is true, sir."

Master: "How much will they charge us here?"

M: "They won't take anything. They are very happy that you have come to the theatre."

Master: "It is all due to the grace of the Divine Mother."

The *Chaitanya Lila* was about to be performed. It was a play about the early life of Sri Chaitanya, who was also known as Nimai, Gaur, Gora, and Gauranga. The curtain rose; the attention of the audience was fixed on the stage.

The first scene depicts a council of Sin and the Six Passions. On a forest path behind them walk Viveka, Vairagya, and Bhakti, engaged in conversation.

Bhakti says to her companions: "Gauranga is born in Nadia. Therefore the *vidyadharis* [demigoddesses], the *munis* [sages], and the rishis have come down to earth in disguise to pay their respects to him." She sings:

> Blest indeed is the earth! Gora is born in Nadia!
> Behold the vidyadharis, coming in chariots to adore him;
> Behold the munis and rishis, who come, allured by the spell
>   of Love.

The vidyadharis, munis, and rishis sing a hymn to Gauranga and adore him as an Incarnation of God.

Sri Ramakrishna watched the scene and was overpowered with divine ecstasy. He said to M.: "Look at it! Ah! Ah!"

Sages:	O Kesava, bestow Thy grace
	Upon Thy luckless servants here!
	O Kesava, who dost delight
	To roam Vrindavan's glades and groves!
Goddesses:	O Madhava, our mind's Bewitcher!
	Sweet One, who dost steal our hearts,
	Sweetly playing on Thy flute!
Chorus:	Chant, O mind, the name of Hari,
	Sing aloud the name of Hari,
	Praise Lord Hari's name!
Sages:	O Thou Eternal Youth of Braja,
	Tamer of fierce Kaliya,
	Slayer of the afflicted's fear!
Goddesses:	Beloved with the arching eyes
	And crest with arching peacock feather,
	Charmer of Sri Radha's heart!
Sages:	Govardhan's mighty Lifter, Thou,
	All garlanded with sylvan flowers!
	O Damodara, Kamsa's Scourge!
Goddesses:	O Dark One, who dost sport in bliss
	With sweet Vrindavan's gopi maids.
Chorus:	Chant, O mind, the name of Hari,
	Sing aloud the name of Hari,
	Praise Lord Hari's name!

As the vidyadharis sang the lines,

> Beloved with the arching eyes
> And crest with arching peacock feather!

the Master went into deep samadhi. The orchestra played on, but he was not aware of the outer world.

Another scene: A guest has arrived at the house of Jagannath Mishra, Nimai's father. The boy Nimai plays about, singing with his friends, in a happy mood:*

> Tell Me, where is My blessed Vrindavan?
> Where is Mother Yashoda?
> Where Father Nanda and Brother Balai?
> Where My twin cows, black and white?
> Tell Me, where is My magic flute?
> My friends Sudama and Sridama?
> Where My Jamuna's bank, My banyan?
> Where My beloved gopi maids?
> Where is Radha, queen of My heart?

The guest closes his eyes while offering food to the Lord. Nimai runs to him and eats the food from the plate. The guest recognizes Nimai as an Incarnation of God and seeks to please him with the Hymn of the Ten Incarnations. Before taking leave of Gauranga's parents he sings:

> Glory to Gora, the Source of Bliss!
> Hail Gauranga, Redeemer of earth!
> Help of the helpless, Life of the living,
> Slayer of fear in the hearts of the fearful!
> Age after age we see Thy play —
> New sports unfolding, moods ever new;
> New waves rolling, new tales to be told.
> Thou who bearest the whole world's burden,
> Shower on us the nectar of Love!
> Take away our grief and affliction:
> Thou in Love's pleasure-cave dost dwell.
> Hope of the suffering! Chastiser of sin!
> Scourge of the wicked! Victory to Thee!

Listening to the hymn, the Master was thrilled with ecstasy.

The next scene is at Navadwip on the bank of the Ganges. After bathing in the holy water, the brahmin men and women engage in worship by the riverside. As they close their eyes, Nimai steals their food offerings and begins to eat them. A brahmin loses his temper and says: "You scapegrace! You rascal! You are taking away my offering for Vishnu. Ruin will seize you." Nimai holds on to the offering and is about to run away.

---

*In this song Gauranga identifies himself with Krishna.

Many of the women love him dearly and cannot bear to have him go away. They call to him: "Return, O Nimai! Come back, O Nimai!" Nimai turns a deaf ear to them.

One of the women, however, knows the irresistible charm that will bring him back. She loudly chants the name of Hari. Immediately he repeats the name of Hari and comes back.

M. was seated beside the Master. Sri Ramakrishna could not control himself. He cried out, "Ah!" and shed tears of love. He said to Baburam and M.: "Don't make a fuss if I fall into an ecstatic mood or go into samadhi. Then the worldly people will take me for a cheat."

Another scene: Nimai is invested with the sacred thread of the brahmins. He puts on the traditional ochre robe of the sannyasi. Mother Sachi and the women of the neighbourhood stand about while he begs for alms, singing:

Drop a morsel of food, I pray, into my begging-bowl;
Alone I roam, a new-made yogi, on the highways of the world.
People of Braja, you I love, and so, time and again,
I come to you; at hunger's call I beg my food from door to door.
The sun is low, and I must seek my home on the Jamuna's bank;
Into its waters fall my tears, as onward murmuring it flows.

The onlookers leave the stage. Nimai stands alone. The gods, in the guise of brahmin men and women, sing his praises.

Men:	Thy body gleams like liquid moonlight;
	Thou hast put on man's dwarfish form.
	O Lord, Thee we salute!
Women:	Bewitcher of the gopis' hearts,
	Thou roamest in the shady groves
	About Vrindavan's vale.
Nimai:	Hail Sri Radha! Glory to Radha!
Men:	The youths of Braja are Thy friends;
	Thou curbest haughty Madan's pride.
Women:	Thy love has made the gopis mad;
	In ecstasy the Jamuna thrills.
Men:	Narayana, Deluder of demons!
	Refuge of the fear-stricken gods!
Women:	O Lover of Braja, Thou dost beg
	The love of Braja's comely maidens!
Nimai:	Hail Sri Radha! Glory to Radha!

Listening to the music, the Master went into samadhi. The curtain fell and the orchestra played on.

A new scene: Srivas and other devotees are engaged in conversation in front of Advaita's house. Mukunda sings:

> Sleep no more! How long will you lie
> In maya's slumber locked, O mind?
> Who are you? Why have you been born?
> Forgotten is your own true Self.
> O mind, unclose your eyes at last
> And wake yourself from evil dreams;
> A fool you are to bind yourself
> So to the passing shows of life,
> When in you lives Eternal Bliss.
> Come out of the gloom, O foolish mind!
> Come out and hail the rising Sun!

Sri Ramakrishna praised the voice of the singer highly.

Another scene: Nimai is staying at home. Srivas comes to visit him. First he meets Sachi. The mother weeps and says: "My son doesn't attend to his household duties. My eldest son, Viswarupa, has renounced the world, and my heart has ached ever since. Now I fear that Nimai will follow in his steps."

Nimai arrives. Sachi says to Srivas: "Look at him. Tears run down his cheeks and breast. Tell, tell me how I can free him from these notions."

At the sight of Srivas, Nimai clings to his feet and says, with eyes full of tears: "Ah me! Revered sir, I have not yet attained devotion to Krishna. Futile is this wretched life! Tell me, sir, where is Krishna? Where shall I find Krishna? Give me the dust of your feet with your blessing, that I may realize the Blue One with the garland of wildflowers hanging about His neck."

Sri Ramakrishna looked at M. He was eager to say something but he could not. His voice was choked with emotion; the tears ran down his cheeks; with unmoving eyes he watched Nimai clinging to Srivas's feet and saying, "Sir, I have not yet attained devotion to Krishna."

Nimai has opened a school, but he cannot teach the students any longer. Gangadas, his former teacher, comes to persuade him to direct his attention to his worldly duties. He says to Srivas: "Listen, Srivas! We are brahmins, too, and devoted to the worship of Vishnu. But you people are ruining Nimai's worldly prospects."

Master (*to M.*): "That is the advice of the worldly wise: Do 'this' as well as 'that.' When the worldly man teaches spirituality he always advises a compromise between the world and God."

Binodini, who acted as Nimai (Chaitanya) in the premier of *Chaitanya Lila*

Banabiharini as Nitai in *Chaitanya Lila*

M: "Yes, sir. That is true."

Gangadas continues his argument with Nimai. He says: "Nimai, undoubtedly you are versed in the scriptures. Reason with me. Explain to me if any other duty is superior to worldly duties. You are a householder. Why disregard the duties of a householder and follow others' duties?"

Master (*to M.*): "Did you notice? He's trying to persuade Nimai to make a compromise."
M: "Yes, sir."

Nimai says to Gangadas: "I am not willfully indifferent to a householder's duties. On the contrary, it is my desire to hold to all sides. But, revered sir, I don't know what it is that draws me on. I don't know what to do. I want to cling to the shore but I cannot. My soul wanders away. I am helpless. My soul constantly wants to plunge headlong into the boundless Ocean."

Master: "Ah me!"

The scene changes: Nityananda has arrived at Navadwip. After a search he meets Nimai, who, in turn, has been seeking him. When they meet, Nimai says to him: "Blessed is my life! Fulfilled is my dream! You visited me in a dream and then disappeared."

The Master said in a voice choked with emotion, "Nimai said he had seen him in a dream."

> Nimai is in an ecstatic mood and becomes engaged in conversation with Advaita, Srivas, Haridas, and other devotees. Nitai sings a song suited to Nimai's mood:

> > Where is Krishna? Where is my Krishna?
> > He is not in the grove, dear friends.
> > Give me Krishna! Bring me my Krishna!
> > Radha's heart knows naught but Him.

At this song Sri Ramakrishna went into samadhi. He remained in that state a long time. The orchestra played on. Gradually his mind came down to the relative plane. In the meantime a young man of Khardaha, born in the holy family of Nityananda, had entered the box. He was standing behind the Master's chair. Sri Ramakrishna was filled with delight at the sight of him. He held his hand and talked to him affectionately. Every now and then he said: "Please sit down here. Your very presence awakens my spiritual feeling." He played tenderly with the young man's hands and lovingly stroked his face.

After he had left, Sri Ramakrishna said to M.: "He is a great scholar. His father is a great devotee of God. When I go to Khardaha to visit Shyamasundar, the father entertains me with sacred offerings such as one cannot buy even for a hundred rupees. This young man has good traits. A little shaking will awaken his inner spirit. At the sight of him my spiritual mood is aroused. I should have been overwhelmed with ecstasy if he had stayed here a little longer."

The curtain rises: Nityananda is walking in a procession on the public road with his companions, chanting the name of Hari. He meets two ruffians, Jagai and Madhai, who are sworn enemies of all religious people. Madhai strikes Nitai with a piece of broken pottery. Nitai is hurt and bleeds profusely, but he pays no heed, inebriated as he is with the love of God.

Sri Ramakrishna was in an ecstatic mood.

Nitai embraces both Jagai and Madhai, and sings a song to the two ruffians:

> Jagai! Madhai! Oh, come and dance,
> Chanting Hari's name with fervour!
> What does it matter that you struck me?
> Dance, dear friends, in Hari's name!
> Sing the name of our Beloved:
> He will embrace you in love's rapture!
> Let the heavens resound with His name!
> You have not tasted true emotion:
> Weep as you chant the name of Hari,
> And you will see the Moon of your soul.
> Hari's name would I lovingly give you;
> Nitai calls you to share His love.

Nimai speaks to Sachi of his desire to enter the monastic life. His mother faints and falls to the ground.

At this point many in the audience burst into tears. Sri Ramakrishna remained still and looked intently at the stage. A single tear appeared in the corner of each eye. The performance was over.

Sri Ramakrishna was about to enter a carriage. A devotee asked him how he had enjoyed the play. The Master said with a smile, "I found the representation the same as the real."

The carriage proceeded toward Mahendra's mill. Suddenly, Sri Ramakrishna went into an ecstatic mood and murmured to himself in loving tones: "O Krishna! O Krishna! Krishna is knowledge! Krishna is soul! Krishna is mind! Krishna is life! Krishna is body!" He continued: "O Govinda, Thou art my life! Thou art my soul!"

The carriage reached the mill. Mahendra fed the Master tenderly with various dishes. M. sat by his side. Affectionately he said to M., "Here, eat a little." He put some sweets in his hands.

With Mahendra and a few other devotees, Sri Ramakrishna left in the carriage for the Dakshineswar temple garden. The Master was in a happy mood. He sang a song about Gauranga and Nitai. M. sang with him:

Gaur and Nitai, ye blessed brothers!
I have heard how kind you are,
And therefore I have come to you....

The Master and Mahendra talked about the latter's intended pilgrimage.

Master (*smiling*): "The divine love in you is barely a sprout now. Why should you let it wither? But come back very soon. Many a time I have thought of visiting your place. At last I have done it. I am so happy."

Mahendra: "My life is indeed blessed, sir."

Master: "You were already blessed. Your father is also a good man. I saw him the other day. He has faith in the *Adhyatma Ramayana*."

Mahendra: "Please bless me that I may have love for God."

Master: "You are generous and artless. One cannot realize God without sincerity and simplicity. God is far, far away from the crooked heart."

Near Shyambazar, Mahendra bade the Master good-bye, and the carriage continued on its way.[8]

*   *   *

This was Ramakrishna's first visit to a Calcutta theatre. With it he sanctified the Bengali stage and blessed its actors and actresses.

Chapter 10

Prahlada Charitra

Girish based *Prahlada Charitra* (The Story of Prahlada) on a beautiful story in the Puranas. The great devotee Prahlada was the son of Hiranyakashipu, king of the demons and archenemy of Lord Vishnu. After Vishnu killed Hiranyaksha, the king's brother, Hiranyakashipu wanted to take revenge on Vishnu by killing him; but he could not track down this imperceptible God. The sage Narada suggested to the demon king that if he wanted to find Vishnu, he should torture His devotees ruthlessly and then Vishnu would appear to protect them. Hiranyakashipu agreed to this suggestion.

Hiranyakashipu's son, Prahlada, was a great devotee of Vishnu and he constantly chanted Vishnu's name. This angered the king, and he engaged two teachers to convince Prahlada to renounce Vishnu. When this failed, he began to torture his own son. He ordered his soldiers to attack Prahlada, but they could not kill him. He had his son thrown under the feet of a mad elephant, but the boy was unhurt. Then he had Prahlada put into a blazing fire, but he was not burnt. Finally, the king ordered his men to tie Prahlada to a big rock and throw him into the ocean from a high peak. But Vishnu rescued the boy and carried him to shore. Enraged, the king questioned his son, "Tell me, where is your Vishnu?"

Prahlada replied, "He is everywhere."

"Is He in this pillar?" asked the king.

"Yes," said Prahlada.

Hiranyakashipu kicked the pillar and broke it into pieces. Immediately Vishnu emerged from it in the form of Nrisimha, the lower half of his body human and the upper half lion. This fearsome being grabbed Hiranyakashipu with His claws and ripped him in half.

Prahlada Charitra's main characters were played by superstars: Amritalal Mitra was Hiranyakashipu and Binodini was Prahlada.

Chaitanya Lila had inaugurated a current of divine love and devotion through the Bengali stage. The people of Calcutta had become bored with exotic Western pastimes and began to seek out entertainment that reflected their own traditional values. In the 1880s Girish made the theatre of Calcutta vibrant. He introduced many songs and dances in his plays. Along with religious plays, he also wrote many satires to entertain people.

Girish wrote *Prahlada Charitra* after *Chaitanya Lila*. This two-act play opened on 22 November 1884 at the Star Theatre in Calcutta. Amritalal Mitra and Binodini charmed the audience with their performances. Westernised audiences did not care for too much singing and dancing, or emotional outbursts, so Girish wrote *Prahlada Charitra* with this in mind. Because *Prahlada Charitra* was a short play, the management added *Bibaha Bibhrat* (The Confusion of Marriage) to the programme. This farce was written by Amritalal Basu, an actor and playwright, and also a friend of Girish. It drew a big crowd.

* * *

Here is M.'s entry for Sunday, 14 December 1884, from *The Gospel of Sri Ramakrishna*:

Sri Ramakrishna arrived at the Star Theatre on Beadon Street in Calcutta to see a play about the life of Prahlada. M., Baburam, Narayan, and other devotees were with him. The hall was brightly lighted. The play had not yet begun. The Master was seated in a box, talking with Girish.

Master (*smiling*): "Ah! You have written nice plays."

Girish: "But, sir, how little I assimilate! I just write."

Master: "No, you assimilate a great deal. The other day I said to you that no one could sketch a divine character unless he had love of God in his heart.

"Yes, one needs to assimilate spiritual ideas. I went to Keshab's house to see the play *Nava-Vrindaban*. I saw a deputy magistrate there who earned eight hundred rupees a month. Everyone said that he was a very learned man; but I found him restless because of a boy, his son. He was very anxious to find a good seat for the boy; he paid no attention to the spiritual conversation of the players. The boy was pestering him with questions: 'Father! What is this? What is that?' He was extremely busy with the boy. You see, he merely read books; but he didn't assimilate their ideas."

Girish: "I often ask myself, 'Why bother about the theatre anymore?'"

Master: "No, no! Let things be as they are. People will learn much from your plays."

The performance began. Prahlada was seen entering the schoolroom as a student. At the sight of him Sri Ramakrishna uttered once or twice the word "Prahlada" and went into samadhi.

During another scene Sri Ramakrishna wept to see Prahlada under an elephant's feet. He cried when the boy was thrown into the fire.

The scene changed. Lakshmi and Narayana were seen seated in Goloka. Narayana was worried about Prahlada. This scene, too, threw Sri Ramakrishna into an ecstatic mood.

After the performance Girish conducted Sri Ramakrishna to his private room in the theatre. He said to the Master, "Would you care to see the farce, *Bibaha Bibhrat* [The Confusion of Marriage]?"

Master: "Oh, no! Why something like that after the life of Prahlada? I once said to the leader of a theatrical troupe, 'End your performance with some religious talk.' We have been listening to such wonderful spiritual conversation; and now to see 'The Confusion of Marriage'! A worldly topic! We should become our old selves again. We should return to our old mood."

Girish: "How did you like the performance?"

Master: "I found that it was God Himself who was acting the different parts. Those who played the female parts seemed to me the direct embodiments of the Blissful Mother, and the cowherd boys of Goloka the embodiments of Narayana Himself. It was God alone who had become all these.

"There are signs by which you can know whether a man has truly seen God. One of these is joy; there is no hesitancy in him. He is like the ocean: the waves and sounds are on the surface; below are profound depths. The man who has seen God behaves sometimes like a madman; sometimes like a ghoul, without any feeling of purity or impurity; sometimes like an inert thing, remaining speechless because he sees God within and without; sometimes like a child, without any attachment, wandering about unconcernedly with his cloth under his arm. Again, in the mood of a child, he acts in different ways: sometimes like a boy, indulging in frivolity; sometimes like a young man, working and teaching with the strength of a lion.

"Man cannot see God on account of his ego. You cannot see the sun when a cloud rises in the sky. But that doesn't mean there is no sun; the sun is there just the same.

"But there is no harm in the 'ego of a child.' On the contrary, this ego is helpful. Greens are bad for the stomach; but *hinche* is good. So hinche cannot properly be called greens. Sugar candy, likewise, cannot be classed with other sweets. Other sweets are injurious to the health, but not sugar candy.

"So I said to Keshab, 'If I tell you more than I have already said, you won't be able to keep your organization together.' That frightened him. Then I said to him, 'There is no harm in the "ego of a child" or the "ego of a servant."'

"He who has seen God finds that God alone has become the world and all its living beings; it is He who has become all. Such a person is called a superior devotee."

Girish (*smiling*): "Yes, God is everything. But the devotee keeps a trace of ego; that is not harmful."

Master (*smiling*): "Yes, there is no harm in that. That trace of ego is kept in order to enjoy God. You can enjoy divine bliss only when you make a distinction between yourself and God — the distinction between the servant and the Master.

"There is also the devotee of the mediocre class: he sees that God dwells in all beings as their Inner Guide. But the inferior devotee says, 'God exists; He is up there,' that is to say, beyond the sky. (*All laugh.*)

"When I saw the cowherd boys of Goloka in your performance I felt that God has become all. He who has seen God knows truly that God alone is the Doer, that it is He who does everything."

Girish: "Sir, I know truly that it is God who does everything."

Master: "I say, 'O Mother, I am the machine and You are the Operator; I am inert and You make me conscious; I do as You make me do; I speak as You make me speak.' But the ignorant say, 'I am partly responsible, and God is partly responsible.'"

Girish: "Sir, I am not really doing anything. Why should I bother about work at all?"

Master: "No, work is good. When the ground is well cultivated and cleared of stones and pebbles, whatever you plant will grow. But one should work without any personal motive.

"There are two types of paramahamsas: the jnani and the premi (lover of God). The jnani is self-centred; he feels that it is enough to have Knowledge for his own self. The premi, like Sukadeva, after attaining his own realization, teaches men. Some eat mangoes and wipe off the traces from their mouths; but some share their mangoes with others. Spades and baskets are needed to dig a well. After the digging is over, some throw the spades and baskets into the well. But others put them away; for a neighbour may use them. Sukadeva and a few others kept the spades and baskets for the benefit of others. (*To Girish*) You should do the same."

Girish: "Please bless me, sir."

Master: "Have faith in the Divine Mother and you will attain everything."

Girish: "But I am a sinner."

Master: "The wretch who constantly harps on sin becomes a sinner."

Girish: "Sir, the very ground where I used to sit would become unholy."

Master: "How can you say that? Suppose a light is brought into a room that has been dark a thousand years; does it illumine the room little by little, or all in a flash?"

Girish: "Then you have blessed me."

Master: "If you sincerely believe it. What more shall I say? I eat and drink and chant the name of God."

Girish: "I have no sincerity. Please give it to me."

Master: "I? Sages like Narada and Sukadeva could have done that."

Girish: "I don't see Narada and Sukadeva. But you are here before me."

Master (*smiling*): "All right. You have faith."

All remained silent. The conversation began again.

Girish: "I have one desire: love of God for its own sake."

Master: "Only the Ishvarakotis have such love. It is not for ordinary men."

All sat in silence. The Master began to sing in an absent-minded mood, his gaze turned upward:

> Can everyone have the vision of Shyama? Is Kali's treasure for everyone?
> Oh, what a pity my foolish mind will not see what is true!
> Even with all His penances, rarely does Siva Himself behold
> The mind-bewitching sight of Mother Shyama's crimson feet.
> To him who meditates on Her the riches of heaven are poor indeed;
> If Shyama casts Her glance on him, he swims in Eternal Bliss.
> The Prince of yogis, the King of the gods, meditate on Her feet in vain;
> Yet worthless Kamalakanta yearns for the Mother's blessed feet!

Girish repeated:

> Yet worthless Kamalakanta yearns for the Mother's blessed feet!

Master (*to Girish*): "One can realize God through intense renunciation. But the soul must be restless for Him, as restless as one feels for a breath of air when one's head is pressed under water.

"A man can see God if he unites in himself the force of these three attractions: the attraction of worldly possessions for the worldly man, the husband's attraction for the chaste wife, and the child's attraction for its mother. If you can unite these three forms of love and give it all to God, then you can see Him at once.

> Cry to your Mother Shyama with a real cry, O mind!
> And how can She hold Herself from you?

"If a devotee prays to God with real longing, God cannot help revealing Himself to him.

"The other day I told you the meaning of bhakti. It is to adore God with body, mind, and words. 'With body' means to serve and worship God with one's hands, go to holy places with one's feet, hear the chanting of the name and glories of God with one's ears, and behold the divine image with one's eyes. 'With mind' means to contemplate and meditate on God constantly and to remember and think of His lila. 'With words' means to sing hymns to Him and chant His name and glories.

"Devotion as described by Narada is suited to the Kaliyuga. It means to chant constantly the name and glories of God. Let those who have no leisure worship God at least morning and evening by wholeheartedly chanting His name and clapping their hands.

"The 'ego of a devotee' begets no pride; it does not create ignorance. On the contrary it helps one realize God. This ego is no more like the ordinary ego than hinche is like ordinary greens. One generally becomes indisposed by eating greens; but hinche removes excessive bile; it does one good. Sugar candy is not like ordinary sweets. Sweets are generally harmful, but sugar candy removes acidity.

"Nishtha leads to bhakti; bhakti, when mature, becomes bhava; bhava, when concentrated, becomes mahabhava; and last of all is prema. Prema is like a cord: by prema God is bound to the devotee; He can no longer run away. An ordinary man can at best achieve bhava. None but an Isvarakoti attains mahabhava and prema. Chaitanyadeva attained them.

"What is the meaning of jnanayoga? It is the path by which a man can realize the true nature of his own Self; it is the awareness that Brahman alone is his true nature. Prahlada sometimes was aware of his identity with Brahman. And sometimes he would see that God was one and he another; at such times he would remain in the mood of bhakti.

"Hanuman said, 'O Rama, sometimes I find that You are the whole and I a part, sometimes that You are the Master and I Your servant; but, O Rama, when I have the Knowledge of Reality, I see that You are I and I am You.'"

Girish: "Ah!"

Master: "Why shouldn't a man be able to realize God in the world? But he must have discrimination and dispassion; he must have the unshakable awareness that God alone is real and all else is unreal and has but a two days' existence. It will not do to float on the surface. You must dive deep."

With these words, the Master sang:

Dive deep, O mind, dive deep in the Ocean of God's Beauty;
If you descend to the uttermost depths,
There you will find the gem of Love....

Master: "You must remember another thing: in the ocean there is danger of alligators, that is to say, of lust and the like."

Girish: "I am not afraid of the King of Death."

Master: "But I am speaking of the danger of the alligators of lust and the like. Because of them one should smear one's body with turmeric before diving in — the turmeric of discrimination and dispassion.

"Some attain knowledge of God in the world. Mention is made of two classes of yogis: the hidden and the known. Those who have renounced the world are 'known' yogis: all recognize them. But the 'hidden' yogis live in the world. They are not known. They are like the maidservant who performs her duties in the house but whose mind is fixed on her children in the country. They are also, as I have told you, like the loose woman who performs her household duties zealously but whose mind constantly dwells on her lover. It is very hard to cultivate discrimination and dispassion. It is not easy to get rid of the idea, 'I am the Master and all these are mine.'... I know a man, whom I shall not name, who used to devote a great deal of time to japa; but he bore false witness in court for the sake of ten thousand rupees. Therefore I say that a man can realize God in the world, too, but only if he has discrimination and dispassion."

Girish: "What will happen to this sinner?"

Sri Ramakrishna sang in a tender voice, turning his eyes upward:

Meditate on the Lord, the Slayer of hell's dire woes,
He who removes the fear of death;
Thinking of Him, the soul is freed from worldly grief
And sails across the sea of life in the twinkling of an eye.
Consider, O my mind, why you have come to earth;
What gain is there in evil thoughts and deeds?
Your way lies not through these: perform your penance here
By meditating long and deep on the everlasting Lord.

Master: "'Sails across the sea of life in the twinkling of an eye.' One attains the vision of God if Mahamaya steps aside from the door. Mahamaya's grace is necessary: hence the worship of Shakti. You see, God is near us, but it is not possible to know Him because Mahamaya stands between. Rama, Lakshmana, and Sita were walking along. Rama walked ahead, Sita in the middle, and Lakshmana last. Lakshmana was only two and a half cubits away from Rama, but he couldn't see Rama because Sita — Mahamaya — was in the way.

"While worshipping God, one should assume a definite attitude. I have three attitudes: the attitude of a child, the attitude of a maidservant, and the attitude of a friend. For a long time I regarded myself as a maidservant and a woman companion of God; at that time I used to wear skirts and ornaments, like a woman. The attitude of a child is very good.

"The attitude of a 'hero' is not good. Some people cherish it. They regard themselves as Purusha and woman as Prakriti; they want to propitiate woman through intercourse with her. But this method often causes disaster."

Girish: "At one time I too cherished that idea."

Sri Ramakrishna looked at Girish pensively.

Girish: "I still have that twist in my mind. Tell me what I should do."

Sri Ramakrishna reflected a minute and said, "Give God your power of attorney. Let Him do whatever He likes."

The conversation then turned to Sri Ramakrishna's young devotees.

Master (*to Girish and the others*): "In meditation I see the inner traits of these youngsters. They have no thought of acquiring house and property. They do not crave sex pleasure. Those of the youngsters who are married do not sleep with their wives. The truth is that unless a man has got rid of rajas and has acquired sattva, he cannot steadily dwell in God; he cannot love God and realize Him."

Girish: "You have blessed me."

Master: "How is that? I said that you would succeed if you were sincere."

Saying this, the Master exclaimed, "Anandamayi!" and went into samadhi. He remained in that state a long time. Regaining partial consciousness, he said, "Where are those rascals?" M. brought Baburam to him. Sri Ramakrishna looked at Baburam and the other devotees and said, still in ecstasy, "The bliss of Satchidananda is indeed good; but what about the bliss of divine inebriation?"

He began to sing:

Once for all, this time, I have thoroughly understood;

From One who knows it well, I have learnt the secret of bhava....

Again he sang:

Why should I go to Ganga or Gaya, to Kasi, Kanchi, or Prabhas,
So long as I can breathe my last with Kali's name upon my lips?...

The Master continued, saying, "While praying to the Divine Mother, I said, 'O Mother, I don't seek anything else: give me only pure love for Thee.'"

Sri Ramakrishna was pleased with Girish's calm mood. He said to him, "This mood of yours is good; the calm mood is the best."

The Master was seated in the manager's room. A man entered and said, "Will you see the farce, 'The Confusion of Marriage'? It is being played now."

Sri Ramakrishna said to Girish: "What have you done? This farce after the life of Prahlada! First sweets and rice pudding and then a dish of bitter herbs!"

After the theatre, the actresses, following Girish's instructions, came to the room to salute Sri Ramakrishna. They bowed before him, touching the ground with their foreheads. The devotees noticed that some of the actresses, in saluting the Master, touched his feet. He said to them very tenderly, "Please don't do that, mother!"

After the actresses had left the room, Sri Ramakrishna said to the devotees, "It is all He, only in different forms."

The carriage was ready at the door. Girish and the others came to the street to see the Master off. As soon as Sri Ramakrishna stepped into the carriage, he went into deep samadhi. Narayan and several other devotees were with him. The carriage started for Dakshineswar.[1]

Chapter 11

Nimai Sannyas

Girish based *Nimai Sannyas* (Nimai's Renunciation) on the life of Nimai Mishra, who became Chaitanya. As a young man, Nimai realized that he had a mission to save humanity from worldly bondage, and that if he wanted to fulfill his goal, he would have to renounce his home, his mother, and his wife. He had a school in his hometown of Navadwip, but he resolved to become a teacher of the world. Thus one night he left home and went to the monastery of Keshav Bharati at Kalna, on the other side of the Ganges, where he took monastic vows and became Sri Krishna Chaitanya. After that, he was on his way to Vrindaban, the playground of Krishna, when his disciples learned that he had become a monk. They then brought him back to Shantipur to meet with his mother, and she gave him permission to live at Puri, the abode of Lord Jagannath on the coast of the Bay of Bengal. His wife, Vishnupriya, chose to lead the life of a nun. For almost twenty-four years, Chaitanya lived in Puri, where he met great men such as Raja Prataprudra, who became his devotee, and Pandit Basudeva Sarvabhauma, who had a vision of Chaitanya as Rama and Krishna, and then realized that he was an incarnation of God.

When *Nimai Sannyas* opened at the Star Theatre on 28 January 1885, the cast included the following:

Nimai — Binodini
Nitai – Banabiharini
Raja Prataprudra — Prabodh Ghosh
Roy Ramananda — Upendra Mitra
Keshab Bharati — Amritalal Mitra
Sarvabhauma — Aghorenath Pathak
Sachi — Gangamani
Vishnupriya — Bhusankumari

Sisir Kumar Ghosh, Girish's neighbour and friend, was the editor of the newspaper *Amrita Bazar Patrika* and a devout Vaishnava. After seeing

Chaitanya Lila, in which Girish dramatized Chaitanya's early life, he was so moved that he asked Girish to continue the story. Sisir Ghosh wanted the spiritual impact of Chaitanya's life, which he deeply felt, to be expressed in a new play, *Nimai Sannyas*.

Amritalal, one of the actors, said of *Nimai Sannyas*: "It was not possible to manifest the deep spiritual feeling through acting, and perhaps it became difficult for the audience to grasp that lofty idea. For this reason, *Nimai Sannyas* did not achieve popularity like *Chaitanya Lila*. The songs in this play were long, but touched the inmost feelings. While seeing the pinnacle of the Jagannath temple of Puri from afar, Nitai and the devotees passionately sang: 'Look, look! There is Krishna who is winking at us!'"[1]

There is a fascinating scene in *Nimai Sannyas* in which Gauranga reveals himself to Pandit Basudeva Sarvabhauma by taking the form of Shadabhuj, a deity with six arms. On Gauranga's body the pandit sees two of Rama's arms and two of Krishna's along with Gauranga's own arms. Binodini, who played the role of Gauranga, later said: "The acting in this particular scene was so inspiring and intoxicating that one would not understand it without seeing the play."[2] According to Abinash Gangopadhyay, Girish's secretary and biographer, Ramakrishna went into samadhi during that scene. Girish was in the audience that day and sat next to the Master. When the play was over, Ramakrishna embraced Girish in an ecstatic mood.[3]

M. did not record the Master's trip to see *Nimai Sannyas*. In fact, there is no entry between 27 December 1884 and 22 February 1885 in *The Gospel of Sri Ramakrishna*. But in the entry for 25 February 1885, M. wrote: "A few days earlier Girish had been very rude to the Master at the Star Theatre; but now he was in a calm state of mind."[4] It can be assumed that the Master went to see *Nimai Sannyas* in late January or February 1885, because the play opened on 28 January 1885. The devotees observed the Master's birthday on 22 February, and Girish was present. On 25 February 1885 M. went with the Master to see the drama *Brishaketu* at the Star Theatre.

Girish observed how the Master's devotees served him with great love and respect, and by contrast, what a terrible life he was leading. He was remorseful, but because of his dissolute lifestyle he was reluctant to offer his service. Girish thought: "I don't know how to serve the guru, but if the Master were born as my son, then perhaps I would be able to serve him with great affection."[5]

Abinash wrote:

One evening Sri Ramakrishna came to see a play [*Nimai Sannyas*]. Girish arranged for the Master's supper in his office at the Star Theatre because it would be too late for him to eat after returning to Dakshineswar. The caterer served hot luchi, curry, and sweets. After the performance the Master had his supper and was about to leave for Dakshineswar. At that time Girish came to the Master, after drinking alcohol, and demanded, "You be my son." Sri Ramakrishna said: "Why should I be your son? I shall be your *Ishta* (Chosen Deity)." Girish insisted and the Master said again: "I shall be your Ishta. My father was extremely pure. Why should I be your son?" Intoxicated, Girish began to use filthy words while speaking to the Master. Enraged, the devotees were ready to punish Girish. The Master stopped them and laughingly remarked: "What kind of devotee is this? What does he say?" Girish continued to abuse the Master.

The devotees escorted the Master to the carriage. Girish followed the Master and lay down on the dirty and muddy street as he bowed down in front of the carriage. The Master left for Dakshineswar.

Girish had no fear at all. As a spoiled son scolds his father and remains unperturbed, knowing that he will be forgiven, so Girish behaved like a favourite, dissolute child of the Master and remained unconcerned about his misbehaviour. He had so much dependence on and faith in the Master's love and affection for him that he had no fear even for a moment that the Master would shun him.

But the Master's devotees were angry. They went to Dakshineswar the next day and told the Master: "We know Girish is a rogue. Why do you go to him?" Some remarked, "Please sever your relationship with him forever." In the meantime Ram Chandra Datta arrived.[6]

Ram recalled:

The next day I went to Dakshineswar and found the Master seated with some devotees. As soon as I entered his room, the Master said, "Hello Ram, do you know that Girish fed me with one and a half luchis and then maligned me along with my parents?"

"What can you do?" I replied.

"If he hits me?"

"You will have to accept it."

"I shall have to accept his blows?"

"I don't find any offence in Girish," I said. "When the cowherd boys of Vrindaban died from the poison of the serpent Kaliya, Krishna jumped on his hood to punish him. Krishna asked, 'Why are you spewing poison?' Kaliya humbly replied, 'Lord, it is You who have given me poison rather than nectar with which to worship you.' Where else will Girish release that poison that was within him? If he said those things to me, I would sue him in court. So you have protected him by absorbing his abusive words."

Immediately the face of the compassionate Master turned crimson, tears trickled from his eyes, and he at once got up to go and visit Girish by carriage. Some devotees suggested that he not go at that time because he might suffer from the scorching sun, but he did not listen to them.[7]

Abinash wrote:

Meanwhile, Girish remained unperturbed. His friends told him that he had committed a terrible offence. Girish said to them: "I have innumerable bad traits. How many shall I restrain? If the Master counts my offences, I shall be a speck of dust." However, Girish was repentant that he had hurt the Master's devotees. He wondered how he would show his face to them.

At that time the Master entered Girish's house with some devotees and said, "Girish, it is God's grace that I have come to your place."

Girish later wrote: "A father disinherits his son because of some offence, but that offence was not considered as an offence to my supreme father. He came to my house and I was blessed to see him. Day by day I began to feel myself small. I was fully convinced that the Master was full of compassion; but I was ashamed thinking of my misconduct. I pondered how the devotees worship him in so many ways. I reproached myself."

On that day Swami Vivekananda took the dust of Girish's feet and remarked: "Blessed are your faith and devotion!"[8]

Swami Adbhutananda recorded his own version of the incident:

I used to accompany the Master to the theatre, where Girish Babu would show him much respect. He used to arrange for a high box seat for the Master and appoint a man to fan him as well. He himself would often come to see the Master on the upper level. On one occasion Girish Babu approached the Master when quite drunk and addressed him affectionately: "You must become my son. I have not been able to serve you in this life, but if you are born again as my son, I can do so. Please promise me that you will be my son."

"What are you saying?" asked the Master. "Why should I be born as your son?" Then Girish Babu became very angry and severely scolded the Master. Hearing him abusing the Master so, I could not hold back my anger. I had a stick in my hand and was ready to hit Girish Babu, but Deven Babu said, "Since the Master is bearing all of this, why should you raise your stick?" I am sure that if Deven Babu had not told me that, I would have given Girish Babu a good blow. I was that angry.

On our way back to Dakshineswar, Deven Babu told the Master what I had almost done. The Master exclaimed: "Wouldn't it have been awful if you had hit Girish? Didn't you notice? After he abused me, he fell to the ground when I got into this carriage and took the dust of my feet. Didn't you see his faith?" And during the trip the Master repeatedly prayed: "O Mother, Girish is an actor. How can he understand Your glory? Mother, please forgive him."

The devotees came to know of the incident at the theatre, and many of them told the Master he shouldn't visit a person such as Girish. Ram Babu also heard about it, and he came to Dakshineswar the following day. As soon as he entered the room, the Master asked him, "Ram, what do you have to say about Girish?"

"Sir," Ram Babu told him, "the serpent Kaliya told Krishna, 'Lord, you have given me only poison; where can I get nectar to offer you?' It is the same with Girish. Where will he get nectar? Why, sir, should you be displeased with him?"

The Master responded, "Then take us in your carriage to Girish's." And the Master, accompanied by Ram Babu, myself, and two others, started for Girish Babu's home in Calcutta.

Meanwhile, Girish Babu had been very repentant. He had refused food and was weeping a great deal. We reached his house a little before evening. Hearing that the Master had come, Girish Babu approached him with tears in his eyes and fell at his feet. Only when the Master said, "All right, all right," did he finally get up.

A long conversation followed. I remember Girish Babu saying: "Master, if you had not come today, I would have concluded that you still had not attained that supreme state of knowledge where praise and blame are equal, and, moreover, that you could not be called a paramahamsa. I would have considered you to be an ordinary man like ourselves. But today I have understood that you are that Supreme One. You will not be able to hide this from me anymore. I shall never desert you. My welfare is now in your hands. Please tell me that you will be responsible for me and that you will save me."[9]

Sri Ramakrishna played two roles: Sometimes he was a chastising father and sometimes a forgiving mother. Like a loving mother, the Master overlooked all of Girish's shortcomings and made him his own.

Whenever the Master practised any sadhana, he dressed, acted, and behaved accordingly. In his boyhood days in his native village, when he had seen any theatrical performance he tried to imbibe the spirit of a character through acting out the part. Swami Turiyananda recalled: "Once some devotees wanted to hear from the Master how Nimai took sannyasa [probably after the devotees saw *Nimai Sannyas*]. To fulfill their wishes, the Master put on his ochre cloth; he completely shaved his head and face; and he began to repeat a mantra with a rosary. Swami Shivananda was also present that day in Dakshineswar."[10]

Chapter 12

Brishaketu

Girish based *Brishaketu* on a story in the Mahabharata concerning Karna, a king well known for his generosity. He gave people whatever they wanted, and never refused any request. He was therefore called Dātā Karna, Munificent Karna.

Lord Vishnu once came to Karna disguised as a brahmin to test his generosity. The brahmin said that he had been fasting and was very hungry. Karna promised to give him whatever he wanted to eat. The brahmin demanded the meat of Karna's only son, a little boy named Brishaketu. He asked Karna and his wife, Padmavati, to butcher their son, without tears and grief, and then cook various dishes with the meat. Brishaketu was playing with his friends at the time and he had a premonition that he would enter the stomach of Lord Vishnu. He returned home and offered himself to his parents, requesting that they fulfill their promise. Meanwhile, the brahmin went to bathe. Brishaketu was killed, and his body was cooked, but the cook discovered that the meat had somehow disappeared from the pot. Karna was bewildered. Then the brahmin appeared with Brishaketu and said to Karna: "Blessed are you, O king. Henceforth you will be known as 'Dātā Karna.'" Karna pleaded with the brahmin, saying: "Lord, please reveal to me Your real form." The brahmin then took the form of Vishnu.

The main characters and cast of *Brishaketu* included the following:

Karna — Upendra Mitra
Vishnu — Aghorenath Pathak
Brishaketu — Bhusankumari
Padmavati — Binodini
Cook — Trailokya Ghosal

Brishaketu, a two-act play, was first performed at the Star Theatre on 16 April 1884. According to Abinash, the actors' and actresses' wonderful performances made the play popular. Jawaharlal Dhar, the stage director, surprised and shocked the audience by portraying the dissection of Brishaketu onstage. This play was later enacted many times at the Minerva Theatre, the Classic Theatre, the Manomohan Theatre, and other venues.

Ramakrishna went to see *Brishaketu* on 25 February 1885 at the Star Theatre. M. recorded in detail the conversations that took place before and after the play. Every one of the Master's actions had deep significance. He not only taught at the temple garden or at devotees' houses but also at the theatre.

*   *   *

M. wrote in *The Gospel of Sri Ramakrishna*:

Sri Ramakrishna was at the house of Girish Ghosh in Bosepara Lane, Calcutta. It was about three o'clock when M. arrived and prostrated himself before him. The Master was going to see a play at the Star Theatre. He was talking with the devotees about the Knowledge of Brahman.

Master: "Man experiences three states of consciousness: waking, dream, and deep sleep. Those who follow the path of knowledge explain away the three states. According to them, Brahman is beyond the three states. It is also beyond the gross, the subtle, and the causal bodies, and beyond the three gunas — sattva, rajas, and tamas. All these are maya, like a reflection in a mirror. The reflection is by no means the real substance. Brahman alone is the Substance and all else is illusory.

"The knowers of Brahman say, further, that it is the identification of the soul with the body that creates the notion of duality. In that state of identification the reflection appears real. When this identification disappears, a man realizes, 'I am He; I am Brahman.'"

A Devotee: "Then shall we all follow the path of reasoning?"

Master: "Reasoning is one of the paths; it is the path of the Vedantists. But there is another path, the path of bhakti. If a bhakta weeps longingly for the Knowledge of Brahman, he receives that as well. These are the two paths: jnana and bhakti.

"One may attain the Knowledge of Brahman by either path. Some retain bhakti even after realizing Brahman, in order to teach humanity. An Incarnation of God is one of these.

"A man cannot easily get rid of the ego and the consciousness that the body is the soul. It becomes possible only when, through the grace of God, he attains samadhi — nirvikalpa samadhi, jada samadhi.

"The ego of the Incarnations returns to them when they come down from the plane of samadhi; but then it is the 'ego of Knowledge' or the 'ego of Devotion.' Through the 'ego of Knowledge' they teach men. Sankaracharya kept the 'ego of Knowledge.'

"Through the 'ego of Devotion' Chaitanyadeva tasted divine love and enjoyed the company of the devotees. He talked about God and chanted His name.

"Since one cannot easily get rid of the ego, a bhakta does not explain away the states of waking, dreaming, and deep sleep. He accepts all the states. Further, he accepts the three gunas — sattva, rajas, and tamas. A bhakta sees that God alone has become the twenty-four cosmic principles, the universe, and all living beings. He also sees that God reveals Himself to His devotees in a tangible form, which is the embodiment of Spirit.

"The bhakta takes shelter under *vidyamaya* [the maya of knowledge]. He seeks holy company, goes on pilgrimage, and practises discrimination, devotion, and renunciation. He says that, since a man cannot easily get rid of his ego, he should let the rascal remain as the servant of God, the devotee of God.

"But a bhakta also attains the Knowledge of Oneness; he sees that nothing exists but God. He does not regard the world as a dream, but says that it is God Himself who has become everything. In a wax garden you may see various objects, but everything is made of wax.

"But a man realizes this only when his devotion to God has matured. One gets jaundice when too much bile accumulates. Then one sees everything as yellow. From constantly meditating on Krishna, Radhika saw everything as Krishna; moreover, she even felt that she herself had become Krishna. If a piece of lead is kept in a lake of mercury a long time, it turns into mercury. The cockroach becomes motionless by constantly meditating on the kumira worm; it loses the power to move. At last it is transformed into a kumira. Similarly, by constantly meditating on God, the bhakta loses his ego; he realizes that God is he and he is God. When the cockroach becomes the kumira everything is achieved. Instantly one obtains liberation.

"As long as God retains the ego in a man, he should establish a definite relationship with God, calling on Him as Master, Mother, Friend, or the like. I spent one year as a handmaid — the handmaid of the Divine Mother, the Embodiment of Brahman. I used to dress myself as a woman. I put on a nose-ring. One can conquer lust by assuming the attitude of a woman.

"One must worship the Adyasakti. She must be propitiated. She alone has assumed all female forms. Therefore I look on all women as mother. The attitude of looking on woman as mother is very pure. The Tantra mentions the *vamachara* [left-hand path] method also. But that is not a good method; it causes the aspirant's downfall. A devotee keeping an object of enjoyment near him has reason to be afraid.

"Looking on woman as mother is like fasting on the ekadashi day without touching even a drop of water; in this attitude there is not the slightest trace of sensual enjoyment. Another way of observing the ekadashi allows the taking of fruit and the like. One can also observe the day by eating luchi and curries! But my attitude is not to touch even a drop of water while I observe the fast. I worshipped the Shodasi [the Divine Mother as a sixteen-year-old girl] as my mother; I looked on all parts of her body as those of my mother. This attitude of regarding God as Mother is the last word in sadhana. 'O God, Thou art my Mother and I am Thy child' — this is the last word in spirituality.

"The sannyasi's way of living is like observing the ekadashi fast without taking even a drop of water. If he clings to enjoyment, then he has reason to be afraid. 'Woman and gold' is enjoyment. If a monk enjoys it, he is swallowing his own spittle, as it were. There are different kinds of enjoyment: money, wealth, name, fame, and sense pleasures. It is not good for a sannyasi to sit in the company of a woman devotee, or even to talk to her. This injures him and others as well. Then others cannot learn from him; he cannot set an example to humanity. A sannyasi keeps his body in order to teach mankind.

"To sit with a woman or talk to her a long time has also been described as a kind of sexual intercourse. There are eight kinds. To listen to a woman and enjoy her conversation is one kind; to speak about a woman is another kind; to whisper to her privately is a third kind; to keep something belonging to a woman and enjoy it is a fourth kind; to touch her is a fifth. Therefore a sannyasi should not salute his guru's young wife, touching her feet. These are the rules for sannyasis.

"But the case is quite different with householders. After the birth of one or two children, the husband and wife should live as brother and sister. The other seven kinds of sexual intercourse do not injure them much.

"A householder has various debts: debts to the gods, to the fathers, and to the rishis. He also owes a debt to his wife. He should make her the mother of one or two children and support her if she is a chaste woman.

"Householders do not know who is a good wife and who is a bad wife, who is a *vidyashakti* and who is an *avidyashakti*. A vidyashakti, a good wife, has very little lust and anger. She sleeps little. She pushes her husband's head away from her. She is full of affection, kindness, devotion, modesty, and other noble qualities. Such a wife serves all, looking on all men as her children. Further, she helps increase her husband's love of God. She doesn't spend much money lest her husband should have to work hard and thus not get leisure to think of God.

"Mannish women have different traits. These are bad traits: squint eyes and hollow eyes, catlike eyes, lantern jaws like a calf's, and pigeon-breast."

Girish: "What is the way for people like us?"

Master: "Bhakti is the only essential thing. Bhakti has different aspects: the sattvic, the rajasic, and the tamasic. One who has sattvic bhakti is very modest and humble. But a man with tamasic bhakti is like a highwayman in his attitude towards God. He says: 'O God, I am chanting Your name; how can I be a sinner? O God, You are my own Mother; You must reveal Yourself to me.'"

Girish (*smiling*): "It is you, sir, who teach us tamasic bhakti."

Master (*smiling*): "There are certain signs of God-vision. When a man sees God he goes into samadhi. There are five kinds of samadhi. First, he feels the *Mahavayu* [spiritual energy] rise like an ant crawling up. Second, he feels It rise like a fish swimming in the water. Third, he feels It rise like a snake wriggling along. Fourth, he feels It rise like a bird flying — flying from one branch to another. Fifth, he feels It rise like a monkey making a big jump; the Mahavayu reaches the head with one jump, as it were, and samadhi follows.

"There are two other kinds of samadhi. First, the *sthita* samadhi, when the aspirant totally loses outer consciousness: he remains in that state a long time; it may be for many days. Second, the *unmana* samadhi: it is to withdraw the mind suddenly from all sense-objects and unite it with God.

(*To M.*) "Do you understand this?"

M: "Yes, sir."

Girish: "Can one realize God by sadhana?"

Master: "People have realized God in various ways. Some through much austerity, worship, and devotion; they have attained perfection through their own efforts. Some are born perfect, as for example Narada and Sukadeva; they are called *nityasiddha*, eternally perfect. There are also those who have attained perfection all of a sudden; it is like a man's unexpectedly coming into a great fortune. Again, there are instances of people's realizing God in a dream and by divine grace."

Saying this, Sri Ramakrishna sang, intoxicated with divine fervour:

Can everyone have the vision of Shyama? Is Kali's treasure for everyone?
Oh, what a pity my foolish mind will not see what is true!...

Sri Ramakrishna remained in ecstasy a few moments. Girish and the other devotees were seated before him. A few days earlier Girish had been very rude to the Master at the Star Theatre; but now he was in a calm state of mind.

Master (*to Girish*): "This mood of yours is very good; it is peaceful. I prayed about you to the Divine Mother, 'O Mother, make him peaceful so that he won't abuse me.'"

Girish (*to M.*): "I feel as if someone were pressing my tongue. I can't talk."

Sri Ramakrishna was still in an indrawn mood; he seemed to be gradually forgetting the men and the objects around him. He tried to bring his mind down to the relative world. He looked at the devotees.

Looking at M., he said: "They all come to Dakshineswar. Let them. Mother knows everything." To a young man of the neighbourhood he said: "Hello! What do you think? What is the duty of man?" All sat in silence. To Narayan he said: "Don't you want to pass the examinations? But, my dear child, a man freed from bondage is Siva; entangled in bondage, he is jiva."

Sri Ramakrishna was still in the god-intoxicated mood. There was a glass of water near him. He drank the water. He said to himself, "Why, I have drunk water in this mood!"

It was not yet dusk. Sri Ramakrishna was talking to Atul, who was seated in front of him. Atul was Girish's brother and a lawyer of the High Court of Calcutta. A brahmin neighbour was also seated near him.

Master (*to Atul*): "All I want to tell you is this. Follow both; perform your duties in the world and also cultivate love of God."

Brahmin: "Can anyone but a brahmin achieve perfection?"

Master: "Why should you ask that? It is said that in the Kaliyuga the sudras achieve love of God. There are the instances of Savari, Ruhidas, the untouchable Guhaka, and others."

Narayan (*smiling*): "Brahmins and sudras — all are one."

Brahmin: "Can a man realize God in one birth?"

Master: "Is anything impossible for the grace of God? Suppose you bring a light into a room that has been dark a thousand years; does it remove the darkness little by little? The room is lighted all at once. (*To Atul*) Intense renunciation is what is needed. One should be like an unsheathed sword. When a man has that renunciation, he looks on his relatives as black cobras and his home as a deep well.

"One should pray to God with sincere longing. God cannot but listen to prayer if it is sincere."

All sat in silence, pondering Sri Ramakrishna's words.

Master (*to Atul*): "What is worrying you? Is it that you haven't that grit, that intense restlessness for God?"

Atul: "How can we keep our minds on God?"

Master: "*Abhyasayoga*, the yoga of practice. You should practise calling on God every day. It is not possible to succeed in one day; through daily prayer you will come to long for God.

"How can you feel that restlessness if you are immersed in worldliness day and night? Formerly Jadu Mallick enjoyed spiritual talk; he liked to engage in it himself. But nowadays he doesn't show that much interest. He surrounds himself with flatterers day and night and indulges in worldly talk."

It was dusk. The lamp was lighted in the room. Sri Ramakrishna chanted the divine names. He was singing and praying. He said, "Chant the name of Hari, repeat the name of Hari, sing the name of Hari." Again he said, "Rama! Rama! Rama!" Then: "O Mother! Thou dost ever enjoy Thine eternal sports. Tell us, O Mother, what is the way? We have taken refuge in Thee; we have taken shelter at Thy feet."

Finding Girish restless, Sri Ramakrishna remained silent a moment. He asked Tejchandra to sit near him. The boy sat near the Master. He whispered to M. that he would have to leave soon.

Master (*to M.*): "What did he say?"

M: "He said he would have to go home."

Master: "Why do I attract these boys to me so much? They are pure vessels untouched by worldliness. A man cannot assimilate instruction if his mind is stained with worldliness. Milk can be safely kept in a new pot; but it turns sour if kept in a pot in which curd has been made. You may wash a thousand times a cup that has held a solution of garlic, but still you cannot remove the smell."

* * *

Sri Ramakrishna arrived at the Star Theatre, on Beadon Street, to see a performance of *Brishaketu*. He sat in a box, facing the south. M. and other devotees were near him.

Master (*to M.*): "Has Narendra come?"

M: "Yes, sir."

The performance began. Karna and his wife Padmavati sacrificed their son to please God, who had come to them in the guise of a brahmin to test Karna's charity. During this scene one of the devotees gave a suppressed sigh. Sri Ramakrishna also expressed his sorrow.

After the play Sri Ramakrishna went to the recreation room of the theatre. Girish and Narendra were already there. The Master stood near Narendra and said, "I have come."

Sri Ramakrishna took a seat. The orchestra was playing in the auditorium.

Master (*to the devotees*): "I feel happy listening to the concert. The musicians used to play on the sanai at Dakshineswar and I would go into ecstasy. Noticing this, a certain sadhu said, 'This is a sign of the Knowledge of Brahman.'"

The orchestra stopped playing and Sri Ramakrishna began the conversation.

Master (*to Girish*): "Does this theatre belong to you?"

Girish: "It is *ours*, sir."

Master: "'Ours' is good; it is not good to say 'mine'. People say 'I' and 'mine'; they are egotistic, small-minded people."

Narendra: "The whole world is a theatre."

Master: "Yes, yes, that's right. In some places you see the play of vidya and in some, the play of avidya."

Narendra: "Everything is the play of vidya."

Master: "True, true. But a man realizes that when he has the Knowledge of Brahman. But for a bhakta, who follows the path of divine love, both exist — vidyamaya and avidyamaya.

"Please sing a little."

Narendra sang:

> Upon the Sea of Blissful Awareness waves of ecstatic love arise:
> Rapture divine! Play of God's Bliss!
> Oh, how enthralling!
> Wondrous waves of the sweetness of God, ever new and ever enchanting,
> Rise on the surface, ever assuming
> Forms ever fresh.
> Then once more in the Great Communion all are merged, as the barrier walls
> Of time and space dissolve and vanish:
> Dance then, O mind!
> Dance in delight with hands upraised, chanting Lord Hari's holy name.

As Narendra sang the words, "Then once more in the Great Communion all are merged," Sri Ramakrishna said to him, "One realizes this after attaining the Knowledge of Brahman; then all is vidya, Brahman, as you said." As Narendra sang the line, "Dance in delight with hands upraised, chanting Lord Hari's holy name," the Master said to him, "Sing that line twice."

After the song Sri Ramakrishna resumed the conversation.

Girish: "Devendra Babu hasn't come. He says in a mood of wounded pride: 'We haven't any stuff inside us, no filling of thickened milk. We are filled only with worthless lentil-paste. Why should we go there?'"

Master (*surprised*): "Does he say that? He never said so before."

Sri Ramakrishna took some refreshments and handed some to Narendra.

Jatin Deva (*to the Master*): "You always say: 'Narendra, eat this! Eat that!' Are the rest of us fools? Are we like straw washed ashore by the flood-tide?"

Sri Ramakrishna loved Jatin dearly. Jatin visited the Master now and then at Dakshineswar and occasionally spent the night there. He belonged to an aristocratic family of Shobhabazar. The Master said laughingly to Narendra, "He is talking about you."

Sri Ramakrishna laughed and showed his affection to Jatin by touching his chin. He said to Jatin, "Come to Dakshineswar; I'll give you plenty to eat." The Master went into the auditorium to see a farce. He sat in a box. He laughed at the conversation of the maidservant. After a while he became absent-minded and whispered a few words to M.

Master (*to M.*): "Well, is what Girish Ghosh says true?"

Girish had lately been speaking of Sri Ramakrishna as an Incarnation of God.

M: "Yes, sir, it must be true. Otherwise why should it appeal to our minds?"

Master: "You see, a change is coming over me. The old mood has changed. I am not able to touch any metal now."

M. listened to these words in wonder.

Master: "There is a very deep meaning in this new mood."

Was the Master hinting that a God-man cannot bear any association with worldly treasure?

Master (*to M.*): "Well, do you notice any change in me?"

M: "In what respect, sir?"

Master: "In my activities."

M: "Your activities are increasing as more people come to know about you."

Master: "Do you see? What I said before is now coming true."

After a few moments he said, "Can you tell me why Paltu can't meditate well?"

Sri Ramakrishna was ready to leave for Dakshineswar. He had remarked to a devotee about Girish, "You may wash a thousand times a cup that has held a solution of garlic; but is it ever possible to get rid of the smell altogether?" Girish was offended by this remark. When the Master was about to leave, Girish spoke.

Girish: "Will this smell of garlic go?"

Master: "Yes, it will."

Girish: "So you say it will."

Master: "All smell disappears when a blazing fire is lighted. If you heat the cup smelling of garlic, you get rid of the smell; it becomes a new cup.

"The man who says he will not succeed will never succeed. He who feels he is liberated is indeed liberated; and he who feels he is bound verily remains bound. He who forcefully says, 'I am free' is certainly free; and he who says day and night, 'I am bound' is certainly bound."[1]

Chapter 13

Daksha Yajna

Girish based *Daksha Yajna* (Daksha's Sacrifice) on a story from the Puranas. King Daksha was one of Brahma's sons. The Divine Mother was born as his daughter, Sati, "the purest one." When Daksha and his wife, Prasuti, wanted to arrange their daughter's marriage, Brahma suggested that Sati should be married to Shiva, but Daksha would not agree to this. Shiva lives in a cremation ground surrounded by ghosts and hobgoblins. He covers himself with ashes and smokes marijuana. According to Daksha, such a person could not be a son-in-law of a king.

Nonetheless, Sati heard of the glory of Shiva from a nun named Tapaswini and fell in love with Him. One day she fervently prayed to Shiva, and when He appeared before her, she offered her betrothal garland to Him. Unaware of this, Daksha arranged a *swayamvara* so that Sati could select her own husband. He invited all of the gods except Shiva. When Sati entered the hall with her garland in hand, the garland disappeared. Daksha was very upset, believing that a ghost had taken the garland. At that moment Shiva entered the hall, wearing that very garland around His neck. He then gave Sati His own garland. Brahma was pleased, but Daksha was unhappy. At last he conceded and unwillingly offered his daughter to Shiva, and the couple left for Shiva's home, Mount Kailasa.

Daksha felt humiliated because his daughter had married a hemp addict, as he regarded Shiva. To regain his self-respect he planned to perform a sacrifice and invite all of the gods, except Shiva. Daksha's ministers and even Vishnu and Brahma advised him to invite Shiva, but he refused. He asked the divine messenger Narada to invite all the rest of the gods. However, Narada secretly went to Kailasa and told Shiva everything. The god was unconcerned, but when Sati heard that her father was going to perform a great sacrifice to which she and her husband were not invited, she decided to attend nonetheless. She wished to repair the relationship between her father and her husband. However, Shiva refused to allow her to go. Sati then revealed Herself to Shiva in each of the ten forms of the Divine Mother, one after another. Shiva finally gave His permission and asked His attendant Nandi to escort Sati in a chariot. Sati went to Daksha's kingdom and met with her mother. Meanwhile, Daksha was busy preparing for the sacrifice. He threatened the sage Dadhichi, saying: "Never utter the name of Shiva. He who chants Shiva's name will go to hell."

Sati arrived just as the sacrifice was beginning. Daksha was displeased to see his daughter and began to speak badly of Shiva. Sati tried to persuade her father not to criticize Shiva, but Daksha went on and on. Finally, Sati could bear no more: She gave up her body on the spot. Nandi returned to Kailasa with the empty chariot and reported everything to Shiva. Enraged, Shiva tore His matted hair and the terrible form of Rudra appeared. Rudra went to Daksha's city and destroyed the king and his sacrifice. Shiva then appeared and picked up Sati's body, and put it over His shoulder. He was about to leave when Prasuti worshipped Shiva's feet with bel leaves. Shiva gave her a boon: "Your husband's head is burning in the fire. However, if you put a goat's head on his body, he will live." Shiva then told Daksha's wife to offer His portion of the sacrifice to a bel tree and disappeared.

The cast of *Daksha Yajna* included the following:

Daksha — Girish Chandra Ghosh
Mahadev (Shiva) — Amritalal Mitra
Dadhichi — Amritalal Basu
Brahma — Nilmadhav Chakrabarty
Vishnu — Upendra Mitra
Narada — Mathuranath Chattopadhyay
Nandi — Aghorenath Pathak
Bhringi — Prabodh Ghosh
Sati — Binodini
Prasuti — Kadambini
Tapaswini — Kshetramani

In Girish's biography Abinash wrote:

Daksha Yajna was a unique play on the Bengali stage, and it attracted all kinds of men, women, and even children, in spite of the fact that it was completely free from humour. The character of Tapaswini in this play was Girish's creation. *Daksha Yajna* was highly appreciated in literary circles because of its excellence and depth. Moreover, its acting was superb. One who saw Girish's performance as Daksha would never forget it.

Daksha Yajna   159

After receiving the boon of Brahma, the creator, Daksha became Prajapati and attained the power of creating beings. Girish's outstanding acting, gestures, and postures would convince anyone that he was truly the creator. Whenever Girish appeared on the stage, the audience would remain motionless watching his lion-like demeanor and strength like a thunderbolt.

A writer remarked: "I saw the acting of Daksha [Girish] in the Star Theatre and listened to his dialogue with Sati: 'One feels dishonour who has honour. You are a beggar; how can you expect honour?' This rude utterance reverberated in my ear for seven days." The audience trembled when Amritalal Mitra, acting in the role of Shiva, came onstage, shouting, 'Who is there? Give me — give me — my Sati!' And when Binodini appeared on the stage in the role of Sati, the audience saw the glowing purity radiating from her face. Binodini methodically displayed her acting skill at the sacrificial place: she showed respect to her father Daksha, vindicated her husband's position, suffered terribly upon hearing her husband criticized, and finally gave up her body. The roles of Dadhichi, Prasuti, Tapaswini, Nandi, Bhringi, Brahma, Vishnu, and other characters were enacted perfectly.

Jawaharlal Dhar, a famous stage director, reflected light on a mirror to show the appearance and disappearance of ten forms of the Divine Mother on the stage. He received much applause from the audience. Beni Madhav Adhikari, the famous music director, put the songs to music, and they were highly appreciated.

It is important to mention here that during this period [1883], Girish would sometimes visit the Kali temple at Kalighat (in South Calcutta) and repeat the Mother's name. He then wrote *Daksha Yajna*. When the rehearsals of the play were over, the dress rehearsal was held at the Natmandir of the Kali temple one night. Girish was pleased to perform before the Divine Mother. Later the play was advertised and performed at the Star Theatre.[1]

Daksha Yajna was first performed on 21 July 1883 at the Star Theatre. Although Ramakrishna saw five of Girish's plays — *Chaitanya Lila, Prahlada Charitra, Nimai Sannyas, Brishaketu*, and *Daksha Yajna* — he saw Girish perform only in this play. Most probably Ramakrishna saw *Daksha Yajna* in the early spring of 1885, because his cancer became evident sometime in April or May. Neither M. nor Abinash wrote anything about the Master seeing this play, but Swami Adbhutananda attended the play with Ramakrishna. He recalled:

> The Master used to take us to the theatre. Once we watched *Daksha Yajna*. He heard Girish Babu [who was acting in the role of Daksha]

saying, "I will completely eradicate the name of Shiva from this world." Immediately the Master said: "What does that rascal say? 'I will eradicate Shiva's name from this world!' What a wonderful teaching that rascal is giving! One should not listen to this kind of thing. Let us go." When Girish Babu heard that the Master wanted to leave the theatre, he immediately rushed to him with his costume on. He requested, "Sir, please listen to the play a little more." The Master said: "What is this? Why are you writing such a thing — 'I will eradicate Shiva's name from this world?' Is it good to write such a thing?" Girish Babu replied: "Sir, just for the sake of the stomach [meaning money] I wrote that thing." However, at the request of Girish Babu the Master watched the play till the end.

I noticed another thing in the theatre. On that night, when the play was over, Girish Babu took the Master to the green room. He then told all the actors and actresses: "All of you bow down to the father [the Master]. All of your sins will be washed away." When the women wanted to touch the Master's feet, he said, "Bow down from a distance." But who was going to listen? All came and touched the Master's feet. After arriving at Dakshineswar, the Master said to us, "Look, my feet are burning." Brother Ramlal brought Ganges water and washed the Master's feet, and only then did that burning subside. The Master could not bear the touch of impure people.[2]

Ramlal, Ramakrishna's nephew, left a vivid eyewitness account:

One day Girish Ghosh came to the Master and asked: "Sir, we are presenting the play *Daksha Yajna* [Daksha's Sacrifice] at the Star Theatre tonight. Would you like to see it?" The Master replied, "Yes, Ramlal and I will go." Then the Master and I hired a carriage and left for the theatre. By mistake we entered through the back way, which was dirty, and found that no one was there. Seeing an actress nearby, the Master said, "Hello, could you inform Girish that some visitors have come from Dakshineswar?" Girish immediately came and fell at the Master's feet and remained on the ground for a few minutes. The Master asked Girish to get up, and when he did his shirt was dirty. The Master began to brush his shirt with his hand and said, "Ah, you have spoiled this clean shirt!"

Girish took us upstairs and arranged for box seats, and then he called the actresses, who at that time were putting on their makeup. They came immediately. Girish told them: "Bow down at the Master's feet. You won't get another chance such as this to purify yourselves." Then the Master said to them: "Enough! O blissful mothers, please get up. You are giving joy to people by your singing and dancing. Now go back to your dressing room for your makeup."

During the first scene Girish appeared onstage in the role of King Daksha and announced, "Today I shall remove the name of Shiva from this world." At this, the Master said to me, "O Ramlal, what is this rascal saying?" When that scene was over, Girish came to the Master and asked with folded hands, "Sir, how did you enjoy the part of King Daksha?" The Master said: "Look, Girish, you were saying, 'I shall remove Shiva's name from this world.' Such words should not come from your lips." Girish replied: "Sir, what can I do? I had to say all these things just for the sake of my stomach." Then the Master said, "Yes, I understand."

Girish left, and the next scene began. When Sati [the wife of Shiva and the daughter of King Daksha] came onstage, the Master went into samadhi. He remained in samadhi till the end of the play, except for a few moments when he exclaimed, "Ah! Ah!" After the play was over I escorted the Master to the carriage, but he was in an intoxicated mood. Girish again came, bowed down to the Master, and asked, "Sir, how did you enjoy the play?" The Master could not talk. We left for Dakshineswar. After regaining normal consciousness, the Master said to me, "Ramlal, tell me about the last part of the play." I told him the story. He said: "Ah, I could not see the whole play. However, after listening to you I am satisfied."[3]

*   *   *

The *Indian Mirror* published this review of *Daksha Yajna*: "The dignified and difficult *panteur* of Daksha was capitally rendered by G.C. who from the fact of being the author of the piece was singularly well-justified to reflect the exact spirit of the role. His impersonation was to apply the remarks of Victor Hugo on Lamaitre's Ruy Blass, 'not a transformation but transfiguration.'"[4]

Hemendra Nath Dasgupta wrote in *Girish Pratibha*:

> We heard from the critics that Girish demonstrated extraordinary skill in acting the role of Daksha. When Girish recited the lines, Daksha's dignity, egotism, and self-importance manifested and overwhelmed the audience.
>
> *Daksha Yajna* is Girish's original creation, although a shadow of Satan fell on this play. Girish depicted Daksha's character with the ethics of some Western philosophers, such as Jeremy Bentham, John Stuart Mill, and others. The goal of these Utilitarians is to do the greatest good to the largest number of people. As Daksha was endowed with the power of creation by his father Brahma, he wanted to eradicate death from this world. According to the Hindu trinity, Shiva is responsible for destruction, so Daksha decided to perform a sacrifice for the eternal happiness of humanity without including Shiva. Daksha did not realize that the "Old order changeth, yielding place to new." He was so proud of the power he had gained from austerity that he wanted to change the inevitable law of nature; he disobeyed Brahma and other gods and sages; and he neglected Shiva and Shakti, which brought about his downfall.[5]

Chapter 14

Sri Ramakrishna: The Patron Saint of the Bengali Stage

*B*y bringing Ramakrishna to his plays, Girish made him the patron saint of the Bengali stage. And through his plays, Girish carried Ramakrishna's message to the red-light districts of Calcutta.

Christopher Isherwood wrote: "In those days, actresses in the Bengali theatre were regarded as no better than prostitutes — a prejudice which also persisted in England until at least the beginning of the nineteenth century....One curious result of their association is that, today, Ramakrishna's picture is to be found hanging backstage in nearly every theatre in Calcutta. The actors bow to it before they make their entrances. By giving his approval to Girish's art and encouraging him to continue practising it, Ramakrishna became, as it were, the patron saint of drama in Bengal."[1]

Nowadays it is no disgrace to go to the theatre, opera, or cinema. On the contrary, one is considered to be uncultured, uneducated, and unsophisticated if one does not attend such cultural events. But in Ramakrishna's time, conservative Hindu society in Bengal, the progressive Brahmo Samaj, and other groups abhorred the stage because they considered the performers to be immoral drunkards, debauchees, and prostitutes. Theatres were therefore considered to be sinful places. Under these circumstances, it was shocking when Sri Ramakrishna Paramahamsa, who was regarded as an illumined soul and even as an avatar, went to see Girish's *Chaitanya Lila* on 24 September 1884 at the Star Theatre in Calcutta. Some conservative and prudish Bengalis considered Ramakrishna's action, and his subsequent visits to the theatre, to be unpardonable.

The first repercussions came from the Brahmos. Hemendranath Dasgupta wrote: "Many people of the Brahmo Samaj stopped visiting Ramakrishna. After Keshab Sen passed away on 8 January 1884,

Sri Ramakrishna: Patron Saint of the Bengali Stage 163

Vijaykrishna Goswami became devoted to the Master. Shivanath Shastri, however, stopped coming to him. Some people asked Shivanath: 'Previously you were devoted to the Master. Why do you not visit him anymore?' Shivanath replied: 'How can I go to see him? He is now connected with the immoral people of the theatre. I can't go to Dakshineswar anymore.'"[2]

One day Ramakrishna talked about Girish with Aswini Datta, a devout Hindu philanthropist.

"Do you know Girish Ghosh?"

"Which Girish Ghosh? The one who is in the theatre?"

"Yes."

"I have never seen him. But I know him by reputation."

"A good man."

"They say he drinks."

"Let him! Let him! How long will he continue that?"[3]

Ram Chandra Datta, a Vaishnava and a staunch devotee of Ramakrishna, did not approve of the Master's visits to the theatre. Girish wrote: "Wherever the Master went, Ram Chandra invariably accompanied him. But when the Master came to the theatre, Ram did not come — but he did have food sent to him [Ramakrishna]. Ram considered the theatre to be a sinful place."[4]

M. recorded in the *Gospel*:

> Sri Ramakrishna was planning to go to a performance of the *Chaitanya Lila* at the Star Theatre. Mahendra Mukherji was to take him to Calcutta in his carriage. They were talking about choosing good seats. Some suggested that one could see the performance well from the one-rupee gallery. Ram said, "Oh, no! I shall engage a box for him." The Master laughed. Some of the devotees said that public women took part in the play. They took the parts of Nimai, Nitai, and others.
>
> Master (*to the devotees*): "I shall look upon them as the Blissful Mother Herself. What if one of them acts the part of Chaitanya? An imitation custard-apple reminds one of the real fruit."[5]

Modern readers may not be bothered by the idea of Ramakrishna's visiting theatres, mixing with drunken actors, and addressing immoral actresses as "Blissful Mother." But for many years he and his disciples had to face opposition and criticism from prominent citizens and from society in general. People spoke out against the Master even after he passed away in 1886.

For example, in August 1896 Max Müller wrote an article on Ramakrishna entitled "A Real Mahatman." A relative of Keshab Chandra

Sen, the famous Brahmo leader, became very jealous. When Max Müller planned to write a biography of Ramakrishna, this man wrote to him in an attempt to change his views. I could not locate the contents of that letter, but Max Müller commented on it in *Ramakrishna: His Life and Sayings*:

> A relative of Keshab Chandra Sen, however, who evidently completely misapprehended what was implied by the influence which I said that Ramakrishna had exercised on Keshab Chandra Sen, [Pratap] Mozoomdar, and others as his disciples, is very anxious to establish the priority of Keshab Chandra Sen, as if there could be priority in philosophical or religious truth. "It was Keshab Chandra," he tells us, "who brought Ramakrishna out of obscurity." That may be so, but how often have disciples been instrumental in bringing out their master? He then continues to bring charges against Ramakrishna, which may be true or not, but have nothing to do with the true relation between Keshab and Ramakrishna. If, as we are told, he did not show sufficient moral abhorrence of prostitutes, he does not stand quite alone in this among the founders of religion. If he did not "honour the principle of teetotalism according to Western notions," no one, as far as I know, has ever accused him of any excess in drinking. Such bickering and cavilings would have been most distasteful both to Keshab Chandra Sen and to Ramakrishna. Both had no words but words of praise and love for each other, and it was a great pity that their mutual relation should have been treated in a jealous spirit, and thereby totally misrepresented.[6]

The Brahmos charged that Ramakrishna "did not show sufficient moral abhorrence of prositutes." When Swami Vivekananda read this, he wrote:

> To this the Professor's rejoinder is very very sweet indeed; he says that in this charge Ramakrishna "does not stand quite alone among the founders of religion!" Ah! How sweet are these words — they remind one of the prostitute Ambapali, the object of Lord Buddha's divine grace, and of the Samaritan woman who won the grace of the Lord Jesus Christ.
>
> Yet again, another charge is that he did not hate those who were intemperate in their habits. Heaven save the mark! One must not tread even on the shadow of a man, because he took a sip or two of drink — is not that the meaning? A formidable accusation indeed! Why did not the Mahapurusha kick away and drive off in disgust the drunkards, the prostitutes, the thieves, and all the sinners of the world? And why did he not, with eyes closed, talk in a set drawl after the never-to-be-varied tone of the Indian flute-player, or talk in conventional language, concealing his thoughts![7]

*   *   *

With their redeeming power, avatars transform people's characters and make sinners into saints. One morning Jesus went to the temple. People gathered around him. While he was teaching them, a group that included teachers of Jewish law and Pharisees brought in a woman who had been caught committing adultery. They said to Jesus: "Teacher, this woman was caught in the very act of committing adultery. In our Law, Moses commanded that such a woman must be stoned to death. Now, what do you say?" They said this to trap Jesus. Jesus kept quiet at first, but when they repeated the question, he replied, "Whichever one of you who has committed no sin may throw the first stone at her." When they heard this, they all left, one by one. Only Jesus remained with the woman. He then asked her: "Where are they? Is there no one left to condemn you?"

"No one, sir," she answered.

"Well, then," Jesus said, "I do not condemn you either. Go, but do not sin again."[8]

"Hatred cannot be conquered by hatred; it can be conquered only by love," said Buddha. Towards the end of his life, Buddha traveled to Kushinagar from Rajagriha and took shelter in the mango grove of the courtesan Ambapali. When she heard of this, she went to visit the Blessed One. As a prudent woman goes forth to perform her religious duties, so she appeared in a simple dress without any ornaments, yet was beautiful to look upon.

Buddha thought to himself: "This woman moves in worldly circles and is a favourite of kings and princes; yet is her heart calm and composed. Young in years, rich, surrounded by pleasures, she is thoughtful and steadfast. This, indeed, is rare in the world.... She, although living in luxury, has acquired the wisdom of a master, taking delight in piety and able to receive the truth in its completeness."

As Buddha presented his teachings, Ambapali's face brightened with delight. She then arose and humbly asked: "Will the Blessed One do me the honour of taking his meal, together with the brethren, at my house tomorrow?" The Blessed One silently gave his consent.

Later, the wealthy people of the area came and invited Buddha to eat with them the next day. Buddha declined, explaining, "I have already promised to dine tomorrow with Ambapali, the courtesan." They departed, saying, "A worldly woman has outdone us; we have been left behind by a frivolous girl."[9]

The next morning Buddha and his disciples went to Ambapali's house. After they had eaten, Ambapali sat at Buddha's feet and offered her mansion and mango grove to his Order, which he accepted. Her whole life was transformed and she became a follower of the Blessed One.

There is a saying: "A church is not a museum for saints. It is a hospital for sinners." It is amazing how love, compassion, and forgiveness are misunderstood by so-called civilized people. When Ramakrishna was criticized for his visits to the theatre, his compassion for the actors and actresses, and his appreciation for their art, his devotees and disciples came forward to defend their guru.

In the beginning, Ram Chandra Datta did not approve of the Master's patronage of the theatre. Later, however, he realized that every one of the Master's actions had deep meaning and significance, and that he had used his redeeming power to save those wayward souls of the stage. In the 1890s Ram began to lecture now and then at the Star, City, and Minerva theatres on Ramakrishna and his teachings. Ram published an article entitled "Society and Morality — Acting" in the first issue of his magazine, *Tattwamanjari*. The writer of the article supported the theatre as a wonderful medium for carrying education to the masses. He wrote: "People are being improved by watching dramas in which the actors and actresses unveil the mystery of spiritual truths. Those who have seen Girish Chandra Ghosh's *Chaitanya Lila, Prabhas Yajna,* and *Buddhadev-Charit* in the Star Theatre are truly uplifted and inspired."[10]

The writer defended employing courtesans by pointing out two facts: first, using male actors in female roles was not natural; second, at that time, most women in mainstream society were not willing or able to perform onstage. Therefore, society should not despise actresses, but rather appreciate their talents and their efforts to lead an honest life: For many of the women, the rigid rules of society had forced them to become courtesans; in addition, many of them were murdered every year. Regardless, many actresses were not prostitutes as such, but were poor women who became mistresses of wealthy men — which was their only means of bettering their condition.

In response to the concern that the characters of young people would be damaged by watching these women act onstage, the writer concluded that youth who have wayward tendencies do not listen to the advice of their parents and school teachers. He stated: "Of course, it is true that evil company encourages evil tendencies. It is better for society if those who have wicked tendencies go to houses of ill fame rather than spread immorality among their own relatives or neighbours."

The actress controversy continued for a long time. Swami Vivekananda had been an uncompromising puritan before he met Ramakrishna. On 6 July 1896 he wrote to Mr. Francis Leggett about his transformation: "At twenty years of age I was the most unsympathetic, uncompromising fanatic; I would not walk on the footpath on the theatre side of the streets in Calcutta. At thirty-three, I can live in the same house with prostitutes and never would think of saying a word of reproach to them. Is it degenerate? Or is it that I am broadening out into the Universal Love which is the Lord Himself?"[11]

Vivekananda wrote to Swami Ramakrishnananda from Switzerland on 23 August 1896:

> Today I received a letter from Ramdayal Babu, in which he writes that many public women attend the Ramakrishna anniversary festival at Dakshineswar, which makes many less inclined to go there. Moreover, in his opinion, one day should be appointed for men and another for women. My decision on the point is this:
>
> 1. If public women are not allowed to go to such a great place of pilgrimage as Dakshineswar, where else shall they go? It is for the sinful that the Lord manifests Himself specially, not so much for the virtuous.
>
> 2. Let distinctions of sex, caste, wealth, learning, and the whole host of them, which are so many gateways to hell, be confined to the world alone. If such distinctions persist in holy places of pilgrimage, where then lies the difference between them and hell itself?
>
> 3. Ours is a gigantic City of Jagannath, where those who have sinned and those who have not, the saintly and the vicious, men and women and children irrespective of age, all have equal rights. That for one day at least in the year thousands of men and women get rid of the sense of sin and ideas of distinction and sing and hear the name of the Lord, is in itself a supreme good.
>
> 4. If even in a place of pilgrimage people's tendency to evil be not curbed for one day, the fault lies with you, not them. Create such a huge tidal wave of spirituality that whatever people come near will be swept away.
>
> 5. Those who, even in a chapel, would think this is a public woman, that man is of a low caste, a third is poor, and yet another belongs to the masses — the less be the number of such people (that is, whom you call gentlemen) the better. Will they who look to the caste, sex, or profession of devotees appreciate our Lord? I pray to the Lord that hundreds of public women may come and bow their heads at His feet; it does not matter if not one gentleman comes. Come public women, come drunkards, come thieves and all — His Gate is open to all. "It is easier for a camel to pass through the eye of a needle than for a rich man to enter the Kingdom of God." Never let such cruel, demoniacal ideas have a place in your mind.[12]

Intolerance, however, was not confined to Bengali society; many Westerners also believed the theatre to be sinful. During Swami

Vivekananda's visit to Paris in 1900, he wanted to hear the famous opera singer Emma Calvé sing *Carmen*; he had known Madame Calvé in America, where she had attended many of his lectures. His Irish disciple Sister Nivedita vehemently objected, as Lizelle Reymond described in *The Dedicated*:

> In Paris Swamiji said to her one day, "I should like to see you in your favourite role."
>
> Calvé blushed as she answered: "It's *Carmen*. Swamiji, you must pardon me, but every evening, in spite of myself, I become that woman when I sing and dance and play my castanets."
>
> "I shall come and hear you," said the Swami.
>
> At this point Nivedita broke into the conversation.
>
> "But that's impossible," she said. "Swamiji, you can't go to the Opera Comique; you will be severely criticized."
>
> The Swami looked at her in astonishment. His only reply was a tender smile.
>
> And, two evenings later, accompanied by Mr. Leggett, he not only went to hear the opera but was taken to the star's dressing room during the intermission. Calvé received him with some embarrassment.
>
> "I wanted to see your *Carmen*, Emma," he said. "Don't think she's a bad woman. She is just true. She does not lie.... And in her violence she expresses her soul. She is of that superb race of women who say to the Divine Mother, after they have prayed to Her, 'Don't listen to my prayers, O Mother of God, for I want to die of my desire.'"[13]

Pravasi and other puritanical magazines in Calcutta continued to criticize the practice of allowing courtesans to perform onstage, but *Rangalaya, Rangamancha, Rangadarshan, Majlish,* and other publications supported the custom. The editor of *Rangadarshan* pointed out to *Pravasi* (a very popular and powerful magazine) that the actresses raised money to support various philanthropic activities benefiting society. For example, in the August 1901 issue, the editor of *Rangalaya* announced: "There will be a Ramakrishna Festival in Kankurgachi Yogodyana for five days. To support this function, there will be a play in the Classic Theatre on Sunday evening. The owner will donate all the proceeds to that cause."[14] A letter was published in the August 1911 issue of *Rangamancha* that read in part: "The Minerva Theatre gave two benefit performances — one for Ramakrishna Mission Sevashrama, Varanasi, and the other for the poor and sick famous poet Rajanikanta Sen. The superstar Tinkari and other actors and actresses did not receive any money for their performances."[15] Miss Josephine MacLeod wrote in a letter on 19 February 1923: "Going in

Sri Ramakrishna: Patron Saint of the Bengali Stage

the evening to a benefit performance at the Star Theatre, for Ramakrishna Mission of Bhubaneswar, near Puri. The great Indian actress Tara coming out of retirement for it."[16]

* * *

It is extremely important to understand how Ramakrishna influenced not only Girish but also his actors and actresses.

Binodini, who performed in the title role in *Chaitanya Lila* as well as many other of Girish's plays, wrote in her autobiography: "I don't care if the whole world looks down upon me, because I know that the pure and venerable Ramakrishna Paramahamsa blessed me. His hopeful and nectar-like message 'Hari guru, guru Hari' — Hari is the guru and the guru is Hari — still reassures me. When I am oppressed by unbearable pain and agony, his forgiving and gracious form appears in my heart and I hear his voice: 'Say — Hari guru, guru Hari.' I don't remember how many times he came to the theatre after *Chaitanya Lila*, but I saw his joyful face many times when he was seated in a box seat of the theatre."[17]

The actor Amritalal Basu wrote: "When the humble actress [Binodini] acted in the role of Chaitanya, the incarnation of the god of Nadia, on the stage, Sri Ramakrishna of Dakshineswar, another incarnation of God, watched that play and made the wretched stage like Vaikuntha [heaven]. We were blessed! The audience was blessed and so was the Mother Earth! The stage of the theatre became a holy place when Sri Ramakrishna watched through his divine eyes the *Chaitanya Lila*, which was enacted on it. To watch *Chaitanya Lila* is no longer considered to be enjoying an amusement, or being educated, or hearing kirtan; it is now considered to be witnessing a divine lila!"[18]

The actor Aparesh Mukhopadhyay wrote: "When the theater was first started, most people believed that those who act onstage are pariahs, or outcastes. Girish once wrote in a drama, 'Who pays respect to a fallen courtesan?' But there was someone who paid respect, and he was none other than a monk who had completely renounced lust and gold! He put his palm on the head of a fallen actress and blessed her, saying, 'May you be illumined.'"[19]

Amar Datta, the editor of *Natya Mandir*, used Ramakrishna's picture on the cover of one of the magazine's issues. Within, he commented:

> We have printed the picture of Bhagavan Sri Ramakrishna on the cover page of the current issue of *Natya Mandir*. Someone may ask why I have used the picture of the avatar Ramakrishna in a magazine that is full of pictures of actors and actresses. Here is my answer: According to the *Natya Mandir* this whole world is a theatre. All human beings act as

actors and actresses on its stage every day. When the fallen ones forget to act in their proper roles according to the will of the Creator, the universal Director descends on the world stage. Thus once a masterly Director was born in a remote place of Bengal. He lived in the holy temple compound of Dakshineswar near Calcutta and attracted the learned and the illiterate, the rich and the poor. He imprinted in the hearts of seekers: This world is apparent and not absolutely real, and the goal of human life is to realize God. No one was deprived of his teaching — be that person a sadhu or a yogi, a sinner or a fallen woman. Incognito, he appeared as a poor and humble human being and mixed with all equally, out of pure love and compassion. The holy feet of this divine being — the saviour of the fallen — touched the national theatre of Bengal. Ordinary people despised the theatre, considering it to be an abode of immoral men and women, but heaven and hell were equal in the eyes of that great deliverer of sinners. So Ramakrishna — the teacher of humankind, the man-god, the compassionate one — came to the theatre. The touch of his holy feet sanctified the stage by wiping out all impurities, enhanced its dignity and beauty, and made it an attractive and wonderful place.[20]

At that time the magazines and papers connected with the Bengali stage gave tremendous importance to Ramakrishna's visits to the theatre. Until Ramakrishna sanctified the theatre with his presence, most Bengalis considered houses of ill repute and theatres to be more or less the same. Ramakrishna's patronage lifted the taboo. Going to see plays became socially acceptable.

The great reformer Ishwar Chandra Vidyasagar fought all his life for women's liberation, but he disassociated himself from the theatre because he disapproved of women performing onstage. Ramakrishna, however, approved of it. Basanta Kumar Ghosh wrote an article entitled "Bengali Women and the Theatre" in *Natya Mandir*: "Being impressed with their artistic skill and performances, Bhagavan Ramakrishna blessed the courtesan actresses. It was a great achievement of an actress [Binodini] who brought a great soul to the theatre and sanctified it."[21]

Those days are gone: Nowadays, upper-class men and women do not hesitate to become actors and actresses, and their family members are proud of them.

In the Hindu tradition, Shiva is sometimes known as Nataraja, the king of actors. Actors and actresses worship Nataraja by their performances so their profession cannot be considered sinful. If Binodini had appealed to the prominent members of Calcutta society thus — "I was born poor, in a red-light district. My mother was a courtesan, so I followed in her footsteps. I know that society hates our profession. God has endowed me

Sri Ramakrishna: Patron Saint of the Bengali Stage

with a talent for acting. Is it wrong if I want to change my profession and become an actress? Is it sinful to act in the role of Chaitanya and bring the audience to a spiritual realm?" — we don't know what they would have answered. We leave Binodini's question to the reader to answer. In this world there are thousands of Binodinis who are used and abused, neglected and persecuted, ill-treated and hated and who are waiting for the right answer.

* * *

Girish remarked: "*Chaitanya Lila* was my all in all. I received the grace of my guru through that play."[22] Through that play the Bengali stage acquired its patron saint. Undoubtedly it was Girish who made Ramakrishna the presiding deity of the Bengali theatre. At that time, Girish was carried away by a great current of devotion. People in the theatre were overwhelmed by his gigantic personality and followed him spontaneously. Girish wholeheartedly believed that on the pretext of seeing a play, the avatar Ramakrishna had come to the theatre to deliver his message to actors and actresses. As manager and director of the theatre, Girish would personally introduce to the Master those performers who had some devotion for him.

When a famous person comes to see a play, it is natural for the cast members to become inspired and act more enthusiastically than they normally would. But they were even more thrilled when Ramakrishna attended a performance. Previously they had been treated as untouchables, but Ramakrishna gave their morale a tremendous boost and helped them achieve recognition and respect in society. The performers would talk about Ramakrishna while dressing and putting on their make-up in the green room. After the play they would assemble in Girish's room. One night at a gathering in the Kohinoor Theatre, the actress Tarasundari said: "With the type of life we have led, there is no deliverance for us."

Girish: "Don't say that, Tara. Don't you remember your aunt Bini [Binodini]? The Master was moved by her acting in the role of Chaitanya and blessed her, saying, 'Mother, may you attain illumination.'"

Abinash: "Binodini is now a devotee and worships Gopala."

Amritalal Basu also had a role in *Chaitanya Lila*, but he avoided Ramakrishna because he thought himself a sinner. Later Girish took him to the Master and changed his whole life, as he described in his memoirs.[23]

After Ramakrishna's passing away, Girish became the Master's representative and guide to the people of the theatre. One day Ram Chandra Datta and Manomohan Mitra, staunch devotees of the Master, went to visit Girish at his home. While smoking a hubble-bubble, Girish said:

"Brother Ram, the Master has possessed me. He is bringing all sorts of people to me. This wayward Raju, a nephew of Akshay Sen, is pestering me to take him to the Holy Mother and to the monastery."

Ram: "You are ordained to do that. But what good will it do if you take him? Don't you see his character?"

Girish: "Yes, you are right. The Master left me all the odd and wicked ones, the drunkards and prostitutes."

Manomohan: "That is the reason the Master attracted you. If you can captivate and change the most nefarious sinner, then others will be captivated easily."

Girish: "Even the courtesans are flocking to me. Before they appear onstage, they bow down to the Master's picture and then take the dust of my feet. If I do not allow them to touch my feet, they get offended and cannot act wholeheartedly. I am now in trouble!"[24]

The tradition of bowing down to Ramakrishna before going onstage still continues in Calcutta. The Master's picture is decorated with a garland every night before a performance and someone waves lights and incense. It is astonishing that even now there are pictures of Ramakrishna in Calcutta theatres, in the green room, in the parlour, and in some actors' private dressing rooms. Even the technical workers of the theatre do not start their work before saluting Ramakrishna. Girish, a man who once called himself an atheist, is responsible for introducing this tradition.

The following story illustrates how deeply Ramakrishna's teachings permeates the red-light districts of Calcutta: A courtesan died in a nursing home a few years ago. Some young people went to a monk of the Ramakrishna Order in Calcutta and informed him that they needed 26,000 rupees to cremate that woman. The swami learned from them who she was and found information about her will and the executor of her estate. He then talked to the executor, a prominent political leader in that area, and was informed that the woman had left everything to the hospital of the Ramakrishna Mission. The swami gave the money to those young people for her cremation and later went to her home with the police. From her house he recovered half a million rupees in cash, half a million rupees worth of jewellery, and a certificate of deposit worth 1 million rupees. The swami also found in her home some books about Ramakrishna as well as his picture.[25]

That unknown courtesan must have been a great soul! She left everything she had to Ramakrishna. Although her profession kept her body in the world, her devotion connected her mind with Ramakrishna — the Man-god — the Saviour of the soul.

Chapter 15

Three Stars: Binodini, Tarasundari, and Tinkari

God is ever present: He is undying and eternally active and infinitely watchful. We ought not to hate anyone. This world will always continue to be a mixture of good and evil. Our duty is to sympathize with the weak and to love even the wrong-doer. The world is a grand moral gymnasium wherein we have all to take exercise so as to become stronger and stronger spiritually. You hear fanatics glibly saying, "I do not hate the sinner, I hate the sin," but I am prepared to go any distance to see the face of that man who can really make a distinction between the sin and sinner.[1] *— Swami Vivekananda*

As the sun shines on all equally, so God's love flows evenly towards saints and sinners. Krishna says in the Gita: "I am the same towards all beings; to Me there is none hateful or dear. Even the most sinful man, if he worships Me with unswerving devotion, must be regarded as righteous; for he has formed the right resolution. He soon becomes righteous and attains eternal peace. Proclaim it boldly, O son of Kunti, that My devotee never perishes."[2]

Ramakrishna told his devotees: "All the sins of the body fly away if one chants the name of God and sings His glories. The birds of sin dwell in the tree of the body. Singing the name of God is like clapping your hands. As, at a clap of the hands, the birds in the tree fly away, so do our sins disappear at the chanting of God's name and glories."[3]

Ramakrishna also said: "He who says day and night, 'I am a sinner, I am a sinner' verily becomes a sinner. One should have such burning faith in God that one can say: 'What? I have repeated the name of God, and can sin still cling to me? How can I be a sinner anymore?' If a man repeats the name of God, his body, mind, and everything become pure."[4]

At another time, he said: "Heinous sins — the sins of many births — and accumulated ignorance all disappear in the twinkling of an eye, through the grace of God. When light enters a room that has been kept dark a thousand years, does it remove the thousand years' darkness little by little, or instantly? Of course, at the mere touch of light all the darkness disappears."[5]

What a reassuring message! Binodini, Tarasundari, and Tinkari — three superstars of the Calcutta theatre — heard Ramakrishna's message. The Master blessed Binodini after seeing her perform the title role in Girish's *Chaitanya Lila* at the Star Theatre. Though Tarasundari and Tinkari did not meet the Master, they heard his message through Girish, their director and mentor. Later they visited Holy Mother at Udbodhan and received her blessings. Swami Brahmananda and other monastic disciples of the Master also guided them in their spiritual paths.

One's birth is in the hands of Providence, but one's karma is one's own responsibility. These three actresses were born in the red-light district of Calcutta and did not know who their fathers were. Their mothers were active in the most ancient profession, and they lived in misery and poverty. Orthodox society shunned them; they were not even allowed to have a formal education. But the acting talent of Binodini, Tara, and Tinkari overcame all these obstacles. Their self-effort and sincerity, patience and perseverance, passion and ambition led them to the pinnacle of success in life. A blazing fire cannot be hidden, nor can a great talent. The French writer Francois La Rochefoucauld (1613-1680), wrote: "Nature has concealed at the bottom of our minds talents and abilities of which we are not aware. The passions alone have the privilege of bringing them to light, and of giving us sometimes views more certain and more perfect than art could possibly produce."[6]

In the 1870s women began appearing onstage in female roles. However, women from respectable families did not become actresses, so theatre owners hired courtesans and other women outside of mainstream society to perform onstage. As a result, hardcore puritans and pseudo-moralists boycotted the theatre. But some liberals defended the practice of hiring courtesans to act because they realized that the theatre provided a wonderful means of spreading Indian art and culture.

Girish's *Chaitanya Lila* revolutionized the Bengali stage. Even orthodox Vaishnavas of Navadwip went to Girish's theatre to see the play, as did Ramakrishna.

One may ask why these particular actresses were so important to Girish. As a jeweller understands the value of a gemstone, so Girish

Three Stars: Binodini, Tarasundari, and Tinkari 175

perceived the potential talent of Binodini, Tarasundari, and Tinkari even when they were teenagers. He loved them as if they were his own daughters. He rescued them from their dark environment, roused their self-esteem and self-confidence, trained them to become great actresses, and through them, he gave life to his imagination of the most important female roles in his plays. By presenting them on the altar of the Bengali stage, he made them celebrities. Finally, he helped them to develop their spiritual life by introducing them to Ramakrishna, Holy Mother, and the disciples of the Master. For their part, these brilliant actresses brought to life the main characters of Girish's plays, generated revenue for the theatre owners, learned how to be independent, and improved their financial condition. They also brought glory to their teacher, Girish, and preserved Indian art and culture by means of their superb acting. And through this, they brought joy to audiences and attracted tremendous crowds to the theatre. Thus they defeated the social proscriptions against their being onstage. Ultimately they earned recognition for their talent, and commanded people's love and respect.

Upendranath Vidyabhusan (1867-1959), a professor, scholar, and art critic, wrote a biography of all three actresses. We are indebted to Upendranath, who was an eyewitness to their careers and left much valuable information about their lives and performances. He also wrote much about the history of the Bengali stage in the last part of the nineteenth and the first part of the twentieth centuries. This chapter is based upon Upendranath's reflections on Binodini, Tarasundari, and Tinkari.

"Rome was not built in a day" — it took time for Binodini, Tarasundari, and Tinkari to become skillful actresses. Genius is a natural, god-given faculty. Of course, this faculty must be encouraged to grow and manifest through good training and practice. Just as a piece of coal may be washed a hundred times and still remain black, so even strenuous effort cannot turn a dullard into a genius. Some actors and actresses just memorize their lines; there are very few who study their characters, identify with them, and become absorbed in the play. Only this type of performer can leave a deep impression in the hearts of the audience.

A brief note is necessary to explain the social status of women like Binodini, Tarasundari, and Tinkari during the last part of the nineteenth century. Although these women were born and lived in the red-light district of Calcutta, they were not prostitutes who generally sell their bodies for money. Instead, they were the mistresses of wealthy men. At that time it was not uncommon for rich men to support mistresses. Though at present, unmarried men and women in many countries live together, in the nineteenth century this was socially unacceptable.

It was necessary for Binodini, Tarasundari, and Tinkari to become the mistresses of men connected with the theatre to obtain financial security, emotional support, and protection from abuse. This also allowed them to pursue their careers without anxiety. At that time society looked down upon them as fallen women and considered them to be untouchable. But times have changed, and so has society. At present these women and their relationships would be accepted. Even conservative societies are becoming more accepting of this lifestyle.

1. Binodini Dasi (1863–1941)

In the 1870s when women were introduced on the Bengali stage, a few actresses attained celebrity status. Binodini became a superstar. She succeeded by dint of tremendous effort and sincerity, hard labour and perseverance, and above all, her extraordinary genius. In the early era of the Bengali stage, Binodini was Girish's right-hand woman. Binodini performed the female lead in almost all of Girish's plays, bringing each role to life through her genius. Binodini wrote of her indebtedness to Girish in her autobiography, *Āmār Kathā* (My Life Story): "Onstage I was the right hand of Girish Chandra Ghosh. As I was his first and main student, I was famous in the theatre world. He was always anxious to fulfill even my smallest request."[7]

Binodini was born at 145 Cornwallis Street (now Bidhan Sarani) in the red-light district of North Calcutta, most likely in 1863. Her mother and grandmother were very poor, but her grandmother had a small house and a few cottages that they rented out. This was their main source of income — but it was meagre, because the cottages were in a slum and their tenants payed only nominal rent. Binodini and her younger brother both grew up without a father and the small family struggled against poverty. The income they received was not sufficient, so the women of the family were forced to sell their jewellery for food, clothing, and other necessities. When Binodini was 6 years old, her grandmother arranged for her 5-year-old brother to marry a 2 1/2-year-old orphan girl. This marriage brought the family a dowry consisting of jewellery that the little girl had inherited from her mother.

People do not understand poverty until they feel the pain of hunger and see their children crying for food. Binodini's grandmother and mother could not bear it anymore. They began to sell the young bride's jewellery, one piece after another, to buy food for the family. Traditionally in Hindu

Three Stars: Binodini, Tarasundari, and Tinkari 177

Binodini (1863–1941) At right: Binodini as Mati Bibi in *Kapalkundala*

society, a bride's jewellery was meant as a sort of insurance policy, to be sold only in case of emergency and not for day-to-day living. One day Binodini's mother attended a neighbour's function, where she begged for some sweets for her children. Her miserly neighbour gave her some stale sandesh. Binodini recalled that it took her a half hour to eat one piece of that sandesh.

Binodini wrote a vivid account of her young brother's death:

> My brother died at a young age leaving my poor mother and our wretched family. My grandmother and mother were completely broken down from grief. We had no money for treatment, so we carried him to a charitable hospital nearby. We two little girls stayed at home and a compassionate woman who was our neighbour gave us food. She would also escort us and carry food to the hospital for my grandmother and mother. Some days she would stay in the hospital and send them home for food. After their return to the hospital, she would again bring us back home. She was a wonderful, generous woman not only to us but to others also.
>
> My brother died in the hospital. That scene is still vivid to me. When we found my brother's condition critical, we all stayed at the hospital. My grandmother was very fond of my brother. She had heard earlier that in the charitable hospital, the doctors dissect human bodies for experiments and do not allow them to be cremated. So as soon as my brother died, my grandmother grabbed the dead body and held it to her chest. She then rushed down the steps from the third floor, and ran towards the cremation ground on the bank of the Ganges. Holding my mother's hand, my sister-in-law and I cried and followed our grandmother. Seeing our condition, the main doctor of the hospital said, "Don't worry. We shall not keep the body." But my grandmother did not listen to him. When my grandmother placed the body on the bank of the Ganges, another doctor came and told us: "Don't cremate the body right now. We have administered a very strong medicine to his body. Please wait. I shall come back soon." My grandmother waited for an hour holding the dead body on her lap, and finally that doctor returned and gave permission for the cremation. Just as the body was placed on the funeral pyre at Kashi Mitra's ghat in North Calcutta, our kind-hearted neighbour arrived. She had gone home to get some money.
>
> Meanwhile, a terrible accident almost took place. My mother developed temporary insanity and was laughing loudly off and on. When my grandmother and the compassionate lady were busy with the funeral arrangements, my mother walked into the Ganges and reached waist-deep water. Holding my mother's cloth, I cried and shouted. Hearing my voice, my grandmother ran and rescued her from drowning. Afterwards, my mother remained half-mad for a long period. She never cried, but

Three Stars: Binodini, Tarasundari, and Tinkari

laughed from time to time. My grandmother was very careful and never allowed anyone to talk to her about her son. One night when we were in bed, my mother suddenly cried out, saying, "O my son, where have you gone?" My grandmother commented: "Uh! I am relieved." I got up and tried to console my mother, but my grandmother said to me: "Keep quiet. Let her cry." She knew this is the way one can unburden one's heart.[8]

At an early age Binodini was married to a little boy, but this marriage was in name only. Many years later, she wrote in her autobiography: "I heard that I was married to a handsome boy a little older than me. I still remember, that boy, my brother and his wife, and I would play with the neighbours' children. People would say that this handsome boy was my husband. But after some days I did not see him anymore. I heard that his aunt took him away and never allowed him to come to us. I later heard that he married again. My grandmother wanted to keep him in our family as he was also born in a poor family."[9]

The mind of a creative genius is always active and tremendous energy flows in her veins. This inborn restlessness and hunger for knowledge forced the little Binodini to seek admission to a free school on Cornwallis Street where she learned how to read and write, and to speak a little English. Observing women in her community, she realized that youth and beauty are transient, so she concentrated on developing her artistic talent.

Binodini wrote: "When I was 9 years old, a young woman named Gangamani moved into a room of our only brick-built house. She did not have any parents, so my grandmother and mother looked after her as their own daughter. Ganga and I became close friends. Ganga was a wonderful singer and later she became a famous actress in the Star Theatre. She was very humble, largehearted, and grateful to our family. My grandmother engaged her to teach me singing."[10]

Some gentlemen would visit Gangamani regularly to hear her sing, and Binodini became acquainted with them. Gangamani told them about Binodini's poor background, so they were very affectionate to this bright, beautiful little girl. Forgetting her music lessons, Binodini loved to hear their stories. Her imagination later helped her to become a successful actress. She also observed the living conditions of her family's tenants, men and women who were not married but who lived together as husband and wife. Sometimes they would fight, and again they would laugh, joke, and eat together. Binodini wrote: "I was then a little girl. Seeing their behaviour I was overwhelmed with fear and wonder. I was disgusted by their way of life. I thought that I would never be so mean in my life. But I did not realize that Providence had set a patch of thick clouds over my head."[11]

Purna Chandra Mukhopadhyay and Brajanath Seth loved Gangamani's music, so they visited her quite often. One day Binodini heard that they were trying to stage a musical drama called *Sitār Bibāha* (Sita's Marriage). Purna had learned about the poor condition of Binodini's family from Gangamani, so he said to her grandmother: "I understand that you have terrible financial difficulties. Why don't you allow your granddaughter to act in the theatre? Now she will get some pocket-money, and later when she is trained, she will draw a good salary."

Her grandmother replied: "Sir, I can't answer right now. Please give me a little time. I shall consult with a few people and then let you know within a couple of days."

Binodini wrote: "My grandmother consulted with three or four people and then agreed to the proposal of Purna Babu. At that time there were two theatres: Bhuban Mohan Niyogi's Great National Theatre and Sharat Chandra Ghosh's Bengal Theatre. Purna Babu then took me to the Great National Theatre and enrolled me there at 10 rupees per month."[12]

Binodini was 11 years old. Her new life commenced, leading her from the dirty slums to the luxurious stage of Calcutta. In this environment she began acting lessons, which were new to her. But she was sincere, passionate, and a quick learner. Instead of cursing poverty, this little girl considered it to be a blessing.

She wrote: "Whenever I thought of the poverty of my family, I felt a desire to improve it. And whenever the sorrowful face of my mother appeared in my mind, my enthusiasm for acting increased to a great extent. At that time there were four famous actresses at the National Theatre: Raja, Kshetramani, Lakshmi, and Narayani. I used to wonder how soon I would be a great actress like them. Seeing my wornout clothes, Raja bought for me two half-sleeved chintz frocks. I was overjoyed. Those two frocks were my only clothes in winter."[13]

When Binodini joined the Great National Theatre, *Beni-sanghar*, a play based on the Mahabharata, was being rehearsed. The manager, director, and others consulted among themselves and gave Binodini a small part, as a confidante of Queen Draupadi. She had to say only a couple of sentences, which she memorized. She was not nervous until the day of the dress rehearsal on the stage. Then came the day of the gala opening: 12 December 1874.

Binodini wrote: "I can't express my feelings of anxiety on that day when I appeared in front of the audience on the stage. Those dazzling lights of the theatre and the steady gaze of the large excited audience made me very nervous. My whole body perspired, my heart beat wildly, and my legs trembled. But the director encouraged me. I was a poor girl and had never had this kind of assignment. When I was very young, my mother taught me, 'When you are afraid, remember Hari, God.' Thinking of God, I went to the stage, and recited those few words wholeheartedly with the proper gestures as instructed by the director. When I was leaving the stage, the audience clapped and shouted joyfully. My body was trembling either out of fear or excitement. As soon as I returned to the greenroom, the director and others patted me. At that time I didn't know what applause meant, so they explained to me that my performance was appreciated."[14]

Binodini conquered the hearts of all who saw her perform. Thus her triumphant career began. The theatre authorities then decided to stage *Hemalata* and cast her in the main role. Hemalata was a princess, so they thought that Binodini's bright, beautiful, and innocent face would match that character. She needed only a little training and makeup. Binodini wrote: "On the opening day of the play [6 March 1875] I was happy and excited putting on the gorgeous dress of the princess. I had never seen such a costume, not to speak of wearing it. However, by the grace of God I acted well in the role of Hemalata."[15]

The Great National Theatre was popular, but it was not making sufficient money to meet its expenses. So the authorities planned to take the theatre party to various cities in the western part of India to make extra money. Binodini refused to go alone, so they raised her salary by five rupees and included her mother in the group. In her autobiography Binodini wrote a complete account of her travels. In March 1875 the group first went to Lucknow and performed *Nildarpan*. There is a scene in this play where an Englishman tries to molest an Indian woman and an Indian man starts hitting him. While this scene was being performed, an English gentleman from the audience became angry and jumped onstage to hit the Indian. There was chaos and confusion. The Indians were afraid to say anything against the English as they were the rulers of the country. The play ended immediately and the party left Lucknow the next morning.

The group went on to Delhi, and then to Lahore. Here Binodini acted in several main roles, such as Radhika in *Sati ki Kalankini*, Kamini in *Navin Tapaswini*, Kanchan in *Sadhabar Ekadashi*, and Phati in *Biye Pagla Buro*. She was then 11 or 12 years old, so the makeup crew had a challenge to present her as a young woman. Sometimes they would tease her, saying, "We shall send you to a blacksmith who will hammer you on his anvil and make you a little bigger."

Binodini wrote: "When I was acting in Lahore, a strange thing happened. Golap Singh, a local wealthy landlord, wanted to marry me and offered plenty of money to my mother. He asked to see our manager and our director, and put them into an embarrassing situation. He was a very influential man there. My mother began to cry and I was scared to death. We had to leave Lahore very quickly."[16] After visiting Vrindaban the party returned to Calcutta.

The Great National Theatre closed after six months because of its financial problems. In December 1876 Binodini got an acting job in the Bengal Theatre at twenty-five rupees per month. The owner, Sharat Chandra Ghosh, loved this talented girl and gave her full freedom and opportunity to grow. Binodini acknowledged him in her autobiography: "Sharat Babu loved me as his own daughter. Having only one mouth, I am unable to express his unbounded affection and noble qualities."[17] Sharat was Binodini's principal acting teacher. He cast her in the main role in the following plays: Manorama in *Mrinalini*, Kapalkundala in *Kapalkundala*, Ayesha and Tilottama in *Durgeshnandini*, and Pramila in *Meghnad-badh*. Bankim Chandra, the author of *Mrinalini*, came to see his play performed at the Bengal Theatre. After seeing Binodini's portrayal of Manorama, he commented: "I depicted the image of Manorama in the book and I never expected that I would ever see her living. Today that notion of mine has been dispelled after seeing Binodini's acting."[18]

In *Durgeshnandini*, a drama based on Bankim's novel, Binodini acted in the roles of Tilottama, a timid daughter of King Birendra Singha, and of Ayesha, the proud daughter of the Muslim king. If one actress was sick, she performed both roles on the same night. Her virtuosity overwhelmed the audience. One evening Binodini dressed as Ayesha and came to the theater. The actress who was supposed to act in the role of Ashmani, a maidservant, was sick and did not show up. The theatre was full of spectators. The manager and director hesitated to ask Binodini to take on another role, but they had no alternative. Finally, Amritalal Basu went to Binodini and said: "My sweet sister, in addition to your role, you will have to act in the role of Ashmani; otherwise we will be in trouble. Please somehow manage this for tonight." Binodini refused several times, but finally agreed.

Binodini related an interesting episode that took place in the auditorium of the Maharaja of Krishnanagore: "I was acting in the role of Pramila in the drama *Meghnad-badh* on horseback. A mud stage had been built. While coming down from the stage, the mud step broke, the horse stumbled, and I also fell down. I was injured and could not get up. The

Three Stars: Binodini, Tarasundari, and Tinkari

stage manager carried me to the greenroom, gave me medicine for pain, and bandaged my knee and waist. There was still a long way before my part ended. Sharat Babu affectionately said to me: 'My sweet child, I know you are in great pain. But please save the play tonight.' His loving and affectionate words reduced half of my pain. Though I was in much pain, I acted that night and returned to Calcutta the next day. I was bedridden for a month. I had a nice time at the Bengal Theatre. I made no demands. I took whatever they gave me. Everyone loved me."[19]

Towards the end of 1877, a new chapter began in Binodini's life. She was then 14 years old. Kedarnath Chaudhury was the owner of the National Theatre and Girish was the manager, playwright, and director, in addition to being one of the actors. One night Kedarnath took Girish to the Bengal Theatre to see Bankim's *Kapalkundala*, in which Binodini was performing the title role. Both were overwhelmed by her talent. Kedarnath commented: "This girl appeared to be the real Kapalkundala and she displayed a sylvan simplicity in her acting."[20]

Girish approached Sharat Ghosh and asked him to release Binodini from the Bengal Theatre and allow her to join the National Theatre, where she would earn a higher salary. The Bengal Theatre was then passing through a financial crisis and Binodini was not receiving her monthly salary. With Sharat's permission, Binodini moved to the National Theatre. Girish became her acting guru, and she worked under him throughout the rest of her career. In the National Theatre, Binodini was favoured by fortune and became an extremely popular actress. She was adored as a queen of the stage and her fame spread throughout Bengal.

Binodini wrote: "In the theatre Girish Babu was my teacher and I was his first and main disciple. I acted in all the main female roles of his plays. He taught me with great care so that I could depict each character flawlessly."[21] In *Meghnad-badh* Girish acted in the roles of Meghnad and Ram. Binodini demonstrated her talent by performing seven roles in that play — Chitrangada, Pramila, Baruni, Rati, Maya, Mahamaya, and Sita — all on the same night. During that period Girish and Binodini performed the roles of the hero and heroine in every play that the National Theatre staged. Binodini wrote: "In *Mrinalini*, Girish Babu became Pashupati and I, Manorama; in *Durgeshnandini*, he was Jagat Singha and I was Ayesha; in *Bishabriksha*, he was Nagendranath and I was Kundanandini; in *Palasir Yuddha*, he was Lord Clive and I was Britannia, and so on."[22]

Human life is not always smooth, and Binodini began to face difficulties. The National Theatre passed through a financial crisis and the ownership changed a few times. Finally, in 1880 it had to be auctioned, and a

Marwari businessman named Prataplal Jahuri bought it. He made Girish the full-time manager and did not change the staff. Girish wrote fourteen plays and Binodini acted in the main female roles as usual. During this time Binodini, now 17 years old, began to live with a wealthy young man. He wanted her to give up the theatre, but she refused. Soon after, she became ill and took leave from the theatre for fifteen days. She went to Varanasi to convalesce, where her illness at first became worse, but gradually she recovered. After one month she returned to Calcutta and rejoined the theatre. Prataplal refused to pay her for the month that she had been away. Binodini wanted to leave the National Theatre, but Girish asked her to be patient.

Towards the end of 1882 friction developed between Prataplal and Girish and the other actors and actresses. Girish was secretly looking for a wealthy investor who would be willing to start a new theatre. Meanwhile, Gurmukh Roy, an affluent young Marwari man, came forward to start a theatre on the condition that Binodini would live with him. He offered all of the money needed to build a theatre, plus a large sum for Binodini. Binodini refused the offer, but Girish and other actors and actresses encouraged her to accept it. After much persuasion Binodini agreed to move in with Gurmukh because his previous lover had gone back home and married. However, she delayed.

Sometimes the life of a celebrity is like a roller coaster. Beauty, talent, and name and fame do not always bring peace and happiness. Binodini began to experience this hard reality. Before Binodini could move in with Gurmukh, her ex-lover came back and asked her to return to him. He offered Binodini thousands of rupees, which she declined. One night after a rehersal Binodini was sleeping in her room. In the early morning she was awakened by a sudden noise, only to see that her ex-lover was standing by her bed, wearing a military uniform and holding a sword. He again asked her to return to him, this time offering more money. When she did not budge, he became very angry.

Binodini wrote: "Suddenly he took the sword and was about to strike my head. My eyes were on the sword. Instantly I hid under my table harmonium, and the sword struck three fingers deep into the harmonium cover. He again struck, and this time it hit the stool as I jumped under it. It was my good luck that I was not killed. When he tried to strike me a third time, I grabbed his sword hand and said: 'What are you doing? If you want to kill me, do it later. First think of your future. It does not matter if my sinful life ends here. Please think about the result of your action and about your family. You will leave this world with the sin of killing a courtesan. Shame, shame! Listen, be calm.' He then threw the sword aside and sat down. After a while he left without saying a word."[23]

Gurmukh then offered Binodini 50,000 rupees and requested her to live with him permanently and not be involved with the theatre anymore. But acting was more important than money to Binodini, so she declined that offer. The theatre was her altar, acting was her worship, and Girish was her guru. Binodini wrote: "At my request a plot of land was taken on lease on Beadon Street, and Gurmukh Roy began to spend money lavishly for the construction of the theatre. After rehearsal we used to go to the construction site and join with the labourers to expedite the work. I used to carry dirt in a basket and fill the back rows where the seats would be. I was overjoyed. During the construction all told me, 'The name of this theatre will be connected with your name, i.e., "B-theatre." After your death your name will be immortalized.'"[24]

The construction of the theatre took one year. Binodini was shocked when she heard that the theatre had been registered as the Star Theatre. The organizers felt that although Binodini was a great actress, people might not come to the theatre if it was named after a courtesan. But Binodini felt betrayed and used by her friends and well-wishers. With a wounded heart she stayed at home for a couple of months. Gurmukh was also upset because Binodini's desire had not been fulfilled. He even threatened to destroy the theatre. Girish mediated between the owner and the staff and convinced Binodini to join the theatre. She had tremendous love and respect for Girish, so she could not refuse. The Star Theatre opened on 21 July 1883 with Girish's *Daksha Yajna*, which is described in Chapter 13. Girish acted in the role of King Daksha, and Binodini performed as Sati. The opening night drew a tremendous crowd: The house was sold out. Girish then wrote two new plays, *Dhruva Charitra* and *Nala-Damayanti*, which were staged at the Star. Binodini acted in the role of Suruchi in *Dhruva Charitra* and Damayanti in *Nala Damayanti*.

Gurmukh Roy remained the owner of the Star for a year. In the early part of 1883 he fell ill and was forced by his relatives and associates in the Marwari community to give up the theatre. Gurmukh decided to sell the theatre. He said to Girish: "I spent an enormous amount of money to build the theatre, but I shall sell it for 11,000 rupees."[25] Girish was delighted to hear this proposal. He told the management group that they could own the Star by paying that relatively small amount. Amritalal Mitra, Hariprasad Basu, Dasu Charan Niyogi, and Amritalal Basu came forward with the money, and the theatre was registered in their names.

Girish easily could have bought the Star, but he had promised his brother that he would never own a theatre.

Gurmukh wanted Binodini to have a share in the ownership, and he said that he would not sell the theatre unless that condition was fulfilled. But Girish knew that the other partners would not agree to this condition, so he told Binodini's mother: "Look, you are women. It is better for you not to get involved in this risky business. I shall not manage this theatre without taking your daughter into account. No one can deny that Binodini is indispensable to the theatre. We shall do our work. Let the owners take the responsibility."[26] Binodini's mother loved and respected Girish, so she at last agreed, but Binodini was hurt. However, she loved the theatre and continued acting with her usual enthusiasm.

In 1883 the International Exhibition attracted many maharajas as well as foreigners to Calcutta. These distinguished visitors wanted to see cultural programmes at night. To entertain them, Girish presented many plays in the Star Theatre. All tickets were sold at the price of box seats, so the owners raised enough money to clear the loan that they had incurred to buy the theatre. Girish staged his most popular plays, including *Nala-Damayanti, Dhruva Charitra, Prahlada Charitra, Sribatsa Chinta,* and *Hirar Phul.* Binodini had leading roles in all of them and attracted a large audience every night.

Chapter 9 presented M.'s accounts of *Chaitanya Lila*, which Ramakrishna went to see at the Star Theatre on 21 September 1884. Binodini was then a young woman of 20 when she played the part of Chaitanya, who was also in his early 20s during the time the play was set. There is no photograph of Binodini dressed in the role of Chaitanya, but Ramakrishna's comment was: "I found the representation the same as the real." This remark is enough for us to visualize how skillfully Binodini transformed herself with makeup, costumes, and her acting talents to become a god-intoxicated man. In her memoirs Binodini described her preparation for that role:

> As our Star Theatre became more famous day by day, Girish Babu took special care to instruct me in various ways so that I might perform better. *Chaitanya Lila* was written and we started rehearsing the new play. Sisir Kumar Ghosh, the editor of *Amrita Bazar Patrika*, was a devout Vaishnava, and he would often attend the rehearsals. As I was a fallen woman, he advised me how to act in the role of that divine character Chaitanya with solemnity and elegance. He repeatedly told me: "Meditate on Gauranga [Chaitanya] in your heart continually. He is the saviour of the lowly and the redeemer of the fallen, and he is compassionate to fallen people." According to his advice I would meditate on Mahaprabhu Gauranga

with fear. I was apprehensive about accomplishing my task. I always prayed to him: "O Lord Gauranga, the saviour of the soul, please bestow grace on me, a lowly, fallen woman."

The night before my first performance in *Chaitanya Lila*, I could hardly sleep. My heart throbbed with anxiety. I rose early that morning, went to bathe in the Ganges, and then I wrote out Mother Durga's auspicious name 108 times. I bowed down to the Lord Gauranga and prayed: "Mahaprabhu, please bestow grace on me and help me so that I can pass this difficult ordeal." I passed the whole day in apprehension and anxiety. Later I learned that my prayer and surrender to him were not in vain. I indeed became the recipient of his grace, which was confirmed and expressed by a large enthusiastic audience. I realized that God was showering grace on me.

There was a scene of Chaitanya's early life in which I slowly entered the stage with this song: "I have no one but Radha. I play the flute calling for Radha." At that time I felt as if a powerful light engulfed my heart. Receiving a garland from a woman flower-seller, I asked her, "What do you see, Malini?" At that time my outward vision turned inward. I could see nothing around me. I perceived the beautiful form of Gauranga in my heart. I experienced that it was Gauranga himself who was speaking and I was listening and echoing his words. I was thrilled with bliss, my body was covered with goose bumps, and I perceived a mist around me. During a scene in which I argued with my teacher, saying: "Sir, who belongs to whom? Everyone is Krishna!" At that time I truly felt, who in this world belongs to whom? In another scene, out of joy and exultation I uttered:

> In Gaya I saw the living Lord Vishnu.
> Millions of souls were
> Sipping divine nectar from His lotus feet.

At that time I felt that someone was speaking those words from my heart. I was nobody. I was then devoid of I-consciousness.

In a scene, after taking sannyasa vows, I went to take leave of my mother, Sachi Devi, saying:

> Dear Mother, cry for Krishna,
> And not for your son Nimai.
> If you cry for Krishna, you will achieve everything;
> But if you cry for Nimai,
> You will lose Nimai as well as Krishna.

Listening to these lines, some of the women in the audience would cry out so loudly that I felt a throbbing in my heart. The heartrending cry of Mother Sachi, the excitement of the audience, and my overflowing emotion would overwhelm me so much that I was beside myself with tears.

During the final scene, after becoming a monk, I sang this song with the kirtan party:

> O Hari, You have bewitched my heart,
> And now You have hidden Yourself somewhere.
> I am alone in this world,
> Reveal Yourself, O my beloved companion,
> And give me shelter at Your feet....

I cannot express in writing the state of my mind when I sang this song. Truly I felt then that I was all alone in this world, with none as my own. My soul would rush to the lotus feet of Hari and take shelter there. During the kirtan I danced in ecstasy. Some days I could not carry the gravity of the role and I fainted on the stage.

One day there was a large audience in the theatre, and while acting I fainted in the middle of the play. We drew unusually large crowds all through the run of *Chaitanya Lila*. However, some days when the foreign visitors would come, the theatre would be packed with many dignitaries. One day Father Eugene Lafont, a respected Christian, came to see the play. Seeing my ecstatic state, he came on the stage when the curtain fell after the play and told Girish Babu, "I want to see her personally." Girish Babu escorted him to my dressing room. When I regained consciousness, I found a tall Englishman with long beard wearing a cloak and trousers caressing my head with his hand. When I sat up, Girish Babu told me: "Salute him. He is Father Lafont, a great pandit." I had heard about him but never met him. I saluted him with folded hands. He stroked my head and asked me to drink a glass of water. After I drank it, I recovered quickly and became normal. On another occasion when I lost consciousness, I felt weak; but this time it never happened. I do not know the cause.

I cannot count how many blessings I received from the great Sanskrit scholars for my performances in the role of Chaitanya. Pandit Mathuranath Padaratna, the most venerable devout Vaishnava of Navadwip, came on the stage and blessed me, his two hands touching my head. It was the sheer grace of Mahaprabhu Chaitanya that I became the recipient of the boundless grace of many learned, spiritual people. But the most remarkable thing that happened in my acting of *Chaitanya Lila* and also in my life was when I received the grace of Sri Ramakrishna Paramahamsadeva, the saviour of the fallen. He came to see the performance of *Chaitanya Lila* and allowed me to take refuge at his feet. When the performance was over, I went to bow down to him in the office of the theatre. He immediately got up and danced ecstatically, and then said to me with a joyful face: "Repeat, mother, 'Hari is the guru; the guru is Hari. Hari is the guru; the guru is Hari.'" He then placed both of his hands on the head of my sinful body, purified it, and said, "Mother, may your spiritual consciousness be awakened." I can't express how his beautiful, loving, forgiving, and compassionate gaze fell on a lowly person like me! Being a saviour of sinners and purifier of the fallen, he personally assured protection to me. Alas! I was truly an unfortunate, wretched woman. I could not recognize him. Once again, I became engulfed in that bewitching maya and made my life a veritable hell. And once, when he had been ill in a house at Shyampukur, Calcutta, I went to see him. Although he was then disease-stricken, he said to me graciously, "Come, sit down, my child." Ah, what a loving, affectionate mood! He was always eager to come forward to forgive this creature of Hell.

Sri Ramakrishna's main disciple Narendranath (who later became known as Swami Vivekananda) came to our theatre hall many times and I had an opportunity to hear this auspicious song in his melodious voice:

> Oh, when will dawn for me that day of blessedness
> When He who is all Good, all Beauty, all Truth
> Will light the inmost shrine of my heart?...

I truly feel blessed that my body was dedicated to the theatre. It does not matter at all if people of the world look down upon me. I received the grace of the most respected and venerable Ramakrishna Paramahamsadeva. His divine hopeful message, "Hari is the guru, the guru is Hari" still brings me hope. When I am afflicted by the unbearable pain and agony of my heart, I see that the all-forgiving, graceful form of Sri Ramakrishna appears within and advises me saying, "Say — Hari is the guru, the guru is Hari!" I do not recall how many times he came to the theatre after the performance of *Chaitanya Lila*, but I saw his graceful and joyful face several times in the theatre box seat.[27]

Binodini mentioned above that she went to see the Master in Shyampukur when he was ill. The disciples who cared for him there had decided that strangers would no longer be allowed to approach the Master, because this might aggravate his cancer. In *Sri Ramakrishna and His Divine Play* Swami Saradananda gave a detailed account of how Binodini met with the Master:

> An amusing incident took place related to the above rules. When the Master lived at Dakshineswar, he went one day to see a religious drama*

---

*Ramakrishna went to the Star Theatre to see the play *Chaitanya Lila* on 21 September 1884. In this play, Binodini portrayed Chaitanya, and the Master blessed her, saying, "Mother, be illumined." — Translator.

in a theatre managed by Girish and praised the performance of the actress who played the lead role. At the end of the play, the actress had the good fortune to take the dust of the Master's feet when he was in ecstasy. From then on she considered the Master to be a living god. She cherished a heartfelt love and respect for him, and she was now looking for an opportunity to see him once more. When she heard of the Master's fatal disease, she was extremely eager to see him. As she knew Kalipada Ghosh, she fervently requested him to help her visit the Master.

Kalipada was a follower of Girish in every respect and considered the Master to be the avatar of this age. He did not believe that the Master's illness would grow worse if a repentant sinner touched his holy feet. He therefore felt no fear and did not hesitate to take the actress to the Master. One evening he secretly advised her to dress like a gentleman, with hat and coat, and took her to the Shyampukur house. He introduced her to us as his friend, took her to the Master, and told him who she really was. We were not then in the Master's room, so they faced no obstacles. When the fun-loving Master learned that the actress had dressed like that to hoodwink us, he laughed heartily. He was pleased by her faith and devotion and praised her courage and cunning. He advised her to cultivate faith in and reliance on God, gave her a few spiritual instructions, and then shortly bade her good-bye. With tearful eyes she bowed down to the Master, placing her head at his feet, then left with Kalipada. The Master told us this story later, and when we saw him laughing and joking about the trick that had been played on us, we could not be angry with Kalipada.[28]

*   *   *

Binodini continued performing at the Star Theatre. After the success of *Chaitanya Lila*, Girish wrote *Nimai Sannyas*, which dramatized the second half of Chaitanya's life. Binodini again played the leading role of Chaitanya. Her performance was highly praised by all, including Sir Edwin Arnold, author of *The Light of Asia*. In Girish's *Buddhadev-Charit*, Binodini acted in the role of Gopa, the wife of Buddha. Girish said that Binodini was not only a gifted actress but also had a special talent for doing her own stage makeup and designing her costumes. For example, as Princess Gopa in the early part of the play, Binodini wore a royal robe and looked gorgeous. But as soon as Buddha renounced the world, Binodini changed her costume and makeup. She appeared on the stage as a half-mad woman, demanding her husband's cloth from Buddha's charioteer so she could worship it. When Binodini transformed herself according to the character she portrayed, it was difficult for the audience to recognize that it was the same woman.

Binodini also performed the role of the courtesan Chintamani in Girish's famous drama *Vilwamangal Thakur* (see Chapter 16). She established her acting talent in comedy as well as in drama and proved to be unique in each. Regardless of the type of role, Binodini devoted 100 percent of her energy, emotion, and sincerity to every performance. For that reason, her acting was natural and expressive and left the audience awestruck.

Ramakrishna passed away in August 1886, and Binodini quit the stage on 1 January 1887. On that day she performed in Girish's *Nala-Damayanti* and *Bellik Bazar*, in the roles of Damayanti and Rangini respectively.[29] She had acted for 12 years, from the age of 11 to 23, in 80 plays and in more than 90 roles.[30]

In her autobiography, Binodini tells some fascinating stories about her time on the stage. For example, the first scene of *Nala-Damayanti* was set on a lake. There were six large lotuses onstage, and six lotus-maidens would sing and dance on them, leaping from one to the other. One night one of these actresses did not show up, so the performance could not begin. People in the audience were growing impatient and began clapping to protest the delay, so Girish asked Binodini to fill in for the missing actress. She was reluctant to do it, but finally yielded when Girish insisted. The other actresses had their hair covered by flower crowns so that they could easily enter and come out of those artificial lotuses. But Binodini had no flower crown covering her head, so her hair became entangled in a cable of the crane that was used to lift her up to the empty lotus. Only part of her face was visible and there was no way she could get down. She was in great trouble. The stage manager shouted, "Her hair is caught." He immediately brought scissors and cut Binodini's beautiful hair in three or four places to release her.

Binodini recalled: "I came backstage and broke down in a fit of tears. I said adamantly, 'I will not act in this role anymore.' Girish Babu came to me, patted me on the back, and began to comfort me, saying: 'You see, this sort of thing happens quite often. You are crying because you lost a few clumps of hair! Do you know that there are some famous actresses in England who have no hair on their heads and not even a single tooth? Why are you crying over a few clumps of hair? Come, let me tell you a story and while I tell it, put on your costume.' Saying so, Girish Babu began his story: 'A famous English actress returned home after a performance: She first took off her costume, then her fancy curly wig, and finally she took her upper and lower dentures out of her mouth. Her daughter, who was 5 or 6 years old, had been watching this entire scene. She then went close to her mother and began to pull on her nose, thinking that her mother's nose and ears must also be glued to her face.' My anger melted. Somehow I suppressed my laughter and said: 'Sir, please stop. It is enough.' Smiling, I returned to the stage. After achieving his purpose, he also left with a smile."[31]

Life rolls on through waves of laughter and tears. Binodini joyfully acted on the stage and gave joy to many people. Finally the time came for Binodini — the beautiful, talented superstar — to depart from the stage of her beloved Star Theatre. Why Binodini left her career is a mystery. Her biographers give various reasons: One states that her lover did not want her to act anymore; another claims that the owners did not pay enough attention to her; yet another that she became upset when Gangamani, a fellow actress and a wonderful singer, got more applause in *Vilwamangal Thakur* in the role of Pagalini than she got in the role of Chintamani. However, Binodini herself wrote: "Eventually it became almost impossible to continue working in the theatre because of various kinds of estrangements and betrayals. Those who had been just like loving brothers, friends, kinsmen, and companions while we were working together, suddenly turned into wealthy, authoritative owners of the theatre. Perhaps it was for that reason, or it was my fault. In any case, I had to take leave from the stage."[32]

Binodini's public life ended and her private life began. She lived with a wealthy, kindhearted man for 31 years. In 1890 she had a daughter who became her solace and succour. Binodini named her Shakuntala and tried to give her a good education. But unfortunately the girl died in 1903. Binodini was brokenhearted. She became seriously ill, and was near death. Her lover engaged several doctors, spent thousands of rupees, and finally saved her life. Binodini faced one tragedy after another. Finally her lover died in 1912,[33] and her happy family life was shattered.

Following Girish's advice, she began to write. She began with her autobiography, which was published in 1912 in Bengali as *Amar Katha*.* In her writings, Binodini never tried to hide her way of life, and at the same time she attacked the so-called respectable men of society who used and exploited courtesans while considering themselves to be innocent.

It is not good to harbour grief for departed loved ones. Each human being comes to this world alone and leaves it alone. As the sun never stops its journey, so the journey of life never stops. After the death of her

---

*The enlarged edition of *Amar Katha O Anyanya Rachana* was edited by Saumitra Chattopadhyay and Nirmalya Acharya and published by Subarnarekha, Calcutta in 1987. In 1998 Rimli Bhattacharya edited and translated the above book into English as *My Story and My Life as an Actress*; it was published by Kali for Women, New Delhi.

Three Stars: Binodini, Tarasundari, and Tinkari — 193

daughter, Binodini adopted a girl and eventually had four grandchildren. She used to sing while accompanying herself with her organ, and sometimes she would go to see a play. All the actors and actresses respected her highly and called her "aunt." She spent her time in writing her autobiography and recording stories from her acting career, which were published serially in *Natya Mandir* magazine. In 1896 she wrote 41 poems that were published under the title *Bāsanā*. She dedicated this book to her mother. In 1905 she wrote *Kanaka O Nalini*, another book of poems that she dedicated to her beloved daughter Shakuntala. Binodini was a wonderful storyteller because she made everything living and vivid.

Binodini had experienced the emptiness and transitoriness of human life, but Ramakrishna had given her some peace. She never forgot Ramakrishna and the blessings he had bestowed on her. Sometimes she would describe her encounters with the Master to visitors. She would also take Tarasundari, who was her neighbour and who later became a famous actress, to Belur Math. Swami Brahmananda always received them with love and affection, fed them, and encouraged them to visit Belur Math frequently.

Pratibha, Tarasundari's daughter, said: "Binodini made a worship room on the third floor of her house. There she installed the images of Radha and Krishna, Gopala, and a Narayana Shila. A brahmin priest would come every day to perform worship. Apart from that worship room, Binodini had a small personal shrine, where she installed a picture of Sri Ramakrishna. She worshipped the Master herself with flowers and sandal paste. She regularly practised her spiritual disciplines and read the Gita."[34]

Binodini was a compassionate, benevolent, and religious woman. The name of her house was "Gopal Kutir" (Baby Krishna's cottage). The last part of her life was completely dedicated to God. Towards the end, she would go every evening to the Ramakrishna Vedanta Math, which was near her home, to visit Swami Abhedananda and attend the vesper service of the Master. Swami Prajnanananda told the present author that he saw her crying in front of the Master's picture. Binodini passed away on 12 February 1941.

2. Tarasundari (1879–1948)

The roots of a lotus lie in foul-smelling mud, but its stem comes through the water, takes the form of a bud, and finally blooms as a beautiful and sweet-smelling flower on the surface of the pond. People do not care for its source, but they enjoy the beauty and fragrance of the blossom. Bees sip nectar from lotuses and give it to human beings in the form

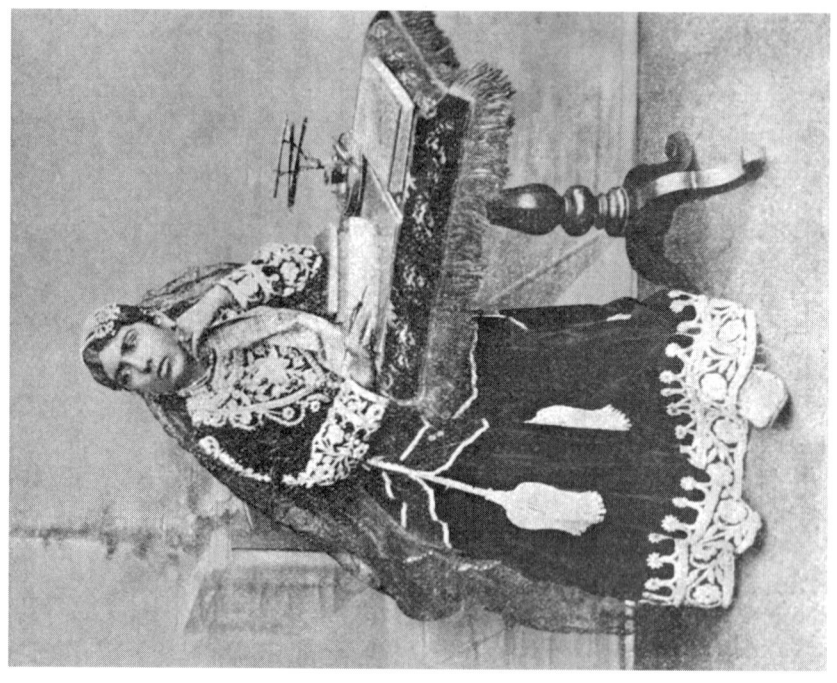

Tarasundari (1879–1948) At right: Tarasundari as Ayesha in *Durgeshnandini*

of honey; devotees pick the lotuses and offer them at the feet of the Lord. The lives of Binodini, Tarasundari, and Tinkari can be compared to those lotuses. They might have been born in a lowly place, but they gave tremendous joy and inspiration to humanity through their beautiful acting.

Tarasundari was born in 1879 in the same red-light district of North Calcutta where Binodini had been born sixteen years earlier. Tarasundari's mother was a poor courtesan and had two daughters, Nrityakali and Tarasundari, whom she raised through tremendous hardship and sacrifice. Tara's mother and Binodini's mother were friends. In 1885 Binodini took Tara to the theatre to make her an actress. She told the little girl: "This is our theatre; this is the stage; this is the greenroom; and look, he is our manager. His name is Girish Chandra Ghosh, and he is a famous actor and playwright."[35]

In *Chaitanya Lila*, there was a role of a boy that had no dialogue. Tara was offered that part, thus making her debut at the Star Theatre at the age of 6. Gopallal Sil, a wealthy man in Calcutta, bought the Star Theatre, remodeled it, and changed its name to the Emerald — costing both Binodini and Tara their jobs.

In 1888, the new Star Theatre was built in Hatibagan and on 25 May it opened with Girish's *Nasiram*. Tara was then 9 years old. She was offered the role of a tribal boy. When her mother objected, two actors and Binodini convinced her to allow Tara to act in the play. Tara's role was small and had very little dialogue. Amritalal Mitra was the stage director, and he became Tara's first acting guru. After memorizing her few lines she began to recite that dialogue according to the director's instruction. Tara enchanted the audience with her lively performance and her simple, pure, innocent face. She also acted in *Swarnalata*, performing the role of Gopala. That performance was also highly appreciated.

In 1888 Girish returned to the Star, and Tara had the opportunity to meet him. One day Girish came to the theatre and saluted the portrait of Ramakrishna with folded hands and closed eyes. Tara imitated Girish and stood near him. Seeing the little girl, Girish asked with a smile, "Who are you?"

"I am Tara," she humbly and joyfully replied.

Girish: "Oh, you act in the role of Gopala?" Smiling, Tara nodded her head. Amritalal Mitra, Tara's teacher, was seated nearby. Girish put his palm on Tara's head and said, "Amrita, look after this girl; her future will be bright."[36] Only a jeweller knows the value of a jewel. The actor Girish saw the potential of the future actress Tara. She received Girish's blessing, which later was fulfilled.

In Girish's *Prafulla*, Girish himself trained Tara to act in the role of Jadav, a boy who was about to be murdered by his uncle (see Chapter 6 for more on the play). Tara's performance was so intense that people in the audience shed tears.

Tara was 10 years old in 1889 when she got her first female role. In Girish's *Haranidhi* she was cast as Hemangini, the spoiled daughter of a wealthy man. This role required singing, which Tara did not know how to do, so Amritalal Basu engaged Ramtaran Sanyal to teach her to sing. Kashinath Chattopadhyay taught her to dance.

When Tara was 13, she performed the roles of Chaitanya in *Chaitanya Lila*, Damayanti in *Nala-Damayanti*, and Gopa in *Buddhadev-Charit*, all of which had been performed previously by Binodini. It is not possible to list here the many characters that Tara portrayed in her career.

The teenage years are very dangerous for a beautiful and successful young woman because various kinds of temptation come to lure her. When Tara was 15 or 16, Amritalal Basu transformed Bankim Chandra's novel *Chandrashekhar* into a drama and cast her in the role of Shaivalini. When Amrita trained her for the role, he said: "Your career depends on this important role. If you can act well, you will be established on the stage forever."[37] Tara's performance as Shaivalini made her a celebrity overnight. It is said that Tara performed for only three nights as Shaivalini and was then lured away from the stage by a wealthy young man named Amarendra Nath Datta. He and Tara moved to his garden house in Bagmari, a suburb of Calcutta.

Without a constant flow of money, savings slowly disappear. Amarendra's family cut off all connection with him, and soon all his money dwindled away. Amarendra then formed The Indian Dramatic Club with the help of Tara and some of his friends. They staged a few plays in different theatres, but they could not make much money. Poverty reveals the reality of life. One day there was no money to buy groceries. Tara asked Amarendra to borrow two rupees from the gardener and buy some food. Shortly after Amarendra had borrowed the money, he met a poor friend who sought help from him. The generous Amarendra gave that money to his friend and passed the day eating fried gram.[38]

Girish's *Karameti Bai* was going on at the Minerva Theatre, with the famous actress Tinkari in the title role. But during the play's run, Tinkari suddenly quit the theatre. Helpless, Girish rushed to Bagmari and asked Tara to act in that role for two nights. Tara could not refuse Girish. After three days of rehearsal, Tara returned to the stage. When the play was over, Girish patted Tara on the back and said: "My child, you have saved my reputation. I bless you that you will be a famous actress of Bengal in the future."[39]

Tara's lover, Amarendra, leased the Emerald Theatre and started the Classic Theatrical Company. On 16 April 1897, the opening play was Girish's *Nala-Damayanti* and Tara acted in the role of Damayanti. As fire cannot be hidden, so the energy of a genius cannot be suppressed. Tara's acting life started up again in full earnest. The Classic Theatrical Company staged several famous plays, including *Haranidhi*, *Tarubala*, *Vilwamangal Thakur*, and Bankim Chandra's *Devi Chaudhurani*. Tara was cast in the main female roles in all of these plays, but she became a star when she acted as the courtesan Chintamani in *Vilwamangal Thakur* and Devi in *Devi Chaudhurani*. She also performed in the role of Gopa in Girish's *Buddhadev-Charit*. However, Tara's happy life drew to an end: An actress named Kusumkumari came between her and Amarendra. Tara cut off all connection with Amarendra and joined the Star Theatre with a salary of 32 rupees per month.[40]

Tara acted in so many roles, in so many plays, that it is not possible to present them all to the reader in this brief life sketch. She left her mark especially on the following roles: Ayesha in *Durgeshnandini*, Shaivalini in *Chandrashekhar*, Shaivya in *Harishchandra*, Saraswati in *Balidan*, and the title role in *Ramanuja*, and *Rezia*.[41]

The *Bengalee* paper advertised *Rezia* and Tara's performance on 15 May 1902[42]:

> AURORA THEATRE
> 9, Beadon Street
> Saturday, 17th May 1902, at 9 p.m.
> REZIA
> The Virgin Queen of Delhi
> By Baboo Manomohan Roy, B.A.
> A Historical Tragedy in Five Acts
> The maiden production of a drawing genius
> Rezia — Sm. Tarasundari
> Blood curdling situation! Dreadful revenge of disappointed lovers.
> A young couple on the bosom of Jamuna.
> Their thrilling last moments.
> The Gloriana of Delhi in Prison.
> The Horrible suicide of Rezia.
> Songs — Each a crystal of poetry
> Dance — A deviation from trodden track.

The Brahmo leader Bipin Chandra Pal saw Tara's performance as Rezia and was so impressed that he wrote about her in his review of the play for the *Hindu Review*. The article included pictures of Tara, which was unthinkable in orthodox society because she was a courtesan. Here is an excerpt:

> But not merely in the refinement and delicacy of their deportment on the stage, but equally also in the quality of their art some of our actresses could well hold their own in competition with the best representatives of the English stage. Those who have seen the part of Rezia as it is played by Sreemati Tarasundaree, will bear out the truth of this statement. Rezia is one of the most complex characters met with in any literature. Shakespeare's Lady Macbeth comes very close to it. But even Lady Macbeth is possibly a shade simpler than Rezia. And Tara's rendering of Rezia has been declared by competent critics, who have seen the best European actresses, to be as good an achievement as the best rendering of Lady Macbeth by the most capable of English actresses.[43]

In 1904 Tara met and fell in love with Aparesh Chandra Mukhopadhyay, a handsome young actor, and from 1904 to 1910 she followed him from one theatre to another. This relationship continued for twenty years. In 1908 Tara and Aparesh had a son, Nirmal.[44] In 1909 Aparesh opened a travelling theatre company called the Bani Theatre, and Tara financed it. The party went to Cuttack in Orissa and gave a few performances, but as it was very hot and there was an epidemic of cholera in the city, the party returned to Calcutta, losing a lot of money. In 1915 Tara and Aparesh had a daughter, whom they named Pratibha.[45]

Generally people think that money and success, name and fame bring happiness in life. Tara had all those things, yet she still felt empty. One day some actors and actresses were in Girish's room in the theatre when he was talking about Ramakrishna. Tinkari asked Girish: "Sir, will Ramakrishna bestow grace on me? I have done so many sinful things in my life."

Girish: "His door is always open to each and all."

Tara was moved to hear this. She asked Girish: "Is Ramakrishna for all? Then is it possible for us to get liberation?"

Girish: "Sri Ramakrishna sees everyone as equal. Yes, everyone's prayer reaches him, and for that reason he is God. There is no difference between rich and poor, queen and actress to him. By God's grace, 'A well-dressed dancing girl [a courtesan] became a saint.'"*

---

*Girish referred to a courtesan who went to tempt Haridas, a disciple of Chaitanya, but failed. She was instead transformed and became a saint.

Three Stars: Binodini, Tarasundari, and Tinkari

Tara: "But the way we lead our lives, there is no deliverance for us."

Girish: "Don't say that, Tara. Didn't you hear the story of your aunt Binodini? The Master was moved by her performance in the role of Chaitanya and blessed her, saying, 'Mother, may you attain illumination.' He is the deliverer of the fallen. He is the refuge of courtesans."[46]

A book consists of many chapters. It would be boring to read the same chapter again and again. Similarly, in human life a person is not content to stay in the same state forever. To this point Tara's spiritual aspect had been overshadowed by the glamour and excitement of her acting career. Now she listened to the call of her Indwelling Self. Ramakrishna, the great magnet, attracted Tara's soul. Tara waited several years after that conversation with Girish, but in 1916 finally went to Belur Math to meet Swami Brahmananda, the spiritual son of Ramakrishna. Tara wrote in her memoirs:

> Ever since I was a little girl I worked on the stage with Girish Chandra Ghosh and heard from him about Sri Ramakrishna. There was a photograph of Sri Ramakrishna in every theatre with which Girish Babu was connected, and the actors and actresses used to bow down to the Master's photograph before they appeared on the stage....
>
> My first visit to Belur Math took place about six years ago [1916]. I was then depressed and restless. Life seemed unbearable to me. I began to seek out places of pilgrimage. In this unhappy state of mind I finally went to Belur Math. Binodini, the finest actress of Bengal at the time, was with me. When I was seven years old she had introduced me to the theatre, and again it was she who introduced me to the monastery.
>
> It was past noon when we came to the Math. Maharaj [Swami Brahmananda] had finished his lunch and was about to go to his room to rest. At that moment we arrived and prostrated before him.
>
> Maharaj said: "Hello, Binod! Hello, Tara! So you have come! You are too late. We have already finished our lunch. You should have let us know that you were coming."
>
> We could see how worried he was about us. He immediately ordered fruit prasad, and arrangements were made to fry luchis for us. We went first to the shrine, then had our prasad, and afterwards were shown around the Math by a swami. Maharaj did not have his rest that day.
>
> We were brought up to revere holy men. But along with respect and faith I felt much fear of them. I was impure — a fallen woman. And so when I touched the holy feet of Maharaj, I did it with great hesitancy, afraid to offend him. But his sweet words, his solicitude and love dispelled all my fear.

Maharaj asked me, "Why don't you come here often?" I replied, "I was afraid to come to the Math." Maharaj said with great earnestness: "Fear? You are coming to Sri Ramakrishna. What fear can there be? All of us are his children. Don't be afraid! Whenever you wish, come here. My child, the Lord does not care about externals. He sees our inmost heart. There should be no fear in approaching Him."

I could not hold back my tears. My lifelong sorrow melted as the tears fell from my eyes, and I realized: Here is my refuge. Here is someone to whom I am not a sinner, I am not an outcast.[47]

On Swami Brahmananda's advice, Aparesh began work on a play about Ramanuja, a great saint of India. He worked closely with Ramakrishna's disciples, first reading the life of Ramanuja written by Swami Ramakrishnananda, then reading aloud each chapter of his play in progress to Swami Saradananda at the Udbodhan house. The swami encouraged Aparesh and explained to him the philosophy of Vishishtadvaita, or qualified nondualism, that Ramanuja had propounded. Swami Brahmananda also advised Aparesh to include a kirtan on Ramachandra in the drama and asked Swami Ambikananda to teach him the tune for it. The play premiered in the Minerva Theatre on 15 July 1916. Aparesh acted in the role of Yamunacharya; Tara performed the title role of Ramanuja. Swami Brahmananda went to see the play and was very impressed with Tara's performance. Tara wrote: "After the play I took the dust of the swami's feet and he blessed me, saying: 'Very well! Excellent acting! May you attain more devotion.'"[48]

Aparesh wrote: "Swami Brahmananda wanted that the theatre should not only be a place of entertainment but also an institution of national education. He used to see the plays in the theatre, and he always encouraged the actors and actresses and prayed for their moral and spiritual welfare. He inspired them so that they could devote their lives for the betterment of society."[49] Both Tara and Aparesh became disciples of Swami Brahmananda.

In 1918 Aparesh became the manager of the Star Theatre and Tara left the Minerva to join him there. Devendra Nath Basu translated Shakespeare's *Othello* into Bengali and it opened on 8 March 1919. Aparesh acted in the role of Iago and Tara, Desdemona. On 16 March the *Bengalee* paper reviewed Tara's performance: "We were assured by more than one critic that the acting of Desdemona approached perfection and that the heroine showed a remarkable power of adaptability which extorted unstinted praise from the audience."[50] In 1920 Tara helped Aparesh to take over the lease of the Star Theatre and both acted in different plays.

Three Stars: Binodini, Tarasundari, and Tinkari   201

They made a good income from the theatre.

Tara's family life went on smoothly with Aparesh and their two children. But after receiving initiation from Swami Brahmananda, a change came over her life. Wealth and luxury slowly became distasteful. On the stage Tara appeared in gorgeous costumes, but at home she wore the most ordinary saris, slept on a blanket on the floor, and ate a vegetarian meal at lunch and some puffed rice and sweets at night. She loved to drink tea and would carry it in a thermos to the theatre.

Swami Brahmananda considered Bhubaneswar in Orissa to be a wonderful place for spiritual disciplines. He bought a large parcel of land there and built a monastery.

Tara recalled:

> I was travelling all around but had no peace of mind. I felt emptiness in my life. I had pain within and was looking for a place where I could get peace and rest. I started my journey to see Jagannath in Puri, but on the way I stopped at Bhubaneswar. I was staying in an inn and heard that Maharaj was in Bhubaneswar, so I went to see him. His love, care, and compassion were unbelievable. He was eager to feed me. He said: "Ah, you have come through this scorching sun; your face is dried up. You have come here to recuperate your health. Don't go out in the sun. Where do you eat? From tomorrow we shall send the Master's prasad (lunch) to you. What do you love to eat? My child, we are poor monks and everything is not available in this place."
>
> I was dumbfounded. What a great monk! Even the worldly attached householders are not so anxious for their children! Who am I? Where is my place in society? My place in society is so low that I received from this world only abhorrence and neglect. I have no father, no true friend or relative in this vast world. Without self-interest no one talks to or looks at me. I have none in this world.
>
> Today Swami Brahmananda — the spiritual son of Sri Ramakrishna, an all-renouncing monk and adorable Maharaj — made me his own by his sincere eagerness, unselfish love, and unexpected care. I have never seen my father but I heard that he died when I was in my mother's womb. I received from Maharaj more than a father's affection. I could not control the tears that flowed, melting all my pent-up sorrow. I felt that I had found a loving and caring soul who did not consider me an untouchable, despicable, fallen woman. I am Maharaj's daughter. He consoled me, saying: "My child, call on the Master. Don't be afraid. The Master came to deliver fallen souls. Chant his name. In the beginning the spiritual disciplines are a little difficult, but eventually the Master will make everything favourable. Don't worry. Don't fear. You will find peace and bliss."[51]

Tara wanted to live near her guru, so she bought a piece of land to the west of the Lingaraja Shiva temple in Bhubaneswar. Maharaj went to see the land. As he stood there, in a meditative mood, he remarked: "It is a wonderful spot for practising spiritual disciplines. This place is very auspicious and Lord Shiva [the Lingaraja Temple] is in the northeast."[52]

Tara and Tinkari sometimes visited the Holy Mother at Udbodhan, Calcutta, but they never entered the Mother's room where the Master's shrine was located. They would bow down to the Master and Mother from outside the door. Holy Mother loved them and always asked them to have lunch. Afterwards, she would give them each a betel-roll. One day when they left, the Holy Mother remarked: "These girls have genuine devotion. Ah! Whenever they call on God, they do it with one-pointed minds."[53]

In 1920 during Holy Mother's last illness Tara visited her quite often. Swami Ishanananda recalled:

> One day at noon Tarasundari, the famous actress of the Star, came to visit Holy Mother. Mother's body was very weak, so she was lying on the floor of her room surrounded by some women. Tara bowed down to her and sat outside her door. She spoke to the Mother softly with great reverence. Mother said: "You act very well in the theatre. It is hard to recognize you when you appear on the stage with your costume and makeup. Why don't you recite something for us." Tara sometimes would act in the role of a man. She saluted the Mother with folded hands and then recited a part of the heroic role of Prabir in *Prabir-Arjun*. Afterwards the Mother said to her, "My child, come another day." Tara again saluted the Mother and left with some prasad in hand.
>
> Another afternoon Tara suddenly arrived in a taxi and brought four or five baskets of various things, such as sweets, curd, mangosteens, oranges, bananas, grapes, pomegranates, pineapples, and other fruits, flowers, bouquets of tuberoses, cloths for Mother, Radhu, Maku, and Nalini, and woolen shoes for Radhu and Maku's children. Mother had a slight fever and she was in bed. Tara bowed down to her from outside the door. Mother asked me to keep those gifts in the middle room. When Tara left with some prasad, Mother asked me to distribute those things to Radhu, Maku, and other people of the household. In the evening Dr. Pranadhan Basu, a Christian physician, came to see her. After examining the Mother the doctor went to Sharat Maharaj's room downstairs. Mother asked me: "Barada, you carry Tara's flowers and the remaining things to the doctor's car. He loves flowers." The doctor prescribed medicine and proper diet and received his fee from Lalit Babu, who was Mother's disciple. While getting in the car, the doctor saw baskets full of fruits,

Three Stars: Binodini, Tarasundari, and Tinkari

sweets, and flowers. He asked who had given all these things. Sharat Maharaj replied: "Mother has presented you with those things." Pleased, the doctor left Udbodhan.[54]

Sometimes an exciting, glamorous life is also exhausting and stressful. To refresh herself Tara would often visit Holy Mother or the disciples of the Master at Udbodhan House. Swami Parameshananda recalled:

> One day at 2:00 p.m., Tarasundari came to visit Swami Saradananda at Udbodhan. She brought a large quantity of sweets and fruits to offer to the Master, and I put them in the storeroom and gave her a small carpet on which to sit on the upper floor near the steps. She pushed away the seat and sat on the bare floor. Swami Saradananda was then resting, so I asked her to wait.
>
> I had seen Girish's play *Prafulla* at the Star Theatre and I told her that I saw her performance in that play.
>
> Tara: "Swami, I am glad that you enjoyed the women's performances in the play. They act in such a way that the audience feels that they are like goddesses. You are a young monk, so you don't know what a sinful life they lead. As they act, tears flow through one eye and a smile shines through the other."
>
> I: "Why don't you recite something for us?"
>
> Tara then began to recite some lines from a tragedy and tears trickled down from her eyes. Her cloth even became wet. She then recited a portion of the title role from Girish's play *Jana*. When Arjuna killed Jana's son, Prabir, in battle, her heart was devastated by grief and she cried profusely. Afterwards, Jana wanted to take revenge. Like the Greek goddess Nemesis, she roared and burst into loud laughter. The whole house reverberated with the sound of that laughter. Thus Tara demonstrated how actresses can cry and laugh alternately.
>
> When Swami Saradananda heard the noise, he got up and washed his face in the bathroom and became ready to receive his visitors. When I entered his room, he asked, "Who has come?" I told him that it was the actress Tara and recounted my conversation with her. The swami then said to me, "Well, you have learned a wonderful lesson from her." He then instructed me to send Tara's offerings of fruits and sweets to the Kali temple.
>
> I then took Tara to Swami Saradananda. She bowed down to him, and sat near the threshold of his room. Swami Saradananda always saluted women by bowing down his head. When they began to talk, I left the room.[55]

Until 1921 Tara continued her acting with tremendous enthusiasm and passion. But when her guru, Swami Brahmananda, died in 1922, she felt renunciation within. She built a house at Bhubaneswar and planned to retire there. She then lost all interest in acting and went into a deep depression. Swami Shivananda heard about her condition and summoned her to Belur Math. She cried for Maharaj, and Shivananda consoled her. He asked her to build a temple on her property in the name of Maharaj. Tara followed the swami's advice. Aparesh named the temple "Rakhal Kunja."[56] (Rakhal was Brahmananda's premonastic name and *kunja* means "garden temple.")

Swami Shivananda went to Bhubaneswar to inaugurate Rakhal Kunja and install the pictures of Ramakrishna, Holy Mother, and Swami Vivekananda on the altar. Later, Swami Subodhananda installed some of the relics of Swami Brahmananda under the altar of Rakhal Kunja with a special ceremony and a homa fire. Tara's dream was fulfilled. She was excited about her place of sadhana, and she spent hours in worship and meditation there. However, she had a desire to offer cooked food to the Master but felt herself unworthy. One day Swami Akhandananda visited Rakhal Kunja and remarked: "Mother Tara, what is this? The Master looks emaciated. Don't you offer cooked food?" Ashamed of her sinful life, Tara replied, "No, swami." Swami Akhandananda advised her to offer cooked food and milk to the Master every day. As Tara listened to the advice of a disciple of Ramakrishna, tears came to her eyes.[57]

Aparesh bought a plot of land to the north of Tara's and built a house there. Gradually a rift took place in Tara and Aparesh's relationship because they lived at a distance from one another. In 1924 their son, Nirmal, passed away at the age of 16. He had been endowed with his mother's artistic talents as well as her devotion, and he had been groomed as his father's successor in the theatre. Tara and Aparesh were terribly grief-stricken. Tara returned to Calcutta, and her relationship with Aparesh came to an end. Aparesh died in 1934.

There is a saying: "The old order changeth yielding place to the new." The Girish era was over and the new era of the Bengali stage began. Tara became the connecting link between the two. During this period an important event took place. In June 1925 Sisir Kumar Bhaduri, a great actor of the new era, invited Tara to perform in the title role of *Jana* in the Manomohan Theatre. He himself acted in the role of Prabir. Tara was then 47 years old and had been absent from the stage for 3 years. Nonetheless, she manifested her talent and spirit and made a deep impression on the audience. Why did she return to the theatre? Perhaps she was trying to assuage her grief at her son's death, or perhaps she was eager to transmit the acting tradition of the old generation to the new one. Tara continued

Three Stars: Binodini, Tarasundari, and Tinkari — 205

acting off and on until 1933. She gave her last performance in her triumphant role as Rezia in the play of the same name.[58]

At the age of 54 Tara finally retired from the stage to live in Rakhal Kunja in Bhubaneswar, where she remained for 12 years. Her daughter, Pratibha, lived with her.

There is no record that Tara had any formal education. She seems to have been a self-made person. She must have educated herself; otherwise she could not have memorized long lines of dialogue for the various characters she portrayed. During this time Tara wrote two poems — *Prabāher Rupāntar* and *Kusum O Bhramar* — which were published in *Saurav* magazine.[59]

Tara spent hours in her shrine, and her method of worship was unique. She had such deep concentration that one day she didn't even notice that there was a fire in her cowshed. The neighbours tried to extinguish the fire, but when they called her they could not break her meditation. Another day at noon Swami Subodhananda went to Rakhal Kunja and found no one around. The door and windows of the temple seemed to be closed and the whole area was quiet. He then observed that a window was partially open. When he peeped through it, he saw Tara dancing in front of Sri Ramakrishna's picture. She was completely oblivious to the world. As she had always given joy to the audience in the theatre by her acting, she was worshipping the Master with her acting and dancing in the same way. Without disturbing her sadhana, Swami Subodhananda returned to the monastery.[60]

The time came for Tara to depart from the world stage. She had made herself ready to go by cutting all worldly ties and attachments and burning all the mementos of her career. The scripture says, *"Vairagyam eva abhayam* — Renunciation alone makes one fearless." The fearless Tara was waiting for the call of her beloved Ramakrishna. When she became seriously ill, Swami Govindananda (Balai Maharaj) of Bhubaneswar suggested that she be taken to Calcutta for treatment. She then left for Calcutta, accompanied by her daughter. Sisir Kumar Bhaduri arranged for her treatment and tried to save her life in every possible way, but she passed away within the week. Pratibha recalled the final moments of her mother's life:

> It was 10:55 a.m. on 19 April 1948, the day after Ramnavami. My mother said to me: "Read the Gita to me. Today I can't read. I will listen." I read one chapter of the Gita. Again she said, "Sing that song 'Raghupati Raghava.'" Sitting on the floor I began to sing that song and my mother was listening. Meanwhile other visitors came there and we all sang loudly

Tinkari (1870–1917)

in chorus: *"Raghupati raghava rajaram, Patita pavana Sitaram."* [O Rama, O Raghava, the king of Raghu dynasty! O Rama, the lord of Sita, the deliverer of the fallen!] Mother at that time vomited some blood. She raised her head, took the spittoon by herself, and spat into it. She again put her head on the pillow. There was a picture of Sri Ramakrishna in front of her. She looked at the Master with wide open eyes and then passed away with a smile.[61]

3. Tinkari (1870–1917)

Every human being is born endowed with three powers of the Atman: *Jnana-shakti*, the power of intelligence; *Ichha-shakti*, the power of will; and *Kriya-shakti*, the power of action. The difference between human beings lies in how these powers are manifest. Tinkari displayed all three powers in her life to such a great degree that she became a superstar on the Bengali stage. She was truly blessed with a God-given talent for acting. There is a saying: "The name does not make one famous; one makes one's name famous." Tinkari made herself famous through her own efforts.

Tinkari was born in 1870 in the same red-light district of Calcutta that Binodini and Tarasundari had been born in. Her mother's financial condition was not too bad, so she did not suffer from lack of food or clothing. As morning shows the day, so Tinkari's talent showed itself when she was a little girl of 4 years old. On hearing a song of a street beggar only once, she would learn it by heart. She would then dance for others and sing the song in her melodious voice. When her neighbours advised her mother to hire a music teacher for Tinkari, she replied: "Am I so fortunate that I can hire a music teacher for my daughter? We manage the household somehow. Where shall I get money to pay the salary of a music teacher?"[62]

Tinkari and her mother lived in one of several rented rooms in a house. One woman who lived downstairs was extremely poor and sometimes had no money to buy food. Tinkari was 10 years old at the time, and she could not bear to see others suffer. She used to share her meals with that woman, without telling her mother. One day her mother caught her and scolded her severely. Her mother said: "From tomorrow you will have to eat in front of me." Tinkari tearfully said to her: "I beg you, mother, don't be so cruel. If we do not do something, that woman will starve."[63] When her mother left, Tinkari cried. This compassion for others made Tinkari a great actress. She could express this intense feeling in her roles onstage, touching the hearts of all who watched her.

A wealthy neighbour once hired a professional lecturer who spoke on scriptural and mythological topics. The topic that day was "The Banishment of Sita," based on a story in the Ramayana. Tinkari went with her mother to listen to the talk. When Tinkari heard that Rama had banished the innocent Sita to the forest, she cried and rushed home alone without listening to the rest of the story. She cried for Sita for a long time and then fell asleep.

The next morning, her mother asked: "Why did you leave without listening to the rest of the story? The speaker said so many spiritual things, and so many people stayed till late at night." Tinkari kept quiet for some time and then finally asked: "Mother, Ramachandra was God. Why was he so cruel?" The mother wisely replied: "It is the play of God. Do we understand everything? We just go there to listen to those stories." This answer did not satisfy her intelligent daughter. "Why is God so cruel?" she asked again. This question arose in her mind repeatedly and she continued to shed tears for Sita.[64]

In the fall of 1881 Girish's *Ravan-badh* [The Death of Ravana] was being performed with much fanfare at the Great National Theatre in Calcutta. One Saturday evening Tinkari's mother and some of her friends decided to go see the play. After her noon nap Tinkari heard that her mother was going to the theatre, and she immediately ran to her, hugged her, and said, "Mother, I want to go with you to see the play." Her mother said: "No, you cannot go with us. I am going with some of my friends. It will not be good for you to see the play with us." Tinkari was then 11 years old. Even in her childhood she had a passion for the theatre.

Tinkari became adamant. When her mother did not yield to her demand, she began to cry profusely. Then the other ladies said to her mother: "Take your daughter to the theatre. Though you are an old lady, you are crazy to see the play, so it is no wonder that this little girl wants to see it." When all her friends agreed, her mother relented and said to Tinkari: "You always give me trouble. All right, now stop crying. Go, have a shower and dress properly if you want to go with me."[65]

Excited, Tinkari bathed, dressed herself, and left for the Great National Theatre with the group. Girish was then acting in the role of Rama. This was the first time Tinkari saw any play and the first time she saw Girish, the famous actor and playwright. She was deeply absorbed in the play. Joy and wonder captured her heart. She returned home with her mother after the play. Her inherent desire to act had been roused.

When Tinkari got up the next morning, she told her mother she wanted to be an actress. At that time Sukumari and Binodini were famous actresses, and their name and fame had spread throughout Bengal. Tinkari's mother was delighted to hear about her daughter's desire. However, she said: "It is wonderful that you want to be an actress, but

Three Stars: Binodini, Tarasundari, and Tinkari

it is very difficult to enter the theatre. You don't know how to sing or dance well. Who will hire you?" Tinkari grabbed both of her mother's hands and said, "I beg you, mother, please try to get an acting job for me in the theatre." Her mother smiled and remarked, "You are my crazy daughter."[66]

It was not easy in those days to become an actress because there were not many theatres in Calcutta. There was extreme competition and one needed a good recommendation to get an audition. Tinkari kept pestering her mother, and for her part, her mother sincerely tried to fulfill her daughter's ambition. Five years passed without any success. Tinkari was 16 when an opportunity finally came. Her mother met a neighbour who was an actor in the Star Theatre, and she asked him to recommend Tinkari to the theatre management. That man replied: "I don't know whether the managers will hire your daughter in the theatre, but I can introduce her to them. If the managers consider your daughter talented, she may get a job. If you wish, you may send her with me one day."[67]

The next day Tinkari dressed nicely and went to the Star Theatre with the neighbour. At that time Girish's *Rupa-Sanatan* (see Chapter 16) was being rehearsed. This play is based on the life stories of two disciples of Chaitanya. Tinkari saw that all the actors and actresses were practising their lines. The neighbour introduced Tinkari to the stage manager, saying: "This girl's mother asked me to enroll her in the theatre. She has a passion for acting." The manager looked at her and asked, "Do you really want to be an actress?" Nervous, Tinkari softly replied, "Yes, sir, I do."[68]

The manager was busy with the rehearsal, so he told her: "Well, come here every day, starting tomorrow. If you can learn acting well, you will be hired as an actress. Please go to that hall and watch the rehearsal." Tinkari went to the hall and sat in a corner, watching as the director trained the actors and actresses. When they saw her, some people were curious and asked her questions, but Tinkari answered carefully, with few words. At midnight Tinkari returned home with her neighbour. Her mother was anxiously waiting for her. As soon as she arrived, she asked her: "Tell me what happened. What did they say? Will they accept you?" Overjoyed, Tinkari replied with a smile: "Yes, mother, they asked me to return to the theatre every day, so I will go." This made her mother happy. Filled with pride for her daughter, she shared this good news with her neighbours.

Sitting in the corner of the rehearsal room, Tinkari patiently observed and learned the gestures and postures, movements and facial expressions of the best actors and actresses. And with her sharp memory she also learned by heart the lines of some important roles.

On 21 May 1887 *Rupa-Sanatan* was first performed, but Tinkari was not cast in any role. She did not mind because she was new and did not yet know how to act. When *Vilwamangal Thakur* was staged later on, she was cast as a confidante of Krishna. Her role called for her to fan Radha and Krishna. This was her first public appearance, and she was happy even though she had no lines. Some days later, Amritalal Basu's satire *Bibaha Bibhrat* (Confusion of Marriage), opened. Tinkari was asked to sit in the bridal chamber without speaking. In *Chorer Upar Batpari* satire, Tinkari was cast as a maidservant carrying a tray of refreshments and water. Slowly she got used to being onstage.

One night during a performance of *Rupa-Sanatan* one of the actresses became sick, so the director asked Tinkari to fill in for her. The minor role required her to sing a song. She sang so well that the audience clapped again and again. The director was pleased and gave Tinkari a rupee to buy some sweets. It is said that Tinkari saved that rupee carefully throughout her life, never spending it even in times of dire need.[69]

In 1887 Gopallal Sil, a Calcutta multimillionaire, purchased the Star Theatre and some adjacent land. He built a new theatre and named it the Emerald Theatre. The former owners of the Star then bought a piece of land in Hatibagan in North Calcutta, where they started to build a new theatre. During the construction period, they planned to go to Dhaka and give some performances. Tinkari intended to go with them but did not tell her mother. However, the neighbour who had taken her to the Star informed her mother of the plan and told her that the theatre company would be leaving within a couple of days.

Surprised, Tinkari's mother said: "She didn't say anything about this. I don't want my daughter to go so far away."

The man replied: "Well, if you don't agree then write a letter today to the manager of the theatre."

Tinkari arrived during this conversation. Enraged, her mother said: "I hear that you have planned to go to Dhaka without consulting me. Have you become so independent after going to the theatre for such a short time? You should be punished. I won't let you go." She then told the neighbour: "Sir, please wait. I am writing a letter stating that my daughter will not go to your theatre anymore. Please remove her name from the register."[70] Tears fell from Tinkari's eyes, but her mother's cruel heart did not soften. Tinkari fervently begged her to change her mind and cried profusely, but could not sway her. The theatre party left for Dhaka without Tinkari. It is said that Tinkari remained in bed for three days without eating.

Three Stars: Binodini, Tarasundari, and Tinkari

Seeing Tinkari broken-hearted, a neighbour woman came to her mother and said: "Your daughter is depressed because you have stopped her acting in the theatre. Will you let your daughter go to the theatre again? A gentleman who is connected with a theatre visits us. I told him about your daughter and he is eager to meet her. If you wish, I can ask him to talk to her." Seeing Tinkari's sorrowful face, her mother agreed to send her again to the theatre.

The neighbour's friend introduced Tinkari to a private theatre company and there she acted in some important roles. But this company did not survive long because the owners fought among themselves. When the company dissolved, Tinkari joined the Bina Theatre, which was owned by Rajkrishna Roy. When a gentleman introduced Tinkari to Rajkrishna, the latter asked: "Those who have seen your acting in the private theatre praise you. Have you performed in any other theatre?" Tinkari told him that she had been connected with the Star and that she had performed a few leading roles in the private company.

Rajkrishna: "Well, I appoint you from today as an actress here. If you work wholeheartedly, I shall give you more opportunities. Your monthly salary will be 20 rupees. Will you accept this offer?"

Tinkari: "Yes, sir, I shall accept it."[71]

Rajkrishna offered Tinkari a high salary at the outset because he recognized her potential. Soon after, he staged *Mirabai* in the Bina Theatre and cast Tinkari in the title role. Mirabai was queen of Chittore, a great devotee of Krishna, and she composed many devotional songs. The audience was overwhelmed by Tinkari's skillful acting, beauty, and wonderful singing.

But Tinkari's popularity brought her trouble. The lustful eyes of some wealthy men in the audience fell on Tinkari, and her mother wanted to use her to get rich. For her part, Tinkari just loved acting and wanted to become a celebrity. Tinkari recalled:

> I was then working as an actress at the Bina Theatre and my monthly salary was 20 rupees. I was 17. At that time *Mirabai* was going on and I acted in the role of Mira. I had just acted two or three nights and then the next night I went for a rehearsal. When I returned home about 11:00 p.m. I saw two well-dressed young men seated in our room. They seemed to be very wealthy because they had several rings with precious stones on their fingers and gold chains around their necks.
>
> Seeing the strangers in my room I stopped at the threshold. They were looking at me lustfully. My mother said, "Come inside." I slowly entered the room and sat near my mother. She introduced me, saying, "This is my daughter." They said: "Yes, we saw your daughter in the

theatre several times. She acts in the role of Mirabai very well. At any rate, whatever you have asked for, we are ready to pay but on condition that your daughter give up the theatre."

I then realized the intention of their visit to my room. Listening to them talk, my face froze. My mother said: "She loves to act in the theatre. She has just started there and has gotten a little fame. She is getting a salary. Anyhow, you continue to visit. Eventually she will give up the theatre." One of them said: "No, it will not work out. Your daughter will be busy with the theatre, so when shall we meet her? You have asked for 200 rupees. We are ready to pay, and moreover we will give her a salary also. You will have to stop her from going to the theatre. If you do not trust us, we are ready to pay six months' salary in advance."

I was angry. I felt that someone should drag them out of my room. I realized my mother's mind had softened by their words, as she was unwilling to give up such a good amount of money. She told them: "Please come tomorrow. We shall make a decision." One of them said: "No, you will have to give us the final word, and then we shall come with the money tomorrow." My mother agreed and asked them to come the next day. They left joyfully and reminded my mother: "We shall come with money tomorrow evening. Ask your daughter not to go to the theatre."

As soon as they left I told my mother firmly, "I will never give up my acting in the theatre, whatever you may say." My mother said: "Don't be obstinate. We should not give up such a big offer. They are extremely wealthy people. If you live with them you will not have to think about the future. They will cover your body with jewellery. What will you get from the theatre?"

I did not change my mind at all. My mother first tried to convince me and then began to scold me. She even threatened to beat me if I did not obey her. Others also advised me to give up the theatre, but I did not pay any heed to them. The next day I left for the theatre and when I returned home I heard that those two men had come. Disgusted, they left after humiliating my mother.

My mother was in a rage. As soon as I entered the house, she took a bamboo stick and beat me right and left. I was in terrible pain and had a high fever. I remained in bed for three days in that condition. When I recovered, I started to go to the theatre as usual, but my mother would not speak to me for many days. Afterwards, she told me again and again to give up the theatre and did not even give me anything to eat for two or three days. But I never gave up the theatre. It is the grace of the Lord that I overcame that temptation."[72]

The famous actor Mahendralal Basu went to see *Mirabai* and was impressed with Tinkari's performance. He offered to double Tinkari's

Three Stars: Binodini, Tarasundari, and Tinkari

salary if she left the Bina and joined the Emerald instead. She accepted. In the Emerald Theatre Tinkari acted in three plays: *Nanda Vidāy*, *Vidyāsundar*, and *Rāslilā*. However, the Emerald was facing financial difficulties, so the authorities were reducing the salaries of their actors and actresses. Tinkari was getting 40 rupees, which was a bit high, so they decided to cut her salary to 25 rupees. Mahendralal conveyed this message to Tinkari and asked her to think about it for a day or two before she made any decision.

Tinkari had tremendous self-esteem and integrity. She could not bear this kind of humiliation. She immediately told Mahendra: "I do not have to consider or consult with anyone regarding this matter. I am telling you my decision right now. Please tell the authorities that Tinkari will not accept a penny less than her stipulated salary." Mahendra liked Tinkari, so he suggested that she accept the proposal and continue her acting. But Tinkari said firmly: "It is better to beg for a living than to accept this kind of humiliation. Please inform the authorities that Tinkari will not work here from tomorrow."[73] Saying so, she left for home.

Tinkari remained without work for quite a long time. However, in 1891 the City Theatre was established in Calcutta. Tinkari was 21, and her talent had not yet been fully developed, but many people in different theatres knew her to be an actress. Nilmadhav Chakrabarty, the manager of the City, came to Tinkari and invited her to join his theatre. He offered the same salary that she would have gotten from the Emerald. Tinkari joined the City the next day.

At the City Theatre, Tinkari acted in several plays, including *Vilwamangal Thakur*, where she was cast as the merchant's wife. In *Chaitanya Lila* she performed in the role of Bhakti, and in *Sadhabar Ekadashi* as Kanchan. People observed some originality and spirit in every character she portrayed. Fortune smiled on Tinkari while she was acting at the City Theatre: She drew the attention of Girish and received his blessing.

The City staged Amritalal Basu's *Bibaha Bibhrat*, and the role of the maidservant was a complex one. Jagattarini was cast in that role, but Tinkari did not like her performance. When she was with the Star, she had seen a famous actress perform that role, and Jagattarini was not as good an actress. She went to Nilmadhav and said: "Sir, if you don't mind I want to tell you something." Then she said: "I think the maidservant's role in the play is not being performed properly. Please allow me to act in that role one night."

Nilmadhav knew that Tinkari was young and did not have sufficient experience to perform in such a role, so he said: "That role is very complex and difficult. You don't understand that role properly, so you just assume you can handle it. It is not possible for you to act in that role."

Tinkari: "Sir, it does not matter whether you give me that role, but allow me to recite the maidservant's lines to you tomorrow." Nilmadhav agreed. The next day Nilmadhav listened to Tinkari recite all the lines of the maidservant. He was not only pleased but amazed. From that day on Tinkari was cast in that role and earned the audiences' praise.[74]

During Durga Puja in October 1891, the City Theatre was hired to perform *Bibaha Bibhrat* at Kalikrishna Tagore's house in Calcutta. Girish sat next to Kalikrishna and watched Tinkari in the role of the maidservant. Afterwards, Girish went to the greenroom. All the actors and actresses took the dust of his feet. Tinkari had heard about Girish's greatness but had never met him face to face. She also took the dust of his feet. The guru and the disciple recognized each other. Girish told Nilmadhav a few things concerning the theatre and then pointed to Tinkari and asked: "In what other roles does this girl act?"

Nilmadhav: "She has had some supporting roles in recent plays."

Girish: "Her features are right for the stage. She has some good stuff. Her voice is also wonderful. It modulates from one tonality to another. Train her. Eventually she will be a great actress. If you give her a little scope, you will see that my words will come true." Girish left, and later what he predicted came to pass.

Tinkari was slim and tall; her complexion, golden; her voice, sweet and strong; her eyes, bright and large. She was vivacious and lively. But her friends would tease her because she was not buxom and curvaceous, as many actresses were. This upset her. She did not realize that in the future her slim figure and strong voice would help her play the role of the heroine in tragedies.

In 1892 Nagendra Bhusan Mukhopadhyay bought the Minerva Theatre and appointed Girish as the manager. With tremendous effort Girish translated William Shakespeare's *Macbeth* into Bengali and decided to stage it at the Minerva. It is said that Girish had never worked so hard on any other drama. He himself selected the actors and actresses for *Macbeth* and the rehearsals began. He gave the role of Lady Macbeth to a famous actress named Pramadasundari, but he was not satisfied with her voice and her performance in the role. He knew that the success of the play depended upon the portrayal of Lady Macbeth. One night when he was returning home after a rehearsal Tinkari came to his mind.

The next day, without consulting anyone, he sent someone to bring Tinkari to the Minerva. Tinkari recalled:

Three Stars: Binodini, Tarasundari, and Tinkari

After lunch I was sleeping. Someone called me and said that a gentleman had come from the theatre to see me. I immediately got up, washed my face, changed my clothes, and met the gentleman. He said: "Girish Babu, the manager of the Minerva, has sent me to you. He wants you at the theatre. This evening a carriage will come to pick you up." I was overjoyed because Girish Chandra, the guru of the Bengali stage, had invited me to see him. I got ready before evening. When the carriage arrived, I found that three or four actresses were inside. As soon as I got in, one of them asked, "Are you going to join the theatre today?"

I replied: "I am not sure. I have been asked to go there."

Another girl asked, "Have you acted in any other theatre?"

"Yes, I work at the City Theatre," I answered.

Meanwhile the carriage arrived at the theatre. They smiled and got down from the carriage and I got out last. I entered the theatre and met that gentleman who had come to our home. He said: "Girish Babu has not yet arrived. Please sit here. I shall let you know when he has arrived."

I quietly sat on one side of that hall. It was a big theatre and there was a lot of activity going on. I saw some actresses repeating their lines holding their long sheets. Meanwhile the actress Pramada arrived. She was exquisitely well dressed. She was highly respected there. Seeing me she asked someone: "Who is this? Is she a newcomer?"

"Yes, she is," replied the other.

Then that gentleman said to me: "Girish Babu has arrived. Please come with me." I followed him and went to a room at the back of the theatre. Slowly I went near Girish Babu and took the dust of his feet. He asked me to sit down. Then he said: "I saw your acting as the maidservant in *Bibaha Bibhrat* at Kalikrishna Tagore's house. I think you have tremendous potential to be a good actress. Please join here today. If you work wholeheartedly I will give you more opportunities. At present you will get 30 rupees per month. If you act well, you will get a raise. Will you accept this offer?" I agreed to his proposal by nodding my head. Then he told that gentleman: "Write a contract for one year for this girl. And from tomorrow please send the carriage to her home regularly." "Yes, sir," replied that gentleman.

By that time the rehearsal had started and Girish Babu hurriedly left. I went to the office with that gentleman, signed the one-year contract, and returned home at 7:00 p.m.

Girish was the manager, director, and playwright. He had cast Pramadasundari as Lady Macbeth, but now he was not happy with her performance. He knew it would be discourteous to remove a famous actress from a leading role, but he had no choice. Tinkari recalled:

After joining the Minerva I went there regularly. Thus five or six days passed. I sat there as a spectator, listening to the rehearsals and watching Girish Babu's direction. I did not get any role. I wondered why they had hired me.

One evening the rehearsal began. Pramada was rehearsing the role of Lady Macbeth. Girish was correcting her again and again, but she could not do it properly. Irritated, Girish Babu said: "No, there is no hope for you to act in this role." He was so grave that no one dared make a sound in that hall. The whole theatre fell silent. After a while, he suddenly said: "Well, this role is not working properly with Pramada. Call that new actress. Let me try her." I was not very far from Girish Babu, so I heard what he said. I was scared! Meanwhile, an actress who was seated close to me said: "Hello, Girish Babu is calling you."

I slowly got up and stood before Girish Babu. He looked at me and said gravely: "Well, you have heard the part that Pramada was rehearsing now. I want to give that role to you. Will you be able to perform it?" I humbly replied: "I don't know, but I can try." Girish Babu took the script from Pramada and gave it to me. He then said: "Recite that part a little. Let me hear how you express it." I took the script from Girish Babu and said: "I shall recite it tomorrow. Let me read the whole script tonight." Girish Babu said: "All right. Read the whole part tonight, and tomorrow I shall make you recite it."

After the rehearsal when I was returning home, Pramada taunted me and said a few harsh words. It roused my tenacity and I decided to perform better than she had done. Anyhow, I came home, ate my supper hurriedly, and then sat with the script. I did not sleep the whole night. I read the script eight or ten times and memorized it. I remembered how Girish Babu had instructed Pramada and corrected her during the rehearsals. Accordingly I practised that role a few times at home.

The next day I went to the theatre, and when my turn came Girish Babu called me. On that day many people were anxious to hear me. Girish Babu said to me: "All right, now you start and let me listen." I began to recite the whole part and by the grace of God I saved Girish Babu's face. Those who were present there remarked that I would be better than Pramada. I had very little education, but by the grace and training of Girish Babu I succeeded in portraying the complicated character of Lady Macbeth. This role made my acting life brighter.

On 28 January 1893 *Macbeth* opened at the Minerva. The house was full. I appeared as Lady Macbeth and Girish Babu, Macbeth. By God's grace and with the guru's blessing I did even better on the stage than during the rehearsals. The audience applauded again and again. I forgot myself and became fully identified with Lady Macbeth. When the play was over, Girish Babu patted my back and said: "After watching your acting, I think that my writing of this play has been a success. Let the Bengalis see that there is also a great actress on the stage here. I did not realize that you would be able to act so wonderfully and flawlessly."

Girish Babu's praise brought tears to my eyes. I fell at his feet. Holding my hand he said: "I bless you that you will be a real actress, and that you act in such a way that the Bengalis will never forget you." From then on my salary was doubled, and all the newspapers in Calcutta wrote about me with praise. At that time *Macbeth* was enacted at the Minerva every Saturday. Acting in this role I became a celebrity and reached the acme of fame."[75]

Girish decided to translate more of Shakespeare's plays into Bengali and stage them. He had spent an enormous amount of money on *Macbeth*. He had even engaged Mr. Williard, a famous English painter, to paint the scenes and Mr. J. Pimm to make the costumes according to the English fashion. *Macbeth* was well received in the beginning, but unfortunately, this kind of English tragedy did not interest the Bengali audience for very long. However, during that period Tinkari received tremendous accolades for her portrayal of Lady Macbeth, next only to Binodini's performance as Chaitanya in *Chaitanya Lila*.

On 5 February 1893, Girish's *Mukul Munjara*, a love story, opened at the Minerva. Tinkari acted in the role of Tara. *The Indian Nation* commented about Tinkari: "The acting was worthy of the play. A magnificent actress appeared as Tara. The heroine of the play, Munjara, played her part well, but seemed to be a little nervous."[76]

Girish then wrote *Abu Hossain*, a comic opera based on a story from *The Arabian Nights*. Abu Hossain was a poor man who awoke to find himself transformed into a Muslim king. Beautiful girls sang and danced for him. The audience enjoyed the comedy, and it made good money for the Minerva, but it sparked some criticism against Girish. The critic of *Anusandhan* (April 1893) complained that the public expected religious and social plays like *Chaitanya Lila* and *Vilwamangal Thakur* from Girish rather than this kind of light comedy. Perhaps this criticism affected Girish, because he then wrote *Jana* (see Chapter 22). Tinkari appeared in the title role. When Prabir, Jana's son, dies on the battlefield, Jana appears on the stage, a madwoman seeking revenge. Tinkari's acting was so realistic that the audience felt she was Nemesis itself embodied. The character of Margaret in Shakespeare's *Richard III* is a mere shadow of Jana.

On 18 May 1895 Girish's *Karameti Bai* opened at the Minerva. The play is based on the story of a woman devotee of Krishna named Karameti, whose life is given in the book *Bhaktamala* (Garland of Devotees). Girish made this drama come alive by combining devotion and knowledge. Tinkari performed in the title role.

Karameti is a Hindu widow who lives like a nun. She is supposed to wear a white sari, with no jewellery. On the opening night of the play, Tinkari's paramour came to watch the play. She knew he was there, so she was reluctant to put on the clothing of a widow and appear before him unadorned. Tinkari thought she would look ugly in that plain white sari, so she refused to get dressed and appear onstage. The musicians were playing the overture, but the curtain was not going up. People in the audience started shouting. Girish got news of this and immediately went to the greenroom and shouted: "Bring a barber. I shall shave my head and act in the role of Karameti. I don't want to flatter anyone. I don't care for an irresponsible actress."[77]

Nagendra Babu, the theatre owner, then learned why Tinkari was reluctant to appear in widow's clothing. He immediately went to the box seat where her paramour was and explained the whole situation to him. The man smiled and left the theatre. Nagendra escorted him to his carriage, apologizing. When Tinkari heard that her lover had left, she immediately got ready to go onstage. As soon as the people in the audience saw Tinkari, they were pleased. Everyone enjoyed her performance.

Very little is known about Tinkari's personal life. As a celebrity she encountered many temptations, but she lived only with that man who had come to see her perform. Tinkari's beauty, affectionate nature, and lively acting captured the heart of one of Girish's friends, a wealthy man of North Calcutta. He proposed marriage to Tinkari, putting her in great difficulty. She hated the idea of sacrificing her career to become a wealthy housewife. She consulted Girish, who was her mentor. Girish told her: "No, you shouldn't be bound by marriage. Money is nothing. You have talent and you will be a great star in the future."

Tinkari rejected the wealthy man's offer, but he just smiled and said to her: "Look, your beauty is transient, and this acting job is also temporary. If you live with me your life will be safe and secure. All right, you go on acting as usual and I shall wait for you."

Rich people are often moody, and some believe that everything can be accomplished through money and power. This man knew that Girish was the obstacle to having Tinkari in his life, so he engaged Golap Singh a notorious ruffian to murder Girish.

One evening the wealthy man invited some close friends, including Girish and Tinkari, to his garden house in Sinthi, a suburb of North

Three Stars: Binodini, Tarasundari, and Tinkari   219

Calcutta. Girish arrived with Tinkari, who brought along her servant, Fakir. Their host then announced that the party would end at midnight. He asked everyone to leave then, except for Girish and Tinkari, as he had some business with them. The whole house reverberated with the joy of dining, drinking, dancing, and singing.

Rajen Chattopadhyay, who was friends with both Girish and the host, arrived late to the gathering. As he entered the garden, he saw some people doing something in a dark corner. Curious, Rajen walked over and found some men digging a pit. He recognized one of the men as Golap Singh. Golap whispered to Rajen: "Please leave this place by midnight. Tonight we will murder Girish, bury him in this pit, and cover it with plants." Rajen knew then that the owner of the house had hired Golap Singh to kill Girish.

Rajen asked: "Where is Fakir?"

"He must be somewhere," answered Golap.

Rajen told him that Fakir must also leave; otherwise he could be a witness. Golap agreed to let Rajen look for him. Rajen located Fakir near the pond and instructed him to go and hire a carriage, and wait for Tinkari and Girish on the street. He then rushed inside the house to join the party. The owner of the garden house was happy to see Rajen and offered him a drink. When Rajen inquired about Girish, the owner replied that Girish and Tinkari were upstairs.

Rajen found Girish and Tinkari eating dinner. Rajen quietly told them the whole story, and Tinkari began to weep. Girish wanted to leave immediately, but Rajen stopped him, saying that four villains were at the gate and that no one could protect him. "I have the grace of my guru," said Girish boldly.

But Rajen had a plan. He said: "There is one way you can escape. This veranda extends from here to the bathroom, and the bathroom has a window without a grill. There is a mango tree between the bathroom and the boundary wall. Go through the window, grab a tree branch, and then go over the wall and jump onto the sidewalk. There you will see Fakir waiting with a carriage." Without losing a minute, Girish, Tinkari, and Rajen followed the escape plan. Thus the murder plot was foiled.[78]

For nearly four years Tinkari worked for the Minerva Theatre, where she earned much money and built her reputation. At one point, Girish and Nagendra Babu had a difference of opinion, so Girish left the theatre. Tinkari followed her acting guru. Afterwards she acted at the various theatres that Girish was involved with, including the Classic, the Grand, the Kohinoor, the National, the Thespian Temple, and the Manomohan. She performed in many plays and was always cast in leading roles. Tinkari left an indelible impression on her audiences when she appeared in the following roles: Pagalini in *Vilwamangal*, Subhadra in *Pandav Gaurav*, Matibibi in *Kapalkundala*, Abhimanyu in *Abhimanyu-badh*, Bimala in *Durgeshnandini*, Prafulla in *Devi Chaudhurani*, and Jijabai in *Chatrapati Shivaji*.

Apart from her acting career, Tinkari was a deeply religious person. Her devotion for God flowed within, yet there was no pompous display. From her childhood she never went to bed without mentally praying to God. Later, when she became well-to-do, some of her tenants would ask her to arrange for a religious festival at her home. Tinkari would demur, responding in this manner: "God has sent us to be born in this sinful place. Under such circumstances is it good to bring Him here? People will laugh at us and remark: 'What kind of devotion is this? These women are making a religious display. Perhaps it is another one of their ways to make money!' We are unfortunate, so it is better to call on God mentally."[79]

Girish was not only Tinkari's acting guru, he also often gave her spiritual advice. One day she asked him: "I committed so many sins in my past life so I was born in a sinful place. Can you tell me what one should do so that one will not have to be born in such a place?"

Girish: "One of the epithets of God is the Redeemer of the Fallen. If one calls on Him with humility and wholeheartedly, He will definitely give shelter to that fallen person."

Tinkari: "Can you teach me how to call on God in the correct way? I pray to God every day, and millions of people like me also call on Him. I am a lowly person. Does my prayer reach God?"

Girish: "Everyone's call reaches His ear equally. That is the reason He is God. To Him there is no sinner or lowly person. He lovingly accepts those who call on Him wholeheartedly. If you call on God, He will definitely give you shelter in His heavenly abode."[80]

Girish inspired many actors and actresses and told them about Ramakrishna, Holy Mother, and the disciples of the Master. Tinkari met Holy Mother for the first time when she went with Tarasundari to the Udbodhan house in Calcutta. Holy Mother had seen Tinkari act in *Vilwamangal Thakur*. Ashutosh Mitra recalled the visit:

> Tinkari, the famous actress, came to visit the Holy Mother, and Sister Lakshmi requested her to sing a song. Tinkari hesitatingly said, "What kind of song may I sing for you?"
>
> Holy Mother: "It will be wonderful if you sing that song of Pagalini [from *Vilwamangal*]." Tinkari had performed in that role. She then got ready to sing.

It was 9:30 a.m. We were then busy working downstairs. Suddenly we heard Tinkari's sweet and melodious voice singing in the *Chayanat* tune, "He [Krishna] travels holding my hand." We stopped our work and went upstairs to listen to her singing. Sharat Maharaj was writing something. He dropped his pen and became absorbed in the music. Yogin-ma was cutting vegetables; she also went upstairs. The cook and servants also stopped what they were doing and went upstairs to listen to the song.

When I went upstairs I noticed that the Holy Mother had finished her worship and was listening to the song, sitting on the floor. Tinkari sat on the little veranda near the entrance to the Master's shrine. We felt that her overflowing devotion was reverberating throughout the entire house through her singing:

> He [Krishna] travels holding my hand.
> Wherever I go, He follows me,
> Even if I don't ask Him to.

The Holy Mother looked at the Master and then closed her eyes. After a while she opened her eyes, but we felt she was indrawn. Her eyes were open but she was not seeing anything. Tinkari continued:

> He wipes my face with great care,
> And intently looks at my face.
> When I smile, He smiles; and when I cry, He cries.
> How lovingly He takes care of me.

The whole house was completely still, as if no one was there. Everyone was overwhelmed and absorbed in an exalted mood. Was it the influence of Tinkari's singing or the Holy Mother's spiritual power? Who could say? Tinkari finished the last lines of that song:

> So I came to know: who says that the Precious One does not exist?
> Come and see for yourself whether it is true or false.
> He is talking to me with great love.

The Holy Mother exclaimed in an ecstatic mood: "Aha! Aha!"

Tinkari finished her singing. The Holy Mother remained in that condition for a while and silence prevailed everywhere. Then she wiped her eyes and said to Tinkari, "What a beautiful song you have sung today, my child!"[81]

On 9 May 1903 Tinkari acted in the role of Annada in Girish's *Bhranti*, which was performed at the Classic Theatre. Girish had selected all the best actors and actresses for this play, and Tinkari gave an excellent performance. After a few nights, however, Tinkari felt ill and had to stop acting. She was 33 years old and had begun to develop diabetes. Her doctor suggested that she give up the theatre because the type of work involved was extremely injurious to her health: Theatrical performances generally continued for five to six hours every night, for many days at a stretch. Though she temporarily withdrew herself from the theatre, acting was a kind of intoxication for her. Her weak body was at home but her mind remained in the theatre. Despite her poor health, she began acting again in 1905 and performed off and on until 1909.

Most probably in 1910, on her doctor's advice Tinkari went to Varanasi for a change. She rested completely for a month, and as a result she recovered her strength to a great extent. The doctors at Varanasi were satisfied, but they advised her to continue her convalescence for a year. She stayed in Varanasi for four months, then considered herself to be normal again. One day after lunch, Tinkari was relaxing on the upper veranda and thinking: "What is the purpose of keeping this body? Why am I spending so much money to protect this body which is giving me so much pain and suffering? This world does not care whether I exist or not; no one will shed a tear if I die. Then why am I struggling to live long?"[82] The more she was thinking in this vein, the more her attachment to her body diminished, and she decided to return to Calcutta.

Meanwhile a minstrel was singing a Baul song on the street, and a young boy, about 4 years old, was dancing and playing a small tabor along with the music. Although Tinkari's mind was occupied with her own thoughts, one line of the song touched her heart. She was eager to hear the whole song. She sent her attendant to invite the minstrel and the little boy to her house, and then asked the man to sing that song again. Seeing that little boy's jubilant and lively dancing, she shed tears of relief for having recovered from that long illness. She gave two rupees to the singer. Later she related the substance of that Baul song: "O Madhava [Krishna], may I be content with whatever sadhana you have sent me to do to fulfill your will. This is my request to you: May my transitory body end performing your work day and night, and may I never indulge in any laziness."[83]

The doctors of Calcutta had asked Tinkari to stay in Varanasi for at least one year, but this Baul song made her realize that God had sent her to this world to be an actress. She should continue acting until she died, and that would be her sadhana. She ordered her attendants to pack her things, and three days later she left for Calcutta.

After arriving in Calcutta she met with Girish, who was then manager of the Minerva. Girish said to her: "You have been acting since you were young, so it is not good for you to stay at home without doing anything.

Three Stars: Binodini, Tarasundari, and Tinkari 223

You should join the theatre, but you must be careful not to overexert yourself."[84] Girish gave her the small role of Badari in his new play, *Tapobal*. The play opened on 18 November 1911 at the Minerva. Tinkari acted until 28 January 1912 and made a deep impression on the audience, but unfortunately her health did not allow her to continue. Eleven days later, on 8 February 1912 Girish passed away. This was a terrible shock to her, as Girish was her beloved guru and guide in life.

After Girish's death Tinkari disconnected herself from the theatre as a regular actress. She lived just another five years. During this period, whenever any theatre manager wanted to stage any of Girish's plays, Tinkari would appear for only a few nights in the role she had performed before. She charged 100 rupees per night at a time when no actress in Bengali stage earned more than 50 rupees on any night.

As Tinkari was a celebrity, she always attracted a large crowd. At the request of the manager, she acted in the Thespian Temple from 7 August to 1 September 1915. And again she acted in the Manomohan Theatre from 22 October 1915 to the early part of 1916. She finally left the stage when she was completely unable to act anymore. In 1917 a carbuncle appeared on one of her upper arms. Then she received treatment from the best doctors in Calcutta, but it did not subside. She was reluctant to have surgery, but she agreed to when the pain became unbearable. An English doctor of the Calcutta Medical College performed the surgery, removing the pus and blood from the carbuncle. For a couple of days she felt better, but septicemia developed and all further treatment was of no avail.

During her final days, the celebrated actress Tinkari prayed: "O Lord, you are my all in all. You have come to take me to your blissful abode. Today I have achieved the goal of my life's sadhana. I hear the heavenly music and I see my guru coming with my respected friends to receive me, singing the song of victory. O Lord, O fulfiller of all desires, O Saviour of fallen souls, your divine touch cleansed all impurities from my life. I feel only love and bliss. My life as an actress was successful. Blessed am I! Good-bye, good-bye! O Lord, you have fulfilled all my desires. O rescuer of the helpless ones, I have realized your infinite grace and compassion!"[85]

On the third day after her operation, the great heroine Tinkari said her final prayer and departed from the world stage at 8:00 p.m. Her body was decorated with flowers and garlands. All of Calcutta's actors and actresses came to pay homage to their friend. Her body was carried to the Nimtala cremation ground, on the bank of the Ganges in Calcutta. At

11:00 p.m. her funeral pyre was made ready with sandalwood, ghee, perfume, myrrh, and incense; the god of fire consumed Tinkari's mortal body and carried her luminous body to the abode of her beloved Lord.

Tinkari had made a will before she passed away. In it she left two houses to the Barabazar Hospital and one house to her paramour's son in gratitude to his father, who had taken care of her. The money that came from selling her jewellery was spent on her funeral expenses and shraddha ceremony. Each of her tenants received 50 rupees from what remained.[86] Tinkari was well known for her generosity. While she was alive no beggar left her home without receiving gifts and assistance.

There is a saying in Sanskrit: *Kirtiryasya sa jivati* — A person who has fame lives forever. Tinkari, Binodini, and Tarasundari were truly talented actresses. They will remain immortal in the history of the Bengali stage.

Chapter 16

Ramakrishna's Influence on Girish's Plays

At the advent of an avatar, or divine incarnation, a renaissance occurs, a new civilization begins, and a cultural revival takes place. Although Christ's public life lasted only three years, his contribution to the world of thought and culture was immense. His life and teachings have been sources of inspiration for countless artists in every field — painters, sculptors, architects, poets, writers, musicians, actors, and dramatists. Two thousand years have passed, and still people are writing books and composing songs about him. Painters and sculptors still strive to depict his form. In the same way, avatars like Rama, Krishna, and Buddha, who lived before Christ, still inspire artists all over the world.

Ramakrishna was born at a critical period in Indian history. Western culture and civilization were spreading rapidly throughout Indian society, and Christian missionaries were working hard to convert the population. Ramakrishna's divine life and his spiritual teachings touched people's hearts and restored their faith in their culture and religious heritage. He had a great influence on many social and religious leaders.

Ramakrishna is a living force even now: His ideas are growing and spreading day by day. His life is like a dazzling diamond with many facets, each one revealing one of his talents. Once Swami Vivekananda remarked: "The artistic faculty was highly developed in Sri Ramakrishna, and he used to say that without this faculty none could be truly spiritual."[1] Although Ramakrishna was mostly in a god-intoxicated mood, his artistic talents permeated his life.

Ramakrishna encouraged and supported the artists, writers, actors, singers, dancers, and musicians who came to visit him. Girish once said, "I learned how to write drama and how to act from Sri Ramakrishna." M., who was a schoolteacher, said, "I learned how to teach in school from Sri

Ramakrishna." And Swami Vivekananda said, "I learned how to reason scientifically from Sri Ramakrishna."[2]

Professor Nalini Ranjan Chattopadhyay has written a book called *Sri Ramakrishna O Banga Rangamancha* (*Ramakrishna and the Bengali Stage*). This book, written in Bengali, describes the tremendous influence that Ramakrishna had on the actors, actresses, and musicians of Bengal. Ramakrishna is worshipped as the patron deity of the stage. Even today many Bengali actors and actresses bow down to his picture before going onstage, continuing a tradition started by Girish. During Ramakrishna's time, the courtesans would act in the theatre because women of good families were reluctant to perform onstage. Ramakrishna gave these actresses his blessings and approval, thereby gaining for them society's approval as well. He acknowledged the talent involved in acting and elevated actresses to a higher status, thereby bringing about a revival of the Bengali stage.

Girish wrote roughly ninety plays, some before meeting Ramakrishna, but most of them afterwards. It is wonderful to see how he incorporated Ramakrishna's ideas into his plays — the ideal of religious harmony, as well as his spiritual teachings on faith, devotion, renunciation, self-surrender — sometimes even his very words. But more important, Girish showed how a real guru rescues his disciples from temptation and sin and transforms their lives. He introduced Swami Vivekananda's spirit of service in some of his plays; and he also created characters based on devotees of the Master, such as Latu and Pagalini. In some plays we watch Girish depict his own character, his grief and pain, his faith and devotion, and his transformation through the guru's grace. Girish was with the Master from September 1884 to August 1886. During that time he received the Master's unbounded love, affection, and grace.

Ramakrishna selected some of his disciples to spread his message. Before he passed away, he wrote on a piece of paper, "Narendra will teach people." He had already told M.: "God binds the Bhagavata pandit to the world with one tie; otherwise, who would remain to explain the sacred book? He keeps the pandit bound for the good of men. That is why the Divine Mother has kept you in the world."[3] When Girish wanted to give up the theatre and become a monk, the Master told him: "No, no! Let things be as they are. People will learn much from your plays."[4]

The theatre and other popular media are very powerful tools for spreading a message to the masses. Girish was a genius: He was not only a superb playwright, but also a great poet and composer of songs, a novelist, essayist, and storyteller. Girish's powers of observation and mimicry, and his capacity to assimilate his guru's ideas and incorporate them in his plays were remarkable. Unfortunately only a few of Girish's plays have been translated into other languages (see Chapter 6). This chapter presents a few passages from some of the plays in which the reader will find Ramakrishna's influence.

Vilwamangal Thakur

Ramakrishna saw Girish's *Chaitanya Lila* in September 1884. In April 1885 he developed cancer, so when Girish's *Prabhas Yajna* was staged in May 1885, he could not go to see it. During the Master's illness, Girish wrote two more dramas: *Buddhadev-Charit* and *Vilwamangal Thakur*. *Vilwamangal Thakur* premiered on 12 June 1886 at the Star Theatre at 68 Beadon Street, when Ramakrishna was alive. The main themes of this drama are love and renunciation. The story is taken from *Bhaktamala* (A Garland of Devotees).

One day when Girish was depressed he went to see the Master. To alleviate his depression, the Master told Girish the story of Vilwamangal and asked him to base a drama on it.[5] The Master described to Girish the nature of a real saint and also the character of a false monk. He himself showed this to Girish by demonstrating the gestures and deportment of a hypocritical monk. Girish depicted this monk in the character of Sadhak in *Vilwamangal Thakur*. He also created a character named Pagalini in this drama. This role was based on an unbalanced woman who would come to Ramakrishna in Dakshineswar and Cossipore and disturb him. The devotees called her Pagalini (crazy woman). Girish had observed her devotion and longing for God, and he dramatized this in that character. He also composed some songs that the character sang in the drama. These songs describe the different stages of sadhana.

After seeing *Vilwamangal Thakur* performed, a philosopher said to Girish: "Sir, the purpose of writing *Vilwamangal* has been fulfilled by one sentence in the drama: 'The result of the vision of Krishna is the vision of Krishna and nothing else.'"[6] If one has the vision of God once, that experience never goes away. After seeing and reading *Vilwamangal* many times, Swami Vivekananda remarked: "Girish's *Vilwamangal* surpasses the plays of Shakespeare. I have never read a book with such lofty ideas."[7] Chandrakanta Basu, a famous writer and critic, said: "*Vilwamangal* is Girish's masterpiece."

* * *

The Main characters:
Vilwamangal, a young and wealthy brahmin
Sadhak, a hypocritical monk

Somagiri, an honest monk
Banik, a merchant
Rakhal, who is Krishna in disguise as a cowherd
Bhikshuk, a thief
Chintamani, a courtesan
Thak, a companion of Chintamani
Ahalya, the wife of Banik
Pagalini, an unbalanced woman

Girish portrayed himself in the character of Vilwamangal, and Ramakrishna was portrayed in that of Somagiri. Here is a brief synopsis of the five-act play:

Act One: It is night. Vilwamangal goes to Chintamani's house, but the door is closed. Chintamani is eating her dinner, so she opens the door after a long time. Vilwamangal is hurt and feels he is being neglected. They argue, but it is clear that they love each other.

The next morning Bhikshuk sings a song that explains to Vilwamangal the nature of love: It flows like the ebb and tide of the ocean. Vilwamangal cannot visit Chintamani that night because his father has died. He hires Bhikshuk to watch the courtesan's house.

Act Two: Sadhak goes to Chintamani's house, where he falls in love with Thak. Sadhak says that he wants to teach Thak about the love of Radha and Krishna. He suggests that she think of herself as Radha and him as Krishna. Sadhak also tells her that he will teach her how to turn copper into gold and become rich. The conversation between Thak and Sadhak is very entertaining. Girish beautifully portrayed how a hypocritical monk enjoys lust and gold while wearing the garb of a monk. Sadhak then tries to persuade Bhikshuk to be his disciple.

Night falls, and a rainstorm sets in. After performing the shraddha ceremony for his dead father, Vilwamangal wants to be with Chintamani, so he leaves home. No boatman dares to ferry him across the river in the storm, so he swims across by holding on to a corpse, thinking it to be a log. He then scales Chintamani's wall by holding on to the tail of a cobra, which he takes to be a rope. The next morning Vilwamangal and Chintamani discover what he has done.

Chintamani tells him: "Really, you are mad with love. You have no shame, no fear. You mistook the snake for a rope, and the corpse for a log. Look, I am a prostitute. We only feign love, but your love is genuine. If you would give your mind to God instead of me, you would see God."

Vilwamangal replies: "You are right. I really am madly in love with you. I have given you my money and everything else. When you sleep, I

Ramakrishna's Influence on Girish's Plays 229

gaze at your face the whole night. When you heave a sigh, I see darkness all around. If I see tears in your eyes, I feel as if someone were piercing my heart with a spear. All along I have worshipped your beauty. Now I see this is all maya."

Thus the courtesan becomes Vilwamangal's first guru.

The next day Vilwamangal renounces his home and his wealth, even his beloved Chintamani. He then begins to search desperately for a guru: "Now I have no one in this world. There must be someone. Within this thick cloud of my mind I can't see anybody, but from my heart someone is telling me, 'I am with you.' Please do Thou reveal Thyself to me. I want to offer my heart and soul to you so that I can have peace. O my Lord, my heart is empty; I see darkness all around; I can't live here anymore. I am alone in this world."[8] Saying this, he leaves.

Chintamani cries out: "Where are you going? What is this? Are you going to renounce me? I see now I have no one."

Act Three: Vilwamangal meets Somagiri, who immediately recognizes him as a god-intoxicated man. Vilwamangal addresses him as "guru," but Somagiri replies that he is not the guru; only Krishna is the guru. Somagiri gives shelter to Vilwamangal and advises him to call on Krishna.

Meanwhile, Chintamani laments: "I am a sinner. I have hurt and betrayed so many people in my life. I am a loveless prostitute. I have known neither how to give love nor how to accept love. If God loves me, shall I be able to accept it?" Thak tries to console her, saying that Vilwamangal will be back — and if he does not return, she can trap another man. However, Chintamani now feels drawn towards renunciation, and she gives some of her jewellery to Pagalini. Thak becomes jealous and plots with Sadhak to steal the courtesan's money and jewellery. She asks Sadhak to put on torn ochre clothes, like a poor monk, and visit Chintamani that evening. He is to address her as "mother" and talk to her about Krishna's love. Then Chintamani will give him some money. The two plan to poison Chintamani later on and take all her wealth.

Elsewhere, Vilwamangal is beginning his sadhana, repeating his mantra day and night and eating food from the garbage with the dogs. He struggles to keep his mind focussed on Krishna. One day he is seated near a pond when he hears the sweet sound of a woman's anklets. He opens his eyes and sees Ahalya, the wife of Banik, who has come to bathe there. Seeing her beauty, Vilwamangal's old desires return. Aghast, he resolves to punish his eyes, which have become his enemies. He follows Ahalya to her house and meets her husband, whom he asks to allow him to see Ahalya privately. Banik is deeply virtuous and a wealthy business man and he thinks that God is testing him, so he does not object. When Vilwamangal and Ahalya are alone together, Vilwamangal asks Ahalya to give him two of her hairpins and then return to her husband. As soon as she leaves, he pushes the hairpins into his eyes, blinding himself. He then leaves the house, asking Krishna to guide him.

That evening Sadhak sneaks into Chintamani's house and puts deadly poison in the courtesan's milk. Thak and Sadhak plan to kill Chintamani and bury her body on the bank of the river. Bhikshuk is hiding behind some bushes and he hears their conversation. He considers warning Chintamani.

Chintamani soliloquizes: "The day is gone and night has come. This is a house of ill-fame and I shall have to sleep alone. If someone kills me for my money then I shall lose this life and the next one. O mind, you injured so many people for money, and now that money has become your enemy. When Vilwamangal was with me, I had no fear or worry. He loved me and protected me. Vilwamangal loved my beauty and that beauty is my enemy. What shall I do now? Who will save a great sinner like me? I shall go to Vilwamangal. He is a holy man and will not hate me. He will take care of my next life. I am a helpless, single woman. Who will guide me?"

Pagalini arrives and comforts her: "My daughter, I have been watching you. Don't worry about food and shelter. Look, even the jackals and the birds eat and have places to live." When Chintamani invites Pagalini to her house, she declines to go because she knows through her yogic power that Thak and Sadhak have plotted to poison her. She tells Chintamani about the plot. Chintamani then throws her keys and jewellery on the floor and leaves for Vrindaban with Pagalini and Bhikshuk. Bhikshuk secretly picks up the jewellery and puts it in his bag.

Act Four: Thak and Sadhak enter Chintamani's room. Her iron safe is installed in the wall. Thak tells Sadhak to break into the safe with an axe because they have no key. While they are breaking into the safe, a police officer and two constables enter the room.

The officer asks: "Who are you? Why are you stealing Chintamani's money and jewellery? I shall arrest you both."

Thak says that she is Chintamani's tenant and niece. Sadhak says that he is Chintamani's godson. Seeing that they don't have a key, the officer orders his men to arrest both of them. He tells them to put Sadhak in prison and bring Thak to his house. The officer plans to take all of Chintamani's money and report that the money was stolen by thieves.

Meanwhile, Sadhak takes out some poison. He gives some to Thak, and they both commit suicide.

On the way to Vrindaban, Pagalini leaves Chintamani and asks her to continue on alone. Bhikshuk, however, continues the journey with her.

One day seeing her husband's grey hair, Ahalya teases Banik: "You are getting old. It is wonderful that you will not be able to marry again."

Banik replies: "You are right. This grey hair reminds me that death is approaching. All these years I have been enjoying lust and gold. I don't enjoy this worldly life anymore. It is time for me to go somewhere."

Ahalya responds: "Wherever you go, I shall go also."

Banik says: "Let us go to Vrindaban."

Rakhal appears. He is pleased that the merchant couple is planning to go to Vrindaban. Rakhal addresses Ahalya as "mother," melting her heart. He introduces himself as a cowherd and says that he found a blind man in the nearby forest who does nothing but cry for Krishna. The man wants to go to Vrindaban. Ahalya thinks that it must be that great soul who took her hairpins and made himself blind. Banik tells Rakhal that they will be going to Vrindaban by boat and they would be happy to take that holy man with them. Rakhal goes to the forest to meet Vilwamangal, and convinces him to go to Vrindaban with them.

Act Five: Chintamani arrives in Vrindaban wearing only a plain sari and without any money or jewellery. She covers her beauty with ashes and is about to cut her hair when Rakhal appears and grabs the scissors.

Chintamani: "Who are you, my boy?"

Rakhal: "I am a cowherd. Do you love Krishna or me?"

Chintamani: "I am a loveless, wretched, fallen woman. I don't know how to love Krishna."

Rakhal: "You are now in Vrindaban. Tell me, do you want Krishna or me?"

Chintamani: "I want Krishna, but I love you."

Bhikshuk arrives and tries to befriend Rakhal. Rakhal tells him that if he wants to be his friend, he will have to give up the bag he carries, in which he is hiding Chintamani's jewellery. Rakhal then leaves.

Pagalini and Somagiri, accompanied by his disciple, reach Vrindaban. Chintamani is happy to see Pagalini because it was she who advised her to come to Vrindaban. Chintamani asks Somagiri: "Is there any hope for me to receive the grace of Krishna?"

Somagiri: "My mother, you have such intense love that Krishna will definitely shower his mercy on you."

Chintamani: "Father, show me the way to attain Krishna."

Somagiri: "Mother, there is a holy man in Vrindaban named Vilwamangal. Take refuge in him."

Chintamani: "Father, you are my guru. I am a great sinner and I ill-treated him innumerable times."

Somagiri: "Mother, he is a great sadhu. A real holy man is always forgiving." Pagalini promises to accompany Chintamani to see Vilwamangal.

Vilwamangal is seated alone in the forest of Vrindaban. He has been there for seven days without food, crying for Krishna and contemplating a fast until death. Rakhal appears with milk in hand and begins to feed him. While Rakhal is giving him milk, Vilwamangal grabs his hand, as he is convinced that Rakhal is Krishna himself.

Rakhal: "What are you doing? Let go of my hand. You're hurting me."

When Vilwamangal loosens his grip a little, Rakhal runs away.

Vilwamangal: "O my beloved Gopala, Krishna! You have snatched your hand away from me. Look, you revealed your love after making me cry. Now I shall tie you in my heart. Let me see how you can run away from there! Although I am blind, I shall catch you."

Rakhal (*standing behind the tree*): "Let me see how you can catch me."

Following the sound of his voice, Vilwamangal moves forward. Rakhal immediately takes the form of Krishna and returns Vilwamangal's sight. The man is overwhelmed by seeing the beautiful divine form of Krishna.

Rakhal says to Vilwamangal: "I hear some people coming. Let me hide myself, but I shall always be with you."

Ahalya and her husband approach Vilwamangal, and then Chintamani, Pagalini, and Bhikshuk arrive.

Vilwamangal: "I have seen the beautiful form of Krishna!"

Somagiri and his disciple then come on the scene.

Somagiri says to his disciple: "Krishna wanted to teach us renunciation through this courtesan and debauchee. (*Pointing to Vilwamangal*) Look, he is the embodiment of renunciation. We shall see Krishna by the grace of Chintamani and Vilwamangal."

Disciple: "Master, I am sorry that I looked down upon them. Now I will bow down to them. Please tell me, what is the result of the vision of Krishna?"

Somagiri: "The result of the vision of Krishna is Krishna *darshan* [the vision of Krishna]."

Chintamani to Vilwamangal: "O monk, look at me. I am your maid, seeking refuge at your feet. Be compassionate to me. If you reject me, I shall kill myself. I have come to you expecting so much — to see Krishna. Be gracious to me."

Ramakrishna's Influence on Girish's Plays 233

Vilwamangal: "Aha! Who has uttered Krishna's name in my ear? (*Seeing Chintamani*) Who is this? My guru who taught me love? Have mercy on me." Vilwamangal bows down to Chintamani.

Chintamani: "O my beloved Master, please don't turn me away. You are a yogi, a great lover of God. You have seen Krishna. Now share your Krishna with me."

Vilwamangal: "O beloved, Krishna is in your heart. Call on him wholeheartedly and you will see him."

Chintamani: "O Krishna, do thou reveal yourself to me. You love your devotees. If you do not reveal yourself to me, your devotee's words will be false. O Rakhal, I did not recognize you, but now I know you are Krishna. Please reveal yourself to me."

At that moment Krishna and Radha appear on the stage. Vilwamangal and Chintamani, Somagiri and his disciple, Pagalini and Bhikshuk, Banik and Ahalya — all see Radha and Krishna.[9]

* * *

Girish ingeniously transformed a short love story into a full-fledged five-act play. In it, he beautifully portrayed how sinners could become saints and how Vilwamangal's and Chintamani's devotion and renunciation helped others to see God. As Somagiri went to see Vilwamangal, so the Master went to see Girish in the theatre.

* * *

The following is a conversation that Girish had with a devotee regarding this play:

A devotee: "You have written so many dramas and created innumerable characters."

Girish: "I could not create a small part of what Ramakrishna has created."

Devotee: "You are really a great actor."

Girish: "My goodness! In acting, I could not even come close to him."

Devotee: "Why?"

Girish: "One day the Master demonstrated how a false monk behaves, and I tried to show this in the character of Sadhak in *Vilwamangal*. Sadhak was trying to make Bhikshuk, a thief, his disciple. Let me give you an example."

Bhikshuk: "Will you maintain silence or talk?"

Sadhak: "I shall talk with those whom I think fit."

Bhikshuk: "Will you light a dhuni fire?"

Sadhak: "Sometimes."

Bhikshuk: "Will you keep a Bhairavi [a woman companion]?"
Sadhak: "Secretly."
Bhikshuk: "Shall I ask people to give you money or not?"
Sadhak: "There will be a pot for the homa fire in front of me, where people will drop money according to their means."
Bhikshuk: "Where will you stay?"
Sadhak: "I shall find a Shiva temple nearby."[10]

Girish continued: "The Master was expert in studying and observing human character. He could imitate exactly the gestures and deportment of both men and women. He said: 'There is a kind of monk who wears a long cloak. He has a necklace of rudraksha beads around his neck strung with a gold or silver string, and in between the beads there are a few precious stones. He behaves as if he is omniscient.' I portrayed the Master's description of a hypocrite monk in the character of Sadhak."[11] Although Girish portrayed himself in the character of Vilwamangal, he acted in the role of Sadhak.[12]

Girish depicted Ramakrishna's spiritual experiences in the following song, which the character of Pagalini sang:

"He [Krishna] wanders with me holding my hand.
Wherever I go, He follows me,
Even if I don't call Him.
He wipes my face with great care,
And intently looks at my face.
When I smile, He smiles; and when I cry, He cries.
How lovingly He takes care of me.
So I came to know: who says that the Precious One does not exist?
Come and see for yourself whether it is true or false.
He is talking to me with great love.[13]

When Vilwamangal came to the ferry ghat to cross the river on a stormy night, he saw Pagalini at the cremation ground and requested her divine help to enable him to meet his beloved Chintamani by crossing the river. Girish wrote this song for Pagalini to sing, which depicts Ramakrishna's longing for the Divine Mother:

Where, friend, where is my Chintamani?*
Tell me where has He gone?
I have gone mad having lost the jewel of my heart.
Look, I have come to the cremation ground
But He is not here.

* Chintamani means "the jewel of thought." Vilwamangal's Chintamani was a courtesan, but Pagalini's Chintamani was Krishna.

In caves and forests, how many days
Have I spent weeping for Him?
Sometimes I besmear my body with ashes,
But the burning of my heart is not thereby allayed.
I roam in this empty world enduring the pain
  of a thunderbolt in my chest;
Still I cannot find His whereabouts.
He is the delight of my heart,
I ever pine for a sight of Him.[14]

When Vilwamangal said that Chintamani was a woman's name, Pagalini replied: "Chintamani is sometimes the Divine Mother Kali and sometimes Krishna. He is Purusha and Prakriti." These are all Ramakrishna's ideas. This drama illustrates how Girish's mind was saturated by Ramakrishna's life and philosophy.

Seeing the setting sun and hearing the vesper music in the Dakshineswar temple garden, Ramakrishna used to cry: "Mother, another day is gone in vain. Still You have not revealed Yourself to me!" Girish depicted this episode of the Master's life and his intense longing in the character of Vilwamangal. In the play, Vilwamangal cried out:

There! The conches and bells are sounding;
The brahmins are performing their evening worship.
I see the day is already over.
Oh! Another day is gone. Still I have not seen Him!...
Reveal Yourself to me! O Compassionate Lord, reveal Yourself to me!
My heart is riven by despair.[15]

Rupa-Sanatan

Girish witnessed Ramakrishna's love for God and unique renunciation, and he depicted this in *Rupa-Sanatan*. The play was first performed on 21 May 1887 at the Star Theatre. It is a five-act play. Like *Vilwamangal*, Girish based *Rupa-Sanatan* on a story from the *Bhaktamala*. In the character of Sanatan, Girish depicted Ramakrishna's love and longing for God, his austerities, renunciation, truthfulness, and steadfastness for the ideal. But this play also revealed the condition of Girish's mind just after Ramakrishna passed away.

Abinash Gangopadhyay, Girish's biographer and secretary, wrote:

In *Rupa-Sanatan*, Girish showed Chaitanya taking the dust of his devotees' feet at Chandrashekhar's house in Varanasi:
  A Vaishnava: "Lord, what are you doing?"

Chaitanya: "I am plunged in grief because of separation from Krishna, so I am putting the dust of His devotees' feet on my body. Thus I shall get the devotees' grace."

When this play was staged at the Star Theatre, some Vaishnava leaders were upset. According to them it is unthinkable that Chaitanya would take the dust of his devotees' feet and smear it on his body. They expressed their anger and even used abusive words to Girish.

Unperturbed, Girish firmly replied: "I have seen with my own eyes that Ramakrishna took the dust of his devotees' feet."

He continued: "I don't write anything without knowing the subject myself. One day at a devotee's house after kirtan and spiritual talk, Sri Ramakrishna took the dust of that place and smeared it on his own body. When the devotees tried to prevent him, the Master said: 'You see, this place has been sanctified by the presence of many devotees, spiritual talk, and singing the glory of God. Where God's name is sung, God Himself comes to listen to it. The dust of this place has truly been purified by the touch of the devotees' feet.'"[16]

* * *

The Main characters:
Chaitanya
Sanatan, prime minister of the Nawab of Bengal
Rupa, one of Sanatan's brothers and also a minister
Vallabha, one of Sanatan's brothers
Ishan, Sanatan's servant
Buddhimanta, a landlord
Jivan, a brahmin
Hussein Shah, the Nawab of Bengal
Ramdin, a jailor
Nasir Khan, a guard
Alaka, Sanatan's wife
Karuna, Rupa's wife
Vishakha, Vallabha's wife

Act One: Sanatan sits on the bank of the Ganges earnestly praying for renunciation. He feels that Chaitanya, whom he has recently met, is calling to him. In the meantime, his servant Ishan arrives and asks him to return home to eat. He also reminds Sanatan that the Nawab has sent messengers to him ten times. Sanatan laments that he is still working as a minister of this Muslim ruler, whereas two of his brothers, Rupa and Vallabha, have left and become disciples of Chaitanya. He decides to resign from his post.

Buddhimanta and Jivan are very jealous of Sanatan and his family's wealth, so they try to damage Karuna's and Vishakha's reputations by spreading rumours that their husbands have become mendicants. This has no effect on the women, however, because they remain as devoted to Chaitanya as are their husbands, and they worship him in their family shrine.

Vallabha comes to see his elder brother, Sanatan, bringing news of Chaitanya and informing him that the Master will call him at the proper time. He also conveys Rupa's request that his fortune be distributed among the poor. Sanatan follows his brother's wish.

Act Two: Jivan delivers a cryptic letter from Rupa to Sanatan. The letter contains only eight syllables — ya, ri; ra, la; I, ram; na, ya — the first and last syllables of each line of this Sanskrit verse:

Yadupateh kva gata mathurapu**ri**
Raghupateh kva gatottarakosa**la**.
Iti vichintya kuru svamanah sthi**ram**
Na sadidam jagat iti avadhara**ya**.

When deciphered, the letter reveals this meaning:

Where now is that Mathura city, where Krishna lived?
Where now is Ayodhya, where Rama ruled?
Thinking of this deeply, make your mind firm;
Know for certain: This world is not real.

This hint is enough for Sanatan to understand what his brother Rupa wishes to convey. Sanatan decides to go to Varanasi, where Chaitanya is staying. He asks Ishan to look after his wife, Alaka, and to distribute his wealth to the poor, setting aside a small amount for Alaka and Ishan himself. But before Sanatan can leave, two messengers from Hussein Shah arrive and forcibly take him to the Nawab. Sanatan tells Ishan to give the news to Alaka, but the faithful servant follows his master instead.

Buddhimanta has been spying on Sanatan and tells the Nawab that Sanatan is pretending to be ill. But the judge informs the Nawab that Buddhimanta cannot be trusted, as he is doing all types of mischief because Sanatan works for a Muslim ruler. The angry Nawab puts some defiled water into Buddhimanta's mouth, thus forcibly converting him to Islam. When people learn of his conversion, he leaves his family and decides to go to Varanasi. Buddhimanta had spread rumours against Vishakha and Karuna, yet now they come to him dressed as nuns. They advise him to chant Chaitanya's name and thereby become free from sin. Karuna tells him: "Touching a philosopher's stone, a piece of iron becomes gold; so also, seeing Chaitanya, a man becomes God." Buddhimanta then begins to chant Chaitanya's name.

When Sanatan is brought before the Nawab, the ruler asks him to concentrate on his work instead of trying to become a mendicant like his brothers. Sanatan refuses to work and says he wants to resign. He tells the Nawab that his mind is focussed on God and so it is not possible to turn it to worldly duties. In response to the Nawab's threats, he says that if he is forced to work, he will kill himself. The Nawab orders his guard to put Sanatan in prison, and tells his doctor to treat him as if he has an illness.

Alaka dresses like a young brahmin pandit, and Ishan takes her to Ramdin, the Hindu jailor. Ishan introduces Alaka, saying that this pandit might change Sanatan's mind. Ramdin allows her to go to Sanatan and tells her to defeat Sanatan in debate by quoting the scriptures that say family life is better than monastic life. Alaka goes alone to Sanatan's cell. Sanatan does not recognize her. The two have a lengthy discussion, but Sanatan is determined to renounce family life. Finally, Alaka reveals who she is. Sanatan then tells her to return home and surrender herself to Chaitanya. Alaka leaves, in tears.

The Nawab comes to the prison and asks Sanatan to look after his kingdom, because he is going to war with the king of Orissa. Sanatan declines, saying that his mind is on God now and he cannot turn it back to the world. The angry Nawab orders the guard to put Sanatan in a dungeon and put his feet in chains. He is also to be given only fried gram and a little water.

Act Three: Alaka, Karuna, and Vishakha meet and plan to rescue Sanatan. Then Ishan arrives but has no news of Sanatan.

Alaka: "Ishan, come with me. If I am a chaste woman and have true love for Chaitanya, I shall rescue my husband."

Alaka again disguises herself as a brahmin pandit and goes with Ishan to Ramdin's office in the jail.

Ramdin: "Hello, pandit. Why do you want to see me? Your luck is bad. But if you could change the mind of the minister, the Nawab will give you a lot of property."

Alaka: "I am not only a pandit, but an astrologer also. I see your luck will change tonight."

Ramdin: "What do you mean? I am a low-paid jailor."

Alaka: "I promise that you will be a millionaire tonight."

Ramdin: "I promise that if I get a million rupees tonight, I shall give you whatever you want."

Alaka: "You have promised! Now take this jewellery. It is worth more than a million rupees."

Ramdin: "Where did you get this jewellery? Who are you?"

Alaka: "I am the wife of Sanatan. Please keep your promise and release my husband, or I shall kill myself with this knife."

Ramdin is in a dilemma. He tells Alaka that there is a Muslim named Nasir Khan who is guarding Sanatan. However, he will try his best to release Sanatan.

Meanwhile, Nasir enters Sanatan's dungeon and asks him: "Sir, you were a minister, and now you are in this dungeon. I hear you talking with someone. I see you are even happier than our Nawab. Can you tell me why you are in this condition?"

Sanatan: "Look, I am a servant of Chaitanya. How can I serve the Nawab? My Lord is always with me."

Nasir: "Sir, I don't see anyone here. Who is this Chaitanya?"

Sanatan: "He is a monk. He saves souls from bondage and distributes God's name to all."

Nasir: "Sir, I am a sinner and a Muslim. You are very respected and also a holy man. I put those chains on your feet. Is there any hope for me?"

Sanatan: "Nasir, you are a devotee. Chant Chaitanya's name and embrace me. He who chants his name becomes holy. It does not matter whether he is a Muslim or a Hindu."

Just then Ramdin and Alaka enter the dungeon. Nasir salutes his superior, Ramdin, and says that he will not work anymore but instead will chant Chaitanya's name. He then leaves. Ramdin is surprised, and he feels the grace of Chaitanya. He realizes that God makes everything favourable for His devotees. He tells Sanatan: "I have come here to release you. Please write on this paper that you will continue your service. Then please leave."

Sanatan: "How can I write a lie?"

Ramdin: "I shall lie for you. The Nawab ordered me to free you as soon as you agree to continue serving him. There is a horse for you. Please leave; otherwise you will die here."

Sanatan: "The Nawab will punish you. Moreover, it is better to die than to lie or deceive others."

Alaka: "O devotee of God, why are you discriminating between truth and untruth now? Lord Chaitanya is calling you. Please leave this place right now."

Sanatan: "Don't delude me anymore, my dear. Once you deluded me and I became involved in worldly life. Please leave me alone."

Alaka asks Ramdin to release Sanatan from his chains and escort him out of the dungeon. She will do the rest. Ramdin calls for Nasir, but Ishan enters instead. Surprised, Ramdin asks Ishan how he got in.

Ishan replies: "I saw a Muslim leaving through the gate, chanting Chaitanya's name. He told me that he was going to see Chaitanya. I asked him for his uniform, and he told me where my master was being held."

Ramdin then unchains Sanatan and takes him outside.

Ishan tells Sanatan: "Lord Chaitanya has called you. Let us go to him quickly."

A boat is waiting for Sanatan and they leave for Varanasi, crossing the Ganges. Alaka becomes a nun like her sisters-in-law and dedicates her life to spreading Chaitanya's name among the masses.*

Act Four: Sanatan and Ishan are travelling through a forest when Sanatan tells his servant: "Ishan, I am having difficulty walking. It is as if someone is pulling me back. I am going to see Lord Chaitanya. Why do I have such difficulty? Ishan, when you come near me, I can't breathe. I am afraid to look at your quilt; I think it is not pure."

Ishan: "Master, it is made with holy cloth marked with the Lord's name."

Meanwhile a man comes across Sanatan and Ishan and invites them to his house to eat and rest. He tells them that this area is infested with robbers. Sanatan notices that Ishan is afraid, and asks him: "Do you have any money with you? Be honest." Ishan replies that he stitched 15 gold coins into his quilt for the expenses of their journey. Sanatan then realizes why he has been having difficulty walking and breathing. The man accompanying them reveals himself to be a robber, and threatens to attack Ishan. Sanatan stops him and says: "Please wait. Take all of my servant's gold coins, but please let him keep one so that he can return home." The robber is touched and he honours Sanatan's request.

He says: "I have been watching you for the last three days. I knew that your servant had money, so I planned to kill you both and take the money. Now that I know you are a real holy man, your life is safe."

---

*Girish here differs from *Bhaktamala* and *Chaitanya Charitamrita*. According to *Chaitanya Charitamrita*, Sanatan buys his freedom from the Muslim jailor by giving him 5,000 rupees. He tells the jailor to inform the Nawab that he had been taken to the Ganges to bathe, and he jumped into it and was drowned. The Muslim jailor took the money, released Sanatan, and helped him to cross the Ganges along with his servant Ishan. Girish's conscience did not approve of this deceit from a devout Vaishnava like Sanatan, so he created the characters of Ramdin, Alaka, and Nasir and released Sanatan from the dungeon in a more dignified way.

Sanatan asks Ishan to return home, keep all the money he gave to him earlier, enjoy his family, and take refuge in Chaitanya. Ishan reluctantly leaves, blaming those 15 gold coins for his misfortune. Sanatan continues walking to Varanasi.

Meanwhile, in Varanasi Chaitanya is staying at Chandrashekhar's house. Rupa and Vallabha arrive and Chaitanya takes the dust of their feet, embarrassing them. Chaitanya explains his action: "Rupa, don't you know that even the gods worship the devotees of Krishna? Human life is precious. One among millions becomes a devotee of Krishna; you are one of them. You two brothers have come. Now where is my Sanatan?"

Rupa: "I have heard that the Nawab became angry and put Sanatan in jail."

Chaitanya: "I am convinced that no power in this world can bind Sanatan. He will come here soon."

Rupa is a great Sanskrit scholar, so Chaitanya asks him to go to Vrindaban and write books on devotional sadhana. Vallabha accompanies him.

Chaitanya later explains why he took the dust of the devotees' feet: "When I become anxious because of my separation from Krishna, I take the dust of the devotees' feet and put it on my body. If I receive the grace of the devotees, then I will definitely receive the grace of Krishna."

Sanatan arrives in Varanasi and meets Chaitanya at Chandrashekhar's house. Chaitanya is delighted by Sanatan's story of how he was released from prison. Sanatan wants to stay with his guru, but Chaitanya asks him to go to Vrindaban and take care of Madanmohan Krishna.

Nasir, Ramdin, and Buddhimanta also come to Varanasi, where they meet Sanatan, who encourages them to see Chaitanya, the incarnation of love. Chaitanya arrives and accepts the three men as his devotees. He asks them to repeat the name of Krishna.

Act Five: Chaitanya is now in Puri; Sanatan is in Vrindaban and has begun his sadhana, and has received the grace of Madanmohan. Rupa has begun to write on Vaishnava philosophy and also compose dramas based on Radha and Krishna.

Jivan has come to Vrindaban, where he encounters Sanatan. He tells him that he fasted for seven days and prayed to Lord Shiva for money. On the seventh night, in a dream a voice told him that his wish would be fulfilled in Vrindaban. Jivan does not recognize Sanatan, who is now a poor mendicant. Sanatan responds: "My goodness! You have come to Vrindaban for money? At any rate, Lord Shiva's words cannot be false. Look, there is a philosopher's stone in the bushes near my cottage. Any metal you touch with it will turn into gold." Jivan picks up the stone and touches his key with it: The key turns into gold. Excited, Jivan asks: "Sir, are you Lord Shiva, playing with me?"

When Sanatan tells him who he is, the latter exclaims: "You must be a god. You must have something more precious than the position of prime minister for the Nawab and this philosopher's stone. Please give me that precious thing." He then throws the philosopher's stone into the nearby river. Sanatan tells him: "I am a poor mendicant. I have only Krishna. Please repeat the Lord's name, 'Krishna, Krishna, Krishna.'" Jivan repeats the Lord's name and his life is changed.

Madanmohan Krishna has been the family deity of the Chaube family. Chaube's wife and son take care of the deity. But in a vision, Madanmohan tells Chaube's wife that he wants to live with Sanatan. So she gives the deity to him. Finally Sanatan has the vision of Madanmohan and Radha.[17]

Kalapahar

Girish based *Kalapahar* on a historical event and his own knowledge of human love. He also incorporated Ramakrishna's teachings into it. *Kalapahar* was first performed on 26 September 1896 at the Star Theatre in Hatibagan, Calcutta. This five-act play is very long, and it has many characters. It is therefore not possible to describe it act by act, as has been done thus far. Instead, what follows is a summary of the plot, with emphasis placed on those sections where Girish introduced Ramakrishna's ideas. In *Kalapahar* he portrays Ramakrishna in the character of Chintamani, a holy man, and Latu (Swami Adbhutananda) in the character of Leto, a disciple.

> *The Main Characters*:
> Kalapahar, a great warrior who had been born a Hindu but converted to Islam. (He is a historical figure.)
> Chintamani, a holy man
> Mukundadev, King of Orissa
> Vireswar, a powerful brahmin
> Saliman, Nawab of Bengal
> Leto, Chintamani's disciple
> Chanchala, Kalapahar's female companion
> Iman, the daughter of Saliman
> Dolena, a friend of Iman

Kalapahar converts to Islam, then destroys many Hindu temples. In his early life he had had doubts about God, so he went to Chintamani. In the following conversation between Kalapahar and Chintamani, Girish incorporated Ramakrishna's ideas about ego, faith, reason, and the existence of God.

Chintamani asks Kalapahar who he is. When Kalapahar tries to introduce himself, Chintamani says: "Look, if you remove the onion skin layer after layer, nothing remains at last. So this 'I' disappears when you search for it."

Kalapahar: "Sir, does God exist?"

Chintamani: "Yes, He does exist. I swear thrice, and I don't know that anything else exists."

Kalapahar: "Where is God?"

Chintamani: "He is in that tamarind tree. He is in your heart. He is everywhere."

Kalapahar: "Have you seen Him?"

Chintamani: "Yes, I have. My guru showed Him to me."

Kalapahar: "Who is the guru?"

Chintamani: "Look, the guru is like a matchmaker. He brings the disciple to God."

Kalapahar: "I see only darkness."

Chintamani: "Correct. Look, if the guru does not illumine the heart, one sees only darkness. How can a tiny human being with a tiny intellect understand the Truth? Take refuge in the guru, who is God in human form. Only the guru can remove your doubts."

Kalapahar: "This is blind faith — conjecture without reasoning. How can I accept that the all-pervading God lives in a human being? Where is the guru? How can I trust him? That guru is also a human being like me."

Chintamani: "You think that the guru is a man like you? The guru is a wish-fulfilling tree. He appears in this world as a human being to help all beings. He who takes refuge in the guru has his ignorance destroyed, and he sees his Chosen Deity by the guru's grace. Perhaps you tried to see God by closing your eyes for a couple of days, and when God did not come you concluded that there is no God and that the scriptures are all wrong."

Kalapahar: "Shall I have to proceed with blind faith like you?"

Chintamani: "Look, don't get angry. Be calm and try to understand your foolishness. You are telling me that my faith is blind, yet I am surrounded by light. You, however, are roaming in darkness like a ghost, full of doubt!"

Kalapahar: "I will not believe anything without reasoning."

Chintamani: "Aha! What an intellect you have! One attains God through faith, and you say that faith is blind. Only a blind person like you speaks that way."

In *Kalapahar* Girish also dramatized Ramakrishna's opinion of occult powers. The character Vireswar is a brahmin who developed eight occult powers by carrying out difficult spiritual disciplines.

Chintamani: "Well, I hear that you have a power that makes whatever you utter come true."

Vireswar: "Yes."

Chintamani: "Well, why don't you say, 'O God, appear before me.' Let me see whether He comes or not."

Vireswar: "What?"

Chintamani: "Aha! You can't do that. Your power can only burn a tree, kill an elephant, or sink a boat. What useless powers you have!"

Vireswar: "What do you say?"

Chintamani: "Look, don't show your angry red eyes to me. You think that you can kill me this moment."

Vireswar: "Yes, I have that power. Do you know why the rulers of Bengal are continually changing? Those who fail to show me proper respect die. My anger kills them."

Chintamani: "I don't care for your power, even if it can kill me. People die from fire, water, swords, disease, snakes, tigers, and so on. In fact, you are acting just like a cobra. I shall consider you great if you can make a person immortal. But I am sure you can't do that, even though you are endowed with eight occult powers."

Vireswar: "Who are you?"

Chintamani: "Never mind who I am. You should rather think of yourself. What have you done with your life? You have acquired some useless powers through sadhana. You have never inquired about God, the Creator of this universe. Get away from here. I don't like your company."

Vireswar: "Sir, don't go away. Listen to me."

Chintamani: "Why should I listen to your rubbish? I would be eager to listen to you if you would tell me something about God."

Vireswar: "Sir, teach me. I don't know God."

Chintamani: "Look, just as Uncle Moon is everybody's uncle, so God belongs to everyone. Call on God."

Vireswar: "Let me tell you a little of my background. I was born a brahmin and then worshipped Mahamaya to obtain wealth, name and fame. To acquire occult powers I practised austerities and sadhana in the cremation ground. Now I am a slave to this power of Mahamaya. How can I escape this bondage?"

Chintamani: "Shun your ego and destroy this power of ignorance. Know for certain, egotism leads to hell. To whom do these powers belong?

They belong to God. But you think these powers belong to you. Just as rainwater flows through a channel, but the water does not belong to the channel, so also you are only a channel for God's power. It is God's will that human beings reap the results of their actions. Now repeat this mantra: 'Tuhun, tuhun, naham, naham — Thou, thou, not I, not I.' This is how you will be freed from bondage and the Divine Mother will be awakened in your heart. Look, I am teaching you. Is it my ego? Brother, this ego does not want to leave. Naham, naham, tuhun, tuhun — not I, not I, but thou, thou, O Lord."

Vireswar accepts Chintamani as his guru.[18]

Later Chintamani says to Vireswar: "What is there to fear? Give me all of your sins."

Vireswar: "What do you say? You will take all my sins and my sufferings! Truly, here is someone who is a saviour of sinners. I have no more fear. My divine sight has been opened. I see God through the light of knowledge."[19]

In this section Girish depicted Ramakrishna's teaching on how lust and gold delude men:

Chintamani: "You are Kalapahar? Correct?"

Kalapahar: "Yes, people say so."

Chintamani: "I hear that you do not listen to any women, so you are *kālā*, deaf; and that you sit in one place like a motionless *pahar*, rock. Now I see your rock is cracked."

Kalapahar: "How do you know that?"

Chintamani: "I saw a girl disguised as a boy escort you to the Nawab's garden where you met some girls and heard some love songs. Now you are meditating on those girls. These actions indicate that your heart is cracked."

Kalapahar: "Have you been following me?"

Chintamani: "I saw where you were going. I know what human beings want."

Kalapahar: "How do you know what human beings want? Are you omniscient?"

Chintamani: "Both of us know that men desire three things in this world: women, money, and fame."

Kalapahar: "Do people perform actions only to fulfill their selfish desires? Don't you know that some people work without any selfish motive?"

Chintamani: "I understand what you mean. You are talking about compassion, helping others unselfishly."

Kalapahar: "Yes, that is correct. Don't you believe in these things?"

Chintamani: "Yes, I do. But let me tell you about compassion. When I give something to someone, I feel that everyone should see me do this. Or if I secretly give a gift or money to someone, I tell all my friends and my family. If someone does not acknowledge a gift, I become angry and remark: 'That fellow is ungrateful, unappreciative, and rude.' I give charity to show off, and I expect praise from the recipient. Do you consider this to be an unselfish action?"

Kalapahar: "Oh, you are amazing!"

Chintamani: "The human mind is a mysterious thing. Once I meditated throughout the night and cried for God with a longing heart, with tears flowing from my eyes. After my meditation was over I thought to myself how nice it would have been if someone could have seen me in that condition. Since then I have understood the nature of this tricky mind. The darkness of coal goes away only when fire enters it. This mind is deceitful, so I silently watch it and restrain it."

Kalapahar: "You are a jnani, a man of wisdom."[20]

Ramakrishna's teaching on "ripe I and unripe I" has been narrated here:

Saliman: "Who are you?"

Chintamani: "Which 'I'? The 'ripe I' or the 'unripe I'?"

Saliman: "I don't understand your 'ripe I' and 'unripe I.'"

Chintamani: "Well, my 'unripe I' says: 'I was born in Bengal as a brahmin. My name is Kalikrishna. I move around. I eat whatever I get and sleep wherever I find a place.' My 'ripe I' says: 'I am a servant of God, a part of God, one with God. I can't speak any further about it. Then I will lose consciousness.'"

Saliman: "Are you a saint?"

Chintamani: "I don't know. I have lost myself. I see that God has become everything. He is in the air, fire, water, earth, space, the stars, moon, and so on. You see, it is something extraordinary."

Saliman: "I don't understand what you're saying."

Chintamani: "How can you understand this? One cannot understand this through the intellect. A salt doll touched the ocean and became one with the ocean. What do you know if you do not know God?"[21]

Girish described Ramakrishna's message on the harmony of religions, universal love, and purity in the following:

Dolena, a companion of Princess Iman, goes to a flower garden to pick flowers for Iman. Leto, a disciple of Chintamani, visits the same garden to pick flowers for the worship of God. Dolena gives a beautiful garland to Leto. Chintamani is delighted by the garland and the flowers, and he wants to use them for the worship. But Leto cautions his teacher that those flowers were touched by a Muslim woman, so they should not be used for worshipping a Hindu god.

Chintamani: "Shame on you, Leto! You still differentiate between Ishwara and Allah? God is one but people call Him by various names. As the same water is called *jal*, aqua, water, *pani*, so also the eternal God is called by people as Allah, God, Ishwara, Jehovah, and Jesus. This perception of difference comes from ignorance. Give up this idea of difference. God has many names, and each name is endowed with infinite power. People develop love for a particular name of God, who fulfills their desires when they call on Him. Muslims, Hindus, and Christians worship the same infinite God. Ignorant people fight among themselves because of their dualistic beliefs."

Iman and Dolena come to see Chintamani.

Iman: "Fakir [holy man], I had a desire to meet you."

Chintamani: "I also wanted to see you. I love those people who are intoxicated with love and forget themselves. You are one of them. "

Iman: Fakir, you love everyone. Will you teach me how to love all? Please don't refuse me. I am a wretched woman."

Chintamani: "Mother, don't think that you are wretched. You are the all-powerful, blissful Mother. You do not know your real nature because you are ignorant."

Iman: "Fakir, I am burning with misery. I am a sinner. I fell in love with a person [Kalapahar] who saved me from a lion. I am a Muslim girl. He is now madly in love with me, but I disappointed him. Please tell me, what shall I do now?"

Chintamani: "My child, the Lord will show you the way."

Iman: "I am not pure. Without purity one cannot call on the pure God."

Chintamani: "My child, don't you know that one who takes God's name becomes free from sin? That person's soul becomes pure. For that reason the prophet declared: 'Come, call on God and you will be free from sins.'"

Iman: "Fakir, your words are very encouraging. Please teach me how to call on God."

Chintamani: "Your mind will teach you. When one longs for God, one learns to call on Him. I see that you long for God. Don't worry. God loves you. He is your Beloved. Pour your love out to Him."

Iman: "How shall I call on God?"

Chintamani: "He has many names — Ishwara, Allah, Khoda. Call on Him according to your aptitude. He will come, listen to you, and will be with you."[22]

Girish portrayed how he gave his power of attorney to Ramakrishna in the following scene:

Chanchala wants to be with Kalapahar, but discovers that he is in love with Princess Iman. Seeking revenge, Chanchala kidnaps Iman and Dolena and takes them to Mukundadev, the Hindu king of Orissa. Kalapahar had previously been Mukundadev's commander-in-chief and had defeated the Muslims. But when he learns that Iman has been kidnapped, he deserts the Hindu leader and converts to Islam. Taking control of the Muslim army, he invades Orissa and destroys Hindu temples. Mukundadev surrenders.

When Chintamani discovers that Chanchala is planning to kill Iman, he tells her: "Listen, don't do such a thing. Give all your pain and misery to me." He cannot stop her. After killing Iman, Chanchala kills herself.

Kalapahar: "I can't bear this burning pain anymore!"

Chintamani: "Give me all of your pain and suffering."

Kalapahar: "Who are you? Why do you want my suffering? You are always with me, O Compassionate One."

Chintamani: "Why do you say that? Call on God. He is the only Compassionate One."

Towards the end of the drama, the Muslim army occupies the Hindu kingdom. Nawab Saliman regrets the bloodshed and he seeks advice from Chintamani.

Chintamani: "Don't be afraid. Call on God. Rule the country impartially. Treat the Hindus and Muslims as equals. Give solace to those who are afraid. Don't be hostile to other religions. Be compassionate to all, so that both the Hindus and Muslims will glorify you."[23]

Purnachandra

Ramakrishna said: "Faithful devotees always feel the all-auspicious Lord in their hearts and are never discouraged, even when facing thousands of dangers."

Girish illustrated this teaching in the life of the title character of his play *Purnachandra*.

Purnachandra is a five-act play, and its themes are ideal renunciation and faith in God. The drama is based on a Hindi story entitled *Puran*

Bhakat (The Devotee Purna). *Purnachandra* was first performed on 17 March 1888 at the Emerald Theatre in Calcutta.

The Main Characters:
Gorakshanath, a perfect yogi
Shalibahan, the King of Sialkot
Purnachandra, son of the king
Sundara, princess of the Punjab
Sari, Sundara's female confidante

Purna is a prince, but he wants to become a monk. He renounces everything and leaves home to become a disciple of the Yogi Gorakshanath. His guru says to him: "Monastic life is a difficult path. You were brought up in luxury in the palace, and this life is full of austerities and hardships. You will have to live on alms, sleep on the open ground or under a tree, and meditate in the forest surrounded by wild animals."

Purna agrees to fulfill all of these conditions, then takes monastic vows. Gorakshanath decides to test him.

Sundara, the princess of the Punjab, is unmarried and looking for a husband. One day she says to her female confidante: "The man who is proud of learning I defeat in argument and make a fool of him. He who is proud of wealth becomes overwhelmed when he sees my treasury. He who is proud of his own beauty becomes my slave when he sees my beauty. A man's pride is his sword, but when most men see my banner from a distance, they drop their sword."

Gorakshanath sends Purna to Sundara to beg for food. When she sees Purna, she falls in love with him. Sundara says to her companion: "Sari, this young yogi is my beloved. I know the signs of a yogi. His mind is absorbed in God and he is free from worldliness."

Sundara offers him a gold coin, but he returns it and asks only for food. She invites him to enter her palace, but he refuses, saying that a monk should not enter such a place.

Sundara then follows Purna with food to meet Gorakshanath. On the way she asks him: "If I ask for something from your guru, shall I get it?"

Purna replies: "My guru is a wish-fulfilling tree. Whatever you ask for, you will get."

After reaching Gorakshanath, Sundara says to him: "Lord, I want this young monk to be my husband."

Gorakshanath immediately tells Purna: "Go with this woman now. Do as I wish."

Purna: "O guru, may my mind be absorbed in you and may I never be deluded by maya."

Sundara: "My desire is fulfilled by the grace of this wish-fulfilling guru."

Purna says to Sundara: "You have lost the nectar of immortality. You have bad luck."

After Sundara, Sari, and Purna have left, one of Gorakshanath's disciples asks him: "Master, what is this? This woman wants to fulfill her worldly desires and you have offered Purna to her."

Gorakshanath responds: "Purna is a real yogi. He is able to pass very difficult tests. Moreover, only a true monk can remain undisturbed by the temptations of beautiful women and great wealth."

By the grace of his guru, Purna maintains his unbroken celibacy: Sundara's beauty, wealth, and humble pleas leave him unmoved.

Purna tells Sundara: "This worldly relationship is momentary; a physical relationship is nothing but slavery. Look, the union between Atman and Atman never breaks. In that plane one enjoys bliss continuously. Offer your heart to Lord Shiva and we will be united in God-consciousness forever. Dissolve your mind in the Atman and shun all worldly relationships. This nondualistic knowledge will remove all perception of multiplicity and you will find no difference between man and woman."

Sundara finally gives up her desire to be Purna's wife. She tells him: "O Lord, may I have that dualistic knowledge birth after birth, so that I can worship you and serve you. I don't want to be an obstacle in your path. I shall not bind you. You go wherever you like. Your happiness is my happiness."

Purna: "O blessed one, I bless you that you may have unflinching devotion to Lord Shiva."

Sundara: "I don't want God. I have no desire other than to serve you. O yogi, I bow down to you. Forgive all my faults."

Purna returns to his guru Gorakshanath, who is delighted that his disciple passed the test.

Sundara begins leading a nun's life and serves Purna's elderly mother.

Girish portrayed Ramakrishna's uncompromising renunciation in this drama.[24]

Nasiram

In the title character of this play Girish portrayed Ramakrishna and his teachings about how lust and love, the animal nature and the divine nature coexist in human beings. Girish also showed how the divine overcomes the bestial. *Nasiram* was first performed on 25 May 1888 at the Star Theatre in Hatibagan, Calcutta. It is a five-act play.

The Main Characters:
Nasiram, a god-intoxicated man
Yogeshnath, King of Bengal
Anathnath, a prince
Kapalik, the guru of the king
Sona, the female companion of the Kapalik
Viraja, a woman posing as a princess

Nasiram is a god-intoxicated man whom people consider to be mad. Regarding himself, Nasiram says: "I want neither to die nor to live. I want neither the palace nor the shade of a tree. I want to eat neither fancy food nor a few grains of rice. I know that one day I am happy and the next day unhappy. These two rascals — good and bad — are companions.

"People call me mad. I have seen those rascals: some are mad after money, some for name and fame, some for women, and some for children. I chant only God's name."

Prince Anath: "Nasiram, don't you have any desires?"

Nasiram: "Show me one thing that one should ask for. Everything in this world is empty, false, and impermanent. Look at this beautiful girl: She will be ashes one day. Your friends and relatives exist today, but you don't know where they will be tomorrow. Today you may be rich; tomorrow you may be a pauper. Clay is money and money is clay. I don't find anything that I want in this world."

Prince Anath: "Don't you want God?"

Nasiram: "He is looking after me, so why should I want Him?"

Prince Anath: "My goodness! You say that God is looking after you?"

Nasiram: "Of course He is. And not only that, He looks after birds and beasts, ants and insects. He provides food and shelter to each and all. I watch Him and enjoy the fun. He plays hide and seek. He is everywhere, supplying everything to all, and people think they are doing everything themselves. If you watch carefully, you will enjoy this worldly fun and frivolities. In every home you will see the puppet show going on."[25]

Anath falls in love with Viraja, a beautiful, clever girl, but his father wants to end their relationship. One day Nasiram taught Anath how one can transform lust into love: "You can have a physical relationship for a long time — but for how long? A relationship based on divine love is everlasting. Try to understand the difference between lust and love: Lust shrinks the mind, but love expands the mind. It is all-pervading, all-encompassing.

"Distribute love in this world. Love all those who are poor, fallen, and wretched. The love of God is unending. Distribute this love as much as you can. My work is over."

Ramakrishna always depended on the Divine Mother, and Girish dramatized this in the character of Nasiram. He taught people to surrender to God. He transformed the lustful king into a devotee of God.

King Yogeshnath: "Nasiram, do you hate me?"

Nasiram: "How can I hate you? I am also a slave to my senses, as you are. Look, I have this wonderful human life; still I do not have that intense love for God. So I ask you to call on God."

King: "Haribol, Haribol! Will Lord Hari accept me?"

Nasiram: "You do your work, and He will do His. O King, if God had not accepted you, how could you chant His name?"

Viraja: "Master, I am a sinner. Will God have mercy on me?"

Nasiram: "What do you mean? It is God's concern to show mercy to the fallen. One of His names is 'saviour of the fallen.' Those who think they are fallen, God also accepts. Simply chant God's name. He will be with you."

A false monk named Kāpālik ruined a young woman's life and made her his mistress. Nasiram is very fond of that innocent woman, Sona, so he decides to save her from this situation. He asks her to chant God's name. But Sona is hurt and asks Nasiram: "Why should I chant Hari's name? Who made me a prostitute? Who forced me to become addicted to alcohol? Who made me helpless? Is it not Hari who did all these things? And now you are asking me to chant Hari's name?"

Nasiram: "If you do not want to chant Hari's name, let me chant while you listen."[26]

Sona's life is eventually transformed and she becomes a great devotee of God.

Hemendra Nath Das Gupta wrote:

> In the play *Nasiram*, the influence of Ramakrishna is more than evident. Through every word and every act of Nasiram, we seem to see Girish sitting at the feet of Ramakrishna and wielding his pen as if at his Master's bidding. Nasiram is mad in the eyes of the worldly-wise. Surely he must be a mad fellow who loves everybody and hates none, not even the most despicable. Nasiram sees even in the worst sinner the great possibilities that may be attained by him, for the human soul is but God in man.[27]

*　　　*　　　*

Ramakrishna's influence is evident throughout Girish's works. The Master asked Girish to continue his acting and writing in order to educate the masses. Girish saw how some wealthy young men became trapped by the courtesans in red-light districts, losing their money, prestige, and manliness, as well as the love of their family and friends.

Girish's drama *Bishad*, based on the story of Queen Madalasa from the Markandeya Purana, opened at the Emerald Theatre on 6 October 1888. King Alarka was a highly spiritual man but through the influence of an evil friend he began leading an immoral life. Girish vividly showed in this drama how Queen Saraswati changed her husband's life through her love, purity, humility, and self-sacrifice.

* * *

This world is a den of miseries; there is no real joy in worldly pleasures. Earthly love is gross and selfish. Divine love is the goal of life, and it alone can save human beings from miseries. Herein lies the liberation of man.

Girish wrote his drama *Jana* based on a story from the *Ashwamedha parvan* of the Mahabharata that vividly portrays Jana's motherhood and Bidushaka's devotion and faith. *Jana* was first performed on 23 December 1893 at the Minerva Theatre. Ardhendu Shekhar Mustafi acted in the role of Bidushaka for a few nights and then left for the Emerald Theatre. Girish took over the role. His performance made a deep impression on the audience.

Ramakrishna said: "You must have heard about the tremendous power of faith. It is said in the Purana that Rama, who was God Himself — the embodiment of Absolute Brahman — had to build a bridge to cross the sea to Ceylon [now Sri Lanka]. But Hanuman, trusting in Rama's name, cleared the sea in one jump and reached the other side. He had no need of a bridge."[28]

In *Jana* Girish depicted this tangible faith and pure love.

We also find the influence of Ramakrishna in other plays of Girish, such as *Pāndava Gaurav*, *Swapner Phul*, *Maner Matan*, *Shankarācharya*, *Ashoka*, and *Tapobal*. Again, Girish based some of his plays on Swami Vivekananda's ideal of serving human beings as God. These plays include *Māyāvasān*, *Bhrānti*, *Balidān*, *Grihalakshmi*, *Shāsti ki Shānti*. One could write a whole book on this topic alone.

Girish received unbounded love and devotion through the grace of Ramakrishna, and this he translated into his life. Through his plays he shared this grace with others.

Ramakrishna at Bengal Photographer's Studio, Calcutta,
10 December 1881

Chapter 17

Reminiscences of Ramakrishna
by Girish Chandra Ghosh

Girish wrote his reminiscences of Ramakrishna for two Bengali magazines: Udbodhan *(April 1905) and* Janmabhumi *(June-July 1909). Swami Aseshananda translated these articles and they were published in* Vedanta and the West *(Hollywood: Vedanta Press), March-April 1953, as one article. This is a reprint of the English translation.*

When the responsibility for writing an article on Sri Ramakrishna fell on me, I thought it would be a very simple thing. But actually, I find the writing extremely difficult. I thought it would be easy, for I have enjoyed his unfathomable love. I have also heard from each disciple how Sri Ramakrishna showered his infinite love on him. Many a time, with enraptured minds, we have discussed among ourselves that great love. Whenever a disciple would recount his personal experiences, immediately as a reaction, a hundred fountains would open up from within and a hundred streams would flow with a gushing torrent. Not so much from the actual words of the disciple, but from the manner of his expression, a sympathetic chord in my heart would be touched, and his experience would become vivid and living before my mind's eye.

A single word of the disciple, a single incident described, would make me feel that I too had heard such words of affection. I too had seen many such acts of compassion. With a single word the disciple would relive the experience and the listener would feel himself to be a participant. But I wonder if my readers will be able to share with equal vividness my own experiences. Shall I be able to convey them in words? Let me ask a question: Can you describe the warmth of affection which you have received from your own mother? For myself, I cannot. I can only exclaim, "Ah, mother's love, mother's love." In every act of my mother, in her every glance and movement, what I have felt is beyond my words to describe. Besides, can anyone really understand a mother's love without becoming a mother? Even were such understanding possible, an understanding of Sri Ramakrishna's love lies far beyond it.

Our relationships in the world are conditioned by maya. Father's love or mother's love can also be said to fall within maya. Usually love prompted by maya desires only the worldly happiness of the son. It seeks only his worldly prosperity and nothing more. Very often it is seen that if the son, for the sake of spiritual enlightenment, pays no attention to worldly duties, he becomes a source of annoyance to his parents. In spite of his possessing good qualities, if the son prefers monastic life to marriage, he becomes an object of displeasure to his parents. They advise him that there is time for everything, and that he should attend to spiritual life after finishing his life in the world and discharging his duties to the world in a proper manner. If the boy does not listen to their advice, they may not say in so many words that their son has gone astray, but will not refrain from saying to friends and relations with a sigh of regret that he is useless and lacking in purpose. There is selfishness in the love of parents. It is seen that the father is partial to an accomplished son. As long as the son is a mere boy and helpless, the parents are unselfish. But most parents expect that in their old age they will be looked after and provided for by their sons. Greater is the love of the mother for the son who has no talents. Father's love or mother's love is very high indeed. But it cannot be said that it is absolutely free from selfishness.

If I stretch my imagination I can have a glimpse of my parents' love. But the love of Sri Ramakrishna — that immaculately pure and absolutely unselfish love — how can I comprehend it? How shall I portray it in words? Without attaining the state of consciousness that is free from the touch of selfishness, free from the delusion of maya, how shall I understand the actions of a person who has broken the bonds of maya and is without faults? If I had attained that condition in which Sri Ramakrishna lived, the condition of being totally free from maya, and if I had had a disciple, I could then have gained the power of understanding Sri Ramakrishna's love in a small measure. But I don't know whether I would have been able to express it. I have grasped to some extent the love of Sri Ramakrishna by listening to the stories which other disciples have narrated to me and by comparing notes which I myself have gathered, but it is not possible to describe the story of the pilgrimage of the soul which a fellow traveller has made and to paint a picture of the longings and aspirations of his heart. I may or may not know the story of my own life, but the story of another man's life is a completely sealed book to me. Therefore in this article I shall tell only my own tale: what I felt about the love of Sri Ramakrishna in relation to me. Beyond that I am helpless. I must speak about myself. My listeners, out of compassion for my pitiable condition, must kindly forgive me.

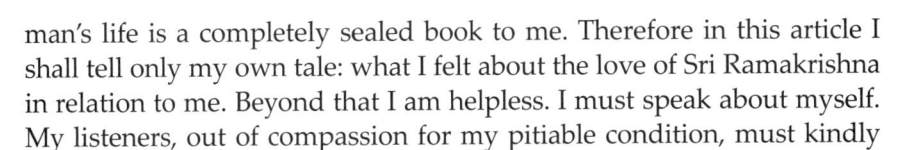

Another thing: Those who went to Sri Ramakrishna were all gentle, good-natured, and virtuous. Boys like Narendra and others, who are considered as his own, visited the Master at an early age, when they were very young. Being drawn by his love, they left their hearth and home and later embraced the monastic life in order to carry out his mission. To describe his love for them will hardly give a correct picture of his love. His affection for these boys, who were pure and spotless and who had taken shelter in him after renouncing everything for his sake, was quite natural. But I too was the recipient of his love. This seems to me something extraordinary. Sri Ramakrishna loved me unstintingly. This was proof of the fact that he was an ocean of unconditional mercy and boundless compassion.

One of the names of God is "Saviour of the Fallen." I, and no one else, can bear witness that he deserved that name. Some of those who have been with the Master may be fickle-minded, but in comparison with my fickle and restless nature they are all saints. They may have a few weaknesses; their feet may have slipped a few times; but in comparison with my Himalayan faults, those shortcomings are nothing. From my early boyhood I was moulded in a different way. I never learned to walk a straight path. I always preferred a crooked way. In spite of my faults, I was the object of his deepest affection. The manifestation of his love was revealed nowhere so clearly as in my case. The readers will get a glimpse of it from the story I shall tell below.

Sri Ramakrishna gave me refuge at a time when I was torn by conflicts and brutal agony of the heart. My early training, lack of a guardian from childhood, wayward youthful tendencies — all these conspired to lead me away from the path. Atheism was the fashion of the day. Belief in the existence of God was considered foolish and a sign of weakness. In my circle of friends if one could prove the nonexistence of God, one received the most extravagant praise and honour. I used to make fun of those who believed in God. After reading a few pages about science I jumped to the conclusion that religion was pure imagination and myth. Priests had concocted it to frighten people into morality and abstention from evildoing. Wisdom lay in accomplishing one's ends by any means, fair or foul. An unworthy act became ignoble when it was discovered and not before that.

It was daylight that made sin. To fulfill one's purpose secretly was a proof of talent. To satisfy one's desire through cleverness was a mark of intelligence. But in a world ruled by Providence such intelligence does not last. Evil days are bound to come. When they come, they teach hard truths. I learned from them one big lesson, that there is no way to hide a wicked deed. There is a saying, "Murder will out." Too true, as I learned. But the deeds had already begun to bear fruit. A terrible future was painted in vivid colours on the canvas of my mind. It was not the end but only the beginning of the episode that darkened my destiny. Punishment had begun, but the way to its escape had not yet been found. Friendless, and surrounded on all sides by enemies who took advantage of my misdeeds to ruin me, I felt that I was adrift on a sea of despair.

At such a crisis I thought: "Does God exist? Does He listen to the prayers of Man? Does He show him the way from darkness to light?" My mind said, "Yes." Immediately I closed my eyes and prayed: "Oh God, if Thou art, carry me across. Give me refuge. I have none." I remembered the words of the Gita: "Those who call on Me only in the days of affliction, to them too I bring succour and refuge." These words sank deep in my consciousness and gave me solace in sorrow. I found the words of the Gita to be true. As the sun removes the darkness of the night, so the sun of hope arose and dispelled the gloom that had gathered thick in my mind. In the sea of trouble I found the harbour of repose. But I had nurtured doubt all these years. I had argued long, saying, "There is no God." Where would the impressions of these thoughts go? I began to reason in terms of cause and effect and argued that such and such a cause had produced such and such an effect, which was instrumental in bringing release from this danger. It is said that doubt dies hard. Again I fell victim to doubt. But I had not the courage to say boldly, "God does not exist."

Desire for inquiry came. Looking into the current of events, sometimes faith, sometimes doubt, emerged. Everybody with whom I discussed my problems said unanimously that without instruction from a guru doubt would not go and nothing could be achieved in spiritual life. But my intellect refused to accept a human being as a guru, for one has to salute the guru with the words, "The guru is Brahma, the guru is Vishnu, the guru is the Lord Maheshwara, the god of gods, etc." How could I say this to a man like me? This was hypocrisy. But the tyranny of doubt was intolerable. Terrible conflicts pierced my heart through and through. That condition can better be imagined than described. Suppose a man, all of a sudden, is forcibly dragged to a dark, solitary room with his eyes covered and kept confined there with no food and drink. What will be the state of his mind? If you can picture his mental condition, you will be able to understand something of my own. There were moments when I was breathless with emotion. Thoughts of despair bit through me like a saw. At other times the memory of the past was revived and the darkness of my heart knew no bounds. Just at this time I saw Sri Ramakrishna passing by our lane to the house of Balaram, the great devotee, and for the first time I felt irresistibly drawn to him. However, I shall describe this meeting later.

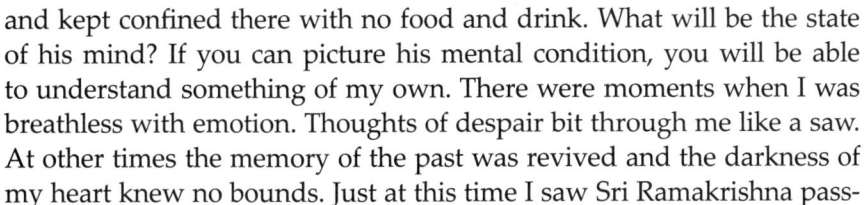

Sometime previously I had read in the "Indian Mirror" that there was a paramahamsa [an illumined soul] who was living in Dakshineswar. Keshab Chandra Sen was visiting him frequently, accompanied by his disciples. With my little understanding I thought that the Brahmos, who had many strange ideas, had created a fake paramahamsa. He could not be the real thing.

A few days passed, and I heard that the paramahamsa would be coming to the house of Dinanath Basu, an attorney of the Calcutta High Court, in our neighbourhood. To satisfy my curiosity and to ascertain what kind of a paramahamsa he was, I went to see him. I returned with irreverence instead of reverence. When I arrived at Dinanath Basu's I saw that the paramahamsa had come and that he was giving instructions to Keshab Sen and others, who were listening with rapt attention. It was dusk. Lights were lit and they were placed in front of Sri Ramakrishna. But he began to make repeated inquiries, saying, "Is it evening? Is it evening?" At this I thought to myself: "What pretention! It is dusk. Lights are burning in front of him. Yet he cannot tell whether it is evening or not." Thinking I had seen enough of him, I left.

A few years later Sri Ramakrishna was to come to the residence of Balaram Basu at Ramkanta Bose's Street. High-souled Balaram had invited many in our neighbourhood to come and visit the Master. I too had an invitation, so I went. After arriving there I found Sri Ramakrishna had already come. A dancing girl was seated by his side in order to sing a few devotional songs for him. Quite a large gathering had assembled in Balaram's drawing room. Suddenly my eyes were opened to a new vision by Sri Ramakrishna's conduct. I used to think that those who consider themselves paramahamsas or yogis do not speak with anybody. They do not salute anybody. If strongly urged, they allow others to serve them. But the behaviour of this paramahamsa was quite different. With the utmost humility he was showing respect to everybody by bowing his head on the ground. An old friend of mine, pointing at him, said sarcastically: "Bidhu has had a previous intimacy with him. That's why he is laughing and joking with her." But I did not like his insinuations. Just at this time Sisir Kumar Ghosh, the well-known editor of *Amrita Bazar Patrika*, arrived. He seemed to have very little respect for Sri Ramakrishna. He said, "Let us go. Enough of him!" I wanted to stay and see a little more, but he insisted and made me come with him. This was my second visit.

Again some days went by. My play, *The Life of Chaitanya*, was being enacted in the Star Theatre. I was strolling in the outer compound of the theatre one day when Mahendra Nath Mukhopadhyay, one of the devotees of Sri Ramakrishna, came and said to me: "Paramahamsadeva has come to see the play. If you allow him a free pass, well and good. Otherwise we will buy a ticket for him."

I replied: "He will not have to purchase his ticket. But the others will have to." Saying this, I proceeded to greet him. I found him alighting from the carriage and entering the compound of the theatre. I wanted to salute him, but before I could do so he saluted me. I returned his salute. He saluted me again. I bowed my head and he did the same to me. I thought this might continue forever, so I greeted him mentally and led him upstairs and offered him a seat in the box. After arranging with an attendant to fan him, I returned home, feeling indisposed. This was my third meeting.

Before I narrate my fourth meeting I must tell you the condition of religion that prevailed in the country at that time. During my school days those who were called "Young Bengal" were the people who were recognized in society as respectable and learned. They were the first products of Western education in Bengal. The majority of them were materialists. A small minority had been converted to Christianity. Some of them accepted the creed of the Brahmo Samaj, but few of them had any respect for Hinduism. Orthodox Hindus were bitterly torn by sectarianism. Conflict between Shaktas and Vaishnavas was very strong. And Vaishnavism too was divided into many sects, each contending for supremacy over the other. Rivalry was growing fast between one sect and another. Moreover, there were other faiths prevalent at the time. Each faith condemned the followers of the other faiths to the darkness of hell. Added to this, many brahmin priests were degenerate. They were completely ignorant of their own scriptures and were not even familiar with the formalities of religion, and yet they acted as priests and preachers. In a word, they lived a most hypocritical life.

On the other hand, the youths of the day, having studied a few pages of English, became iconoclasts at heart. The materialists were considered the most enlightened people on earth because of their erudition and scholarship, and so their words were accepted as the supreme authority. The sign of scholarship was not to believe in God. Under such circumstances, the young educated people lost all faith in their own religion. But there would be a discussion now and then among ourselves about the existence of God. Occasionally I would attend the services of the Brahmo Samaj, and would sometimes visit the one in our neighbourhood, but I arrived at no conclusion. Whether God existed or not I was doubtful. If He existed, which religion should I follow? I argued much, deliberated much, but could not find any solution.

This made me uneasy. Then one day I prayed, "Oh Lord, if Thou art, show me the way." But there was egotism in my heart, and I thought: "All the necessities of material life, such as air, water, and light, are abundantly supplied by nature and available for man to enjoy. Why should not religion, so essential for eternal life, be equally available? To me, it seems neither natural nor within my reach, and therefore it must be false. Materialism must be true." Thus I passed fourteen long years in a fog of gloom.

Then came evil days which allowed me no rest. There was darkness within; there was darkness without — darkness everywhere. I thought: "Is there any escape? I have seen people taking refuge in Taraknath Shiva when they suffer from some incurable disease." My condition too was very serious. To get release from my trouble was almost impossible. At this juncture, would it do me good if I prayed to Taraknath Shiva, the protector of His devotees? Let me test it! I made an honest attempt to resign myself to the will of the Lord, and my attempt was successful. A network of danger was pierced through in no time. A firm conviction arose that God was not unreal.

I was saved from the present danger, but was this the way to ultimate salvation? Terrible conflict was raging in my mind, and I was uncertain which way to turn. I had seen the glory of Taraknath. Why not call on Him again? Gradually, faith in God began to grow in me. But people said that no liberation is possible without a guru. Furthermore, I was told that one must look upon the guru as God. My reason found this hard to accept. The very idea was revolting to me, for nothing seemed more blasphemous than to think of a man as God. I must trudge on alone without a human guru. I would pray to Taraknath. Let Him be my guru. I had heard of some people to whom the Lord had appeared as guru in a vision and who had thus received their spiritual instruction without a human intermediary. If He would shower such grace on me, I would be saved. Otherwise

I was helpless. But I had not seen Taraknath. What should I do then? Let me chant His name in the morning and then see what happens.

At this time I became acquainted with a painter who was a Vaishnava. I don't know if it was true or not, but he said to me one day: "I offer food to the Deity every day, and I am convinced by certain signs that He accepts it. Until one is initiated by a guru such a rare privilege will not happen in one's life." My mind became restless. I took leave of him, went to my room, closed all the doors, and began to weep.

Three days later I was sitting on the porch of a friend's house, which was at an intersection, and I saw Sri Ramakrishna slowly approaching, accompanied by Narayan and a couple of other devotees. No sooner had I turned my eyes towards him than he saluted me. I returned his salute. Then he went on. For no accountable reason my heart felt drawn towards him by an invisible string. As soon as he had gone a short distance, I felt an urge to follow him. I could not keep calm, for the attraction I felt was not of this earth. It was something for which no former experience had ever prepared me. It was something unique, which no words could describe. Just at that moment a person, whose name I do not recall, brought me a message from him and said, "Sri Ramakrishna is calling you." I went.

Sri Ramakrishna went on to Balaram's, and there I followed him. Balaram was lying on a couch, seemingly ill. The moment he saw Sri Ramakrishna he got up quickly and with great reverence prostrated himself before him. After an exchange of a few words with Balaram, Sri Ramakrishna suddenly exclaimed, "I am all right, I am all right." So saying, he went into a state of consciousness which seemed very strange to me. Then he remarked, "No, no, this is not pretense, this is not pretense." He remained in this state for a while and then resumed his normal state. I asked him, "What is a guru?" He answered: "Do you know what the guru is? He is like a matchmaker. A matchmaker arranges for the union of the bride with the bridegroom. Likewise a guru prepares for the meeting of the individual soul with his Beloved, the Divine Spirit." Actually, he did not use the word matchmaker, but a slang expression, more forceful. Then he said: "You need not worry. Your guru has already been chosen." I asked, "What is the mantram?" He replied, "The name of God." And as an example he told the following story.

"Ramananda used to bathe in the Ganges early every morning. On one of the steps of the ghat a weaver by the name of Kavir was lying, and as Ramananda came down the steps his feet accidentally touched the body of Kavir. Being conscious of the divine presence in all, he uttered the word 'Rama.' Kavir, on hearing this name from the lips of a holy man, took it to be his mantram, and by chanting it he eventually realized God."

Then the talk drifted to the theatre, and he said: "I liked your play very much. The sun of knowledge has begun to shine upon you. All the blemishes of your heart will be washed away. Very soon devotion will arise to sweeten your life with profuse joy and peace." I told him that I had none of those qualities and that I had written the play only with the idea of making some money. He kept quiet. Then he said, "Could you take me to your theatre and show me another play of yours?" I replied, "Very well, any day you like." He said, "You must charge me something." I said, "All right, you may pay eight annas." Sri Ramakrishna said, "That will allow me a seat in the balcony, which is a very noisy place." I answered: "Oh no, you will not go there. You will sit in the same place that you sat last time." He said, "Then you must take one rupee." I said, "All right, as you please." Our talk ended.

Soon after this, Haripada and I saluted Sri Ramakrishna and came out of Balaram's house. On the way Haripada asked me, "What do you think of him?" I replied, "A great devotee." My heart was filled with unspeakable joy, for it seemed as though my search for a guru had ended. For did not Sri Ramakrishna say that my guru had already been chosen?

Looking back at my former objections to a guru, I understood the pride and vanity which had lain behind my rationalizations. I had thought: "After all, the guru is a man. The disciple is also a man. Why should one man stand before another with folded palms and follow him like a slave?" But time after time in the presence of Sri Ramakrishna my pride crumbled into dust. Meeting me at the theatre, it had been he who first saluted me. How could my pride remain in the presence of such a humble man? The memory of his humility created an indelible impression on my mind.

A few days after my visit with him at Balaram's, I was sitting in the dressing room of the theatre when a devotee came to me in a hurry and said with some concern, "Sri Ramakrishna is here in his carriage." I replied: "Very well. Take him to the box and offer him a seat." But the devotee answered, "Won't you come to greet him personally and take him there yourself?" With some annoyance I said: "Does he need me? Can't he get there himself?" Nevertheless I went. I found him alighting from the carriage. Seeing his serene and radiant face, my stony heart melted. I rebuked myself in shame, and that shame still haunts my memory. To think that I had refused to greet this sweet and gentle soul! Then I conducted him upstairs. There I saluted him, touching his feet. Even now I do not understand the reason, but at that moment a radical change came over me and I was a different man. I offered him a rose, which he accepted. But he returned it again, saying: "Only a god or a dandy is entitled to flowers. What shall I do with it?"

There was a special room on the second floor of the Star Theatre, which was intended for the visitors of the dress circle to sit in during the concert. Sri Ramakrishna came there, and a good number of devotees joined him. He started conversing with me. He spoke of several things while I listened longingly. I felt a spiritual current passing, as it were, through my body from foot to head and head to foot. All of a sudden Sri Ramakrishna lost outer consciousness and went into ecstasy, and in that mood he started talking with a young devotee. Many years earlier I had heard some slandering remarks against him, made by a very wicked man. Suddenly I remembered those words, and at that moment Sri Ramakrishna's ecstasy broke and his mood changed. Pointing towards me, he said, "There is some crookedness in your heart." I thought: "Yes, indeed. Plenty of it — of various kinds." But I was at a loss to understand which kind he was particularly referring to. I asked, "How shall I get rid of it?" Sri Ramakrishna replied, "Have faith!"

Time rolled on. One afternoon I went to the theatre and saw on my desk a slip of paper with a note that Sri Ramakrishna would be going to Ram Chandra Datta's house at Madhu Roy's Lane, Calcutta. After reading that note I felt in my heart the same kind of strong urge to go to meet him as I had felt on that day when I saw the Master coming while I was sitting on the porch of a friend's house in our neighbourhood. I was very eager to go. But again I considered, "Should I go to a stranger's house without an invitation?" But the pull of the invisible string was strong. I had to go. I went as far as Anath Babu's market and stopped. Then I thought again, "No, I must not go." But I was helplessly drawn. I would go a few steps and then stop. I hesitated even after coming very near to the house of Ram Chandra.

At last I reached the gate. Ram Chandra was sitting there and ushered me in. It was evening. Sri Ramakrishna was dancing in ecstasy in the courtyard. There was singing accompanied by a drum, and the devotees were dancing in a circle around Sri Ramakrishna. The words of the song were: "Nadia is shaken by the surging waves of divine love emanating from the heart of Gauranga." The courtyard seemed a sea of bliss. Tears filled my eyes. Sri Ramakrishna suddenly became still, absorbed in samadhi. The devotees began to take the dust of his feet. I wanted to do the same, but I could not, as I was shy. I was thinking of what others might say if I went to Sri Ramakrishna and took the dust of his feet. No sooner had this thought crossed my mind than Sri Ramakrishna, coming down from samadhi, began dancing again. While dancing he came before me and stood still, once more absorbed in samadhi. Now there was no longer any hesitation on my part to touch his feet. I took the dust of his feet.

After the music Sri Ramakrishna came and sat in the drawing room, and I followed him. Then he began to talk to me. I asked him, "Will the crookedness go out of my heart?" He said, "Yes, it will go." Again I asked him the same question, and he gave the same reply. I repeated it once more, and he said the same thing. But Manomohan Mitra, an ardent devotee of his, said to me rudely: "Enough. He has already answered you. Why do you bother him again?" I turned towards him to answer sharply, for no one who criticized me ever escaped the lash of my tongue. But I controlled myself, thinking: "Manomohan must be right. He who does not believe when told once will not believe even if he is told a hundred times." I bowed down before Sri Ramakrishna and returned to my theatre.

One night, in a happy and drunken mood, I was visiting a house of prostitution with two of my friends. But suddenly I felt an urge to visit Sri Ramakrishna. My friends and I hired a carriage and drove out to Dakshineswar. It was late at night, and everyone was asleep. The three of us entered Sri Ramakrishna's room, tipsy and reeling. Sri Ramakrishna grasped both my hands and began to sing and dance in ecstasy. The thought flashed through my mind: "Here is a man whose love embraces all — even a wicked man like me, whose own family would condemn me in this state. Surely this holy man, respected by the righteous, is also the saviour of the fallen."

After these meetings with Sri Ramakrishna I began to wonder: "Who is this man who speaks to me with such intimacy and makes me feel that he is my very own? No longer do I fear my own sins, for I feel sure he would not condemn me. Though he seems to know me through and through, a confession might do me great good. I must take shelter at his feet, for he alone can bring me peace."

I went to Dakshineswar and found Sri Ramakrishna seated on the southern porch of his room. He was talking with a young devotee named Bhavanath. I prostrated myself before Sri Ramakrishna and mentally recited the verse "The guru is Brahma, the guru is Vishnu, the guru is the Lord Maheshwara, the god of gods." He said: "I was just talking about you. And if you don't believe me, ask Bhavanath!"

After a while he started to give me some spiritual advice. I stopped him, saying: "I won't listen to any advice. I have written cartloads of it myself. It doesn't help. Do something that will transform my life." Hearing these words, Sri Ramakrishna was highly pleased. Ramlal, his nephew, was present. Sri Ramakrishna asked him to recite a particular hymn, which ran thus: "Go into solitude and shut yourself in a cave. Peace is not there. Peace is where faith is, for faith is the root of all." I saw a smile playing on the lips of Sri Ramakrishna, and I felt at that moment that I was freed from all impurities. And at that moment my arrogant head bowed low at his feet. In him I found my sanctuary and all my fear was gone. I prostrated myself before him and was about to return home. He followed me as far as the northern porch. There I asked him, "Now that I have received your grace, am I to continue the same kind of work that I have been doing?" Sri Ramakrishna replied, "Yes, why not?" From his words I understood that my connection with the theatre would not hurt my spiritual life.

My heart was filled with joy. I felt as if I were born anew. I was a totally changed man. There was no more doubt or conflict in my mind. "God is real. God is my sanctuary. I have found my refuge in this God-man. Now I can easily realize God." Thoughts like these cast their spell on me night and day. While awake or while dreaming, the same mood persisted: "Fearless am I! I have found my very own. The world can no longer bind me, for even the greatest fear, the fear of death, is gone."

Meanwhile, I would hear from various devotees that the Master had spoken affectionately of me. If anybody would criticize me, Sri Ramakrishna would say: "It is not true. You do not know. He has tremendous faith."

Sri Ramakrishna would come to the theatre now and then to visit me, bringing some sweets for me from Dakshineswar. He would first taste them and then give them to me. Immediately my mood would change, and I would feel like a little child, fed by a loving parent.

One day when I arrived at Dakshineswar, Sri Ramakrishna was just finishing his noonday meal. He offered me his dessert, but as I was about to eat it, he said: "Wait. Let me feed you myself." Then he put the pudding into my mouth with his own fingers, and I ate as hungrily and unselfconsciously as a small baby. I forgot that I was an adult. I felt I was a child of the mother and the mother was feeding me. But now when I remember how these lips of mine had touched many impure lips, and how Sri Ramakrishna fed me, touching them with his holy hand, I am overwhelmed with emotion and say to myself: "Did this actually happen?

Or was it only a dream?" I heard from a devotee that Sri Ramakrishna saw me as a little baby in a divine vision. And whenever I was with him, I would actually feel like a child.

Although I had come to regard Sri Ramakrishna as my very own, the scars of past impressions were not so easily healed. One day, under the influence of liquor, I began to abuse him in most unutterable language. The devotees of the Master grew furious and they were about to punish me, but he restrained them. Abuse continued to flow from my lips in a torrent. Sri Ramakrishna kept quiet and then silently returned to Dakshineswar. There was no remorse in my heart. As a spoiled child might carelessly berate his father, so did I abuse Sri Ramakrishna without any fear of punishment. Soon my behaviour became common gossip, and I began to realize my mistake. But at the same time I had so much faith in his love, and felt his love was so infinite, that I did not fear for a moment that Sri Ramakrishna could ever desert me.

Many of the devotees wondered why the Master put up with all my wickedness and suggested that he sever all connection with me. Ram Chandra Datta alone pleaded on my behalf and said to him: "Sir, he has worshipped you with abuse, according to his nature. The serpent Kaliya asked Lord Krishna, 'Since you have given me poison, how can I offer you nectar?'" Sri Ramakrishna said, "Just listen to what Ram says." But as the others continued to condemn me, the Master said abruptly: "Get me a carriage. I must go to see Girish!" My affectionate spiritual father then came to my house and blessed me by his presence.

As the days passed on I began to feel more and more remorse for my conduct towards this gentle holy man, who was the very soul of love. Thinking of the other devotees who worshipped him with adoration, I was full of self-reproach. It was in this state of depression that Sri Ramakrishna found me a few days later, and in an ecstatic mood he said: "Girish Ghosh, don't worry. People will be amazed at your transformation."

From my early childhood it had been my nature to do the very thing that I was forbidden to do. But Sri Ramakrishna was a unique teacher. Never for one moment did he restrict me, and that in itself worked like a miracle in my life. Whenever any lustful thought would arise in my mind, it would quickly fade. My head would bow low before Brahman and Shakti, and Sri Ramakrishna would appear in my mental vision. Behind the degenerate words and actions of worldly people, I felt the eternal play of God. Again, it was my habit to tell occasional lies. Though Sri Ramakrishna was very strict with regard to truthfulness and would not allow anyone to tell an untruth even in fun, when I approached him to confess my guilt, he replied: "You need not worry. Like myself, you are above truth and falsehood." Yet afterwards, when even a thought of telling a lie arose in my mind, the mental image of Sri Ramakrishna would again appear before me, and no untruth could escape my lips.

Sri Ramakrishna has taken full possession of my heart and bound it with his love. But such a love cannot be measured by any earthly standard. If I have acquired any virtues, it is not through my own efforts, but solely due to his grace. He literally accepted my sins and left my soul free. If any of his devotees would speak of sin and sinfulness, he would rebuke him saying: "Stop that. Why talk of sin? He who repeatedly says, 'I am a worm, I am a worm,' becomes a worm. He who thinks, 'I am free, I am free,' becomes free. Always have that positive attitude that you are free, and no sin will cling to you."

The significance of the word "guru" has dawned on me gradually. It was a slow process, but its effect was deeply penetrating. Now I have realized that the guru is everything. He is my all in all. Through him my life has been blessed. To this redeemer of my soul I have paid little homage. In a drunken state I have abused him. When given the opportunity to serve him, I have ignored it. But I have no regrets. In my attempts to escape all discipline I found myself disciplined without knowing it. Such is my guru's grace — an infinite ocean of mercy, not conferred because of merit, nor withheld because of sin, but lavished on saint and sinner alike. With a love transcending reason, he has given me sanctuary, and I have no fear. Hail Sri Ramakrishna![1]

Chapter 18

Conversations with Ramakrishna

This chapter presents conversations between Ramakrishna, Girish, and others that took place between 22 February 1885 and 23 April 1886. In these dialogues, recorded by M. in The Gospel of Sri Ramakrishna, *the reader will witness how the wild, bohemian Girish was transformed into a wonderful devotee.*

22 February 1885

Sri Ramakrishna was sitting on the northeast veranda outside his room at Dakshineswar. It was about eight o'clock in the morning. Many devotees, including Narendra, Rakhal, Girish, Baburam, and Surendra were present. They were celebrating the Master's birthday, which had fallen on the previous Monday. It was Girish's belief that God Himself had been born in the person of Sri Ramakrishna.

Girish (*to the Master*): "Your ways are like Krishna's. He too pretended many things to His mother Yasoda."

Master: "True. It was because Krishna was an Incarnation of God. When God is born as a man He acts that way. You see, Krishna easily lifted the hill of Govardhan with His hand, but He made Nanda believe that He found it very hard to carry a footstool."

Girish: "Yes, sir, I have understood you now."

Master (*to Girish*): "I look on Narendra as Atman. I obey him."

Girish: "Is there anyone you don't obey?"

Master (*smiling*): "He has a manly nature and I have the nature of a woman. He is a noble soul and belongs to the realm of the Indivisible Brahman."

Girish went out to have a smoke.

Narendra (*to the Master*): "I had a talk with Girish Ghosh. He is indeed a great man. We talked about you."

Master: "What did you say about me?"

Narendra: "That you are illiterate and we are scholars. Oh, we talked in that vein!" (*Laughter.*)

Mani Mallick (*to the Master*): "You have become a pandit without reading a book."

Master (*to Narendra and the others*): "Let me tell you this: really and truly I don't feel sorry in the least that I haven't read the Vedanta or the other scriptures. I know that the essence of the Vedanta is that Brahman alone is real and the world illusory."

Girish entered the room.

Master (*to Girish*): "Hello! What were you saying about me? I eat, drink, and make merry."

Girish: "What should we have been saying about you? Are you a holy man?"

Master: "No, nothing of the sort. Truly I do not feel I am a holy man.

Girish: "I am not your equal even in joking."

The evening worship was over. One or two devotees were still in the temple garden. Narendra had left. Sri Ramakrishna was pacing the veranda northeast of his room. M. stood there looking at him. Suddenly he said to M., "Ah, how sweet Narendra's music is!"

Girish Ghosh came and stood by Sri Ramakrishna, who had started to sing:

Is Kali, my Mother, really black?
The Naked One, of blackest hue,
Lights the Lotus of the Heart....

Sri Ramakrishna was filled with divine fervour. Standing with one arm resting on Girish's body he sang:

Why should I go to Ganga or Gaya, to Kasi, Kanchi, or Prabhas,
So long as I can breathe my last with Kali's name upon my lips?
What need of rituals has a man, what need of devotions anymore,
If he repeats the Mother's name at the three holy hours?
Rituals may pursue him close, but never can they overtake him....

Then he sang:

Once for all, this time, I have thoroughly understood;
From One who knows it well, I have learnt the secret of bhava.
A man has come to me from a country where there is no night,
And now I cannot distinguish day from night any longer;
Rituals and devotions have all grown profitless for me.
My sleep is broken; how can I slumber anymore?
For now I am wide awake in the sleeplessness of yoga.

> O Divine Mother, made one with Thee in yoga-sleep at last,
> My slumber I have lulled asleep for evermore.
> I bow my head, says Prasad, before desire and liberation;
> Knowing the secret that Kali is one with the highest Brahman,
> I have discarded, once for all, both righteousness and sin.

As Sri Ramakrishna looked at Girish, his ecstatic fervour became more intense. He sang:

> I have surrendered my soul at the fearless feet of the Mother;
> Am I afraid of Death anymore?
> Unto the tuft of hair on my head
> Is tied the almighty mantra, Mother Kali's name.
> My body I have sold in the market-place of the world
> And with it have bought Sri Durga's name....

Intoxicated with God, Sri Ramakrishna repeated the lines:

> My body I have sold in the market-place of the world
> And with it have bought Sri Durga's name.

Looking at Girish and M. he said, "'Divine fervour fills my body and robs me of consciousness.'

"Here 'consciousness' means consciousness of the outer world. One needs the Knowledge of Reality and Brahman.

"Bhakti, love of God, is the only essential thing. One kind of bhakti has a motive behind it. Again, there is a motiveless love, pure devotion, a love of God that seeks no return. Keshab Sen and the members of the Brahmo Samaj didn't know about motiveless love. In this love there is no desire; it is nothing but pure love of the Lotus Feet of God.

"There is another kind of love, known as *urjhita bhakti*, an ecstatic love of God that overflows, as it were. When it is awakened, the devotee 'laughs and weeps and dances and sings.' Chaitanyadeva is an example of this love. Rama said to Lakshmana, 'Brother, if anywhere you see the manifestation of urjhita bhakti, know for certain that I am there.'"

Girish: "Everything is possible through your grace. What was I before? And see what I am now."

Master: "You had latent tendencies; so they are manifesting themselves now. Nothing happens except at the proper time. Take the case of a patient. Nature has almost cured him, when the physician prescribes a herb and asks him to drink its juice. After taking the medicine he is completely cured. Now, is the patient cured by the medicine, or does he get well by himself? Who can tell?

"Lakshmana said to Lava and Kusa: 'You are mere children; you don't know Rama's power. At the touch of His feet, Ahalya, who had been turned into a stone, got back her human form.' Lava and Kusa said: 'Revered sir, we know that. We have heard the story. The stone became Ahalya because of the power of the holy man's words. The sage Gautama said to her: "In the Tretayuga, Rama will pass this hermitage. You will become a human being again at the touch of His feet."' Now, who can tell whether the miracle happened in order that the sage's words should be fulfilled or on account of Rama's holiness?

"Everything happens by the will of God. If your spiritual consciousness has been awakened at this place, know that I am only an instrument. 'Uncle Moon is everybody's uncle.' All happens by the will of God."

Girish (*smiling*): "Did you say 'by the will of God'? What I am saying is the very same thing." (*All laugh.*)

Master (*to Girish*): "By being guileless one can speedily realize God. There are several kinds of people who do not attain divine knowledge. First, a man with a perverse mind; he is not guileless. Second, one who is very fastidious about outer purity. Third, a doubting person."[1]

1 March 1885

Girish had been visiting Sri Ramakrishna for some months. The Master said that none could fathom the depth of Girish's faith. And his longing for God was as intense as his faith was deep. At home, he was always absorbed in the thought of Sri Ramakrishna. Many of the Master's devotees visited him; they talked only about Sri Ramakrishna. But Girish was a householder who had had varied experiences of worldly life, and the Master knew that Narendra would renounce the world, that he would shun "woman and gold" both mentally and outwardly.

Master (*to Narendra*): "Do you visit Girish frequently? No matter how much one washes a cup that has contained a solution of garlic, still a trace of the smell will certainly linger. The youngsters who come here are pure souls — untouched by 'woman and gold.' Men who have associated a long time with 'woman and gold' smell of the garlic, as it were. They are like a mango pecked by crows. Such a fruit cannot be offered to the Deity in the temple, and you would hesitate to eat it yourself. Again, take the case of a new pot and another in which curd has been made. One is afraid to keep milk in the second pot, for the milk very often turns sour.

"Householder devotees like Girish form a class by themselves. They desire yoga and also bhoga. Their attitude is that of Ravana, who wanted to enjoy the maidens of heaven and at the same time realize Rama. They are like the asuras, the demons, who enjoy various pleasures and also realize Narayana."

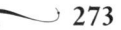

Narendra: "But Girish has given up his old associates."

Master: "Yes, yes. He is like a bull castrated in old age. In Burdwan I once saw an ox moving about the cows. I asked a bullock-cart driver: 'What is this? An ox? How strange!' He said to me: 'True, sir. But it was castrated in old age, and so it hasn't altogether shaken off the old tendencies.'

"In a certain place there sat some sannyasis. A young woman happened to pass by. All continued as before to meditate on God, except one of them, who cast sidelong glances at her. Before becoming a monk he had been the father of three children.

"If you make a solution of garlic in a cup, won't it be hard to remove the smell from it? Can a worthless tree like the babui produce mangoes? Of course such a thing may become possible through the occult powers of a yogi; but can everyone acquire such powers?

"When have worldly people time to think of God?"...

Narendra: "Nowadays Girish Ghosh thinks of nothing but spiritual things."

Master: "That is very good. But why is he so abusive? Why does he use such vulgar language to me? In my present state of mind I cannot bear such rudeness. When a thunderbolt strikes near a house, the heavy things inside the house are not much affected; but the window-panes rattle. Nowadays I cannot bear such roughness. A man living on the plane of sattva cannot bear noise and uproar. That is why Hriday was sent away. It was the Divine Mother who sent him away. During the later part of his stay he went to extremes; he became very rough and abusive. (*To Narendra*) Do you agree with Girish about me?"

Narendra: "He said he believed you to be an Incarnation of God. I didn't say anything in answer to his remarks."

Master: "But how great his faith is! Don't you think so?"[2]

11 March 1885

After school-hours M. returned to Balaram's house and found the Master sitting in the drawing-room, surrounded by his devotees and disciples. Among them were Girish, Suresh, Balaram, Latu, and Chunilal. The Master's face was beaming with a sweet smile, which was reflected in the happy faces of those in the room. M. was asked to take a seat by the Master's side.

Master (*to Girish*): "You had better argue this point with Narendra and see what he has to say."

Girish: "Narendra says that God is infinite; we cannot even so much as say that the things or persons we perceive are parts of God. How can Infinity have parts? It cannot."

Master: "However great and infinite God may be, His Essence can and does manifest itself through man by His mere will. God's Incarnation as a man cannot be explained by analogy. One must feel it for oneself and realize it by direct perception. An analogy can give us only a little glimpse. By touching the horns, legs, or tail of a cow, we in fact touch the cow herself; but for us the essential thing about a cow is her milk, which comes through the udder. The Divine Incarnation is like the udder. God incarnates Himself as man from time to time in order to teach people devotion and divine love."

Girish: "Narendra says: 'Is it ever possible to know all of God? He is infinite.'"

Master (*to Girish*): "Who can comprehend everything about God? It is not given to man to know any aspect of God, great or small. And what need is there to know everything about God? It is enough if we only realize Him. And we see God Himself if we but see His Incarnation. Suppose a person goes to the Ganges and touches its water. He will then say, 'Yes, I have seen and touched the Ganges.' To say this it is not necessary for him to touch the whole length of the river from Hardwar to Gangasagar. (*Laughter.*)

"If I touch your feet, surely that is the same as touching you. (*Laughter.*) If a person goes to the ocean and touches but a little of its water, he has surely touched the ocean itself. Fire, as an element, exists in all things, but in wood it is present to a greater degree."

Girish (*smiling*): "I am looking for fire. Naturally I want to go to a place where I can get it."

Master (*smiling*): "Yes, fire, as an element, is present more in wood than in any other object. If you seek God, then seek Him in man; He manifests Himself more in man than in any other thing. If you see a man endowed with ecstatic love, overflowing with prema, mad after God, intoxicated with His love, then know for certain that God has incarnated Himself through that man.

(*To M.*) "There is no doubt that God exists in all things; but the manifestations of His Power are different in different beings. The greatest manifestation of His Power is through an Incarnation. Again, in some Incarnations there is a complete manifestation of God's Power. It is the Shakti, the Power of God, that is born as an Incarnation."

Girish: "Narendra says that God is beyond our words and thought."

Master: "That is not altogether true. He is, no doubt, unknowable by this ordinary mind, but He can indeed be known by the pure mind. The mind and intellect become pure the moment they are free from attachment to 'woman and gold.' The pure mind and pure intellect are one and the same. God is known by the pure mind. Didn't the sages and seers of olden times see God? They realized the All-pervading Consciousness by means of their inner consciousness."

Girish (*with a smile*): "I defeated Narendra in the argument."

Master: "Oh, no! He said to me: 'When Girish Ghosh has so much faith in God's Incarnation as man, what can I say to him? It is not proper to meddle with such faith.'"

Girish (*with a smile*): "Sir, we are very free and easy with our words. But M. is sitting there with his lips shut tight. What in the world is passing through his mind? What do you say about it, sir?"

Master (*with a laugh*): "There is a common adage that tells people to beware of the following: a man with a loose tongue, a man whose mind cannot be fathomed even by an expert diver, a man who sticks the sacred tulsi-leaf in his ears as a sign of holiness, a woman wearing a long veil to proclaim her chastity, and the cold water of a reservoir covered with green scum, by bathing in which one gets typhoid fever. These are all dangerous things. (*With a smile*) But it is different with M. He is a serious man." (*All laugh.*)

Chunilal: "People have begun to whisper about M.'s conduct. The younger Naren and Baburam are his students, as are Naran, Paltu, Purna, and Tejchandra. The rumour is that he brings these boys to you and so they neglect their studies. The boys' guardians hold M. responsible."

Master: "But who would believe their words?"

Girish (*at the sight of Naran*): "There! Who told him about this? Now we realize that M. is at the root of all the mischief." (*All laugh.*)

Master (*smiling*): "Stop! Hold your tongue. There is already an evil rumour about him."

The drawing-room was full of devotees. The Master wanted to hear some songs. At his request Tarapada sang about Krishna:

> O Kesava, bestow Thy grace
> Upon Thy luckless servants here!
> O Kesava, who dost delight
> To roam Vrindavan's glades and groves!
> O Madhava, our mind's Bewitcher!
> Sweet One, who dost steal our hearts,

Sweetly playing on Thy flute!
(Chant, O Mind, the name of Hari,
Sing aloud the name of Hari,
Praise Lord Hari's name!)
O Thou Eternal Youth of Braja,
Tamer of fierce Kaliya,
Slayer of the afflicted's fear!
Beloved, with the arching eyes
And crest with arching peacock feather,
Charmer of Sri Radha's heart!
Govardhan's mighty Lifter, Thou,
All garlanded with sylvan flowers!
O Damodara, Kamsa's Scourge!
O Dark One, who dost sport in bliss
With sweet Vrindavan's gopi maids.
(Chant, O mind, the name of Hari,
Sing aloud the name of Hari,
Praise Lord Hari's name!)

Master (*to Girish*): "Ah! It is a beautiful song. Did you write it?"

A Devotee: "Yes, sir, he wrote all the songs for his play, the *Chaitanya Lila*."

Master: "This one has really hit the mark."

The devotees pressed M. to sing; but M. was shy and asked them in a whisper to excuse him.

Girish (*to the Master*): "Sir, we can't find a way to persuade M. to sing."

Master (*annoyed*): "Yes, he can bare his teeth at school, but shyness overpowers him when he is asked to sing!"

M., feeling greatly distressed, remained speechless.

Suresh Mitra, a beloved householder disciple of the Master, was seated at a distance. The Master cast an affectionate glance at him and said to him, pointing to Girish, "You talk of having lived a wild life but here is one you could not surpass."

Suresh (*with a smile*): "Yes, sir, he is my elder brother in that respect." (*All laugh*.)

Girish (*to the Master*): "Well, sir, I didn't have any education during my boyhood, but still people say I am a learned man."

Master: "Mahimacharan has studied many scriptures. A big man. (*To M.*) Isn't that so?"

M.: "Yes, sir."

Girish: "What? Book-learning? I have seen enough of it. It can't fool me anymore."

Master (*with a smile*): "Do you know my attitude? Books, scriptures, and things like that only point out the way to reach God. After finding the way, what more need is there of books and scriptures? Then comes the time for action....

"The almanac forecasts the rainfall for the year. You may squeeze the book, but you won't get a drop of water — not even a single drop." (*Laughter.*)

Girish (*smiling*): "What did you say, sir, about squeezing the almanac? Won't a single drop of water come out of it?" (*All laugh.*)

Master (*with a smile*): "The pandits talk big, but where is their mind fixed? On 'woman and gold,' on creature comforts and money. The vulture soars very high in the sky, but its eyes are fixed on the charnel-pit. It is continually looking for charnel-pits, carcasses, and dead bodies.

(*To Girish*) "Narendra is a boy of a very high order. He excels in everything: vocal and instrumental music and studies. Again, he has control over his sense-organs. He is truthful and has discrimination and dispassion. So many virtues in one person! (*To M.*) What do you say? Isn't he unusually good?"

M.: "Yes, sir, he is."

Master (*aside to M.*): "He [meaning Girish] has great earnestness and faith."

M. looked at Girish, and marvelled at his tremendous faith. Girish had been coming to Sri Ramakrishna only a short time and had already recognized his spiritual power. To M. he seemed a familiar friend and kinsman, related to him by the strong bond of spirituality. Girish was one of the gems in the necklace of the Master's devotees.

Gradually it became dusk. The shadow of evening fell on Calcutta. For the moment the noise of the busy metropolis was stilled. Gongs and conch-shells proclaimed the evening worship in many Hindu homes. Devotees of God set aside their worldly duties and turned their minds to prayer and meditation. This joining of day and night, this mystic twilight, always created an ecstatic mood in the Master.

Girish invited the Master to his house, saying that he must go there that very night.

Master: "Don't you think it will be late?"

Girish: "No, sir. You may return anytime you like. I shall have to go to the theatre tonight to settle a quarrel there."

It was nine o'clock in the evening when the Master was ready to start for Girish's house. Since Balaram had prepared supper for him, Sri

Ramakrishna said to Balaram: "Please send the food you have prepared for me to Girish's. I shall enjoy it there." He did not want to hurt Balaram's feelings.

As the Master was coming down from the second floor of Balaram's house, he became filled with divine ecstasy. He looked as if he were drunk. Narayan and M. were by his side; a little behind came Ram, Chuni, and the other devotees. No sooner did he reach the ground floor than he became totally overwhelmed. Narayan came forward to hold him by the hand lest he should miss his footing and fall. The Master expressed annoyance at this. A few minutes later he said to Narayan affectionately: "If you hold me by the hand people may think I am drunk. I shall walk by myself."

Girish's house was not far away. The Master passed the crossing at Bosepara Lane. Suddenly he began to walk faster. The devotees were left behind. Presently Narendra was seen coming from a distance. At other times the Master's joy would have been unbounded at the thought of Narendra or at the mere mention of his name; but now he did not even exchange a word with his beloved disciple.

As the Master and the devotees entered the lane where Girish lived, he was able to utter words. He said to Narendra: "Are you quite well, my child? I could not talk to you then." Every word the Master spoke was full of infinite tenderness. He had not yet reached the door of Girish's house, when suddenly he stopped and said, looking at Narendra: "I want to tell you something. 'This' is one and 'that' is another." Who could know what was passing through his innermost soul at that moment?

Girish stood at the door to welcome the Master. As Sri Ramakrishna entered the house, Girish fell at his feet and lay there on the floor like a rod. At the Master's bidding he stood up, touching the Master's feet with his forehead. Sri Ramakrishna was taken to the drawing-room on the second floor. The devotees followed him and sat down, eager to get a view of the Master and listen to every word that fell from his lips.

Many of his devotees were in the room: Narendra, Girish, Ram, Haripada, Chuni, Balaram, and M. Narendra did not believe that God could incarnate Himself in a human body. But Girish differed with him; he had the burning faith that from time to time the Almighty Lord, through His inscrutable Power, assumes a human body and descends to earth to serve a divine purpose.

The Master said to Girish, "I should like to hear you and Narendra argue in English."

The discussion began; but they talked in Bengali. Narendra said: "God is Infinity. How is it possible for us to comprehend Him? He dwells in every human being. It is not the case that He manifests Himself through one person only."

Sri Ramakrishna (*tenderly*): "I quite agree with Narendra. God is everywhere. But then you must remember that there are different manifestations of His Power in different beings. At some places there is a manifestation of His avidyasakti, at others a manifestation of His vidyasakti. Through different instruments God's Power is manifest in different degrees, greater and smaller. Therefore all men are not equal."

Ram: "What is the use of these futile arguments?"

Master (*sharply*): "No! No! There is a meaning in all this."

Girish (*to Narendra*): "How do you know that God does not assume a human body?"

Narendra: "God is 'beyond words or thought.'"

Master: "No, that is not true. He can be known by the pure buddhi, which is the same as the Pure Self. The seers of old directly perceived the Pure Self through their pure buddhi."

Girish (*to Narendra*): "Unless God Himself teaches men through His human Incarnation, who else will teach them spiritual mysteries? God takes a human body to teach men divine knowledge and divine love. Otherwise, who will teach?"

Narendra: "Why, God dwells in our own heart; He will certainly teach us from within the heart."

Master (*tenderly*): "Yes, yes. He will teach us as our Inner Guide."

Gradually Narendra and Girish became involved in a heated discussion. If God is Infinity, how can He have parts? What did Hamilton say? What were the views of Herbert Spencer, of Tyndall, of Huxley? And so forth and so on.

Master (*to M.*): "I don't enjoy these discussions. Why should I argue at all? I clearly see that God is everything; He Himself has become all. I see that whatever is, is God. He is everything; again, He is beyond everything. I come to a state in which my mind and intellect merge in the Indivisible. At the sight of Narendra my mind loses itself in the consciousness of the Absolute. (*To Girish*) What do you say to that?"

Girish (*with a smile*): "Why ask me? As if I understood everything except that one point!" (*All laugh.*)

Master: "Again, I cannot utter a word unless I come down at least two steps from the plane of samadhi. Sankara's Non-dualistic explanation of Vedanta is true, and so is the Qualified Non-dualistic interpretation of Ramanuja."

It was late at night: Girish asked Haripada to call a cab, for he had to go to the theatre. As Haripada was about to leave the room the Master said with a smile: "Mind, a cab. Don't forget to bring one." (*All laugh.*)

Haripada (*smiling*): "Yes, sir. I am going out just for that. How can I forget it?"

Girish: "That I should have to go to the theatre and leave you here!"

Master: "No, no. You must hold to both. King Janaka paid attention to both religious and worldly duties and 'drank his milk from a brimming cup.'" (*All laugh.*)

Girish: "I have been thinking of leaving the theatre to the youngsters."

Master: "No, no. It is all right. You are doing good to many."

Narendra said in a whisper, "Just a moment ago he [meaning Girish] was calling him [meaning Sri Ramakrishna] God, an Incarnation, and now he is attracted to the theatre!"

It was late in the evening. The night was dark. The devotees stood by the carriage that had been brought to take the Master to Dakshineswar. They helped him in gently, for he was still in deep ecstasy. The carriage moved down the street and they looked after it with wistful eyes.[3]

6 April 1885

Sri Ramakrishna seated himself in the drawing-room on the ground floor of Devendra's house. The devotees sat around him. It was evening. The room was well lighted. The younger Naren, Ram, M., Girish, Devendra, Akshay, Upendra, and some other devotees were present. As the Master cast his glance on a young devotee, his face beamed with joy. Pointing to the devotee, Sri Ramakrishna said to the others: "He is totally free from attachment to land, wife, and money, the three things that entangle one in worldliness. The mind that dwells on these three cannot be fixed on God. He saw a vision, too. (*To the devotee*) Tell us, what did you see?"

Devotee (*laughing*): "I saw a heap of dung. Some were seated on it, and some sat at a distance."

Master: "It was a vision of the plight of the worldly people who are forgetful of God. It shows that all these desires are disappearing from his mind. Need one worry about anything if one's mind is detached from 'woman and gold'? How strange! Only after much meditation and japa could I get rid of these desires; and how quickly he could banish them from his mind! Is it an easy matter to get rid of lust? I myself felt a queer sensation in my heart six months after I had begun my spiritual practice. Then I threw myself on the ground under a tree and wept bitterly. I said to the Divine Mother, 'Mother, if it comes to that, I shall certainly cut my throat with a knife!'

(*To the devotees*) "If the mind is free from 'woman and gold,' then what else can obstruct a man? He enjoys then only the Bliss of Brahman."

Sashi had recently been visiting Sri Ramakrishna. He was studying at the Vidyasagar College for his Bachelor's degree. The Master began to talk about him.

Master (*to the devotees*): "That boy will think of money for some time. But there are some who will never do so. Some of the youngsters will not marry."

The devotees listened silently to the Master.

Master: "It is hard to recognize an Incarnation of God unless the mind is totally free from 'woman and gold.' A man asked a seller of egg-plants the value of a diamond. He said, 'I can give nine seers of egg-plants in exchange, and not one more.'"

At these words all the devotees laughed. The younger Naren laughed very loudly. Sri Ramakrishna noticed that he had quickly understood the implication of these words.

Master: "What a subtle mind he has! Nangta also could understand things that way, in a flash — the meaning of the *Gita*, the *Bhagavata*, and other scriptures.

"Renunciation of 'woman and gold' from boyhood! Amazing indeed! It falls to the lot of a very few. A person without such renunciation is like a mango struck by a hail-stone. The fruit cannot be offered to the Deity, and even a man hesitates to eat it.

"There are people who during their youth committed many sins, but in old age chant the name of God. Well, that is better than nothing.

"The mother of a certain Mallick, who belonged to a very noble family, asked me if prostitutes would ever be saved. She herself had led that kind of life; that is why she asked the question. I said: 'Yes, they too will be saved, if only they cry to God with a yearning heart and promise not to repeat their sins.' What will the mere chanting of Hari's name accomplish? One must weep sincerely."

The kirtan began to the accompaniment of drums and cymbals. The singer was a professional. He sang about Sri Gauranga's initiation as a monk by Keshab Bharati:

Oh, what a vision I have beheld in Keshab Bharati's hut!
Gora, in all his matchless grace,
Shedding tears in a thousand streams!...

Sri Ramakrishna went into ecstasy when he heard the song. The musician sang again, describing the suffering of a milkmaid of Vrindavan at her separation from Sri Krishna. She was seeking her Krishna in the madhavi bower:

> O madhavi, give me back my Sweet One!
> Give me, give me back my Sweet One!
> Give Him back, for He is mine,
> And make me your slave forever.
> He is my life, as water is to the fish;
> O madhavi, you have hidden Him in your bosom!
> I am a simple, guileless girl,
> And you have stolen my Beloved.
> O madhavi, I die for my Sweet One;
> I cannot bear to live without Him.
> Without my Madhava I shall die;
> Oh, give Him, give Him back to me!

Now and then Sri Ramakrishna sang with the musicians, improvising lines:

> How far from here is Mathura,
> Where dwells the Beloved of my soul?

Sri Ramakrishna went into samadhi. His body was motionless. He remained in that state a long time.

Gradually he came down to the consciousness of the outer world. Still in a spiritual mood, he began to talk, sometimes addressing the devotees, sometimes the Divine Mother.

Master: "Mother, please attract him to Thee. I can't worry about him anymore. (*To M.*) My mind is inclined a little to your brother-in-law.

(*To Girish*) "You utter many abusive and vulgar words; but that doesn't matter. It is better for these things to come out. There are some people who fall ill on account of blood-poisoning; the more the poisoned blood finds an outlet, the better it is for them. At the time when the upadhi of a man is being destroyed, it makes a loud noise, as it were. Wood crackles when it burns; there is no more noise when the burning is over.

"You will be purer day by day. You will improve very much day by day. People will marvel at you.

"I may not come many more times; but that doesn't matter. You will succeed by yourself."

The Master's spiritual mood became very intense. Again he talked to the Divine Mother.

Master: "Mother, what credit is there in making a man good who is already good? O Mother, what wilt Thou accomplish by killing one who is already dead? Only if Thou canst kill a person who is still standing erect wilt Thou show Thy glory."

A Devotee: "Ram Babu has been writing about you."

Master (*smiling*): "What is he writing?"

Devotee: "He is writing an article on 'The Bhakti of the Paramahamsa.'"

Master: "Good! That will make Ram famous."

Girish (*smiling*): "He says he is your disciple."

Master: "I have no disciple. I am the servant of the servant of Rama."

Girish saluted the Master and took his leave.[4]

12 April 1885

Sri Ramakrishna was sitting with the devotees in Balaram's drawing-room in Calcutta. M. arrived at three o'clock. Girish, Balaram, the younger Naren, Paltu, Dwija, Purna, Mahendra Mukherji, and many other devotees were there. Shortly Trailokya Sannyal, Jaygopal Sen, and other members of the Brahmo Samaj arrived.

Sri Ramakrishna was describing to the devotees the various incidents of his sadhana and the phases of his spiritual realization....

Girish Chandra Ghosh used to say now and then that he could cure illness by the strength of the Master's name.

Master (*to Girish and the other devotees*): "People of small intellect seek occult powers — powers to cure disease, win a lawsuit, walk on water, and such things. But the genuine devotees of God don't want anything except His Lotus Feet. One day Hriday said to me, 'Uncle, please ask the Mother for some powers, some occult powers.' I have the nature of a child. While I was practising japa in the Kali temple, I said to Kali, 'Mother, Hriday asked me to pray to You for some occult powers.' The Divine Mother at once showed me a vision. A middle-aged prostitute, about forty years old, appeared and sat with her back to me. She had large hips and wore a black-bordered sari. Soon she was covered with filth. The Mother showed me that occult powers are as abominable as the filth of that prostitute. Thereupon I went to Hriday and scolded him, saying: 'Why did you teach me such a prayer? It is because of you that I had such an experience.'

"People with a little occult power gain such things as name and fame. Many of them want to follow the profession of guru, gain people's recognition, and make disciples and devotees. Men say of such a guru: 'Ah! He is having a wonderful time. How many people visit him! He has many disciples and followers. His house is overflowing with furniture and other things. People give him presents. He has such power that he can feed many people if he so desires.'

"The profession of a teacher is like that of a prostitute. It is the selling of oneself for the trifle of money, honour, and creature comforts. For such insignificant things it is not good to prostitute the body, mind, and soul, the means by which one can attain God. A man once said about a certain woman: 'Ah! She is having a grand time now. She is so well off! She has rented a room and furnished it with a couch, a mat, pillows, and many other things. And how many people she controls! They are always visiting her.' In other words, the woman has now become a prostitute. Therefore her happiness is unbounded. Formerly she was a maidservant in a gentleman's house; now she is a prostitute. She has ruined herself for a mere trifle.

(*To Girish, M., and the others*) "I have the nature of a child. Hriday said to me, 'Uncle, ask the Mother for some occult powers.' At once I went to the temple to ask Her about them. At that time God had put me in such a state that I had to listen to those who lived with me. I felt like a child who sees darkness all around unless someone is with him. I felt as if I should die unless Hriday was near me. You see, I am in that state of mind just now. While I am speaking to you my inner spirit is being awakened."

Sri Ramakrishna then described to Girish, M., and the other devotees his own experience of mahabhava.

Master (*to the devotees*): "My joy after that experience was equal to the pain I suffered before it. Mahabhava is a divine ecstasy; it shakes the body and mind to their very foundation. It is like a huge elephant entering a small hut. The house shakes to its foundation. Perhaps it falls to pieces....

"In that state I felt as if a ploughshare were passing through my backbone. I cried out: 'Oh, I am dying! I am dying!' But afterwards I was filled with great joy."

The devotees listened breathlessly to these experiences of the Master.

Master (*to Girish*): "But it isn't necessary for you to go so far. My experiences are for others to refer to. You busy yourself with five different things, but I have one ideal only. I do not enjoy anything but God. This is what God has ordained for me. (*Smiling*) There are different trees in the forest, some shooting up with one trunk and others spreading out with five branches. (*All smile.*)

"Yes, my experiences are for others to refer to. But you should live in the world in a spirit of detachment. You will no doubt have dirt on your body, but you must shake it off as the mudfish shakes off the mud. You may swim in the black ocean of the world, but your body should not be stained."

Girish (*smiling*): "But you too had to marry." (*Laughter.*)

Master (*smiling*): "Marriage is necessary for the sake of samskara. But how could I lead a worldly life? So uncontrollable was my divine fervour that every time the sacred thread was put around my neck it dropped off. Some believe that Sukadeva also had to marry — for the sake of samskara. They say he even had a daughter. (*All laugh.*)

"'Woman and gold' alone is the world. It makes one forget God."

Girish: "But how can we get rid of 'woman and gold'?"

Master: "Pray to God with a yearning heart. Pray to Him for discrimination. 'God alone is real and all else illusory' — this is discrimination. One strains water through a fine sieve in order to separate the dirt from it. The clear water goes through the sieve leaving the dirt behind. Apply the sieve of discrimination to the world. Live in the world after knowing God. Then it will be the world of vidya.

"Just see the bewitching power of women! I mean the women who are the embodiment of avidya, the power of delusion. They fool men, as it were. They take away their inner substance....

"If a woman says to her husband, 'Go there,' he at once stands up, ready to go. If she says, 'Sit down here,' immediately he sits down.

"All are deluded by 'woman and gold.' But I do not care for it at all. And I swear to you that I do not know anything but God."

A Devotee: "Sir, a new sect named 'Nava Hullol' has been started. Lalit Chatterji is one of the members."

Master: "There are different views. All these views are but so many paths to reach the same goal. But everyone believes that his view alone is right, that his watch alone keeps correct time."

Girish (*to M.*): "Do you remember what Pope says about it?

'Tis with our judgments as our watches, none
Go just alike, yet each believes his own."

Master (*to M.*): "What does it mean?"

M.: "Everyone thinks that his own watch keeps the correct time. But different watches do not give the same time."

Master: "But however wrong the watches may be, the Sun never makes a mistake. One should check one's watch with the sun." ...

Master: "If you want to realize God, then you must cultivate intense dispassion. You must renounce immediately what you feel to be standing in your way. You should not put it off till the future. 'Woman and gold' is the obstruction. The mind must be withdrawn from it."...

Girish was reading a life of Keshab written by Trailokya of the Brahmo Samaj. In it Trailokya said that at first Sri Ramakrishna had been very much opposed to the world but that after meeting Keshab he had changed his mind and had come to believe that one could lead a spiritual life in the world as well. Several devotees had told the Master about this. They wanted to discuss it with Trailokya. Those passages in the book had been read to the Master.

Noticing the book in Girish's hand, Sri Ramakrishna said to Girish, M., Ram, and the other devotees: "Those people are busy with the world. That is why they set such a high value on worldly life. They are drowned in 'woman and gold.' One doesn't talk that way after realizing God. After enjoying divine bliss, one looks on the world as crow-droppings. At the very outset I utterly renounced everything. Not only did I renounce the company of worldly people, but now and then the company of devotees as well. I noticed that the devotees were dropping dead one by one, and that made my heart writhe with pain. But now I keep one or two of them with me."

Girish left for home, saying he would come back.

Trailokya arrived with Jaygopal Sen.

Girish returned. Sri Ramakrishna introduced him to Trailokya. He asked them to talk to each other.

It was about dusk. Sri Ramakrishna was surrounded by the devotees.

As evening came on, lamps were lighted in the drawing-room and on the veranda. Sri Ramakrishna bowed to the Divine Mother and began to chant the name of God. The devotees sat around and listened to his sweet chanting. They wanted to discuss with Trailokya his remarks about the Master's change of opinion on worldly life. Girish started the discussion.

Girish (*to Trailokya*): "You have written that, after coming in contact with Keshab, Sri Ramakrishna changed his views about worldly life; but it isn't true."

Master (*to Trailokya and the other devotees*): "If a man enjoys the Bliss of God, he doesn't enjoy the world. Having tasted divine bliss, he finds the world insipid. If a man gets a shawl, he doesn't care for broadcloth."

Trailokya: "I referred to those who wanted to lead a worldly life. I didn't mean renouncers."

Master: "What are you talking about? People talk about leading a religious life in the world. But if they once taste the bliss of God they will not enjoy anything else. Their attachment to worldly duties declines. As their spiritual joy becomes deeper, they simply cannot perform their worldly duties. More and more they seek that joy. Can worldly pleasures and sex pleasures be compared to the bliss of God? If a man once tastes that bliss he runs after it ever afterwards. It matters very little to him then whether the world remains or disappears.

"After the bliss of God nothing else tastes good. Then talk about 'woman and gold' stabs the heart, as it were. (*Intoning*) 'I cannot enjoy the talk of worldly people.' When a man becomes mad for God, he doesn't enjoy money or such things."

Trailokya: "But, sir, if a man is to remain in the world, he needs money and he must also save. He has to give in charity and —"

Master: "What? Do you mean that one must first save money and then seek God? And you talk about charity and kindness! A worldly man spends thousands of rupees for his daughter's marriage. Yet, all the while, his neighbours are dying of starvation; and he finds it hard to give them two morsels of rice; he calculates a thousand times before giving them even that much. The people around him have nothing to eat; but what does he care about that? He says to himself: 'What can I do? Let the rascals live or die. All I care about is that the members of my family should live well.' And they talk about doing good to others!"

Trailokya remained silent. M. said aside to Girish, "Then what he has written is not true."

Girish (*to Trailokya*): "Then what you have written is not true."

Trailokya: "Why so? Doesn't he [meaning Sri Ramakrishna] admit that a man can lead a spiritual life in the world?"

Master: "Yes, he can. But such a man should first of all attain Knowledge and then live in the world. First he should realize God. Then 'he can swim in a sea of slander and not be stained.' After realizing God, a man can live in the world like a mudfish. The world he lives in after attaining God is the world of vidya. In it he sees neither woman nor gold. He finds there only devotion, devotee, and God. You see, I too have a wife, and a few pots and pans in my room; I too feed a few vagabonds; I too worry about the devotees — Habi's mother for instance — when they come here."

A Devotee (*to Trailokya*): "I have read in your book that you do not believe in the Incarnation of God. You said so in connection with Chaitanya."

Trailokya: "Why, Chaitanya himself protested against the idea of Divine Incarnation. Once, in Puri, Advaita and the other devotees sang a song to the effect that Chaitanya was God. At this Chaitanya shut the door of his room. Infinite are the glories of God. As he [meaning Sri Ramakrishna] says, the devotee is the parlour of God. Suppose a parlour is very well furnished; does that mean that the master of the house has exhausted all his power and splendour in that one parlour?"

Girish: "He [meaning Sri Ramakrishna] says that prema alone is the essence of God; we need the man through whom this ecstatic love of God flows. He says that the milk of the cow flows through the udder; we need the udder; we do not care for the other parts of the cow — the legs, tail, or horns."

Trailokya: "The milk of God's prema flows through an infinite number of channels. God has infinite powers."

Girish (*to Trailokya*): "Do you believe in the Incarnation of God?"

Trailokya: "God incarnates Himself through His devotees alone. There cannot be a manifestation of infinite powers. It simply isn't possible. It is impossible for any man to manifest infinite powers."

Girish: "You can serve your children as 'Brahma Gopala.' Then why isn't it possible to worship a great soul as God?"

Master (*to Trailokya*): "Why all this bother about infinity? If I want to touch you, must I touch your entire body? If you want to bathe in the Ganges, must you touch the whole river from Hardwar down to the ocean?

"'All troubles come to an end when the ego dies.' As long as a trace of 'I-consciousness' remains, one is conscious of difference. Nobody knows what remains after the 'I' disappears. Nobody can express it in words. That which *is* remains. After the 'I' disappears one cannot say that a part manifests through this man and the rest through another. Satchidananda is the ocean. The pot of 'I' is immersed in it. As long as the pot exists, the water seems to be divided into two parts: one part inside the pot and the other part outside it. But when the pot is broken there is only one stretch of water. One cannot even say that. Who would say that?"

After the discussion Sri Ramakrishna became engaged in pleasant conversation with Trailokya.

Master: "You are happy. Isn't that so?"

Trailokya: "But I shall become my old self again as soon as I leave this place. Here I feel very much the awakening of spiritual consciousness."

It was about nine o'clock in the evening. Balaram took Trailokya to another room and gave him refreshments. Sri Ramakrishna began to tell the devotees about Trailokya and people of his views.

Master (*to Girish, M., and the other devotees*): "Do you know what these people are like? They are like a frog living in a well, who has never seen the outside world. He knows only his well; so he will not believe that there is such a thing as the world. Likewise, people talk so much about the world because they have not known the joy of God.

(*To Girish*) "Why do you argue with them so much? They busy themselves with both — the world and God. One cannot understand the joy of God unless one has tasted it. Can anybody explain sex pleasure to a five-year-old boy? Worldly people talk about God only from hearsay. Children, hearing their old aunts quarrelling among themselves, learn to say, 'There is my God,' 'I swear by God.'

"But that doesn't matter. I don't blame such people. Can all comprehend the Indivisible Satchidananda? Only twelve rishis could recognize Ramachandra. All cannot recognize an Incarnation of God. Some take him for an ordinary man, some for a holy person, and only a few recognize him as an Incarnation."

The devotees listened breathlessly to these words about the mystery of Divine Incarnation.[5]

24 April 1885

Sri Ramakrishna was about to go to the house of Girish, who had arranged a festival to celebrate the Master's coming. The Master came down from the second floor of Balaram's house with M. and a few other devotees. Near the gate he saw a beggar chanting the name of Rama, and he stood still. He fell into a meditative mood and remained standing a few minutes. He said to M., "He sings well." A devotee gave the beggar four pice.

Sri Ramakrishna entered Bosepara Lane. Laughing, he said to M.: "What are these people saying? 'There comes Paramahamsa's battalion!' What these fools say!" (*All laugh.*)

Sri Ramakrishna entered Girish's house. The latter had invited a large number of devotees to join the festival. Many of them were present. They all stood up to receive the Master, who, smiling, took his seat. The devotees sat around him. Among them were Girish, Mahimacharan, Ram, and Bhavanath, and also Baburam, Narendra, Jogin, the younger Naren, Chuni, Balaram, M., and the other devotees who had accompanied the Master from Balaram's house.

Master (*to Mahimacharan*): "I said to Girish about you, 'There is one — very deep. You are only knee-deep.' Now you must help me check up on what I said. I want to see you two argue. But don't compromise." (*All laugh.*)

Girish and Mahimacharan started their discussion. Soon Ram said: "Let them stop. Let us have some kirtan."

Master (*to Ram*): "No, no! This has a great deal of meaning. They are 'Englishmen.' I want to hear what they say."

Mahimacharan contended that all could become Krishna by means of sadhana. Girish said that Sri Krishna was an Incarnation of God. However much a man practised sadhana, he could never be an Incarnation.

Mahima: "Do you know what I mean? Let me give an illustration. The bel-tree can become a mango-tree if only the obstructions are removed. It can be done by the practice of yoga."

Girish: "You may say whatever you like, but it cannot be done either by the practice of yoga or by anything else. Only a Krishna can become Krishna. If anybody has all the attributes of another person, Radha for instance, then he is none other than that person — Radha herself. If I see in a person all the attributes of Krishna, then I shall conclude that I am seeing Krishna Himself."

Mahimacharan could not argue well. At last he had to accept Girish's views.

Mahima (*to Girish*): "Yes, sir, both views are right. God has willed the path of knowledge. He has also willed the path of bhakti. (*Pointing to Sri Ramakrishna*) As he says, by different paths people ultimately reach one and the same goal."

Master (*aside to Mahima*): "You see, what I said was right, wasn't it?"

Mahima: "Yes, sir. As you say, both paths are right."

Master (*pointing to Girish*): "Haven't you noticed how deep his faith is? He forgot to eat his refreshments. Like a dog, he would have torn your throat if you hadn't accepted his view. But we have enjoyed the discussion. You two have known each other and I myself have learnt many things."

Girish (*to the Master*): "Sir, what is *ekangi prema*?"

Master: "It means one-sided love. For instance, the water does not seek the duck, but the duck loves water. There are other kinds of love: *sadharani*, *samanjasa*, and *samartha*. In the first, which is ordinary love, the lover seeks his own happiness; he doesn't care whether the other person is happy or not. That was Chandravali's attitude toward Krishna. In the second, which is a compromise, both seek each other's happiness. This is a noble kind of love. But the third is the highest of all. Such a lover says to his beloved, 'Be happy yourself, whatever may happen to me.' Radha had this highest love. She was happy in Krishna's happiness. The gopis, too, had attained this exalted state." ...

Girish conducted Sri Ramakrishna and the devotees to the roof, where the meal was served. There was a bright moon in the sky. The devotees took their seats. The Master occupied a seat in front of them. All were in a joyous mood.[6]

9 May 1885

It was about three o'clock in the afternoon. Sri Ramakrishna sat in Balaram's drawing-room in a happy mood. Many devotees were present. Narendra, M., Bhavanath, Purna, Paltu, the younger Naren, Girish, Ram, Binode, Dwija, and others sat around him.

Narendra: "How can I believe, without proof, that God incarnates Himself as a man?"

Girish: "Faith alone is sufficient. What is the proof that these objects exist here? Faith alone is the proof."

A Devotee: "Have philosophers been able to prove that the external world exists outside us? But they say we have an irresistible belief in it."

Girish (*to Narendra*): "You wouldn't believe, even if God appeared before you. God Himself might say that He was God born as a man, but perhaps you would say that He was a liar and a cheat."

The conversation turned to the immortality of the gods.

Narendra: "What is the proof of their immortality?"

Girish: "You wouldn't believe it even if the gods appeared before you."

Narendra: "That the immortals existed in the past requires proof."

M. whispered something to Paltu.

Paltu (*smiling, to Narendra*): "What need is there for the immortals to be without beginning? To be immortal one need only be without end."

Master (*smiling*): "Narendra is the son of a lawyer, but Paltu of a deputy magistrate." (*All laugh.*)

The discussion continued. Narendra was arguing. He was then slightly over twenty-two years of age.

Narendra (*to Girish, M., and others*): "How am I to believe in the words of scripture? The *Mahanirvana Tantra* says, in one place, that unless a man attains the Knowledge of Brahman he goes to hell; and the same book says, in another place, that there is no salvation without the worship of Parvati, the Divine Mother. Manu writes about himself in the *Manusamhita*; Moses describes his own death in the Pentateuch.

"The Samkhya philosophy says that God does not exist, because there is no proof of His existence. Again, the same philosophy says that one must accept the Vedas and that they are eternal.

"But I don't say that these are not true. I simply don't understand them. Please explain them to me. People have explained the scriptures according to their fancy. Which explanation shall we accept? White light coming through a red medium appears red, through a green medium, green."

A Devotee: "The Gita contains the words of God."

Master: "Yes, the Gita is the essence of all scriptures. A sannyasi may or may not keep with him another book, but he always carries a pocket Gita."

A Devotee: "The Gita contains the words of Krishna."

Narendra: "Yes, Krishna or any fellow for that matter!"

Sri Ramakrishna was amazed at these words of Narendra.

Master: "This is a fine discussion. There are two interpretations of the scriptures: the literal and the real. One should accept the real meaning alone — what agrees with the words of God.

The conversation again turned to Divine Incarnation.

Narendra: "It is enough to have faith in God. I don't care about what He is doing or what He hangs from. Infinite is the universe; infinite are the Incarnations."

As Sri Ramakrishna heard the words, "Infinite is the universe; infinite are the Incarnations," he said with folded hands, "Ah!"

A Devotee: "The Brahmos say that a man should perform his worldly duties. He must not renounce them."

Girish: "Yes, I saw something like that in their paper, the *Sulabha Samachar*. But a man cannot even finish all the works that are necessary for him in order to know God, and still he speaks of worldly duties."

Sri Ramakrishna smiled a little, looked at M., and made a sign with his eye, as if to say, "What he says is right."

Master: "A man attains Brahmajnana as soon as his mind is annihilated. With the annihilation of the mind dies the ego, which says 'I,' 'I.'

"Each ego may be likened to a pot. Suppose there are ten pots filled with water, and the sun is reflected in them. How many suns do you see?"

A Devotee: "Ten reflections. Besides, there certainly exists the real Sun."

Master: "Suppose you break one pot. How many suns do you see now?"

Devotee: "Nine reflected suns. But there certainly exists the real sun."

Master: "All right. Suppose you break nine pots. How many suns do you see now?"

Devotee: "One reflected sun. But there certainly exists the real sun."

Master (*to Girish*): "What remains when the last pot is broken?"

Girish: "That real sun, sir."

Master: "No. What remains cannot be described. What *is* remains. How will you know there is a real sun unless there is a reflected sun? 'I-consciousness' is destroyed in samadhi. A man climbing down from samadhi to the lower plane cannot describe what he has seen there." ...

Bhavanath (*smiling*): "Ordinary men are like the third-class passengers on a railway train. When the doors of their compartments are locked, they have no way to get out."

Girish: "If a man is so strongly tied hand and foot, then what is his way?"

Master: "He has nothing to fear if God Himself, as the guru, cuts the chain of maya."[7]

14 July 1885

About eleven o'clock the devotees saluted the Master and were departing one by one.

Master: "You may all go. (*Pointing to Narendra and the younger Naren*) It will be enough if these two stay. (*To Girish*) Will you eat your supper at home? You may stay a few minutes if you want to. You want a smoke! But Balaram's servant is just like his master. Ask him for a smoke; he won't give it! (*All laugh.*) But don't go away without having your smoke."

Girish had brought with him a bespectacled friend. The latter observed all these things and left the place. Sri Ramakrishna said to Girish: "I say this to you and to everyone: Please do not force anybody to come here. Nothing happens except at the right time."[8]

15 July 1885

Sri Ramakrishna was talking with the devotees in the small room in Balaram's house. Mahendra, Balaram, Tulasi, Haripada, Girish, and other devotees were sitting on the floor.

Girish (*smiling*): "I am examining your horoscope."

Master (*smiling*): "I was born on the second day of the bright fortnight of the moon. My horoscope shows the positions of the sun, the moon, and Mercury at the time of my birth. There are not many more details."

Girish: "You were born under Kumbha [Aquarius]. Rama and Krishna were born under Karkat [Scorpio] and Brisha [Taurus], and Chaitanya under Simha [Leo]."

Master: "I had two desires: first, that I should be the king of the devotees; and second, that I should not be a dry sadhu."

Girish (*smiling*): "Why did you have to practise spiritual discipline?"

Master (*smiling*): "Even the Divine Mother had to practise austere sadhana to obtain Siva as Her husband. She practised the panchatapa. She would also immerse Her body in water in wintertime, and look fixedly at the sun. Krishna Himself had to practise much sadhana. I had many mystic experiences, but I cannot reveal their contents. Under the bel-tree I had many flaming visions. There I practised the various sadhanas prescribed in the Tantra. I needed many articles — human skulls, and so forth and so on. The Brahmani used to collect these things for me. I practised a number of mystic postures.

"I had another strange experience: if I felt egotistic on a particular day, I would be sick the following day."

M. sat motionless as a picture on canvas, hearing about these unique visions of the Master. The other devotees also were spellbound. There was a dead silence in the room.[9]

1 September 1885

It was the sacred Janmasthami Day, the birthday of Krishna. Ram and other devotees had brought new clothes for Sri Ramakrishna. He put them on and looked charming.

Girish Ghosh arrived in a carriage with one or two friends. He was drunk. He was weeping as he entered the room. He wept as he placed his head on Sri Ramakrishna's feet.

Sri Ramakrishna affectionately patted him on the back. He said to a devotee, "Prepare a smoke for him."

Girish raised his head and said with folded hands: "You alone are the Perfect Brahman! If that is not so then everything is false.

"It is such a pity that I could not be of any service to you." He uttered these words with a tenderness that made several devotees weep.

Girish continued: "O Lord! Please grant me the boon that I may serve you for a year. Who cares for salvation? One finds it everywhere. I spit on it. Please tell me that you will accept my service for one year."

Master: "People around here are not good. Some may criticize you."

Girish: "I don't care. Please tell — "

Master: "All right. You may serve me when I go to your house — "

Girish: "No, it is not that. I want to serve you here."

Girish was insistent. The Master said, "Well, that depends on God's will."

Referring to the Master's throat trouble, Girish said: "Please say, 'Let it be cured.' All right, I shall thrash it out. Kali! Kali!"

Master: "You will hurt me."

Girish: "O throat, be cured! (*He blows at the throat like an exorciser.*) Are you not all right? If you aren't cured by this time, you certainly will be if I have any devotion to your feet. Say that you are cured."

Master (*sharply*): "Leave me alone. I can't say those things. I can't ask the Divine Mother to cure my illness.

"All right. I shall be cured if it is the will of God."

Girish: "You are trying to fool me. All depends on your will."

Master: "Shame! Never say that again. I look on myself as a devotee of Krishna, not as Krishna Himself. You may think as you like. You may look on your guru as God. Nevertheless, it is wrong to talk as you are talking. You must not talk that way again."

Girish: "Please say you will be cured."

Master: "Very well, if that pleases you."

Girish was still under the influence of drink. Now and then he said to Sri Ramakrishna, "Well, sir, how is it that you were not born this time with your celestial beauty?"

A few moments later he said, "I see, this time it will be the salvation of Bengal."

A devotee said to himself: "Why Bengal alone? It will be the salvation of the whole world."

Girish said, addressing the devotees: "Does any of you understand why he is here? It is for the liberation of men. Their suffering has moved him to assume a human body."

The coachman was calling Girish. He got up and was going towards the man. The Master said to M.: "Watch him. Where is he going? I hope he won't beat the coachman!" M. accompanied Girish.

Presently Girish returned. He prayed to Sri Ramakrishna and said, "O God, give me purity that I may not have even a trace of sinful thought."

Master: "You are already pure. You have such faith and devotion! You are in a state of joy, aren't you?"

Girish: "No, sir. I feel bad. I have worries. That is why I have drunk so much liquor."

A few minutes afterwards Girish said: "Lord, I am amazed to find that I, even I, have been given the privilege of serving the Perfect Brahman. What austerities have I practised to deserve this privilege?"

Sri Ramakrishna took his midday meal. On account of his illness he ate very little.

The Master's natural tendency of mind was to soar into the plane of God-Consciousness. He would force his mind to be conscious of the body.

But, like a child, he was incapable of looking after his body. Like a child he said to the devotees: "I have eaten a little. I shall rest now. You may go out for a little while." Sri Ramakrishna rested a few minutes. The devotees returned to the room.

Girish: "The guru and the Ishta. I like very much the form of the guru. I am not afraid of him. Why should it be so? I am afraid of ecstasy. At the sight of ecstasy I run away."

Master: "He who is the Ishta appears in the form of the guru. The aspirant practises meditation on a corpse. When he obtains the vision of his Chosen Ideal, it is really the guru who appears to him and says, 'This is that,' that is to say, he points out to the disciple his Ishta. Uttering these words, the guru disappears into the form of the Ishta. The disciple no longer sees the guru. In the state of perfect jnana, who is the guru and who is the sishya [disciple]? 'That creates a very difficult situation; there the teacher and the disciple do not see each other.'"

A Devotee: "Guru's head and disciple's feet."

Girish (*joyously*): "Yes! Yes! It is true."

Navagopal: "But listen to its meaning. The disciple's head belongs to the guru; and the guru's feet belong to the disciple. Do you understand?"

Girish: "No, that is not the meaning. Haven't you seen the child climbing on the head of the father? That is why the disciple's feet are mentioned."

Navagopal: "But then the disciple must feel like a young baby."

Master: "There are two classes of devotees. One class has the nature of the kitten. The kitten depends completely on its mother. It accepts whatever its mother does for it. The kitten only cries, 'Mew, mew!' It doesn't know what to do or where to go....

"There is another class of devotees. They have the nature of the young monkey. The young monkey clings to its mother with might and main. The devotees who behave like the young monkey have a slight idea of being the doer.

"The farther you advance, the more you will see that there are other things even beyond the sandal-wood forest — mines of silver and gold and precious gems. Therefore go forward."[10]

18 October 1885

Sri Ramakrishna was talking with M. about Dr. Sarkar. M. had been at the doctor's house the previous day to report the Master's condition.

Master: "What did you talk about?"

M.: "Dr. Sarkar is keenly interested in Girish Ghosh. He always asks me whether Girish has given up drinking. He keeps a sharp eye on him."

Master: "Did you tell Girish about that?"

M.: "Yes, sir, I did. And I also told him about giving up drinking."

Master: "What did he say?"

M.: "He said: 'Since you all say so, I take your words as the words of the Master himself. But I won't promise anything.'"

Master (*joyously*): "Kalipada told me that he had altogether given up drinking."

It was afternoon. Dr. Sarkar arrived accompanied by his son Amrita and Hem. Narendra and other devotees were present.

In Dr. Sarkar's opinion, God created men and ordained that every soul should make infinite progress. He would not believe that one man was greater than another. That was why he did not believe in the doctrine of Divine Incarnation.

Doctor: "I believe in infinite progress.... Incarnation! What is that? To cower before a man who excretes filth! It is absurd. But if you speak of a man as the reflection of God's Light — yes, that I admit."

Girish (*smiling*): "But you have not seen God's Light."

Dr. Sarkar was hesitating before giving a reply. A friend who sat near him whispered something into his ear.

Doctor (*to Girish*): "You too have not seen anything but a reflection."

Girish: "I see It! I see the Light! I shall prove that Sri Krishna is an Incarnation of God or I shall cut out my tongue!"

Master: "All this is useless talk. It is like the ravings of a delirious patient. A delirious patient says, 'I shall drink a whole tank of water; I shall eat a whole pot of rice.' The physician says: 'Yes, yes. You will have all these. We shall give you whatever you want when you are convalescent.'

"There are signs of Perfect Knowledge. One is that reasoning comes to an end."[11]

22 October 1885

[Sri Ramakrishna had been moved to a house in Shyampukur, Calcutta.]

It was Thursday evening, a few days after the Durga Puja. Sri Ramakrishna sat on his bed in his room on the second floor, with Dr. Sarkar, Ishan, and other devotees....

The conversation turned to the performance of a drama by Girish Ghosh called *The Life of Buddha*. The doctor had seen the play and been much pleased with it.

Doctor (*to Girish*): "You are a very bad man. Must I go to the theatre every day?"

Master (*to M.*): "What does he say? I don't quite understand."

M.: "The doctor liked the play very much."

Master (*to Ishan*): "Why don't you say something? (*Pointing to the doctor*) He does not believe that God can incarnate Himself in a human form."

Ishan: "What shall I say, sir? I don't like to argue anymore."

Master (*sharply*): "Why? Won't you say the right thing?"

Ishan (*to the doctor*): "Our faith is shallow on account of our pride."

Master (*to the doctor*): "It is very difficult to understand that God can be a finite human being and at the same time the all-pervading Soul of the universe. The Absolute and the Relative are His two aspects. How can we say emphatically with our small intelligence that God cannot assume a human form? Can we ever understand all these ideas with our little intellect? Can a one-seer pot hold four seers of milk?"

Doctor: "I accept as much as I want to. All difficulties come to an end if only God reveals His true nature to the seeker. Then there can be no confusion. How can I accept Rama as an Incarnation of God? Take the example of His killing Vali, the monkey chieftain. He hid Himself behind a tree, like a thief, and murdered Vali. This is how a man acts, and not God."

Girish: "But, sir, such an action is possible only for God."

Doctor: "Then take the example of His sending Sita into exile."

Girish: "This too, sir, is possible only for God, not for man."

Master (*laughing*): "It is not mentioned in his 'science' that God can take human form; so how can he believe it? (*All laugh.*)

"Listen to a story. A man said to his friend, 'I have just seen a house fall down with a terrific crash.' Now, the friend to whom he told this had received an English education. He said: 'Just a minute. Let me look it up in the newspaper.' He read the paper but could not find the news of a house falling down with a crash. Thereupon he said to his friend: 'Well, I don't believe you. It isn't in the paper; so it is all false.'" (*All laugh.*)

Girish (*to the doctor*): "You must admit that Krishna is God. I will not let you look on Him as a mere man. You must admit that He is either God or a demon."

Master: "Unless a man is guileless, he cannot so easily have faith in God. God is far, far away from the mind steeped in worldliness. Worldly intelligence creates many doubts and many forms of pride — pride of learning, wealth, and the rest. (*Pointing to the doctor*) But he is guileless."

Girish (*to the doctor, with a smile*): "You have already spent three or four hours here. What about your patients?"

Doctor: "Well, my practice and patients! I shall lose everything on account of your paramahamsa!" (*All laugh.*)[12]

23 October 1885

It was evening. Sri Ramakrishna was seated on his bed, thinking of the Divine Mother and repeating Her hallowed name. The devotees sat near him in silence. Latu, Sashi, Sarat, the younger Naren, Paltu, Bhupati, Girish, and others were present. Ramtaran of the Star Theatre had come with Girish to entertain Sri Ramakrishna with his singing. A few minutes later Dr. Sarkar arrived.

Doctor (*to the Master*): "I was much worried about you last night at three o'clock. It was raining. I said to myself, 'Who knows whether or not the doors and windows of his room are shut?'"

"Really?" said Sri Ramakrishna. He was much pleased at the doctor's love and thoughtfulness for him.

Girish (*to the devotees*): "Pandit Shashadhar said to him [meaning the Master]: 'Please bring your mind to bear on the body during samadhi. That will cure your illness.' And he, the Master, saw in a vision that the body was nothing but a loose mass of flesh and bones."

Master: "Once, a long time ago, I was very ill. I was sitting in the Kali temple. I felt like praying to the Divine Mother to cure my illness, but couldn't do so directly in my own name. I said to Her, 'Mother, Hriday asks me to tell You about my illness.' I could not proceed any farther. At once there flashed into my mind the museum of the Asiatic Society, and a human skeleton strung together with wire. I said to Her, 'Please tighten the wire of my body like that, so that I may go about singing Your name and glories.' It is impossible for me to ask for occult powers."

Ramtaran began to sing:

Behold my vina, my dearly beloved,
My lute of sweetest tone;
If tenderly you play on it,
The strings will waken, at your touch,
To rarest melodies.
Tune it neither low nor high,
And from it in a hundred streams
The sweetest sound will flow;
But over-slack the strings are mute,
And over-stretched they snap in twain.

Doctor (*to Girish*): "Is it an original song?"
Girish: "No, it is an adaptation from Edwin Arnold."
Ramtaran sang from the play, *The Life of Buddha*:

We moan for rest, alas! but rest can never find;
We know not whence we come, nor where we float away.
Time and again we tread this round of smiles and tears;
In vain we pine to know whither our pathway leads,
And why we play this empty play.

We sleep, although awake, as if by a spell bewitched;
Will darkness never break into the light of dawn?
As restless as the wind, life moves unceasingly:
We know not who we are, nor whence it is we come;
We know not why we come, nor where it is we drift;
Sharp woes dart forth on every side.
How many drift about, now gay, now drowned in tears!
One moment they exist; the next they are no more.
We know not why we come, nor what our deeds have been,
Nor, in our bygone lives, how well we played our parts;
Like water in a stream, we cannot stay at rest;
Onward we flow for evermore.

Burst Thou our slumber's bars, O Thou that art awake!
How long must we remain enmeshed in fruitless dreams?
Are you indeed awake? Then do not longer sleep!
Thick on you lies the gloom fraught with a million woes.
Rise, dreamer, from your dream, and slumber not again!
Shine forth, O Shining One, and with Thy shafts of light
Slay Thou the blinding dark! Our only Saviour Thou!
We seek deliverance at Thy feet.

As Sri Ramakrishna listened to the song he went into samadhi.

Girish (*to the doctor*): "Well, sir, does it ever happen to you that, though you do not intend to come here, you are drawn as if by a subtle force? I feel that way; that is why I am asking you."

Doctor: "I don't know whether I feel that. But the heart alone knows the promptings of the heart. (*To Sri Ramakrishna*) Besides, there isn't much use in speaking about it."[13]

26 October 1885

It was about one o'clock in the afternoon when the doctor and M. entered the Master's room on the second floor. Sri Ramakrishna sat there, smiling as usual, completely forgetful of the fatal illness, which was eating his life away. Among the many devotees in the room were Girish, the younger Naren, and Sarat.

Master: "Once I said to Mathur Babu: 'Don't think that I have achieved my desired end because you, a rich man, show me respect. It matters very little to me whether you obey me or not.' Of course you must remember that a mere man can do nothing. It is God alone who makes one person obey another. Man is straw and dust before the power of God."

Doctor: "Do you think I shall obey you because a certain fisherman obeyed you?... Undoubtedly I show you respect; I show you respect as a man."

Master: "Do I ask you to show me respect?"

Girish: "Does he ask you to show him respect?"

Doctor (*to the Master*): "What are you saying? Do you explain it as the will of God?"

Master: "What else can it be? What can a man do before the will of God?"

Doctor: "If everything is done by the will of God, then why do you chatter? Why do you talk so much to bring knowledge to others?"

Master: "He makes me talk; therefore I talk. 'I am the machine and He is the Operator.'"

Doctor: "You say that you are the machine. That's all right. Or keep quiet, knowing that everything is God."

Girish (*to the doctor*): "Whatever you may think, sir, the truth is that we act because He makes us act. Can anyone take a single step against the Almighty Will?"

Doctor: "But God has also given us free will. I can think of God, or not, as I like."

Girish: "You think of God or do some good work because you like to. Really it is not you who do these things, but your liking of them that makes you do so."

Doctor: "Why should that be so? I do these things as my duty."

Girish: "Even then it is because you like to do your duty."

Doctor: "Suppose a child is being burnt. From a sense of duty I rush to save it."

Girish: "You feel happy to save the child; therefore you rush into the fire. It is your happiness that drives you to the action. A man eats opium being tempted by such relishes as puffed rice or fried potatoes." (*Laughter.*)

Master: "A man must have some kind of faith before he undertakes a work. Further, he feels joy when he thinks of it. Only then does he set about performing the work. Suppose a jar of gold coins is hidden underground. First of all a man must have faith that the jar of gold coins is there. He feels joy at the thought of the jar. Then he begins to dig. As he removes the earth he hears a metallic sound. That increases his joy. Next he sees a corner of the jar. That gives him more joy. Thus his joy is ever on the increase. Standing on the porch of the Kali temple, I have watched the ascetics preparing their smoke of hemp. I have seen their faces beaming with joy in anticipation of the smoke."

Doctor: "But take the case of fire. It gives both heat and light. The light no doubt illumines objects, but the heat burns the body. Likewise, it is not an unadulterated joy that one reaps from the performance of duty. Duty has its painful side too."

M. (*to Girish*): "As the proverb goes: 'If the stomach gets food, then the back can bear a few blows from the host.' There is joy in sorrow also."

Girish (*to the doctor*): "Duty is dry."

Doctor: "Why so?"

Girish: "Then it is pleasant." (*All laugh.*)

M.: "Again we come to the point that one likes opium for the sake of the relishes that are served with it."

Girish (*to the doctor*): "Duty must be pleasant; or why do you perform it?"

Doctor: "The mind is inclined that way."

M. (*to Girish*): "That wretched inclination draws the mind. If you speak of the compelling power of inclination, then where is free will?"

Doctor: "I do not say that the will is absolutely free. Suppose a cow is tied with a rope. She is free within the length of that rope, but when she feels the pull of the rope —"

Girish (*to the doctor*): "How do you know that free will exists?"

Doctor: "Not by reasoning; I feel it."

Girish: "In that case I may say that I and others feel the reverse. We feel that we are controlled by another." (*All laugh.*)[14]

27 October 1885

It was half past five in the afternoon when Dr. Sarkar came to the Master's room at Syampukur, felt his pulse, and prescribed the necessary medicine. Many devotees were present, including Narendra, Girish, Dr. Dukari, the younger Naren, Rakhal, M., Sarat, and Shyam Basu.

Girish and Dr. Sarkar began to talk about the Science Association established by the latter.

Master: "Will you take me there one day?"

Doctor: "If you go there you will lose all consciousness at the sight of the wondrous works of God."

Master: "Oh, indeed!"

Doctor (*to Girish*): "Whatever you may do, please do not worship him as God. You are turning the head of this good man."

Girish: "What else can I do? Oh, how else shall I regard a person who has taken me across this ocean of the world, and what is still more, the ocean of doubt? There is nothing in him that I do not hold sacred. Can I ever look on even his excreta as filthy?"

Doctor: "This question of excreta doesn't bother me. I too have no feeling of repugnance. Once a grocer's child was brought to my office for treatment. His bowels moved there. All covered their noses with cloths; but I sat by his side for half an hour without putting a handkerchief to my nose. Besides, I cannot cover my nose when the scavenger passes by me with a tub on his head. No, I cannot do that. I know very well that there is no difference between a scavenger and myself. Why should I look down on him? Can't I take the dust of his [meaning Sri Ramakrishna's] feet? Look here."

The doctor saluted Sri Ramakrishna and touched the Master's feet with his forehead.

Girish: "Oh, the angels are saying, 'Blessed, blessed be this auspicious moment!'"

Doctor: "What is there to marvel at in taking the dust of a man's feet? I can take the dust of everybody's feet. Give me, all of you, the dust of your feet."

The doctor touched the feet of all the devotees.

Narendra (*to the doctor*): "We think of him [meaning the Master] as a person who is like God. Do you know, sir, what it is like? There is a point between the vegetable creation and the animal creation where it is very difficult to determine whether a particular thing is a vegetable or an animal. Likewise, there is a stage between the man-world and the God-world where it is extremely hard to say whether a person is a man or God."

Doctor: "Well, my dear young friend, one cannot apply analogies to things divine."

Narendra: "I do not say that he is God. What I am saying is that he is a godlike man."

Doctor: "One should suppress one's feelings in such a matter. It is bad to give vent to them. Alas! No one understands my own feelings. Even my best friend thinks of me as a stern and cruel person. Even people like you will perhaps one day throw me out after beating me with your shoes."

Master: "Don't say such a thing! They love you so much! They await your coming as eagerly as the bridesmaids in the bridal chamber await the coming of the groom."

Girish: "Everyone has the greatest respect for you."

Doctor: "My son and even my wife think of me as a hard-hearted person. My only crime is that I do not display my feelings."

Girish: "In that case, sir, it would be wise for you to open the door of your heart, at least out of pity for your friends; for you see that your friends cannot otherwise understand you."

Doctor: "Will you believe me when I say that my feelings get worked up even more than yours? (*To Narendra*) I shed tears in solitude.

(*To Sri Ramakrishna*) "Well, may I say something? When you are in ecstasy you place your foot on others' bodies. That is not good."

Master: "Do you think I know at that time that I am touching another with my foot?"

Doctor: "You feel that it is not the right thing to do, don't you?"

Master: "How can I explain to you what I experience in samadhi? After coming down from that state I think, sometimes, that my illness may be due to samadhi. The thing is, the thought of God makes me mad. All this is the result of my divine madness. How can I help it?"

Doctor: "Now he accepts my view. He expresses regret for what he does. He is conscious that the act is sinful."

Master (*to Narendra*): "You are very clever. Why don't you answer? Explain it all to the doctor."

Girish (*to the doctor*): "Sir, you are mistaken. He is not expressing regret for touching the bodies of his devotees during samadhi. His own body is pure, untouched by any sin. That he touches others in this way is for their good. Sometimes he thinks that he may have got this illness by taking their sins upon himself.

"Think of your own case. Once you suffered from colic. Didn't you have regrets at that time for sitting up and reading till very late at night? Does that prove that reading till the late hours of the night is, in itself, a bad thing? He [meaning Sri Ramakrishna] too may be sorry that he is ill. But that does not make him feel that it is wrong on his part to touch others for their welfare."

Dr. Sarkar felt rather embarrassed and said to Girish: "I confess my defeat at your hands. Give me the dust of your feet." He saluted Girish.

Doctor (*to Narendra*): "Whatever else one may say about him [meaning Girish], one must admit his intellectual powers."

Narendra (*to the doctor*): "You may look at the thing from another standpoint. You can devote your life to scientific research without giving a thought to your health or comfort. But the Science of God is the grandest of all sciences. Isn't it natural for him to risk his health to realize Him?"

Doctor: "All religious reformers, including Jesus, Chaitanya, Buddha, and Muhammed, were in the end filled with egotism. They all said, 'Whatever I say is alone true.' How shocking!"

Girish (*to the doctor*): "Now, sir, you are committing the same mistake. You are accusing them all of egotism. You are finding fault with them. For that very reason you too can be accused of egotism."

Dr. Sarkar remained silent.

Narendra (*to the doctor*): "We offer worship to him bordering on divine worship."

At these words the Master laughed like a child.[15]

6 November 1885

It is the dark night of the new moon. At seven o'clock the devotees make arrangements for the worship of Kali in Sri Ramakrishna's room on the second floor. Flowers, sandal-paste, vilwa-leaves, red hibiscus, rice pudding, and various sweets and other articles of worship are placed in front of the Master. The devotees are sitting around him. There are present, among others, Sarat, Sashi, Ram, Girish, Chunilal, M., Rakhal, Niranjan, and the younger Naren.

Sri Ramakrishna asks a devotee to bring some incense. A few minutes later he offers all the articles to the Divine Mother. M. is seated close to him. Looking at M., he says to the devotees, "Meditate a little." The devotees close their eyes.

Presently Girish offers a garland of flowers at Sri Ramakrishna's feet. M. offers flowers and sandal-paste. Rakhal, Ram, and the other devotees follow him.

Niranjan offers a flower at Sri Ramakrishna's feet, crying: "Brahmamayi! Brahmamayi!" and prostrates himself before him, touching the Master's feet with his head. The devotees cry out, "Jai Ma!", "Hail to the Mother!"

In the twinkling of an eye Sri Ramakrishna goes into deep samadhi. An amazing transformation takes place in the Master before the very eyes of the devotees. His face shines with a heavenly light. His two hands are raised in the posture of granting boons and giving assurance to the devotees; it is the posture one sees in images of the Divine Mother. His body is motionless; he has no consciousness of the outer world. He sits facing the north. Is the Divine Mother of the Universe manifesting Herself through his person? Speechless with wonder, the devotees look intently at Sri Ramakrishna, who appears to them to be the embodiment of the Divine Mother Herself.

The devotees begin to sing hymns, one of them leading and the rest following in chorus.

Girish sings:

Who is this Woman with the thick black hair,
Shining amidst the assembly of the gods?
Who is She, whose feet are like crimson lotuses
Planted on Siva's chest?
Who is She, whose toenails shine like the full moon,
Whose legs burn with the brightness of the sun?
Who is She, who now speaks soft and smiles on us,
And now fills all the quarters of the sky
With shouts of terrible laughter?

Again:

O Mother, Saviour of the helpless, Thou the Slayer of sin!
In Thee do the three gunas dwell — sattva, rajas, and tamas.
Thou dost create the world; Thou dost sustain it and destroy it;
Binding Thyself with attributes, Thou yet transcendest them;
For Thou, O Mother, art the All....

Gradually Sri Ramakrishna came back to the consciousness of the outer world. He asked the devotees to sing "O Mother Syama, full of the waves of drunkenness divine." They sang:

O Mother Syama, full of the waves of drunkenness divine!
Who knows how Thou dost sport in the world?
Thy fun and frolic and Thy glances put to shame the god of love....

When this song was over, Sri Ramakrishna asked the devotees to sing "Behold my Mother playing with Siva." The devotees sang:

Behold my Mother playing with Siva, lost in an ecstasy of joy!
Drunk with a draught of celestial wine, She reels, and yet She does not fall....

Sri Ramakrishna tasted a little pudding to make the devotees happy, but immediately went into deep ecstasy.

A few minutes later the devotees prostrated themselves before the Master and went into the drawing-room. There they enjoyed the prasad.[16]

16 April 1886

[On Friday, 11 December 1885, Sri Ramakrishna had been moved to a beautiful house at Cossipore, a suburb of Calcutta.]

The moon was shining brilliantly, flooding the garden paths, the trees, and the water of the lake with its white rays. Girish, M., Latu, and a few other devotees were seated on the steps leading to the lake. The house stood to the west of the lake. A lamp burnt in the Master's room on the second floor. Sri Ramakrishna was sitting on his bed. There were several devotees in the room.

A few minutes later Girish and M. were strolling along a garden path lined with flowering plants and fruit-trees.

M.: "How beautiful this moonlight is! Perhaps nature has had the same laws from time out of mind."

Girish: "How do you know that?"

M.: "There is no change in the uniformity of nature. European scientists have been discovering new stars through the telescope. There are mountains on the moon; they have seen them."

Girish: "It is difficult to be sure of that. It is hard for me to believe it."

M.: "Why? The mountains have been observed through the telescope."

Girish: "How can you be sure that they have been rightly observed? Suppose there are other things between the moon and the earth. Light passing through them may conjure up such visions."

Girish, Latu, and M. went to Sri Ramakrishna's room and found him sitting on the bed. Sashi and one or two devotees had been tending the Master. Baburam, Niranjan, and Rakhal also entered the room. It was a large room. Some medicines and a few other accessories were kept near the bed. One entered the room by a door at the north end.

That evening Sri Ramakrishna was somewhat better. The devotees saluted the Master and sat down on the floor. The Master asked M. to bring the lamp near him. He greeted Girish cordially.

Latu: "M. wept bitterly last night at the sight of some books that had belonged to his dead child. His wife is almost mad with grief. She sometimes treats her other children violently. She creates a scene at home because he spends the night here now and then."

Sri Ramakrishna seemed worried to hear of this.

Girish: "It is nothing to be wondered at. Even after receiving the instruction of the Bhagavad Gita, Arjuna fainted from grief at the death of his son Abhimanyu."

The devotees were sitting about, and M. was fanning Sri Ramakrishna.

Girish (*to the Master*): "Deven Babu has decided to renounce the world."

On account of his illness Sri Ramakrishna could hardly talk. Touching his lips with his finger, he asked Girish, by signs, "Who will feed his wife and children?"

Girish: "I don't know."

The other devotees remained silent.

Girish: "Sir, which is wiser — to renounce the world regretfully, or to call on God, leading a householder's life?"

Master (*to M.*): "Haven't you read the Gita? One truly realizes God if one performs one's worldly duties in a detached spirit, if one lives in the world after realizing that everything is illusory.

"Those who regretfully renounce the world belong to an inferior class.

"Do you know what a householder jnani is like? He is like a person living in a glass house. He can see both inside and outside."

Again there was silence in the room.

Girish (*to the Master*): "Sir, my mind is now on a very lofty plane. Why does it come down again?"

Master: "That always happens when one leads a worldly life. Sometimes the householder's mind goes up; sometimes it goes down. Sometimes he feels a great deal of devotion; sometimes he feels less. This happens because he lives in the midst of 'woman and gold.' Sometimes a householder contemplates God or chants His name, and sometimes he diverts his mind to 'woman and gold.' He is like an ordinary fly, which now sits on a sweetmeat and now on filth or rotting sores.

"But it is quite different with sannyasis. They are able to fix their minds on God alone, completely withdrawing them from 'woman and gold.' They can enjoy the Bliss of God alone. A man of true renunciation cannot enjoy anything but God. He leaves any place where people talk of worldly things; he listens only to spiritual talk. A man of true renunciation never speaks about anything but God. The bees light only on flowers, in order to sip honey; they do not enjoy anything else."

Master (*to M.*): "A man needs the grace of God to fix his whole mind on Him."

Master (*to Girish*): "Rakhal has now understood what is good and what is bad, what is real and what is unreal. He lives with his family, no doubt, but he knows what it means. He has a wife. And a son has been born to him. But he has realized that all these are illusory and impermanent. Rakhal will never be attached to the world.

"He is like a mudfish. The fish lives in the mud, but there is not the slightest trace of mud on its body."

Girish: "Sir, I don't understand all this. You can make everyone pure and unattached if you want to. You can make everyone good, whether he is a worldly man or a sannyasi. The Malaya breeze, I believe, turns all trees into sandal-wood."

Master: "Not unless there is substance in them. There are a few trees, the cotton-tree for instance, which are not turned into sandal-wood."

Girish: "I don't care."

Master: "But this is the law."

Girish: "But everything about you is illegal."

The devotees were listening to this conversation in great amazement. Every now and then the fan in M.'s hand stopped moving.

Master: "Yes, that may be true. When the river of bhakti overflows, the land all around is flooded with water to the depth of a pole.

"When a man is inebriated with divine love, he doesn't abide by the injunctions of the Vedas. He picks durva grass for the worship of the Deity, but he doesn't clean it. He picks whatever he lays his hands on. While gathering tulsi-leaves he even breaks the branches. Ah! what a state of mind I passed through!

(*To M.*) "When one develops love of God, one needs nothing else."

M.: "Yes, sir."

A crazy woman used to accompany Vijay Goswami to the Kali temple at Dakshineswar and sing for Sri Ramakrishna. Her songs were about Kali. She also used to sing the songs of the Brahmo Samaj. The devotees called her "Pagli" and tried to keep her away from the Master.

Master (*to Girish and the others*): "Pagli cherishes the attitude of madhur towards me. One day she came to Dakshineswar. Suddenly she burst out crying. 'Why are you crying?' I asked her. And she said, 'Oh, my head is aching!' (*All laugh.*) Another day I was eating when she came to Dakshineswar. She suddenly said, 'Won't you be kind to me?' I had no idea of what was passing through her mind, and went on eating. Then she said, 'Why did you push me away mentally?' I asked her, 'What is your attitude?' She said, 'Madhur.' 'Ah!' I said. 'But I look on all women as manifestations of the Divine Mother. All women are mothers to me.'

Thereupon she said, 'I don't know all that.' Then I called Ramlal and said to him: 'Ramlal, listen to her! What is she talking about — this "pushing away mentally"?' Even now she keeps up that attitude."

Girish: "Blessed indeed is Pagli! Maybe she is crazy. Maybe she is beaten by the devotees. But she meditates on you twenty-four hours a day. No matter how she meditates on you, no harm can ever befall her.

"Sir, how can I express my own feelings about it? Think what I was before, and what I have become now by meditating on you! Formerly I was indolent; now that indolence has turned into resignation to God. Formerly I was a sinner; now I have become humble. What else can I say?"

Master (*to Girish*): "'Woman and gold' alone is the world. Many people regard money as their very life-blood. But however you may show love for money, one day, perhaps, every bit of it will slip from your hand.

"They alone make good use of their money who spend it for the worship of God or the service of holy men and devotees. Their money bears fruit.

"I cannot eat anything offered by physicians. I mean those who traffic in human suffering. Their money is blood and pus."

Sri Ramakrishna mentioned two physicians in this connection.

Girish: "Dr. Rajendra Dutta is a generous person. He doesn't accept a penny from anybody. He gives away money in charity."[17]

23 April 1886

It was afternoon. Many devotees were sitting in the Master's room. Narendra, Sarat, Sashi, Latu, Nityagopal, Girish, Ram, M., and Suresh were present.

Kedar came in. This was his first visit to the Master for some time. While staying in Dacca, in connection with his official duties, he had heard of Sri Ramakrishna's illness. On entering Sri Ramakrishna's room he took the dust of the Master's feet on his head and then joyously gave it to the others. The devotees accepted it with bowed heads. As he offered it to Sarat, the latter himself took the dust of Sri Ramakrishna's feet. M. smiled. The Master also smiled, looking at M. The devotees sat without uttering a word. Sri Ramakrishna seemed about to go into an ecstatic mood. Now and then he breathed heavily as if trying to suppress his emotion. He said to Kedar, by a sign, "Argue with Girish."

Girish said to Kedar: "Sir, I beg your pardon. At first I did not know who you were. That is why I argued with you. But now it is quite different."

Sri Ramakrishna smiled.

The devotees had brought various food offerings for the Master and placed them in front of him. Sri Ramakrishna put a grain on his tongue and gave the plate to Surendra. He asked Surendra to distribute the prasad to the devotees. Surendra went downstairs with the offerings.

M. was fanning Sri Ramakrishna. The Master said to him, "Won't you eat anything?" He sent M. downstairs.

It was about dusk. Girish and M. were strolling near the small reservoir in the garden.

Girish: "I understand that you are writing something about the Master. Is it true?"

M.: "Who told you that?"

Girish: "I have heard about it. Will you give it to me?"

M.: "No, I won't part with it unless I feel it is right to do so. I am writing it for myself, not for others."

Girish: "What do you mean?"

M.: "You may get it when I die."[18]

Chapter 19

The Power of Attorney

Ramakrishna accepted Girish's "power of attorney" and saved him from his self-destructive life. This act was significant for both men: Ramakrishna revealed his redemptive powers and Girish showed all human beings that one can be freed from sin by completely surrendering to God.

When a person is completely incapable of dealing with his or her legal or business affairs, due to disability or illness, he or she gives the power of attorney to a highly trusted person. The power of attorney is "a legal instrument authorizing one to act as the attorney or agent of the grantor either generally for the management of a specified business or enterprise or more often specifically for the accomplishment of a particular transaction."[1]

In the last stage of spiritual life, one's ego vanishes and self-surrender arises. God takes responsibility for devotees who have become egoless and can no longer manage their own affairs. As babies depend completely on their parents, so at this stage devotees depend only on God. When Arjuna surrendered to Krishna, the latter said: "Abandon all dharmas and come to Me alone for shelter. I will deliver you from all sins; do not grieve."[2] Christ also said: "Come unto me, all ye that labour and are heavy laden, and I will give you rest."[3]

In *The Gospel of Sri Ramakrishna*, M. describes how Ramakrishna taught his devotees to give their power of attorney to God. Although Ramakrishna knew some English words, in lieu of "power of attorney" he used the Bengali words *ām-moktāri* (according to the Bengali *Gospel* recorded by M.), and *vakalmā* (according to the Bengali *Lilaprasanga* written by Swami Saradananda). Before the British came to India, the Muslims ruled India for several centuries and introduced many Arabic, Urdu, and Farsi words in their legal system. *Vakalmā* is an Arabic word and the word *ām-moktāri* is of Farsi origin. Gradually those Arabic and Farsi words were incorporated into Bengali and other Indian languages.

The Power of Attorney   313

On 8 April 1883 a man who had lost his son came to Ramakrishna for consolation. The Master said to him: "What can you do? Be ready for Death. Death has entered the house. You must fight him with the weapon of God's holy name. God alone is the Doer. I say: 'O Lord, I do as Thou doest through me. I speak as Thou speakest through me. I am the machine and Thou art the Operator. I am the house and Thou art the Indweller. I am the engine and Thou art the Engineer.' Give your power of attorney to God. One doesn't come to grief through letting a good man assume one's responsibilities. Let His will be done.

"House, wife, and children are all transitory; they have only a momentary existence. The palm-tree alone is real. One or two fruits have dropped off. Why lament?

"God is engaged in three kinds of activity: creation, preservation, and destruction. Death is inevitable. All will be destroyed at the time of dissolution. Nothing will remain. At that time the Divine Mother will gather up the seeds for the future creation, even as the elderly mistress of the house keeps in her hotchpotch-pot little bags of cucumber seeds, 'seafoam,' blue pills, and other miscellaneous things. The Divine Mother will take Her seeds out again at the time of the new creation."[4]

On 27 December 1883 a devotee said: "We do not have time to pray to God."

Master: "That is true. Nothing comes to pass except at the right time....

"Surrender everything at the feet of God. What else can you do? Give Him the power of attorney. Let Him do whatever He thinks best. If you rely on a great man, he will never injure you.

"It is no doubt necessary to practise spiritual discipline; but there are two kinds of aspirants. The nature of the one kind is like that of the young monkey, and the nature of the other kind is like that of the kitten. The young monkey, with great exertion, somehow clings to its mother. Likewise, there are some aspirants who think that in order to realize God they must repeat His name a certain number of times, meditate on Him for a certain period, and practise a certain amount of austerity. An aspirant of this kind makes his own efforts to catch hold of God. But the kitten, of itself, cannot cling to its mother. It lies on the ground and cries, 'Mew, mew!' It leaves everything to its mother. The mother cat sometimes puts it on a bed, sometimes on the roof behind a pile of wood. She carries the kitten in her mouth hither and thither. The kitten doesn't know how to cling to the mother. Likewise, there are some aspirants who cannot practise spiritual discipline by calculating about japa or the period of meditation.

All that they do is cry to God with yearning hearts. God hears their cry and cannot keep Himself away. He reveals Himself to them."[5]

On 2 February 1884, a devotee asked Ramakrishna, "Sir, what is the way?"

Master: "Discrimination between the Real and the unreal. One should always discriminate to the effect that God alone is real and the world unreal. And one should pray with sincere longing."

Devotee: "But, sir, where is our leisure for these things?"

Master: "Those who have the time must meditate and worship. But those who cannot possibly do so must bow down whole-heartedly to God twice a day. He abides in the hearts of all; He knows that worldly people have many things to do. What else is possible for them? You don't have time to pray to God; therefore give Him the power of attorney. But all is in vain unless you attain God and see Him."[6]

On 19 October 1884 a member of the Brahmo Samaj who was a court judge, said: "Sir, I am a sinner. How can I say that God dwells in me?"

Master: "That's the one trouble with you Brahmos. With you it is always sin and sin! That's the Christian view, isn't it? Once a man gave me a Bible. A part of it was read to me, and it was full of that one thing — sin and sin! One must have such faith that one can say: 'I have uttered the name of God; I have repeated the name of Rama or Hari. How can I be a sinner?' One must have faith in the glory of God's name."

Judge: "Sir, how can one have such faith?"

Master: "Have passionate love for God. Pray to God in secret and with yearning, that you may have that passionate attachment and devotion to Him. Shed tears for Him. A man sheds a jugful of tears because his wife is sick or because he is losing money or because he is worrying about getting a job. But tell me, who ever weeps for God?"

Trailokya: "Sir, where is people's leisure? They must serve their English masters."

Master: "Well, then give God the power of attorney. If a man entrusts his affairs to a good person, will the latter do him any harm? With all the sincerity of your heart resign yourself to God and drive all your worries out of your mind. Do whatever duties He has assigned to you."[7]

In spiritual life, it is necessary to surrender to God completely in order to give Him the power of attorney. Giving Ramakrishna his power of attorney helped Girish overcome the grief that he suffered from after his wife and son passed away. As far as we know, Ramakrishna only took Girish's power of attorney, because he knew that there was no hypocrisy in Girish's self-surrender. News spread that the Master had accepted the power of attorney for Girish and relieved him of all of his responsibilities. This meant that Girish no longer had to practise spiritual disciplines — the Master would do everything for him. It is the nature of human beings to follow the easiest method they can find. Some of the Master's devotees began to imitate Girish without understanding the serious implications of what he had done.

*   *   *

In *Sri Ramakrishna and His Divine Play,* Swami Saradananda explained the mystery of the power of attorney:

[It seems] after he had visited the Master a few times, Girish Chandra Ghosh completely surrendered to him one day and asked, "Sir, what shall I do from now on?"

The Master: "Do just what you are doing now. Hold on to God with one hand and to the world with the other. Afterwards, when one side [the world] falls to pieces, whatever is ordained to happen will happen. At a minimum, think of God in the morning and evening." After saying this the Master looked at Girish as if waiting for his reply.

Girish thought sadly: "The type of work I do does not allow me to keep fixed hours for bathing, eating, or sleeping. I shall surely forget to remember God in the morning and evening. This is a difficult situation. If I disobey my guru's order, I will incur sin — which will cause me harm. So how can I make that promise? It is definitely wrong to fail to keep one's promise to a person in this world. How much worse it will be if I cannot keep my promise to a person whom I have accepted as my spiritual guide."

Girish was hesitant to express these thoughts. Again he reflected: "The Master did not ask me to do a very difficult task. If he had asked someone else to do this, that person would have gladly agreed to it right away." What could Girish do? As he reflected on his own outgoing tendencies, he realized that it was beyond his capacity to practise even that little spiritual discipline daily. Again, as he examined his own nature, he felt suffocated at the mere thought of being bound forever to a particular vow or to a rule; he knew he would have no peace of mind until that rule was broken. This had happened all through his life. He had no problem doing good or bad according to his will, but the moment he felt that he was under any sort of compulsion to do any work, his mind would rebel and turn away from doing it. Realizing his own powerless and helpless condition, he humbly kept quiet, unable to say either "I shall do so," or "I cannot." How could he shamelessly declare that he would not be able to perform such an easy task? And if he did admit this, how would the

Master and others react? They probably wouldn't understand his utterly helpless condition, and might think, without expressing it, that his silence was mere pretension.

Finding Girish silent, the Master read his mind and said, "Well, if you cannot do that, then remember God before you eat and before you sleep."

But Girish remained silent. He wondered how he could do even that. Some days he ate lunch at 10:00 a.m. and some days at 5:00 p.m., and the same irregularity continued with his dinner. Again, sometimes he was troubled with litigation. On those days he would not realize that he was eating at all. He would then be anxiously thinking: "I have not received confirmation that the fee I sent to the barrister reached him on time. If he cannot appear in court as scheduled, it will be a disaster," and so on. In truth, if such an occasion occurred — and it was not impossible — then on that day he would certainly forget to think of God.

Alas, the Master was asking him to do such a simple thing and he was unable to agree to do it. Girish was in an embarrassing situation, but he remained calm and silent even though a tempest of anxiety, fear, and despondency was blowing in his mind. The Master looked at Girish again and said to him with a smile: "So you are unwilling to agree even to this. All right. Give me your power of attorney." Immediately the Master went into ecstasy!

This was to his liking and Girish felt greatly relieved. In addition, thinking of the Master's infinite compassion, his heart swelled with overwhelming love and faith in him. Girish thought: "What a relief! I will not be trapped by the bondage of rules, which are like dreadful tigers to me. Now whatever I do, I shall have firm faith that the Master will save me somehow or other through his infinite divine power." This was the way Girish at that time understood the power of attorney, which meant surrendering all of his responsibility to the Master. He thought that he would not have to make any effort to give up anything or to practise spiritual disciplines; rather, the Master would use his own power to remove all worldly thoughts from his mind.

At that time Girish did not realize that he had willingly put a noose of love around his own neck that was a hundred times stronger than the bondage of rules, which he considered unbearable. Neither did he understand completely, nor did he have the power to foresee, that no matter what came into his life — good or bad, praise or blame, joy or suffering — he would be able to do nothing but silently bear it. All other thoughts disappeared from his mind, and he felt only the infinite grace of Sri Ramakrishna. And his ego swelled a hundredfold because of this relationship with Sri Ramakrishna. He thought: "Let people say whatever they like about me; let them look down upon me; the Master is mine always and in all circumstances. What else is needed? Of whom should I be afraid?" He did not know then that according to the devotional scripture such an ego is a kind of spiritual practice that comes to a person as a result of great fortune. However, Girish was now reassured. While he was eating, lying, or sitting, he had only one thought: "Sri Ramakrishna has taken full responsibility for me." He could not realize that this thought was constantly making his mind meditate on Sri Ramakrishna and putting the Master's impression on his every action and thought, changing him radically. He was very happy, because he knew that Sri Ramakrishna loved him and that he was more than his own.

The Master always taught, "Never disturb another's faith," and he would behave with each devotee accordingly. Knowing of Girish's new attitude of self-surrender, the Master began to train him with this in mind. One day while in the Master's presence, Girish said "I shall do this," regarding a trifling matter. Immediately the Master said: "What is this? You must not talk in that dogmatic way. Suppose you fail to do it! Say 'I shall do this if God wills.'" Girish understood: "That's right. When I have given all of my responsibilities to God and He has accepted them, I shall be able to do that work if He thinks that I should and that it is good for me." Henceforward, he began to shun the idea of ego and such expressions as "I shall do," "I shall go," and so on.

Thus the days rolled on. The Master passed away. Girish faced grief and pain as he also lost his wife and son. But at every point his mind reminded him as before: "Sri Ramakrishna has allowed these things to happen because they are good for you. You gave your responsibility to him and he accepted it. He did not give you any written assurance regarding the path on which he would lead you. Now he is leading you along this path, considering it to be easy for you. You have no reason to refuse it nor any right to complain. Did you make an empty promise when you gave him the power of attorney and transferred your responsibility to him?" Thus as time passed Girish began to understand more and more the hidden meaning of the power of attorney. Did he now comprehend its whole meaning? When asked about this, Girish replied: "There is still much to understand! Did I realize then that there was so much mystery in the power of attorney? Now I see that there is a limit to the time one must spend practising meditation, japa, and austerities, but the work of a person who has given the power of attorney is unending. Now he has to watch every step and with every breath determine whether he is depending on God and performing those actions by His power or by the power of his own rascal ego!"

Various thoughts arise in our minds in the context of the power of attorney. We find in the religious history of the world that some great teachers like Jesus and Chaitanya sometimes gave assurances of this kind to a few people. Ordinary gurus do not have the ability to accept that responsibility, nor do they have the right to do so. Ordinary teachers or monks can at best instruct others by giving them a mantra or a specific spiritual practice, which can help them to make spiritual progress. Or by leading a pure life, they can inspire others to become more pure. When a person who is entangled in worldly bondage and is completely helpless is instructed to do a certain thing, that person says in despair: "How can I do that? If you give me the power, I can try." It is beyond the capacity of an ordinary guru to help such a person. It is impossible for one person to say to another, "I am taking on the responsibility for your bad karma, and I shall accept its consequences on your behalf." When spirituality declines in human hearts, God incarnates out of compassion, suffers on behalf of the people, and redeems them from the whirlpool of maya. Although He does that, He does not completely absolve humanity. He makes individuals put forth some self-effort so that they may learn. As the Master used to say: "By the grace of the avatars, a person finishes the sufferings of ten lives in one."

One day when the Master was being treated [for throat cancer] at Shyampukur in Calcutta, he saw that his subtle body had left his gross body and was moving around. The Master said: "I saw some wounds on the back of its [his gross body's] throat. I wondered why this had happened. The Divine Mother then showed me: People commit all kinds of sins and then touch this body. And out of compassion for their misery, I take on the results of their evil deeds. That is why I have this (*pointing to his throat*). Otherwise, why should this body suffer from disease? It has never done anything wrong." We were dumbfounded. We wondered at the fact that one could make a person advance in spiritual life by accepting the results of that person's bad karma! Hearing the Master's words, some thought out of love for him: "Alas! Why have we touched the Master after committing all sorts of sinful acts such as lying, cheating, and so on? He is suffering so much from this cancer and undergoing this excruciating pain because of us! We will never again touch the Master's divine body."

It seems as though it would be easy to give the power of attorney, as if one were handing an object over to another. Human beings are slaves to their passions, so they seek opportunities to satisfy themselves even while practising religion. Constantly they look for ways in which they may have both worldly pleasures and divine bliss. They consider sense enjoyments to be sweet, like nectar. If they even consider having to give them up, they see emptiness all around. They wonder how they can live without them. So they get excited when they hear that one can give the power of attorney in the spiritual world, and they think of this as a wonderful thing. They say: "Let us enjoy worldly pleasures to our heart's content by any means — such as stealing, cheating, or robbing — and let Chaitanya, Jesus, or Sri Ramakrishna look after our happiness in the hereafter. Someday we shall die." They do not understand that such a thought is nothing but the deception of a wicked mind. They do not realize that in this way they are continually deceiving themselves. They are just rushing headlong towards destruction, putting blinders over their eyes so that they will not have to see the terrible forms of their own wicked deeds. They cannot envision the day when someone will remove those blinders and force them to understand that they are in great danger. Ultimately they will realize that nobody accepts the power of attorney for hypocrites. Ah, human beings! How many ways you deceive yourselves and think that you have won! And hail Mahamaya, the great enchantress! What an illusion You have created in human minds!

Is the power of attorney so easily given? The condition of giving the power of attorney arises as a result of zeal and perseverance; only then does a person give it. At that time God accepts responsibility for him or her. Only after people have run around seeking happiness in this world, only to find that they have been clutching at shadows; only after they have practised meditation, japa and austerities, only to realize deep within themselves that the Infinite God cannot be bought by means of those spiritual disciplines; only after they have resolved to make a path through a mountain by indomitable self-effort, only to feel utterly helpless — only then do they cry piteously: "Where are you, Lord? Please protect us." And only then does God accept their power of attorney.

But I do not like to practise spiritual disciplines or pray to God; I love to follow my wanton impulses. And if anybody protests against this, I say: "What is wrong? I have given the power of attorney to God. He is making me act that way — what can I do? Why does He not change my mind?" This kind of attitude towards the power of attorney just deceives others as well as oneself. It leads a person to lose both here and hereafter.

This subject can be understood better if it is discussed from another standpoint. All right, we understand that you have given the power of attorney and have no need to practise spiritual disciplines or to pray to God. But if you truly give the power of attorney, the feeling of God's infinite compassion will constantly rise within the deepest recesses of your heart. You will feel as if you had been drowning in the ocean of worldliness, and that now God in His mercy has rescued you. When you experience that, just imagine how much your love and devotion for Him will flow. Your heart will be filled with love and gratitude; you will constantly think of Him and repeat His name. And you will not need anybody to remind you to do so. Even a vicious creature like a snake becomes a pet to the one who gives it shelter, and it will not bite anyone in that household. Is your heart worse than a snake that it still has not been filled with gratitude and love for Him who has accepted responsibility for you here and hereafter? Therefore, after giving the power of attorney, if you find that you do not like to call on God, you have not truly given the power of attorney and He has not taken responsibility for you either. Do not deceive yourself by saying, "I have given the power of attorney" and then imposing the sins of your wrongdoings on the sinless, immaculate God. Such an ominous attitude would be very harmful to you. Please remember the Master's story of the brahmin who killed a cow.

With great effort and care, a brahmin created a beautiful garden. He planted various kinds of flowering plants and fruit trees, and his joy knew no bounds when he saw their luxuriant growth. One day, finding the gate open, a cow entered the garden and began to eat the plants. The brahmin was away on business. When he returned, he saw that the cow was eating his plants. In a rage he attacked the cow with a staff and hit her on a vital spot, killing her instantly. Now the brahmin became afraid: He had just killed a cow, which to a Hindu is the gravest of all sins. The brahmin had studied a little Vedanta, and he had learned that each of the human senses performs its respective functions by means of the power of a particular deity. For example, the eyes see with the power of the sun god, the ears hear with the power of the wind god, the hands work with the power of Indra [the king of gods], and so on. Remembering this, the brahmin thought: "Then I am not the one who killed the cow. My hands move by the power of Indra, so it is Indra who has killed the cow." Thus firmly convinced, the brahmin was reassured.

Now the sin of cow killing came to enter the brahmin's body, but his mind drove the sin away, saying: "Get away, you have no place here. Indra has killed the cow, so go to Him." The sin then went to seize Indra. Indra told the sin: "Please wait awhile. Let Me go and talk to the brahmin a little; then you can take Me." Indra then assumed a human form and entered the brahmin's garden. He saw the man nearby tending to his trees and plants. As Indra walked slowly towards the brahmin, He began to praise the beauty of the garden so that the brahmin could hear. Indra said: "Ah! What a beautiful garden! These trees are planted with great taste! Each one is in its proper place." As He thus talked about the garden, Indra reached the brahmin and asked: "Sir, do you know whose garden this is? Who has planted these trees so neatly and artistically?" Listening to this praise of his garden, the brahmin replied joyfully: "Sir, this is my garden. I have planted all these trees. Please come, let me show you around." He showed Indra his garden in detail and told Him many stories about the plants. Then inadvertently they came to the spot where the dead cow was. Startled, Indra asked: "Oh God! Who has killed this cow?" So far the brahmin had said about his garden, "I have done this; I have done that." And now when he was asked who had killed the cow, he was terribly embarrassed and kept quiet. Then Indra reassumed His real form and said to the brahmin: "You hypocrite! You have done what is best in the garden, yet it is I who have killed the cow! Is that so? Now accept the sin of your cow killing." With that Indra disappeared and the sin seized the brahmin's body.[8]

* * *

Girish used to say: "For one who has a guru, no sin can touch him and he doesn't need to practise any sadhana."[9] Girish expressed this idea of the power of attorney in the following scene from his play on Shankaracharya (5:2):

Shantiprada: "Oh my guru, please give me a little power so that I can understand properly."

Shankara: "My child, it is necessary to practise sadhana. First practise sadhana and then you will understand."

Shantiprada: "Please, you do sadhana for me. You are asking me to control my mind by practising sadhana. I can't do that. My mind works fine, but the moment I try to control it by closing my eyes, the whole world seems to revolve. Tell me, how I can practise sadhana with such a mind? This I have understood, and I like this attitude: 'The root of meditation is the guru's form; the root of worship is the guru's feet; the root of the mantra is the guru's word; and the root of liberation is the guru's grace.' I bow down to you with this hymn; now, you do whatever you like."

Shankara: "My child, you have realized the truth. One attains this conviction after the practice of many sadhanas. The knowledge of Brahman is now in your hands."[10]

Girish's faith increased a thousandfold after giving his power of attorney to the Master. Kiran Chandra Datta recalled Girish's heroic attitude: "I heard him say: 'Do you know that servant of seven generations?* I hired Him without paying Him any monthly salary. Whenever I call, He comes immediately. Listen, His name is God.' Whoever calls on God finds Him. Whether in the past, present, or future, if one calls on God, He reveals Himself to that person. Girish developed this intense faith after giving [Ramakrishna] his power of attorney."[11]

---

*Girish meant that as a hereditary servant obeys his master, so God obeys His devotee.

Chapter 20

Days with Ramakrishna

It is said that if a person takes one step towards God, God takes ten steps towards that person. It was not just that Girish sought out Ramakrishna; to a greater extent it was Ramakrishna who searched for Girish, as he was meant to play a vital role in his divine drama.

Long before he met Girish, Ramakrishna had a vision concerning him: "One day, when I was meditating in the Kali temple, I saw a naked boy skipping into the temple. He had a tuft of hair on the crown of his head, and was carrying a flask of wine under his left arm and a vessel of nectar in his right hand. 'Who are you?' I asked. 'I am Bhairava [the chief of Shiva's hosts],' he replied. On my asking the reason for his coming, he answered, 'To do your work.' Years later when Girish came to me, I recognized that Bhairava in him."[1]

When the Master's devotees asked him not to associate with Girish because of his drunkenness and wayward life, Ramakrishna replied: "Girish's life will not be affected by those shortcomings that you are talking about. He is born as a part of Bhairava. He will delight in celestial maidens, behave like the villain Ravana, and again worship Lord Rama."[2]

Girish hated hypocrisy. Being bold and strong in character, he did not find it necessary to hide his weaknesses, and he despised those who attempted to do so. It takes tremendous courage to unite mind and speech, especially to one's discredit. Girish would say, "I have drunk so many bottles of wine that if you were to place one bottle on top of another they would reach the height of Mount Everest."[3] It is true that Girish drank a great deal, and he had once been addicted to opium. He also visited brothels. But one should not think that he was a seducer, an exploiter, a cheat, or given to cruelty. His strength of character kept him above such evils.

One night Girish and a friend were drinking and talking about the Master. At 11:00 p.m. Girish suddenly decided to visit Ramakrishna in

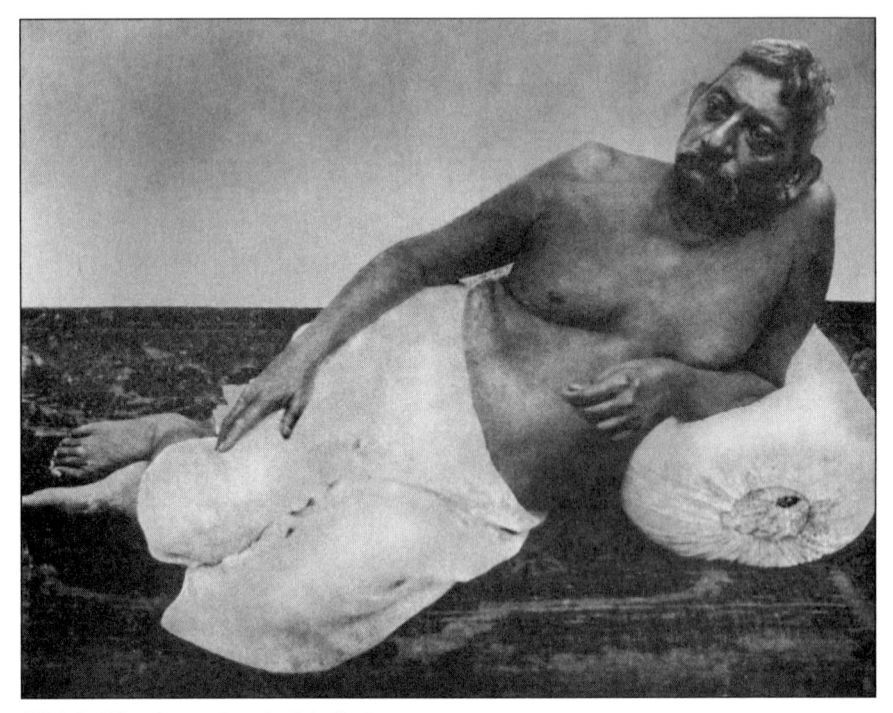

Girish Ghosh resting in his living room

Dakshineswar. He and his friend went to Ahiritola Ghat, hired a boat, and reached Dakshineswar after midnight. The Master slept very little, and at that time he was seated on his bed in a god-intoxicated mood. The door was open. Girish and his friend entered the room and bowed down to Ramakrishna, who immediately realized that they were both drunk.

In ecstasy, the Master got up and, taking their hands, began to dance and sing:

> I drink no ordinary wine, but Wine of Everlasting Bliss,
> As I repeat my Mother Kali's name;
> It so intoxicates my mind that people take me to be drunk![4]

The Master seemed to be more intoxicated than Girish. The intoxication continued for two hours. At last Girish became sober. He bowed down to the Master and returned to Calcutta by boat. On the way Girish said to his friend: "Have you noticed the Master's compassion for a wretched fellow like me? He is God. There is no doubt about it. He has incarnated to deliver horrible sinners like me."[5]

One day a devotee complained to Ramakrishna about Girish's drinking and begged him to ask Girish to give it up. But Ramakrishna sternly replied: "Why do you trouble your head about him? He who has taken charge of him will look after him. Girish is a devotee of the heroic type. I tell you, drinking will not affect him."[6]

Ramakrishna never forbade Girish to drink, because he knew that it takes time to change deep-rooted habits. It was the silent influence of his love that ultimately worked miracles.

Girish saw his life changing under Ramakrishna's influence, yet he could not fathom the nature of this great soul. One day he asked the Master, "Who are you, sir?" Ramakrishna replied: "Some say I am Ramprasad [a poet-saint of Bengal], others that I am Raja Ramakrishna. I simply live here."[7]

Girish gradually became convinced that Ramakrishna was an incarnation of God, and he started to spread this idea among his fellow devotees. On a certain occasion Ramakrishna asked Girish: "Hello! What were you saying about me? I eat, drink, and make merry."

Girish: "What should we have been saying about you? Are you a holy man?"

Master: "No, nothing of the sort. Truly, I do not feel that I am a holy man."

Girish: "I am not your equal even in joking."[8]

In the same vein, Girish related that Ramakrishna had once asked Jogin (later Swami Yogananda) what he thought of him. The young man had replied, "You are neither a householder nor a sannyasin [monk, in any exclusive sense]." Ramakrishna was greatly pleased and exclaimed, "What an extraordinary statement you have just made!"[9] The Master was happy that his disciple had recognized his divine nature, which is beyond all limitations and all stages of life.

To a great extent, progress in spiritual life depends on the intensity of one's effort. Yet it takes time to eradicate past *samskaras* [impressions from previous lives]. In Girish's case, however, his faith and love were so intense that his life was transformed very quickly. In spite of this, when speaking about Girish to another devotee, Ramakrishna once remarked, "You may wash a thousand times a cup that has held a solution of garlic; but is it ever possible to get rid of the smell altogether?" Girish heard about this and his feelings were hurt. He went to Ramakrishna and asked, "Will this smell of garlic go?"

"Yes, it will."

"So you say it will."

"All smell disappears when a blazing fire is lighted. If you heat the cup smelling of garlic, you get rid of the smell; it becomes a new cup."[10]

Jogin used to run errands for the Master. One day Ramakrishna needed some candles for his room, so he asked Jogin to go to Calcutta and get some from Girish. When Jogin arrived, he found Girish drunk. He told Girish that the Master had sent him to get a few candles. Immediately Girish said: "Why a few? Take a box of candles." He then asked his servant to get a box of candles from a shop. Meanwhile, Girish began to use abusive words against Ramakrishna, yet from time to time he faced Dakshineswar and bowed down to him. Jogin was frightened. He had never come across a drunken devotee. He took the candles, however, and upon returning to Dakshineswar, reported everything in detail to the Master. Ramakrishna did not show any indignation; rather, he said to Jogin: "You saw his bad side, how he scolded me. Did you not also see his good side — how much love and devotion he had for me and how he bowed down to me? Girish is in a special class of devotee — a very high class — but his path is different from yours."[11]

One day Ramakrishna asked Girish to massage his feet, allowing him the opportunity to give him the loving and personal service that an intimate disciple would generally do. Girish wrote later: "I was unwilling. I thought, 'What nonsense! Who is going to sit and massage his feet?!' But now when the memory returns I become overwhelmed with remorse. It is only the thought of his infinite love that gives me solace."[12]

Gradually, however, Girish began to notice how other devotees were serving the Master with love and respect, and by contrast, what a terrible life he was leading. He felt bad, but because of his dissolute lifestyle he was reluctant to offer his service.

One morning Girish went to Balaram Basu's house and found Balaram cleaning rice. Balaram was a wealthy landlord and had many servants, but nevertheless he was doing this menial work himself. Girish was amazed and asked Balaram the reason for this. Balaram replied: "The Master is coming today, and he will have his lunch here. So I am cleaning the rice myself."

Girish was impressed by Balaram's devotion, and it saddened him that he could not also serve the Master in that way. He returned home and thought to himself: "Indeed, God comes to the homes of those who have devotion like Balaram. I am a wretched drunkard. There is no one here who can receive the Master properly and feed him." Girish lay down on his bed. At 1:30 p.m. he heard a knock at his door. Opening it, he found the Master standing there. "Girish, I am hungry," he said,

"Could you give me some food?" And yet Ramakrishna had finished his meal at Balaram's house only a little while earlier! As there was no food in his house, Girish asked the Master to wait. He then sent his servant Ishan to a restaurant where he purchased some fried bread and potato curry and brought them back. Girish then placed the food on a plate in front of the Master. This food was coarse and hard to digest — not at all the kind of food usually served to the Master. But Ramakrishna ate it with great joy.[13]

Swami Brahmananda once commented that, among all of the Master's disciples, Swami Vivekananda and Girish had the greatest intellectual powers. Yet Girish's intellect could not stand up to the power with which the Master conveyed the incomprehensible nature of Brahman. One day the Master told him: "What do you know about the knowledge of Brahman? The great sage Narada saw the infinite ocean of Satchidananda from a distance and returned; the ever-pure Sukadeva touched that Ocean only three times; and the great god Shiva drank only three handfuls of its water and lost consciousness." Girish clapped his hand to his forehead and exclaimed: "Stop, sir! Say no more. My head is reeling."[14]

One day Girish asked Ramakrishna to give him a spiritual vision. "Do not desire such visions," was the reply. "For even if you have them, you may not believe what you see."[15] Girish later understood the import of those words, for he realized that his doubting mind would have considered such an experience to be some kind of illusion.

Once Girish heard the Master say: "If a passionate desire arises and persists during meditation, stop and begin to pray. Earnestly pray to the Lord that this desire be removed, that it not be fulfilled. Any desire coming up in meditation, particularly a repressed one, gradually becomes intensified. And if one or more of our passions are involved, the results can be most disquieting."[16]

Girish wrote: "Sri Ramakrishna instructed everyone to abstain from telling lies. I told him: 'Sir, I tell numerous lies. How shall I be truthful?' He replied: 'Don't worry about that. You are above truth and falsehood.' When I feel tempted to tell lies, I at once visualize the Master's form, and lies will not come out. Sri Ramakrishna has full sway over my heart — he has it by the power of his love. Lust, anger, and all the terrible passions vanish if one feels this transcendental love of his — no other spiritual practice is required. This realization is the highest goal of human life."[17]

Once Girish wanted to test Ramakrishna's grace and his spiritual powers. With this in mind, he went to a brothel, intending to spend the night there. But at midnight he experienced an unbearable burning sensation all over his body, and he immediately returned home. The next morning he went to Dakshineswar and told Ramakrishna the whole story. The Master listened and then told him firmly: "Rascal, do you think you have been caught by a poisonless water snake and will be able to escape? You have been bitten by a real cobra. After three cries you will be silenced." Girish's faith in Ramakrishna was strengthened. He was coming to believe that the Master was a saviour of souls, like Chaitanya, who redeemed the two villains, Jagai and Madhai.[18] On another occasion, again wanting to test his guru, Girish deliberately tried to think a worldly thought in the Master's presence, but he found that he could not.[19]

What is dharma? "Unite the mind and speech," said Ramakrishna. It is common for human beings to try to hide the dark side of their character and present to society only their positive attributes. This is hypocrisy, and Girish hated it with his whole being. He knew his shortcomings very well and was not afraid to confess them publicly. Before giving the power of attorney to the Master, he would be concerned at times about his karma and how it would affect his future. He asked Ramakrishna, "Sir, what will happen to me?"

In response, the Master told the following story: "A wealthy landlord had two sons: The elder one was learned, disciplined, and obedient to his father and helped with the household work; while the younger one did not finish his schooling and instead was involved with the theatre, yatra, and music. He would come home only for two meals and to sleep after midnight. He saw his mother during meals but avoided his father. The landlord asked his wife: 'I don't see our younger son. Why does he not come to me?'

"The wife replied: 'You know my dear, he is illiterate and wayward. So he is afraid to come to you.'

"The husband responded: 'Please tell him to come see me. I shall not scold him.'

"One day the mother asked her younger son to see his father, and assured him that he would not be scolded. Reluctantly, he went to see his father, walking behind his mother. The father said to him: 'Hello, come here. Will you go with me to our garden house in the country?' 'Yes, I shall go with you, father,' replied the younger son. The father then ordered his elder son to arrange the trip.

"The father took both of his sons in the carriage and left for the garden house. On arrival, the elder one walked through the garden and showed his father the fruit orchard, vegetable garden, flowerbed, and other things there. Meanwhile, the younger son went to the gardener, got a fishing rod from him, and began to fish in the pond. At 4:00 p.m. the father asked his elder son, 'Where is your brother?' 'Perhaps he has gone fishing,' he replied. The father said: 'Call him here. The refreshments have arrived. Let us all eat together.' The elder son went to call his brother, but he replied, 'Brother, forgive me. I can't go now. Let me first catch a fish and then I shall come.' When the father heard this, he angrily said, 'Wherever that boy goes, he creates problems.' He went to him, snatched the fishing rod from him, and broke it into pieces. He then took his younger son by the hand and brought him to the cottage. They ate the refreshments, then returned home by carriage. The younger son might have been wayward, but the father did not leave him there."

The Master then said to Girish: "You are my younger son and Naren is my elder one. I cannot leave you alone. Both of you will be with me in the end."[20]

On 28 July 1885, Ramakrishna went to the Calcutta home of a wealthy man named Nanda Basu to see his collection of pictures of gods and goddesses. Ramakrishna was greatly impressed and said to Nanda: "Though you are a householder, you have still kept your mind on God. Is that a small thing? The man who has renounced the world will pray to Him as a matter of course. Is there any credit in that? But blessed indeed is he who, while leading a householder's life, prays to God. He is like a man who finds an object after removing a stone weighing twenty maunds." *

On this occasion, Nanda Basu served sweets to Ramakrishna and then offered him betel-leaf on a tray. But the other guests had already taken some from that tray, so the Master would not accept any. Nanda noticed this and questioned him about it. Ramakrishna replied: "Before I eat anything, I offer it to God. It is a notion of mine." It is the custom that something can be offered to God only if no one else has partaken of it beforehand. Nanda was somewhat proud of his knowledge of Vedanta philosophy. Trying to evaluate Ramakrishna's actions intellectually, he said, "But the betel-leaf would have gone to God all the same." He said further: "You are a paramahamsa. Why do you abide by the injunctions or prohibitions of the scriptures? They are meant for ignorant people." Ramakrishna smiled and again remarked, "It is just a notion of mine."[21]

Nanda concluded from this that Ramakrishna had not attained the highest nondualistic state of realization, which is beyond the pairs of

---
*A maund is approximately eighty-two pounds.

opposites and the law of causation. Girish came to know of this and felt bad. He was convinced that the Master had not revealed his divine nature to Nanda because of the man's pride of learning. Wanting to test this idea, Girish invited Ramakrishna to his house. Without any comment, Girish brought in a tray of betel-leaf, took one himself, and then offered the tray to the Master. The Master immediately understood Girish's intent and, with a smile, took a betel-leaf from the tray. Overcome with joy, Girish saluted the Master again and again, then explained the whole story to the others present.[22] He who makes the rules can also change them. Girish's love had set aside all rules of religious observance. Moreover, great teachers observe scriptural rules in order to set an example for others, and not for their own benefit.

Thus, Girish came to have firm faith in the Master's redemptive powers. Once an ordinary-looking man came to visit Ramakrishna but did not show him respect. Considering him to be a rustic fellow, Girish said to him: "Hello sir, what are you looking at? If you want liberation, take the dust of his [*pointing to the Master*] feet." Embarrassed, the Master said to Girish: "What are you talking about? Don't you know he is my uncle-in-law?" (According to Hindu custom a son-in-law is supposed to show respect to his father- or uncle-in-law.) Girish kept quiet. But Narendra interjected: "No, sir, he should take the dust of your feet." Girish later remarked: "I was relieved that Narendra took my side."[23]

Once Girish and Devendra Nath Majumdar planned to visit the Master at Dakshineswar. Devendra was Girish's friend, and Girish dictated his dramas and songs to him. On the way Devendra asked Girish, "Can you suggest some kind of sweet that I can buy for the Master?"

Girish replied: "Buy whatever you like. After all, we shall eat them."

Devendra: "My goodness! The Master won't touch our food today at all."

Girish: "Don't worry! Buy the sweets and come to the carriage." Devendra bought two rupees' worth of rasagollas and then they came to Dakshineswar. Both entered the Master's room and found him coming down from samadhi, saying, "I shall eat a rasagolla." Devendra immediately placed the jar of rasagollas in front of the Master and he ate some with great delight. Girish and Devendra looked at each other overwhelmed. They later had some prasad.[24]

The power of faith can create miracles. Girish was well known for his faith in the Master. Once a servant of his, a poor boy from Orissa, slipped while cleaning the bathroom floor and dislocated his right elbow. His arm swelled and he was in great pain. Even though Girish took him to the doctor, his injury would not heal. After a few days Girish told the boy, "Pray to the paramahamsa of Dakshineswar and mentally promise to offer him rasagollas after you have recovered." The servant followed Girish's instructions. The next day he fell again in the same bathroom, again landing on his right side. This forced his dislocated elbow back into place and his pain subsided. After he had finished bathing, he went to Girish and said, "Sir, I want to go to Dakshineswar and offer rasagollas to the paramahamsa." Girish exclaimed: "What happened? I heard that you fell and injured your right arm again." "It is true, sir," the servant replied. "But when I got up after my fall, I discovered that my arm was set back in place, and my pain subsided considerably." Thinking of the Master, Girish bowed down to him again and again and said: "Who says, Master, that you do not answer our prayer? Who says that you don't aid those who have taken refuge in you?" Girish then bought two rupees' worth of rasagollas and sent his servant to Dakshineswar.[25]

In 1885 during the Dashahara Festival, which involves the worship of the Ganges, Ramakrishna asked Girish to bathe in the holy river. Girish was reluctant to do so. It is a common belief that anyone who bathes in the Ganges becomes pure. Girish considered this idea to be mere superstition. The Master finally persuaded him by saying, "If you [being a great devotee] do not follow these religious customs, who else will?" Girish obeyed and later he would bathe in the Ganges on auspicious occasions. One day, however, the thought occurred to him that if the Master had taken on his power of attorney, why should he need to bathe in the Ganges to be purified? Again, he wondered why the Master had asked him to do so. His analytical mind soon found an answer: When sinners bathe in the Ganges, the goddess Ganges absorbs their sins and makes them pure. However, when holy people bathe, She gains virtue by offering peace and delight to them. He concluded that through the Master's grace he had become so pure that the redeeming power of Mother Ganges would increase a hundredfold when he bathed.[26]

Girish recalled: "Although I had solved the problem by reasoning, a vestige of misgiving remained in my mind. My past impressions and doubting mind continued to agitate me. But when I closed my eyes and thought of the Master, I saw him smiling, his face joyful. Without further thought I descended into the Ganges and said to Her: 'Mother Ganges, by the grace of the Master I am bathing in Your water to purify You.' Saying so I dipped my body into the Ganges and got up. I felt a wonderful bliss in my heart. From then on, whenever I bathed in the Ganges, the same thought would arise."[27]

Where there is love, there is faith. Girish's passionate love for Ramakrishna endowed him with what the Master himself described as "one hundred and twenty-five percent faith." Girish loved to tell his friends about Ramakrishna and to bring them to the Master to be blessed. Knowing this, the Master one day prayed aloud to the Divine Mother: "Mother, I cannot talk so much. Give a little power to Kedar, Ram, Girish, and Vijay, so that people may go to them first, learn a little, and at last come here [to me] to have their spiritual awakening in a word or two."[28]

In the spring of 1885 the cancer that was to prove fatal began to develop in Ramakrishna's throat. In September the devotees moved him from Dakshineswar to Shyampukur, Calcutta. There he was closer to his doctor and could be better cared for by the devotees who served him, supported him, and spent time with him during the last months of his life.

That year the special worship of the Divine Mother Kali was celebrated on 6 November 1885. Ramakrishna said to one of his disciples: "It is good to make some arrangements for the worship. Please speak to the devotees about it."[29] The devotees made the necessary arrangements. That evening, nearly thirty people assembled in the Master's room. Girish described what happened then: "Sri Ramakrishna sat down to perform the worship, surrounded by flowers, fruits, and all the various articles for worship. Suddenly he turned to me and said: 'It is the Divine Mother's day. One should sit and meditate like this.' I do not know what took hold of me at that point. I just rushed forward and, chanting 'Jai Sri Ramakrishna [Victory to Sri Ramakrishna],' offered flowers at his feet. The others in the room did the same. Sri Ramakrishna immediately went into samadhi, his hands assuming gestures symbolizing fearlessness and the bestowal of boons."[30]

Swami Saradananda described this Kali Puja in detail:

> It was the month of November, and the auspicious day of Kali Puja [Friday, 6 November 1885] was approaching. There was still no visible improvement in the Master's condition.
>
> Devendra wished to buy an image of Mother Kali and perform worship to Her. He thought that it would be an extremely joyful occasion if he could fulfill that desire in the presence of the Master and his devotees, so he asked if he could perform the worship at the Shyampukur house. The devotees advised him to abandon the idea because the excitement, enthusiasm, and commotion surrounding the ritual might exhaust the Master. Devendra considered the devotees' response reasonable, so he gave up the idea. But the day before Kali Puja, the Master told some of

his devotees: "Collect everything that is needed for worship on a small scale. Tomorrow we shall have Kali Puja." Delighted, they began consulting with the others. Because they received no further instructions from the Master, they discussed among themselves various ways of accomplishing their task and could not come to any agreement on whether the worship would have sixteen items or five, whether they would offer cooked food, who would perform the worship, and so on. Finally they decided to procure sandal paste, flowers, oil lamps, incense, fruits, and sweets, and then await the Master's instructions. But the Master gave no further directions that day nor did he on the day of worship.

Evening arrived with the sunset. At 7:00 p.m. the devotees found the Master seated silently on his bed, as on other days. He said nothing further about the worship. They cleared some space on his right and placed the worship articles there. Some devotees had seen the Master occasionally worship his own form with sandal paste and flowers when he lived in Dakshineswar. Today they had come to the conclusion that the Master intended to worship himself as a symbol of Universal Consciousness and the embodiment of Divine Power, or to perform the worship of his own Self as identified with the Divine Mother according to the scriptures. It is therefore not surprising that they placed the worship articles next to his bed. The Master watched them do that, but raised no objection.

When everything had been brought to his room, someone lit the lamps and burnt the incense, filling the whole room with light and fragrance. Seeing the Master still sitting quietly, the devotees sat near him. Some looked at him intently, awaiting his direction; some began to meditate on the Divine Mother. Time passed, and the Master remained silent. He neither came forward to perform the worship himself, nor did he ask any of us to do it.

The young devotees were present, along with Mahendra, Ram, Devendra, Girish, and some senior devotees. The Master sometimes said that of his devotees Girish had "one hundred and twenty-five percent" faith. Most of the devotees were puzzled by the Master's silence about the worship. But because Girish had such abundant faith in the Master, he was suddenly struck by this idea: "The Master does not need to worship the Divine Mother for his own sake. If his pure love has inspired him to perform the worship, why would he sit there quietly, doing nothing? That does not seem right. Were these arrangements made for the devotees to worship the Divine Mother in the Master's living form and be blessed? It must be so." He was overwhelmed with joy at that thought and immediately took flowers and sandal paste from a tray and offered them at the feet of the Master, saying, "Victory to the Mother." A thrill passed through the Master's body, and he went into deep samadhi. His face became luminous and a divine smile played upon it. His hands assumed the gestures symbolizing fearlessness and the bestowal of boons that are seen in images of Kali, thus indicating that the Mother was revealing Herself within him. These events happened so quickly that the devotees seated nearby thought Girish had offered flowers after seeing the Master in samadhi. To those who were a little farther away it appeared as if a luminous form of the Devi had suddenly appeared before them, taking possession of the Master's body.

The devotees' joy knew no bounds. Each one took flowers and sandal paste from the tray, uttered a mantra according to his mood, and worshipped the Master's feet. The room was filled with joyous shouts. Some time passed in this way. When the Master slowly regained partial consciousness, the sweets and fruits gathered for worship were placed before him. He partook of some and blessed the devotees that they might attain the highest devotion and knowledge. They ate some of the Master's prasad, then sang devotional songs and hymns to the glory of the Divine Mother until midnight.

Thus, the devotees worshipped the Divine Mother that year in a unique way and experienced an unprecedented bliss that remained forever vivid in their hearts. And whenever they later became oppressed by difficulties in their lives, that image of the Master appeared before them, his serene face illumined with a divine smile and his hands bestowing blessings and fearlessness, reminding them that they were under God's protection.[31]

As Ramakrishna's health continued to deteriorate, his doctor advised him to move outside of the city, where the air would be better. Consequently, a beautiful garden house was found in Cossipore, and the move was made on 11 December 1885. An arrangement was made whereby the Master's householder disciples would contribute money for his treatment and his food, and to pay the rent. The young unmarried disciples, the nucleus of the future monastic order, would manage the household, including shopping and caring for the Master. After a while some of the householder disciples noticed that expenditures were gradually increasing. They accused the young men of carelessness and asked that an account book be strictly maintained. The young disciples, however, were offended by this and decided not to accept any more money. When the tension increased and the situation became critical, Girish came forward with a solution: He simply set fire to the account book in front of everyone. Then he told the householder disciples to each contribute according to his capacity, and he would make up the deficit. To the monastic disciples he said: "Don't worry. I shall sell my house if necessary and spend every bit of money for the Master."[32]

On 1 January 1886, Ramakrishna felt strong enough to take a walk in the garden. It was a holiday, and many devotees had come from Calcutta to visit him that afternoon. He began walking slowly through the garden, and some devotees followed him. Suddenly Ramakrishna said to Girish, "Well, Girish, what have you found in me that you proclaim me before all as an Incarnation?" Falling to his knees before the Master and saluting him with folded hands, Girish responded with great emotion: "Who am I to speak of Him? Even the sages Vyasa and Valmiki could find no words to measure His glory!"

Ramakrishna was deeply moved. He blessed Girish and the assembled devotees, saying: "What more need I tell you? I bless you all. Be illumined!" Then he went into samadhi and began to bless the devotees, touching them one by one. With each touch he instilled a spiritual awakening in their hearts.[33] Excited, Girish ran to the house and called everyone to the courtyard to receive the Master's grace. He entered the kitchen and found the cook making chapatis (a flatbread). He dragged the cook to the Master to be blessed.[34]

Afterwards the Master returned to his room and told his nephew: "Ramlal, my hands and feet are burning. Please bring some Ganges water and sprinkle it on me." Ramlal recalled: "He was extremely restless. I asked, 'What happened?' He replied: 'I came into this world secretly with a few close devotees, and now Ram [Ram Chandra Datta] is spreading my name. He brings all sorts of people here and asks me to touch and bless them. How much burden can I carry? I got this disease [cancer] by taking the sins of these people upon myself. Look, I shall not stay in this world any longer.' I consoled him: 'No, no. You will not have to receive any visitors or touch anybody.' Then I brought the Ganges water and washed his hands and feet, and gradually he calmed down."[35] Holy Mother once remarked that the Master developed cancer because he had taken on Girish's sins.

One day not long after this, Gopal Ghosh (later Swami Advaitananda) told the Master that he cherished a desire to distribute ochre cloths and rudraksha rosaries to monks. Ramakrishna pointed to his young disciples and said: "Why not give them to these boys? They are full of the spirit of renunciation. You won't find better monks anywhere." Gopal had twelve pieces of cloth and twelve rosaries, which he handed over to the Master. Then Ramakrishna himself distributed them among eleven of his young disciples. Thus, the Master himself laid the foundation of the future Ramakrishna Order. One cloth and one rosary were left, and the Master asked that they be kept for Girish; for, indeed, he was second to none in his spirit of renunciation.[36]

After receiving the ochre cloth from the Master, Girish had a dilemma. He pondered: "I lead a worldly life. I go to the theatre every night and sometimes I even perform onstage. What shall I do with this ochre cloth? But I cannot ignore the behest of the Master." He then wrapped that ochre cloth around his head to make a turban, and went to the Master and bowed down. The Master said to Girish with a smile: "That is enough for you."[37]

On 16 April 1886 Girish went to see Ramakrishna at the Cossipore garden house. It is always a joy to see loved ones when one is ill. In the *Gospel* M. described a fascinating scene that took place depicting Ramakrishna's love in action:

> That evening the Master did not feel so bad. The devotees came and after bowing down sat on the floor in front of the Master. The Master asked M. to bring the lamp near him so that he could see the devotees well. The Master greeted Girish affectionately: "Are you quite well? (*To Latu*) Prepare a smoke for him and bring him a betel-leaf." A few moments later he said again, "Bring him some refreshments."
>
> Latu: "I have given him a betel-leaf. They are going to bring some refreshments from the shop."
>
> The Master was seated. A devotee brought a few garlands of flowers. The Master put them around his neck one by one. The Lord dwelt in the Master's heart; perhaps he worshipped Him. The devotees watched him with wonder. He took two garlands from his neck and gave them to Girish as his blessing. The Master asked now and then, "Have the refreshments arrived?" He was anxious to feed Girish.
>
> Refreshments for Girish — warm kachuris, puris, and other sweets — arrived from the famous Fagu's shop, which is located in Baranagore bazar. The Master had all the refreshments placed before him; he took a grain and handed over the plate to Girish. Girish accepted the rest as prasad. The Master had cancer and it was not possible for him to eat that food. Generally we love to feed our guest with food that we ourselves like. He remarked: "Very crispy and warm kachuris."
>
> Girish sat in front of the Master's bed and ate. Girish would need water to drink. There was water in an earthen jug in the southeastern corner of the Master's room. It was summer — the month of Vaisakh. The Master said, "Here is good water."
>
> The Master was very ill. He had no strength to stand. And what did the disciples see to their amazement? They saw him leave the bed and, completely naked, he was crawling forward from the bed like a child. He wanted to pour the water himself. The devotees were breathless! Sri Ramakrishna poured the water from the jug. He poured a little water on

his hand to see if it was cool. He felt that the water was not all that cool. Finally, realizing that no better water was available, he reluctantly gave it to him. Girish was eating the refreshments. The devotees were sitting around. M. was fanning the Master.

Girish enjoyed the refreshments. The Master encouraged him to eat more kachuris because they are more tasty than puris and they enhance the quality of rajas.

Girish went to the small terrace to rinse his hands. The Master said to M.: "Girish has eaten a lot of kachuris. Go and tell him not to eat anything else tonight." Like a loving father, the Master was thinking of Girish's welfare. Entering the room again, Girish sat in front of the Master and chewed a betel-leaf. Despite his sore throat, the Master instructed Girish on how to live in this world.[38]

Girish did not visit Ramakrishna very often at Cossipore because he could not bear to see him ill. One day when Girish was visiting, the Master had just finished eating some farina pudding. The unwashed cup with the remnant of the pudding, mixed with the discharge from his throat cancer, was still on the floor, and some tiny ants were eating it. Pointing to the cup, Ramakrishna said to Girish: "Look! And still people call me an avatar!" Girish immediately remarked: "Sir, now even those ants will get liberation. For what other reason should you have this disease?"[39]

Ramakrishna passed away on Monday, 16 August 1886. A devotee brought the sad news to Girish, but Girish would not believe him. He said to the man: "This is a lie. The Master cannot die."

"Sir, I have come from that place."

"You had better go back there."

"But I have seen him with my own eyes."

Girish covered his eyes with his hands and retorted: "You say whatever you want. I have not seen it with my own eyes, so I do not believe it."[40]

Girish later said: "I heard of the Master's passing away, but I did not go to Cossipore to see him. I knew it would be hard for my weak mind to maintain faith in the Master's immortal nature if I were to see his dead body. Moreover, my eyes would stand against my faith and would tell me: 'Sri Ramakrishna is dead. Did you not see it with your own eyes?' For this reason I intentionally kept a conflict between my eyes and my ears about the Master's passing away. If my ears tell me, 'Sri Ramakrishna is dead,' I shall tell them: 'You have heard so many rumours about the Master. Are you going to believe everything you hear?' Let people say whatever they want. I did not witness the Master's death, so I do not believe it."[41] Not only that, he never saw the two pictures of Ramakrishna's body that were taken after his death.[42]

Girish had the firm conviction that the Master was God Himself, and that his body was eternal and full of pure consciousness. Disease or death could not touch him. Because he had been born as a human being, he acted as a human being, and death was also a part of his divine play.

Soon after the Master's passing, misfortune again descended upon Girish. He lost his two daughters; his second wife died in 1888; and a few years later a young son, who had been very devoted to the Holy Mother, also passed away. In one of his dramas, Girish summed up his feelings: "Life is painful. The world is empty. A beautiful flower garden has withered away."[43]

Girish's hedonistic spirit had been subdued by Ramakrishna's spiritual touch. His life was now completely changed. For the last twenty years of his life he did not drink.[44] And yet his previous life no doubt contributed greatly to his success as an actor and a dramatist. The intensity with which his gigantic heart had felt grief, joy, despair, and hope made it possible for him to portray the characters in his dramas vividly. He used to say that the poet and the playwright could imbue their writings with life and feeling only if they themselves had had firsthand experience of all facets of life. He once said: "Who can criticize the portrayal of characters in my plays? I have studied the lives of all types of people, from the prostitute to the paramahamsa [illumined soul]."[45]

Chapter 21

Girish and Vivekananda

Society, friendship, and love are divine gifts. Close friendship usually develops between contemporaries, but even though Girish was nearly twenty years older than Swami Vivekananda, they behaved as if they were the same age and became close friends. Despite the years that separated them, they had mutual love and respect. Seldom has there been such an open and frank relationship between two great souls. They teased each other, argued and debated various issues. People enjoyed their friendly squabbles and lively conversations. Both men were geniuses and were extremely creative; both were cynics and at the same time lovers of God; both were proud of their physical and intellectual powers; both had struggled and sought a guru. Where self-effort ends, divine grace begins. Providence finally brought them both to Ramakrishna, whose pure love and spiritual power overwhelmed them. Both of these rebellious souls became disciples of Ramakrishna.

Girish once related an incident regarding Ramakrishna's love for Narendra (as Vivekananda was then known): On special occasions, nonvegetarian food is offered to Mother Kali in the Dakshineswar temple. One day the Master saved a bowl of meat curry for Narendra. A few of the devotees asked for some of that prasad, but the Master refused to share it with anyone. When Narendra arrived, the Master was pleased to feed him all of the meat curry.[1]

It is amazing to learn how Girish, a man of faith and devotion, faced Vivekananda, a man of reasoning and knowledge.

Swami Saradananda wrote:

> Under the influence of Western education and of the Brahmo Samaj, Vivekananda would make some caustic remarks about the followers of God with form. Sometimes the Master would set up a lively debate between him and some devotees of God with form, and then enjoy the

Swami Vivekananda in San Francisco, 1900

fun. On these occasions almost no one could withstand Vivekananda's fluent argumentation. His keen intellect and sharp reasoning left his opponents speechless, and some of them also felt hurt when this happened. Sometimes the Master would joyfully mention this to others: "The other day Narendra cut the arguments of so-and-so into pieces! What an outstanding intellect!"

But one day Swamiji was silenced while arguing with Girish, a follower of God with form. On that occasion we felt that the Master took Girish's side in order to strengthen and nourish his faith.[2]

Girish later joyfully said: "Out of grace, the Master allowed me to win on that day. Otherwise, who could defeat Narendra? When Narendra became quiet, the Master humorously told me, 'Take a written statement from Narendra that he has been defeated today.'"[3]

Girish openly proclaimed Ramakrishna to be an incarnation of God, and he tried to persuade everyone to share his conviction. Of course, Girish's case was unique. With none of his sincerity, some devotees went about declaring that they had given Ramakrishna the power of attorney in spiritual matters like Girish had done, and therefore had no need to practise any spiritual disciplines. Narendra realized the dangers of the path these devotees were taking. He cautioned Girish to be more guarded in his speech, and then told the young disciples: "The effusion of sentiment which is not attended by a corresponding transformation of character and which is not strong enough to destroy the cravings of lust and gold by awakening in the heart an enthusiasm for the vision of God is neither deep nor of any real value in the realm of spirituality."[4]

Many years after Ramakrishna had passed away, Kumudbandhu Sen questioned the morality of the young people who went to the theatre, because the actresses were courtesans. Girish replied:

> Some actresses bowed down to the picture of Ramakrishna in the green room of the theatre and humbly prayed to him to remove the pain of their penitent hearts. One day some of those girls came to see me in this hall when Vivekananda (long before he left for America) was present. I told them: "If you call on Sri Ramakrishna sincerely and take refuge in him, then you have nothing to fear." But Swamiji protested. He said this was bigotry, blind faith, and fake devotion. Excited, I began to glorify the Master's name and said that he was the deliverer of the lowly and the fallen. Those who repeat the Lord's name even once should not have any fear in this world. When I continued this way, Swamiji took me outside the room and said: "G.C., why are you preaching this dangerous doctrine? I know the greatness of the Master's name. I know he was the

saviour of the fallen, and he came to save the weak, the fallen, and suffering humanity. But I love purity. Please preach the fiery mantra of purity." I saw Swamiji's tearful eyes and his divine form is still vivid in my eyes.[5]

Girish also recalled: "One evening Narendra and I were meditating under a mango tree at the Cossipore garden house. I was about to enter into a deep concentration when the mosquitoes began to disturb me. I tried to slap them away, but they continued attacking me. I opened my eyes and found Narendra seated in a lotus posture. I did not want to leave the place without him. I called to him but got no response; then I gently touched him, with no response either. I noticed his body was covered with mosquitoes like a blanket. I was amazed by his lack of body-consciousness, but frightened because he did not respond. Finally I pulled him down to the ground and after a great effort brought him back to consciousness. He said with a smile: "G.C., why are you so afraid?"[6]

Girish described Narendra's longing for God and love for the Master:

"One morning Narendra came to my house and sat leaning against the wall. He was absorbed in deep thought. He had no body-consciousness, nor did he have any awareness of the external world. I was dumbfounded by the expression on his face. After a brief silence he said: 'G.C., I won't be able to realize God. I have renounced everything and forgotten everything, but cannot forget that mad brahmin of Dakshineswar. He is my obstacle.' I could not understand his high spiritual state, so I kept quiet."[7]

Narendra always shared his mental condition with Girish. Swami Saradananda recalled:

> Swamiji paid the fee for his law examination, but the next day he thought: "What am I doing? The Master will not live long. My life will be in vain." Anxious, he rushed barefooted to the Cossipore garden house. At that time his family was in straitened financial conditions. He borrowed money for a few months' household expenses from M. and gave it to his mother, saying, "Please don't disturb me for some time."
>
> Girish's brother saw him rushing to Cossipore like a madman and asked, "What happened?"
>
> "My 'I' died," replied Swamiji. Then he privately described his mental condition to Girish.[8]

Girish's play *Buddhadev-Charit* was performed at the Star Theatre on Beadon Street in September 1885. Narendra saw the play and was inspired by Buddha's renunciation. He used to sing this song from the play:

We moan for rest, alas! But rest can never find;
We know not whence we come, nor where we float away.
Time and again we tread this round of smiles and tears;
In vain we pine to know whither our pathway leads,
And why we play this empty play.

We sleep, although awake, as if by a spell bewitched;
Will darkness never break into the light of dawn?
As restless as the wind, life moves unceasingly:
We know not who we are, nor whence it is we come;
We know not why we come, nor where it is we drift;
Sharp woes dart forth on every side.

How many drift about, now happy, now drowned in tears!
One moment they exist, the next they are no more.
We know not why we come, nor what our deeds have been,
Nor, in our bygone lives, how well we played our parts;
Like water in a stream, we cannot stay at rest;
Onward we flow for evermore.

Burst Thou our slumber's bars, O Thou that art awake!
How long must we remain enmeshed in fruitless dreams?
Are you indeed awake? Then do not longer sleep!
Thick on you lies the gloom fraught with a million woes.
Rise, dreamer, from your dream, and slumber not again!
Shine forth, O Shining One, and with Thy shafts of light
Slay Thou the blinding dark! Our only Saviour Thou!
We seek deliverance at Thy feet.[9]

Mahendra Nath Datta, Swamiji's brother, recalled this song: "Sometimes at midnight in the worship hall of their house on Gour Mohan Mukherjee Street in Calcutta, Swamiji used to sing the above song, which was sung to Buddha by two celestial maidens. His voice was so sweet and melodious that some members of the household would lie awake listening to it, giving up their sleep. He sang with such feeling that those who heard it were transported to a higher realm. This song was sung quite often in the Baranagore monastery."[10]

One day Narendra visited Girish and met the actor Amritalal Mitra, who had performed the role of Buddha in Girish's play. Narendra, shaven-headed and barefoot, was reclining against a wall while reading a newspaper. Soon a judge, one of Girish's longtime acquaintances, came into the room and asked Girish: "Was Buddha an atheist? I read in some English books that he did not believe in God."

"Ask him," Girish replied, pointing to Narendra. "Who is he?" asked the judge. Girish joked, "He is a beggar waiting here for a little food." Girish took a puff from his hubble-bubble and smiled.

The judge asked Narendra: "You there, was Buddha an atheist?"

Narendra replied, "Why don't you ask this person? He pointed to Amritlal and said, "He performs in the role of Buddha."

Amritlal humbly responded: "Sir, I don't know all those things. I am an uneducated person, an actor by profession."

This amused Girish, but irritated the judge. He said to Narendra: "Hey, tell me what you know about Buddha."

Narendra covered his face with the newspaper and replied: "Yes, Buddha was an atheist. This was reported in the paper *Haire Maja Shanibar* — Blessed is Saturday!" (This was a paper for drunkards.)

The judge angrily reproached Narendra: "What do you do? Why don't you work? Aren't you ashamed to enjoy Girish's food? Don't you see that everyone is laughing at you?"

Narendra lowered the paper and responded: "Are they watching me or you? People are laughing at your ignorance!"

The judge was furious and left in disgust. Girish had achieved his goal, teaching this proud man a lesson.[11]

Girish based his play *Vilwamangal Thakur* on a story from the *Bhaktamala*. Narendra had read this story before he went to the Star Theatre to see the play. When the play was over and the audience had left, Girish brought Narendra to the stage and introduced him to the actors and actresses. Inspired by the play, Narendra picked up a tanpura and began to sing devotional songs. Tears trickled from his closed eyes, and his voice was at times choked with devotion. It seemed as if he was visualizing his beloved Lord and calling to Him as he sang. The theatre became a temple that night as a current of devotion flowed. The atmosphere became heavy with spirituality and longing for God.

The actresses, however, were restless and felt very uncomfortable. They stood at a distance and listened to Narendra's songs with folded hands. Narendra was absorbed in a divine mood, forgetting where he was. He had completely lost track of time. But Girish was concerned. He took the tanpura away from Narendra and interrupted his ecstasy. He then took Narendra by the hand, led him to his carriage, and brought him to his home in Baghbazar. The next day the actresses scolded Girish: "What have you done? Why did you bring such a powerful spiritual person to the theatre? As you know we are fickle-minded dancing girls. It would have been a horrible sin if we had had any sensual feeling for him.

We have already ruined our present life, and this sin would have doomed us for our next life."

Girish was pleased to hear them. Their words increased his love and respect for Narendra.[12]

Swami Vivekananda read Girish's *Vilwamangal Thakur* many times, and he said that each time he found new light in it. While in America, Vivekananda gave a short lecture on the play, which we present here:

> This is a story from one of the books of India, called "Lives of Saints." There was a young man, a brahmin by birth, in a certain village. This man fell in love with a bad woman in another village. There was a big river between the two villages, and this man, every day, used to go to that girl, crossing this river in a ferry boat. Now, one day he had to perform the obsequies of his father, and so, although he was longing, almost dying to go to the girl, he could not. The ceremonies had to be performed, and all those things had to be undergone; it is absolutely necessary in Hindu society. He was fretting and fuming and all that, but could not help it. At last the ceremony ended, and night came, and with the night, a tremendous howling storm arose. The rain was pouring down, and the river was lashed into gigantic waves. It was very dangerous to cross. Yet he went to the bank of the river.
>
> There was no ferry boat. The ferrymen were afraid to cross, but he would go; his heart was becoming mad with love for the girl, so he would go. There was a log floating down, and he got that, and with the help of it, crossed the river, and getting to the other side dragged the log up, threw it on the bank, and went to the house. The doors were closed. He knocked at the door, but the wind was howling, and nobody heard him. So he went round the walls and at last found what he thought to be a rope, hanging from the wall. He clutched at it, saying to himself, "Oh, my love has left a rope for me to climb." By the help of that rope he climbed over the wall, got to the other side, missed his footing, and fell, and the noise aroused the inmates of the house, and the girl came out and found the man there in a faint. She revived him, and noticing that he was smelling very unpleasantly, she said, "What is the matter with you? Why is this stench on your body? How did you come into the house?"
>
> He said, "Why, did not my love put that rope there?" She smiled, and said, "What love? We are for money, and do you think that I let down a rope for you, fool that you are? How did you cross the river?" "Why, I got hold of a log of wood." "Let us go and see," said the girl. The rope was a cobra, a tremendously poisonous serpent, whose least touch is death. It had its head in a hole, and was getting in when the man caught hold of its tail, and he thought it was a rope. The madness of love made him do it. When the serpent has its head in its hole, and its body out, and you catch

hold of it, it will not let its head come out; so the man climbed up by it, but the force of the pull killed the serpent. "Where did you get the log?" "It was floating down the river." It was a festering dead body; the stream had washed it down and that he took for a log, which explained why he had such an unpleasant odour.

The woman looked at him and said, "I never believed in love; we never do; but, if this is not love, the Lord have mercy on me. We do not know what love is. But, my friend, why do you give that heart to a woman like me? Why do you not give it to God? You will be perfect." It was a thunderbolt to the man's brain. He got a glimpse of the beyond for a moment. "Is there a God?" "Yes, yes, my friend, there is," said the woman. And the man walked on, went into a forest, began to weep and pray: "I want Thee, Oh Lord! This tide of my love cannot find a receptacle in little human beings. I want to love where this mighty river of my love can go, the ocean of love; this rushing tremendous river of my love cannot enter into little pools, it wants the infinite ocean. Thou art there; come Thou to me." So he remained there for years.

After years he thought he had succeeded, he became a sannyasin and he came into the cities. One day he was sitting on the bank of a river, at one of the bathing places, and a beautiful young girl, the wife of a merchant of the city, with her servant, came and passed the place. The old man was again up in him, the beautiful face again attracted him. The Yogi looked and looked, stood up and followed the girl to her home. Presently the husband came by, and seeing the Sannyasin in the yellow garb he said to him, "Come in, sir, what can I do for you?" The Yogi said, "I will ask you a terrible thing." "Ask anything, sir, I am a Grihastha (householder), and anything that one asks I am ready to give." "I want to see your wife." The man said, "Lord, what is this! Well, I am pure, and my wife is pure, and the Lord is a protection to all. Welcome; come in sir."

He came in, and the husband introduced him to his wife. "What can I do for you?" asked the lady. He looked and looked, and then said, "Mother, will you give me two pins from your hair?" "Here they are." He thrust them into his two eyes saying: "Get away, you rascals! Henceforth no fleshy things for you. If you are to see, see the Shepherd of the groves of Vrindaban with the eyes of the soul. Those are all the eyes you have." So he went back into the forest. There again he wept and wept and wept. It was all that great flow of love in the man that was struggling to get at the truth, and at last he succeeded; he gave his soul, the river of his love, the right direction, and it came to the Shepherd. The story goes that he saw God in the form of Krishna. Then, for once, he was sorry that he had lost his eyes, and that he could only have the internal vision. He wrote some beautiful poems of love. In all Sanskrit books, the writers first of all salute their Gurus. So he saluted that girl as his first guru.[13]

In 1888 Girish's second wife died, leaving behind their young boy. Girish believed fervently that the Master had been born as his son, fulfilling his request. Girish therefore was especially solicitous of his young son. The toddler was eager to be held by the Master's devotees, but would not go to others. He would sit calmly, with closed eyes, in front of Ramakrishna's portrait. One day he began to cry before the photo of the Master; it was clear that he wanted it. When it was brought down, many ants were found behind the picture. A towel was used to clear away the ants and the child became calm. Soon after this incident, he became seriously ill and emaciated. Girish engaged all the best doctors and took him to Madhupur, a health resort, for a change. When the child cried from pain, someone would chant God's name to calm him, and he would fall asleep. This behaviour convinced Girish that the Master had definitely fulfilled his wish. One day Girish called on Narendra and said: "Naren, all my efforts to save this child are of no avail. If the child can be saved by my giving up custody, I am ready to do it now. You initiate him into sannyasa and take him into your monastic order." Swamiji honoured Girish's sincere request and whispered the sannyasa mantra into the ears of the boy. But when Swamiji left to perform austerities, the child died. He was three years old.[14]

One evening Girish and Narendra were invited to Balaram Basu's house in Calcutta for dinner. Girish later recalled that occasion: "Narendra and I sat side by side at the dining table. At the end of the meal, mangoes were served: I got sweet mangoes, but Narendra got sour ones. Piqued, Narendra said to me: 'Rascal G.C., you are getting all of the sweet mangoes and I have only the sour ones. You must have prearranged this.' I replied: 'We are householders. We have come to this world to enjoy ourselves. You are a monk. You are supposed to beg for your food from door to door. It is your good fortune that you have gotten the bad, sour mangoes.' Thus our quarrel began and we laughed heartily. Narendra was a great debater, but I was not so bad either. I greatly enjoyed quarrelling with him. It was really sweet!"[15]

Girish remained silent for a while. Then his facial expression changed and he became somber: "What an inauspicious time it was when we met! We never had any opportunity to exchange sweet words: we teased and quarreled with each other, berating each other. I could not rest until I had quarreled with Narendra because this would relieve the heaviness of my heart. Seldom do we find a person like Narendra in this world. It was a great joy talking to him. Inside he was full of sweetness, so it did not matter whether he spoke sweetly or harshly."[16]

Swamiji's brother Mahendra once described the repartee between Girish and Narendra: "Nobody dared to argue with Narendra, except for Girish, who was well versed in English literature and had a prodigious memory and strong common sense. With a view to revealing the depth of each other's wisdom, they would playfully tease or chastise each other. Excited, Girish would burst out: 'Keep quiet, rascal! You are a beggar — a vagabond monk!' Narendra would retort with a smile: 'Rascal, you are a clown! You only know how to make nautch-girls dance at the theatre. Do you have any brains?' Thus they enjoyed themselves and entertained others."[17]

Both Girish and Swami Vivekananda believed that Ramakrishna was an incarnation of God. However, sometimes Vivekananda would play the devil's advocate to goad Girish into an argument. One day their topic of debate was whether God could take a human form. Swamiji baited Girish, attacking his belief in his guru's divinity: "Look, G.C., whatever you may say, the infinite Brahman cannot enter into a human body, which is only three and a half cubits tall." Girish responded: "Yes, it is possible. Why not?" Then they began to argue, and neither one would yield. Gradually the argument became louder and louder. The more calmly Swamiji put his counter arguments, the more excited Girish became. Finally Girish slapped the floor and shouted: "You rascal, keep quiet! I have seen the infinite God take finite form in the Master." Immediately Swamiji got up and embraced him.[18]

It is wonderful to see how the disciples of Ramakrishna loved their guru. Pointing to Girish, Swamiji said to his brother disciples: "At least my guru has one disciple who can never be brought down from his immovable mountain of faith."[19]

Vivekananda greatly appreciated Girish's talent, but he remarked that he was greater as a poet than as a playwright. Swamiji started *Udbodhan*, the Bengali magazine of the Ramakrishna Order, and appointed Swami Trigunatitananda to be the editor. When Swamiji was visiting the West in 1899, Trigunatita gave him some pencils and paper so that he could write articles for the *Udbodhan*. But Swamiji was so busy that he could not write. He suggested to Trigunatita: "Do one thing: From time to time visit G.C., who lives nearby, and bring a pencil and notebook. When he sees you, he will begin to talk about the Master and religious topics. Listen carefully and write down his words, then expand them as articles to publish in the *Udbodhan*."[20]

*   *   *

In May 1893 Swami Vivekananda left for America to represent Hinduism at the Parliament of Religions in Chicago. He returned to Calcutta almost four years later, in February 1897. When Swamiji arrived he went to Pashupati Basu's house in North Calcutta, where Girish and other brother disciples received him cordially. Swamiji told Girish: "G.C., I carried your Thakur [Ramakrishna] to the other side of the ocean." When Girish was about to take the dust of Swamiji's feet, he said, "What are you doing, G.C.? That would harm me." He then himself bowed down to Girish.[21] During another conversation, Swamiji said: "I met many great pandits in the West. But when I challenged them, they were totally defeated. You are the only person whom I have not been able to defeat." Embarrassed, Girish said: "Oh, no! Don't say that to me, brother!"[22]

In March 1897 the anniversary of Ramakrishna's birth was observed in the Dakshineswar temple garden. A huge crowd attended the festival. When Swamiji saw Girish in the crowd near the Panchavati, he bowed down to him and said, "G.C., what a difference between those days and these!" Swamiji meant that only a few people had come to pay respect to the Master when he was alive, and now a large number of people attended the festival celebrating the day he was born. Girish replied: "Yes, you are right. But I have a desire to see more of his divine play." After a short conversation, Swamiji took his Western disciples to show them the bel tree and other important places in Dakshineswar.

Girish always preached the greatness of the Master and his disciples. He said to the devotees: "One day Haramohan [Mitra] told me that he saw in a newspaper that some people had spread a slanderous rumour against Swamiji in America. I said to him: 'If I see with my own eyes that Naren is doing anything wrong, I will consider that my eyes are defective. I will pull them out. He is the kind of butter that has been collected before sunrise; it never gets mixed with water. Those who see faults in him will go to hell.'" Girish was overwhelmed when Swami Niranjanananda told him about Swamiji's grand receptions from Colombo to Calcutta on his return to India from the West.[23]

On 1 May 1897 Swami Vivekananda established the Ramakrishna Mission in the presence of the Master's monastic and householder disciples at Balaram Basu's house in Baghbazar, Calcutta. He delineated the aims and objectives of the Mission. Everyone present approved them, including Girish. Later Swamiji went to Girish's house nearby to chat with him.

Swamiji: "Look G.C., nowadays the thought constantly arises in my mind that I should do this and that and scatter the Master's message all over the world. But I think that this may create another religious sect in India. So I am extremely cautious about it. Sometimes I think, let there be another sect. But again I think: no, it is not right. The Master never disturbed anyone's spiritual beliefs. Samesightedness was his ideal. As I consider this, I often suppress my thoughts. What do you say?"

Girish: "What can I say? You are the instrument in his hand. Whatever he makes you do, you must do. I don't know about all those things you have just mentioned, but I see that the Master's power is working through you. And I see it with open eyes."

Swamiji: "I think that we act according to our own will. But in my experience, whenever there is any danger or difficulty, want or deficiency, the Master reveals himself and guides me in the right direction. I cannot see any limit to the Master's power!"

Girish: "The Master said, 'If you understand everything, all of your activities will vanish at once.' Who will then work? And who will make others do the work?"

Then the discussion drifted to America. Swamiji enthusiastically described its prosperity, its people's good and bad qualities, their wealth, and so on. Girish intentionally changed the topic, as he later explained to others: "The Master told me that if Swamiji talks about his personal spiritual experiences, that will rouse his intense renunciation and longing for God. As a result if he experiences his true nature and knows who he is, he will immediately give up his body."[24]

Once at Balaram's house in Calcutta Swamiji was giving a lesson on the Rig Veda to one of his disciples when Girish arrived. Swamiji was in the process of explaining how creation evolved from sound. He turned to Girish and said: "Well, G.C., you do not care to study all this. You have spent your life with Krishna and Vishnu!"*

Girish responded: "What shall I study, brother? I have neither time nor intelligence enough to fully comprehend such things. But during this lifetime, with the Master's grace, I shall cross the ocean of maya, bidding farewell to your Vedas and Vedanta. It's because he wants to do a lot of preaching through you that he made you study all those books. I don't need them." Saying this, Girish touched the big volume of the Rig Veda with his head and repeatedly exclaimed: "Victory to Ramakrishna in the form of the Veda!"

While Swamiji was thinking, Girish continued: "Look, Naren, let me tell you something. You have studied enough of the Vedas and Vedanta.

---

*An allusion to the dramas that Girish wrote, in which Krishna, Vishnu, and other characters of Hindu mythology play prominent parts.

Have you found anywhere in them a way for us out of the profound miseries in this country — all this grief and starvation, all of these horrible sins of abortion and adultery? Do your Vedas have any way to solve these problems? Here is a woman who used to be wealthy enough to feed many people every day, but now she has had nothing to eat for the last three days. Here is an innocent housewife abused and killed by thugs. Here is a woman driven by shame to have an abortion. Here is a widow cheated and robbed by her relatives."

While Girish continued narrating this painful portrait of Indian society, Swamiji remained silent. Tears began to flow from his eyes. He got up and left the room.

Girish then told Swamiji's disciple: "Did you see? What a great and loving heart! I respect your Swamiji not as a Vedic scholar, but for the great heart that made him retire weeping just now at the thought of the sorrows of his fellow beings. Did you notice how the Vedas and Vedanta disappeared from his mind as he listened to the suffering of others?"

Swamiji returned and said to Girish: "Look, G.C., if I need to be born a thousand times to remove the sufferings of the world, surely I will accept this fate. I will do anything to relieve the misery of a single soul. What good is it to attain one's own liberation? One should take all beings along that path. Can you tell me why I feel this way?"

Girish: "Well, that is why the Master considered you to be the greatest receptacle among his disciples."[25]

During Ramakrishna's birthday celebration in February 1898, Girish went to Belur Monastery to attend the festival. Swamiji was pleased to see Girish. He smeared Girish with *vibhuti* [sanctified ashes], put rosaries around his neck and arms, set a matted wig on his head, and wrapped an ochre robe around his waist. After all this Girish looked like Shiva. Then Swamiji told the assembled devotees: "The Master used to say, 'Girish is an incarnation of Bhairava [a companion of Shiva].' There is no difference between him and us." Then Swamiji said to Girish: "G.C., you will have to tell us about the Master today. (*Addressing the audience*) Please sit down and be quiet."

Girish was so overwhelmed with spiritual emotion that he could not speak for a while. Finally he said: "What shall I say about our all-merciful Master? I feel his infinite grace. He has allowed an insignificant person like myself to sit here with all-renouncing sannyasins." As he said this, Girish's voice became choked with emotion and he could say nothing else that day.[26]

As mentioned in Chapter 20, when Ramakrishna passed away, Girish did not go to see his body. But when Swami Vivekananda breathed his last on 4 July 1902, Girish went to Belur Math the next day and sat on the bank of the Ganges to watch Vivekananda's cremation. Brokenhearted, Girish lamented: "Naren, you were supposed to live and spread the glory of the Master by telling people the story of my transformation. But fate has destroyed this dream of mine. I am an old fellow [he was 19 years older than Swamiji], and yet I have had to live to see this terrible scene. You are the Master's son and you have gone to him. You have departed too soon and left us in a pitiable condition. How unfortunate we are!"[27]

Chapter 22

Girish and Holy Mother

During Ramakrishna's lifetime Girish publicly declared him to be an avatar. As for Holy Mother, he held her in high esteem as the wife of his guru and cherished great respect for her. One day he was pacing back and forth on the roof of his house with his second wife when Holy Mother was on the roof of Balaram's house nearby. Girish's wife noticed her and said to him, "Look, there is the Mother walking on the roof." Girish at once turned his face away and replied: "No, no. My eyes are sinful. I won't look at her that way; I cannot be a sneak."[1] Immediately he went downstairs.

It is said that the exceptional good fortune of his second wife brought Girish his fame, his wealth, and the grace of the Master. Girish and his second wife had three children: two girls and a boy. When his son was born, his wife became very ill. Girish arranged for her treatment, which continued for a year. But finally she died on 26 December 1888. Grief-stricken, Girish tried to occupy himself by studying mathematics and caring for his little son. Girish had once asked the Master to be born as his son, so he believed that his boy was Ramakrishna reincarnated. He served the boy wholeheartedly. Girish bought for him new clothes, cups, glasses, and plates; and he did not allow anyone else to use those things. Holy Mother always took the boy on her lap whenever she met him.

In 1890 Holy Mother was staying at Sourindra Thakur's house at Baranagore. Girish was still grieving for his wife, and Swami Niranjanananda knew this. He insisted that Girish visit the Mother. Girish paid his first visit to Holy Mother at Baranagore with his three-year-old son. The little boy could not speak at that time and expressed himself through inarticulate sounds and gestures. He had seen Holy Mother before. Anxiously he pointed at the upper floor where the Mother lived and simply said: "Ooh! Ooh!" An attendant of the Mother took him upstairs and he rolled on the ground before her. Presently he came down and began to pull at his father's hand. Girish burst out crying and said: "How can I go

353

Holy Mother Sarada Devi, Calcutta, circa 1905

to the Mother? I am a great sinner." The boy would not leave him alone. Finally he took his son in his arms and climbed the stairs, his body trembling and tears flowing from his eyes. Finally he fell flat at the Mother's feet and said: "It is through him that I have seen your sacred feet."[2] The boy died not long afterwards.

In his early life Girish tried to use alcohol to relieve the grief caused by his first wife's death. Now he was determined to use divine intoxication to relieve his grief over the loss of his second wife and his son.

Kumudbandhu Sen wrote in his reminiscences:

Whenever Girish Ghosh referred to Sri Ramakrishna and the Holy Mother, his manner of expression was extraordinarily superb and was different from that of the other devotees. His deep reverence for and strong faith in their divinity and unbounded grace were expressed in his utterances, and he inspired those who happened to listen to him. Later he told me that at first he and other lay devotees of Sri Ramakrishna could not recognize the greatness of the Holy Mother. He said: "We used to pay our respectful tribute to her as the spiritual consort of our Master. We looked upon him alone as our guide, friend, father, and mother — all combined. It was Niranjan [later Swami Niranjanananda] who opened my eyes. In the midst of the grim tragedies of life, stricken with grief and sorrow, I felt for a time quite perplexed and could not console my disturbed mind. During my bereavement, Niranjan often came to me and tried to divert my mind by his spiritual talk.

"One day I told him, 'Brother Niranjan, it is a pity that I cannot now see Sri Ramakrishna, who is my shelter, my only refuge.' Niranjan interrupted me, saying: 'Why! Mother is there. Is there any difference between the Master and Mother? Can you imagine Narayana without Lakshmi, Shiva without Parvati, Rama without Sita, and Krishna without Radha or Rukmini?' I was taken aback. I told him, 'What do you say — the Master and Mother are one and the same?' Niranjan replied: 'Well, you believe that Sri Ramakrishna is an avatar, God incarnate in human form. Do you mean to say that he took an ordinary woman (*jiva*) as his spiritual partner in his divine life? You must remember the words of our Master, "Brahman and Shakti are one and the same — though in manifestation they appear to us as two." Mother is Shakti, the Shakti of Purna-Brahma Ramakrishna.'

"His words cleared my vision and I could at once recognize the Divine Mother — the Mother of the Universe — incarnated as the Holy Mother for the salvation of mankind. I felt a strong urge to go to Jayrambati and see our Holy Mother, who alone could wipe away my tears and remove my sorrow over my recent adversities. Niranjan approved of my suggestion and offered to accompany me there. But Balaram Basu vehemently opposed this proposal, as he did not like the idea that I should disturb the Holy Mother with my worldly problems and miseries. At that time Swami Vivekananda was away from Calcutta and the matter was referred to him by Niranjan. Getting his approval we started for Jayrambati. I could hardly express my joy when I first went to Kamarpukur. To me the cottage where Sri Ramakrishna was born was like a Rishi's holy hermitage; the scenery and its surrounding environment were enchanting. Thence we proceeded to Jayrambati. There, during my stay, I directly asked the Mother, 'Well, Mother, are you my real mother or an adopted mother?' The Mother said, 'Yes, I am your real mother.'"

Further, Girish Ghosh told us in forceful language, pregnant with deep emotion: "Yes, Mother — the Divine Mother — has appeared as a poor village girl, living in a remote hamlet, away from the din and bustle of a town where life reflects only the formal and artificial ways of worldly-wise and sophisticated men and women. I did not ask for anything from Mother. As soon as I went to her all my sorrow and misery vanished completely, and I felt a supreme serenity of mind which I had never experienced before. Oh! Those days were spent in heavenly bliss and joy."

One day at the Mother's place at Jayrambati, a minstrel [Haridas Vairagi of Deshra] came and sang a Bengali song to the accompaniment of a broken violin. A free English rendering of the song is given below:

> O Uma, my darling, what good tidings I hear!
> People say you are adored in Varanasi as Annapurna. Is it true?
> O Gauri, when I married you to Shiva,
> He went as a beggar from door to door for a morsel of food.
> But today how glad I am to hear
> You are now Queen of the World, seated by His side.
> And they called my naked Shiva a madman:
> How much abuse I had to bear from everyone!
> Now I hear that doorkeepers guard His palace
> And god's like Indra, Chandra, and Yama hardly can see Him.
> Shiva used to live in the Himalayas;
> Many a day He got His food by begging;
> Now He rules over Varanasi and is as rich as Kuvera.
> Is it you who have brought Him all this good fortune?
> No doubt He is very rich now,
> Else why should Gauri be so proud?
> She does not cast her eyes even upon her own children,
> And turns her face away from Radhika.

When the minstrel finished singing the song, Girish Ghosh, Swami Niranjanananda, and others who heard it could not restrain their tears. The Mother too, with all her women companions, was shedding tears. It recalled the story of the early life of the Holy Mother, when Sri Ramakrishna was often referred to as the "mad son-in-law" by the people of Jayrambati and its neighbourhood, when her own parents repented giving her in marriage to Sri Ramakrishna, and her neighbours pitied her and expressed sorrow at her "miserable" fate. She did not and could not then protest, and she humbly suffered all those humiliating remarks in silence, though she knew in her innermost heart that her husband was a god-intoxicated man, far above ordinary people. She then tasted divine bliss whenever she came in contact with him. She did not go to anybody's house and she never attended any social function lest people should make humiliating remarks about her husband and blame her for her ill luck. Now that Sri Ramakrishna is revered as a prophet and an avatar and is worshipped in many places, people come to her for her *darshan* even in that remote village, which is situated in an out-of-the-way place. The Holy Mother is now regarded by many devotees as the Mother of the Universe.

The song drew tears from the eyes of the listeners as it aptly applied to and conjured up a vision of the early life of Sri Ramakrishna and Sri Saradamani Devi (the Holy Mother). I heard from Girish Ghosh that for over an hour all remained spellbound and their eyes glistened with tears. But those happy days came to an end.

Holy Mother used to travel back and forth between her Calcutta and Jayrambati residences. One day we heard that Mother was leaving for Jayrambati after Kali Puja. On the day of her departure Girish Ghosh came to bid her farewell. He did not utter a word, and with a serious countenance he called Yogananda and went directly to the Holy Mother. We all followed him. Full of emotion and deep reverence, he prostrated at the feet of the Holy Mother and with folded hands said: "Mother, when I come to you I think that I am a little child coming to its own mother. Had I been a grown-up son, then I would have served my mother. But it is quite the opposite. You serve us and we do not serve you. You are going to Jayrambati to serve the people, even by cooking food for others in that village kitchen. How can I serve you, and what do I know about service of the Divine Mother?"

Girish's voice was choked and his whole face was red with emotion. He again said: "Mother, you know our minds, which we ourselves do not know. We cannot go to you. It is through your grace and kindness that you come here to see your children. Whenever you wish to come here, please do not hesitate for a moment and we, your children, will always be happy to see our Mother and shall deem it a privilege to render you whatever service you will graciously allow us to offer."

Girish then addressed us who were standing behind him: "It is difficult for human beings to believe that God may incarnate in a human form like any of us. Can you realize that you are standing before the Mother of the Universe in the form of a village woman? Can you imagine the Divine Mother doing all kinds of domestic and social duties like any ordinary woman? Yet she is the Mother of the Universe — *maha-maya, maha-shakti* — appearing on earth for the salvation of all creatures and at the same time exemplifying the ideal of true motherhood."

His words made a deep impression on all present, and the whole atmosphere was charged with serene sublimity and calmness. Yes, it was then a veritable paradise, pervaded with spiritual bliss and benediction. We accompanied the Mother to the railway station. She blessed us all as we touched her feet in salutation.[3]

Swami Bodhananda left a vivid account of Girish's visit to Jayrambati in 1891, which is presented here in an abridged form:

Our party consisted of Swami Niranjanananda, Swami Subodhananda, Girish, Kanai [later Swami Nirbhayananda], Kalikrishna [later Swami Virajananda], and myself. Girish also took a cook and a servant with him. After breakfast at Girish's house we left for the Howrah railway station and then reached the Burdwan station at noon. We had our lunch there and bought luchis, fried potatoes, halwa, and sweets for our supper and some special sweets to offer to the Master in Kamarpukur. Five bullock carts were hired and we started our journey just before evening. We crossed the Damodar River, which was almost dry. After crossing the river by bullock cart, we finished our supper. At 10:00 p.m. we resumed our journey, but shortly after, the jerking motion of the cart made Girish's stomach upset. We were then in the middle of a vast meadow. Swami Niranjanananda stopped all the carts and asked the drivers to unfasten the bullocks from the carts. Within an hour Girish fell asleep and then in the morning he felt normal.

We resumed our journey and reached Uchalan (16 miles from Burdwan) at 10:00 a.m. We went to an inn and had lunch. After resting we had tea. We again bought luchis, fried potatoes, and halwa for supper. The drivers drove the whole night, covering 16 miles from Uchalan to Kamarpukur. We arrived there at 9:00 a.m. and met Brother Ramlal and Sister Lakshmi, the Master's nephew and niece. We took a bath in the Haldarpukur, had the prasad of Raghuvir, and spent the night at Kamarpukur. The next morning we left for Jayrambati, which is 4 miles from Kamarpukur. Girish went by palanquin, and the rest of us walked along the mud road. We arrived in Jayrambati at 11:00 a.m. Girish took a bath in the Talpukur and went to visit the Holy Mother wearing his wet cloth and carrying a mango in his hand. He fell flat on the courtyard and bowed down to the Mother. This scene is still vivid in my memory.

I had a great opportunity to associate closely with Girish in Jayrambati. We lived in the same room; we ate together, walked together, and talked freely. When he was in the mood, he would sing some devotional songs in praise of the Divine Mother.

Because of the many guests in Jayrambati, Holy Mother was extremely busy from morning till 11:00 p.m. taking care of our food, sleeping arrangements, and so on. Although Girish's cook and servant worked, the Mother had to supervise everything. It was not easy to get milk early in the morning in Jayrambati, but the Mother would go to the villagers and collect some milk so that we could have tea. We had breakfast with puffed rice, sandesh, and tea; and then after a bath we had some prasad. Mother served lunch with eight or nine kinds of preparations, as well as curd and sweets. In the afternoon we had tea and snacks, and at supper luchi, rice, vegetables, and sweets.

Girish would listen to the dialect of the illiterate farmers and imitate their language. He considered hiring a farmer and bringing him to Calcutta to act in one of his plays. After staying for two weeks in Jayrambati, everyone returned to Calcutta except for Swami Niranjanananda and Girish. The Mother looked after us as her own children. I still remember that I rolled chapatis a few times and the Mother baked them. It was her grace that I could be near her. Those are unforgettable memories![4]

Swami Nikhilananda, author of *Holy Mother*, supplied some more information about Girish and Holy Mother:

After arriving at Jayrambati, Girish took his bath and bowed down to Holy Mother. His body was shaking with emotion. Casting his eyes upon her, he exclaimed with surprise: "Ah, you are that Mother!" He suddenly recalled a vivid dream of many years before, when he had been bedridden from cholera. A luminous goddess wearing a red-bordered sari appeared to him and offered him some sacred prasad, which soon cured him. He now recognized Holy Mother as that deity and felt that she had always been looking after him as his guardian angel. To verify this, Girish asked her: "What kind of Mother are you?" Immediately Holy Mother replied: "Your real Mother, not just the wife of your guru, not a foster mother, not a vague sort of mother. Your real Mother."[5]

Girish spent a happy and carefree time at Jayrambati, wandering about freely with the villagers in the meadows, and drinking in the beauty of the sunset in the open fields. Soon his fame spread throughout the area and he would sing now and then to entertain the simple villagers. One day while Girish was singing for the villagers, Holy Mother heard him singing this song:

Gopala crawls off from the queen
Lest she should catch hold of him.
He casts at her a furtive glance.
As she eagerly cries, "Stop, stop!"
Gopala crawls farther off.[6]

One day at Jayrambati Girish had a heated discussion with Kalikumar, one of the Mother's brothers, regarding whether Holy Mother was an ordinary human being or a goddess. Kalikumar naturally regarded her as his sister and said: "It is you who call her the Divine Mother or the Mother of the Universe. But we were born from the same womb. I do not understand what you say." "What are you talking about?" replied Girish firmly. "You are the son of an ordinary brahmin, born and reared in a village. You have forgotten the duties of your caste, such as worship and study, and are now living as a farmer. If a man promises you a bullock for your plough, you will run after him for at least six months. Is it not possible for Mahamaya, who can make the impossible possible, to appear as your sister and hoodwink you for the rest of your life? Listen to me. If you want liberation in this life or afterwards, go immediately to the Mother and take refuge at her feet. I urge you to go at once."

Girish's words always carried great power. Kalikumar went to Holy Mother and clutched her feet, begging for her grace. She said: "Kali, what are you doing? I am your sister. What are you saying?" Kalikumar returned to Girish the same person he was before. Girish asked him to go back, but he would not. Girish once remarked that Holy Mother's brothers must have performed bone-breaking austerities in a previous life to have obtained her as their sister.[7]

Holy Mother always wore a veil when she was with the monastic disciples and male devotees of the Master, except for Swamis Adbhutananda and Advaitananda and a few others. When Girish ate his lunch at Jayrambati, the Mother would say to him from behind her veil: "My son, please have a little more rice. You will feel hungry if you eat such a small amount of food." Girish was overwhelmed by Holy Mother's affection. Observing her shyness and unwillingness to talk to her male devotees, Girish once told her: "Mother, the Master has become a *chhabi* [a picture] and you have become a *bauma* [a bashful bride who wears a long veil]."[8] Girish meant that people now see the Master only in a picture, so the Mother should not maintain so much distance from and formality with her children.

Girish later recalled his days in Jayrambati: "What infinite affection did I see in the Mother! She was my real mother. She kept her vigilant eyes on every minute detail. One day in Jayrambati I saw the Mother going to the pond with a piece of soap, a bed sheet, and a pillow cover. When I went to bed that night I found that my pillow cover and bed sheet had been beautifully washed. Tears trickle from my eyes when I think of her affection."[9]

Because of the bereavements he had suffered, Girish realized the emptiness of family life. During his visit to Jayrambati he approached Holy Mother for her permission to embrace the monastic life. But the Mother did not give her consent to his request and suggested instead that he continue his literary and acting careers. Girish then gave up the idea of becoming a monk. Shortly after this, Girish took the opportunity to spend a few days in Kamarpukur, and the Mother joined his party. His long association with the Holy Mother and his visits to the sacred places of Jayrambati and Kamarpukur finally brought solace to Girish's broken heart. He returned to Calcutta and resumed his acting career with fresh vigour and a clearer spiritual outlook.

Girish often visited Holy Mother when she was in Calcutta. Once Holy Mother was returning from a long stay in Jayrambati. Swamis Brahmananda and Premananda went to Howrah Station to receive her. The train was three hours late, but the swamis and her devotees waited. When the train arrived, Yogin-ma and Golap-ma helped Mother out of the train and the swamis rushed to take the dust of her feet. Golap-ma was the Mother's guard and caretaker. In her high-pitched voice she scolded Swami Brahmananda: "Maharaj, have you no sense whatsoever? The Mother has just gotten off the train, tired and exhausted from the heat. If you make such a fuss about prostrating, how can I restrain the others?" The venerable swamis felt remorseful and stepped back. The Mother was then driven to Udbodhan House in a carriage, and she went upstairs to rest.

A little later, Swamis Brahmananda and Premananda decided to go to Udbodhan House to confirm that proper arrangements had been made for her. Girish arrived soon after they did and asked them about Holy Mother. When Golap-ma heard Girish's voice, she came downstairs and said to him: "My words beat a retreat, Girish Babu, before your grotesque devotion. You have come to see Mother! She is tired and exhausted. She is supposed to have some rest now, but you have come to disturb her."

Girish retorted: "You are a boisterous woman! I had thought that the Mother's heart would be soothed seeing her children's faces after such a long time. Yet this woman is teaching me devotion to the Mother! Phew!" Girish and Swamis Brahmananda and Premananda then went upstairs to pay their respects to Holy Mother. They bowed down to her and she blessed them. Girish's love and devotion overruled Golap-ma's decrees. After Girish had left, full of joy, Golap-ma complained to Holy Mother about his rude words. Holy Mother replied: "I have warned you many times about criticizing my children."[10]

In 1907 Girish decided to perform Durga Puja at his home, and he and his sister Dakshina wanted Holy Mother to be present on that occasion. However, Holy Mother was then at Jayrambati and had been intermittently suffering from malarial fever. Swami Saradananda wrote to the Mother about Girish's desire, and the gracious Mother agreed to come to Calcutta. At that time there were riots in Calcutta and there was a blackout at night in the city. M. and Lalit Chattopadhyay left Calcutta and went to the Vishnupur railway station, where they met Mother who had travelled there by bullock cart. Their train arrived at Howrah Station that night.

Holy Mother, accompanied by Radhu and her mother, got into Lalit's waiting carriage. M., Lalit, and some devotees escorted them, sitting on the top of the carriage or standing on the footboard. Mother stayed at Balaram's house, which was close to Girish's house.

Durga Puja began a few days after they arrived, and it continued for four days. Mother attended the puja at Girish's house from beginning to end. In addition, many devotees came to Balaram's house to pay their respects to her. Despite her poor health she sat for hours to fulfill her devotees' wishes. Thus two days passed. It was decided that Holy Mother should rest and not attend Sandhi Puja, which takes place between the *ashtami* and *navami* pujas (the eighth and ninth days of the worship). This special ceremony happened to fall at midnight that year. Girish was upset when he heard this, and he decided to stay in his room while the worship was going on. However, when the time of Sandhi Puja came, Holy Mother changed her mind. She covered herself with a chadar, walked through the narrow lane, and knocked at the back door of Girish's house, saying: "I have come." Girish's maidservant opened the door and news of the Mother's arrival spread. Girish hurriedly went to the worship hall, bowed down to the Mother, and joyfully remarked: "I thought that my worship of the Divine Mother would be incomplete. Meanwhile the Mother has tapped on the door and announced, 'Here I have come.'" After four days of worship and Holy Mother's presence, Girish felt that Mother Durga had graciously accepted his worship. On that auspicious occasion Girish had invited his friends and relatives, as well as the actors and actresses of his theatre, who all received the blessings of the Holy Mother.[11]

* * *

Aparesh Mukhopadhyay, an actor and playwright, wrote: "A man sees the outer form of a man, but God sees inside him, and I witnessed this truth: The Holy Mother, the spiritual consort of Ramakrishna, came to a theatre in Calcutta and embraced an actress who was a courtesan. Thus she demonstrated that God's grace does not discriminate between good and thorny plants, between good and bad human beings, and does not care for the injunctions and prohibitions of the empirical world. We saw that divine grace only purifies all — irrespective of caste and creed."[12] The ever-pure Holy Mother accepted and blessed some of the actresses in Girish's theatre. As Ramakrishna gave respectability to the Bengali stage by watching a performance of *Chaitanya Lila*, so also the Holy Mother saw several of Girish's plays and saw him act as well.

It was probably in the last part of the nineteenth century that the Holy Mother saw one of Girish's plays for the first time. She went to see *Daksha Yajna* performed at the Minerva Theatre at 6 Beadon Street in Calcutta. Ramakrishna had also seen this play. Girish acted in the role of Daksha, as mentioned in Chapter 13. Brahmachari Akshay Chaitanya wrote, "Holy Mother went into ecstasy seeing the play of *Daksha Yajna*."[13]

Several years later Girish invited the Holy Mother to see *Vilwamangal Thakur*, a popular devotional play that was described in Chapter 16. Holy Mother went to see it at the Minerva Theatre on Wednesday, 25 January 1905. Girish arranged a royal box seat for the Mother and engaged an attendant to fan her with a large palm-leaf fan. Girish acted in the role of a hypocritical monk who was trying to teach Thakmani, a female confidante of the courtesan Chintamani, how to love Krishna. As she watched Girish's performance, Holy Mother commented with a smile, "Why are you behaving like this in your old age?" And again, observing the one-pointed love of Vilwamangal, the Mother exclaimed, "Aha! Aha! What a wonderful love!"[14]

Holy Mother went to the Minerva Theatre again on 1 March 1905 to see *Jana* performed. Girish based this play on the Mahabharata; it was first performed on 23 December 1893. Jana, a highly powerful and spiritual soul, was the wife of Niladhvaja, the virtuous king of Mahishmati. This royal couple had a son named Prabir. Prince Prabir was a great hero and had been made invincible by the grace of Shiva. In the play King Yudhishthira performs the horse sacrifice, in which his horse roams through all of the kingdoms, and their rulers pay their allegiance to him. Arjuna was protecting the horse. But, instead of paying obeisance to Yudhishthira, the heroic Prince Prabir captured the horse and kept it for himself. War between Arjuna and Prabir was inevitable. Prabir won the first battle. To protect Arjuna, Krishna schemed to tempt Prabir with Rati, the goddess of lust. She took away Prabir's power, and the next day he was killed. Krishna later blessed Niladhvaja and Jana.

In this play, Girish introduced the role of a jester, whose part he took himself. He portrayed himself in that role, criticizing and using abusive words against Krishna — but at the same time showing deep devotion to him. He had once treated his guru, Ramakrishna, the same way. As Holy Mother watched Girish's performance, she laughed. Swami Saradananda asked, "Mother, why are you laughing?" Mother replied: "I see Girish's own character reflected in that role. I know he is endowed with deep faith and he believes that one can have liberation by calling on God — and again he abuses God."[15]

Holy Mother's next visit to the Minerva Theatre was on 22 April 1906. She saw the play *Chaitanya Lila*, which the Master had seen on 21 September 1884.

Ashutosh Mitra wrote:

> Last night Holy Mother went to see *Chaitanya Lila*. Girish arranged for this play to be performed for one night after a long time and offered a royal box seat to the Mother. The roles of two villains — Jagai and Madhai — were enacted by Ardhendu Shekhar and Girish. Bhushan Kumari, a famous actress, had retired from the stage, but she acted in the role of Chaitanya without any remuneration because of Holy Mother. Sushilabala acted in the role of Nitai, a disciple of Chaitanya. Both actresses came and bowed down to the Mother before the play started. Holy Mother later commented: "That girl [Bhushan] was full of devotion; otherwise one cannot act in that role. She looked and dressed like the real Chaitanya. Who could tell that she was a woman?" About Jagai and Madhai, the Mother remarked: "Where will you find devotees like them? Likewise, where can one find devotees like Ravana and Hiranyakashipu? Girish used to scold the Master, and at the same time he had so much devotion for him. They came to this world like that. Is it easy to become a devotee? Does devotion come automatically?"[16]

On Sunday, 12 September 1909, Holy Mother went to the Minerva Theatre to see *Pandava Gaurav*, "The Glory of the Pandavas." Girish based this drama on the story of Dandi, the king of Avanti, and Urvasi, a celestial nymph. Urvasi was disrespectful to the sage Durvasa, so he cursed her, saying that she would be a beautiful woman at night and a mare during the day. She would be released from the curse when the eight divine powers came together. One night Dandi went out to hunt and met Urvasi. He fell in love with her, although she told him her whole story.

Girish connected this legend with Krishna and other characters of the Mahabharata. Just before the war described in the Mahabharata, Krishna wants Dandi to give him the mare, who is really Urvasi. Dandi leaves his kingdom and runs away with the horse. At last he takes refuge with the Pandavas, who are devoted to Krishna. Bhishma says: "The pole star of this world of maya is dharma, and the essence of dharma is to protect a person who has sought refuge." A conflict arises between the Pandavas and Krishna that is averted only when the gods and the Divine Mother appear, manifesting all of the eight divine powers. Urvasi is thus freed from the curse and returns to heaven. In this drama, Girish performed the role of Kanchuki, an old brahmin minister in Dandi's court.

Swami Shantananda recorded in his reminiscences:

> I was then serving Holy Mother at Udbodhan House in Calcutta. One day Girish came to see her and invited her to see him act. Holy Mother agreed. She, Radhu, Maku, and other women devotees went in one carriage; Lalit Chattopadhyay, Dr. Kanjilal, and I went in another carriage. Girish was extremely happy that the Mother had come to see his performance, and was busy trying to make the play perfect. He arranged a special box seat for the Mother and we sat next to her. The Mother silently watched the play. When Kanchuki appeared on the stage, the Mother commented: "Oh, that is Girish. He has dressed very well with wonderful make-up. It is hard to recognize him."
>
> The companions of the goddess sang this closing song:
>
> > Look, look, at the charming Divine Mother;
> > Who says that She is a black woman?
> > Open your eyes and see how Her beauty makes the world
> >   luminous.
>
> The Mother calmly watched the play. I observed that when the song was sung she became absorbed in deep meditation, and she remained in that ecstatic state for some time. The Mother saw the entire play, and when we returned to Udbodhan it was 1:30 a.m.[17]

There was a benefit performance for the Ramakrishna Mission in Varanasi at the Minerva Theatre on 12 July 1910. On that occasion Holy Mother saw two of Girish's plays: *Vilwamangal Thakur* and *Jana*.

According to Akshay Chaitanya, the Holy Mother went to see *Kalapahar*, another play by Girish, at the Manomohan Theatre at 68 Beadon Street on 1 September 1915, a few years after Girish passed away (on 8 February 1912). Girish had based *Kalapahar* on a historical incident, but added devotional elements and Ramakrishna's teachings to it (see Chapter 16).

In September 1918 Holy Mother went to see *Ramanuja* performed at the Minerva Theatre. This play, about a saint and philosopher of the 11th century, was written by Aparesh Chandra Mukhopadhyay, an actor, playwright, and a close associate of Girish. Pravrajika Bharatiprana, an attendant and disciple of Holy Mother, wrote: "Holy Mother, Golap-ma, Yogin-ma, I, and many others went to see the play *Ramanuja* at the Minerva Theatre. Aparesh arranged special seats for us. The Mother was happy to see the play. There was a scene in which the guru tells Ramanuja during initiation: 'Never tell this mantra to others. He who hears this mantra will be liberated. If you share this mantra with others, you will go to hell.' For the benefit of humanity, the great soul Ramanuja disobeys his guru and loudly shouts that mantra to others. Seeing that scene, the Mother went into samadhi. The famous actress Tarasundari acted in the role of Ramanuja. After that scene she came to bow down to the Mother, but found that she had no outer consciousness. After Golap-ma's repeated calls, the Mother regained partial consciousness. Then Tara bowed down to her. The Mother hugged Tara, considering her to be Ramanuja. When the play was over all of the actresses came and bowed down to the Mother. Later they came to Udbodhan to pay their respects to her."[18]

Kshirod Prasad Vidyavinod, a famous playwright and a devotee of the Mother, wanted her to see *Kinnari*, a musical play. On Sunday, 18 September 1918, the Mother went to see it with Swami Saradananda.[19]

As a mother's heart never discriminates between her good and bad children, so the Holy Mother loved the stage actresses although they came from questionable backgrounds. Holy Mother appreciated their talents in acting and music, as well as their sincere devotion for her. She had been born and brought up in a conservative and orthodox brahmin family, but she understood the importance of the theatre: It carries art and culture, religion and philosophy, history and tradition to the masses. The puritans of society gradually became silent when Ramakrishna, Holy Mother, and Swami Vivekananda each visited theatres and gave recognition to the actors and actresses, who were previously treated like outcastes by society.

*   *   *

Girish's talent and magnetic personality attracted many people whom he brought to the Master and Holy Mother. He was extremely generous with his support of the Master, Mother, and the disciples of Ramakrishna.

Girish and Holy Mother

Later, Holy Mother recalled some incidents regarding Girish: "It was Suresh [Surendra Nath] Mitra who gave money regularly to support the monastery. Girish also gave something. He bore all my expenses for a year and a half while I was at Nilambar Babu's house at Belur. Earlier he was a wretch and used to move in bad company, running a theatre. But he was a man of great faith, so he received the Master's unbounded grace. The Master gave him liberation. Once the Master said: 'Girish was born as a part of Shiva.'"[20]

On another occasion the Mother said: "The Master's disease was due to accepting the sins of others. He said: 'I have this cancer because I took on Girish's sins. He would not have been able to bear the suffering of his sinful actions.' The Master had the power to die at will. He could have easily given up the body in samadhi. But he endured all that pain in order to 'unite his young disciples.'"[21]

On 11 February 1912 the Holy Mother said to a devotee: "Alas, Girish is dead. Today is the fourth day. His relatives came here to invite me to their house to attend the ritual. He is no more; so I did not feel the need to go there. Ah! A veritable Indra [king of the gods] has fallen! Oh, what tremendous faith and devotion he had for the Master!"[22]

368 Girish Chandra Ghosh

Front row, left to right: Tarak Datta, Akshay Sen, Girish Ghosh, Swami Adbhutananda, M. (Mahendranath Gupta)
Middle Row: Kalipada Ghosh, Devendra Majumdar, Swami Advaitananda
Back row: Devndra Chakrabarty, *unknown*, *unknown*, Abinash Mukhopadhyay, Mahendra Kaviraj, Vijay Majumdar

Chapter 23

Girish and the Monastic Disciples of Ramakrishna

*G*irish was much older than most of the monastic disciples of Ramakrishna; only Swami Advaitananda was his senior. But despite their youth, Girish had deep respect for his monastic brothers. The scriptures say, *gurubat guru-putreshu* — respect the son of a guru like the guru. So Girish loved these monastic children of the Master as he did his own guru. For their part, the monks revered Girish immensely. They held him in high esteem because they had seen how the Master loved him, and how he had changed Girish's life. So the householders and the monks enjoyed a wonderful brotherly relationship, as was clear in how they interacted.

The monastic disciples sometimes teased Girish: "You write and perform as prompted by your own desires, and yet you claim that the Master gave you the task of saving the fallen people of the world. Don't you feel ashamed to talk like that?" But Girish would boldly reply: "Wait, brothers! When I meet Sri Ramakrishna again I shall tell him that I won't act in the role of a villain anymore. The next time let his monastic disciples play the villains and I shall play the part of a noble character." Girish truly believed that the Master brought different types of devotees to the world to play specific roles in his divine drama.[1]

Faith is the first step in spiritual life. But at first it is a preliminary faith. This then turns into complete faith. Thus faith is the means and faith becomes the end. Girish's spiritual journey centred on faith. He believed wholeheartedly that one can attain God through faith alone, and no other spiritual disciplines are necessary. However, he observed that other devotees of the Master first developed firm faith in their guru, and then performed meditation and austerities to obtain higher spiritual experiences. This behaviour confused Girish, and he sometimes argued with them.

Although Girish was respectful of his monastic brothers, he sometimes questioned their spiritual practices. He told them:

369

Well, brothers, sometimes I hear you lament that you have not achieved anything, and sometimes I see you run to the mountains and fast there for something — but I really don't understand why. Also, I notice that you seem to be even more convinced than I am that the Master is an incarnation of God. This really amazes me. You must perceive something higher about the Master than I do, and for that reason you are trying to attain full realization of whatever that is. Fortunately, after studying mesmerism and hypnotism, I concluded that I did not trust Ramakrishna to give me a strange or supernatural vision, which would put me into an ocean of confusion. If the Master had given me a vision, I would have thought that he had somehow hypnotized me, and thus cheated me. If that had been the case, I am sure it would have been difficult for me to hold onto the faith that the Master is an incarnation of God. I know you want to have spiritual visions. In addition, you believe that the Master is an incarnation of God! Perhaps you are great receptacles, so you can harmonize those contradictory ideas. So I console my mind: "That is not your path. Don't try to see that supernatural stuff." But I have such faith that if I have a fancy to attain bhava, a vision, or samadhi, I will forcefully demand those from the Master, and he will immediately impart those to me by his power.[2]

The monastic disciples of the Master were overwhelmed by Girish's simple, steady, and one-pointed devotion to the Master. In his later years, Girish came to understand that his monastic brothers visited holy places and performed spiritual practices in order to reconcile the Master's words, the scriptures, and their own visions and experiences.

After his youngest son's death, Girish temporarily withdrew himself from the theatre and spent most of his time with the Master's monastic disciples. It brought him tremendous joy to talk with them about the divine glory and infinite grace of the Master. His passionate devotion to his guru made him forget time and space, hunger and thirst, grief and pain. One day Swami Niranjanananda went to Girish's and said: "If the Master made you a sannyasin, then why are you living at home? Let us go to the monastery." Girish responded: "I am ready to do whatever you say, considering your words to be those of the Master. But I have no power to become a monk by my own will because I have given my power of attorney to the Master."

Swami Niranjanananda: "Then I say, please renounce everything and come this moment." Without a second thought, Girish left home, barefooted, wearing a single cloth. However, when he arrived at the monastery the other disciples realized that it would be hard for Girish to live on alms, as he had lived a comfortable life for many years. They also did not think it was necessary for a staunch devotee like him to ruin his health by leading an itinerant life. They convinced Girish to change his mind, and then they advised him to visit Kamarpukur and Jayrambati with Niranjanananda. Girish accepted their advice, considering it as coming from the Master.[3]

Sometimes Girish would visit the monastic disciples of Ramakrishna when they were living at the Alambazar monastery. As one hemp smoker loves another, so the monks were excited when Girish visited them to talk about the Master. To make their renunciation more fervent the disciples would sometimes perform a special worship ceremony called a *homa* fire. While pouring oblations into the flames, they would imagine all of their desires being burnt into ashes. They did not, however, allow any householder devotees to be present during these ceremonies. After Girish's second wife and his young son died, the monks gave him permission to attend one of their homa ceremonies. He observed the ceremony, and when the monks poured their oblations into the fire, Girish got up and poured his own oblations, imagining that his past samskaras and desires were being burnt. Afterwards, Girish sat silently absorbed in his own thoughts. Suddenly, he became extremely excited and began talking about the Master's love and compassion. Then his mood changed: He stopped talking and became grave. Without disturbing his mood, the disciples continued to talk about the Master's divine life. Only one monk noticed that Girish got up and spat on the ashes of the homa altar three times. Girish then came back and began to talk about the Master with doubled enthusiasm.

Later, that monk privately asked Girish why he had done such a strange and blasphemous thing. Surprised, Girish said to him: "Oh, you saw that? Listen, Brother, while I was talking about the Master, I realized that he had not asked me to perform a homa ritual. I did it out of my own will. I dared to pour some ghee into the fire in order to get rid of my samskaras and desires. I have become guilty of having faith in the fire god and in myself rather than in the Master. Alas! Why, I thought, did I have such a foolish idea? I fervently prayed to the Master, confessed my misdeed, and begged his forgiveness. But this rascal mind is so mischievous! It directed my attention to all of you, and said: 'You should not feel guilty for pouring oblations. Look, your monastic brothers do not feel that way; rather, they are feeling great spiritual bliss.' Then my divine conscience arose within me by the Master's grace and made me understand that my brothers were performing that ritual according to the behest of the Master, so they were not wrong. But the Master had not asked me to do that, so this is why I felt guilty for performing it.

"Then I mentally bowed down to you again and again, and a terrible repugnance arose in my mind towards those ashes as a result of my misdeed. At that time it was as if someone forced me to spit on the altar, and this gave me peace. Brother, don't be upset about my strange behaviour. In that way I scorned my bad judgement and action. Please have mercy on your weak brother and bless me that I may not commit the error of following you again."

When the other monks heard Girish's story, they did not blame him at all. Rather they said that this indicated that he had wholeheartedly taken refuge in the Master.[4]

Chapter 21 described the close relationship that Girish enjoyed with Swami Vivekananda. The rest of this chapter provides details about his relationship with the Master's other monastic disciples, and their reminiscences concerning him.

Swami Brahmananda

Girish told the following story about Swami Brahmananda's extraordinary spiritual power:

> Compared to myself, Rakhal [Swami Brahmananda] is only a young boy. I know that the Master regarded him as his spiritual son, but that is not the only reason I respect him. Once I was suffering from asthma and various kinds of ailments. As a result, my body became very weak and I lost faith in Sri Ramakrishna. With a view to getting rid of that dry spell, I engaged pandits to read the Gita and the Chandi to me. But still I had no peace of mind. Some brother disciples came to see me, and I told them about the unhappy state of my mind, but they only kept silent. Then one day Rakhal came and asked me, "How are you?" I replied: "Brother, I am in hell. Can you tell me the way out?" Rakhal listened to me and then burst into laughter. "Why worry about it?" he said. "As the waves of the ocean rise high, then go down again, and again rise, so does the mind. Don't be upset. Your present mood is due to the fact that it will lead you to a higher realm of spirituality. The wave of the mind is gathering strength." As soon as Rakhal left my house, my doubt and dryness disappeared and I got back my faith and devotion.[5]

Swami Saradananda

Girish could not bear hypocrisy. One day he told Saradananda [Sharat] the following story: "Look Sharat, my brother Atul had a daughter who was ill. Atul brought a monk from somewhere and arranged for him to stay in our shrine annex. That fellow would enjoy our food and give some medicine to my niece. I didn't object because it was his [Atul's]

Girish and the Monastic Disciples of Ramakrishna

daughter. One afternoon I could not bear it anymore. I saw that no one was around. I then quietly went to the monk and said: 'Well, holy man, I understand you give medicine to sick people. But do you know that you have a terrible worldly disease [that is, desire for money and fame]? Why don't you focus on curing your own disease?' Saying this I quickly and quietly returned to my room so that nobody could see me. The monk left the next day."[6]

Once Girish asked Swami Vivekananda to write a biography of Ramakrishna. But Swamiji declined, saying that he was incapable of doing this. He said, "Shall I make the image of a monkey while trying to make that of Shiva?" On another occasion Swamiji said, "Sharat will write." Later, after Swamiji's passing, Girish asked Saradananda to write about Ramakrishna's divine life, his sadhana, and his message. He feared that in the future some less knowledgeable people might present the Master in a narrow, incorrect way. This might eventually lead to the creation of a cult, and defeat the purpose of his incarnation. There was cause for such apprehension: It was well known that Girish had given his power of attorney to the Master, who took complete responsibility for him. Later some people started imitating Girish, but they only deceived themselves because they did not understand the importance of self-surrender.

Saradananda started working on *Sri Sri Ramakrishna Lilaprasanga* (Sri Ramakrishna and His Divine Play), first writing "Sri Ramakrishna as a Guru," which became the third and fourth parts of that book. In the beginning of the third part, Saradananda explained the mystery of the "power of attorney" that the Master had accepted from Girish. Before publication, Saradananda read the chapter to Girish, who wholeheartedly approved it (see Chapter 19).[7]

Mahendra Nath Datta wrote:

> One day at noon Sharat Maharaj [Swami Saradananda] and I went to Girish's house in Baghbazar. He had just finished his lunch and was beginning to smoke his hubble-bubble while reclining on a bolster. We sat near him. Girish's *Vilwamangal* was then the talk of the town. Sharat Maharaj asked: "Well, Vilwamangal left Chintamani out of renunciation. Then why did he become infatuated again with the wife of the merchant? Once one has renunciation, how can one's mind again come to a lower plane?"
>
> Girish replied with a smile: "Look, Sharat, you are young; you have not properly understood the plot. A man develops initial renunciation on the spur of the moment or because of a little excitement: This is not real renunciation. Vilwamangal left home and Chintamani in the beginning;

that was raw renunciation. That excitement diminished when he faced suffering. Then his past habits and memories returned vigorously. During this period some people return home to their old habits. At that time if he comes in contact with a real guru, his mind again realizes the transitoriness of the world and he develops real renunciation. This renunciation is permanent and does not come from momentary excitement. It leads to the attainment of God. Initial renunciation comes from anger or worldly suffering; it has no relation with God. For that reason in the beginning of *Vilwamangal*, I showed a lot of commotion and a wave of excitement. But after getting a second blow, Vilwamangal developed passion for God. He then became silent and outwardly calm. He sincerely longed for God. His mouth stopped and his heart began to speak. Such things happen in the lives of spiritual aspirants." We were dumbfounded, and we realized how deeply Girish understood human character.[8]

One day Girish told Swami Saradananda the following story concerning his maidservant: "In 1869 there was an epidemic of dengue fever in Calcutta. All members of our household were in bed with body ache and fever. Our maidservant was doing all the work and she was very upset. While sweeping with a broom, she was grumbling: 'O hopeless God, I would like to beat you with this broom. You have given fever to all and they are comfortably lying in bed. And I am continuously working from morning onward. You don't think of me at all. I would like to beat you with this broom seven times.' Saying so, she hit the broom seven times on the floor. After a while, she said, 'Let me lie down and take a little rest.' As soon as she lay down, she contracted fever and body ache. She then began to chide God: 'O unfortunate one, you were waiting to give ears to my words. The moment I asked for fever, you immediately gave it to me. When I pray for so many good things, you put cotton in your ears and do not listen. You only listen to the bad prayers. Well, let me get well, and I shall beat you again.' We listened to her complain to God and smiled from bed."[9]

Girish was very fond of the Master's monastic disciples. Once when he invited Saradananda to have lunch with him, the cook was late in serving the meal. Girish began to show the swami how two big tomcats fight for food: He lay down on his stomach, raised his face up, and began to snatch the imaginary food from the floor with his right hand. From time to time he opened his mouth and cried, "*mao, mao, mao!*" Girish's mimicry was so perfect that Saradananda laughed heartily.[10]

Every afternoon many people visited Girish, as he was a great entertainer and a wonderful host. He also had encyclopedic knowledge. While drinking tea, he would talk about science, history, and Ramakrishna. Saradananda quite often would join him at that time. If someone disagreed with Girish, he would say with due respect, "Whatever you say is all right, but there is more to say about it." Saradananda learned this technique from Girish. Saradananda would also say: "There are more things in heaven and earth, Horatio, than are ever dreamt of in your philosophy."[11]

Swami Adbhutananda

Girish had a very open and wonderful relationship with Adbhutananda (also known as Latu Maharaj), the unlettered disciple of the Master. Latu recalled:

> One day Girish Ghosh saluted the Master by raising his folded hands to his forehead. The Master immediately returned the salutation by bowing from the waist. Girish Babu saluted the Master again. The Master saluted Girish Babu with an even deeper bow. At last, when Girish Babu prostrated flat on the ground before him, the Master blessed him. Later Girish Babu would say: "This time the Lord has come to conquer the world through prostrations. In his incarnation as Krishna it was the flute; as Chaitanya, the Name. But the weapon of his powerful Incarnation this time is the salutation." The Master used to say: "Learn to be humble. The ego will be thus removed."[12]
>
> Once Girish Babu came to Dakshineswar quite drunk. The Master told me: "Go and see if he left anything in his carriage. If you find something, bring it here." I did as I was told and found a bottle of wine and a glass. I brought both to the Master. When the devotees saw the wine bottle, they began to laugh, but the Master said to me: "Keep the bottle for him. He will want it for a final drink." Just see how liberal the Master was towards his devotees![13]
>
> When the Master was ill in Cossipore, he said to me: "O Leto, Girish has come. Prepare tobacco for him." Again he said: "Go quickly to Fagu's shop in Baranagore and bring hot crispy *kachuri* for Girish." I followed the Master's order. On that day the Master served Girish Babu with a glass of water. Girish Babu had a great desire to serve the Master for a year. In fact the Master took his service for a full year. Girish Babu used to tell us: "The Master blessed me in my old age. If he would have blessed me when I was young, then I could have shown you what monastic life is." Only he who has one hundred twenty-five percent faith can speak that way! That kind of statement does not fit in your mouth or in mine.[14]

Holy Mother told Adbhutananda about Vivekananda's success in the Parliament of Religions in Chicago in 1893. Girish also talked with Adbhutananda about Swamiji's travels. Girish said: "Latu would often come to my place and listen eagerly to every word about Swamiji's triumphant activities in America. His attitude was like a child's, full of faith and enthusiasm. When I told him that Swamiji's speech had been considered the best, he laughed gleefully like a boy and said: 'It is bound to be so. Didn't the Master say that in him eighteen powers were working in their highest form? It cannot be otherwise. Can the Master's prediction be false?' One day he was so beside himself with joy that he cried out: 'Please write to him, "Fear not, the Master is protecting you."'"[15]

Once Girish remarked to a devotee, "If you want to see a monk such as the Gita describes, go and see Latu." The devotee did not know what Girish meant. Girish said: "I see you have not read the second chapter of the Gita. The nature of a person of steady wisdom is described there. You can see all those qualities exemplified in Latu's character."[16]

The section that Girish refers to is: "When a man completely casts off all the desires of the mind, his Self finding satisfaction in Itself alone, then he is called a man of steady wisdom. He who is not perturbed by adversity, who does not long for happiness, who is free from attachment, fear, and wrath, is called a man of steady wisdom." (2:55-56)

Girish always appreciated the purity and renunciation of the Master's disciples. He told the following story: "In 1897 Latu went with Swami Vivekananda to visit various places of northern India. When they were in Kashmir, Swamiji hired a houseboat. The boatman and his family used one corner of the boat as their home. But Latu was not prepared for this. He was the first of the party to get onto the boat, but the moment he saw a woman on board, he jumped out again. Swamiji understood the situation, but no matter how much he tried to persuade him, Latu insisted that he must not share a boat with a woman. At last Swamiji said: 'I am here with you. What is there to fear? Nothing will happen to you.' Only then did Latu agree."[17]

Girish's house, like Balaram Basu's, was a meeting place for the Master's disciples. For a time, Latu and some other disciples lived at Balaram's house, which was near Girish's. They would share their memories of their Master, and sometimes also chat and tease each other. One day Swami Brahmananda said: "As soon as you assume a body, you suffer from disease and misery. These are the taxes for having a body; none can escape from them." Soon afterwards a hornet flew through the window and stung Brahmananda beneath his ear. Girish immediately took a bit of lime from his betel-roll box and applied it to the injured spot. When the pain subsided a little, Latu humorously said, "Rakhal, now you are paying tax." Everyone laughed.[18]

Saradananda needed some money to pay the debt that he had incurred to build the Udbodhan house for Holy Mother. Once he jokingly said to Adbhutananda: "Sadhu, why don't you repeat your mantra: '*Taka dharma, taka karma, taka hi paramantapah. Yashya grihe taka nasti, tasya grihe kuchu nai — sudhu thak-thak-thak-thak.* — Money is religion, money produces action, money is the supreme thing. He who has no money in his house, his house is empty: there is only a *thak thak* sound.'"

Adbhutananda replied: "It is the duty of a householder to earn money. If he cannot earn money, how will he maintain his family? Is it good to be a wretched, poor householder?"

Saradananda went to Girish's house some days later. Adbhutananda was there. In the course of conversation, Saradananda said to Girish: "I took out a large loan to buy the Mother's Udbodhan house. I don't know what to do. I shall not be able to keep my word if I cannot pay the interest on that loan."

Adbhutananda then said with a smile: "Sharat, now you see the power of my money mantra! It is creating anxiety even for a great monk like you. Now tell me whether you believe in my mantra or not."

Saradananda replied in jest: "Can you give me a guarantee that the money will come if I believe in your mantra?"

Adbhutananda: "Of course, it will come. First accept this mantra."

Saradananda: "Look, Sadhu, I hope your words will not prove false."

Adbhutananda: "No, Sharat, you will see the power of the mantra."

Saradananda then said to Girish: "You have heard what this sadhu said. You are the witness."

Girish said with a smile: "I don't like to be a witness. Let me fulfill the words of this sadhu." Saying so, Girish took some money from his pocket and gave it to Saradananda.[19]

Girish wrote a play, *Kalapahar*, in which he depicted a character like Adbhutananda's. Someone told the swami about this. One day when Girish said something, Adbhutananda remarked with a smile: "Shape your mind; control your mind; never give license to your mind. Think before you say anything. Brother, be careful."

Girish replied, "Well, sadhu, you are speaking by hints and insinuations!"

Adbhutananda: "It is better to speak that way; otherwise you will write another *Kalapahar*."[20]

Adbhutananda recalled:

Girish Babu used to say: "I am not afraid of God, but I am scared of hypocritical devotees. They don't understand me, but they are expert in giving me trouble. God knows everything about me; I can't hide anything from Him. I am in His shelter, so how can I live being afraid of Him?" This is true. If you are afraid of God, you cannot love Him. Where there is fear, there is no love.[21]

It is hard for ordinary people to understand Girish Babu's complex character. His life did not appear to be pure, and it was mysterious. If a man tries to imitate him, he may ruin his life. The Master used to say, "Girish has one hundred twenty-five percent faith." Sometimes [in 1904] I did not get any sleep for four or five days [because of excessive japa and meditation]. Girish Babu could understand this by seeing my eyes. He would then tell me many stories, and listening to his wonderful stories I would fall asleep. Thus he would give me rest for four or five hours. What a relief! Girish Babu would call me, "Sadhu — a holy man."[22]

One day I went to visit Girish Babu in his house. As soon as he saw me, he said: "Brother Latu, I see the Master clearly. Look, he is seated under that tree. Look, the Master is there." In later years his mind was full of Ramakrishna. Just imagine his wonderful life! It is amazing how the Master's grace transformed his life![23]

After Swami Ramakrishnananda's passing away in 1911, Adbhutananda told Girish that he would like to move to Varanasi. Girish told him: "Look, Sadhu, you are planning to run away. But who will let you go?" As it happened, he was unable to go to Varanasi until after Girish died in 1912.

During Girish's last illness Adbhutananda did not go to see him. Some devotees made some remarks about it. And he did not go even when Girish asked him to. Once when a devotee asked him the reason for this apparent apathy, he replied, "I can't bear to see Girish Babu suffer." This one simple sentence reveals his deep love for Girish. But he would get news of Girish from the devotees twice a day. The day Girish passed away, Adbhutananda would not speak to anybody. The next day, however, he talked about Girish continuously. Following are some of his reminiscences:

> One day the Master asked Girish Babu to massage his feet, but he declined. At that time Girish Babu did not have sufficient faith in the Master. However, when he developed intense faith in the Master, he did not get a chance to serve him because the Master passed away shortly thereafter. Later his conscience tormented him. Then he went to Kamarpukur and stayed there for some months. Every evening he would go to the Master's bedroom and sit there — hoping that the Master would ask him for a massage. Afterwards he returned to Calcutta.
>
> Once the Master told Girish Babu: "If someone frankly tells Mother Ganges one's weaknesses, She forgives all shortcomings." The Master's

advice penetrated Girish Babu's mind in such a way that every day he would inform Mother Ganges of all his faults. The day he could not go to the Ganges, he expressed himself while facing in that direction. Thus he became pure.

The Master never forbade Girish Babu to do anything. One day someone said to the Master, "If you tell him not to drink, he will listen." To this, the Master said: "No, no, it is not necessary for me to tell him anything. He will be able to raise himself from all his defects."

One day Brahmachari Nandalal said that the Master had taken only Girish's power of attorney and no one else's. In reply, Girish Babu said: "Look, Nandalal, don't say such a thing. He has taken responsibility not only for Girish but for all. In a moment he can liberate millions of Girishes like me."[24]

Swami Yogananda

Mahendra Nath Datta, Swamiji's brother, recalled:

In the summer of 1891 Swami Yogananda was staying at Balaram's house in Calcutta. He was lying down and suffering from a terrible headache. His eyes were red. He told me: "Please go to Girish and inform him that I have severe pain in my head and it is hard for me to bear it." I immediately went to Girish, who was then about to take his bath. When I reported Swami Yogananda's condition to him, he said: "I am coming soon. You make a light tea right now and give it to him to drink. It will cure his headache." I returned to Balaram's and made tea and offered it to the swami without milk and sugar. As soon as the swami drank the tea, his headache subsided to a great extent. The swami sat up and told me the reason for his headache: "For the last few days I have been repeating my mantra day and night continually. I think that is the reason I had this terrible headache." Meanwhile Girish came and asked him, "How is your headache?" Yogananda replied, "That light tea has almost cured my headache." Girish jokingly remarked, "Did you notice, rascal, the effect of my homeopathic medicine?" They continued to tease each other.[25]

Six months before Swami Yogananda's death, Ramakrishna appeared before him. Yogananda said: "Master, I don't want to be born again. The lesson of this life is enough for me. Please give me final liberation."

The Master replied, "You will have to come once more."

"No, I won't come," Yogananda said. "Please release me forever."

Immediately Ramakrishna disappeared. Yogananda went through six months of physical suffering, hoping that the Master would grant his request.

Knowing Yogananda's resolution, Girish at last said to him: "Brother, don't you know that you have been suffering terribly these last six months? Your pain is causing pain to all of us. Please agree to the Master's will. Don't refuse to come back with the Master.... Look here, Jogin! Don't seek nirvana. Don't think of the Master as pervading the entire universe, the sun and the moon forming his eyes. Think of the Master as he used to be to us, and thus thinking of him, go to him." At this Yogananda said: "What! I have been suffering in bed for the last six months? All right. May the Master's will be done. I am his servant. Whatever he asks me to do, I will do." Saying so, Yogananda fully resigned himself to the Master.[26] He passed away in samadhi shortly after, on 28 March 1899.

Swami Ramakrishnananda

The Ramakrishna Math was established in Baranagore in October 1886. In 1892 it was moved to Alambazar, near Dakshineswar. Swami Ramakrishnananda set up the shrine in Alambazar and followed the same routine as he had in Baranagore. One summer night when he was lying in his room and fanning himself with a palm-leaf fan, he felt that the Master too must be suffering from the heat. At once he entered the shrine and stood near the bed of the Master, fanning him till dawn.

Once Girish remarked about Ramakrishnananda: "Shashi is *asana-siddha* [perfect in sitting]; otherwise it would be impossible for someone to worship Mother Jagaddhatri for a twenty-four hour stretch, sitting in one place." Later someone asked Ramakrishnananda how he was able to do this. He replied modestly, "Devotion can accomplish anything."[27]

In 1911 Ramakrishnananda was dying from tuberculosis and was being cared for in the Udbodhan house. Towards the end the swami expressed a desire to see the Holy Mother, who was then in Jayrambati. Swami Dhirananda was sent to bring her, but she could not come, perhaps for two reasons: first, she knew that she could not bear to witness Ramakrishnananda's death; second, there was not enough room in Udbodhan for her to stay. However, the swami was blessed with a vision of the Holy Mother on the night before he passed away. Ramakrishnananda exclaimed, "Ah, Mother has come."

On the morning of Ramakrishnananda's last day, Pulin Mitra, a famous singer and disciple of Brahmananda, came to see him. Ramakrishnananda expressed his vision in a Bengali line, *Pohalo dukha rajani* (the night of misery is over), and asked Pulin to take it to Girish to compose a song. Girish recalled: "By the grace of Sri Ramakrishna, I completed the composition immediately. Pulin Mitra sang it before him. He was greatly moved and was satisfied with the composition." Here is a translation of the song that Girish composed:

> The night of misery is over.
> The terrible nightmare of ego is gone forever.
> The illusion of life and death is no more.
> Lo, the light of knowledge is dawning, and the Mother Divine is smiling.
> The Mother is bestowing the boon of fearlessness.
> Sing victory in a loud voice.
> Blow the trumpet to proclaim the conquest of death.
> Let the name of the Mother vibrate all over the world.
> The Mother says: "Weep no more. See the feet of Ramakrishna.
> Then all worries will vanish, all pain will go.
> Son, look by my side: The Saviour of the world is standing,
> His eyes full of grace and compassion."

Pulin sang this song for a long time and Ramakrishnananda listened with rapt attention. It seemed that the song gave him peace because it corresponded with his vision. After this he desired to hear another, "A Song on Samadhi" composed by Swami Vivekananda. Pulin sang that also. Ramakrishnananda was in an ecstatic mood for the entire morning. Doctor J.N. Kanjilal checked him and found that his condition had improved. The swami drank a small amount of sanctified water that had been offered to the Master, and for the last three hours of his life he was in samadhi. At 1:00 p.m. he began to perspire, his face was flushed, the hair of his body stood on end, and his gaze was fixed between his eyebrows. Swami Ramakrishnananda left his body while in samadhi at 1:10 p.m. on Monday, 21 August 1911.[28]

Swami Subodhananda

When he was not travelling, Subodhananda lived in the Alambazar monastery with his brother disciples. The monastery was extremely poor. One day Saradananda and Subodhananda went to Girish to ask for money. When Girish was approached, he said gruffly, "Where is any money?" Subodhananda replied jokingly: "Sharat Maharaj will grab you, and I shall break your box and take the money." Girish extended his hand to Subodhananda and said, "First try to bend my finger." Girish was extremely strong. When Subodhananda failed to bend his finger, Girish said to his secretary, "Abinash, please give the monks whatever money I have in the box." Girish fed the swamis and told

Subodhananda: "I am a wild horse. Only the best jockey can handle me. Khoka [Subodhananda's nickname], I see you will be able to deal with me."[29]

Swami Shivananda

Swami Shivananda one day reminisced about Girish: "It was to save the sinners and the afflicted that the Master incarnated. If anyone takes shelter in him with all sincerity, he passes his merciful hand over the supplicant and wipes away all his sins. By his divine touch one immediately becomes sinless. What is needed is sincere love for him and absolute surrender to him. Girish had committed many sins, but the Master was impressed by his devotion and so accepted him as his own. That is why Girish used to say at the end of his life, 'Had I known there was such a huge pit in which to throw one's sins, I would have committed many more.' The Master is full of compassion. He is a veritable ocean of mercy."[30]

Swami Premananda

Swami Premananda reminisced: "The Master lived in this world after giving the power of attorney to the Divine Mother; and Girish gave the power of attorney to the Master. The power of attorney means transferring full responsibility for one's activities to another person. Seeing his own weaknesses, Girish surrendered to the Master for his spiritual welfare. It is an extremely difficult thing to do. One cannot give the power of attorney as long as one has an iota of ego."[31]

Girish believed that the Master had the power to redeem sinners, but one must experience the results of his or her own karma, nonetheless. A surgeon does not operate on a cataract until it is fully developed. In this connection, Premananda recalled the following incident, which took place in the theatre:

> Girish asked the Master to bless one of his friends. The Master told that person: "You are full of impurities and crookedness. Go to the Ganges and confess all of your sinful acts to Her while standing in throat-deep water, which will make you sinless. I cannot even sit on a carpet that you have touched." Girish's friend did not follow the Master's advice. One day the Master visited Girish's theatre. After the performance, the actresses began bowing down to him as he sat in an ecstatic mood, his feet hanging down before him. Girish thought that this would be a great chance for his friend to touch the Master's feet. But as soon Girish's friend came close, the Master's ecstasy broke and he pulled his feet up under his legs. Girish's plan failed. The Master's body was full of consciousness and he was omniscient.[32]

Girish and the Monastic Disciples of Ramakrishna

In 1910 Premananda was in Varanasi, and Girish also went there for a change of climate. During that period Premananda visited Girish every day. He wrote to Ramakrishnananda on 4 December 1910:

> Girish Babu is now in Varanasi. He is gradually recovering from his illness, and we visit him every day. Ah, what a change has come in his nature! The Master said to him, "People will be amazed seeing you." That prophecy has been fulfilled. He tells us many wonderful things about his life and the Master. His magnanimity and steadfast devotion to the Master are remarkable. He is humble and does not care for name and fame at all. I have not seen such noble traits even in many monks. I see clearly that he has become gold by touching the philosopher's stone [the Master]. He cherishes unselfish, pure love and affection for us. He is 68 years old, but his nature is like that of a boy. He gets excited and intoxicated when he talks about the Master and Swamiji. Even his servants have become devotees of the Master. This is all due to the grace of the Master![33]

Swami Turiyananda

Turiyananda reminisced:

Even a man like Girish Babu was accepted by Sri Ramakrishna. The Master could mix with all types of people. We try to mould everyone according to our own ideas, but he took each person from where he was and pushed him forward. He never disappointed anyone by failing to mould that person according to his or her own light. He had a unique relationship with each devotee and maintained it through the years. Often he would teach them through humour. Ah, what a teacher! Where can one find another like him?

    Girish Babu used to say: "My younger brother would take hold of my father's hand when he walked, but I used to sit on his lap. I would say all sorts of things to Sri Ramakrishna, but he was never displeased with me. Often when I was dreadfully intoxicated, I would go to him. Even then he would receive me cordially and say to Latu: 'See if there is anything in the carriage. If he wants to drink here, how can I provide it?' He knew there must be a bottle in the carriage. Then he would gaze into my eyes and completely destroy the effect of the intoxication. I would say, 'Why, you have spoiled the effect of a whole bottle!' He used to inquire about the past of each person who came to him, but he never asked me anything about my past life. Nevertheless, I told him the whole story. He never forbade me to do anything. Is it for nothing that I adore him so much?"

Sri Ramakrishna used to say, "If a water snake bites a frog, it produces no effect, but if the frog is bitten by a cobra the poor thing expires before it can croak thrice."

There were few sins in which Girish Babu had not indulged. He once said to us, "I have drunk so much wine in my life that if the wine bottles were placed one upon another, they would stand as high as Mount Everest." He was a poet, so he spoke poetically like that. Truly speaking, he did drink a lot. When he was asked by the Master to repeat the name of God morning and evening, he refused to do so. He said: "I am not sure I can do it. I do not know in what condition or where I may be at those hours." Then Sri Ramakrishna asked him to remember God before meals. "That also I cannot promise you," replied Girish Babu. "I am often engrossed in lawsuits and have to attend to all sorts of things. I can't even do that." At this Sri Ramakrishna said, "Then give me the power of attorney."

Referring to this conversation later, Girish Babu said to us: "I readily agreed to give him the power of attorney, but later on I realized how difficult it was. I had told him I wouldn't be able to repeat the name of God even once in the evening, but afterwards I found I could not do the least bit of work without remembering Him at every step."

In one day Girish Babu gave up his fifteen-year habit of taking opium. He said the first three days he suffered tremendously; his entire body became inert. By the fourth day, he was all right. Later in life he did not even smoke.

Sri Ramakrishna was knowledgeable on a variety of subjects. Girish Babu once said to him, "You are my superior in every respect — even in wicked things." At this the Master said: "No, no, it is not so. Here [*meaning himself*] there are no samskaras [past impressions]. There is a world of difference between knowing something by actual experience and learning about it through study or observation. Experience leaves impressions on the mind which are very difficult to get rid of. This is not the case with knowledge through study or observation."

Once Girish Babu asked the Master, "Why did you have to practise [spiritual disciplines] so much?" The Master replied: "You know, there is eternal union of Hara [Shiva] with Gauri. Still, why did she practise so much austerity? It was to set an example for others. If I do so much, others will do at least one-sixteenth part of it. Isn't that so?"

The Master once said to Girish: "What are you saying about knowledge of Brahman? Sukadeva saw and touched the Ocean of Brahman. And Shiva drank only three handfuls of Its water and became a *shava* [corpse]." Girish Ghosh clasped his head and exclaimed: "Stop, sir, say no more. My head is reeling."

A householder devotee once had a wonderful experience. He had drunk freely and was very excited. Stopping his carriage before a house of ill repute, he went upstairs. But at the top of the staircase he found Sri Ramakrishna standing in front of the door! He fled in shame. Unless God saves us, there is no way out. Blessed are those who have no evil tendencies in their minds. They alone are saved. None can escape this attraction by personal exertion. But as Sri Ramakrishna used to say, "If you are sincere, Mother will set everything right."

Generally, people try to show their good side. They want to make a good impression, rather than trying to be good themselves. The first thing we learned from Sri Ramakrishna was to pay no attention to the opinion of others. He used to say: "Spit on public opinion! Look towards God and try to please Him!" Swamiji was also like that.[34]

Swami Abhedananda

Swami Abhedananda recalled:

A crazy woman used to visit the Master at Cossipore. She had a sweet voice, and when she would sing the Master went into ecstasy. One of her songs was:

> Come! Come, Mother! Doll of my soul! My heart's Delight!
> In my heart's lotus come and sit, that I may see thy face.
> Alas! sweet Mother, even from birth I have suffered much;
> But I have borne it all, thou knowest, gazing at thee.
> Open the lotus of my heart, dear Mother! Reveal thyself there.

The devotees were overwhelmed listening to her song. The woman was very obstinate and unpredictable, however. Whenever she had a chance, she would run upstairs to the Master's room. The Master forbade her to come there as she had adopted the same attitude towards him as the gopis had had towards Krishna. Finding that the disciples would not permit her to visit the Master, she eventually stopped coming. Girish Chandra Ghosh was inspired by this woman, and he depicted her in the character of the madwoman in his drama *Vilwamangal*.[35]

Swami Vijnanananda

Swami Vijnanananda recalled:

One day [Janmashtami (Krishna's birthday), 18 August 1884] Girish Ghosh came to visit the Master at Dakshineswar. I was also there. That evening Girish sang a song to the Master from his play *Chaitanya Lila*: "O Keshava, bestow thy grace upon thy luckless servants here. O Keshava, who dost delight to roam Vrindaban's glades and groves!" The Master went into ecstasy, embraced Girish, and sat on his lap. Tears of joy flowed from the Master's eyes. After a while Girish left for Calcutta. Since it was too late for me to return home, the Master said to me: "It is late. You will not have to return home. Stay here tonight." So I decided to pass the night at the temple garden of Dakshineswar. Some time later the Master gave me some luchis [fried bread] and sweets, which were prasad of the Divine Mother. Sri Ramakrishna made a bed for me and set up the mosquito curtain. I fell asleep as soon as I lay down. At midnight I woke up and found the Master walking around my bed, saying, "Mother, Mother." I was dumbfounded and could not understand what was going on. That night Sri Ramakrishna blessed me.[36]

Chapter 24

Girish and the Devotees of Ramakrishna

*L*ife is lonely and painful without loved ones. We are not born with friends and foes; we make friends when we bind each other with love. A true friend steadfastly and unselfishly stands beside us at times of joy and sorrow, plenty and famine, peace and war. Although unselfish love is rare in this world, the avatars and some great souls have shown us how to live in this world selflessly with love and joy, peace and tranquility.

During his last days, Jesus's disciple John lived in Ephesus. He was too old and infirm to speak in the church every Sunday. But every Sunday the devotees of Jesus would carry him in a chair to the entrance of church, where he would meet with the congregation. The enthusiastic audience would request John, "Please tell us something about Jesus." John would say in his feeble voice: "Love one another." Every Sunday he gave the same message, until one day someone asked, "Have you not heard anything else from Jesus?" John replied: "What else is there to say? That is the final message. Whatever is needful in life is there in that message, 'Love one another.'"

As a thread ties together all the pearls in a necklace, so God connects all beings. Ramakrishna said: "Sometimes God acts as the magnet and the devotee as the needle. God attracts the devotee to Himself. Again, sometimes the devotee acts as the magnet and God as the needle. Such is the attraction of the devotee that God comes to him, unable to resist his love."[1]

This chapter describes how Girish and the householder devotees of the Master interacted with each other and shared their memories of the Master. Although they were not related by blood, they developed deep spiritual relationships by the grace of the Master. These relationships became strong and solid by means of their mutual love and respect.

387

Girish Chandra Ghosh

Back view of Girish's house. He lived in the upper room.

Despite his complex character, Girish commanded both love and respect from everyone in the Master's circle for several reasons: First, the Master singled him out among the devotees for his unflinching devotion; second, Girish was a very famous actor and playwright; third, he was a creative genius and had a charismatic personality; and fourth, he was older than most of the Master's devotees and disciples. In the divine drama of Ramakrishna Girish played an important role. He attracted many people who found his company to be inspiring and reassuring.

M. (Mahendra Nath Gupta)

M. recalled:

The Master went to see the play *Chaitanya Lila* in September 1884. We went with him. Girish Ghosh arranged a box seat for the Master and engaged a man to fan him with a big palm-leaf fan. The Master asked, "How much will they charge?" "Nothing," I replied. "They are happy that you have come to see the performance." Then the Master said joyfully, "I chant Mother's name, so they do all these things for me." It is amazing that he was reluctant to take any credit for himself. The Mother was doing everything.

Girish and the Devotees of Ramakrishna

Sri Ramakrishna went on another occasion to see Girish's performance at the Star Theatre. He gave him a rupee since he did not want to see it for free. Putting the money on his head, Girish began to dance. He regarded it as prasad from the Master and preserved it in his shrine.

One day while going to Balaram's house, the Master passed near the home of Girish Ghosh, who was then seated on his veranda. Pointing to him, Narayan, a young devotee, said to the Master, "There is Girish Ghosh, who wrote *Chaitanya Lila*." As the Master was by nature humble, he saluted Girish with folded hands. Girish followed the Master to Balaram's. There the Master said to him: "The play is well written. Many people will derive joy from it." Girish replied: "Sir, I am an unworthy person. I do not deserve such a compliment. Wherever I sit, the earth becomes impure seven cubits deep." Immediately the Master entered into an ecstatic state and sang this song:

> If only I can pass away repeating Durga's name,
> How canst thou then, O Blessed One,
> Withhold from me deliverance,
> Wretched though I may be?
> I may have stolen a drink of wine, or killed a child unborn,
> Or slain a woman or a cow,
> Or even caused a brahmin's death;
> But, though it all be true,
> Nothing of this can make me feel the least uneasiness;
> For through the power of thy sweet name
> My wretched soul may still aspire
> Even to Brahmanhood.

Listening to this song, Girish felt consoled. The Master blessed him. After that Girish would inquire about when the Master was coming to Calcutta and would wait for him at the homes of his hosts. Gradually his life began to change. One day he and his friend went to Dakshineswar by carriage. Both were dead drunk. Holding onto the Master, Girish began to sing, "O Lord, where is your sweetheart Radha?" Later the Master said: "What faith Girish has! It is so deep that it cannot be measured."

* * *

It was not an accident that the Master went to the theatre. It was so destined. It was an important chapter of the avatar's divine play. One of the epithets of God is *patitapavan*, the Saviour of the fallen. This aspect of the Master was manifested there. God goes to devotees, wherever they live. The magnet attracts the needle, and again the needle attracts the magnet. God knows what is in others' minds. He listens to the call of the devotees' hearts. As parents take back their wayward children, so God goes to His wanton devotees and brings them back to Him.

At that time many people scorned the theatre because courtesans would act in the plays. A member of the Brahmo Samaj remarked, "When the actors and actresses of the theatre began to visit Sri Ramakrishna, we stopped visiting him." The Brahmos behaved like good boys. But God sees inside the devotees, and pays no attention to their outer behaviour. When the devotees are in deep trouble, they call on God wholeheartedly. Girish's inner call reached the Master's ear, so the Master himself went to bring Girish back to his fold. Can a father reject his own son?

Chaitanya Lila was Girish's *naivedya*, an offering of worship, and he reached God through it. How much devotion he expressed in this play! An ordinary person could not have written such a drama. There are many playwrights, but how many have such sincere devotion to God? In Girish's writing two important things are present: his literary skill and his exuberant devotion. You won't find such high ideals in Shakespeare.

Girish was a heroic devotee. It is said that he had practised severe austerities in his early life. He would bathe in the Ganges every day, eat boiled rice and ghee, and continually chant Shiva's name. Like an ascetic, he did not shave or cut his hair, and he walked barefooted. He thought that he would see God by practising these kinds of disciplines, but it did not work out. Without God's grace, none can see Him. Attaining the Master's grace was the last chapter of Girish's life.

Girish could not attain God by practising austerities. When self-effort failed, he took the opposite direction. He joined the theatre and began acting and writing plays. In that environment he became addicted to drinking and developed other bad habits. It is said that he remarked: "If God Himself comes to me as a guru and pulls me, only then will I return to Him. Otherwise Girish will continue to lead his wanton life." As a heroic devotee, he did not want to hide anything. He drank publicly and paid no attention to others' opinions. Through such things one tries to prove one's manliness, though in a perverse way. Not many can act like this.

Girish took a rather perverse path, and his true devotional nature remained hidden. Whatever he might have done, Girish as a devotee was pure, immortal, awakened. Gradually a battle began between Girish the superb playwright and Girish the supreme devotee. The latter eventually won. Like a loving father, the Master lifted up Girish, his self-absorbed son. The Master went to the theatre to perform this great task. This gave him a new name, *patitapavan*, Saviour of the fallen. But the Master also saved many other wayward people in the theatre in addition to Girish....

When Girish was reluctant to continue acting in the theatre, the Master said to him: "Please continue as you are doing. This theatre also spreads the Divine Mother's message. People will learn much from your plays."

Girish and the Devotees of Ramakrishna

To some people Girish was a lion among men, but with the devotees he behaved like a child. He had a great heart. Whenever we visited him, he would give up his work and talk to us. He had tremendous humility and longing. That is why the Master said, "Girish has one hundred twenty-five percent faith." Girish recognized the Master to be an avatar and began to talk about it to others.

God is same-sighted: "He maketh His sun to rise on the evil and on the good." Seeing Girish's redemption, others felt assurance and hope, and they gradually began to rectify themselves. Even courtesans started to better themselves through his grace.

Buddha, Christ, and Chaitanya also took on this role. Christ had a devotee named Mary Magdalene. She belonged to a very wealthy family. When her parents died she moved in the wrong direction, but she had devotion within. When later she became repentant, Christ went and rescued her. After his crucifixion, Christ appeared first to Mary Magdalene, which proved how much love he had for her. Buddha redeemed the life of Ambapali; and during his itinerant days, Chaitanya transformed the life of a rich courtesan. This is the duty of the avatars. They come to uplift devotees to the spiritual plane. Avatars see inside human beings. When they see purity and devotion within, they induce those people to return to their fold. Ordinary people cannot understand this divine play of the avatars.

*   *   *

One day the Master asked Girish to immerse himself in the Ganges and pray, "O all-purifying Mother Ganges, please bless me." Girish unwillingly did what the Master said. But after dipping into the Ganges, his mind became filled with bliss. Such was the greatness of Mother Ganges! The Master said, "In this Kali Yuga, Ganges water is the veritable manifestation of Brahman."

Another time Girish asked the Master, "Why do I feel depressed from time to time?" The Master replied: "As long as you are in the world, the cloud of maya will arise. Don't be afraid of it. It is the nature of the mind to move sometimes up and sometimes down." Girish said: "Sir, you have the power to make everybody pure and unattached, whether one is a householder or a monk. You are beyond all laws." What faith he had! The Master said to him: "Yes, it is possible. Exuberant devotion transcends all scriptural injunctions." Here the Master gave himself away. Who could admit such a thing except an avatar? Whatever Girish asked for from the Master he received. He said to the Master, "Sir, what I was and what I have become — just by thinking of you!"

The Master didn't give importance to a person's external behaviour; he saw the interior. Once he said, "I can see the inside of each person as one sees an object through a glass case." He could see not only the present life of a person but his past and future lives too. Though Girish's external life was to some extent unconventional, basically he was a spiritual person.

Once the Master visited Girish's house. Girish bought some refreshments at the market and served them on plates that were put directly on the carpet where the devotees were seated. Balaram Basu, a staunch devotee of the Master, was also present. Girish's style of service upset Balaram, because in his opinion it was not the proper way to serve the Master. Sri Ramakrishna looked at Balaram and told him with a smile: "This is the custom here. When I go to your house, you may serve me in your way." Balaram was an orthodox Vaishnava devotee.[2]

M. also said: "Girish Ghosh once said to the Master: 'Sir, my servant was down with a fever for six days. Your prasad cured him.' At once the Master scolded him: 'Fie on you! What a small-minded person you are! You are asking for pumpkins and gourds from God! You should ask for immortality from Him.'"[3]

On 6 December 1884 Bankim Chandra Chattopadhyay, a famous Bengali writer, met Ramakrishna at Adhar Sen's Calcutta residence. The Master invited Bankim to visit him at Dakshineswar and the latter accepted. Kumudbandhu Sen recorded M.'s reminiscences of this event:

> Girish knew Bankim very well, so the Master sent me with Girish to Bankim's. Bankim had promised the Master at Adhar's that he would visit the Master at Dakshineswar, so I was sent to find out the date of his visit. We went to Bankim's Calcutta residence and as soon as he heard of our arrival, he came and received us cordially. Girish and Bankim began to talk about their writings, and I stood there and listened to them.
>
> The age difference between Girish and Bankim was 8 or 10 years, and both were literary men. They became absorbed in their discussion. I was then 30 years old. I listened to them attentively. When their conversation was over, I mentioned the Master's invitation. Girish then said: "You wanted to visit Dakshineswar, so the Master has sent us to ask when it would be convenient for you to go there." Bankim replied: "I have a great desire to visit him. The other day I felt tremendous joy seeing him at Adhar's. Not only do I have a desire to see him at Dakshineswar, I am also eager to bring him to my home here. Now I am extremely busy with my work; I am unable to tell you now when I shall get time to go there. Whenever I find an opportunity, I shall let you (*pointing to Girish*) know." Unfortunately, Bankim's wish was not fulfilled.[4]

After the crucifixion of Jesus, his disciples came together in order to protect themselves from persecution. They would meet at a devotee's

Girish and the Devotees of Ramakrishna 393

house at night, make their plans, and talk passionately of the greatness and glory of Christ. Just as Christ's disciples were united by their love for him and for each other, so Ramakrishna's disciples and devotees were bound with a cord of unselfish love. Mahendra Datta wrote: "One day Girish invited M. to his house for dinner. While eating, Girish said: 'This food is sanctified with bliss and love! It is a great joy to have the company of the Master's devotees and to eat together!' In fact, the devotees had so much love for one another that they would visit each other's homes and dine without any invitation. Each one felt that the other's home was his own home and the other's food was pure and sanctified. They felt so much attraction for each other that they would feel a pang of separation if they did not see a particular devotee for a few days. They loved to be together and talk about the Master."[5]

Once, while Girish was pondering his own death, he thought: "Well, death is slowly approaching. What will happen after death? I do not know where I shall go." Girish was thinking in this way when M. came to visit him. M. started to talk with Girish about the Master. Suddenly, in an inspired mood, Girish said to M.: "Brother, could you beat me with your shoes? I am not joking. I am serious." M. smiled and asked the reason for such a request. Girish replied: "To tell you the truth, I deserve a shoe-beating. Sri Ramakrishna is sitting within my heart and is always protecting me. Yet I wonder what will happen to me after death!"[6]

Many years earlier, when Sri Ramakrishna was suffering from cancer, Girish went to see him at the Cossipore garden house. On 23 April 1886 M. recorded in the *Gospel*:

> It was about dusk. Girish and M. were strolling near the small reservoir in the garden.
> Girish: "I understand that you are writing something about the Master. Is it true?"
> M.: "Who told you that?"
> Girish: "I have heard about it. Will you give it to me?"
> M.: "No, I won't part with it unless I feel it is right to do so. I am writing it for myself, not for others."
> Girish: "What do you mean?"
> M.: "You may get it when I die."[7]

However, M. published four volumes of *Sri Ramakrishna Kathamrita* between 1902 and 1910. After reading the first three Girish wrote to M. on 22 March 1909: "If my humble opinion goes for anything, I not only fully endorse the opinion of the great Swami Vivekananda but add in a loud voice that the *Kathamrita* has been my very existence during my protracted illness for the last three years.... You deserve the gratitude of the whole human race to the end of time."[8]

Devendra Nath Majumdar

Devendra and Girish had been friends long before they met Ramakrishna. Once the Master went to see one of Girish's plays at the Star Theatre, where Girish had arranged a special seat for him. Devendra and Latu accompanied him. After the performance, Girish, who was drunk, humiliated the Master and used abusive language. Latu became furious and Devendra stopped him from hitting Girish. The next day Devendra went to Girish's house and said to him: "When you drink you lose control of yourself and talk nonsense. You should go to Dakshineswar and apologize to the Master." But Girish replied: "No, I shall not go to Dakshineswar. And I shall not apologize either. Whatever qualities he gave to me I offered back to him. I've been fasting and crying all day. Doesn't he know it? If he is an avatar, doesn't he realize what I am suffering? He will have to come here. Otherwise I shall not eat any food. I shall starve to death." It was raining. At four o'clock in the afternoon Ramakrishna came to Girish's house with Ram Chandra Datta. Girish fell at the Master's feet, and Ramakrishna blessed him.[9]

One evening when Swami Vivekananda was returning from Dakshineswar with Devendra, he said to him: "Look at the Milky Way. It is just like a stream of milk. Do you know that every moment millions of suns and moons are being formed within it? That is the source of the stars. Just imagine what an inconceivable Being is the ruler of this vast universe! And a tiny man with his limited intellect is trying to fathom and comprehend Him! Is He so easily obtainable?" After listening to Swamiji, Devendra was absorbed in the thought of the Infinite. He then concluded that it was not possible for a man to realize God. This greatly troubled him, and he could not sleep for three days. At last he went to Girish and told him the cause of his anxiety. Girish said to him: "But it is also true that the ruler of this universe, from whom this cosmic creation evolves, incarnates Himself in a human body and gives liberation to sinners like us." Devendra was relieved to hear this.[10]

In 1893 Girish became the director of the Minerva Theatre and hired Devendra as a cashier and supervisor. Devendra was a faithful worker. When Girish noticed that his handwriting was good and that he could write quickly, Girish also engaged him to take dictation. Several of Girish's dramas were thus written down by Devendra. Girish had sincere love and respect for Devendra, regardless of the fact that Devendra was his employee. If necessary, as a friend and well-wisher, Devendra would scold Girish and point out his mistakes, and the latter would humbly confess his error.[11] To err is human. A weak man does not admit to mistakes, nor does he want to change his way. A strong man, however, admits his mistakes boldly and corrects himself accordingly. Girish was a strong man of many good qualities.

Nag Mahashay

Durga Charan Nag, known as Nag Mahashay, was a great lay disciple of Ramakrishna and a close friend of Girish. He was an embodiment of humility, and his austerities defy description. The Bhagavata says, "He who has controlled the tongue has controlled everything." To curb his desire for delicacies, Nag Mahashay did not use salt or sugar on his food. Once he lived for two or three days only on rice bran. He often abstained from food and water for days. He also gave up shirts and shoes and wore only a plain cloth and a cotton shawl. Observing his austerities and self-effacement, Girish remarked, "Nag Mahashay has knocked on the head of his rascal ego so severely that it cannot raise its hood anymore."[12]

Towards the end of Nag Mahashay's life, when his reputation as a holy man drew people to his home in Deobhog [in Bangladesh] to seek his company, he frequently left home secretly to visit Calcutta. The first place he went upon reaching Calcutta was the Kalighat temple, where he would bow down to the Divine Mother. Then he would leave his cloth bundle at his Calcutta residence and go straight to Girish to pay his respects. He once said of Girish: "If one is in the company of Girish Babu for even five minutes, one is freed from worldly delusion. He has such keen insight that he can see at a glance the innermost recess of a man's heart, and by virtue of this powerful insight he was able to recognize the Master as an avatar."[13]

Girish had tremendous love and regard for Nag Mahashay. He knew that Nag Mahashay did not accept gifts, but in spite of that one day he gave him a blanket. Out of his deep respect for Girish, Nag Mahashay put the blanket on his head and went home. A devotee went to visit him later that day and found him seated, with the blanket on his head. When Girish heard of this, he found a tactful way of taking it back so that Nag Mahashay might not suffer any further discomfort.[14]

Years before, when Ramakrishna had introduced Nag Mahashay to Swami Vivekananda, he said: "This man has genuine humility. There is no hypocrisy in it." Humility was one of the main traits of his character. "I and mine" are the warp and woof of maya, which bind the soul, and these were totally obliterated in his personality. Girish once humorously remarked that the great enchantress, Mahamaya, was in trouble when she tried to bind Swami Vivekananda and Nag Mahashay: "As she tried to trap Vivekananda he became bigger and bigger, and at last he became so big that all Her fetters were too short and She had to let him go. And when She attempted to trap Nag Mahashay, he began to make himself smaller and smaller until he had at last reduced himself to such a degree that he could easily slip through the holes of Her net."[15]

One day Nag Mahashay was at Girish's house with other disciples and devotees of Ramakrishna. They were speaking about the Master when Swami Niranjanananda turned to Nag Mahashay and said: "Well, sir, our Master used to say that one who thinks of himself as mean and wretched actually becomes so. Why then do you always think of yourself as so low and degraded?" Nag Mahashay replied: "Ah, I see with my own eyes that I am low and degraded. How can I think that I am Shiva? You can think like that. Girish Babu can say that he is Shiva. You have such great devotion for the Lord. Where is such devotion in me? If you all help me, if the Master grants me his grace, my life will be blessed." The utter sincerity and humility of his words silenced Niranjanananda. He could neither contradict him nor pursue the subject any further. Girish later said, referring to the incident: "If a man is sincere, and if all idea of egotism has really vanished from his mind, he attains the state of Nag Mahashay. The earth becomes blessed by the very touch of the feet of such great men."[16]

Once Nag Mahashay came to visit Girish and the latter asked him about his father: "Sir, is there any difference in religious views between you and your father?"

Nag Mahashay replied: "No, there is no more difference between us. My father also repeats his mantra day and night. But he is still attached to me."

Girish: "It is his good fortune that he loves a great soul like you."

Shaking his head like a boy, Nag Mahashay said: "Sir, what will it avail? My father is rowing an anchored boat. How far will his mind go repeating the mantra while having attachment for his son?" Girish and others were moved as they listened to this wonderful devotee of the Master.[17]

Girish told this story about Nag Mahashay: "Once at the Cossipore garden house the Master expressed a wish to eat an amalaki, but it was not the season for that fruit. When Nag Mahashay heard about the Master's wish, he left home in search of an amalaki in the suburbs of Calcutta.

He continually searched for three days and finally found a few for the Master. The Master's wish or words were like the words of the Vedas. Practising severe austerities and looking for an amalaki were equal to him. Such devotion for the guru is rare in this world, and it will remain an ideal forever."[18]

Shashi Bhusan Ghosh

Shashi Bhusan Ghosh, a devotee and a biographer of Ramakrishna, asked Girish, "Did you ever hear the Master say, 'If a person takes one step towards God, God comes ten steps towards him?'"

Hearing this Girish became excited. He slapped the floor and replied loudly: "Shashi, I never heard those words spoken by the Master. Neither do I know nor do I care for those words. But this I definitely know, that I did not take a single step. The Master himself took ten steps towards me and blessed me."[19]

Ram Chandra Datta

Girish and Ram Chandra Datta were staunch devotees of Ramakrishna and both believed that he was an avatar.

Girish wrote:

I first met Brother Ram when the Master was visiting him at his Simla residence in Calcutta. Then I met him at Dakshineswar, and he took me to the secluded Panchavati. He had heard from Deven Majumdar that I considered the Master to be an avatar. He was excited because he also had the same opinion about the Master. Brother Ram was excited and expressed his belief in a choked voice: "Do you understand, Brother Girish? This time all three — Sri Chaitanya, Nityananda, and Advaita — are united in the form of Sri Ramakrishna. Love, devotion, and knowledge are equally manifested in this present Incarnation."

From that day on I became his dearest friend and we met frequently. He would come to the theatre and talk to me only about the Master. Whatever I said he accepted wholeheartedly without any question. If anybody contradicted my statement, Brother Ram would vehemently attack him and say: "What! You want to contradict Brother Girish? The Master has said, 'Girish has one hundred twenty-five percent faith and intelligence.'" I observed that Brother Ram was an extremely wise and skillful person. Day and night he would think about what he could do for the Master, how he could preach the Master's message and serve him. The Master said, "Ram is very devoted to me." Inviting the Master, Brother Ram would arrange a festival in his house as well as in other devotees' houses. When he invited the Master to his own home, he used to consult me about the menu and what delicacies should be offered to the Master.[20]

In September 1885 Ramakrishna moved to Shyampukur, in the northern part of Calcutta, for his cancer treatment. Ram took an active part in the arrangements that were made for the Master's care. As the day of Kali Puja approached, the Master expressed a desire to celebrate the occasion with a worship of the Divine Mother and asked the devotees to collect the necessary materials. Accordingly, they procured flowers, fruits, sweets, sandal paste, incense, and candles. When the auspicious time came, they placed those things in front of the Master, thinking that he would perform the worship. There was no image. The devotees sat around the Master silently waiting, but he remained absorbed in meditation. All of a sudden the thought came to Ram's mind: "It is needless for the Master to perform worship. We shall worship him." Ram whispered this idea to Girish, who responded: "What do you say? Is the Master waiting to accept our worship?" Immediately Girish took some flowers and offered them to the Master, saying, "Victory to Sri Ramakrishna! Victory to Mother!" The hair of the Master's body stood on end and he entered into samadhi. His face was radiant with a divine smile. The rest of the devotees also offered flowers to the Master and were blessed.[21]

Girish recalled an event that occurred a few months later at Cossipore: "The day the Master became the Kalpataru [the wish-fulfilling tree], Brother Ram was beside himself. My brother Atul said: 'On that day I received the blessings of the Master by the grace of Ram. I was standing on one side and watching the whole thing. Ram grabbed my hand and pulled me in front of the Master, who then touched me.' Atul and other devotees were deeply moved by Brother Ram's love and compassion.[22]

Ram Datta wrote *Sri Sri Ramakrishna Paramahamsadever Jivanvrittanta*, a short biography of Ramakrishna in which he included a chapter entitled "Girish, a heroic devotee." Ram wrote:

> Girish was extremely religious, but he did not care for so-called Hinduism. His character was complex. He was not only an alcoholic but would take all kinds of drugs, such as hemp, opium, and so on. Once a devotee asked the Master to tell Girish to give up drinking. The Master replied: "Why do you have such a headache over him? He who is his guide will decide whether he should give up drinking or not. Moreover, he is a heroic devotee. Drinking will not do him any harm."
>
> The Master highly praised Girish's devotion, but this irritated him. He would say: "Master, I don't care for advice. I want to see action. I am

now as I was before." Afterwards, one evening he began to drink with a couple of his friends, who then passed out. But he belched once and his drunkenness was gone. He drank a second bottle, and then a third. His stomach was full of alcohol but still he was not intoxicated. At first he was surprised, then he was disgusted and he stopped drinking. Girish was a very obstinate person. No one could stop him once he decided to do something. The Master knew his nature, and for that reason he never forbade him to drink.

Girish's devotion was incomparable. We noticed how the Master was exceedingly happy whenever he saw Girish. The Master remarked that he had never seen another man as intelligent as Girish. After giving Ramakrishna his power of attorney, Girish did not practise any spiritual disciplines. His mind dwelt in Ramakrishna, and this gave him peace. He became a man of divine wisdom, as was evident in his dramas — *Buddhadev-Charit, Vilwamangal, Nasiram, Rupa-Sanatan*, and so on. We know that his dramas opened the door of religion in the hearts of many people.[23]

Purna Chandra Ghosh

The following conversation with Purna Chandra Ghosh was recorded by Kumudbandhu Sen:

One evening I was talking to Purna about Girish's love and devotion for the Master. In the course of conversation I said, "Last night Girish mentioned something wonderful." Purna asked curiously, "What did he say?" I replied that Girish had said this: "Who could understand Sri Ramakrishna? Do you think the Master's disciples have understood him? But those who have tasted a drop of his love have realized that the Master's pure divine love was above the world and even beyond any paternal love. God can hide everything except his unbounded love. The disciples and the devotees get intoxicated with a little of that love. Otherwise, who, however great he may be, can comprehend the infinite nature of God?"

As soon as I told him what Girish had said, Purna's face became red and his eyes filled with tears. Grabbing my hand, he took me from his room to the junction of Shyampukur Street and Cornwallis Street [now Bidhan Sarani] and said to me in a choked voice, "Here — here I experienced that love of the Master." I had never before seen Purna so emotional. Outwardly he had always been very calm and serious by nature. That night, when I saw his radiant face in the streetlight, I was speechless. He then said, his voice still choked with emotion: "It is true, Girish Babu is right. Who can understand the Master? Who can measure his unmotivated, unconditional love? I was a mere boy. What did I know about him? His superhuman love made me convinced that he was God incarnate."[24]

In 1911, Purna visited Girish during his last illness. Seeing Purna, a beloved disciple of the Master, Girish forgot his pain and suffering. Both talked about Ramakrishna for some time. When Purna was about to leave, Girish said to him: "Brother, bless me so that I may remember the Master with every breath. Glory to Sri Ramakrishna!" Purna humbly replied: "The Master is always looking after you. Please bless us." The next day Purna told a devotee that the Master would not keep Girish Babu in this world much longer — Girish Babu would return to the Master very soon. Purna's words came true.[25]

Chapter 25

Further Glimpses of Girish

"When a true genius appears in the world," wrote Jonathan Swift, "you may know him by the sign that the dunces are all in confederacy against him."[1] This is exactly what happened to Girish. His bohemian lifestyle was questioned and attacked, and his genius was misunderstood and misinterpreted. In addition, the death of his dearest ones and subsequent doubts about God's existence nearly devastated him. Yet despite all of these difficulties, he never gave up. He fought heroically at every step of his life. Public criticism was like champagne to him. His passion for playwriting and acting energized him and gave expression to his creativity. Finally, self-effort and grace worked together in Girish's life, and the goddess of fortune gradually made everything favourable for him.

Girish was like a brilliant-cut diamond, with many facets. Abinash Gangopadhyay and other writers recorded different aspects of Girish's genius. People enjoy watching fireworks with their star-like bursts of various colours. So also, it is hoped that the reader will equally enjoy glimpses of Girish's brilliant mind and sharp intellect, his experiences and wisdom, his intelligent conversation and frankness, his likes and dislikes, his commonsense and concentration, and his affection and empathy with others.

Writing a Play

During his life Girish encountered grief after grief. He tried to find relief from his pain by drinking alcohol, visiting brothels, performing onstage, composing poems, and associating with his guru, Ramakrishna. But the more Girish was tormented by grief, the more his genius became manifest. Once he said: "Without being stricken with grief and pain in life, it is hard to develop the poetic faculty — especially for writing plays. A playwright experiences the truth by undergoing various circumstances. A real poet does not write anything that he has not experienced himself. By God's grace, I came in contact with all types of characters in this world — from the prostitute to the all-venerable paramahamsa [illumined soul]. This world is a big stage, and the theatre is its microscopic form."

Girish used to say: "The best art is when art is concealed. Writing a play is the most difficult of all forms of writing. And next to that is writing history."[2]

Once Devendra Nath Basu, a cousin of Girish, asked him: "Before writing a play, some playwrights imagine the whole plot of the play, and others the main characters. What do you do?"

Girish replied: "I first imagine the character of the hero, and then I create events to manifest that person's character."[3]

Genius

Girish said: "A genius does not walk on the same path that has been trodden by others. Previously a ship would take six months to reach India from England, after encircling Africa. But a genius created the Suez Canal and reduced the six-month journey to six weeks. Now, due to advances in technology, a boat reaches England from India in three weeks.

"A poet or a playwright is a worshipper of simplicity and truth. A real playwright does not hide any of his feelings from the public; and he candidly describes the human characters he witnesses in this world. Who is happy when someone points out his faults? So, quite often a playwright — a teacher of people — is reproached by the public. Seldom do fame and fortune smile on him. The truths that the playwright realizes through his transcendental vision are not understood by his contemporaries. Later, when the time comes for the masses to understand those truths, they appreciate the playwright. The misfortune of a genius is being born ahead of his or her time. The main goal of a playwright is to point out the good and bad traits of human character. But sometimes people mistakenly take the criticisms personally, and as a result, the playwright often has to endure censure, enmity, and even persecution."

Once Girish was extremely hurt by just such an incident and he expressed this in a poem: "Low-class people criticize me, but I never wrote a single line slandering anybody."[4]

The Theme and Dialogue in a Play

Girish remarked: "When the mind becomes muddled with intense anxiety, one's thinking and speech also become muddled. Under such circumstances, an expert playwright puts muddled ideas and language on the lips of a particular character. When Hamlet was pondering whether suicide was proper or not, he burst out, 'To take arms against a sea of troubles.' This one sentence clearly expressed the idea in Hamlet's mind."[5]

Realization of One's Imagination

When Girish was writing *Chaitanya Lila*, he arose one night and in a half-asleep state saw the large round face of Balaram coming towards him, addressing his brother Krishna in a song, "Hare-re-re-re." Based on this vision, Girish wrote the opening song of Nitai with the word "Hare-re-re-re."[6] Girish's imagination was so intense that it turned into a realization.

How to Write a Play

Girish had such a great reputation as a playwright that other dramatists would come to him for suggestions and opinions about their own works. Once while Girish was recuperating from an asthma attack, his friend Surendra Nath Roy read his drama *Behula* to him. In the opening scene of the drama, Surendra depicted Chand Sadagar and his wife, Sanaka, lamenting the deaths of their seven sons from snakebites. After listening to each of the laments, Girish told Surendra to stop reading and asked: "Now read Chand's lament as Sanaka's and Sanaka's lament as Chand's." Surendra followed Girish's instructions. Then Girish asked, "Do you find any inconsistency?"

"No, I don't," Surendra replied.

Girish then said: "Listen, dear friend, as you have started to write dramas, you should be extremely careful. It is very difficult to write a drama. It requires a wide range of knowledge about the world and keen insight regarding human character. Just now you have said that the mother's lamentation and father's lamentation are the same, but they should be completely different. Look, when a son dies the mother bemoans his death expressing her grief in a particular way, whereas the father does not grieve in that manner. Both are grieving, but their expressions, language, and gestures are different. A playwright should always remember that a drama is an imitation of our lives in this world."[7]

"I Am My Own Rival"

Girish was very worried whenever one of his new plays was warmly received by the public. He said, "I used to think about how I could write a new one that would be loved even more by the audience."

He was more motivated to write when a drama was not well received. He would say: "This time I will produce something new. You see, my

Girish Chandra Ghosh

problem is that I am my own rival. There is no playwright in the Bengali theatre, except I, whose life is fully dedicated to the theatre and who has taken a vow to satisfy and give joy to the public. I make great efforts every time so that I can defeat myself. I always try to write a new play that will surpass the previous one."[8]

The Constituents of Genius

Girish said: "A genius is endowed with the power of memory, the power of imagination, and the power of will more than ordinary people. But he should have full control over those powers. Otherwise, if the power of imagination is beyond his control, he may go mad. One should have such a strong memory that as one writes, all of one's past experiences automatically arise in the mind. For example, during the Mahabharata war the great hero Karna could not remember the powerful weapon he had to use against Arjuna, and he was killed as a result. Finally, if one does not have steady willpower, one's imagination does not yield any result."[9]

Love for the Daredevil

Girish thought highly of boys who were tough, stubborn, and adventurous. He remarked: "If these daredevil boys are handled and guided properly, they can do more work than gentle, well-mannered boys. If there is any trouble in the community, the former group appears first. If anyone dies in a poor and helpless family, these boys immediately come forward to carry the dead body for cremation. One finds genuine manliness in them."[10]

Simplicity of Language

Once Pandit Mokshada Charan Samadhyayi, a well-known Bengali scholar, came to visit Girish at his home. After discussing various topics, they talked about literature. The pandit said to Girish: "Your writing is so simple that even women with little education can understand it. This is the beauty and characteristic of your language. When we write, our language becomes mixed with Sanskrit words, so ordinary people cannot easily understand it. Can you give me some advice so that I can write lucidly?"

Smiling, Girish said: "Sir, you are a great scholar. How can I give you any advice? But I can tell you a secret."

The pandit asked eagerly, "What is it?"

Girish replied: "Please write in the language that is used by the children and women in your home. You will see, it will be easy for people to understand, and the reader will not have to open the dictionary again and again."[11]

Ability to Compose Quickly

One day when Girish was going to his office, one of his friends approached him, saying: "I am sending some lichees to a relative. Please write a poem about lichees that I can send along with them." Girish immediately wrote a humorous six-line poem in Bengali on lichees.[12]

Years later, when Girish was working at the Minerva Theatre, it was decided one Saturday night that there would be a new musical drama on the following Saturday. The next day, Sunday, Girish began writing *Mani-haran*, a two-act musical based on Krishna's life. That night *Prafulla* was being performed in the theatre, and he was acting in the role of Yogesh. He asked his secretary to wait in the greenroom with some paper and a pencil, and a man was appointed to call him every time he was expected to appear onstage. As the play progressed, Girish alternated between appearing onstage to act in his role and dictating *Mani-haran* to his secretary in the greenroom. Thus by the time *Prafulla* was over, the new musical had been written. Later that night, he composed songs for the new musical, and then he went home.[13]

No Excuses

Girish was a man of action. He used to say, "I want work to be done. I don't want excuses." He was annoyed with anyone who made excuses for not doing his or her job. Before opening a new drama, he would distribute lists of responsibilities to the cast and crew. If someone suddenly did not show up, or mentioned problems and difficulties and had not followed his guidance, he would say, "Your excuse is wonderful, but remember, the company will still sustain a loss."[14]

Painter and Poet

Girish said: "The poet also paints a picture just as the painter does. In my writing, I always tried to depict the exact picture of people, places, and environments."[15]

Paradise Regained

Girish said: "Most people are fond of Milton's great epic, *Paradise Lost*, and do not care to read his *Paradise Regained*. But I am truly indebted to the latter. If I had not read *Paradise Regained*, I could not have written *Chaitanya Lila* the way I did." Girish had written *Chaitanya Lila* before he met Ramakrishna, and it was the first of his plays that the Master saw.

On English and French Novelists

Girish once advised someone: "One should first read the novels of Fielding, Scott, Dickens, Thackeray, and so on. The French novelists' power of story-writing is superb. As the English novelists are expert in depicting characters, so the French novelists (Dumas, Hugo, and others) are superb in creating stories. But Victor Hugo was endowed equally with a tremendous imagination and a talent for creating characters and stories. If this great novelist had also had a sense of humour, he could have been considered more or less equal to a poet like Shakespeare."[16]

Respect for the Authors of the Hindu Scriptures

Girish had tremendous respect for the authors of the Hindu scriptures. About them he said: "They developed so many thoughts of a high level that are inaccessible to the ordinary human intellect. The array of arguments they presented in favour of atheism did not arise in the minds of the renowned atheistic philosophers of Europe. The Hindu philosophers refuted their own arguments for atheism, and finally established the idea of God's existence. I observed that the authors of the scriptures left for me beforehand the answers to all my objections in their thoughtful arguments. Nowhere else have I come across such arguments for and against atheism, all of which arose in the minds of those authors long ago. How wonderfully they gave their conclusions."[17]

On Autobiography

Once when someone asked Girish to write his autobiography, he replied: "It is not an easy thing to do. The great sage Vyasa described his life story without hiding anything. When one can get the courage to expose all one's shortcomings, then only should one venture to write one's autobiography. Otherwise, while writing an autobiography the author becomes his own lawyer. He always tries to justify his own defects and proclaim his noble qualities."[18]

The Importance of Debate

Girish said, "A person may be a famous and powerful writer, but I never accept that person's conclusions without mentally deliberating back and forth." By using this method while reading, Girish acquired such a keen ability to debate that it was almost impossible to defeat him.

During debates Girish never showed any arrogance, but would lose himself in the subject. Knowing his keen power of argument, Ramakrishna would sometimes encourage Girish to debate with some of the devotees.

Thus one day Girish had a war of words with Mahima Charan Chakrabarty, a scholarly devotee of the Master. However, after debating for only a short while, Mahima Charan was compelled to accept Girish's view.

After Girish left the room, the Master said to Mahima Charan: "Did you notice that Girish forgot to drink water?* If you had not accepted his view, he would have continued to attack you." Later in his life, Girish no longer cared for debates. He wrote in his play *Shankaracharya*, "Arguments are necessary to destroy the argumentative intellect."[19]

On Seeking Peace

One day Girish asked his secretary, Abinash: "If you pleased God and He offered a single boon to you, what would you ask for? What do you want from Him?"

Abinash replied: "May my mind dwell in dharma." He also mentioned some other things.

Girish then said: "You are planning and speaking after careful consideration. You see, people seek money, name and fame, and so on for peace. They think that by having those things they will get peace. Every man seeks peace. In whatever condition a man may be, he always looks for peace. There is no prayer other than for peace."[20]

Presence of Mind

Another day Girish asked Abinash: "Suppose you live in a village. If robbers attack you with clubs, what would you do?" When Abinash could not answer, Girish told him: "You see, at that time most people try to run away and the robbers hit them immediately. But when one falls into such a dangerous situation and the robber raises his club, one should rush towards the robber, grab him around the waist, and thrust one's head into his stomach. Then one should pick up a handful of dust and throw it into the eyes of the robber. One will then find the perfect opportunity to run away from the robber."[21]

On Rewards for Good Actions

After reading a novel, Abinash once said to Girish: "Sir, the beauty of this novelist's writing is that the hero is rewarded immediately whenever he works unselfishly. The author has tactfully encouraged people to perform good deeds."

Girish gravely replied: "I don't consider it proper for an author to induce people to do good actions by promising them a reward. In the

---

* Girish asked for water before beginning his argument, but forgot his thirst while debating.

real world we find that some get results by doing good actions, but others may not get any result in this life. A great writer should always try to place this high ideal in front of people: The performance of a good deed is for the sake of the good deed itself and not for a good result. There are some people in this world who expect rewards for their good deeds. And if they don't get any, they lose interest in doing good. This kind of writing that you have mentioned increases a false expectation in such people. But when they see that it is different in the field of action, they then lose faith in religion also."[22]

The Value of Time

Girish never liked misusing other people's time. For example, when a creditor would come to his house, Girish would open his money box and give him the money owed. Then he would ask his servant to give the creditor a smoke. Or if he did not have the cash, he would immediately ask him to return at a particular date and time. Girish said: "I don't like to detain that person and give him money after chatting for a couple of hours, or saying, 'Please come another day.' But I have no objection if we first finish his business and then we talk for three hours at leisure."[23]

Expiation

One day a brahmin pandit told Girish: "One should pray to God regarding one's sinful actions. This is the code of Hindu law for the expiation of sin."

Girish responded: "God has already forgiven us before we pray to Him. We commit so many mistakes at every step in our lives. Would it be possible for human beings to remain at peace for a moment if He were counting our mistakes?"[24]

His Deep Empathy

One afternoon after lunch Girish was seated in his parlour when his neighbour Manilal Mukhopadhyay came to see him. Observing his sorrowful expression, Girish asked him why he was sad. He then learned that Manilal's eldest son had recently drowned in the Ganges. Girish consoled him, talking to him for a long time. When Manilal left, Girish went to bed as usual. But he soon hurriedly came back to the parlour and sat down. When asked why he had left his bed so quickly, Girish replied: "You see, while lying in bed I was thinking of Manilal's son. All of a sudden it came to my mind how that drowning boy must have struggled for breath, and then while thinking of his condition I felt as if I were suffocating. I could no longer stay inside the mosquito curtain, because I was panting for breath. So I left my bedroom and came to the parlour."[25]

Power of Memory

Girish had an extraordinarily powerful memory. He could recite by memory many passages from the Ramayana, Mahabharata, the works of Milton, and some sections of Shakespeare's dramas. When he would see a man whom he had met many years earlier, he could immediately repeat verbatim their last conversation. Whatever books he read, he could later vividly remember the page numbers and lines of important passages.

One day Girish's friend Giridhari Basu said to him: "Every day you give homeopathic medicines to so many patients. Why don't you write down their names and medications in a notebook?"

Girish replied, "I remember them all, so it is not necessary to write them down."

Giridhari asked, "Can you tell me the names of the medicines that you prescribed for my mother's illness eight years ago?" When Girish recited the names of those medications he was dumbfounded.

Girish never studied books by underlining important sentences. He once told someone: "It restricts one's memory when the books are read with underlinings. Look, illiterate servants go to the market and buy groceries. They do not write down anything, but after shopping they submit accounts of every item without any mistake. Whereas you go to the market with a list, and still you make mistakes."[26]

National Pride

In 1911 the Mohan Bagan soccer team of Calcutta defeated the British team and won the Indian Football Association shield. This news made Girish so happy and excited that he forgot his old age and illness. When asked why he was so excited, Girish replied: "Previously no one could imagine that in a physical competition the Bengali boys could stand against the British. But today our boys have defeated the English soldiers in soccer. This event will enkindle hope that one day they will be able to defeat the British by physical strength. It is not an easy task. This victory of the I.F.A shield has made the Bengali race advance by ten years."[27]

About Eating and Sleeping

Girish was straightforward about his lifestyle. He used to say: "If you want to keep your body fit, then eat when you are hungry and sleep when you are sleepy. In this respect, don't feel shy or hesitant, or comply with any kind of etiquette."

Mahendra Nath Datta said: "Girish Babu's brain and body were in excellent condition till the last. He never neglected his stomach. While talking to people in his parlour, he would suddenly say, 'Please wait, let me eat something.' And he would ask his servant Ishan to bring some refreshments. When they were brought, he would immediately begin to eat in front of everybody. After a while he would say, 'Let me have a little rest.' Saying this, he would recline on his bolster. After 15 minutes he would sit up and begin to talk again."[28]

How to Tell a Story

Seldom does one find a person like Girish, who knew so many stories. Whenever Girish would express grief, joy, or anger in the stories he presented onstage, his audience would experience those moods as well. But Girish himself remained free from grief, joy, and anger. He said: "One should keep oneself separate from what one says. If one is overwhelmed, then the theme of the story becomes spoiled. The secret of writing or telling a story is this: The storyteller should first minutely observe the subject of the story, and then tell the story slowly, using his mental eye to visualize the action. If one is emotionally agitated, one cannot express the theme properly."

Girish developed to perfection his power of expression, whether it was in writing, storytelling, acting, or any other form. When he would tell funny stories, others would roll on the floor with laughter, but he would remain calm and show no external expression. He had the power to divide his mind in two.[29]

Rejoicing in Life

Girish said: "I have never done any work that did not give me joy and excitement. If I had not received bliss in searching for God, or if Sri Ramakrishna's company had not given me joy and happiness, I would not have gone in that direction at all."[30]

Chapter 26

Interviews and Reminiscences

Girish once told someone who wanted to write his biography: "A biography is not necessary. Those who want to know me will find me in my writings."[1] In the 1920s Hemendra Nath Dasgupta began writing *Girish Pratibha* (Girish as a Genius), a comprehensive and descriptive biography. For help he went to Devendra Nath Basu, Girish's cousin and a famous writer. Devendra quoted Emerson in reply: "Great geniuses have the shortest biographies. Their cousins can tell you nothing about them. They live in their writings."[2] Despite all of this, in 1928 Hemendra completed *Girish Pratibha*, a wonderful biography of Girish Chandra Ghosh in Bengali.

Girish was very inspiring, and those who came in contact with him even once could never forget him. He was a wonderful conversationalist. This chapter presents some personal interviews with and reminiscences of Girish.

An Informal Meeting with Girish

In 1907 Girish was the director of the Kohinoor Theatre. One day before rehearsals he was seated in his office with some actors and actresses, including Aparesh Mukhopadhyay, Purna Chandra Ghosh, Kshetra Mitra, Tinkari, Tarasundari, Kiranshashi, Kiranbala, Sushilabala, and others. Girish was talking about Ramakrishna, and everyone was listening with rapt attention. A great soul was uplifting their minds by talking about spiritual life.

Kshetra: "Sir, please tell us something more — something new."

Girish: "What do you want to know?"

Kshetra: "Please tell us about actors and actresses of England."

Girish: "No, not today. I shall tell you about them another day. We have started to talk about the Master today — let it continue."

Aparesh: "Well, whom do you think is the greatest among the disciples of the Master?"

Girish: "What? It seems you are ready to receive initiation from one of them. Look, by the grace of their guru, the minds of all of them are absorbed in God. It is not proper to compare them with each other."

Kshetra: "Wasn't Swami Vivekananda the foremost and most famous among them?"

Girish: "Kshetra, don't say anything about him. He was beyond description. He conquered the world. Nirvikalpa samadhi lay in the palm of his hand. It was the Master who engaged him to work for the good of humanity."

Tinkari: "Sir, will Ramakrishna bestow grace on me? I have done so many sinful things in my life."

Girish: "His door is always open to each and all."

Tarasundari: "Is Ramakrishna for all? Then is it possible for us to get liberation?"

Girish: "All are equal in the eyes of Sri Ramakrishna."

Tinkari: "I committed many sins in my past life, so I was born in a sinful place. Could you tell me what one should do so that one will not have to be born in such a place?"

Girish: "One of the epithets of God is the Redeemer of the Fallen. If one calls on Him with humility and wholeheartedly, He will definitely give shelter to that fallen person."

Tinkari (*with choked voice*): "Can you teach me how to call on God in the right way? I pray to God every day and millions of people like me also call on Him. I am a lowly person. Does my prayer reach God?"

Girish: "Everyone's call reaches His ear equally and that is the reason He is God. To Him there is no sinner or lowly person. He lovingly accepts those who call on Him wholeheartedly. You call on God, and He will definitely give you shelter in His heavenly abode, just as He forgave Jagai and Madhai — two villains. By God's grace, 'A well-dressed dancing girl became a saint.'"*

Tarasundari: "But the way we have led our lives, there is no deliverance for us."

Girish: "Don't say that, Tara. Didn't you hear the story of your aunt Binodini? The Master was moved watching her act in the role of Chaitanya and blessed her, saying, 'Mother, may you attain illumination.'"

Abinash: "Binodini is now engaged in worshipping Gopala [baby Krishna]."

---

*Girish is referring to the story of a courtesan who went to tempt Haridas, a disciple of Chaitanya, but failed. She was instead transformed and became a saint.

Girish: "All of you, remember that He is the Lord of the lowly. He will not refuse or disappoint anyone."

With tearful eyes and choked voice, Girish began to recite: "O Refuge of the lowly, as the rain falls on the earth evenly, so You distribute grace in this world, whether it is asked for or not. One may steal a poor widow's money, kill an embryo, commit adultery with other women; one may give up one's wife and children, become a drunkard and tyrant, and lead a wretched life — still, O Saviour of the Fallen, Your door is open for such people."

Tinkari: "Sir, let me ask you something: Can the money that we have earned in an immoral way be used for a noble cause?"

Girish: "Of course it can. But don't give charity seeking a result."

Tinkari: "I wish to give some money to help poor people."

Girish: "Well, that is a wonderful intention. The Master will be pleased with you."

Tarasundari: "Sir, is it possible to do anything without seeking a result?"

Girish: "Why not? You will have to give up your ego. You will have to think that you are nobody and that the Master is all in all. You will have to remember God in the waking, dreaming, and sleeping states. You perform your actions and leave the fruit to God."

Kiranshashi: "We are very low, insignificant creatures."

Girish: "The Master used to say, 'If a man always thinks of himself as a worm, he becomes a worm.' Always remember that you also are a daughter of Jagaddhatri, the Mother of the Universe. Her loving compassionate eyes are watching you."

Aparesh: "Sir, it is by your grace that all people in the theatre have become devotees of Ramakrishna."

Girish placed his hands on his head and bowed down in front of a picture of Ramakrishna.

Sushilabala: "Sir, I have a question: We become proud when we do something for others. We think that our action will give us virtue and happiness. Is this good?"

Girish: "It is wonderful to do good to others. But don't expect any result that will bring you virtue and happiness. It will be a right action when you can give up that expectation of happiness. All of you should remember that wherever you may have been born, you are destined to do good to others without seeking any result. The goal of our actions is public welfare."

All: "What a lofty idea!"

Girish: "This is true *Balidan* — self-sacrifice! There is no higher duty than this. And everyone has a right to perform it."

Just then the bell for the rehearsal was rung, and the joyful gathering ended.[3]

A Meeting of Two Great Souls

Generally people consider the theatre to be a place for recreation or amusement. Girish transformed it into a temple. Whatever dramas he wrote he offered to the Lord. Girish used the theatre to educate people in the religious traditions of India, to awaken an Indian national consciousness, to reestablish and reinvigorate an Indian national education, and to attempt to reverse the degradation that existed then in society.

In June 1911 Girish was not well. Deshbandhu Chittaranjan Das, a well-known barrister and national leader, came to visit him at his Baghbazar residence. Girish joyfully received Chittaranjan and his secretary, Lalit Mohan Sen. Chittaranjan raised the topic of Girish's dramas and even recited some passages from some of his plays.

Girish: "I didn't know you had read my dramas so thoroughly."

Chittaranjan: "I am one of your ardent devotees."

Girish: "Don't you know that I am *noto* (actor) Girish — I have no place in society."

Chittaranjan: "You are far above society. It is extremely rare to find a *jnani* [man of wisdom] and devotee like you. I strongly believe that you have preserved the tradition of the Vaishnava poets."

Girish: "Sir, I am not a seer but I see you are a great yogi and a great soul. Your karma will be wiped out. As Sri Ramakrishna used to say to me, 'People will be amazed seeing you.'"

Chittaranjan: "Please bless me."

Girish: "God will bless you. Yes, I remember your poem *Baravilasini*. It was written with great love and sympathy. It manifested your wonderful poetic faculty."

In the meantime Dani, Girish's son, arrived and Girish introduced him to Chittaranjan. With great respect Dani saluted Chittaranjan.

Chittaranjan (*to Dani*): "I saw your acting as Osman and Tarasundari's as Ayesha in Bankim Chandra's *Durgeshnandini*. It was outstanding. I want to see your performance again on another night."

Dani (*humbly*): "Yes, sir. It will be my pleasure."

Girish: "Of course, you will see his acting, but you will have to forgive me. It will not be possible for me to act in the role of Birendra Singha in that play."

Chittaranjan took his leave. Girish looked at him intently for a long time and found in him an ideal man.[4]

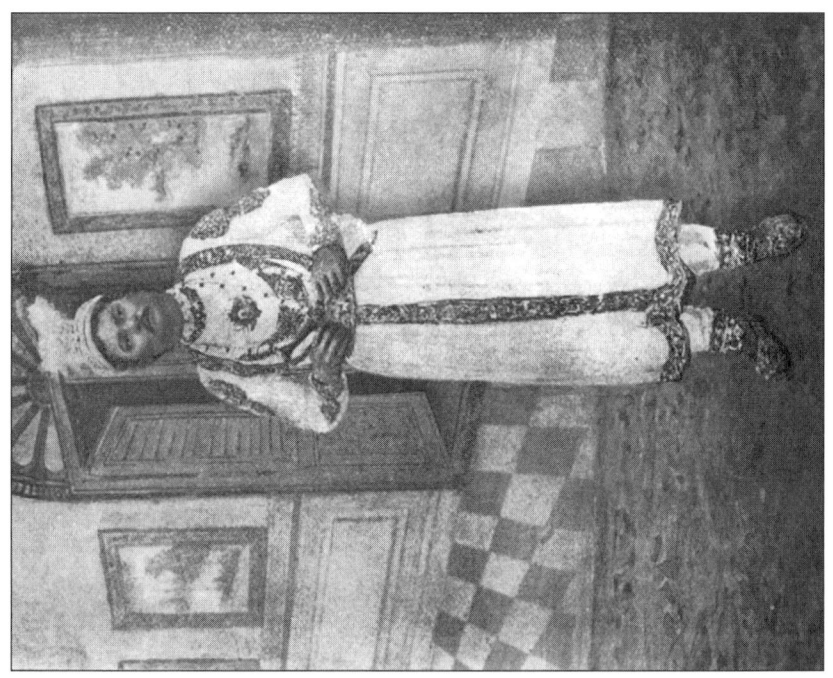

Surendranath Ghosh (Dani), Girish's son. At right: Surendra Nath acting in costume

From the Minutes of the Ramakrishna Mission

Swami Vivekananda inaugurated the Ramakrishna Mission on 1 May 1897 at Balaram Basu's house in Calcutta. Girish was present on that occasion. During the weekly meetings of the Ramakrishna Order, the monastic and householder disciples of Ramakrishna would recount their memories of their Master. Girish attended many of those meetings and recounted his personal reminiscences of the Master. Sometimes he commented on the activities of the Order and answered questions. Following are notes and interviews from the minutes of the Ramakrishna Mission.

Seventh Meeting: 6 June 1897

Girish Chandra Ghosh spoke about the work of Swami Vivekananda, emphasizing that Swamiji was spreading the teachings of Ramakrishna without the least thought of making himself the originator of the ideas he was disseminating.

He continued as follows: "You are all aware of the dynamic message and activities of Swami Vivekananda. He has been disseminating the teachings of Sri Ramakrishna everywhere. One day Swamiji said, 'Whoever chants the name of my Thakur [Ramakrishna] need never fear death.'

"He wants the Master's disciples to remain perfectly pure. Before leaving for other parts of the world, he repeatedly saluted me and requested my blessings so that he might fulfill his heart's desire, because he considered me one of the Master's beloved children.

"In the Gita, when Arjuna was overpowered by tamas, Sri Krishna spoke inspiring words to him again and again. Similarly, by his bold message, 'Thou art Brahman,' Swamiji aroused rajas in the people steeped in tamas.

"In his lecture, 'The Sages of India,' he has extolled the divine love found in the lives of Sri Krishna and the gopis [the cowherd girls of Vrindaban]. In this, Swamiji has illustrated the highest expression of devotion possible.

"His deep love for the disciples of the Master reveals how deeply he loves and adores Sri Ramakrishna. This boundless love expressed itself one day, just before he was starting for Darjeeling, when he told me, 'I can lay down my life, even at this moment, in the service of the Master.'

"Through words and deeds [precept and practice] he strove to spread the teachings of the Master so that the entire world would benefit by the spiritual message of Sri Ramakrishna. I call ignorant anyone who thinks Swami Vivekananda is separate or different from Sri Ramakrishna."[5]

Fourteenth Meeting: 25 July 1897

Girish reminisced about his association with Ramakrishna: "Four or five days after I sought refuge at the feet of Sri Ramakrishna, he asked me, 'What have you achieved?' I answered that I had achieved fearlessness. On hearing this he laughed. What it means to take refuge at his feet is not easy to describe, because it is not easy to describe *him*. Even after seeing Sri Ramakrishna so much, I am unable to say definitely what he really is or what his distinctive aspects are. I have seen him manifest himself differently at different times. During the festival at Panihati,* for instance, I saw the Master's various spiritual moods. Since that time, I cannot say whether he is *Purusha* or *Prakriti*. He told me that even he did not know whether he was Purusha or Prakriti [male or female].

"Like a mother he was affectionate to me and would feed me; and like a father, he was a man of knowledge and an ideal devotee. It is hard, therefore, to describe him. Even to form a concept or idea within oneself is difficult. However, I am personally convinced that he is the giver of shelter and protection.

"I do not know what the scriptures say about God, but I believe that if Sri Ramakrishna was able to love me as he did in the same way that I love myself, then he must be God. He loved me in this way.

"I never had a true friend; but *he* is one because he transformed my faults into virtues. In a way, I feel he loved me *more* than I loved myself.

"I have known another thing about him. Whoever was able to see his own fault and admit it, has been blessed and made better by him. Through contact with him, as with the philosopher's stone, even a great sinner's heart would be transmuted into gold. He gave refuge to such a sinner, if the latter was meek and humble.

"Sometimes his utterances were difficult to understand. For instance, he would see a prostitute standing nearby and address her as the Divine Mother. Or he would refer to Varanasi as 'the golden Varanasi.' But then, by his mere glance everything could become gold — this his intimate devotees will tell you.

"When I wrote the play *Vilwamangal*, several of his devotees questioned me about it. I told them I had learned the art of playwriting from Sri Ramakrishna. Narendra [Swami Vivekananda] has said that he learned science from Ramakrishna, and Mahendra Nath [M.] says Sri Ramakrishna taught him the art of teaching. How it is possible to express Ramakrishna's many moods and aspects? How can one say what they

---

*A holy place near Calcutta where Ramakrishna went several times to attend the annual Vaishnava festival held there.

are? I am only able to say this much: that whosoever takes refuge at the feet of Sri Ramakrishna will attain peace. Of this there is no doubt. All spiritual desires of such a person will be fulfilled.

"Now, who is this Ramakrishna? Whether he is an avatar [divine incarnation] or not, I do not know. But if the functions of an incarnation are to bestow grace and compassion on all and protect and liberate those who surrender themselves [to God] — then I say that Sri Ramakrishna is undoubtedly God incarnate.

"Sri Ramakrishna is the giver of infinite peace and happiness. How shall I think of him? His worship transcends formal observances. Coming to the theatre, he fed me with sweets. When I abused him, he would embrace me. The only way to worship him is to call on him by repeating his holy name.

"This morning Rakhal Maharaj [Swami Brahmananda] told me to speak to you for one hour. By seeking refuge in them [the direct disciples], I have dared to deliver this speech. If I depend on them, there is no fear anymore. In conclusion, let me say this: Sri Ramakrishna is the embodiment of compassion and the loving ruler of our hearts. If we call on him our hearts will be freed from ignorance and iniquity."[6]

After the lecture Girish answered the following questions.

Question: "What is the power of attorney?"

Girish: "The power of attorney is to offer all responsibility to God, as one transfers the right to manage one's worldly affairs to another person."

Question: "Is God's grace conditional or unconditional?"

Girish: "Unconditional."

Question: "Does grace come as the result of one's previous life's action?"

Girish: "Grace dawns from His grace."

Question: "Is Sri Ramakrishna a householder or a renunciant?"

Girish: "He did everything without attachment. A jiva (individual soul) is under maya but maya is under God. He incarnates in every age and does whatever is necessary."

Question: "What is virtue and what is vice?"

Girish: "Spiritual practices, such as japa and meditation, lead to liberation, so they are virtuous deeds. And the actions which bind people in this world are bad deeds."

Question: "Why do we have the propensity to karma?"

Girish: "It comes by the samskaras (impressions) of our past lives. There is no answer to the origin of samskaras because karma is beginningless."

Question: "How can we end this flow of worldly karma?"

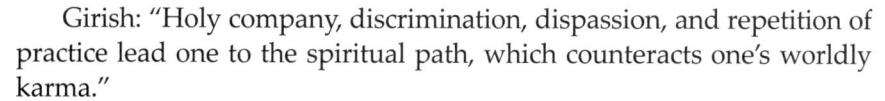

Girish: "Holy company, discrimination, dispassion, and repetition of practice lead one to the spiritual path, which counteracts one's worldly karma."

Question: "Why are we afraid of death?"

Girish: "The authors of the scriptures say that the death pain is terrible and we have had the experience of it in previous lives. So we are afraid of it."

Question: "How can we get rid of this fear?"

Girish: "By sadhana and liberation. It is difficult for ordinary people. One can conquer the fear of death by attaining samadhi through chanting God's name."[7]

Sixteenth Meeting: 8 August 1897

Girish spoke on "Prarabdha Karma": "We hear in the scriptures that karma is beginningless, and in practical life we see there is no end to karma. Now, how can we get release from the bondage of karma? Whatever we do in this life, its result will come to us either in this life or the next. As it is said, one should do good actions; then there will be no fear of bondage. Regarding this, Sri Ramakrishna once said, 'Undoubtedly, to establish a temple is a virtuous deed, but if that man thinks that he is its founder, he will have to come back to enjoy the fruit of his action.'

"One will have to experience the result of one's karma whether it is happiness or misery. Sometimes one suffers doing good karma. Suppose a man helps his friend with money, and then if the latter is ungrateful, the former becomes angry and upset. But if one performs action without any desire or expectation, then one can avoid such consequences. One should work for work's sake. We need an exemplar of an ideal karma yogi; otherwise we cannot move forward in this path of karma.

"One day I went to Sri Ramakrishna and found him crying profusely, and he said: 'Nitai [Chaitanya's disciple] walked door to door and distributed love, but my body is so fragile that I cannot go to the devotees' houses without a carriage.' On another occasion the Master said, 'I will do good to others, even by taking sago pudding.' He worked unselfishly without any expectation. To me, Sri Ramakrishna is an ideal role model of unselfish action."[8]

Seventeenth Meeting: 15 August 1897

Girish spoke before the group on the topic "What is God?" He said among other things: "Once I requested Sri Ramakrishna to 'show me something,' that is, to give me a spiritual vision.

"But he said, 'Do not desire such visions. For even if you have them, you may not believe what you see.' Later I realized the import of his words. For undoubtedly if I saw someone standing in front of me, holding a mountain in his hands, for instance, I should think it some kind of magic, some illusion.

"The life and teachings of Sri Ramakrishna are most appropriate for this age. Persons with little or no faith in God went to see him. He treated them with loving consideration, offered them refreshments, and then talked to them about God. In his presence no one felt like contradicting him or arguing about the existence of God. He made all feel the 'actuality' of God.

"People were impressed with the fact that he never asked for money or gifts. His was a life of unquestionable purity. His attitude was liberal and universal. He would say: 'All paths are true. Follow whichever manifestation of the divine that you love.' Whoever has witnessed his samadhi knows for certain that God is real and ever-present.

"Vain arguing never arose while we were in his company. At that time, however much I tried, I could never think of myself as an atheist. Though I would vacillate between scepticism and faith, ultimately, by his grace, I found myself accepting everything.

"Formerly, I thought faith the property of a weak mind. But after seeing him, I realized its great power. Through his *darshan* [holy company], I have been freed from all doubts. He once said to me, 'Do that which you feel within yourself, and have firmly decided upon.' Through his words he gave me faith, and my agnostic, materialistic attitudes were transformed into spiritual ones. To what other cause can I attribute my faith? God cannot be realized through reason and logic. A mere lamp will not help one see the sun. The aspirant must approach an illumined teacher who has himself realized God.

"Sometime or other in our lifetime the mind turns to God; if not in happy times, then in times of sorrow or suffering or at the moment of death. If we want to know God there is no other way than to go to God Himself — that is, to a man of God, a man in whom God is most manifest. Where is he found? If the seeker is earnest enough, if he yearns longingly for the Lord, then God Himself will see that his devotee finds such a man. Sri Ramakrishna would say, 'He who sincerely seeks will find a teacher.'

"In order to realize God, one must first cultivate humility. Most of us are filled with egotism, for we think to ourselves, 'What need have I of a guru?' But in Ramakrishna's presence, this sort of egotism disappeared. He would be the first to salute a person with his hands together. The one and only means to attain God is to take refuge in the guru. Although you may lack faith now, you can all be transformed by the grace of the guru."

A member of the audience addressed the following questions to Girish.

Question: "What did Sri Ramakrishna mean by the expression 'to commit theft within one's own heart?'"

Girish: "I think it a mistake to make any claim to thoroughly understand Sri Ramakrishna — and in only one way. But let me tell you what I have been privileged to understand. The expression which you have quoted means that one should meditate on and worship the Lord according to one's own devotional temperament. Once Ramakrishna asked Swami Yogananda, 'Hello, what do you think of me?' Yogananda replied, 'You are neither a householder nor a sannyasin [in any exclusive sense].' Sri Ramakrishna was greatly pleased, and exclaimed, 'What an extraordinary statement you have just made!'"

Question: "What is your view regarding the belief that Sri Ramakrishna is an avatar?"

Girish: "It annoys me even to consider any other man as possessing his divinity! When I went to see him once, I had just left a house of ill-repute — and yet he offered me a seat. Once he came to see me at that profane theatre of mine, carrying sweets! And just for me!

"I have never received such love from anyone. To me, Sri Ramakrishna is the Lord; he is God-incarnate. A single utterance of his removed the doubts of a lifetime from my mind. Even now, if I see doubts begin to stir, I think of him. Immediately they vanish and do not rise again. I find that it is not difficult to obey him, love him, and worship him. But, indeed, it is difficult to forget him."[9]

Nineteenth Meeting: 29 August 1897

The topic of the meeting was self-effort.

Girish spoke: "Which is true, we ask ourselves — God's grace or self-effort? Sri Ramakrishna used to say that both were effective, that both were true. I met Sri Ramakrishna for the first time at the house of Dinanath Basu. It was at night. I heard the Master exclaim: 'What, isn't it dusk yet? Is it still daylight?' My first reaction to these words was one of scepticism. I thought his spiritual state a pretense, and returned home with that feeling. I was not then aware that persons endowed with ecstatic love of God could actually be so indrawn as to be oblivious to day or night."

A member of the audience addressed the following questions to Girish.

Question: "What is your concept of the avatar?"

Girish: "An avatar is an embodiment of love and compassion. I have never found such love as what the Master had for me. He picked me up even from the theatre [which was considered at that time a sinful place]. He said: 'I am not confined to any particular place. I have only compassion. I lost everything except compassion for humanity.' He who possesses such compassion for all beings I consider an avatar. The Master said, 'If I be born thousands of times to deliver only one person, even that I consider efficacious and worthwhile.' The best proof of an avatar is his own words. When Ramachandra was incarnated, he was recognized only by seven sages. If he does not let anyone know, none can know him."

Question: "Did Sri Ramakrishna bestow his compassion on everyone who went to him?"

Girish: "I believe this to be true. At times, what seemed harsh to us or cruel always turned out to be unfailingly benevolent and beneficial. On a certain occasion, Sri Ramakrishna asked Shashi [Swami Ramakrishnananda] not to ride with him in the carriage. He refused to let him even enter the carriage. At the time I thought this terribly unkind. But see how wonderfully Shashi has turned out! I have seen many such instances."[10]

Twenty-Fourth Meeting: 17 October 1897

Girish spoke on "The Glory of the Divine Name": "In the external as well as the internal world, one can expedite the result of a slow action by a fast action. We see that one person can memorize something in one hour that another person cannot memorize in many hours. As it is true in acquiring learning, so it is in the field of religion. Pure thoughts purify the impure mind. The result comes quickly if one strives intensely. A worldly atheist suddenly realized that God exists and that one can find Him by calling on Him sincerely. This faith dawned in his heart and the world became dull and insipid to him. His heart was attracted to the path of God, and finally God became his all in all. At the time of death, a degenerate brahmin became sinless by thinking of the all-purifying goddess Ganges. If the scriptures are true, this kind of human hope is auspicious and beneficial."

Question: "If a man is close to death or is critically ill and he chants God's name and becomes sinless, then why does he again get engaged in bad actions after recovering from the illness?"

Girish: "You see, he chanted God's name out of fear, but he couldn't develop a taste or love for His name. He did not know that even a great sinner becomes free by chanting God's name. If he were convinced of this,

his mind would be drawn to God day by day, and the intensity of his worldly desires would gradually become less and less.

"Everyone, even the lowly, has a right to chant God's name. God tests our faith by giving us some troubles. But the heart becomes more pure by the fire of repentance than by telling one's beads with ego for years. When one develops a taste for God's name, one experiences God's grace and attains humility. This experience is the dawn of knowledge."

Question: "The result of chanting a divine name comes from faith and not from the name."

Girish: "Those great souls whose hearts are absorbed in God are alone capable of explaining the glory of the divine name. Faith develops from chanting God's name, and then that faith produces infinite results. Liberation is not possible without cessation of karma. Only a competent person finds the result of chanting God's name. It is not that God is unattainable; it is that we are incompetent."

Question: "If one attains liberation by chanting God's name once, then why does another person who had been chanting the divine name his whole life not get the same result?"

Girish: "There is theft in the chamber of his heart. An exorcist wants to drive away a ghost using mustard seeds, but the ghost already entered the mustard seeds beforehand. He chants God's name just to impress people. But when that hypocrite suffers at the time of death, he will wholeheartedly take refuge in God's name and also get its result."

Question: "Many people chant God's name. Will all of them get the result?"

Girish: "Of course! The divine name is very effective. You see, we love an object that is familiar to us. Similarly, devotion will dawn when we develop knowledge of God."[11]

Twenty-Fifth Meeting: 24 October 1897

After the meeting a question-and-answer session followed.

Question: "What was the need for Sri Ramakrishna's advent as an avatar?"

Girish: "Before Sri Ramakrishna came, religious ideals and practices were in turmoil. For instance, if someone hides a key in a remote corner of a marketplace, how easily do you think it can be found? Similarly, prior to the advent of Ramakrishna it had become impossible to find the key to the realization of God in the welter of scriptures, sects, and creeds. Sri Ramakrishna's incarnation was needed to bring order and harmony to the various religions. It was he who said: "Every form of true faith in God is a true path to the one and only goal. All religions are true if they lead to God, and if one is sincere and earnest at heart, one can attain Him by following any religion."

Question: "What did Sri Ramakrishna say regarding renunciation?"

Girish: "He said that true renunciation is to give up attachment to those desires and objects that are obstacles to God-realization. There is no need to renounce the world externally. One may live in the world so long as one remains in close communion with God. The object of renunciation is to join oneself to God."

Question: "What are the ways to worship God?"

Girish: "Pray, meditate, and chant His name. Nothing else is necessary. And let those who can, perform ritual worship. The reward of ritual is love and the joy of God, and the best method to attain Him is to intensely desire to realize Him. Sri Ramakrishna used to say to me: 'Never be a lazy devotee. Feel that you can and will attain God in this very life; nay, at this very moment. Practise with this sort of forcefulness.'"

Question: "How do we attain such devotion?"

Girish: "Through constant prayer."

Question: "Please describe the night of the Kali puja when offerings were made at the feet of Sri Ramakrishna by the devotees."

Girish: "While Sri Ramakrishna was living in Shyampukur [in North Calcutta], Kali puja was performed. He sat down to perform the worship, surrounded by flowers, fruit, and all the other various articles. Suddenly he turned to me and said: "It is the Divine Mother's day. One should sit and meditate like this." I do not know what took hold of me at that point. I just rushed forward, and chanting 'Jaya Sri Ramakrishna,' offered flowers at his feet. The others in the room did the same. Sri Ramakrishna went into samadhi, his hands assuming the gestures symbolizing fearlessness and the bestowal of boons.

"When Sri Ramakrishna was present, no desire was felt other than the desire for God. I purposely tried to introduce other thoughts in my mind one day. But no worldly desires could arise."[12]

Twenty-Ninth Meeting: 21 November 1897

Girish read a paper on "Karma". Following is the gist of it:

"Sri Ramakrishna ignored his own health and comfort in order to guide aspirants along the spiritual path. His sympathetic heart felt the pain and suffering afflicting all other beings. Therefore, he always expressed his readiness to be born again and again, if need be, to help others towards God. He would say: 'If the heart is not freed from the bondage of worldly desires and attachments, it will do no good to withdraw prematurely from all work and worldly responsibilities and put on an ochre cloth. This will bring benefit neither to this life nor to the life hereafter. One may be able to deceive oneself and others in the world, but in spiritual life it only raises a veil between the self and God.'

"Truly, one is plunged in maya and ignorance if one works with attachment. Sri Ramakrishna would say: 'If a passionate desire arises and persists during meditation, stop and begin to pray. Earnestly pray to the Lord that this desire be removed, that it not be fulfilled. Any desire coming up in meditation, particularly a repressed one, gradually becomes intensified. And if one or more of our passions are involved, the results can be most disquieting.'"[13]

Thirty-Eighth Meeting: 30 January 1898

The subject was a teaching of Ramakrishna: "Tie the knowledge of nonduality in a corner of your cloth and then do as you please."

Girish spoke: "Some people interpret the above teaching to mean that there is no virtue or vice; do whatever you like. This kind of understanding is not an indication of the knowledge of nonduality. A true nondualist does not consider anything his own. He who can fearlessly serve a leper with his own hand is a knower of Advaita [nondual Brahman]. But he who has a sense of ego does not have this knowledge of Oneness.

"This knowledge dawns on that person who has purified his mind through good action. Good action means to serve others without any motive. This purifies the mind and destroys selfish desires. Even a person who is eager to preach his own religious view has self-interest. The truth of Advaita Vedanta has not revealed itself to him.

"We should know our true nature. We are all parts of that nondual Reality. We are all one. We are not different from each other. This human body is the temple of that nondual God, and He is the true nature of all human beings. The greatest worship is to worship living human beings. Worship the living gods instead of worshipping images of wood and clay.

"Once the angel Gabriel was visiting the world with a list of God's true devotees in his hand. A man asked him: 'I don't practise religion, or worship God, but I love human beings. Is my name on your list?' Gabriel opened the list and found that man's name at the top.

"Some say if you have nondualistic knowledge, you can do whatever you like and you will not incur any sin. But a true knower of nondual Brahman cannot commit any sinful act, because his mind is devoid of impure thoughts. While doing good to humanity, we do good to ourselves. Compassion dwells in every human heart. One can achieve this divine quality by relinquishing cruel selfishness. If one wishes to cultivate compassion in one's heart, one's resolution comes true by the grace of God and one's guru."[14]

'A Man of Faith and Genius'
Sister Devamata*

My life in Calcutta brought me in contact with people rather than with places. Although I spent some time there, I saw little of what the casual traveller sees. Buildings, parks and scenic streets seemed to me of small value compared with the less usual opportunity of knowing men and women of eminence and achievement in Indian life. One I especially enjoyed meeting was the noted Bengali dramatist, Girish Chandra Ghosh, familiarly known as Girish Babu. A gifted actor also, he is called the Garrick of the Bengali stage as well as the Shakespeare of the Bengali drama.

The measure of his gift as a player is given in this incident. Vidyasagar, the scholar and philanthropist, was at Girish Babu's theatre one night when the actor was depicting a profligate. In a scene where he was abusing a woman, Vidyasagar became so stirred by the vividness of the portrayal that he took off his sandal and threw it at the actor. It struck him and rebounded on the stage. Girish Babu picked it up, placed it on his head, and with a bow to the audience declared he had never received a more gratifying tribute.**

His productivity was phenomenal. He wrote in all seventy plays, some of them being composed, as it were, by one continuous stroke of the pen. One of the greatest, a six-act drama entitled *Vilwamangal the Saint* was written in twenty-eight hours of uninterrupted labour. Another remarkable literary production is his play on Gautama Buddha. Both of these have been translated beautifully into English by Swami Paramananda [a disciple of Vivekananda]. Many of his subjects are taken from the religious history of India and are so powerful in their effect that now and then a listener in the audience, moved to the depths by the life of some spiritual hero portrayed on the stage, has passed directly from the door of

---
*An American devotee, named Laura F. Glenn, who later became a nun of Ananda Ashrama, California.
**There is another version: Vidyasagar threw his slipper at Ardhendu Shekhar Mustafi, Girish's co-actor, in the Nildarpan play. Ardhendu was acting in the role of an Englishman who was torturing an Indian woman. That scene enraged Vidyasagar so much that he reacted in that way.

the theatre to the solitary seclusion of the forest, renouncing everything. I had personal acquaintance with two such instances and the impression in both cases persisted.

Girish Babu possessed a deeply religious nature; but as a boy he found no satisfying phase of faith to feed it and because of this he lived through many dark years of doubt and profligacy, during which the drama became his creed and the playhouse his temple. It was Sri Ramakrishna who led him back to boyhood faith and requickened his spiritual ardour. This is the account of their meeting as Girish Babu himself gave it to me:

> The first time I saw Gurumaharaj [Ramakrishna] was in the house there at the end of the lane. He had just come out of samadhi and he was asking, 'Is it evening?' I thought: This man must be either mad or a fraud, for here is the lamp burning, it is dark outside and he asks, 'Is it evening?' The next time I saw him was at Balaram Babu's house. Then one day someone came and said the Paramahamsa wished to come to my theatre and what would I charge. I told the person I would not take any money from him, but the disciples would have to pay. When he arrived at the theatre I meant to be at the entrance to receive him, but he had got down from the *Gari* (carriage) before I came. As he saw me he made *pranam* (bowed down), then when I tried to make *pranam*, again he bowed and so for two or three times. Then I thought: It is useless to keep this up with an insane man; so I led him to a box and as people said he had fits of unconsciousness I gave him a *punkah* [fan] man; then I came away home and thought no more about him.
>
> But there had risen a great trouble in my mind. People said that one could not attain realization without a *guru* (spiritual teacher), yet I did not see how anyone could take initiation from a human being. It seemed as if God could be the only real guru. I grew so disturbed about it that at last I prayed for help. One day Sri Gurumaharaj came to Balaram Bose's house and sent for me. I told him my trouble and he said to me, 'You have your guru.' I was very much pleased and thought: I was right after all. I do not need anyone outside. My guru is inside myself.
>
> After that I felt an irresistible desire to go to Dakshineswar. It was as if some unseen power were drawing me and one day I went there. Gurumaharaj was sitting alone in his room with Bhavanath. As I entered he looked at me and said: 'I was just talking of you to Bhavanath.' Then it came into my mind that anyone who could take so much trouble to seek me out must be very good, and after that I never had any doubt that he was my guru.
>
> He was a mother to me and a father to his disciples for sometimes he would scold them, but he forgave everything in me. From the time I was

a little child I was very obstinate and whenever anyone told me I must not do anything, at once I would want to do it. But he never forbade me to do anything. He took me just as I was. Somehow I could never do anything wrong, because the thought that he might be displeased held me back. But if he had told me I must not do it, I should not have felt that way.

Once someone told me that unless a man was absolutely truthful he could not hope to realize the Truth. This troubled me because I did not always tell the truth, so I went to him [the Master] about it. But the moment I mentioned it to him, he said quickly: 'You need not worry about that. Whatever you do now will be right.' I did not go often to Dakshineswar but he came very frequently to my house and that was another proof to me that he was a real mother.

I had been in Calcutta only a short time when a note came from Girish Babu expressing regret that he was not able to call upon me because of illness and asking if I would not come to see him. The first time I went Swami Saradananda took me. They were close friends and Swami Saradananda paid him daily visits. We turned from the main street into a narrow lane running between high blank walls and closed at the end by Girish Babu's wide entrance doorway. We passed through this, went along a short hall, across a large court, up an outdoor staircase, over a roof terrace and into a narrow low-studded room on the second storey. There between a window opening on the court and one over the entrance door, on a rug, half reclining against a round bolster, lay the great dramatist like a fallen giant, mighty even in his physical distress. He was a sufferer from asthma and his breath came in quick short gasps.

He was a man of powerful build, tall and stately in his bearing. His voice, though hoarse, was still deep and resonant; his enunciation, that of the trained and cultured actor. Swami Saradananda left us and Girish Babu plied me with questions about Swami Ramakrishnananda, about Swami Paramananda and his work in the West, about my own religious experiences. Then he began to speak to me of Sri Ramakrishna. I have rarely seen such ardour of discipleship. His face shone with it, his breath grew deep again and one could sense the burning glow in his heart. He told me of their meeting, of the indulgent mother-love the Master had always given him; how in the beginning when he had tried to shock him by a song or word, the Master had merely laughed, as at a wayward child.

Now and then as he talked, he would wave a greeting to some friend passing in the street at the end of the lane and I understood why he had chosen that small room above the entrance and the place between the windows. It kept him in touch with those who were still actively moving through the world while he had fallen by the wayside. Many a comrade, I was told, went out of his way to cross the little lane and give an answering wave of the hand to his, for he had many staunch friends and admirers.

Faith and genius created an extraordinary mingling of qualities in his character and lent to it impelling force. The strain of lawlessness that ran through it seemed merely to accentuate the highlights of productive power and unfaltering trust. His faith once restored could not be shaken. It triumphed over gasping breath, over death even. A description of his going came to me in a letter from Swami Premananda.

> "The saddest news from India now is the passing away of Babu Girish Chandra Ghosh," the swami wrote. "This year his asthma was giving him trouble from the beginning of the winter. Towards the close of January some improvement was apparent, but on the full moon day of the next week there was a relapse. The end, however, was evident only in the last two days — not even that, only for the last thirty hours. He himself gave up the struggle twenty-four hours before with the ejaculation: 'Why still this clinging to matter! Master, remove this intoxication of the flesh.' A short time after he had spoken these words, he grew quiet, then he went into a state of coma and passed out twelve hours later."[15]

Reminiscences of Girish Chandra Ghosh
Mrs. Gray Hallock[*]

Girish Chandra Ghosh, who died in February 1912, was a Hindu disciple of Sri Ramakrishna, and an exponent of the Vedanta, a religion and philosophy as old as India, which he worked into his fascinating dramas. So far as I know, there are as yet no translations of his complete works; otherwise his name would, I think, be even better known than Tagore's.

In India, G.C. as he was affectionately called in Sri Ramakrishna's circle, is still remembered and revered as a saint and a genius. There is a G.C. Society and a park in Calcutta is named after him — for the charm of his personality is utterly unforgettable by those who knew him well.

The great yellow river was alive with small craft almost half across its width. Ghats and white buildings gleamed between palm trees on the opposite shore against the deep blue of India's clear warm winter sky. It was a day of religious festival. In the grounds of the Math or Hindu Monastery, founded by Vivekananda, the scent of blossoming mango trees was almost overpowering. Marigolds in the grass were trodden underfoot (as we tread daisies) by the great crowd of *babus* [gentlemen] who had come from Calcutta by river, and garlands of these flowers

[*] A personal friend and admirer of Girish Chandra Ghosh.

strung like beads by their heads, without stems or foliage, festooned the portraits of Ramakrishna the Master, and of Vivekananda the disciple here venerated, set out like shrines under a large *shamiana* or tent. The garden and field was so crowded with visitors that the mass of humanity even surged in and out of the monastery, changing the usual peacefulness of this spot to the semblance of a fair.

The poor from surrounding villages, sitting cross-legged in rows on the grass, were being fed by Vivekananda's sannyasins (monks), their salmon-coloured robes or *chadars* distinguishing them from the bareheaded, white *dhoti*-clad, umbrella-carrying *babu* visitors. These were mostly Bengali gentlemen, but here and there were men from the South or from the Hills, whose sympathies had drawn them to this annual festival. Here and there, under awnings, were groups of religious singers known as Sankirtan parties. In another place an improvising musician with matted hair, ash-strewn, was dancing and reciting in a frenzy of devotion, or what he intended to appear as such. Elsewhere pictures of Hindu gods, goddesses, and saints, and pious books were for sale. Everywhere heat and dust and the raucous voices of chattering, gesticulating Bengalis.

In this environment, so utter a contrast to the quiet upper room with which I came to associate him, I first saw Girish Chandra Ghosh. A friend conducted me through this chaos of sights and sounds. Among a group, a little distance away, stood an elderly man of commanding appearance and bearing. He had a Roman type of face, and was the very evident centre of attraction in this little group under the trees. There must have been some witty repartee that raised a laugh from the others. With a smile, throwing his silk chadar or shawl toga-fashion across one shoulder, the Roman figure strode away from the others.

"Who is that?" I asked. "That is Girish Chandra Ghosh, poet, dramatist, disciple of Sri Ramakrishna. I brought you to this part of the grounds to show him to you, but you have picked him out yourself. Shall I introduce you?" asked my guide, an American doctor.

"I would prefer not to meet him in this noisy place. Can you not take me to see him someday at his own house?" For I knew that my escort was *persona grata* there.

"Perhaps it can be arranged. You are quite right; this is no time or place for any real talk."

The tall figure was lost in the press, but there remained an impression of a physique and dignity seldom seen in India, and of a face Roman rather than Hindu, with keen grey eyes, iron-grey hair, and extraordinarily large ears. I knew nothing about him at this time except that he was called "the Bengali Shakespeare," and that he was a bhakta (mystic) devoted to his Master and his memory.

A few weeks later I was taken to see this Indian poet in his own setting. Girish had consented to receive me, and through the northern quarter of crowded Calcutta bazars we turned from a narrow lane into a short blind alley. At the end of it there faced us a typical native house of the better sort. Beside the entrance was a stone seat, and the house had an upper floor with a row of long iron-barred, open windows. In this upper room several men were seated on the floor about Girish, who always occupied a position at one end, facing the long windows that looked down into the little alley a few feet below. He must have seen us coming and wished to do us a courtesy, for when we entered the courtyard, crossed it, and were ascending a little stone stair in the wall to the roof (whence that upper room was reached), Girish stood before us, descending and saluting us in the beautiful Hindu way, with folded hands. It is the attitude familiar to us in the saints who stand beside Madonna and Child in the old masters. In India it is the usual greeting. With most persons it may have degenerated into a mere salute but the meaning of this gesture is really a sanctification, for the word that accompanies it, or is understood by the action, means, "I worship the Divine in thee." Is there any more beautiful greeting imaginable? I returned G.C.'s greeting, and realized that it is rare in the East for a host and an old man to rise to receive a woman. We followed him up the stone stair and across the roof that gave a glimpse of fading pink on sky and river and palm trees to the north.

The upper room we entered was long and narrow, with windows on both its sides, looking into the courtyard of the house, and on to the little alley that led to the entrance of the house. At one end a door led to the roof we had traversed, another at the opposite end led to an inner chamber — G.C.'s bedroom. The floor of the larger room was covered with a drugget, and bolsters were strewn about for guests to lean against. Bookcases lined the walls. At G.C.'s elbow was a pile of magazines and papers. Near him stood a medicine chest and some small brass bowls containing spices which were handed round among the visitors at intervals. A native punkah [fan] of matting hung across the ceiling, and a boy sat on the balcony overlooking the courtyard of the house, working the cord it swung by. There is something infinitely soothing and hypnotic in that slow, monotonous creaking. No electric fan can compare with it for soporific influence.

We found several Bengali gentlemen already with G.C. to whom my presence was something of a shock and embarrassment. I had just enough knowledge of oriental etiquette to leave shoes at the door, and had sufficiently acquired the habit of sitting cross-legged and to let myself down more or less gracefully into that attitude. I had a sense of feeling at home with Girish at once. His smile was very winning, his English perfect, his voice capable of conveying many shades of feeling. It is twenty years and more since I last saw him, but the personality is sharp and clear to me as when I saw him often, reclining at one end of this upper room. Strength, physical, mental, and spiritual, was the keynote of the impression he made. The term "mild Hindu" did not in the least apply to him, for it conveys the effeminacy characteristic of most Hindu men. Yet Girish never used his powers destructively. Sentimentality, patriotic or artistic, held no appeal for him. No fool or knave could stand unrecognized in his presence. I never heard any political or disloyal talk there.

In this house G.C. lived with an older widowed sister and his son. His wife and daughter had passed away some years before. Girish had been more or less wild in his youth. His saintliness, which was of the robust order, dated only from the time he came in contact with Sri Ramakrishna and the latter's death. I met Girish at a moment when I was greatly disillusioned and needed to meet just such a soul to save me from turning my back on much that appealed to me in India, but was so obscured by surface rubbish.

India has many saints, *soi-disant* [so-called], but it has few *men*. And here was a man of whom in his closing years I could feel the manliness and strength, the sweetness and tolerance and devotion of spirit. If you heard rumours of a wild youth, it was merely, as you looked at the fine old Roman face, to think how handsome he must have been. What a magnificent lover he must have been — fierce, delicate, poetic, tenderly masterful, as a woman would have the man of her choice; taking her and her love as his birthright; assertive, not deliberate, yet humble by the strength of his love; aggressive in affection yet not in ownership! My respect went out to this old man who had had something to renounce, whose very strength sent him first to the devil and then, with equal impetus, to God. My reverence went out to him at once, as to the saint I had been looking for in a land of saints. There is so much mawkish sweetness among religious devotees in India. All mystics stand in danger of sentimentality. But here was one who had genius and fire, who was not half dead nor atrophied, one who had renounced the world, the flesh, and the devil, knowing their charm, and yet lived actively and beneficently in the midst of life; who used his genius for his time and his people, yet knew that fame is a bubble and laid his work at the feet of his God. A saint, this, who meditated and had realized God — yet had time and compassion enough to help the small troubles of his world, who went to Calcutta slums with righteous indignation and medicines, who scolded and annihilated evil, but loved the sinner and gave spiritual, mental, and physical comfort in a brotherly way. A saint, this, with a love of God that does not crowd out God's children; his heart set on God, yet his brain, its servant, inspired to write great dramas and poems.

At the end of each day Girish gave free access to friends who cared to talk with him, and firmly he guided the conversation to only such topics as were worthwhile. He was to me a living exponent of that saying of the mediaeval mystic, Meister Eckhart, that "what a man takes in by contemplation, he must give out in love." He was that rare "mystic who can be practical." Those who sought him regarded him as a master of mysticism before they thought of him as a master of rhetoric, yet they came to him, also, for advice in matters frankly worldly. He led that busy life which can always find leisure.

I spent many hours in that room at sunset. He made me always welcome literally and metaphysically. I sat at his feet and came to regard him with the affection of a daughter. It is difficult to recall all the details of that first meeting, for the privilege became a habit, but never a commonplace. Girish had his moods, like all sensitive souls. Sometimes gay and playful, you might also find him silent, grave, almost tragically serious, full of the sense of "Maya" — the impermanence of what seems so real. That first time I was at his house he was at his best. I could forget myself even with a number of *babus* furtively watching me. I saw only G.C. as he liked to be called because Vivekananda had so dubbed him. The others, beside Girish, were merely furniture till I could individualize them, and see how they venerated and tried to serve him.

Girish never quenched frankness or spontaneity. This was a great boon to me at the time, for I was leading a life of tremendous isolation and self-repression. To go to him was freedom to be myself, say what I thought, without fear of criticism. I never felt I had better not express a thought or question. He dealt patiently and sympathetically with stupid questions, repressed and depressing moods, understanding and respecting the problem he knew I had to meet.

But G.C. could be angry. He did not suffer fools gladly. I have seen him berate a friend or a servant with flashing eye. I rejoiced in this positiveness, this definite expression. He could sympathize and tolerate, but not weakly compromise. He said his say — then at once restored that person to his favour. And that has always seemed to me the only anger that is ethical. State the grievance, hit from the shoulder if you must — then leave the other to deal with it as he will, but reinstate him at once. If he sulks, that is not your affair. You are as much his friend as before, and you are ready to be treated by the same heroic method of swift, honouring plain speech and expect the same rapid closing and forgetting of the incident.

A thing that struck me was an action that I afterwards found to be a habit with G.C. As the short twilight deepened into the blue tropical night a servant came to light a hanging lamp. No matter if he was talking at the moment, Girish would stop, raise folded hands to his forehead in a gesture of worship, and murmur a salutation to Ramakrishna. It was the same if a bell were rung somewhere. I came to know that he set himself the time of candle-light and the sound of a bell as sentinels for a momentary remembrance of God. Perhaps this was not original, but he was the only Hindu in whom I ever observed it. It greatly impressed me as a simple and genuine application of the teaching of his Master that "worship is constant remembrance." And did not Christian Brother Lawrence teach the same?

I once complained to Girish that his friends, if I asked them a question about Hindu customs, mythology, or literature, always murmured the replies with heads bent down into their clothing without looking at me. "I find it impossible," I told him, "to carry on a conversation that way, yet I feel they know so much about things I want to learn here. Why are they so awkward about it?"

Girish laughed heartily. He had never been out of India, yet he seemed Western in his understanding of my objection to this foolish embarrassment and self-consciousness, so noticeable, then, when Hindu men met Western women in India.

"Yes, it is absurd, Little Sister! But they are shy and not used to ladies who talk with men freely and at ease. And this is their idea of respect. You startle them by being interested in the things we talk about here: religion, philosophy, metaphysics. You must remember that a Hindu must not look in the face of any woman but his mother, wife, sister, or daughter. It would be considered rude for him to do so."

"With us," I replied, "it is considered rude and shifty *not* to look at the person you are speaking to, and we are taught to answer clearly. *You don't act so!*"

The old man smiled. "Shall I tell you how to put them at their ease with you? In India, if you can *establish* a relationship, it is accepted. Why don't you tell them you are their sister?"

So at the next visit to Girish I addressed the five or six men present. I told them I had come a long way to see India, to learn all I could, that I wished they would help me by talking to me freely, as do men and women in the West, and that I hoped they would henceforth regard me as their sister, since our dear Girish himself so honoured me. There was an immediate transformation. Faces came out of chadars and I saw their chins for the first time. After this, on arrival and departure, I even got smiles and little acts of courtesy especially from G.C.'s secretary and a Hindu doctor who frequented the house much and was greatly devoted to Girish. The talk was now not only between Girish and them, or between Girish and myself; it became general and gradually they addressed me. The first time this happened, Girish gave me a delighted wink and chuckled. And once he told me that if I was learning anything from his friends, they also were certainly learning something through me of Western men and women. And the reader must remember that I write of the India of a quarter of a century ago. Yet how slowly do things of custom change in the immemorial East!

Reverence for others was one of G.C.'s characteristics. I never saw him permit anyone to touch his feet, a salute common in India towards a spiritual giant. I recall how greatly his proud humility struck me, when, in his presence, I saw a very much lesser man complacently accept such homage from a member of G.C.'s group of companions, and this reverence for others showed itself in his courtesy and patience towards the most insignificant individual present. Often a messenger would come to him for medicine (he was something of a homeopathic doctor) for some poor sufferer in the bazar. Then he would drop his brilliant talk, ignore his admiring circle, turn to his medicine chest, and inquire about symptoms. Sometimes he would leave us and go to satisfy himself about the case, or send a reassuring message with the medicine. His diploma as a physician was his faith in regarding himself as merely an instrument in the hands of his Master for the relief of suffering. I have seen him take a medicine in his folded hands and offer it in worship and supplication for blessing before giving it to the sick one. And the faith of the patient in Girish was equally great. So he often made good cures.

For financial, mental, and domestic distress his sympathy was ever ready also.

His views as a Vedantist empowered him to ignore caste rules. At one time he was ill with asthma and acute indigestion, and became interested in my ideas on diet. I doubted if he would eat of anything not prepared by brahmin hands, but I prepared and took him some simple dishes, and to my delight he ate them and with relish. But it was because he had accepted me. Anyone who sought Truth was his brother or sister, and therefore no *Mlechchha* (foreigner). How great in Girish this un-Hindu sense of brotherhood was can only be estimated by those who know from experience that the most broad-minded and Veda-quoting Hindu will keep up fences and reserves of caste between himself and a *Mlechchha*, even if that foreigner should dress, think, eat, and live according to orthodox Hindu custom.

Once G.C. came and ate a European lunch with me in my rooms at a Calcutta boarding-house. How it must have shocked his orthodox friends! I can see him now, as he appeared that day on my veranda, in a long white *dhoti*, a clean white linen coat, a silk chadar, and a cane. A tall old man, spare but powerful of frame, he held himself with almost military bearing and a great easy dignity. At first he had some difficulty with the fork, but my Mohammedan "boy" stood behind his chair and whispered opportune directions in Bengali, and I am sure that had I had the bad manners to smile Girish would have entered into my amusement about his awkwardness at a memsahib's table. To that little visit I owe an excellent little snapshot of him.

A sense of humour was his; keen, delicate wit, and repartee. It was a delight to hear him tell a story. It brought out his dramatic instinct and his beautiful English. For he told me many legends and often illustrated some point in our conversation with a mythological tale. He was a born actor.

Of his own inner life and mystical experiences, Girish could seldom be brought to speak. Much is conveyed in the beautiful metaphor in which he once replied to an inquiry as to his realization of God in meditation. "For three days I saw all this" (with a comprehensive sweep of his arm) "as the dress of the Mother." Most of Ramakrishna's disciples had learned from him to speak of God in His aspect of Mother as well as Father. And the universe, to G.C., had become the mere Maya-garment expressing and yet hiding the immanence of God. Returning one day from Belur Math, the monastery up the Ganges founded by Vivekananda, and leaving the boat at Annapurna Ghat, I ascended the steps to the streets of Baghbazar and met Girish on his way home from the riverside. After some talk he went to his house in the company of a mutual friend who afterwards told me that on his short walk Girish stopped with folded hands at every wayside shrine — and there are many such in these busy native quarters. "I dare not omit it," he had said, in explanation of the delay, and in him this was no slavery to custom but the mystic's desire to think of God at every opportunity. He felt the privilege of worship must not be denied to the soul so easily distracted by the kaleidoscopic external life. His spiritual make-up seemed to me a happy combination (and one of which India has crying need) of the bhakti and karma paths — the mystic and the practical path of service. Of merely psychic matters, which he considered hindrances to, rather than indications of, spirituality, I never heard him speak.

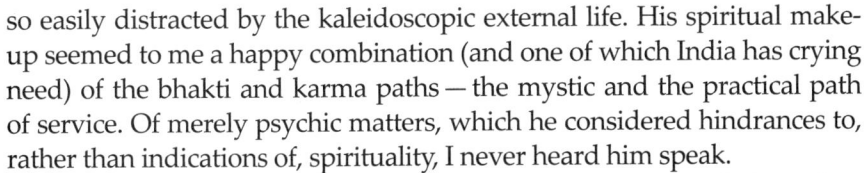

On my return to the West the letters from Girish were a help and an inspiration. As they became rarer, I jotted down notes to help me preserve my memories of him and our talks. Just before these notes were brought up to the date of my leaving India came the news of his death. Afterwards they sent me an unfinished letter found in his rooms. The Hindu friend of G.C.'s circle, who found it and often helped the secretary, wrote to me as follows:

> Through his last illness the great soul, so far as I could glean, had only one theme — to meet the Beloved in His indwelling and everlasting glory, free from all relativity. His ideal being to have no desire of his own, giving himself up entirely to the will of God, he justified himself in having even this wish, by his impatience to realize Him apart from all form. His last audible words were these: 'Now that you have come, dispel all my illusions and let me go! Let me go!' For the period that I had the privilege to sit at his feet, I cannot but feel eternally grateful. I feel how great would have been my ignorance without his enlightening and loving gifts from day to day. How now to fill the blank? I could sit beside him and keep silence and listen for a hundred lifetimes, and not think it enough! How then am I to be resigned after this brief span of his helpful companionship? Is it not worse than the loss of many fortunes? But the comparison is stupid. A legacy is a spoilt piece of paper when the fortune is lost, but the legacy which Girish Babu has left on the pages of our minds will not fail to bring a harvest year after year. He has his well-earned rest. Of that abode we know little, but we do know that we are no less dear to him there than we were here.
>
> I enclose a letter he started to you. I hoped he might finish it by dictating to me, but he grew too weak.

Any personal elements in this article have only been included as tribute to a great soul. I can present G.C. only in relation to myself, so hope to be forgiven frequent references to the writer. One who has travelled far is often questioned as to what was found most impressive. What most impressed me in India was Girish Chandra Ghosh, the biggest soul I have met. It was he who taught me and helped me to *realize* that what happens to us matters little, but that our *attitude* towards what happens to us is of immense importance.[16]

Reminiscences of Girish Chandra Ghosh
Kumudbandhu Sen* (1879–1962)

The "Convention of Religions of India" was held on 9, 10, and 11 April 1909 at Town Hall in Calcutta. Sarada Charan Mitra, a judge of the Calcutta High Court, was the president of the convention. He requested Girish Chandra Ghosh and Sisir Kumar Ghosh to write on "The Vaishnava Religion," and both agreed. On 6 April 1909, at the suggestion of Sarada, I went to Girish with a request for him to compose a song of harmony for the convention. In the morning when I went to his house, he was not there. I was told that he had gone for a walk on the bank of the Ganges. I went there and found him near the Baghbazar ghat. I noticed him pacing, absorbed in deep thought. After saluting him, I stood facing him. Seeing me, he asked: "Hello, why are you here?"

I replied: "Our 'Convention of Religions of India' will be held on the 9th, and it is our desire that you compose a song about harmony."

Girish: "Who will sing it?"

I: "Pulin Bihari Mitra."

Pulin was a member of the Vivekananda Society and a great devotee of Sri Ramakrishna. His voice was sweet and melodious. He was then a famous singer of Bengal and some of his songs had been recorded by the Gramophone Company.

Girish: "Look, I cannot promise anything. If the Master wishes, it will be done."

I: "I don't want to hear your excuses. You will have to compose a song."

Girish (*smiling*): "If I had that power, you would not have to insist. I could compose that song right now. You know, I cannot do anything by my own wish. If it is the Master's wish then it will be done. Since it is the wish of you all, the wish-fulfilling Master may fulfill it."

I took leave of Girish and went directly to Sarada and informed him of everything. He said: "I have special regard for Girish's words. His inside and outside are the same."

I: "Do you know Girish well?"

Sarada: "Of course, I do. His younger brother, Atul, was my classmate. Since my student days I have respected Girish as my elder brother. I visited him many times and listened to his stories. His life has been completely changed by the grace of Sri Ramakrishna."

Sarada continued: "I saw Sri Ramakrishna. He was a wonderful man! Seeing his eyes, one could feel they were beaming with intelligence. His

---

*A disciple of Swami Brahmananda and a scholar. He was closely connected with the disciples and devotees of Ramakrishna.

form was such that once one saw it, one could not forget it. In this present age, Ramakrishna is a great spiritual giant."

In the evening I was working on the convention at Sarada's house. Suddenly Girish called from outside: "Where is Kumud? Where is Kumud?" I was surprised to see him. He then handed over a piece of paper and said, "Here is your song." Sarada received him cordially and requested him to sit in his parlour. Girish sat down and then said to Sarada: "Kumud requested me to compose a song for the convention. I know he is busy so I have come myself to give it to him." Sarada said: "We are sorry to give you trouble, but I am fortunate to see you." After visiting a few minutes, Girish left.

I then read that song* to Sarada who praised it immensely. He said: "This song expresses the aim of our convention nicely. Girish's songs are unique. They are full of our national ideas and their rhymes are beautiful and sweet."

After the convention Dr. Kanjilal and I went to visit Girish. Girish said: "I heard that the convention was a grand success. I couldn't believe that it would take such a great shape. You see, the heart-strings of India are attuned to religion, and when one strikes there it reverberates everywhere. All Indians — Hindus, Muslims, and Christians — feel an electric current in their veins in the name of religion. They know that religion is their own soul."[17]

Sunday, 18 April 1909: I was busy with the aftermath of the religious convention so I could not visit Girish for a few days. I went to see him today at 4:00 p.m. Some familiar and unfamiliar visitors were in his parlour. Seeing me, Girish said: "I am glad to see you. Everyone was praising your reading of the article. And see, you were reluctant to read it."

I: "It would have been better if Amar [Amarendra Nath Datta, a famous actor] had read it."

Girish: "No, it would not. You see, each one has expertise in one's own area. A person may be a good actor, but that does not mean he can be a good reader or a reciter, especially this kind of article."

I: "I had no objection to reading your article. But Dr. Kanjilal said that

---

*The ocean, mountains, planets, and light may be with form or formless,
They appear equally in the heart of a contemplative one as God.
Ignorance and ego limit God with a name and a place,
And create hatred, division, sophistry, and confusion.
Where peace dwells, wrangling comes to create delusion,
But seeing the loving form of a sadhu, people float in the ocean of love.
Where holy people meet, there heaven dawns.
Let this religious conference remove all hatred and quarrels of humanity.

I would have to rehearse before you prior to reading it aloud, to which I objected."

Girish: "You didn't need to have a rehearsal. I just wanted to see whether you had any difficulty reading the handwriting. When you read a couple of lines, I realized that you would not have to read anymore and I asked you to go."

A gentleman (*to Girish*): "What article are you talking about?"

Girish: "At the request of Sarada Mitra I wrote a paper on the *Gauriya Vaishnava Religion*, which was read during the Convention of Religions at the Town Hall. Kumud read it on my behalf and people appreciated his reading."

In the meantime Atul, Girish's brother, entered the room. He had attended the convention. He remarked, "That paper was excellent."

Girish: "Have you heard any other comments? What did Sarada say?"

I: "I did not hear anything from Sarada, but others remarked that your article was devoid of philosophical discussion, reasoning, or argument. It was emotionally stirring."

Girish: "That is correct. There is no place for philosophical discussion, reasoning, or argument in the Gauriya Vaishnava religion. This Vaishnava religion is the religion of love. Love is the gem of sadhana and an object of devotional mood or emotion. The goal of this religion is to taste the bliss of love."[18]

*   *   *

I: "Some people say that the theatre is a sinful place because of its association with courtesan actresses. If young men go to the theatre, their moral character will go down, and they will be perverted and degenerated."

Girish: "Look, I want to say something to those who think we are injecting sin into society by allowing courtesans and illiterate bohemians to act in the theatre. Courtesans and illiterate bohemians exist in every society. Is it an effective means of social reform to drive them away from society or to hate them? Jesus, Buddha, Chaitanya, and other great prophets did not teach people to abandon or hate them. Rather, they uplifted the lives of those fallen people of society.

"I don't boast that I imitated those great teachers of the world, but I am guiding those courtesans on to a new path. Treading this path of acting, they will be able to lead, if they wish, a pure life. They will get a chance to think higher thoughts; and they will desist from alluring men who go to the red-light district. Those whom people hate as bohemians or villains also belong to our society. They are our own countrymen. Yet people want to reform them through hatred! I just opened an easy path for them to earn money. When they act, they think high ideas, repeat inspiring dialogue, and express wonderful moods. Can you tell me what these puritan social reformers have done to change their lives?

"It is true that association with those courtesan actresses is risky and dangerous, because they are reflectors of lust. But if their numbers increase every year, then what is the remedy? From a personal standpoint one should always shun evil company, but from a social standpoint one should not abandon or hate them. Theatre is an important element of national life. It is the main institution for spreading any kind of idea.

"Look, when I got shelter at the feet of the Master, I quite often felt an urge to give up the theatre. But the Master forbade me, saying: 'No, no, don't give it up. Let things go on as usual. This theatre is giving a great service to society.' I couldn't understand the purport of his words at that time. Now I think that I am not doing anything for myself; I am doing the Master's work. My plays are spreading his ideas, and the theatre is the refuge of fallen men and women. They live in a deceitful world, no doubt, but when they come to the theatre to act, they get a taste of a different world. This is a great gain. Some actresses bow down to the picture of Ramakrishna in the greenroom of the theatre and humbly pray to him to remove the pain of their penitent hearts."

* * *

I: "I think if you would have visited the West, you could have made a lot of improvement to the theatre."

Girish (*with a smile*): "My goodness! I don't need to go to the West. Even that which I have in my brain I cannot give to our people because of their apathy, and now who will accept Western ideas? Look, this is my conviction: As fruits and flowers grow from each country's soil, seed, water, and air, so language and art manifest according to the idea and sadhana of each race. Although Shakespeare is my role model, I have my own original and distinct ideas. In my plays there are impressions of our country's traditions, our upbringing and environment, our manner of thinking and learning, our ideals and spirit, which are fused with our flesh and bone. I met Sri Ramakrishna and Swami Vivekananda and came in close contact with them. As a result, their influences are reflected in some of my plays also."

I: "Sir, some say that some of the characters in your plays are overdrawn."

Girish: "Those who say that have not thoroughly studied human character. I never wrote anything that I have not witnessed myself. As a writer, I have never cheated people. I have tried to promulgate whatever I have felt deeply, realized in practical life, and known as supreme truth in my life. I have never taken any credit for this. The Master told me that these plays would benefit many people, and I believe that wholeheartedly. I trust the Master's words. So I know that whatever I do is his work. If it is the Master's work, it will definitely benefit human beings. This is my faith — this is my conviction. I don't do anything by my own power. Do you understand?"

I: "Do you feel inspiration when you write a play?"

Girish: "What do you mean by feeling? I have seen that someone writes holding my hand."

Girish went into his own room and came back after a couple of minutes. He said: "Look, whatever I have depicted in *Shankaracharya* is just right. I wrote it out of inspiration. The Master said, 'All jackals howl alike.' All great teachers preached the same truth. But seeing Swamiji, I understood Shankara's character.

"While I was in Varanasi I completed *Shankaracharya* and then sent it to Calcutta for rehearsals. There is an old Shankara Monastery in a secluded garden, which was close to my rented house. A beautiful stone image of Shankara is inside that temple. I took the complete manuscript of *Shankaracharya* to that temple, touched Shankara's feet with it, and then sent it to Calcutta. I had a strong belief that this play would be highly appreciated. In this play I exactly depicted Shankara's true life and his mode of preaching Vedanta. I didn't write it; it was written out of inspiration."

Girish said that he used to take all kinds of intoxicating drugs and liquor but now he had completely given up those things.

I: "Don't you feel now and then the desire to have intoxicating drugs and liquor as before?"

Girish: "No, by the grace of the Master I have no more desire to have those things. I have done many wrong things in my life. I have committed all sorts of sins. Now those sinful actions are the objects of my glory. I stood in front of the Master with all my dirty flaws. The Master showed the path to his sinless, virtuous children. By contrast, my life was full of all sinful actions — adultery, deception, drinking, and whatnot. Besmeared with all these blemishes and stains, I boldly stood in front of the Master and said: 'Lord, I have no glory — no pride of my own. But I have this pride and vainglory that there is no sin that I have not committed. Now if you wish, accept me, washing away all the impurities and stains of my character; otherwise there is no hope for me.'

"The Master listened to my prayer. So, out of his unconditional grace, he took my power of attorney. Listening to stories of my past sins many times, he made me understand that those are nothing but child's play and he filled my heart with bliss. Now I see whatever intoxicating things that you may take cannot be compared to even an iota of that divine intoxication, or the intoxication of recollecting the Master. Disregarding this joyful intoxication, people are ruining their lives taking drugs, alcohol, and other rubbish. Let all Indians and the people of the world be intoxicated with this divine bliss and get rid of those worldly intoxicants. As long as people are addicted to the poisonous intoxicants of alcohol, marijuana, hemp, opium, and other drugs, it will be impossible to awaken the national consciousness."[19]

* * *

Girish: "The other day Arabinda Ghosh [a national leader and philosopher] came to see me. I asked him about his ideas on Sri Ramakrishna and Swami Vivekananda."

I: "What did he say?"

Girish: "I found he had faith in Ramakrishna. Then I said to him, 'Don't you think we should follow Ramakrishna's ideal and Swamiji's teachings to uplift and regenerate India?"

I: "What did he answer?"

Girish: "He kept quiet. He just calmly listened to what I said."[20]

* * *

I: "The other day I read an article *Rup O Arup* (Form and Formless) written by Rabindranath Tagore in the *Pravasi* magazine. Without mentioning Ramakrishna's name, he clearly referred to Ramakrishna and attacked his idea [of God with form]."

Girish was surprised and asked, "Why?"

I: "Referring to how human beings are caught and bound by the idea of form, Rabindranath wrote that he had heard a famous worshipper of Shakti express a desire to see a lion in the zoo, because 'the lion is a carrier of the Divine Mother.'* Rabindranath said that there is nothing wrong in imagining the Shakti (Power) as a lion, but the glory of imagination disappears if one sees a lion as Shakti."

Girish: "Well, the Master did not see the lion as Shakti."

I: "Ramakrishna said, 'The lion is the carrier of the Divine Mother.'"

---

*Ramakrishna described his own experience: "I was taken to the Zoological Garden. I went into samadhi at the sight of the lion, for the carrier of the Mother awakened in my mind the consciousness of the Mother Herself. In that state who could see the other animals? I had to return home after seeing only the lion." — *The Gospel of Sri Ramakrishna*, 391

Girish: "Does it mean that the lion is the form of the Divine Mother? You said that Rabindranath had mentioned that 'there is nothing wrong in imagining the Shakti (Power) as a lion, but the glory of imagination disappears if one sees a lion as Shakti.' It seems he could not express it properly. Do the Hindus imagine the lion as the Divine Mother? They don't worship the lion either."

I: "Rabindranath blames image worship* and considers it to be a great obstacle to man's spiritual progress. He does not admit image worship to be an expression of a spiritual mood. He says that the form or creation that manifests *Satyam-Shivam-Sundaram* — the Truth, the Beauty, and the Good is not bound nor is it one. Rather, it is continuously flowing and many. He says that man goes downward when he limits the Truth, the Beauty, and the Good to a particular form or rite within space, time, and circumstances."

Girish: "The Hindus consider the divine image as the eternal form of God because it manifests the Truth, Beauty, and Good. This form is neither bound nor one. It represents infinite forms of the Infinite. The Hindus do not worship this image as a form of matter; they worship the formless One in that form. They imagine a conscious form on the clay, stone, or metallic image. Worship is nothing but imagination, which is dynamic, and its power is manifold. Everyone is aware that God knows the inmost thoughts of all beings. Without love there is no worship. People worship God through love and imagination. It is not a relation between matter and physical eyes. What is mental worship or meditation?

"It is really surprising that a thoughtful poet like Rabindranath did not have any inkling of the Formless in the form and the Unmanifest in the manifest. His attack on the Master's sadhana and experience is meaningless and fanciful imagination. The Master would see that all objects of the world are the manifestation of Brahman. He was immersed in samadhi most of the time. He would feel pain if someone walked over the green grass, and he would immediately merge into the Formless Ocean of Consciousness when he saw any divine form, temple, or special manifestation of Shakti. The Brahmo devotees recognized him as a Shakta, Vaishnava, and Vedantin yogi, so it was improper for Rabindranath to refer to the Master only as a Shakti worshipper.

"Keshab Chandra Sen was a great soul and a follower of the formless God. He even imitated the nonsectarian ideas of the Master and incorporated them in his New Dispensation (Navavidhan Brahmo Samaj). It is an imprudent remark to say that the Master was only a Shakta devotee.

---

*Rabindra Nath Tagore belonged to the Brahmo Samaj, which taught that God is formless but has attributes.

The experience of a poet and the realization of Brahman are not the same thing. Based on his experience, Rabindranath made a comment that is completely wrong. The Master told Shivanath Shastri: 'I have seen the carrier of the Divine Mother. What more is there to see?' Rabindranath understood the Master's words according to his mental makeup. The Master used to see the manifestation of the Cosmic Power in everything in this universe, and he experienced *Sarvam khalu idam Brahma* — everything is verily Brahman. Now Rabindranath has pointed out a defect in this experience of the Master! He may be a great poet, but this is nothing but his meddling."

I: "But there is nothing wrong in discussing it."

Girish: "If you want to discuss a particular event pertaining to the Master, you must first study his whole life. Without knowing anything about him, you have taken a sentence out of context and given a distorted interpretation. That is not considered to be a search for truth. As Rabindranath is a poet, he worships every day the forms found in nature. A poet composes poems about the Infinite Lord imagining forms of nature: Is this not a worship of the form? According to one's capacity, some are absorbed in contemplating small forms and some the Cosmic form. If one wants to reach the Formless Ocean of Consciousness, one will have to go through the form and worship the form. The form manifests in every sound and rhythm. Then it becomes boundless and vast, and finally merges into the Formless.

"Some people talk about knowledge. One day I got a glimpse of that knowledge from the lips of the Master. He said: 'The knowledge of Brahman is the infinite Ocean of bliss and consciousness. Listening to the sound of that Ocean's waves, Narada was overwhelmed; Shuka stood near the shore and became stupefied; and the great god Shiva drank only three handfuls of Its water and lost consciousness.' When the Master said this, I started to have an idea of the Infinite and my head began to reel. Even my worst enemy will not doubt my intellectual power, but I could not conceive the idea of that unbounded, infinite, cosmic Brahman. When I was about to express to the Master my inability to think further, I saw him standing before me in samadhi. Who has known him? Who can understand him? It is true realization and not artificial intellectual jugglery." Saying so, Girish's face turned red.

Girish continued: "Look at this cosmic universe: when we look at the vast, unbounded space, we feel ourselves smaller than little ants. And we try to ascertain whether there is any Creator of this universe! We dare to measure the power of the all-powerful! We try to make people understand the One who is smaller than the smallest and greater than the greatest, who is omnipotent, omniscient, and omnipresent, and who is the substratum of all ideas and forms! Who can measure that infinite One? Ramprasad sang:

> How are you trying, O my mind, to know the nature of God?
> You are groping like a madman locked in a dark room.
> He is grasped through ecstatic love: how can you fathom Him without it?

"Who can make Him understand and who can understand Him? Reclining on an easy chair, one cannot understand Sri Ramakrishna. He was the embodiment of spirituality. If one is not attuned to ecstatic love, one cannot grasp the Master's spiritual mood."

I: "Ramanuja, Chaitanya, Madhavendra Puri, Rupa, Sanatan, Ramprasad, and other great teachers of India acknowledged God with form. And some served and worshipped divine images. Rabindranath wants to say that those saints were stuck with the form and could not grasp the Truth, the Beauty, and the Good. From this standpoint he made that criticism of the Master's spiritual mood."

Girish: "The Master was the embodiment of all spiritual moods and he practised all kinds of sadhana. Hindus, Muslims, Christians, Shaktas, Vaishnavas, and followers of God with form and without form — all were overwhelmed observing his wonderful moods. The great teachings of the Master in this age are: The harmony of religions; all religions are worshipping the same God; all religions are true; God can be attained through all religions. Love and peace are India's message to the world. The future civilization of the world will be based on this message. Revolt, disrespect, and hatred towards another's religion will not succeed in this age. Whether a man is a Hindu, Brahmo, Christian, or Muslim, he will have to transcend the boundary of narrowness and embrace everyone with love. A person may be a monk, a poet, a philosopher, or a politician, but if he cannot recognize this living form of supreme love, he will not be able to give the true message for this age or to contribute anything permanent to the world's civilization."

Girish then became silent and sat there motionless. We also sat there quietly for a while and then left for home.[21]

* * *

Girish once told me: "When I went to the Master I was proud that there was no sin in the world I had not committed. The other disciples of the Master were pure, sincere, and innocent. They were great receptacles of spirituality. Yet the Master still gave a horrible sinner like me shelter at his holy feet."

There are many stories about Girish that I heard from him and that are not yet published in any book. He first saw the Master at Dina Basu's house but was not at all impressed. But gradually the Master attracted him. I heard from Girish that his real transformation occurred after the following incident:

One night Girish was drinking with a friend and some prostitutes in a brothel in Calcutta when suddenly, on a whim, they decided to go to a garden house for some fun. A carriage was hired. When the driver asked, "Where will you go?" Girish replied, "Rani Rasmani's garden at Dakshineswar." It was then midnight.

At 2:00 a.m., they arrived at the gate of the Dakshineswar Kali temple. As the gate was locked, they began pushing at it and shouting. Sri Ramakrishna himself then came and opened the gate for them. He was naked like a child and was holding his cloth under his arm. Seeing Girish, the Master said: "My son, you are in a joyful mood! I see that you are in a very happy mood!" Then the Master began to dance, singing: "Haribol! Haribol! Haribol!" [Repeat the name of the Lord.] Girish and his friends were so drunk that they were hardly conscious of anything. At dawn, when Girish became somewhat sober, he found that he and his friends were dancing while holding on to the Master. Sri Ramakrishna was also dancing in a god-intoxicated state, and they were all chanting, "Haribol! Haribol!" and weeping profusely. Coming to his senses, Girish thought: "The Master is truly the saviour of the fallen. All of us — drunkards, debauchees, and prostitutes — have come here, and this god-intoxicated man has danced with us. It is amazing!"

There was no motive behind the Master's behaviour. Out of sheer joy this great soul made these drunkards and prostitutes god-intoxicated by chanting the name of God. Girish looked around and found that some of the local villagers and temple employees were also there chanting and dancing and clapping their hands. Then Girish saw that the Master was silent and not moving. He was in samadhi. Some people carried him to his room.

Girish told me that he feared people would recognize him, so he and his companions hurriedly left the place.

This incident convinced Girish that God truly exists. What else could explain the power behind this great soul's love that made him spend the night with these fallen people, chanting the name of God? Is it ever possible, he thought, for one to acquire such love without realizing God? If the Master did not have divine power he could never have remained unperturbed in the presence of the prostitutes. While Girish was pondering these things, he became terrified thinking of his past sins.

Girish said to me: "I then wondered: 'What is my way out now? I have committed all kinds of sins in this world. If God exists, then I have no place even in hell, because even in that place there is no sinner like me. The Master is proof that God truly exists. It is because God exists that such a great soul can be overwhelmed with divine love.' Then I felt a pain that was like the stings of thousands of scorpions on my body. This is absolutely true. These are not mere words. Unable to bear that pain, I rushed to the Master at Dakshineswar. Reaching there, I found the Master seated in the Panchavati. Tears were pouring from his eyes like water pouring out of a syringe. Water was running from his nose also. His tears had made the ground wet, and he was smearing the mud on his body.

"Seeing this amazing sight I was overwhelmed. I slowly approached him and asked, 'Sir, what are you doing?' Looking at me he replied: 'You see, the devotees come here, so I am rubbing the dust of their feet on my body. I am devoid of devotion. Perhaps by getting the dust of the devotees' feet I may acquire some devotion.' Stunned, I thought, 'If this is how one acquires devotion, then I shall not be able to make it in millions of births.' Then the pain I had been feeling increased a hundredfold.

"I then asked, 'Sir, who are you?' He replied: 'Some call me Ramakrishna and others, the young priest. Whatever people call me, I am that.' After saying this, the Master begged for my pain and suffering. I told him: 'Sir, do you know who I am? I have committed all kinds of sins in this world.' But the Master again begged me for my pain and suffering, and then he touched my heart with his palm. Immediately my whole body cooled down and all my pain and suffering disappeared."

Sometimes Girish would talk to us about the Master till midnight. He would become so excited then that he would shout: "Ramakrishna! Ramakrishna! O my mind, chant Ramakrishna's name." The whole room would reverberate with those words. Again, sometimes he would say: "The hearts of human beings are hard! They do not melt. God's name does not melt a human heart, but it melts even stone and iron. Look, I received His love, but still my heart has not melted." Saying this, he would slap his chest.

While writing *Chaitanya Lila*, Girish read that when Chaitanya cried for God, tears flowed from his eyes like water from a syringe. Girish considered this to be mere poetic fancy. But when he saw the Master crying that day, he no longer doubted it.[22]

Memoirs of Girish Chandra Ghosh
Dilip Kumar Roy (1897–1980)

In his famous book Smriticharan, *Dilip Kumar Roy wrote about Girish, M., and other disciples of Ramakrishna. Dilip's father, Dwijendralal Roy, was a famous Bengali poet and playwright. Dilip's cousin Nirmalendu Lahiri was a celebrated actor and associated closely with Girish and M. He became a sincere devotee of Ramakrishna. Dilip had the great fortune to meet Girish and M. and also many savants of Bengal when he was in his teens. He later became a great musician, poet, writer, artist, and mystic. The following are some reminiscences summarized and translated from Dilip's writings.*

Brother Nirmal lived with our family and was a staunch devotee and follower of Girish Babu. But some of my father's friends spoke ill of Girish Babu's character, and this made Brother Nirmal upset. He left our home after writing this note to my father: "I love Girish Babu. I adore Girish Babu. But I am sorry I can't say the same about your flawless friends who run him down — who are not fit to lace his shoes."

Debkumar Roy Chaudhury, the biographer of Dwijendralal Roy, left the following account:

> Girish Babu came to attend a meeting. Dwijendralal received him cordially and said, "It is our great fortune that you have come despite your ill health."
>
> Girish Babu (*humbly with a smile*): "No, no, you do not have to say that. I have come today not only to honour your invitation, but also to tell you something personally. Let me tell you frankly: Some people are trying to create a misunderstanding and strained relationship between us. I know well that whatever they say to me about you is not true, and I also believe that you disregard what slander they say to you about me. Of course, I wrote many dramas and only a madman would say that every one of them was successful. But will you not admit that a few turned out all right?"
>
> Dwijendralal: "My goodness! Such a statement does not suit you. In this respect [writing a play] you are my guru. In fact, I learned to write a few plays by imitating you."
>
> Girish Babu: "What do you say, sir? You are being humble. I have great expectations for you. In the future you will be the greatest playwright in Bengal, and I have no doubt about it."
>
> Dwijendralal changed the subject, and said: "Is it possible that I shall believe any gossip against you? I know the intention of those who come to tell me that kind of hearsay — at least I have that much intelligence."

Girish Babu (*joyfully*): "Wonderful! This is what I wanted to hear from you. Look, we cannot disregard or undermine each other. Let our good relationship remain forever. Let people say what they want to say; we should not pay any attention to it."

I was playing tennis when Girish Babu was talking with my father. When I entered our parlour after the game, however, Girish Babu was about to leave. I bowed down to him.

Girish Babu: "Are you not Mantu [Dilip's nickname]?"

I (*humbly*): "Yes, sir."

Girish Babu (*affectionately*): "I am extremely pleased to hear from Nirmal about your faith and devotion. You are fortunate that you have received his [Ramakrishna's] grace at such a young age."

Father (*startled*): "Grace! Whose grace?"

Girish Babu (*saluting with folded hands*): "Whose grace? He who came in this age as a God of love to deliver us. Dwiju Babu, what shall I say to you about him — he was not a man."

Saying so, Girish's eyes became moist. My father was also moved and he bowed his head out of respect.

When Girish Babu left, my father asked: "What did Nirmal say about you to Girish Babu?"

I (*hesitantly*): "I really don't know. Perhaps it was because I visited Dakshineswar and Belur Math with him."[23]

* * *

At first Girish Babu came into my life as a playwright, but Brother Nirmal taught me to see him from a new angle — as a devout knower of Truth. After reading *The Gospel of Sri Ramakrishna*, I became curious to know more about Girish Babu, but I learned to love him under Brother Nirmal's instruction. With overflowing love and respect he used to tell me many incidents about Girish Babu.

Brother Nirmal: "You see, the Master did not give any advice to Girish Babu. He said that Girish would overcome his own shortcomings. The Master took full responsibility for Girish Babu and accepted his power of attorney."

I: "What is 'power of attorney'?"

Brother Nirmal: "It is some sort of letter of legal authority. Through it one surrenders responsibility for managing one's own affairs. When a person transfers to another the power or right to manage his worldly affairs, the latter does all business transactions, gives receipts, writes letters, and signs all documents on that person's behalf."

I (*surprised*): "What do you say, Brother? Girish Babu gave Sri Ramakrishna the responsibility for taking care of his next life!"

Brother Nirmal: "Sri Ramakrishna was Girish Babu's guru, so he took responsibility for his disciple. Do you know what Girish Babu said to me this morning?"

I: "Please tell me."

Brother Nirmal: "You can't keep anything secret. Promise that you will not divulge these secrets."

I: "Please trust me."

Brother Nirmal: "All right, listen: Girish Babu told me that he saw Mother Kali in Sri Ramakrishna. I swear this is true. He further said today: 'Nirmal, what more shall I say about the compassion of the Master? People often say that the Master produced Vivekananda. Is that not his wonderful glory? But, my child, let me tell you that the greatest proof of the Master's glory is not Vivekananda — it is I — because Vivekananda was a great receptacle. It may be difficult to make a big fire from a small spark by fanning it, but it is possible. Whereas, my child, only a philosopher's stone can transform an iron rod into gold. Likewise the Master transformed me into a beautiful divine image from a lump of clay. You see, from his childhood the Master was a natural artist, and later he became the saviour of the lowly and deliverer of sinners.'

"Mantu, believe me, I am telling you the truth. While saying those words, tears began to trickle from Girish Babu's eyes. It happened this morning."

I had so many discussions with Brother Nirmal about Girish Babu and I regret that I did not record them in my diary. If I had recorded the stories about Girish Babu's great, catholic, and pure character, I could tell his ungrateful countrymen about his faith, devotion, and genius, which they have almost forgotten.

I realized the greatness of Girish Babu through Brother Nirmal, and my father was also influenced to some extent. He highly praised Girish Babu's genius as a playwright and actor, but did not care much about his devotion, faith, and love for his guru. When Brother Nirmal left our home, my father began to read *The Gospel of Sri Ramakrishna* and he would sometimes talk to me about Girish's devotion for Sri Ramakrishna. Up to this point he had respected Girish Babu as a dramatist and actor, but gradually he discovered Girish Babu as a holy person, a devotee, and a staunch follower of his guru.

When Girish Babu visited our home, he blessed me and invited my father to see his play, *Shankaracharya*. This was his last religious drama. After releasing this play [15 January 1910], Girish Babu did not live long.

However, I went with my father to see *Shankaracharya*. While watching the play, I was amazed by my father's facial expressions. In the theatre he said off and on: "Aha! Aha!" He could not say anything else. I was delighted, and realized that the Master's gospel had worked on my father.

I was then a teenaged boy. It was through the Master's grace that my atheistic environment was swept away by the current of simple devotion. Ramakrishna became all in all in my life. The nectar of his gospel made my passion for literature, drama, and music seem dull and insipid. In this respect, one day I asked Brother Nirmal, "How has such an impossible thing happened?" He smiled and replied, "I shall ask Girish Babu and then answer your question." After returning from visiting Girish Babu, Brother Nirmal told me: "After listening to your question, Girish Babu smiled and quoted this verse of the Gita (2:29): 'Some look on the Self as a wonder; some speak of It as a wonder; some hear of It as a wonder; still others, though hearing, do not understand It at all.'"

I did not go to anybody about this problem of mine because my mind accepted Girish Babu's words. I interpreted his statement in my own way and repeated it mentally: Who can understand Him whose every action is wonderful?[24]

Reminiscences of Girish Chandra Ghosh
Srishchandra Matilal* (1875–1934)

I did not have the good fortune to see Sri Ramakrishna during his life on earth, nor did I meet Vivekananda. Whatever I have learned of Sri Ramakrishna is what I heard from Girish Chandra Ghosh and felt in the atmosphere created by his life and association with the Master.

Whenever I listened to Girish tell of Sri Ramakrishna's wonderful grace and love, I used to feel that my life had been wasted. Although I could have seen the Lord on earth, I lost that opportunity because of my own ignorance. I used to tell Girish how much I regretted this, and he would say: "Look here! You are more blessed than we. Do you know why? You have become a devotee of the Master just by hearing his name. Don't you remember what Jesus said: 'Blessed is he that cometh in the name of the Lord?'" For the moment I would find consolation in such words, but some regret continued to lie hidden in the corner of my heart.

My first introduction to Swami Brahmananda was at the house of Girish Chandra. Although I had seen Maharaj before at Belur Math, at Dakshineswar, and at Balaram Mandir, there was no opportunity for close acquaintance until that day at Girish's home.

*A disciple of Holy Mother Sarada Devi and a biographer of Girish Chandra Ghosh.

As far as I can remember, that afternoon Maharaj and Girish Chandra were talking about Sri Ramakrishna. A number of devotees were present. I arrived with a basket of sweets [sandesh]. Girish remarked: "See how the Lord provides for his own." He asked me to offer the sweets to Maharaj. I prostrated and placed the basket before him.

Maharaj wanted to know who I was. Girish introduced me and asked a servant to bring a glass of water. Maharaj closed his eyes, offered the sweets and the water to the Master, and then accepted one or two sweets. He said: "Oh, these sweets are wonderful! Distribute them to everybody." They were passed to the devotees. Girish said to me: "Blessed you are!" There was some conversation afterwards. It turned dark, and Maharaj left for Balaram Mandir.

After Maharaj had gone, I asked Girish: "Why do I feel so blessed? Why did I receive his grace even before I asked for it?"

Girish replied: "You see, you cannot explain these things. Sri Ramakrishna attracts a devotee and leads him to the right teacher."

Atul, Girish's brother, was present. He remarked: "Sri Ramakrishna said that Rakhal [Swami Brahmananda] was his spiritual son. Even a son who is no good inherits some of his father's qualities. And in Rakhal many of Sri Ramakrishna's qualities are manifest. You have not seen the Master, but you can get some idea of him by seeing his son."

Girish added: "Sri Ramakrishna used to say, 'You will achieve everything if you come here.' Do you understand what he meant by 'here'? It means to come to him and to his intimate disciples."

Whether I understood everything or not, this I know: when I went home that night, my heart was filled with bliss and with a peace not previously experienced.[25]

Chapter 27

Departure from the World Stage

Girish's acting and writing flowed over the Bengali stage almost uninterruptedly from 1867 to 1912, when he realized that his lifeboat was nearing the shore. Girish had been born with indomitable energy and great talent, and he used them to their full extent. He had a successful life, and as he neared the end, he had no regrets.

A hero remains a hero in all circumstances: Among Ramakrishna's devotees Girish was a heroic devotee; and on the stage he usually played the role of a hero whether he was the main character or in a supporting role. His life was focussed and he knew his mission very well. In praise and blame a yogi remains unperturbed, so Girish was never affected by either applause or criticism. The British hated him, but the Bengalis loved him. His magnetic personality overwhelmed even his critics, and whenever he joined a particular theatre, his own hand-picked actors and actresses followed him just as bees follow their queen.

Towards the end, Girish pondered what he had achieved in his life: He received the grace of his guru, Ramakrishna, and surrendered to him completely by giving him the power of attorney. He spread the gospel of the Master to all who came in contact with him, even those of the red-light district. He acquired tremendous popularity as an actor, playwright, director, writer, and storyteller. He helped found the Bengali stage and set it on a strong footing. He turned the theatre into a medium for spreading socio-religious culture, and he used his plays to awaken national feeling and the political consciousness of British-subjugated India. He developed the theatrical profession and helped poor actors and actresses make a good living in a respected career. He created hope and strength in the minds of the fallen and downtrodden. Girish had so many facets to his character that he was a source of inspiration for everyone from drunkards to devotees. Truly, he had a full and interesting life.

Girish was not simply an actor and playwright; he also had encyclopedic knowledge and a powerful intellect. Every day he would receive visitors and converse with them on various subjects, including art and acting, literature and science, politics and medicine, psychology and scriptures, and his encounter with Ramakrishna, as well as the story of his own rebellious, wanton, and exciting life. He had a talent for communicating with all types of people. Mahendra Datta wrote: "There were 10 or 12 Girish Ghoshes who lived in his body. But the real Girish Ghosh was an extremely simple, straightforward person, endowed with a childlike devotional nature."[1]

Girish's memory was phenomenal. He could recite long passages from Byron and Shakespeare, and he was able to explain the intricate themes of Shakespeare's works and shed new light on them. One day he lamented to Mahendra Datta: "Do you know my condition? I have a gigantic brain but a very small body. I have the ability to understand a subject and also the power of visualizing the idea, but I am unable to act on my understanding. So I feel bad that I cannot always carry out what I understood."[2] It is like that famous saying, "My spirit is willing but the flesh is weak."

Girish dearly loved his only surviving son, Surendra "Dani," who became a successful actor. Once Amarendra Nath Roy, a great admirer of Girish, went to see *Vilwamangal Thakur*, in which Surendra performed in the title role. The next day Amarendra went to Girish and told him that he was disappointed by Surendra's performance. Girish immediately called Surendra and asked why he had acted so poorly while Amarendra was in the audience. Embarrassed, Surendra replied: "I was not well yesterday. Moreover, there was not much of a crowd, so I did not put much effort into my performance."

Girish told him: "Listen, when you act in my play, don't pay any attention to the audience. Rather, identify yourself with the character I created. If your body and mind are not well, ask someone else to act on that day. Never ruin your good reputation. Learn another thing: If one wise and appreciative spectator is in the theatre, think that one thousand are there. When I act, I don't let my mind dwell on the audience. I focus it on revealing the character in the play."[3]

In 1895 Surendra became very ill. Girish was extremely anxious. He arranged treatment for him and bought all of the medicines that he needed. One evening he told his visitors: "You see, I did what was to be done for Dani's [Surendra's] treatment. And I did something else at noon.

I went to the shrine room when no one was there. I bowed down to the Master and told him: 'Master, Dani is my only living son. Please cure him of this illness.' Then I started scolding the Master, vilifying his family for fourteen generations. I was mad at him! Angrily I said: 'If you are an avatar, please cure my son. Otherwise, I shall abuse you with the filthiest language.' Now you will see, my son will definitely be cured."[4] Saying this, Girish burst into laughter. His visitors were amazed at his steadfast faith in and dependence on the Master. Dani recovered shortly after this.

This kind of behaviour was possible only for Girish as he was unique and of a heroic temperament. Once a devotee entered the Kali temple of Dakshineswar and began to scold the Divine Mother as he had seen Girish do, but Ramakrishna forbade him because it was not his nature. Swami Vivekananda also cautioned the devotees: "Look, never imitate G.C."[5] Swamiji acknowledged Girish's divine nature and greatness, but knew that his unconventional way of life should not be blindly followed by others, because it might lead them in the wrong direction.

Girish's younger brother, Atul, told him: "Brother, the Master would call you 'Bhairava' — the guardian angel of Shiva — and I strongly believe that you are. Some people believed that if they drank alcohol like you they could also write play after play. And what was the result? They began drinking in order to write plays and finally ended up as alcoholics. Some thought that if they dressed carelessly like you and paced back and forth, they would get great ideas. Alas! Those people remained careless and devoid of any ideas. Others tried to imitate you and mix freely with the actresses in the theatre, but they only became libertines. You, however, have remained my same dear elder brother as before."[6] Atul's words are an important testimony to Girish's complex character, which was misunderstood by many.

Girish never wanted an easygoing, dull, idle life. He loved excitement, and he cared deeply about others. Early one morning in 1904 Girish was returning home from the Classic theatre after a performance. It was 2:30 a.m. As he entered his house, he heard someone crying nearby, so he sent his servant to inquire. When the servant returned, he reported a bullock cart driver was lying in the street under his cart and weeping. He was suffering from fever and chills, and he had no warm clothing or coverings, so he was trying to keep himself warm under the cart. Girish could not sleep that night, and in the morning he took a blanket and some medicine to that man.

As mentioned in Chapter 3, when Girish was working as an accountant for the John Atkinson Company, he studied homeopathy and became a very successful practitioner, curing many sick people. After the incident just described, he resumed his practice. He continued to treat the poor till the end of his life, accepting no payment. One day Devendra Babu asked him why he had started practising homeopathy. Girish replied: "Nowadays I don't need to work hard in the theatre, so I have plenty of time on my hands. If I sit idle, I shall pass my time either talking about myself or about others. This practice helps me avoid gossiping and it also helps poor people."[7]

At this time Girish was writing *Bhranti*, and he expressed his frame of mind through the dialogue of the character Rangalal, a successful physician: "It is true that this world is like an ocean, which has no limit or boundaries. But there is a polestar in this world and that is *compassion*. One cannot become a king or an emperor by following the path that compassion shows, but it makes the mind calm. Its effect is tangible and it needs no logic or argument."[8]

As acting was Girish's profession, so homeopathy was his hobby. Before selecting any medicine, a homeopathic doctor needs to know every detail of the patient's physical and mental condition. Then the doctor determines the proper diagnosis. Girish was a successful doctor because of his analytical mind and he was able to help many patients who suffered from chronic ailments. Every morning and evening many poor — and sometimes even wealthy — people would come to Girish for medicine. He treated them for free and sometimes also gave money to poor people who needed it to buy proper food.

Jnanendra Nath Kanjilal was a successful allopathic doctor and a surgeon. He was devoted to Girish but he did not believe that homeopathy was effective. He told Girish, "One cannot be a good physician without understanding pathology." One evening while Dr. Kanjilal was visiting Girish he started coughing.

Girish: "You are coughing so much. Why don't you take my homeopathic medicine?"

Kanjilal: "I can take the medicine, but if I am cured I shall not admit that your homeopathic medicine has cured me."

Smiling, Girish said: "All right. You will not have to admit the effect of my medicine."

Kanjilal took the medicine and left. The next day he admitted that he had stopped coughing, but would not give credit to the homeopathic medicine. After Girish passed away, Dr. Kanjilal changed his profession and began to practise homeopathy. He remarked: "If I had started homeopathy during Girish Babu's lifetime, I could have learned so many things from him. It would have made him happy."[9]

Even when he was advanced in years, Girish would fast during the annual Shiva-ratri celebration in honour of Lord Shiva. Once someone asked him: "You are old and not well. Why should you fast?"

Girish replied, "I get something."

"What?"

"A vision."

"A vision of whom — Lord Shiva or Sri Ramakrishna?"

"I get a vision of the Master."

"Does he talk to you?"

"No," he said, then added, "That is the last wish of my life."[10]

In the fall of 1905 Girish developed asthma. Despite his mental and physical exhaustion, he continued to act and write plays as usual. His doctor advised him to leave Calcutta during the winter and stay in Varanasi for a change of climate. Accordingly, Girish spent the winters of 1909 and 1910 in Varanasi, and thus avoided severe attacks of asthma. As described in Chapter 6, Girish wrote some parts of *Shankaracharya* and *Tapobal* while he was in Varanasi.

On 29 January 1910 Swami Vivekananda's birth anniversary was observed at the Ramakrishna Advaita Ashrama in Varanasi. Despite his illness Girish wrote a long and valuable article, "Vivekanander Sadhanphal" (The Result of Vivekananda's Sadhana) in Bengali, and it was read at a public meeting held for the celebration. In the article Girish described how Ramakrishna taught according to the temperament of each individual. For example, Ramakrishna advised some of his disciples to renounce everything and devote their whole lives to God-realization, while he told others to treat people as God and serve them. Both paths will lead to the same goal, and Vivekananda attained perfection in each one. The monks of the Ramakrishna Order follow their leader's ideal: The monks of the Ramakrishna Mission Home of Service worship the living gods in the hospital, and the monks of the Ramakrishna Advaita Ashrama worship the same God in the temple. Girish's article concludes: "Vedanta philosophy is based on samesightedness. It is not a matter of study but of realization. As I know myself, so I should know that you and I are the same. This realization depends on sadhana. For that reason, Swami Vivekananda, the great disciple of Sri Ramakrishna, established these two centres [in Varanasi] on the basis of equality. Therefore, let us all say in one voice: 'Victory to Ramakrishna! Victory to Vivekananda!'"[11]

It is hard for a creative genius to remain idle. Srish Chandra Matilal, a great admirer, asked Girish to write a drama about the sage Vishwamitra. Girish agreed to do so and borrowed a copy of the Ramayana from the

Ramakrishna Mission Home of Service library. He then began to write his last complete play, *Tapobal* (The Power of Austerity). He finished writing it in Varanasi, and it opened on 18 November 1911 at the Minerva Theatre. (See Chapter 6 for more on this play.)

In the spring of 1911 Girish returned to Calcutta for the last time. He had attained such a state of mind that disease, pain, and grief could not subdue his spirit. Even during his asthma attacks he would say with a smile: "Look, I have no sympathy for this ungrateful body. I have given it good food for its nourishment, taken care of it with comforts and all sorts of things — yet this very body has courted this terrible asthma! Truly speaking, I don't want this disease to be cured. Every attack of asthma reminds me of the impermanence of the body." Then he prayed, "Lord, you are gracious. May I have this faith until death."[12]

Ramakrishna had asked Girish to continue acting and writing, and Girish did so until the end of his life. On 15 July 1911, he gave his last performance. It was advertised in the paper that Girish would perform the role of Karunamay in *Balidan*, to be performed at the Minerva Theatre. He reached the theatre in the evening in a heavy rain. When the hall opened only a few people came, and the ticket sales totaled less than 50 rupees. The owner, Mahendra Nath Mitra, said to Girish: "The weather is very bad today, and moreover the ticket sales are low. It will be all right if you don't act on this cold night and risk your health." But despite the bad weather, people slowly began arriving for Girish's performance, and the ticket sales rose to 400 rupees. Then Girish said: "I will not deprive those who have come to the theatre, ignoring this cyclonic weather and rain. It may ruin my health, but I am helpless."[13] Alas! Who knew that it would be the last night he acted onstage?

His role required that he come onstage bare-chested several times. But the weather and the strain together aggravated his asthma, and afterward he suffered greatly. Later some people told him: "It would have been better if you had not acted that night. We earnestly forbade you, but you wouldn't listen to us."

Girish: "It would have been improper if I had not performed that night. Moreover, acting is not subject to my will because I gave the power of attorney to the Master. At his command I wrote the play and managed the theatre."

A well-wisher responded: "But the Master didn't ask you to act if it was going to ruin your health."

Girish: "He didn't forbid me either. It would be an insult to the Master if I had disappointed that audience."

A well-wisher: "Well, you could easily have skipped that particular night, and performed another night."

Girish: "What will happen if I cannot act anymore? Sacrifice yourself — that is the teaching of *Balidan*. Look, so many people came despite that terrible storm and they would have been disappointed!"

A well-wisher: "You see, now your health is permanently damaged."

Girish: "This body does not belong to me; it belongs to the Master. As long as he wants to keep it, it will remain."[14]

Thus he always obeyed the command of his guru, Ramakrishna. He used to meet people while sitting in his large living room, which faced west. His visitors were monks and brahmacharins, friends and strangers, actors and actresses. As a fragrant flower attracts bees, so Girish attracted many admirers. They found in him a source of joy and inspiration and a fountain of devotion and wisdom. And they received from him solace and succour. Despite the pain of his disease, his face would shine whenever the discussion turned to Ramakrishna. The memory of the Master gave him peace and joy.

One day Girish said: "Look, I have done so many things to make this body comfortable. But it is so ungrateful — it has invited this terrible disease and is giving me pain."

A visitor: "Don't you want to be cured of this disease? Why don't you ask the Master about it?"

Girish: "Truly speaking, I don't want this disease to be cured. Rather, it always reminds me of the Master. If he wishes, it will be cured, and if he does not, it will not be cured."

While speaking in this vein, his face glowed. Then he burst out: "Victory to Ramakrishna! O Lord, you are all-auspicious. May I never forget you."

A visitor: "How do you feel now?"

Girish: "Now I feel good, as if I have no disease."

A visitor: "Do you call on God?"

Girish: "The Master said: 'The guru merges into the Chosen Deity.' The Master was God. I constantly think of him and see him in all gods and goddesses."[15]

Although Girish was very ill and stopped going to the theatre, he invited actors and actresses to his home and trained them to act in *Tapobal*. In October 1911, all of Girish's poems were collected and printed under the title *Pratidhwani* (An Echo). On the cover page, Girish quoted this line of the great English poet Percy Bysshe Shelley: "Our sweetest songs are those that tell of saddest thought." Girish dedicated this book to Manindra

Chandra Nandi, the Maharaja of Kashimbazar, who was very fond of his poetry.

Sister Nivedita (Miss Margaret Noble), an Irish disciple of Vivekananda, lived near Girish. The two were close friends. Before leaving for Darjeeling on 22 September 1911, Nivedita went to see Girish and had a long talk with him about Ramakrishna and Vivekananda. *Tapobal* was then being rehearsed in Girish's house. Nivedita was eager to know about the play and expressed her desire to see it. Unfortunately Nivedita died in Darjeeling on 13 October 1911. Grief-stricken, Girish dedicated *Tapobal* to her:

> Dear pure Nivedita, you always rejoiced when my new dramas were staged. My new play [*Tapobal*] is now being performed in the theatre, but where are you? When I was lying ill, before you left for Darjeeling, you tenderly said to me, "May I see you well again on my return." I am still alive, my child. Why don't you come to see me? I hear that you remembered me on your deathbed. You are now in the divine abode. If you still remember me, please accept this tearful gift of mine. — Girish Chandra Ghosh.[16]

Once, while Girish was pondering his own death, he thought: "Well, death is slowly approaching. What will happen after death? I do not know where I shall go." Girish was thinking in this vein when M. (Mahendra Nath Gupta, the recorder of *The Gospel of Sri Ramakrishna*) came to visit him. M. started to talk with Girish about the Master. Suddenly, in an inspired mood, Girish said to M.: "Brother, could you beat me with your shoes? I am not joking. I am serious."

M. smiled and asked the reason for such a request.

Girish replied: "To tell you the truth, I deserve a shoe-beating. Sri Ramakrishna is sitting within my heart and is always protecting me. Yet I wonder what will happen to me after death!"[17]

Another time Girish said to his brother disciples, with his usual vigour: "Do you think I cannot get rid of this ordinary disease? I can. I can prove it to you. If I roll on the ground of the Panchavati at Dakshineswar and forcefully pray to the Master, this disease will go away. But I know the Master is all-merciful. It is his will that I am undergoing this disease, grief, pain, and suffering. Everything is for my good. This feeling, by his grace, is so strong in my mind that I have no inclination to pray that my disease be cured. Sri Ramakrishna is a wish-fulfilling tree. Whenever I have prayed for anything, I have gotten it."[18]

Ramakrishna's touch had gradually awakened God-consciousness in Girish, and Girish's great faith and devotion made it even stronger.

It was as if he was possessed by an all-powerful spiritual force. The mysterious effect of the power of attorney did not allow him to lead his life as he had before. Once someone asked Girish, "How did you give up drinking?" Girish replied: "I didn't give it up intentionally. It was the Master who made me give up drinking. Although he didn't forbid me, I used to think constantly that the sinless Master had taken all my responsibilities. Why should I burden him with my sins by committing more sin?"[19]

Long ago, Ramakrishna made a prediction about Girish: "You will be purer day by day. You will improve very much day by day. People will marvel at you. I may not come many more times, but that doesn't matter. You will succeed by yourself."[20] People were truly amazed by Girish's transformation. Towards the end of his life, Girish said: "I find that it is not difficult to obey him [the Master], love him, or worship him. But indeed it is difficult to forget him."[21]

When people would lament their ill luck at not having had the chance to meet Ramakrishna, Girish would reply, "As Mother Ganges flowed in a hundred streams in order to redeem the Sagara dynasty,* so the exuberant love of Sri Ramakrishna is flowing through hundreds of devotees in order to eventually redeem the world."[22]

In the fall of 1911, Girish received ayurvedic treatment from Shyamadas Vachaspati, a famous physician in Calcutta. In the initial stages he received some benefit, but he was not cured. His body was so weak that the doctor did not suggest he go to Varanasi as he had done the previous two winters. During the winter the people of Calcutta burned coal in order to cook their food, and the whole city remained covered with thick smoke for several hours every evening. This terrible pollution was killing Girish. During the months of March and April 1910, Girish had temporarily moved to a friend's house on the outskirts of Calcutta. His friend again offered his house to Girish during the winter months of 1911 and 1912. But Girish could not accept the offer because malaria had struck that area.

---

* In ancient times, King Sagara wanted to perform a horse sacrifice in order to attain supremacy and merit. This rite involved setting a horse free, but heavily guarded, to wander around at will for a year. If in that time no one had defeated the soldiers and stolen the horse, all the lands that it had wandered in would belong to the king performing the sacrifice. King Sagara's sons were guarding the horse, but it got away from them. They later found the horse at the hermitage of a sage. Sagara's sons accused the innocent sage of stealing the horse, and that accusation brought about their ruin. Bhagirath, the great-great-grandson of Sagara, brought the Ganges down from heaven to earth in order to save his departed ancestors.

Departure from the World Stage   463

Girish again came under homeopathic treatment. His friend Dr. Satish Barat, and Dr. W. Younan, a famous European homeopathic doctor, together began to treat Girish. They did not tell him the name of the medicines that they had prescribed, but when Girish would suggest a medicine, they were surprised to find it on their lists. Girish began to recover, but his body was weak, so the doctors suggested that he have a carriage ride every day. During January 1912 he felt better, and people hoped that as the winter was almost over, he would not have further asthma attacks.

After the death of his second wife, Girish had stopped sleeping in their bedroom. He used a wooden partition to divide his large living room upstairs, and he made his bedroom there. This living room was connected with so many memories: It was his study, his dispensary, and the room where he received his visitors. Every day many people would come to talk to him about Ramakrishna, spiritual life, and their problems, and they left at peace and reassured. This living room was also the playground of Girish's imagination, where he wrote most of his plays, poems, songs, and articles. Most important, it had been blessed by the touch of the holy feet of Ramakrishna. In this holy place the great poet Girish breathed his last.

On Saturday, 3 February 1912 Girish ate lunch and went to bed for a rest. After a while, he called to his secretary, Abinash, "Are you going out?"

"No, I am not," replied Abinash.

Girish: "Please don't go out, even if it is necessary. I am not feeling well." At 4:00 p.m. he asked Abinash to take his temperature. It was 102°. Abinash informed Girish's brother, Atul, who immediately reported this to the doctors, and they prescribed medicine accordingly. On Monday they were encouraged when his temperature went down to 98° degrees, and then to 97° on Tuesday, and 96° on Wednesday. Abinash said, "It is amazing that your temperature is going down every day!" Smiling, Girish replied, "You see, I will collapse soon."[23]

Gradually it became difficult for Girish to lie down because it was hard for him to breathe. He spent the nights of Monday and Tuesday without any sleep and continued having difficulty breathing. Most of the time he was either seated on his bed or reclining on his pillow. On Wednesday morning at 2:00 a.m., he said to Abinash, who was caring for him: "Listen to me: Please go to sleep and let others look after me. If you become sick, I shall be in trouble."[24]

Abinash lay down but could not sleep. Suddenly at 3:00 a.m. Girish loudly repeated the name of Ramakrishna three times. Abinash shivered because he had never heard such a plaintive cry from Girish. Abinash felt that Girish was saying to his Chosen Deity, Ramakrishna: "Master, it is enough! Give me peace, peace, peace!" Abinash got up and attended him. He was convinced that Girish would depart very soon. At 4:00 a.m. Abinash called for Atul, who immediately came to his brother. Girish said to him, "I don't understand why I am not getting any sleep." Atul called Dr. Bepin Behari Ghosh and Dr. J.N. Kanjilal and reported his brother's condition. They carefully examined him and gave him some medication, but it did not help. Girish passed Wednesday without any sleep. He talked to his visitors as usual and commented: "What is this? I can't sleep while sitting."

Surendra, Girish's son, had gone with the Minerva Theatre troupe to Faridpur (now in Bangladesh) to perform in a play. Atul sent a telegram to Surendra on Wednesday evening, asking him to return to Calcutta immediately. While semiconscious, Girish said, "Send Dani — a message."

Atul: "Yes, I have sent a telegram to him." Girish remained silent. The whole of Wednesday night passed that way. The doctors brought oxygen. Girish inhaled it a few times and then refused to take it anymore.

On Thursday morning Girish said, "Move me from my bed and change my bed sheet." It was done. At 9:00 a.m. he began saying, "Let me go."

"Where will you go?" Abinash asked.

Girish replied, "My car has come." Dr. Brown from Calcutta Medical College came, examined Girish, and talked to him. He left, saying, "His condition is critical." At noon Devendra, Girish's cousin, gave Girish a glass of water, which he held himself and drank. Devendra also fed him a few slices of an orange, and asked him to lie down, but he refused. Devendra asked, "Shall we inform the Holy Mother about your illness?" Girish looked at Devendra for a while and then said: "Look, I don't understand what you are saying. Everything is confusing." Off and on he continued saying: "Let me go." "Destroy my worldly intoxication." "Ramakrishna."[25]

At 8:00 p.m. Surendra arrived from Faridpur and rushed to his father. He plaintively called, "Father, Father." Girish blessed his son by putting a shaky hand on Surendra's head and then asked for a little water. There was pomegranate juice next to his bed. Surendra gave him that juice and Girish drank a little and then nodded his head. Girish had told Surendra before he left for Faridpur that he had something to tell him. Now Surendra reminded him: "Father, please tell me what you wanted to say." Girish said something in a feeble voice that no one could understand. He fell into a coma and the doctors realized that his last hour had come.

Departure from the World Stage 465

Although it was raining that afternoon, many people came to see Girish. The news of his critical condition had spread all over Calcutta by Thursday morning. At 11:00 p.m. Swami Saradananda and the devotees of Ramakrishna, Girish's relatives, and various actors and actresses came to visit Girish. They began to sing "Ramakrishna Haribol" in glorification of his guru. The song reverberated throughout the neighbourhood. At 1:20 a.m., on Friday, 9 February 1912 (according to the Bengali calendar, Thursday, 25 Magh 1318 or 8 February 1912) Girish Chandra Ghosh breathed his last and merged with his guru, Ramakrishna.

Girish's last words were: "Master, you have come. Please destroy my worldly intoxication. Victory to Sri Ramakrishna! Let us go."[26]

Girish left the stage of the world as he had left the stage of the theatre — with the flourish and heroism of a seasoned actor. Like a drama in itself, the story of his miraculous transformation has travelled from person to person, place to place, and country to country. His acting, writing, love for art, compassion for the poor and the fallen, and above all, his faith in his guru, have made him immortal.

The morning after his death thousands of people assembled to have a last glimpse of Girish. His bed was beautifully decorated with flowers and garlands; the name "Ramakrishna" was written with sandal paste on his forehead. Finally, his body was taken outside. The rush of photographers and musicians was out of control, and they were asked to go to the cremation ground as there was not enough room for them. The funeral procession slowly moved to Kashi Mitra's cremation ground on the bank of the Ganges in the western part of Calcutta.

Many distinguished people of Calcutta came to pay their homage to the great poet, actor, and playwright Girish Chandra Ghosh, including: Swami Saradananda, Bhupendra Nath Basu, Matilal Ghosh (editor, *Amrita Bazar Patrika*), Ramendrasundar Trivedi (editor, *Sahitya Parishat Patrika*), Panchkari Bandyopadhyay, Suresh Chandra Samajpati, Dinesh Chandra Sen, Nagendra Nath Basu (editor, *Vishwakosh*), Dr. R.G. Kar, Kshirod Prasad Vidyavinod (a famous playwright), and the owners, actors, and actresses of Calcutta theatres. On Saturday, 10 February 1912, all of the theatres of Calcutta were closed in honour of Girish.

Girish's body was placed on the funeral pyre and the crowd began to sing "Ramakrishna Haribol." Abinash described the scene: "Hundreds of people touched their heads to Girish's feet. Some took flowers from his cot with devotion as offered flowers to God. I have never seen such a scene in my life. Seeing the ocean of human beings, I realized that the Bengali people had learned to appreciate the noble qualities of a great soul."[27]

Girish at cremation ground, Calcutta.
His son, Surendra (in short sleeves), stands by his head.

Gradually the fire god engulfed Girish's body with a thousand blazing tongues. A gentle breeze from the Ganges spread the fragrance of sandalwood, ghee, incense, and camphor all around. By 3:00 p.m., Girish's mortal body was reduced to ashes. Some monks of Belur Math gathered Girish's remains in a copper urn and carried it to the monastery. When the Vivekananda temple was built in Belur Math, the urn was placed on the altar next to Vivekananda's statue. It is still there.

Where does the soul go after death? What happened to that famous bohemian Girish after he left the body? Holy Mother talked about this on the day Girish passed away. Some devotees asked her, "Mother, those who become unconscious before death, do they not attain final beatitude?" To this, the Mother gave a wonderfully rational answer. She said, "The thought that he had at the time he became unconscious leads a man to that destination." On the 8th at 6:00 p.m., Girish apparently became unconscious after saying, "Victory to Ramakrishna! Let us go!" Before that he was saying off and on, "Let us go! Let us go!" Someone reminded Girish, "Please chant the Master's name." Girish replied, "Do I not know that?"

Holy Mother remarked: "At the time of death, Girish's mind was absorbed in the thought of the Master — the Ocean of Consciousness. You see, these devotees are parts of the Master — someone is his hand, someone his feet, someone his hair, and so on."[28]

Girish's genius was not really understood or appreciated by the people of Bengal. Deshbandhu Chittaranjan Das remarked: "The Bengalis could not recognize the greatness of Girish Chandra Ghosh. It will take some time. Just as Shakespeare was recognized by the English people only after 100 years of his passing away, so also a day will come when our people will recognize and appreciate Girish's genius and will finally be proud to honour him. Some day Westerners will come here to learn more about Girish's genius and the beauty and depth of his writings."[29]

At the beginning of this book, Girish is shown introducing himself as a sinner. Towards the end of his life, when Swami Vishuddhananda went to see Girish for the first time, the latter welcomed him, saying: "Come, come, see me. Just see, what I was and what I am now. The Master made me a *god*. He transformed me through love and not by scolding. How can I express his love? When you see me, you will get faith and understand what the Master was. Chaitanya Mahaprabhu delivered Jagai and Madhai. They were two villains, but compared to me they were nothing! The Master gave shelter to a horrible sinner like me. If I had known that there was such a large dustbin to dump all my sins in, I would have enjoyed more pleasures in my life. Look at me, I am Ramakrishna's miracle!"[30]

References

Biographical Introduction

1. Christopher Isherwood, *Ramakrishna and His Disciples* (Methuen & Co.: London, 1965), 38-39.
2. Ibid., 154-55.
3. Ibid., 248.
4. Ibid., 248.
5. Ibid., 249-50.
6. Ibid., 250.

Chapter 1
"I am a Sinner"

1. M., *The Gospel of Sri Ramakrishna*, trans. by Swami Nikhilananda (Ramakrishna–Vivekananda Centre: New York, 1969), 679-82.
2. Swami Chetanananda, ed. & trans., *Ramakrishna as We Saw Him* (Vedanta Society: St. Louis, 1990), 207.
3. *Gospel*, 1026.
4. Hemendra Nath Dasgupta, *Sri Sri Ramakrishnadev O Bhakta-Bhairav Girishchandra*, 44.
5. *Vedanta and the West* (Vedanta Society: Hollywood), March-April 1953, 56-57.
6. Tryon Edwards, comp., *The New Dictionary of Thoughts* (Standard Book Company: New York, 1966), 617.

Chapter 2
Early Life and Adulthood

1. Abinash Chandra Gangopadhyay, *Girishchandra* (Dey's Publishing: Calcutta, 1977), 16.
2. Hemendra Nath Dasgupta, *Girish Pratibha* (Calcutta, 1929), 2.
3. *Girishchandra*, 14-15.
4. Ibid., 2.
5. Ibid., 3.
6. Ibid., 20.
7. Ibid., 20.
8. Ibid., 32.
9. *Girish Pratibha*, 6.
10. *Girishchandra*, 20.
11. Ibid., 105.
12. Ibid., 24.
13. Ibid., 27.
14. *Girish Pratibha*, 21.
15. Ibid., 21.
16. *Girishchandra*, 97.
17. Mahendra Nath Datta, *Vivekananda Swamijir Jivaner Ghatanavali* (Mahendra Publishing Committee: Calcutta, 1966), 2:64-65.
18. *Girishchandra*, 43.
19. Shankari Prasad Basu, ed. *Thakur Ramakrishna O Swami Vivekananda* (Mandal Book House: Calcutta, 1981), 43-44; Achintya Kumar Sengupta, *Ratnakar Girishchandra* (Anandadhara Prakashan: Calcutta, 1964), 19-20.
20. *Udbodhan*, 15:139-41.
21. *Girish Pratibha*, 19.
22. Swami Nikhilananda, ed. *Vivekananda: The Yogas and Other Works* (Ramakrishna-Vivekananda Centre: New York, 1953), 870.
23. *Vishwavani*, 36:198-99.
24. Ibid., 199-200.

Chapter 3
As an Accountant

1. Abinash Chandra Gangopadhyay, *Girishchandra* (Dey's Publishing: Calcutta, 1977), 94-95.
2. Ibid., 117; *Udbodhan*, 14:721.
3. *Udbodhan*, 15:138-39.
4. *Girishchandra*, 119-20.
5. Ibid., 121-22; Achintya Kumar Sengupta, *Ratnakar Girishchandra* (Anandadhara Prakashan: Calcutta, 1964), 20-21.

Chapter 4
As an Actor

1. Kiran Chandra Datta, *Girishchandra* (Calcutta University, 1954), 21.
2. Abinash Chandra Gangopadhyay, *Girishchandra* (Dey's Publishing: Calcutta, 1977), 46.
3. Ibid., 46.
4. Ibid., 93-94.
5. Ibid., 48.
6. Achintya Kumar Sengupta, *Ratnakar Girishchandra* (Anandadhara Prakashan: Calcutta, 1964), 6-7.
7. *Girishchandra*, 55.
8. Hemendra Nath Dasgupta, *Girish Pratibha* (Calcutta, 1929), 26.
9. *Bartlett's Familiar Quotations* (14th edition, 1968), 558.
10. *Girishchandra*, 57.
11. *Girish Pratibha*, 60.
12. *Girishchandra*, 65.
13. Ibid., 78-82.
14. Ibid., 81-82.
15. Ibid., 89-90.
16. Ibid., 91.
17. Ibid., 111.
18. Ibid., 112.
19. Ibid., 128-29.
20. Ibid., 133-35.
21. Ibid., 136-37.
22. Ibid., 137.
23. Ibid., 137-38.

Chapter 5
As a Playwright and Actor (1)

1. Abinash Chandra Gangopadhyay, *Girishchandra* (Dey's Publishing: Calcutta, 1977), 148-49.
2. Ibid., 150-53.
3. Ibid., 154-56.
4. Ibid., 156-57.
5. Ibid., 157.
6. Ibid., 177.
7. Ibid., 176-77.
8. Ibid., 176.
9. *Udbodhan*, 14:123.
10. Ibid., 14:718.
11. Sister Devamata, *Days in an Indian Monastery* (Ananda Ashrama: La Crescenta, 1927), 268.
12. Swami Jnanatmananda, *Mahat Smriti* (Udbodhan Office: Calcutta, 1977), 43.
13. *Girishchandra*, 325.
14. Ibid., 177.
15. Ibid., 171.
16. Aparesh Chandra Mukhopadhyay, *Rangalaye Tirish Batsar* (Papyrus: Calcutta, 1991), 64.

Chapter 6
As a Playwright and Actor (2)

1. Kiran Chandra Datta, *Girishchandra* (Calcutta University, 1954), 59.
2. Mahendra Nath Datta, *Girishchandrer Mana and Shilpa* (Calcutta University, 1942) 3-4.
3. Ibid., 4-5.
4. Abinash Chandra Gangopadhyay, *Girishchandra* (Dey's Publishing: Calcutta, 1977), 213.
5. Ibid., 216.
6. Ibid., 231-34.
7. *Girish Rachanavali* (Sahitya Samsad: Calcutta, 1996), 3:483-546.
8. Amarendra Nath Roy, *Girish-Natya-Sahiter Vaishishtya* (Calcutta University, 1956), 48.
9. *Girishchandra*, 266.

References

10. Ibid., 267.
11. Ibid., 290.
12. Ibid., 309-10.
13. *Mana and Shilpa*, 7-8, 23-24.
14. *Girishchandra*, 320-21.
15. Ibid., 325-26.
16. Ibid., 113-14.
17. Ibid., 329-30.
18. Hemendra Nath Dasgupta, *Girish Pratibha* (Calcutta, 1929), 68.
19. *Rachanavali*, 1:631-704.
20. Aparesh Chandra Mukhopadhyay, *Rangalaye Tirish Batsar* (Papyrus: Calcutta, 1991), 88-90.
21. *Girishchandra*, 367.
22. Ibid., 370.
23. Ibid., 371.
24. Peary Mohan Mukhopadhyay, *Smriti Tarpan* (Mahendra Publishing Committee: Calcutta, 1964), 92-93.
25. *Girishchandra*, 376.
26. Ibid., 377.
27. Ibid., 413.
28. Ibid., 381.
29. Ibid., 382.
30. Ibid., 383.
31. *Rangalaye*, 123.
32. Achintya Sengupta, *Ratnakar Girishchandra* (Anandadhara Prakashan: Calcutta, 1964), 169.
33. *Girishchandra*, 389-90.
34. Ibid., 392-93.
35. *Girish Pratibha*, 567.

Chapter 7
As a Director

1. Nalini Ranjan Chattopadhyay, *Sri Ramakrishna O Banga Rangamancha* (Mandal Book House: Calcutta, 1978), 20.
2. Dhan Gopal Mukerji, *The Face of Silence* (E.P. Dutton & Co.: New York, 1926), 214-16.
3. Abinash Chandra Gangopadhyay, *Girishchandra* (Dey's Publishing: Calcutta, 1977), 411.
4. Ibid., 422-23.
5. Aparesh Chandra Mukhopadhyay, *Rangalaye Tirish Batsar* (Papyrus: Calcutta, 1991), 85-86.
6. Ibid., 95-96.
7. Ibid., 119-21.
8. Kiran Chandra Datta, *Girishchandra* (Calcutta University, 1954), 39.
9. *Banga Rangamancha*, 34.
10. *Girish Rachanavali* (Sahitya Samsad: Calcutta, 1996), 3:820-23.
11. Ibid., 3:823-25.
12. Ibid., 3:827.
13. Ibid., 3:829-46.
14. Kumudbandhu Sen, *Girishchandra* (Calcutta University, 1936), 83.
15. Upendranath Vidyabhusan, *Tinkari, Binodini O Tarasundari* (Rama Prakashani: Calcutta, 1985), 92-93.
16. Hemendra Nath Dasgupta, *Girish Pratibha* (Calcutta, 1929), 630-31.
17. Ibid., 630.
18. Ibid., 636-37.
19. Ibid., 637.
20. Ibid., 637.
21. Hemendra Nath Dasgupta, *Sri Sri Ramakrishnadev O Bhakta-Bhairav Girishchandra*, 83.
22. *Girish Pratibha*, 75.

Chapter 8
From Atheist to Devotee

1. Abinash Chandra Gangopadhyay, *Girishchandra* (Dey's Publishing: Calcutta, 1977), 99-100.
2. Ibid., 100.
3. Ibid., 100.
4. Ibid., 100.
5. Ibid., 101.
6. *Dictionary of Thoughts*, 35.
7. *Girishchandra*, 179.
8. Ibid., 180.
9. Ibid., 180.
10. Ibid., 181.
11. Ibid., 181-84.
12. Ibid., 184-85.

13. Ibid., 185.
14. Ibid., 185-86.
15. *Udbodhan*, 15:200-202.

Chapter 9
Chaitanya Lila

1. Abinash Chandra Gangopadhyay, *Girishchandra* (Dey's Publishing: Calcutta, 1977), 197-98.
2. Srishchandra Matilal, *Bhakta Girish Chandra* (Dey's Publishing: Calcutta, 2003), 41-42.
3. Ibid., 42.
4. *Girishchandra*, 198.
5. Ibid., 198.
6. Peary Mohan Mukhopadhyay, *Smriti Tarpan* (Mahendra Publishing Committee: Calcutta, 1964), 93-94; Mahendra Nath Datta, *Vivekananda Swamijir Jivaner Ghatanavali* (Mahendra Publishing Committee: Calcutta, 1967), 3:71-72.
7. M.,*The Gospel of Sri Ramakrishna*, trans. by Swami Nikhilananda (Ramakrishna–Vivekananda Centre: New York, 1969), 546.
8. Ibid., 550-57.

Chapter 10
Prahlada Charitra

1. M., *The Gospel of Sri Ramakrishna*, trans. by Swami Nikhilananda (Ramakrishna–Vivekananda Centre: New York, 1969), 677-83.

Chapter 11
Nimai Sannyas

1. Abinash Chandra Gangopadhyay, *Girishchandra* (Dey's Publishing: Calcutta, 1977), 210.
2. Ibid., 54.
3. Ibid., 210.
4. M.,*The Gospel of Sri Ramakrishna*, trans. by Swami Nikhilananda (Ramakrishna–Vivekananda Centre: New York, 1969), 702.
5. *Girishchandra*, 223.
6. Ibid., 223-24.
7. Ramchandra Datta, *Sri Sri Ramakrishna Paramahamsadever Jivanvrittanta* (Yogodyana: Calcutta, 1950), 142-44.
8. *Girishchandra*, 224.
9. Swami Chetanananda, *How a Shepherd Boy Became a Saint: Life and Teachings of Swami Adbhutananda* (Vedanta Society: St. Louis, 2000), 45-47.
10. Swami Kamaleswarananda, *Ramakrishna Parikar* (Calcutta, 1977), 88.

Chapter 12
Brishaketu

1. M., *The Gospel of Sri Ramakrishna*, trans. by Swami Nikhilananda (Ramakrishna–Vivekananda Centre: New York, 1969), 699-706.

Chapter 13
Daksha Yajna

1. Abinash Chandra Gangopadhyay, *Girishchandra* (Dey's Publishing: Calcutta, 1977), 188-89.
2. Chandra Shekhar Chattopadhyay, *Sri Sri Latu Maharajer Smritikatha* (Udbodhan Office: Calcutta, 1953), 157-58.
3. Swami Chetanananda, ed. & trans., *Ramakrishna as We Saw Him* (Vedanta Society: St. Louis, 1990), 49.
4. Hemendra Nath Dasgupta, *Girish Pratibha* (Calcutta, 1929), 561.
5. Ibid., 68, 507-11 (adapted).

Chapter 14
Sri Ramakrishna: Patron Saint of Bengali Stage

1. Christopher Isherwood, *Ramakrishna and His Disciples* (Methuen & Co.: London, 1965), 292, 254.

References   473

2. Hemendra Nath Dasgupta, *Sri Sri Ramakrishnadev O Bhakta-Bhairav Girishchandra* (Calcutta, 1953), 32.
3. M., *The Gospel of Sri Ramakrishna*, trans. by Swami Nikhilananda (Ramakrishna–Vivekananda Centre: New York, 1969), 1026.
4. Devipada Bhattacharya, ed. *Girish Rachanavali* (Sahitya Samsad: Calcutta, 2002), 5:291.
5. *Gospel*, 546.
6. Max Müller, *Ramakrishna and His Sayings* (Advaita Ashrama: Calcutta, 1951), 66-67.
7. *The Complete Works of Swami Vivekananda* (Advaita Ashrama: Calcutta, 1966), 4:418-19.
8. Bible: *St. John*, 8:2-11.
9. Paul Carus, *The Gospel of Buddha* (Publications Division of Government of India: New Delhi, 1961), 183-87.
10. Nalini Ranjan Chattopadhyay, *Sri Ramakrishna O Banga Rangamancha* (Mandal Book House: Calcutta, 1978), 67-68.
11. *The Complete Works of Swami Vivekananda* (Advaita Ashrama: Calcutta, 1968), 6:366.
12. Ibid., 6:369-70.
13. Lizelle Raymond, *The Dedicated* (The John Day Company: New York, 1953), 222.
14. *Banga Rangamancha*, 72-73.
15. Ibid., 73.
16. Ibid., 73.
17. Binodini Dasi, *Amar Katha O Anyanya Rachana* (Subarnarekha: Calcutta, 1987), 47; *Banga Rangamancha*, 74.
18. *Banga Rangamancha*, 74.
19. Ibid., 74-75.
20. Ibid., 75.
21. Ibid., 75-76.
22. Ibid., 77.
23. Ibid., 77-78.
24. Ibid., 78-79.
25. Told by a swami (who wishes to be anonymous) to the author in the summer of 2004.

Chapter 15
Three Stars — Binodini, Tarasundari, and Tinkari

1. *The Complete Works of Swami Vivekananda* (Advaita Ashrama: Calcutta, 1970), 1:80.
2. *Gita*, 9:29-31.
3. M., *The Gospel of Sri Ramakrishna*, trans. by Swami Nikhilananda (Ramakrishna–Vivekananda Centre: New York, 1969), 181-82.
4. Ibid., 138.
5. Ibid., 616.
6. *Dictionary of Thoughts*, 654.
7. Upendranath Vidyabhusan, *Tinkari, Binodini O Tarasundari* (Rama Prakashani: Calcutta, 1985), 1.
8. Binodini Dasi, *Amar Katha O Anyanya Rachana* (Subarnarekha: Calcutta, 1987), 14-16.
9. Ibid., 16-17.
10. Ibid., 17.
11. Ibid., 18.
12. Ibid., 18.
13. Ibid., 18-20.
14. Ibid., 20-21.
15. Ibid., 22.
16. Ibid., 24.
17. Ibid., 27.
18. Amit Maitra, *Rangalaye Banganati* (Ananda Publishers: Calcutta, 2004), 92.
19. *Amar Katha*, 30-31.
20. Ibid., 31.
21. Ibid., 33.
22. Ibid., 33.
23. Ibid., 42.
24. Ibid., 43-44.
25. Abinash Chandra Gangopadhyay, *Girishchandra* (Dey's Publishing: Calcutta, 1977), 192.
26. *Amar Katha*, 47.

27. Ibid., 47-51.
28. Swami Saradananda, *Ramakrishna and His Divine Play*, trans., Swami Chetanananda (Vedanta Society: St. Louis, 2003), 901.
29. *Amar Katha*, 151.
30. Ibid., Introduction, 15.
31. Ibid., 104.
32. Ibid., 52.
33. Ibid., Introduction, 26.
34. Nalini Ranjan Chattopadhyay, *Girishchandra O Anyanya Prasanga* (Udbodhan Office: Calcutta, 2002), 95.
35. Ibid., 120.
36. Upendra/*Tara*, 61.
37. Ibid., 68.
38. *Girish O Anyanya*, 124.
39. Upendra/*Tara*, 70.
40. *Girish O Anyanya*, 126-27.
41. Upendra/*Tara*, 79.
42. *Rangalaye Banganati*, 245.
43. Ibid., 246.
44. Ibid., 247.
45. Ibid., 248.
46. *Girish O Anyanya*, 130-31.
47. Swami Chetanananda, *God Lived with Them* (Vedanta Society: St. Louis, 1997), 116-17.
48. Nalini Ranjan Chattopadhyay, *Sri Ramakrishna O Banga Rangamancha* (Mandal Book House: Calcutta, 1978), 103.
49. Ibid., 103.
50. *Rangalaye Banganati*, 252.
51. Swami Chetanananda, ed., *Swami Brahmanander Smritikatha* (Udbodhan Office: Calcutta, 2003), 489-91.
52. *Banga Rangamancha*, 211.
53. Ashutosh Mitra, *Srima*, 177.
54. Swami Ishanananda, *Matri Sannidhey* (Udbodhan Office: Calcutta, 1968), 214-16.
55. From Swami Dhireshananda's diary.
56. *Girish O Anyanya*, 139-40.
57. Ibid., 140-41.
58. *Rangalaye Banganati*, 258.
59. Ibid., 259.
60. *Banga Rangamancha*, 211-12.
61. Ibid., 212.
62. Upendra/*Tinkari*, 96.
63. Ibid., 152-53.
64. Ibid., 153-54.
65. Ibid., 97.
66. Ibid., 98.
67. Ibid., 99.
68. Ibid., 99.
69. Ibid., 102.
70. Ibid., 104-05.
71. Ibid., 106-07.
72. Ibid., 115-19.
73. Ibid., 107-08.
74. Ibid., 110-12.
75. Ibid., 125-29.
76. *Rangalaye Banganati*, 220.
77. Upendra/*Tinkari*, 134.
78. *Rangalaye Banganati*, 233; Achintya Sengupta, *Ratnakar Girishchandra* (Anandadhara Prakashan: Calcutta, 1964), 159-64.
79. Upendra/*Tinkari*, 155-56.
80. Ibid., 156.
81. *Srima*, 209-10.
82. Upendra/*Tinkari*, 157.
83. Ibid., 157-58.
84. Ibid., 159.
85. Ibid., 164.
86. Ibid., 165.

Chapter 16
Ramakrishna's Influence on Girish's Plays

1. *The Complete Works of Swami Vivekananda* (Advaita Ashrama: Calcutta, 1970), 5:259.
2. *Vedanta and the West* (Hollywood), 186:56.
3. Swami Chetanananda, *They Lived with God* (Vedanta Society: St. Louis, 1989), 195.
4. M., *The Gospel of Sri Ramakrishna*, trans. by Swami Nikhilananda

(Ramakrishna–Vivekananda Centre: New York, 1969), 677.
5. Nalini Ranjan Chattopadhyay, *Sri Ramakrishna O Banga Rangamancha* (Mandal Book House: Calcutta, 1978), 108-09.
6. Hemendra Nath Dasgupta, *Sri Sri Ramakrishnadev O Bhakta-Bhairav Girishchandra* (Calcutta, 1953), 54.
7. Abinash Chandra Gangopadhyay, *Girishchandra* (Dey's Publishing: Calcutta, 1977), 215.
8. *Bhakta Bhairav*, 54.
9. *Girish Rachanavali* (Sahitya Samsad: Calcutta, 1996), 4:261-99.
10. *Bhakta Bhairav*, 58-59.
11. Ibid., 59.
12. *Banga Rangamancha*, 111.
13. *Rachanavali*, 4:274.
14. Ibid., 4:268-69.
15. Ibid., 4:293-94.
16. *Girishchandra*, 217-18.
17. *Rachanavali*, 3:175-207.
18. Ibid., 3:315-20.
19. Ibid., 3:271.
20. Ibid., 3:223-24.
21. Ibid., 3:226-27.
22. Ibid., 3:246-49.
23. Ibid., 3:266-70.
24. Ibid., 1:129-68.
25. Ibid., 4:235-36.
26. Ibid., 4:251-52.
27. *Prabuddha Bharata*, 1933:194.
28. *Gospel*, 87.

Chapter 17
Reminiscenses of Ramakrishna

1. *Vedanta and the West* (Vedanta Society: Hollywood), March-April 1953.

Chapter 18
Conversations with Ramakrishna

1. M., *The Gospel of Sri Ramakrishna*, trans. by Swami Nikhilananda (Ramakrishna–Vivekananda Centre: New York, 1969), 691-99.
2. Ibid., 709, 711.
3. Ibid., 725-36.
4. Ibid., 739-42.
5. Ibid., 743-60.
6. Ibid., 762-68.
7. Ibid., 768-77.
8. Ibid., 809.
9. Ibid., 813-14.
10. Ibid., 840-44.
11. Ibid., 849-52.
12. Ibid., 856-66.
13. Ibid., 870-76.
14. Ibid., 889-94.
15. Ibid., 898-906.
16. Ibid., 928-30.
17. Ibid., 954-58.
18. Ibid., 972-73.

Chapter 19
The Power of Attorney

1. *Webster's Third New International Dictionary*, (Merriam-Webster: Springfield, 2002).
2. Bhagavad Gita, 18:66.
3. Bible: *Matthew*, 11:28.
4. M.,*The Gospel of Sri Ramakrishna*, trans. by Swami Nikhilananda (Ramakrishna–Vivekananda Centre: New York, 1969), 209.
5. Ibid., 368-69.
6. Ibid., 385.
7. Ibid., 627-28.
8. Swami Saradananda, *Sri Ramakrishna and His Divine Play*, trans. Swami Chetanananda (Vedanta Society: St. Louis, 2003), 388-96.
9. Hemendra Nath Dasgupta, *Girish Pratibha* (Calcutta, 1929), 112.
10. Ibid., 112.
11. Kiran Chandra Datta, *Girishchandra* (Calcutta University, 1954), 127.

Chapter 20
Days with Ramakrishna

1. Advaita Ashrama, *The Disciples of Ramakrishna* (Calcutta, 1955), 400.

2. Kiran Chandra Datta, *Girishchandra* (Calcutta University, 1954), 123; Hemendra Nath Dasgupta, *Sri Sri Ramakrishnadev O Bhakta-Bhairav Girishchandra*, 43.
3. Christopher Isherwood, *Ramakrishna and His Disciples* (Methuen & Co.: London, 1965), 252.
4. M., *The Gospel of Sri Ramakrishna*, trans. by Swami Nikhilananda (Ramakrishna–Vivekananda Centre: New York, 1969), 95.
5. *Bhakta Bhairav*, 35.
6. Ramchandra Datta, *Sri Sri Ramakrishna Paramahamsadever Jivan-vrittanta* (Yogodyana: Calcutta, 1950), 144.
7. Advaita Ashrama, *Life of Sri Ramakrishna* (Calcutta, 1943), 447-48.
8. *Gospel*, 694.
9. *Vedanta and the West* (Hollywood), 187:58.
10. *Gospel*, 706.
11. Swami Chetanananda, *God Lived with Them* (Vedanta Society: St. Louis, 1997), 229-30.
12. *Disciples of Ramakrishna*, 403.
13. Swami Chetanananda, *They Lived with God* (Vedanta Society: St. Louis, 1989), 277.
14. Ibid., 277-78.
15. Ibid., 278.
16. Ibid., 278.
17. Ibid., 278.
18. Abinash Chandra Gangopadhyay, *Girishchandra* (Dey's Publishing: Calcutta, 1977), 219.
19. *They Lived with God*, 278.
20. Kiran Datta/*Girishchandra*, 124-25.
21. *They Lived with God*, 279.
22. Ibid., 279.
23. Mahendra Nath Datta, *Vivekananda Swamijir Jivaner Ghatanavali* (Mahendra Publishing Committee: Calcutta, 1964), 1:10.
24. Srishchandra Matilal, *Bhakta Girishchandra* (Dey's Publishing: Calcutta, 2003), 89.
25. Ibid., 51-52.
26. *They Lived with God*, 280.
27. Matilal/*Girishchandra*, 65.
28. *They Lived with God*, 280.
29. Ibid., 280.
30. Ibid., 280-81.
31. Swami Saradananda, *Sri Ramakrishna and His Divine Play*, trans. Swami Chetanananda (Vedanta Society: St. Louis, 2003), 891-92.
32. *The Lived with God*, 281.
33. Ibid., 281.
34. Akshay Kumar Sen, *Sri Sri Ramakrishna Punthi* (Udbodhan Office: Calcutta, 1949), 607.
35. Swami Chetanananda, ed. & trans., *Ramakrishna as We Saw Him* (Vedanta Society: St. Louis, 1990), 55-56.
36. *They Lived with God*, 281-82.
37. Kiran Datta/*Girishchandra*, 127.
38. Adapted from the *Gospel*, 955-57.
39. *They Lived with God*, 282.
40. Ibid., 282.
41. Ibid., 282.
42. *Udbodhan*, 15:354.
43. *They Lived with God*, 283.
44. Ibid., 283.
45. Ibid., 283.

Chapter 21
Girish and Vivekananda

1. Mahendra Nath Datta, *Vivekananda Swamijir Jivaner Ghatanavali* (Mahendra Publishing Committee: Calcutta, 1967), 3:66-67.
2. Swami Saradananda, *Sri Ramakrishna and His Divine Play*, trans. Swami Chetanananda (Vedanta Society: St. Louis, 2003), 436-37.
3. Srishchandra Matilal, *Bhakta Girishchandra* (Dey's Publishing: Calcutta, 2003), 57.
4. His Eastern and Western Disciples, *Life of Swami Vivekananda* (Advaita Ashrama: Calcutta, 1965), 126.

5. Kumudbandhu Sen, *Smritikatha: Srima Sarada, Swami Vivekananda O Ramakrishna Mandali* (Ramakrishna-Vivekananda Ashrama: Howrah, 2001), 89.
6. *Ghatanavali*, 1:3.
7. Ibid., 1:82-83.
8. Swami Chetanananda, ed. *Swami Saradanander Smritikatha* (Udbodhan Office: Calcutta, 2006), 332-33.
9. M., *The Gospel of Sri Ramakrishna*, trans. by Swami Nikhilananda (Ramakrishna–Vivekananda Centre: New York, 1969), 871-72.
10. *Ghatanavali*, 3:80-81.
11. Ibid., 1:77-79.
12. Ibid., 1:109-10.
13. *The Complete Works of Swami Vivekananda* (Advaita Ashrama: Calcutta, 1970), 1:485-88.
14. Abinash Chandra Gangopadhyay, *Girishchandra* (Dey's Publishing: Calcutta, 1977), 251-52.
15. *Ghatanavali*, 3:67-68.
16. Ibid., 3:67-68.
17. Ibid., 1:105-06.
18. Brahmagopal Datta, *Jivanmukta Kiranchandra*, 5.
19. Kiran Chandra Datta, *Girishchandra* (Calcutta University, 1954), 14.
20. Ibid., 14-15.
21. Hemendra Nath Dasgupta, *Sri Sri Ramakrishnadev O Bhakta-Bhairav Girishchandra* (Calcutta, 1953), 85.
22. *Udbodhan*, 47:70.
23. Sharat Chandra Chakrabarty, *Swami-Shishya Samvad* (Udbodhan Office: Calcutta, 1963),1:33-34.
24. Ibid., 1:57-58.
25. Ibid., 1:73-84.
26. Ibid., 1:109-10.
27. *Prabuddha Bharata*, 108:373.

Chapter 22
Girish and Holy Mother

1. Swami Nikhilananda, *Holy Mother* (Ramakrishna-Vivekananda Centre: New York, 1962), 271-72.
2. Ibid., 272.
3. *Prabuddha Bharata*, 1952: 263-65.
4. Swami Chetanananda, ed., *Matridarshan* (Udbodhan Office: Calcutta, 1990), 14-17.
5. *Holy Mother*, 272-73.
6. Ibid., 273.
7. Ibid., 123.
8. Swami Chetanananda, ed., *Swami Brahmanander Smritikatha* (Udbodhan Office: Calcutta, 2003), 506.
9. Hemendra Nath Dasgupta, *Sri Sri Ramakrishnadev O Bhakta-Bhairav Girishchandra* (Calcutta, 1953), 76.
10. *Holy Mother*, 274.
11. Swami Gambhirananda, *Sri Sarada Devi, Holy Mother* (Ramakrishna Math: Chennai, 1955), 222-23.
12. *Udbodhan*, 107:328.
13. Ibid., 107:328.
14. Ibid., 107:328.
15. *Bhakta Bhairav*, 77-78.
16. Ashutosh Mitra, *Srima*, 193-94.
17. *Matridarshan*, 30-32.
18. Ibid., 74-75.
19. *Udbodhan*, 107:330.
20. *Mayer Katha* (Udbodhan Office: Calcutta, 2004), 39.
21. Ibid., 197-98.
22. Ibid., 9.

Chapter 23
Girish and the Monastic Disciples of Ramakrishna

1. *Udbodhan*, 15:351.
2. Ibid., 15:363-64.
3. Ibid., 15:355-56.
4. Ibid., 15:367-69.
5. Swami Chetanananda, trans., *A Guide to Spiritual Life* (Vedanta Society: St. Louis, 1988), 22-23.
6. Mahendra Nath Datta, *Vivekananda Swamijir Jivaner Ghatanavali* (Mahendra Publishing Committee: Calcutta, 1964), 2:65-66.

7. Swami Chetanananda, *God Lived with Them* (Vedanta Society: St. Louis, 1997), 335.
8. Mahendra Nath Datta, *Saradananda Swamijir Jivaner Ghatanavali* (Mahendra Publishing Committee: Calcutta, 1948), 44-45.
9. Ibid., 54-55.
10. Ibid., 113-14.
11. Ibid., 178-80.
12. Swami Chetanananda, ed. & trans., *Ramakrishna as We Saw Him* (Vedanta Society: St. Louis, 1990), 86-87.
13. Ibid., 91.
14. Chandrasekhar Chattopadhyay, *Sri Sri Latu Maharajer Smritikatha* (Udbodhan Office: Calcutta, 1953), 254-55.
15. *Ramakrishna as We*, 420.
16. *God Lived with Them*, 417.
17. *Latu Smritikatha*, 318.
18. Ibid., 428.
19. Ibid., 429.
20. Ibid., 430.
21. Swami Siddhananda, *Satkatha* (Udbodhan Office: Calcutta, 1974), 171-72.
22. *Satkatha*, 241.
23. Ibid., 176-77.
24. *Latu Smritikatha*, 435-37.
25. *Ghatanavali*, 1:233-34.
26. *God Lived with Them*, 240.
27. Ibid., 280.
28. Ibid., 307-08.
29. Ibid., 545-46.
30. *Ramakrishna as We*, 130.
31. Swami Omkareswarananda, *Premananda* (Ramakrishna Sadhan Mandir: Deoghar, 1952), 2:16.
32. Brahmachari Akshay Chaitanya, Premananda-Premakatha (Nababharat Publishers: Calcutta 1975), 130.
33. Hemendra Nath Dasgupta, *Sri Sri Ramakrishnadev O Bhakta-Bhairav Girishchandra* (Calcutta, 1953), 92.
34. *Ramakrishna as We*, 206-08.
35. Ibid., 225.
36. Ibid., 247.

Chapter 24
Girish and the Devotees of Ramakrishna

1. M., *The Gospel of Sri Ramakrishna*, trans. by Swami Nikhilananda (Ramakrishna–Vivekananda Centre: New York, 1969), 471.
2. Swami Nityatmananda, *Srima Darshan* (General Printers and Publishers: Calcutta, 1967), 6:130, 7:156, 1:108-09, 3:86, 2:107, 5:210-11, 276-79, 4:39-40.
3. Swami Nityatmananda, *Srima Darshan* (General Printers and Publishers: Calcutta, 1967), 1:42.
4. Kumudbandhu Sen, *Smritikatha: Srima Sarada, Swami Vivekananda O Ramakrishna Mandali* (Ramakrishna-Vivekananda Ashrama: Howrah, 2001), 161-62.
5. Mahendra Nath Datta, *Vivekananda Swamijir Jivaner Ghatanavali* (Mahendra Publishing Committee: Calcutta, 1964), 2:69.
6. Swami Chetanananda, *They Lived with God* (Vedanta Society: St. Louis, 1989), 313.
7. *Gospel*, 973.
8. M., *Sri Sri Ramakrishna Kathamrita* (Kathamrita Bhavan: Calcutta, 1951), 3:vii-viii.
9. *They Lived with God*, 335-36.
10. Ibid., 338.
11. Ibid., 315; Mahendra Nath Datta, *Bhakta Devendranath* (Mahendra Publishing Committee: Calcutta, 1956), 16-17.
12. *They Lived with God*, 236.
13. Ibid., 244.
14. Ibid., 244.
15. Ibid., 245.
16. Ibid., 245-46.
17. *Ghatanavali*, 2:96.
18. Ibid., 2:97.
19. Brahmagopal Datta, *Smritichayan* (Calcutta, 1983), 4.

References 479

20. Girish Chandra Ghosh, *Thakur Sri Ramakrishna O Swami Vivekananda*, ed., Shankari Prasad Basu (Mandal Book House: Calcutta, 1981), 50-52.
21. *They Lived with God*, 106.
22. *Smritikatha: Srima Sarada, Swami Vivekananda O Ramakrishna Mandali*, 55.
23. Ramchandra Datta, *Sri Sri Ramakrishna Paramahamsadever Jivanvrittanta* (Yogodyana: Calcutta, 1950), 141-47.
24. *They Lived with God*, 452.
25. Ibid., 456.

Chapter 25
Further Glimpses of Girish

1. John Gage Allee, comp., *Webster's Encyclopedia of Dictionaries* (Ottemheimer Publishers, 1978), 875.
2. Abinash Chandra Gangopadhyay, *Girishchandra* (Dey's Publishing: Calcutta, 1977), 411.
3. Ibid., 412.
4. Ibid., 412.
5. Ibid., 411-12.
6. Ibid., 413.
7. Ibid., 413.
8. Ibid., 414.
9. Ibid., 414.
10. Ibid., 414.
11. Ibid., 415.
12. Ibid., 415.
13. Abinash Chandra Gangopadhyay, ed., *Girishchandra: Girish Prasanga, Girish Gitavali* (Bengal Medical Library: Calcutta, 1913), 162-63.
14. Ibid., 170.
15. *Girishchandra*, 416.
16. Ibid., 416.
17. Ibid., 416-17.
18. Ibid., 417.
19. Ibid., 417.
20. Ibid., 418.
21. Ibid., 418.
22. Ibid., 419.
23. Ibid., 419.
24. Ibid., 420.
25. Ibid., 420.
26. Ibid., 421.
27. Ibid., 422.
28. *Girish Rachanavali* (Sahitya Samsad: Calcutta, 1996), 3:70; Peary Mohan Mukhopadhyay, *Smriti Tarpan* (Mahendra Publishing Committee: Calcutta, 1964), 44-45.
29. Mahendra Nath Datta, *Vivekananda Swamijir Jivaner Ghatanavali* (Mahendra Publishing Committee: Calcutta, 1967), 3:69.
30. Hemendra Nath Dasgupta, *Girish Pratibha* (Calcutta, 1929), 27.

Chapter 26
Interviews and Reminiscenses

1. Hemendra Nath Dasgupta, *Girish Pratibha: Introduction* (Calcutta, 1929), 1.
2. *Girish Pratibha, Preface*, 1.
3. Hemendra Nath Dasgupta, *Sri Sri Ramakrishnadev O Bhakta-Bhairav Girishchandra* (Calcutta, 1953), 86-90.
4. Ibid., 99-100.
5. *Vedanta and the West* (Hollywood), 186:49-50.
6. Ibid., 186:55-57.
7. *Ramakrishna Mission's Minute Book*, 19.
8. Ibid., 26.
9. *Vedanta and the West*, 187:56-59.
10. Ibid., 187:59-60.
11. *Minute Book*, 52-53.
12. *Vedanta and the West*, 187:60-62.
13. Ibid., 187:62-63.
14. *Minute Book*, 72.
15. Sister Devamata, *Days in an Indian Monastery* (Ananda Ashrama: La Crescenta, 1927), 267-73.
16. *Prabuddha Bharata*, 1936:651-57.
17. *Sarada* (Yogeswari Ramakrishna Math: Howrah, 1959), 4:16-20.
18. Ibid., 4:193-94.
19. Kumudbandhu Sen, *Smritikatha: Srima Sarada, Swami Vivekananda O Ramakrishna Mandali* (Ramakrishna-Vivekananda Ashrama: Howrah, 2001), 86-91.

20. Ibid., 91.
21. Ibid., 91-94.
22. Swami Sambuddhananda, *Jeman Suniachi* (Sri Ramakrishna Ashrama: Belanagar, 1970), 128-32.
23. Dilip Kumar Roy, *Smriticharan* (Surakavya Samsad: Calcutta, 1987), 191-205.
24. Ibid., 205-12.
25. *Vedanta and the West*, March-April, 1960.

Chapter 27
Departure from the World Stage

1. Mahendra Nath Datta, *Vivekananda Swamijir Jivaner Ghatanavali* (Mahendra Publishing Committee: Calcutta, 1964), 3:74-75.
2. Ibid., 76.
3. *Sarada* (Yogeswari Ramakrishna Math: Howrah, 1961), 6:292.
4. *Ghatanavali*, 3:77-78.
5. *Udbodhan*, 57:291.
6. Srishchandra Matilal, *Bhakta Girishchandra* (Dey's Publishing: Calcutta, 2003), 74.
7. Abinash Chandra Gangopadhyay, *Girishchandra* (Dey's Publishing: Calcutta, 1977), 352.
8. Ibid., 352-53.
9. Ibid., 355-56.
10. *Udbodhan*, 52:291.
11. *Girish Rachanavali* (Sahitya Samsad: Calcutta, 2002), 5:280-87.
12. *Girishchandra*, 419-20.
13. Ibid., 398.
14. Hemendra Nath Dasgupta, *Sri Sri Ramakrishnadev O Bhakta-Bhairav Girishchandra* (Calcutta, 1953), 102.
15. Ibid., 102-04.
16. *Girishchandra*, 404.
17. *Udbodhan*, 15:366-67.
18. Ibid., 15:359.
19. *Bhakta Bhairav*, 103.
20. M., *The Gospel of Sri Ramakrishna*, trans. by Swami Nikhilananda (Ramakrishna–Vivekananda Centre: New York, 1969), 741.
21. *Vedanta and the West*, 187:59.
22. *Udbodhan*, 53:506.
23. *Girishchandra*, 406.
24. Ibid., 407.
25. Ibid., 408.
26. *Udbodhan*, 14:118.
27. *Girishchandra*, 410.
28. *Sarada*, 4:169.
29. Amarendra Nath Roy, *Girish-Natya-Sahityer Vaishishtya* (Calcutta University, 1956), 77.
30. *Yogakshema*, comp. Bimal Kumar Bhattacharya and Lalit Kumar Mukhopadhyay (Calcutta, 1979), 45; Swami Vishuddhananda, *Sat Prasanga* (Ramakrishna Mission: Shilong, 1959), 2:50-51

Index

GC = Girish; Rk = Ramakrishna; HM = Holy Mother; SV = Swami Vivekananda
Page numbers followed by "n" indicate a footnote.

Abedhananda, Swami (Kali), 193; on Rk, crazy woman, 385
Abhimanyu (Arjuna's son), 54, 308
Abinash, 43, 89; on Binodini and Gopala, 171, 412; on *Brishaketu*, 147; comparing GC, A. S. Mustafi, 88–90; on *Daksha Yajna*, 158–59; and GC, 407–8; on GC and Rk monks, 381; on GC and Shiva, 70; on GC at Varanasi, 80; on GC dictating, 69; on GC's absorption, 78; GC's biographer, 8; on GC's cremation, 465; at GC's death, 463–64; on GC's playwriting, 53–54; GC's secretary, 8, 53; on Rk in samadhi, 143
Adbhutananda, Swami (Latu): GC depicting, 242; GC praises, 376; at GC's death, 378; on "money mantra", 377; on M.'s grief, 307; praises GC, 375–78; provoked by GC, 145; and Rk, 159–60; saw HM without veil, 360
Adhikari, Beni Madhav (music director), 119, 159
Advaitananda, Swami (Brother Gopal): giving cloths, rosaries for monks, 335; saw HM without veil, 360; senior to GC, 369
Akhandananda, Swami: instructing Tara, 204

Amarendra (actor), 439; Classic Theatre, closed, 73; Emerald Theatre, leased, 197; hiring GC, 68; Tara, relationship with, 196–97
Amrita Bazar Patrika (newspaper), 142, 186, 260, 465
Aparesh: author, play on Ramanuja, 200; on GC leading actors to Rk, 413; with GC, on Rk's disciples, 411; his memoirs, 55, 90; on HM embracing actress, 363; HM seeing play of, 366; leasing Star Theatre, 200; named Tara's temple, 204; on police censorship, 79; praises GC's methods, 90–91; relationship with Tara, 198, 201; rift with Tara, 204; on Rk's respect, actresses, 169; tutored by Sharat, Maharaj, 200
Arjuna, 308, 312, 363–64, 416
Arnold, Sir Edwin, 300; author, *The Light of Asia*, on life of Buddha, 58; praises GC, 58; praises Binodini, 190
art: GC on theatre as origin of arts, 97; Rk, teaching arts to disciples, 441; theatre and Indian art, culture, 174–75, 366
Aseshananda, Swami, 255
Asiatic Society: GC, member of, 29, 75, 95; Rk, on his visit to, 299
atheism, 11, 13, 28, 110, 112, 115, 257, 406

481

Atkinson, John (American businessman), 39; liked GC's work, 34; partner, Atkinson Tilton Co., 34
Atkinson Tilton Co.: GC, accountant for, 34–35, 41, 64
Atul (Girish's brother), 8, 27, 440; on GC owning theatre, 47; at GC's death, 463–64; lawyer, Calcutta High Court, 152; monk treating daughter, 372–73; praises GC, 456; praises Maharaj, 453; published GC's work, 7; Rk blessing him, 398; Rk instructing, 152–53; Sarada's classmate, 438
Aurangazeb, Emperor, 78, 80
avatar (*see also* Incarnation of God): Amar Datta on avatar Rk, 169; GC accepting Rk as, 21; GC on Rk as, 391, 418, 422; inspiring artists, 225; Kalipada on Rk as, 171; on Rk as, 357

Baburam. *See* Premananda, Swami
Balaram, 355; devotees and, 376; devotion for Rk, 326; on GC serving Rk, 392; HM and, 362; Rk and, 259, 262–63, 427; Rk Mission, started at, 349, 416; Yogin and, 379
Balaram (Krishna's brother): GC's vision of, 403
Banabiharini (actress), 119, 129, 142
Bandyopadhyay, Gurudas (judge): praises GC's *Macbeth*, 65
Bandyopadhyay, Surendra Nath: praises GC's *Chatrapati*, 79; praises GC's *Siraj-ud-Daulla*, 76
Bankim, 50, 55; with GC, M., 392; praises Binodini, 182; writings of: *Bishabriksha*, 47; *Chandrashekhar*, 196; *Devi Chaudhurani*, 197; *Durgeshnandini*, 44, 47, 76, 182, 414; *Kapalkundala*, 44, 53, 70, 183; *Mrinalini*, 45, 71
Baring, T. G., Earl of Northbrook: Governor General of India, 43
Basu, Amritalal (actor): author, satire *Bibaha Bibhrat*, 134, 210, 213; buying Star Theatre, 185; Dadhichi in *Daksha Yajna*, 158; dramatizing *Chandrashekar*, 196; GC bringing to Star, 96; on GC finding religion, 114; GC taking to Rk, 171; Hiranyakashipu in *Prahlada Charitra*, 133–34; persuading Binodini, 182; praises Binodini, 169; praises *Chaitanya Lila*, 121; praises GC, 73; taking GC's dictation, 53
Basu, Balaram. *See* Balaram
Basu, Devendra Nath (GC's cousin): GC hired, 65; with GC, on playwriting, 402; with GC, treating friend, 116; GC's biograper, 411; at GC's death, 464; taking GC's dictation, 53; translating Shakespeare's *Othello*, 200
Basu, Kalinath: friend of GC, 110–11; with GC at Brahmo Samaj, 111; member, Brahmo Samaj, 111; and servant's theft, 111; signed Temperance pledge, 111
Basu, Mahendralal (actor), 95; hiring Tinkari, 212–13
Basu, Nanda: Rk refusing betel-leaf, 329–30
Belur Math, 436; Binodini, Tara at, 193, 199; GC at Rk festival, 351; GC at SV's cremation, 352; GC's relics at, 467; Tara at, 204
Bengal Theatre, 92, 180; Binodini at, 182–83; Sharat Ghosh founded, 44
Bengalee (magazine): advertising, Rezia, 197; praises GC, 38, 77, 79, 81–82; praises Tara, 200
Bernhardt, Sarah (actress), 92, 94
Bhagavata, 26, 121n, 395
Bhaktamala (Garland of Devotees), 218, 227, 235, 344
bhaktiyoga (bhakti), 124, 213, 283, 290, 437; Rk on, 138, 148, 151, 271, 309
Bibaha Bibhrat (play; Confusion of Marriage), 134–35, 210, 213–15
Binodini (actress), 128, 176–93, 177; autobiography, 192; Bankim praises, 182; brother's death, 178; death, 193; Fr. Lafont blessing, 188; meditating on Gauranga, 186–87; meeting theatre folks, 179–80; mentoring Tara, 195; at National Theatre, 184; Nimai in *Chaitanya Lila*, 119; Nimai in *Nimai Sannyas*, 142; onstage, hair entangled,

191; on Padaratna's blessing, 188; Padmavati in *Brishaketu*, 147; Prahlada in *Prahlada Charitra*, 133; praises GC, 96; praises S.C. Ghosh, 182; retiring from stage, 192; on Rk blessing, 169; on Rk blessing her, 174, 189n; Sita in *Ravan-badh*, 51; title role, *Kapalkundala*, 71, 182–83; worships Rk's picture, 193
Bodhananda, Swami, 358
Brahmajnana. *See* jnanayoga
Brahman (All-pervasive Spirit), 253, 291; Ganges water as, 391; as incomprehensible, 327; on mystery of incarnation, 348; as one with Shakti, 122–23, 355; as one's true nature, 138; Rk on, 148, 154, 445; as sole reality, 270–71
Brahmananda, Swami, 418, 452; building math, 201; caring for actresses, 199–200; death, 203–4; encouraged Aparesh, Tara, 200–201; and GC, 81; GC on his power, 372; Golap-ma scolding, 361; guiding actresses, 174, 193; praises GC, SV, 327; receives HM at train, 361; relics at Tara's temple, 204; Rk's spiritual son, 453; on suffering, 376
Brahmo Samaj, 111–12, 114; faulting Rk on fallen, 164; no concept of bhakti, 271; Rk's ideas incorporated, 444; and SV on God with form, 339; theatre, shunning Rk over, 162, 390
Brishaketu: son of King Karna, Mahabharata, 147–48
Brishaketu (GC's play), 147–56
British, 38, 454; ban GC's plays, 45, 79; Calcutta, presence in, 10–12; and censorship, 45; soccer, Bengal team defeating, 409; victory at Palasi, 75–77
Buddha: GC's *Buddhadev-Charit*, teachings in, 57–58; redeeming Ambapali, 165–66
Byron, Lord, 41–42, 96, 455
Calcutta: British theatres in, 38–39; capital, British Raj, 10, 38; GC in theatres, 57; GC's birth in, 12; park named for GC, 429; Prince of Wales at, 45; rioting, blackout at night, 362; Western influence on, 28; and widow marriage, 80

Calvé, Mme. Emma (opera singer), 168
Chaitanya (*see also* Gauranga): associates of, 118; birth name, 118; birthplace, Navadwip, 118; epithet of, 118; GC, on nature of, 119; role, *Rupa-Sanatan*, 120–22; title role, *Chaitanya Lila*, 118–31; transformed ruffians, 118
Chaitanya Lila (GC's play), 81, 92, 118–32; changed Bengali stage, 174
Chatrapati Shivaji (GC's play), roused nationalism, 78–79
Chattopadhyay, Bankim Chandra. *See* Bankim
Chattopadhyay, Lalit (HM's disciple), 202, 362, 365
Chattopadhyay, Prof. Nalini Ranjan: on Rk's influence on theatre, 226
Chattopadhyay, Rajen: saved GC's life, 219
Chattopadhyay, Ramlal (Rk's nephew). *See* Ramlal
Chaudhury, Kedarnath: leases National Theatre, 47; praises Binodini, 183; takes GC's dictation, 53
Chintamani (courtesan): role, *Vilwamangal Thakur*, 191–92, 197, 228–35, 363, 373
Chintamani (holy man): role, *Kalapahar*, based on Rk, 242–48
Chosen Deity (Chosen Ideal), 120, 144, 243, 296, 460, 464
Chowringhee Theatre, 38
Christ Jesus, 312; disciple John's message, 387; lifts fallen, 165; redeemer, Mary Magdalene, 391; Rk's disciples and his, 392–93
Christianity, 439, 446; missionaries influence, 12–13, 110, 225; Rk on preaching sin, 314; "Young Bengal," few converted, 260
City Theatre: Ram lectures on Rk, 166; Star Theatre actors moving to, 64; Tinkari at, 213–15
Classic Theatre, 70–71; GC, Dramatic Director, 68; Muslims protesting GC's *Satnam*, 79–80
Clive, Lord Robert: victory at Palasi, 75

Convention of Religions of India, 438–40
Cossipore garden house: GC at, 336–37, 393; Rk as Kalpataru, 398; Rk moved to, 307, 334; SV at, 342

Daksha, King: son of Brahma, role, *Daksha Yajna*, 157–61
Daksha Yajna (GC's play), 157–61; HM at, 363
Dakshineswar (temple garden), 144, 235, 392; GC at, 265; Rk festival, 167, 349; Rk moved from, 332
Das, Deshbandhu Chittaranjan (national leader): praises GC, 414, 467
Das, Upendranath: author, Gajadananda, banned by British, 45
Dasgupta, Hemendra Nath: biographer, *Girish Pratibha*, 411; on Brahmos on Rk at theatre, 162; on GC's acting, 161; on GC's character, 97; on Rk's influence, GC's *Nasiram*, 252
Dasi, Binodini. *See* Binodini
Datta, Amar (editor, *Natya Mandir*): putting Rk on cover, 169
Datta, Amarendra Nath. *See* Amarendra
Datta, Aswini Kumar: with Rk, on GC, 20
Datta, Mahendra Nath (brother of SV), 57, 76; on GC as devotee, 455; with GC, curing Yogin, 379; on GC shocking Vaishnavas, 121; on GC, SV bantering, 348; on GC's health, 410; on GC's mannerisms, 69; at GC's with Sharat, 373; on Rk devotee's love, 393; on SV's singing, 343
Datta, Michael Madhusudan (playwright), 50; author, poem *Meghnadbadh*, 45, 51, 54; forming public theatre, 44; praises GC, 43; playwright, *Krishnakumari*, 43; playwright, *Mayakanan* (A Garden of Maya), 44; playwright, *Ratnavali*, 40; playwright, *Sharmistha*, 40, 44; for women onstage, 44, 92
Datta, Ram Chandra. *See* Ram Chandra Datta
death: fear of, 419; GC on Rk and fear of, 416; GC ponders, 393, 461; of GC's relatives, 29, 70; HM on GC's, 467

Devamata, Sister: on GC, Sharat, 428; on GC's playwriting, 53
Devendra (Deven), 52, 397; GC on his renouncing, 308; GC's friend, 394–95; preparing for Kali worship, 332–33; Rk and, 280; with Rk and GC, 330; stopping Latu, hitting GC, 145; taking GC's dictation, 53
Dhar, Jawaharlal (stage director), 147, 159
Divine Mother (Kali), 313, 365; GC calls on, 120; GC identifies HM with, 356–62; GC worships, 113–15; GC's rehearsal at Kalighat, 159; on GC's scolding of, 456; GC's vision of, 117; Rk as handmaid of, 149; Rk depends on, 252; Rk on, 294–95; Rk on theatre and, 390; Rk prays to, 141, 152, 299; on Rk seeing lion, 443–45; Rk talks to, 281–83; Rk worshipped as, 305–6, 332–34, 398, 424; on Rk's power of attorney to, 382
drama: in Indian tradition, 56; in Western tradition, 56
Dramatic Performance Control Bill: restricting theatres, 45
Durga Charan Nag: Niranjan on his humility, 396; relationship with GC, 395–97; Rk on his humility, 395–96; searching for amalaki, 396–97
Durga (Divine Mother), 47, 271, 389; Binodini invoking, 187; Durga Puja, 31, 58; GC's Durga Puja, 362

East India Company: British power in India, 75, 77–78, 91
Emerald Theatre, 253; Amarendra Datta leased, 197; GC, manager, 60; original Star renamed as, 59, 195, 210; Tinkari acting at, 213

Fribarger & Co.: GC, accountant for, 35–36

Gadadhar (*see also* Ramakrishna), 10
Gangamani (actress), 119, 142; living with Binodini's family, 179–80; Pagalini in *Vilwamangal Thakur*, 192

Ganges, 274, 422, 462n; Binodini's brother's cremation at, 178; death on banks of, 30–31; GC, bathing, Tarpan to parents, 111–12; GC purifies Mother Ganges, 331; Ramlal puts water on Rk's feet, 160, 335; Rk on confessing sins to, 378–79, 382; Rk on GC bathing in, 331, 391
Gangopadhyay, Abinash Chandra. *See* Abinash
Garrick, David (actor, playwright), 97; comparing GC to, 81, 426
Gauranga: Binodini meditating on, 186–88; epithet of Chaitanya, 118; toothmarks on prasad, 120
George III, King, 97
Ghosh, Atul Chandra. *See* Atul
Ghosh, Girish Chandra. *See* Girish
Ghosh, Gopal. *See* Advaitananda, Swami (Brother Gopal)
Ghosh, Kalipada. *See* Kalipada
Ghosh, Nilkamal (GC's father), 34; advising friends, 24; death, 28; and employees, 23–24; teaches GC self-reliance, 28
Ghosh, Purna Chandra (Purnachandra). *See* Purna
Ghosh, Raimani (GC's mother): death of, 27; devoted to God, 23; offering to Vishnu, 24
Ghosh, Sharat Chandra: Bengal Theatre, owner, 44, 180, 182–83; love for Binodini, 182; put women onstage, 92
Ghosh, Sisir Kumar: editor, *Amrita Bazar Patrika*, 142; with GC, slighting Rk, 260; on GC writing *Nimai Sannyas*, 143; with GC, writing paper for Convention, 438; mentored Binodini, 186
Ghosh, Surendra Nath (GC's son), 8, 415, 466; actor, known as Danibabu, 29; fame for Pashupati in *Mrinalini*, 73; GC berating Rk for his cure, 455–56; on GC healing pet bird, 116; GC telling, give best effort, 455; at GC's death, 464; published GC's works, 7; Shankara in *Shankaracharya*, 81; Siraj in *Siraj-ud-Daulla*, 75; title role, *Mirkasim*, 77

Girish, 48, 49, 61, 72, 89, 324
[*Subentries following general entries:* HM; Personal traits; Religion; Rk; Rk's disciples; Theatre; Plays; Roles]

accountant, Atkinson Tilton Co., 34–35, 41; advising Abinash, 407–8; advises on Hindu customs, 434–35; associate, Nirmal Lahiri, 449–52; on autobiographies, 406; biographical sketch, 10–18; biography, *Girish Pratibha*, 411; birth, 23; cremation, 465, 466, 467; Curriculum Vitae, 82–86; daily routine, Varanasi, 80–81; death of relatives, 29, 70; destroys Durga image, 31; early schooling, 26; eating neighbour's chickens, 32; family tree, 27; final days, 463–65; griefs, late in life, 338; on his genius, 401; house, 388; humorous stories of, 374; influence on Dilip Roy, 449–52; and Madhusudan Datta, 54; member, Asiatic Society, 29, 75; murder plot against, 218-19; occult healing, 115–16; policeman harassing, 32; practising homeopathy, 29–30, 457; praises Chittaranjan Das, 414; relics at Belur Math, 467; resigns, Parker Co., 37, 47; shocks Vaishnavas, 121; on soccer win and national pride, 409; trapped in ravine, 36; on writing simply, 404; on "Young Bengal", 260

Girish — and HM
cured by HM, in a vision, 31–32, 359; Durga Puja, HM at his, 362; first visit, 353; on HM as Divine Mother, 355–58; on HM as his real mother, 360–61; HM on not renouncing, 361; on HM's greatness, 355; on HM's nature, 360; on HM's veil, 360; not watching HM, 353; visit, 32, 355–62
Girish — Traits
boldness, 30; debater, 406–7; devotional, 390; dissolute, 29–30; doubt, longing for God, 13; empathy, 408; an enumerating, 21; expressiveness, 410; extolling bravery, 27; faith, 322;

Girish Chandra Ghosh

Girish — Traits (*continued*)
flaunting faults, 323; genius unappreciated, 467; hated hypocrisy, 30, 111, 323; love of literature, 26; power of memory, 409; power of visualization, 57; saintliness, 462; seeker of bliss, 410; sensitivity, 26; sins, 323; willfulness, 25

Girish — and Religion
at Brahmo Samaj, 111–12, 261; calling on God, 258; on Chaitanya, 119; disillusionment, 112; Divine Mother, vision of, 117; and Dr. Sarkar, 298; on faith and humility, 420; in Ganges, Tarpan to parents, 111–12; purifies Mother Ganges, 331; on God as redeemer, 412; on Hindu philosophers, 406; on intoxications, 443; and Mahimacharan, 289–90; on need for guru, 258, 427; on not needing prayer for sins, 408; on power of attorney, 316–17, 384, 418; on power of God's name, 422–3; on prarabdha karma, 419; prays to Shiva, 261; on a race's sadhana, 441; song, paper for Convention, 438–40; at Tarakeswar, Shiva Ratri, 113; and Trailokya, 286–88; vision of Balaram, Krishna's brother, 403; warning on visions, 370; worshipping Shiva, 70

Girish — and Rk
attracted to Rk, 259; berating Rk to cure son, 455–6; cleansed by Rk, 266; on curing Rk's cancer, 294–95; at Dakshineswar, 265; death, 465; discussion with, 273–78; gives Rk power of attorney, 8, 20, 88, 248, 315, 384, 399, 443, 454, 459, 462; held Rk festival, 289; at Kalpataru day, 335; mind filled with Rk, 378; mystified by Rk, 417; no self-will left, 370, 438; on not viewing Rk's body, 337; put Rk's ideas in plays, 226; at Ram's, 264; refuses to apologize to Rk, 394; reminiscing on Rk, 255–68; on Rk accepting all faiths, 446; on Rk as all in all, 268; on Rk as avatar, 171, 269, 391, 418, 421–22; on Rk as bhaktiyogi, 397; on Rk as jnanayogi, 397; on Rk as Kalpataru, 398; Rk at, 278; with Rk at Chaitanya Lila, 117; with Rk at Star Theatre, 19, 135, 260; with Rk, Cossipore, 336–37, 393; Rk, discussion with, 283–89; Rk feeding, 336; on Rk forgiving his abuse, 146; on Rk improving all people, 309; Rk inviting him, 262; on Rk, life and teachings, 420; Rk on bathing in Ganges, 331, 391; Rk on GC as part of Shiva, 367; on Rk on God knowledge, 425, 445; on Rk on human nature, 234; on Rk removing his suffering, 448; on Rk, saviour of fallen, 21, 447; on Rk seeing lion, 443–45; on Rk subduing his pride, 263; on Rk taking dust, devotees feet, 236; on Rk taking sins of, 367; on Rk teaching playwriting, 225; on Rk to be born as son, 145; Rk warning on visions, 327, 419–20; on Rk's acting, 233; on Rk's advent, 423; on Rk's horoscope, 293; on Rk's love, 256–57; on Rk's mercy, 442–43; on Rk's respect for all, 259; on Rk's training, 422; Rk's vision, GC as Bhairava, 267, 323, 351, 456; saluting Rk's picture, 195; servant healed, 331; on SV doing Rk's work, 350; vision of Rk, 458; worshipping Rk as Kali, 305, 332–33, 424

Girish — and Rk's Disciples
asks about Shashi, 428; asks M. for shoe-beating, 393, 461; asks M. for writings on Rk, 311, 393; asks Sharat, write life of Rk, 373; asks SV, initiate young son, 347; defeats SV, 341; GC on SV meditating, 342; on getting sweet mangoes, 347; with Golap-ma, 361–62; Latu and, 375–78; mutual love and respect, 369; praises Shashi's worship, 380; Ram comparing to Kaliya, 267; song for Shashi, 380–81; spits on homa, 371–72; SV, discussion with, 350; SV, dispute with, 291–93; with SV, on God, 278–79; on SV, spreading Rk's teachings, 416; on SV's anguish,

350–51; at SV's cremation, 352; on SV's greatness, 412; on SV's sadhana, 458; on Yogin and Rk's will, 380

Girish — and Theatre
on actress as child, Divine Mother, 413; on actresses seeking redemption, 440–41; based plays on Indian epics, 57, 118; building new Star Theatre, 60; Classic Theatre, Dramatic Director, 68; composing plays, 405; criticized for comedies, 217; directing style, 88–90; director, Minerva Theatre, 394; dislike of excuses, 405; founder, Baghbazar Amateur Theatre, 41; on giving best effort onstage, 455; hired to manage Minerva, 64; his influence on cultural life, 454; his writing genius, 226; on human nature, 373–74; irregular blank verse, "GC's metre", 51; leased Great National Theatre, 45; *Macbeth* manuscript lost, 34–35, 64; *Macbeth*, second translation, 64; manager, National Theatre, 47; mentored by Mrs. Lewis, 39; Minerva Theatre, quitting, 65; National Theatre, director, 54, 183; on not owning theatre, 47, 186; onstage, burnt, 71–73; portrayal, fake monk, 228; praises Tinkari, 214; prompting players from novel, 44, 70; recruiting Binodini, 183; staging *Macbeth*, 214; on theatre, origin of arts, 97; on training actors, 460; on translating *Macbeth*, 25, 34–35; on writing drama, 403; writing of *Siraj-ud-Daulla*, 75

Girish — Plays of
Abhimanyu-badh (Death of Abhimanyu), 54; *Agamani*, Uma's visit to parents, 47; *Akalbodhan*, Rama's worship of Durga, 47; *Balidan*, against dowry system, 73; *Bishabriksha*, on Bankim's novel, 47; *Bishad*, on Markandeya Purana, 60, 253; *Brishaketu*, on Mahabharata, 147–48; *Buddhadev-Charit*, on Arnold's *The Light of Asia*, 57–59; *Chaitanya Lila*, on life of Chaitanya, 118–32; *Chanda*, on Todd's History of Rajasthan, 63; *Chatrapati Shivaji*, on life of Shivaji, 78–79; comedy, *Aladin*, 51; *Daksha Yajna*, on story of Shiva, 157–61; *Dhruva Charitra*, on life of Dhruva, 185–86; drama, *Ananda Raho* (Be Happy), 51; drama, *Ravan-badh* (Death of Ravana), 51; *Durgeshnandini*, on Bankim's novel, 47, 76; *Hara-Gauri*, on Puranas, 73; *Haranidhi*, 63; *Hirak Jubilee*, for Victoria's Diamond Jubilee, 66; historical drama, *Satnam*, 79–80; historical drama, *Siraj-ud-Daulla*, 75–77; *Jhansir Rani*, abandoned, censorship, 79; *Kalapahar*, on Rk's life, teachings, 66, 242–8, 365–66, 377; *Kapalkundala*, on Bankim's novel, 53, 70; *Lakshman-Varjan* (Forsaking of Lakshman), 54; *Maya-avasan* (The End of Maya), on SV's philosophy, 66; *Meghnad-badh*, on M. M. Datta's poem, 45; *Mirkasim*, sequel to *Siraj-ud-Daulla*, 77; *Mrinalini*, on Bankim's novel, 45, 71; musical, *Basar*, 76; musical, *Deldar*, 68; musical drama, *Mayataru* (Mystical Tree), 51; musical drama, *Mohini Pratima* (Image of Love), 51; *Nasiram*, on Rk's teachings, 250–52, 399; *Nimai Sannyas*, later life of Chaitanya, 142–43; *Palasir Yuddha*, on Navin Sen's poem, 45–47; *Parasya Prasun*, on Arabian Nights, 66; *Prafulla*, 60; *Purnachandra* (Devotee Purna), 60, 248–50; *Ramer Vanabash* (Exile of Rama), 54; *Rupa-Sanatan*, on Chaitanya's disciples, 59, 209–10, 235–42, 399; satire, *Bellik Bazar*, 58; *Shankaracharya*, life of Shankara, 81; *Shasti ki Shanti?*, on widow marriage, 80; *Sita-haran* (Abduction of Sita), 54; *Sitar Vanabash* (Banishment of Sita), 53; *Sitar Vibaha* (Sita's Marriage), 54; *Tapobal* (Power of Austerity), 81–82; *Vilwamangal Thakur*, from *Bhaktamala*, 227–35; *Yaisa-ka-Taisa*, on Moliere's *L'Amour Medicin*, 78

Girish — Roles
Aurangazeb, *Chatrapati Shivaji*, 78; Birendra Singha, *Durgeshnandini*, 77, 414; Chintamani, *Kalapahar*, 242; Daksha, *Daksha Yajna*, 68, 158; Kalikinkar, *Maya-avasan*, 66; Kanchuki, *Pandava Gaurav*, 68; King Bhimsingha, *Krishnakumari*, 43; Lalit, *Lilavati*, 42; Lord Clive, *Siraj-ud-Daulla*, 47, 65, 183; Meghnad and Rama, *Meghnad-badh*, 68; Mirjafar, *Mirkasim*, 77; Mr. I.I. Wood, *Nildarpan*, 43; Nimchand, *Sadhabar Ekadashi*, 38, 41; Pashupati in *Mrinalini*, 45, 71; Rama, *Ravan-badh*, 51; Rama, *Sitar Vanabash*, 53; Sadhak, *Vilwamangal Thakur*, 227; title role, *Macbeth*, 64; Vetal, *Ananda Raho*, 51; Visvamitra, *Sitar Vibaha*, 54; Yogesh, *Prafulla*, 68
Girish Pratibha: biography of GC, 161, 411
Golap-ma: and GC, 361–62; HM's attendant, 361; at play with HM, 366; recalls HM to awareness, 366; reproved by HM, 362
Gospel of Ramakrishna (by M.), 122, 269; influenced Dilip Roy, 450–52; power of attorney discussed, 312–15
Goswami, Vijaykrishna. *See* Vijay
Great National Theatre: Binodini at, 180–84; GC leased, 45; renamed, National, 45; Tinkari attending, 208
Gupta, Mahendra Nath. *See* M.
Gurmukh, Roy: Binodini, his mistress, 184–86; built Star Theatre, 184–85; sold Star Theatre, 185–86

Hallock, Mrs. Gray (GC's friend): GC advises, Hindu customs, 434–35; on GC saluting shrines, 434–35; on GC's impressiveness, 430, 437; on GC's medical treatments, 435; on GC's moods, 433; on GC's sense of humor, 436; on GC's strengths, 432
Hanuman: Rama's devotee, 138, 253
Haridas (Chaitanya's disciple), 130, 198n

Haripada (devotee), 263, 278, 280, 293
Hazra, Pratap Chandra: and Rk, 122–23
Hiranyakashipu (demon king): father of Prahlada, 133
Holy Mother (Sarada), 354; accepts Tara's gifts, 202; actresses visit, 174, 202–3, 220–21; blesses actresses, 363; brother clutches feet, 360; cares for devotees, 359; cures GC through vision, 31–32, 359; eulogises GC, 367; on GC bearing expenses, 367; GC on her as Divine Mother, 355–58; GC on her veil, 360; on GC's death, 467; at GC's Durga Puja, 362; GC's esteem for, 353; GC's first visit, 353; as GC's real mother, 356–60; GC's son's devotion to, 338, 353; on Golap-ma scolding Maharaj, 361–62; at Howrah Station, 361; at Manomohan Theatre, 365–66; at Minerva Theatre, 363–66; at musical play, 366; praises actresses' devotion, 202; relationship with "mad" Rk, 356–57; on Rk on GC as part of Shiva, 367; on Rk taking GC's sins, 335, 367; Sharat builds Udbodhan for, 377; Shashi's vision of, 380; on SV at Parliament of Religions, 375; tells GC not to renounce, 361
Hriday, 273, 299; Rk's dependence on, 284; telling Rk, ask for occult powers, 283–84
Hugo, Victor, 161, 406; author, *Hunchback of Notre Dame*, 94

Incarnation of God (*see also* avatar): Dr. Sarkar on, 297–98; GC accepting Rk as, 325; as teacher, GC on, 279; GC on Rk as, 155, 341, 370; GC, SV accepts Rk as, 348; Rk on, 274–75; Rk on recognizing, 281; SV on infiniteness of, 292; Trailokya on, 287–89
Indian Mirror: review, *Daksha Yajna*, 161
Ishan: role in *Rupa-Sanatan*, 236–38, 240–41
Ishan (GC's servant), 121, 327, 410
Ishan (Rk's devotee): and Dr. Sarkar, 297–98

Isherwood, Christopher: biographical sketch, GC, 10–18; lecturing on GC, 8; on Rk as patron saint of stage, 162
Ishta (*see also* Chosen Deity): 144, 296
Ishvarakotis: Rk on, 137–38
Ishwar Chandra V.: disapproves women onstage, 44; GC dedicates play to, 53–54; social reformer, 92, 170; throws sandal at GC onstage, 426

Jagannath (Lord of the Universe), 201; on Chaitanya at Puri, 142–43; on Rk Mission, Math as City of, 167
Jahuri, Pratapchand: bought (Great) National Theatre, 47; gave GC free rein, 50; hired GC, 47; provided for National Theatre, 54; refuses Binodini pay, 184; rift with GC, 184
japa: GC on, 418; on Latu's, 378; Rk on, 280; Yogin on, 379
Jatin Deva (devotee), 155
Jayrambati: GC at, 32, 64, 355–62
jnanayoga (jnana), 154, 250; GC on Rk as jnanayogi, 397; GC on Rk on, 425, 445; Rk on, 138–39, 148–49, 271, 292, 327, 384
Jogin. *See* Yogananda, Swami

Kalapahar: title role, *Kalapahar*, 242–8
Kalapahar (GC's play), 242–8, 365–66, 377
Kali (Divine Mother), 114n, 309; food offering to, 339; GC seeing in Rk, 451; Kalighat, GC at, 113–14, 159; name as mantra, 271; Rk praying to, 283; Rk worshipped as, 305, 332–34, 398, 424
Kalighat, 113, 159
Kalipada, 297; helping Binodini see Rk, 190; on Rk as avatar, 190
Kamarpukur, 10; GC at, 64, 358, 361, 371, 378
Kanjilal, Dr. Jnanedra Nath: became homeopathist, 457; at GC's death, 464; checks Shashi, last day, 381; visits GC, 439
Karna, King: in Mahabharata, 147, 153
Keshab, 114, 259, 271; Brahmo's on relations with Rk, 162–64; incorporating Rk's ideas, 444; leader, Brahmo Samaj, 111; Trailokya Sannyal wrote life of, 286
Keshab Bharati: gave Chaitanya monastic vows, 142, 281
Khoka. *See* Subodhananda, Swami
Kohinoor Theatre, 77, 171, 219; GC, director of, 411; GC joining, 78
Krishna, 23, 187, 350n, 403, 416; Binodini, devotee of Gopala, 193; GC and Dr. Sarkar on, 297–98; GC and Mahimacharan on, 290; GC compared to Kaliya, 144–46, 267; GC compares Rk to, 269; Gita passage, 9, 113, 173, 312; King Dandi, enmity with, 68; leaves Vrindaban for Mathura, 26; Nimai's devotion to, 118–19, 127, 130; Radhika meditating on, 149; Ram with Rk at birthday of, 294; Rk's devotion to, 131–32; role in *Jana*, 364–65; role in *Vilwamangal Thakur*, 227–33; SV slighting Gita and, 292
Krishnakishori (GC's sister): arranged GC's marriage, 28; guardian, GC, brothers, 28
Kumudbandhu Sen: on GC composing song, 438–9; on GC's devotion, 355, 399; organizer, Convention of Religions, 438; reminisces on GC, 438–48; theatre, disapproved of, 341
Kusumkumari (actress), 53, 96; came between Tara, Amarendra, 197; GC telling of value, all roles, 70

La Rochefoucauld, Francois, 174
Lady Macbeth: Bernhardt in role, 94; role of Rezia compared to, 198; Tinkari in role, 64, 96, 214–17
Lafont, Father Eugene: blesses Binodini, 188; GC visited, 95
Lahiri, Nirmalendu (Nirmal; actor): associate of GC, M., 449; taught Dilip Roy devotion to Rk, 449–52
Lakshmi, Sister (Rk's niece), 220
Latu. *See* Adbhutananda, Swami
Lewis, Mrs. G.B.W. (actress), 39
Lilavati (play): author, Dinabandhu Mitra, 42

Lord Auckland (Governor General), 11
M. (Mahendranath Gupta), 163; associate, Dilip Roy, 449; bringing boys to Rk, 275; dining at GC's, 393; on Dr. Sarkar and GC, 296–97; escorting HM on train, 362; with GC and Dr. Sarkar, 302; GC asking for his writings, Rk, 311, 393; GC asking for shoe-beating, 393, 461; with GC, disputing Trailokya, 286–8; with GC, inviting Bankim to Rk's, 392; with GC, on science, 307; on GC's faith, 277; Latu on his grief, 307; loaned SV money, 342; on power of attorney, in *Gospel*, 312–15; recorder, *Gospel of Rk*, 21; on Rk as avatar, 155; with Rk, at Star Theatre, 122–32, 143, 153–56; Rk chiding for not singing, 276; Rk giving sweets to, 132; on worship of Rk, 305

Macbeth: GC staging, 64, 214–17; GC's first translation, 34; GC's second translation, 35, 64

Mahabharata, 54, 365; GC's liking for, 26, 29, 409

Maharaj. See Brahmananda, Swami

Mahendra, 260; Rk at his flour mill, 122, 131–32; with Rk, Star Theatre, 123, 163

Mahimacharan (devotee): dispute with GC, 407; and GC, 289–90; Rk on his learning, 276

Majumdar, Devendra Nath. See Devendra

Manomohan Theatre, 148, 204; Tinkari at, 219

mantra, 112, 396; Latu, Sharat, on "money mantra", 377; Mother Kali, name as, 271; name of God as, 262–63; Ramanuja shouts to all, 366

Master. See Ramakrishna

Matilal, Srishchandra (biographer, GC): 458; reminiscences on GC, 452–53

Minerva Theatre, 200; GC at, 64–65, 75–85, 405; GC, manager, 214–15, 394; HM at, 363–66; Ram at, lecturing on Rk, 166; Tinkari at, 214–17, 219, 222–23

Mirjafar: Siraj-ud-Daulla's general, 75–77

Mirkasim: Mirjafar's son-in-law, 77–78

Mirkasim (GC's play): roused nationalism, 79; sequel to *Siraj-ud-Daulla*, 77–79

Mishra, Jagannath (Chaitanya's father), 118–19, 125

Mitra, Amritalal (actor): buying Star Theatre, 185; directed GC's *Nasiram*, 195; Hiranyakashipu in *Prahlada Charitra*, 133–34; Keshab Bharati in *Nimai Sannyas*, 142; Madhai in *Chaitanya Lila*, 119; Mahadev in *Daksha Yajna*, 158–59; meeting SV at GC's house, 343–44; on *Nimai Sannyas*, 143; star of stage, 96; taking GC's dictation, 53; taught Tara acting, 195

Mitra, Ashutosh: on HM at theatre, 220, 364

Mitra, Dinabandhu (playwright), 50, 55; author, drama *Sadhabar Ekadashi*, 38; author, play *Nildarpan*, 42–43; praises GC in *Lilavati*, 42

Mitra, Manomohan: chiding GC, bothering Rk, 265; with Ram at GC's, 171–72

Mitra, Pulin Bihari: sang at Convention of Religions, 438; singing GC's song for Shashi, 380–81

Mitra, Sarada Charan (judge): on his respect for GC, 438; president, Convention of Religions, 438–39

Mitra, Surendra Nath. See Surendra

Moliere, 97; GC's *Yaisa-ka-Taisa*, on *L'Amour Medicin*, 78

Mukerji, Dhan Gopal: author, life of Rk *The Face of Silence*, 87–88

Mukerji, Mahendra. See Mahendra

Mukhopadhyay, Aparesh. See Aparesh

Mukhopadhyay, Gopal Chandra: GC cures him, 115–16

Mukhopadhyay, Hridayram. See Hriday

Mukhopadhyay, Jagadananda: hosted Prince of Wales, 45

Mukhopadhyay, Mahendra Nath. See Mahendra

Mukhopadhyay, Purna Chandra, 180

Müller, Max, 163–64; author, *Rk: His Life and Sayings*, 164

Mustafi, Ardhendu Sekhar (actor), 41, 114; Bidushaka in *Jana*, 253; on his

directing, 88–89; Jagai in *Chaitanya Lila*, 364; Karunamay in *Balidan*, 74
Nag Mahashay. *See* Durga Charan Nag
Nagendra Bhusan Mukhopadhyay: bought Minerva Theatre, 64, 214; coaxes Tinkari to act, 218; rift with GC, 65, 219
Narada, 133, 137; Rk on, 138, 151, 327, 445; role, *Daksha Yajna*, 157–58
Narayan (devotee), 152, 278
Naren (younger), 275; Rk praises, 281
Narendra: *See* Vivekananda, Swami
Narisundari (actress): praises GC, 96–97
Nasiram (GC's play): on Rk's teachings, 250–52
National Theatre, 46; Binodini at, 184; GC, manager, 50, 54; Great National renamed as, 45; ownership problems, 47
Natya Mandir (magazine), 81, 193; on Rk on cover, 169–70
Navadwip: Chaitanya's birthplace, 120; Vaishnavas at GC's plays, 120–21, 174, 188
Neri, Phillip (Christian saint), 17
Nikhilananda, Swami: biography of Holy Mother, 359
Nildarpan (play): author, Dinabandhu Mitra, 42; GC, friends staging, 43; ruckus in Lucknow at, 181
Nilmadhav Chakrabarty (actor): Brahma in *Daksha Yajna*, 158; hiring Tinkari, 213–14; Jagannath Mishra in *Chaitanya Lila*, 119; manager, City Theatre, 64
Nimai Sannyas (GC's play), 142–43
Niranjanananda, Swami (Niranjan): chides Nag Mahasay, 396; on HM's greatness, 355; at HM's with GC, 64, 355–59; on SV's return, India, 349; tells GC to renounce, 370–71; telling GC, visit HM, 353; worships Rk as Kali, 305
Nityananda (associate of Chaitanya), 397; role, *Chaitanya Lila*, 118–19, 130–31
Nivedita, 86; on GC's plays, 461; on SV at Opera Comique, 168
Niyogi, Bhuban Mohan: and Great National Theatre, 44–45, 47, 180

Noble, Margaret: *See* Nivedita
Padaratna, Pandit Mathuranath: blesses Binodini, 188; salutes GC, 120
Pagalini (Pagli): crazy woman, disturbing Rk, 226–27, 309–10, 385; role based on, 226–27, 385
Pagalini (role): crazy woman, *Vilwamangal Thakur*, 227–35; Gangamani as, 192; Narisundari as, 97; Tinkari as, 220
Pal, Bipin Chandra (Brahmo leader): on Tara as Rezia, 198
paramahamsa: GC on Rk as, 146, 259–60, 331; Rk on, 136
Paramananda, Swami: GC asks about, 428; translated GC's plays, 426
Parker Co.: GC, accountant for, 36–37, 47
Parker (English businessman): GC's friend, 36–37; on GC's resignation, 47; liked GC's work, 36; and Parker Co., 36
power of attorney, 62, 331, 341, 418; Bengali phrases for, 312; comparing guru, avatara on, 318; on effecting, 318–20; on GC giving to Rk, 248; GC on Rk accepting all, 379; legal definition of, 312; parable, cow killer blames Indra, 320–21; Rk on, 312–22; Rk to Kali, GC to Rk, 382
Prahlada: devotee of Vishnu, 133; Rk on, jnani and bhakta, 138; son of Hiranyakashipu, 133
Prahlada Charitra (GC's play): on life of Prahlada, 133–35
Pramodini Sarkar (GC's first wife), 28–29, 34–35
Pratibha (Tara's daughter), 193, 198, 205
Pravasi (magazine), 168, 443
Premananda, Swami (Baburam): on GC's death, 429; at GC's in Varanasi, 383; with HM at Howrah Station, 361; on power of attorney, 382; on Rk not blessing GC's friend, 382
Prince of Wales (later Edward VII): at Calcutta, 45
Puranas, 68, 82, 133, 157; GC writings based on, 53–54; GC's liking for, 29; Markandeya Purana, 253
Puri (abode of Jagannath), 142–43, 201, 288

Purna (Purnachandra), 411; on GC's final illness, 400; on GC's remarks on Rk, 399–400
Purnachandra (GC's play): on renunciation, faith in God, 248–50

Radha, 126, 228, 233, 290; GC on Chaitanya, 119
Rakhal. *See* Brahmananda, Swami
Ram Chandra Datta, 283, 335; biographer, Rk, 398–99; comparing GC to Kaliya, 144, 146, 267; disapproving, Rk at theatre, 163, 166; with GC, 171–72; GC with Rk and, 264; lecturing on Rk, 166; relations with GC, 397–99; on Rk redeeming actors, 166
Rama: on bhakti, 271; Dr. Sarkar on, 298; freeing Ahalya, 272; sun sign of, 293; role, *Lakshman-Varjan*, 54; on Sita, 140
Ramakrishna (the Master; *see also* Gadadhar), 254; on avatar with GC, 274–75; on being with GC, SV, 329; on bhaktiyoga, 138, 148, 151, 271, 309; blesses actresses, 93; blesses Binodini, 188–89; on Brahman, Shakti as same, 122–23; on Brahmo's preaching of sin, 314; in charge of GC's life, 328–29; chides M. for not singing, 276; at Devendra's, 280; disapproves occult powers, 116–17; and Dr. Sarkar, 298; on ekadashi, 150; encourages artists, 225; encourages GC, 15, 134; on faith, 301–2; feeds GC, 266; on food rules, 329–30; on forms of love, 290; and GC, 13–22, 135; on GC giving power of attorney to, 18, 315–16; at GC's, 148, 278; on GC's faith, 277; on GC's "garlic smell", 156; GC's vision of, 458; on giving God power of attorney, 314, 384; on God as magnet, 387; on God-vision, 151; and Hazra, 122–23; on householder vs. sannyasi, 308; instructs Atul, 152–53; on Ishvarakotis, 137–38; on jnanayoga, 138–39, 148–49, 271, 292, 296, 327, 384; as Kalpataru, 335, 398; on lust and greed, 310; on a magazine cover, 169; on mahabhava, 284; on Mahamaya and God vision, 140; on Rakhal's non-attachment, 309; moved to Cossipore, 307, 334; on not forbidding GC, 379; on overcoming sin, 173; patron saint of stage, 171; pours water for GC, 336; praises Nag Mahasay, 395; refuses to be born as GC's son, 144; on religious views, 285; removes GC's suffering, 448; restores India's religion, culture, 225; on sadhana, 294; on self-effort vs. surrender, 313; at Star Theatre, 14, 122, 134–41, 143, 148, 153; takes on sins, 318; on teachers, like prostitutes, 284; tells GC bathe in Ganges, 391; theatre visits as part of lila, 389; and Trailokya, 287, 288; training methods, 422; vision, GC as Bhairava, 267, 323; vision, occult powers as filth, 283; warning GC on visions, 419–20; warns SV about GC, 272–73; on worldly, like frog in well, 289; on worship of Shodasi, 150; worshipped as Kali, 305, 332–34, 398, 424
Ramakrishnananda, Swami (Shashi), 378; GC asking of, 428; GC on Rk training, 422; GC wrote song for at death, 380; HM, his vision of, 380–81; mahasamadhi, 381; nursing Rk, 307; Rk on him, 281; wrote life of Ramanuja, 200
Ramanuja: propounder, qualified non-dualism, 200, 279; shouting mantra to all, 366
Ramanuja (play): author, Aparesh, 200, 366
Ramanuja (role): Tara as, 197, 200, 366; title role, *Ramanuja*, 366
Ramayana: GC based plays on, 51, 53–54, 81, 207–8; GC's liking for, 26, 29, 409
Ramlal (Rk's nephew), 266, 310, 335; and Rk, 160–61
Ramprasad (Bengali poet-saint), 325, 446
Rangalaya (journal): for women acting, 92–93, 168
Rezia (play): author Manomohan Roy, 197

Rezia (role): Tara as, 197–98, 205; title role, *Rezia*, 197–98
Roy, Amarendra Nath: criticizes S.N. Ghosh's acting, 455
Roy Bahadur, Raja Chandranath: gave GC royal regalia, 43
Roy, Dilip Kumar (Mantu): GC tells of Rk, 449–52; memoirs on GC, *Smriticharan*, 449–52
Roy, Dwijendralal (poet, playwright): author, historical drama *Rana Pratap*, 74, 90; Dilip's father, 449; GC tells of Rk, 449–52
Roy, Surendra Nath: on GC on writing drama, 403
Rupa (Chaitanya's disciple): role, *Rupa-Sanatan*, 236–37, 241
Rupa-Sanatan (GC's play), 235–42; depicted Rk's love of god, 235

Sachi (Chaitanya's mother), 118–19
Sachi (role): in *Chaitanya Lila*, 119, 126–27, 131, 187; in *Nimai Sannyas*, 142
Sadhak: fake monk, *Vilwamangal Thakur*, 86, 227–31, 233–34
sadhana (spiritual discipline), 113, 290; GC on each race's, 441; GC on need for, 321; love, its gem, 440; and occult powers, 244; Rk on, 150–51; Rk on Tantric, 294; on Rk's, 146; on SV's, 458; Tinkari, treating acting as, 222–23
Sagara, King, 462n
Sahitya Samsad: GC's publisher, 7–8
Samadhyayi, Pandit Mokshada Charan: asks GC's advice on writing, 404
Samajpati, Suresh Chandra: editor, *Sahitya* magazine, 75; eulogises GC, 465
Sanatan (Chaitanya's disciple): role, *Rupa-Sanatan*, 235–42
Sannyal, Trailokya. *See* Trailokya
sannyasa: Rk on, 146; SV initiates GC's son into, 347
sannyasi, 309; GC praises, 351; Niranjan on GC as, 370; one glancing at women, 273; Rk gives rules for, 150; Rk on carrying Gita, 292; Rk on thinking of God, 308; SV's sannyasis feed poor, 430;

Yogin on Rk as, 325, 421
Sans Souci Theatre, 38
Saradananda, Swami (Sharat): asks GC for money, 381–82; on Binodini at Rk's, 189; eulogises GC, 465; and GC, 372–75; on GC defeating SV, 339–41; and GC, on renunciation, 373–74; at GC's, 78; at GC's with Devamata, 428; on "money mantra", 377; on power of attorney, 315–21, 373; sings for dying GC, 465; on SV on God with form, 339; and Tara, 203; tutors Aparesh, 200; on worshipping Rk as Kali, 332–34
Sharat. *See* Saradananda, Swami
Sarkar, Akshay: praises *Bellik Bazar*, 59
Sarkar, Dr. Mahendralal, 42, 95; and GC, 297–98, 301–5; treats Rk, 296, 302
Sarkar, Navin Chandra (GC's father-in-law): accountant, Atkinson Tilton Co., 34; GC's guardian, 28
Shashi. *See* Ramakrishnananda, Swami
Sati: role, *Daksha Yajna*, 157–58, 161
Satnam (GC's play): closed, Muslim protests, 79–80
Sen, Keshab Chandra. *See* Keshab
Sen, Navin Chandra: author, poem *Palasir Yuddha*, 45; praises GC, 47
Sen, Paresh Chandra, 89
Shakespeare, 39, 92, 97, 198, 217, 455; comparing GC to, 426, 431; depicts European society, 56; GC translates *Macbeth*, 64–65, 214; role model to GC, 441; SV ranks GC with, 227; translating of *Othello*, 200
Shakti (Divine Mother's power): Rk on Brahman, Shakti as same, 122–23, 355; Rk on propitiating, 149; on Rk seeing lion, 443–44
Shankara: SV's life gave GC insight on, 442
Shankaracharya (GC's play), 407, 451–52; GC on power of attorney in, 321; GC touches manuscript to image of, 442; on life of Shankara, 81
Shashadhar, Pandit: on Rk curing own illness, 299
Shastri, Shivanath. *See* Shivanath

494   Girish Chandra Ghosh

Shiva (Siva), 202, 241–42, 294, 306, 323, 327, 356, 456; GC at Shiva-ratri, 458; GC worshipping, 70, 113, 261; knower of Brahman, 384; Nataraj, presiding deity, theatre, 45, 170; Rk on GC as part of, 367; enmity towards Daksha, 157–58; SV comparing GC to, 351

Shivaji: Maharashtrian hero, 78–79; title role, *Chatrapati Shivaji*, 78–79

Shivananda, Swami, 146; inaugurates Tara's temple, 204; on Rk, GC's saviour, 382; and Tara, 204

Shivanath, 445; disapproves Rk connection with actors, 163

Shyampukur house: Binodini at, 189–90; Kali puja at, 424; Rk at, 318; Rk moved to, 297, 332, 398

Sil, Gopallal: bought Star Theatre, renamed Emerald, 59, 195, 210; electric lights for Emerald, 59; hired GC, 59–60; leased away Emerald, 60

Siraj-ud-Daulla (GC's play): historical drama, 75–77, 91; roused nationalism, 76, 79

Siraj-ud-Daulla (Muslim Nawab): title role, *Siraj-ud-Daulla*, 75–76

Somagiri: true monk, *Vilwamangal Thakur*, 113, 228–29, 231–33

Star Theatre, 63, 120, 134, 143, 264; Aparesh leasing, 200; building of, 59, 184–86, 195; Ram at, lecturing on Rk, 166; Tinkari at, 209

Subodhananda, Swami: asks GC for money for math, 381–82; on GC dictating dramas, 53; installed Rakhal's relics, 204; on Tara's worship of Rk, 205

Sukadeva (Shuka), 137, 285; Rk on as born perfect, 151; Rk on as jnani, 327, 384, 445; staying in the world, 136

Surendra (Suresh): distributes Rk's prasad, 311; Rk on his wild life, 276; supports Rk math, 367

Sushilasundari (actress): on GC's genius, 96

Swamiji: *See* Vivekananda, Swami

Tagore, Dwijendra Nath: on GC's blank verse, 51

Tagore, Rabindranath, 429; disapproves women onstage, 92; member, Brahmo Samaj, 444n; on Rk's spirituality, 443–46

Tantra, 149, 291, 294

Tapobal (GC's play), 81–82, 459; dedicated to Nivedita, 461

Tara; Tarasundari (actress): 193–207, 194; Amarendra's mistress, 196–97; Aparesh, relationship with, 198, 201, 204; asking of Rk, 412; becoming mistress, 175–76; Binodini mentoring, 195; building temple, 204; buying land, 202; Chintamani in *Vilwamangal Thakur*, 197; death, 205–7; despairs, 171; GC telling of Rk, 174; leasing Star Theatre, 200; and Maharaj, 199; Maharaj initiating, 201; retiring from stage, 205; son's death, 204; stage debut, 195; training as actress, 175; at Udbodhan, 202-3

The Statesman (English newspaper): praises GC, 76, 77, 79

Tilak, Balgangadhar (nationalist): praises GC's play *Siraj-ud-Daulla*, 76

Tinkari (actress), 87, 168, 206; asks about Rk, 198, 412; becomes mistress, 175–76; at Bina Theatre, 211; at City Theatre, 213; death, 223; at Emerald Theatre, 213; empathy, 207; fears over lover, 218; followed GC job to job, 219; GC praises, 214; GC taught to act, 96; on GC's death, 223; with GC at murder plot, 218-19; helps poor, 413; on her acting talent, 207; with HM, 175, 202, 220; left estate to hospital, 224; at Manomohan Theatre, 223; at Minerva Theatre, 219; mother selling her favours, 211; rejects marriage proposal, 218; on singing touching her, 222; at Thespian Temple, 223; in training, 209; at Varanasi, 222

Todd, James: author, *History of Rajasthan*, 63

Trailokya, 314; and GC, 286–88; member, Brahmo Samaj, 283, 286

Trigunatitananda, Swami: editor, *Udbodhan*, 348

Turiyananda, Swami, 88; on GC, Rk, 383–85; on Rk as sannyasi, 146

Udbodhan: HM's residence, 361, 365; on Sharat building, 377
Udbodhan (magazine): publishing GC on Rk, 255; on SV's starting of, 348

Vaishnavas, 440, 446; and GC on Chaitanya, 236; liked GC's plays, 120–22, 174; sectarian strife and, 260; toothmarks on prasad, 120, 262
Varanasi, 241, 356; GC at, 80–81, 97–98, 383, 458–59; GC on Rk's revering, 417; Tinkari at, 222
Victoria, Queen: GC's Hirak Jubilee for, 66
Vidyabhusan, Upendranath: biographer of actresses, 175; on GC's methods, 95
Vidyasagar, Pandit Ishwar Chandra. *See* Ishwar Chandra V.
Vijay, 309, 332; at *Chaitanya Lila*, 120; devotion for Rk, 162–63
Vijnanananda, Swami: on GC with Rk's, 385–86
Vilwamangal: title role, *Vilwamangal Thakur*, 227–35
Vilwamangal Thakur (GC's play), 220, 227–35; GC and Sharat on, 373–74; SV lecturing on, 345–46; SV on, surpasses Shakespeare, 227
Vishnu, 147; as Nrisimha killing Hiranyakashipu, 133
Vishuddhananda, Swami: on GC as Rk's miracle, 467
visions: GC warning on, 370; GC's of Balaram, Krishna's brother, 403; GC's of Divine Mother, 117; GC's of HM, cured by, 31–32; GC's of Rk, 458; Rk on God-vision, 151; Rk warning GC on, 327, 419–20; Rk's, GC as Bhairava, 267, 323; Rk's of prostitute in filth, 283; Shashi's of HM, 380–81; of worldly people, 280
Vivekananda, Swami (Narendra; Swamiji), 340; anguish for others, 350–51; on Brahmo criticism of Rk, 164; on dangers, GC's path, 341–42, 456; defends sinners, 173; establishes Rk Mission, 349, 416; and GC, 278–79, 291–93, 347; GC on his meditation, 342; on GC's devotion to Rk, 18; GC's play inspires, 342–43; on GC's talks on Rk, 348; on God with form, 339–41; his life, inspires GC, 442; on his puritanism, 166; initiates GC's son, 347; lectures on GC's play, 345–46; on not writing Rk's life, 373; on Rk as godlike, 303; with Rk, GC, Star Theatre, 153–55; on Rk's artistic talent, 225; sings at theatre, 344; taking dust, GC's feet, 145, 349; with proud judge, 343–44
Vrindaban, 93, 231, 241; Krishna, leaves for Mathura, 26

Yogananda, Swami (Jogin; Yogin): GC curing, 379; mahasamadhi, 380; Rk to, on GC's traits, 326; on Rk's sannyas, 325, 421; on Rk's will, 380
Yogin. *See* Yogananda, Swami
Yogin-ma, 221; and HM at theatre, 366; HM's attendant, 361
Young Bengal: Western educated youth, 260

Works by Swami Chetanananda

Books

Ramakrishna and His Divine Play, by Swami Saradananda
  (*Translated by Swami Chetanananda*)

God Lived with Them: Life Stories of Sixteen Monastic Disciples of Sri Ramakrishna

They Lived With God: Life Stories of Some Devotees of Sri Ramakrishna

How to Live with God: In the Company of Ramakrishna

Ramakrishna as We Saw Him

Ramakrishna: A Biography in Pictures
  (*Biographical Introduction by Swami Smarananada*)

Sarada Devi: A Biography in Pictures
  (*Biographical Introduction by Swami Smarananada*)

Vivekananda: East Meets West (*A Pictorial Biography*)

Vedanta: Voice of Freedom

Meditation and Its Methods: by Swami Vivekananda
  (*Edited by Swami Chetanananda*)

A Guide to Spiritual Life — Spiritual Teachings of Swami Brahmananda

Spiritual Treasures: Letters of Swami Turiyananda

How a Shepherd Boy Became a Saint: Life and Teachings of Swami Adbhutananda

Avadhuta Gita: The Song of the Ever-Free
  (*Translated by Swami Chetanananda*)

CDs

(*Sanskrit Chants with English translation*)

Echoes of the Eternal: Peace, Bliss, and Harmony

Breath of the Eternal: Awakening, Reflection, and Illumination

DVDs

Ramakrishna (*A Documentary*)

The Parables of Ramakrishna (*40 Parables of Ramakrishna*)

Vivekananda as We Saw Him (*A Documentary*)